Michael Wolff
Essay on the Principles of Logic

Michael Wolff

Essay on the Principles of Logic

A Defense of Logical Monism

Translated by
W. Clark Wolf

DE GRUYTER

This work, originally published in German as *Abhandlung über die Prinzipien der Logik* in 2004, appeared in two further editions, each expanded and revised, in 2009 and 2023, recently with the subtitle: *Eine Verteidigung des logischen Monismus.* © 2004 Verlag Vittorio Klostermann GmbH, Frankfurt am Main.

ISBN 978-3-11-162480-8
e-ISBN (PDF) 978-3-11-078493-0
e-ISBN (EPUB) 978-3-11-078510-4

Library of Congress Control Number: 2022952387

Bibliographic information published by the Deutsche Nationalbibliothek
The Deutsche Nationalbibliothek lists this publication in the Deutsche Nationalbibliografie; detailed bibliographic data are available on the internet at http://dnb.dnb.de.

© 2024 Walter de Gruyter GmbH, Berlin/Boston
This volume is text- and page-identical with the hardback published in 2023.
Typesetting: Integra Software Services Pvt. Ltd.

www.degruyter.com

Preface to the English Edition

The view defended in this book can be summarized in essence as follows: there are strictly universal logical principles presupposed by the various modern systems of 'classical' and 'non-classical' deductive logic. The universal validity of these principles stems solely from the meaning of the logical vocabulary used in their formulas, and this meaning can be determined by analytically discoverable definitions of the logical constants belonging to that vocabulary.

I call this view logical monism. For according to it there is exactly one system of deductive logic which can make explicit the logical principles which the other systems presuppose as valid in different ways. Logical monism is opposed to what today is called 'logical pluralism', since according to that view the different systems of deductive logic have an equal claim to validity, so that it is a question of mere choice which system is to be preferred to others. In what follows, however, a criticism of logical pluralism will not be my explicit topic.[1] Rather, my aim here is to show in detail that and why logical monism is tenable. Some preliminary remarks may suffice to explain my intention a little more precisely.

The idea of logical monism, as I understand it, goes back to Kant. For he understood logic as the "science of the rules of understanding in general" and assumed it to concern either the "general" or the "particular use of understanding", which is why he divided it into a general logic and into (an indeterminate number of) special logics; in doing so, he called that logic general which "contains the absolutely necessary rules of thinking, without which no use of understanding takes place, and it therefore concerns these rules without regard to the difference of the objects to which it may be directed" (Kant, *CPR* B 76).[2] Accordingly, Kant assumed that special logics presuppose the rules of the general logic as valid.

Now the *modern* logical systems were still unknown to Kant, and by "general logic" he could only mean the traditional syllogistic, going back to Aristotle. We must thus ask whether one is justified in relating Kant's division of logic to the systems known today, since he could not comment on them directly and knew nothing about their relation to the syllogistic.

As far as his appreciation of the syllogistic as *general* logic is concerned, he saw its "advantage" in its "own limitation" of being "the science that exhaustively presents and strictly proves nothing but the formal rules of all thinking [. . .]" (*CPR* B viii–ix). Because of its limitation, general logic is "justified in abstracting – is even obliged to abstract – from all objects of cognition and all the distinctions between them"; for in it, "the understanding has to do with nothing further than itself and its

---
1 It is the topic of my article, Wolff 2013.
2 For what follows, compare also: *CPR* B vii–ix, 76–78, and 82–86; cf. Ak. 4: 387–88.

own form" (*CPR* B ix). To this advantage it owes its success (*CPR* B ix) and the "secure path of a science", which it has taken "from the earliest times" (*CPR* B vii–viii). "As general logic it abstracts from all contents of the cognition of the understanding and of the difference of its objects, and has to do with nothing but the mere form of thinking"; as "pure logic it has no empirical principles," which is why it "draws nothing from psychology" but is a "proven doctrine" in which "everything [. . .] must be completely certain *a priori*" (*CPR* B 78, modified).[3] As a logic that abstracts "from all content of cognition (whether it be pure or empirical)" it is "merely formal logic" (*CPR* B 170; cf. 77) and as such not an "organon" (i.e., an instrument) for bringing forth cognitions, but only a "canon" (i.e., a norm) "of the understanding and reason" (*CPR* B 77).[4] For, mere "agreement with the general and formal laws" of general logic never guarantees truth, but concerns "only the form of truth" and is not a sufficient, but only a "negative condition" ("the *conditio sine qua non*") "of all truth" (*CPR* B 84–85, cf. 824).

As far as *special* logics are concerned, Kant expected them to be an "organon of this or that science" and to contain "the rules for correctly thinking about a certain kind of objects"; however, "if one will offer the rules for how a science of [these objects] is to be brought about," one must already know these objects "rather well" (*CPR* B 76). For this reason, Kant regarded special logics as "the latest to be reached in the course of human reason, once the science is already long complete and requires only the final touch for its improvement and perfection" (*CPR* B 76). For him, special logics are projects for the future, projects in the making at best.

Kant could have had mathematics in mind as an example of a science that requires a special logic. Thus, in his "Transcendental Doctrine of Method," he outlines the algebraic procedure of inferring from n to $n + 1$ as a method of mathematical "demonstration". It is known today as "mathematical induction"; Kant calls it "symbolic construction" (*CPR* B 762).[5] Though it was fundamental for the theory of natural numbers, the problem of how to justify it was considered an unsolved since the 17th century. It was Frege, in his *Begriffsschrift* of 1879 (in which he established the first modern system of logic), who provided the key to the solution by deriving the principle of mathematical induction from the axioms of this system (see Frege 1879/1967, Part III, §§ 23–27).

---

[3] The *Cambridge Edition of the Works of Immanuel Kant* leaves out "certain [*gewiß*]" in Kant's text, and thereby eliminates the idea that the universal validity of general logic must *a priori*, i.e., independent of all experience, rule out uncertainty and wavering regarding its principles.
[4] '*Organon*' was the traditional name for Aristotle's logical writings, '*Canon*' the title of Epicurus' treatise on logic, as Kant was well aware.
[5] For details see my 1995, 211–19.

Obviously, the system founded by Frege should be regarded neither as 'general' nor as 'formal' logic in Kant's sense.[6] For it is based on axioms that consist of (logically) true judgments, which are formulated in a symbolic language modeled on that of arithmetic. Frege therefore let his axioms (as well as all theorems derived from them) begin with '⊢', which means: "It is a fact that . . . ".[7]* This sign is followed in the formulas of each axiom or theorem by the formula of a truth function whose arguments are "judgeable contents"[8] and which (for any interpretation of its descriptive signs) has the value *True*. This function value is computable with truth tables. The validity of the rules for deriving theorems from axioms is also based on the computable truth of truth functions.[9] These form, together with the axioms, the "core" of a "boundless multitude of laws" derivable from them, in which "the content of all these laws is included, albeit in an undeveloped state" (Frege 1879, 25, § 13 [1967, 29]). Frege's logic is therefore a system of laws which, just like algebraic equations, contain (true) judgments about facts of "pure" (i.e., non-empirical) thought. Since truth always already "concerns" the "content" of "cognition" (Kant, *CPR* B 83),[10] this logic is neither general nor formal in Kant's sense: it cannot abstract from the truth of the content of its axioms or theorems, nor can it abstract from all distinctions between objects. For even functions of the form Φ (ν), with which objects are ascribed a "property" or a "relation" to other objects, are judgeable contents to which reference is made in truth functions (Frege 1879, 18, § 10 [1967, 24]).

Frege's use of functional expressions of different kinds was made possible by a state of research in pure mathematics that allowed the simplest algebraic truths such as $x + x = 2x$ to be treated as functions whose arguments can stand for anything countable (i.e., for any given objects) and whose value is always a truth value. Therefore, Frege's system (as well as the 'classical' logic that emerged from it) may be called an organon in Kant's sense, namely a cognitive tool that pure mathematics needs in order to claim to be an *a priori* demonstrative, exact science. In this sense it is a *special*, mathematical logic: an organon of arithmetic, which can be used like a calculus.

---

[6] The synonymy of 'formal' and 'symbolic' logic is not a feature of Frege's terminology. It was introduced by Russell (1903, 10).
[7] Frege 1879, 2, Part I, § 2 (1967, 11–12), and Part II, §§ 13–22. For the following cf. Frege 1879/1967, Part I, §§ 1–12 and II, §§ 13–22.
*Translator's note [= TN]: References to existing English translations of original sources will be included next to the original references, within parentheses. Some slight modifications may be made to fit the context without explicit mention.
[8] Frege 1879, 2, § 2 (1967, 11–12), and Frege 1879, 5, § 5 (1967, 13).
[9] Frege 1879, 8–10, § 6 (1967, 15–17), and Frege 1879, 21–22, § 11 (1967, 25–27).
[10] According to Frege, the truth value of a judgment constitutes its *extensional content* (its 'meaning'), while the thought it contains constitutes its *intensional content* (its 'sense').

General logic, which Kant had in mind as a 'canon', differs from such a system in that it contains no truths, but only rules for the "logical use of the understanding in general"; this consists in subordinating and coordinating concepts in judgments and conclusions without contradiction (*CPR* B 92–94).[11] It consists therefore in actions by which one arranges possible concepts as in a pyramid of terms (see below §§ 1, 4 and 6).[12] If in such a pyramid letters represent the terms, the relations between these correspond to the forms of the Kantian table of judgments and the forms of inference in Aristotle's *Prior Analytics* (see Part I, Section 1 below). No truth can be rendered with these forms, not even if one transforms valid forms of inference into forms of judgment (e. g., if one converts the form of syllogisms according to *modus Barbara* into the correct form of true hypothetical judgments: 'If every α is a β, then if every γ is an α, then every γ is a β'). Judgment forms such as these, while logically valid, do not express a truth, but (to use Kant's term) only a "form of truth" (*CPR* B 84).[13] As forms, they contain only "formal laws" (*CPR* B 84) or forms of logical truth. Agreement with them is not a sufficient but only a general and necessary condition for truth.

The universal validity of rules of the categorical or hypothetical syllogistic is based solely on the meaning of the logical vocabulary that occurs in syllogisms. Thus, the hypothetical conjunction 'if p, then q' merely indicates that q follows from p (*CPR* B 98–99), and this means that p and 'not q' represent incompatible propositions. It is due to this meaning that, e.g., an inference is valid according to *modus ponendo ponens*, so that, given 'if p, then q', q follows *logically* from p. This logical consequence is thus not a function of the truth values of the judgeable contents of p and q.

Likewise, syllogistic negations ('not p') are not truth functions. For they have the task "solely of preventing error" (*CPR* B 737; 97). That is, there are cases in which 'not p' is compatible with 'not not p', i.e., cases in which the negation of a false judgment admits the possibility of being negated itself. For example, the negation of a universal affirmative judgment has the form 'not every α is a β'. It leaves

---

[11] Cf. also Kant's *Dissertation* (1770), Ak. 2: 393–94.

[12] What Kant calls "logical use of the understanding in general" (*usus intellectus logicus*) refers to the same actions that Plato described in his dialogue *Sophist* as "*dihairēsis*" and "*synagogē*" of concepts. This description "undoubtedly influenced Aristotle in his invention of the syllogism" (Kneale & Kneale 1975, 10; cf. 44 and 67).

[13] To illustrate this with an example of Kant's (cf. "The False Subtlety of the Four Syllogistic Figures" (1762), Ak. 2: 48): According to *modus Barbara*, from the assumptions (1) 'Everything rational is a spirit' and (2) 'All human souls are rational' it logically follows that (3) 'All human souls are spirits'. Provided there are no spirits, the counterfactual proposition 'If (1) were true, then if (2) were also true, (3) would also be true' is true. But about objects and what *is* true of them, it says nothing sufficient. Whether objects (like, e.g., spirits) exist at all cannot be judged by general logic alone (as Kant understands it).

undecided whether α is an empty or a non-empty term, i.e., whether 'not some α is a β' or 'some α is not a β' holds. Moreover, a negative universal affirmative is compatible with its subcontrary opposite, i.e., with a judgment of the form 'some α is a β', thus also with the negation of its contradictory opposite ('not not some α is a β'). This means there are cases in which negations of the form 'not p' and 'not not p' are compatible with each other (and in which then 'neither p nor not p' does not involve any contradiction either).

The semantic analysis of the logical vocabulary of the syllogistic is the task of Part I of this book. This analysis shows that not only has Frege's attempt to let true judgments take the place of "Aristotelian modes of inference" (Frege 1879, 10, Part I, § 6 [1967, 17]) by derivation from axioms failed but so has the attempt at a "systematic derivation of traditional Aristotelian inferences" from principles of the calculus of classes, carried out by Hilbert and Ackermann (1967, 57–63, II, § 3 [1950, 48–54]). Instead, the opposite of these attempts turns out to be true: the language of the syllogistic is suitable to replace the logical vocabulary of modern 'classical' logic, so long as one postulates the validity of certain rules which can be formulated in the syllogistic language but are invalid within the syllogistic. In this case the principles of 'classical' logic can be derived from principles of syllogistic. One can also extend the language of syllogistic by transforming functional expressions of the form $\Phi(v)$ (for properties of or relations between objects) into appropriate expressions for specified contents of concepts or of propositions. It is also the task of Part I to show how this can be done.

Part II begins by showing that it is possible to establish basic rules and rules for deduction which are valid on the basis of analytically obtained definitions of the syllogistic vocabulary, and that is possible to derive on this basis all the rules of the assertoric and modal syllogistic for which Aristotle has given or sketched validity proofs in his *Prior Analytics*. Moreover, this Part shows that the validity of syllogistic rules is implicitly presupposed in modern 'classical' logic. This is done by proving that its axioms and basic rules can be derived from syllogistic principles, so long as one postulates the validity of four rules (see § 72) which can be expressed in syllogistic language though without being valid in syllogistic logic. In this way, Part II confirms Kant's assumption that Aristotelian logic is a general logic, insofar as its rules underlie even modern 'classical' logic.

However, the logic founded by Frege – as well as the modified version in the *Principia Mathematica* by Russell and Whitehead – does not contain modal logic, but avoids the use of modal expressions like 'necessary', 'possible', 'compatible' etc. These are indispensable for ordinary logical thinking and occur already in the syllogistic because the meaning of the assertoric-logical vocabulary depends on their use.[14] Therefore one must regard 'classical' logic as a special logic for two reasons: first, because it does not contain a modal logic; and second, because its principles can be derived from syllogistic principles if one postulates four pseudo-syllogistic rules as valid.

In a similar way, one must consider the 'non-classical' logics as special logics. These include the systems of intuitionistic logic, (paraconsistent) relevance logic, 'free'[15] logic, and axiomatic modal logic.[16] These systems (as well as those resulting from their mutual combination) are special logics in the same sense as 'classical' logic is. The task of the appendices at the end of this book is to justify this thesis. Here I will explain it only briefly.

First, each of the four 'non-classical' systems are built on only one of the syllogistic subsystems. Intuitionistic logic and relevance logic are merely alternatives to 'classical' propositional logic, and 'free' logic is merely an alternative to 'classical' predicate logic; axiomatic modal logics are merely modal complements either to 'classical' propositional logic or to its two alternatives.[17] *Second*, the 'non-classical' systems have in common that they (unless they presuppose 'classical' propositional logic and merely add a modal propositional logic, like Lewis' systems of axiomatic modal logic) do not presuppose as valid each of the four pseudo-syllogistic postulates from § 72. Yet in modern modal logic as well, certain axioms have been introduced which (analogous to the postulates of § 72) presuppose rules whose validity can only be postulated, because though they are expressible in the modal syllogistic language, they are not valid in the modal syllogistic. In this way it becomes evident that the logical vocabulary used in the systems of 'non-classical' deductive logic, just as that used in 'classical' logic, can be translated into the language of the syllogistic. This language is thus a universal language of deductive logic.

---

[14] Even to explain the meaning of the logical vocabulary of the assertoric syllogistic, modal expressions are needed. Note, for example, Aristotle's semantic explanation of 'being predicated of all' and 'being predicated of none' as used as logical vocabulary in universal affirmative or negative categorical judgments (see *Analytica priora* 1. 1, 24 b 28–30).

[15] 'Free' is here the commonly used abbreviation for 'free of existence assumptions with respect to terms.'

[16] I do not count many-valued logics as 'non-classical' in the strict sense. They can be regarded as (hybrid) variants of 'classical' logic, since they differ from it only in that they allow, apart from the truth values of true and false, intermediate values for 'neither true nor false', from which function values can be calculated with truth tables. They presuppose the invalidity of the principle of bivalence and thus a change of the meaning of 'true' and 'false' (and of 'truth value'). See *Appendix 8*. However, the function value of a many-valued 'truth' function in all cases where none of its arguments is an intermediate value is the same as its value in two-valued 'classical' logic.

[17] On the controversial sense of an axiomatic quantified modal logic, see *Appendix 7*.

The systems of 'non-classical' logic can be built up as axiomatic systems just like 'classical' logic. But the validity of their axioms and derivation rules cannot be calculated by truth tables. The meaning of the logical vocabulary in the different systems of 'non-classical' logic thus differs from the meaning it has in 'classical' logic. For in 'non-classical' logic this vocabulary is not used truth-functionally but receives its meaning by the respective system of axioms and rules of derivation. What it means in each case to be logically true or derivable depends on this.

The relationships between the different systems of modern deductive logic (including insofar as they can be related to the axiomatic systems of mathematics which have developed since Peano) have become the subject of mathematical logic in the 20th century, which therefore has (as Gödel [1944, 125] describes it) "two quite different aspects": On the one hand, it has become a "section of mathematics treating of classes, relations, combinations of symbols, etc. instead of numbers, functions, geometrical figures, etc."; on the other hand, "it is a science prior to all others," which contains "the principles underlying all sciences"; "in this second sense," it is in accordance with the "idea of a logical calculus really sufficient for the kind of reasoning occurring in the exact sciences."

Whether and to what extent this very broad concept of mathematical logic strikes a chord with Kant's assumption that the logic of the particular use of understanding is an organon of this or that science is a question I do not deal with in this book. It is clear, however, that even according to this concept mathematical logic cannot be identified with general logic in the Kantian sense, i.e., in the sense of logical monism.

* * *

The text of the present book – including the above preface – corresponds to that which will be published next spring (2023) in a third and improved edition under the title 'Abhandlung über die Prinzipien der Logik' by Vittorio Klostermann (Frankfurt am Main). Among the changes and improvements that this edition contains over the earlier ones, many have been prompted by questions from the translator, William Clark Wolf, about the best possible translation of a dark German expression. I am grateful to him for his careful work on this book and not least for his philosophical interest to which it owes its existence.

Bielefeld, March 22, 2022.   Michael Wolff

Contents

Preface to the English Edition —— V

Introduction —— XIX

I Analytical Part: Analysis of Logical Languages

Section One
The Language of the Syllogistic —— 3
1   The Language of the Assertoric Syllogistic —— 3
        § 1 Syllogistic Propositional Schemata —— 3
        § 2 In Search of a Universal Language of Deductive Logic —— 5
        § 3 The Logical Vocabulary of the Assertoric Syllogistic —— 6
        § 4 Additions to the Logical Vocabulary of the Assertoric Syllogistic —— 8
        § 5 Categorical Form —— 12
2   The Language of the Modal Syllogistic —— 15
        § 6 The Logical Vocabulary of the Modal Syllogistic —— 15
        § 7 The Indispensability of the Logical Vocabulary of the Modal Syllogistic —— 22
3   Analysis of Expressions of Negation —— 24
        § 8 The Bivalence Principle —— 24
        § 9 The Principle of Excluded Middle —— 25
        § 10 Truth-Functional and Non-Truth-Functional Negation —— 27
        § 11 The Strong Logical Square of Assertoric Opposition —— 31
        § 12 The Weak Logical Square of Assertoric Opposition —— 33
        § 13 The Logical Square of Modal Opposition —— 34
4   Symbolic Abbreviations —— 36
        § 14 Syllogistic and Non-Syllogistic Modal Expressions —— 36
        § 15 Other Expressions in the Language of Elementary Syllogistic —— 38

Section Two
The Language of the Calculus of Classes —— 41
1   A Translation Program —— 41
        § 16 The Vocabulary of the Calculus of Classes —— 41
        § 17 The Strong Logical Square of Assertoric Opposition in the Language of the Calculus of Classes —— 43

2   The Problem of Implicit Existence Assumptions —— 46
           § 18 The Problem of the Empty Class —— 46
           § 19 Alternative Theories —— 47
3   Limits of the Language of the Calculus of Classes —— 50
           § 20 Grounds for a Modification of the Translation Program —— 50
           § 21 The Null Class and Empty Conceptual Scopes —— 54
           § 22 Translation of Class-Logical Propositional Schemata into the Language of the Syllogistic —— 58
           § 23 Reduction of Class-Logical Modes of Inference to Syllogistic Modes of Inference —— 63
           § 24 Advantages of a Transformation of the Language of the Calculus of Classes into the Language of the Calculus of Functions —— 65

Section Three
The Language of the Logical Calculus of Functions —— 72

1   A Translation Program —— 72
           § 25 The Representation of Concept Expressions with Functional Expressions —— 72
           § 26 The Function Theory of Concepts —— 74
           § 27 Grammatical and Logical Predicates —— 78
           § 28 Remarks on the Function Theory of Concepts —— 84
2   Examination of the Translation Program —— 90
           § 29 Subordination of Concepts in the Language of the Calculus of Functions —— 90
           § 30 Truth Functions and their Reduction to Non-truth-functional Forms —— 92
           § 31 An Extension of the Language of the Syllogistic —— 102
           § 32 The Categorical Form in the Language of the Calculus of Functions —— 105
           § 33 The Logical Form of Singular Propositions —— 110
           § 34 Quantifier Rules and the Weak Logical Square —— 115
           § 35 The Assumption of Non-Empty Domains —— 118
3   Limits of the Language of the Logical Calculus of Functions —— 125
           § 36 A Formal Language of Non-Pure Thinking —— 125
           § 37 Reference to Intuition and Symbolic Construction —— 129
           § 38 The Problem of Synthetic Propositions A Priori in Arithmetic —— 133

4   The Vocabulary of the Universal Language of Deductive Logic —— 135
           § 39 Non-Syllogistic Basic Rules in the Language of Syllogistic —— 135
           § 40 The Dispensability of an Expression for Logical Conjunction
               in the Elementary Language of Syllogistic —— 139

II Synthetic Part: Construction of the Logical Calculus of Functions from the Elements of the Syllogistic

           § 41 General Preliminary Remark —— 145

Section One
Rules for Deriving Rules —— 149
1   Principles —— 149
           § 42 Notation —— 149
           § 43 Definitions —— 150
           § 44 Basic Rules —— 153
2   Derived Rules —— 154
           § 45 Rules Derived From the Basic Rules —— 154

Section Two
Hypothetical and Disjunctive Syllogistic —— 158
1   Preliminary Remark —— 158
2   Principles —— 159
           § 46 Notation —— 159
           § 47 Definitions —— 160
           § 48 Basic Rules —— 164
3   Derivation of Formulas of the Hypothetical and Disjunctive
           Syllogistic —— 165
           § 49 Derived Rules —— 165
           § 50 Conditionalization —— 174

Section Three
Categorical Syllogistic —— 178
1   Preliminary Remark —— 178
2   Principles —— 178
           § 51 Notation —— 178
           § 52 Definitions —— 178
           § 53 Basic Rules —— 182
3   Derived Rules —— 184

§ 54 Rules of the Strong and Weak Logical Squares —— 184
§ 55 Conversion Rules —— 187
§ 56 Categorical Syllogisms —— 189
§ 57 Universally Valid Propositional Schemata —— 201

Section Four
Modal Syllogistic —— 203
1   Preliminary Remark —— 203
2   Principles —— 204
       § 58 Notation —— 204
       § 59 Definitions —— 204
       § 60 Basic Rules —— 210
3   Derived Rules —— 212
       § 61 Modal Consequence Rules —— 212
       § 62 Modal Conversion Rules —— 219
       § 63 Modal Syllogisms —— 225

Section Five
Contentful Syllogistic Inference —— 261
       § 64 Notation —— 261
       § 65 Comments on the Notation —— 263
       § 66 Examples of Contentful Syllogistic Inference —— 264
       § 67 Abbreviation Rules —— 267
       § 68 Examples of Contentful Syllogistic Inference (Continued) —— 268
       § 69 Further Abbreviation Rules —— 270

Section Six
Derivation of Formulas within the Framework of a System Extended Beyond the Limits of Elementary Deductive Logic —— 271
1   Principles and Metalogical Rules —— 271
       § 70 Notation —— 271
       § 71 Definitions —— 271
       § 72 Postulates —— 272
       § 73 Metalogical Rules —— 275
2   Derived Formulas —— 277
       § 74 Derivation of Truth-Functional Rules —— 277
       § 75 Derivation of Truth-Functional Laws —— 281
       § 76 Contentful Inference —— 286

Section Seven
Provability and Derivability within the Logical Calculus of Functions —— 293
   § 77 Notation —— 293
   § 78 An Axiomatic System of the Logical Calculus of Functions —— 294
   § 79 Definitions —— 296
   § 80 Theorems of the Calculus of Functions —— 297
   § 81 Soundness and Completeness —— 301

Conclusion —— 306
   § 82 Principles and Rules on Which the Complete System of the
      Calculus of Functions Depends —— 306
   § 83 Logical Form: A Review of the Results Attained —— 308
   § 84 Stages in the History of Logic —— 310

Appendix 1
On the Completeness of a Syllogistic without Logical Conjunction —— 315

Appendix 2
Mathematical Induction without Higher-Level Predicate Logic —— 321

Appendix 3
Reduction of Truth-Functional Expressions to Non-Truth-Functional
Expressions —— 329

Appendix 4
Compatibility and Incompatibility —— 333

Appendix 5
Modern Non-Syllogistic Systems of Modal Logic in Their Relationship to Modal
Syllogistic —— 337

Appendix 6
Non-Classical Systems of Logic in Their Relationship to the Logical Calculus of
Functions —— 351

Appendix 7
The Barcan Formula —— 357

Appendix 8
On Bivalence —— 359

Appendix 9
Absolute Logical Constants —— 365

Index of Symbols Used —— 369

Outline of the Rules Used Mainly in the Proofs of Part II —— 371

Index of Metalogical Rules Used in the Proofs of Part II —— 373

Index of Syllogistic Rules Used Directly in the Validity Proofs of Assertoric Syllogisms (in § 56) —— 375

Index of Modal-Syllogistic Rules Used Directly in the Validity Proofs of Modal Syllogisms (in § 63) —— 377

Index of Logical Rules Used Directly for the Derivation of Truth-Functional Rules and Laws (in § 74 and § 75) —— 379

Bibliography —— 381

Subject Index —— 387

Name Index —— 395

Introduction

Even if one is not prepared to accept that the analysis of language is the only or most important method of philosophy, one can still agree to a view which Gottlob Frege, one of the founding fathers of analytic philosophy, expressed in the following way. It is, he says,

> one of the tasks of philosophy to break the domination of the word over the human spirit by laying bear the misconceptions that through the use of language often almost unavoidably arise concerning the relations between concepts and by freeing thought from the means of expression of ordinary language which only burden it [. . .]. (Frege 1879, vi–vii [1967, 7])

By the "use of language," Frege means here the use of *natural* language.

But one can, or rather should, also connect the task of philosophy to the use of *non-natural* languages, especially to the use of formal languages which are applied in logic to rules of inference and to portray what Frege calls, in the passage just cited, "relations between concepts." Already from his perspective logic had "hitherto always followed ordinary language and grammar too closely" (Frege 1879, vii [1967, 7]). Hence, he saw that the use of formal-logical languages was open in part to the same critique as the use of natural languages; their vulnerability to critique was what provided him with the justification for inaugurating a new kind of formal-logical language – the concept-script (*Begriffsschrift*).

However, although we can find in Frege's writings numerous critical remarks on the language of the syllogistic going back to Aristotle as well as the "Boolean formal language," something like a systematic analysis of these languages is still absent from them. A systematic comparison of the capability of these languages with the capability of the concept-script – or with the capability of languages which are in use instead of the concept-script in modern deductive logic – has not (as far as I know) been undertaken until now, or at least not with the necessary thoroughness.

In Part I of this essay, in §§ 1–40, I will subject the *formal* languages of deductive logic to a systematic analysis and a systematic comparison of their merits. This comparison will especially bear on the capability of these languages to present *conceptual relations* (which Frege mentions in the quote just cited).

Part II, §§ 41–84, presupposes the analysis of Part I of this essay. In these paragraphs, a clear and precise presentation of the systematic structure of deductive logic will be given, and this in a language which is able to portray logical relations between *any* concepts. In this language, all rules and laws of deductive logic can be presented. It will emerge that syllogistic rules are distinguished by the fact that their validity depends only on the meaning of the logical vocabulary of this language.

I do not wish to put questions pertaining to the *historical* relationship between syllogistic and modern, mathematical logic at the center of the following investigations. (I will go into these issues only in passing, at the end of Part II, § 84.) I would rather like to be guided by the systematic question whether the language of syllogistic can be reduced to a more elementary, non-syllogistic language. In order to be able to answer this question – in the negative (to anticipate my answer) – it will be necessary at first to describe precisely the logical vocabulary with which the language of syllogistic represents conceptual relations.

– The question of *what* concepts really *are* will not be systematically treated in this book. Frege believed that a 'real definition' could not be given to determine 'the essence of concepts'. But he pointed out that the grammatical distinction between proper names (*nomina propria*) and substantives (*nomina appellativa*) corresponds in some way to the distinction between object-designators and concept words. Concept words are accordingly expressions which "come with the indefinite article and with words like 'all', 'some', 'many', etc." Thus, the expression 'square root of four' in the proposition 'There is at least one square root of four' corresponds to "the concept square root of 4."[18] At a later point (§§ 33–35) it will be necessary for me to go into Frege's views on proper names and concept expressions. For now, it may suffice to mention that I use the word 'concept' in this book so that it designates precisely what a concept word or a concept expression is used to indicate. Concept words and concept expressions should be understood as expressions that can be preceded by the definite or indefinite article or a word like 'all', 'some', 'many', etc. This usage corresponds to a use of the word 'concept' which is not only to be found in Frege but was also common practice in the traditional syllogistic. –

My application of the method of logico-semantic language analysis to the languages of logic will show that the view held by Frege, Hilbert, and others – that the logical vocabulary of the syllogistic is replaceable, without change in meaning, by truth-functional and quantified expressions, or by expressions of the calculus of classes – is untenable, since truth-functional expressions are equivalent to *complex* expressions, and class-logical and quantificational expressions to *nonformal* syllogistic expressions. The logical vocabulary of the syllogistic suffices, as can be proved, to render all valid rules and laws of deductive logic, including modal logic. On the other hand, the rules and laws formulated only within the language of a modern system of the calculus of functions or calculus of classes (to which "classical" predicate logic belongs) prove not to be universally valid, since their validity does not depend exclusively on the meaning of the logical vocabulary they use. These systems implicitly presuppose the validity of the syllogistic and are derivable from it so long as, in addition to the *universally valid* syllogistic

---

18 See Frege's letter to Liebmann from August 1900 in Frege 1976, 150 (1980, 92–93).

rules (and in addition to the necessary transformation rules with which complex and non-formal syllogistic expressions are translatable in other logical languages), certain *non*-universally valid rules (on which ultimately depend the divergence of these different logical systems) are formulated and accepted as valid in the syllogistic language. Part II of this essay will show extensively how this derivation is to be rigorously and seamlessly carried out, following a method already developed in the school of Aristotle.

I Analytical Part: Analysis of Logical Languages

Section One
The Language of the Syllogistic

1 The Language of the Assertoric Syllogistic

§ 1 Syllogistic Propositional Schemata

I understand by a *syllogistic propositional schema* an expression which is suited to present relations between concepts as they occur within a concept pyramid. Let α, β, γ, etc. be concepts of various generality, and let there be an order between them such that β and γ divide the concept α, so that they are subordinated to it and are at the same time coordinated with each other. In the same way, let δ and ε be subordinated to the concept β and coordinated with each other. Then the order just described is based on α, as a higher concept to β and γ, being the most general concept, while δ and ε, as lower concepts to β, are less general than α or β.[19] The hierarchy of these five concepts can be presented in a diagram which resembles a fragment of a pyramid

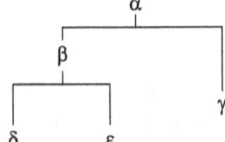

Figure 1

When one represents the conceptual relations portrayed in this diagram with expressions that resemble propositions except that all concept expressions are replaced with 'α', 'β', 'γ', 'δ', and 'ε', i.e., with concept variables, then the resulting expressions are those I will call syllogistic propositional schemata. As we can easily see from the relations illustrated in Figure 1, these are expressions like:
(1) 'every β is an α,'
(2) 'every γ is not a β,'
(3) 'some α is a γ,'
(4) 'some α is not a δ,'

---

[19] One already finds examples of conceptual hierarchies in Plato's dialogues. The investigations of conceptual hierarchies carried out in Plato's *Sophist*, 218e–221c, were especially important for the emergence of syllogistic. Cf. Kneale & Kneale 1975, 9–10, 44, and 67.

(5) 'if some α is an ε, then that α* is a β,'
(6) 'if some α is a β, then that α is not a γ,'
(7) 'either some α is a β, or that α is a γ,'
(8) 'if some α is a β, then either that α is a δ, or that α is an ε.'

These propositional schemata can be appropriately called '*syllogistic*' schemata insofar as they represent judgment forms which are of fundamental interest for the syllogistic theory of deductive inference.[20]

The syllogistic has always taken a special interest in such judgment forms because there are deductive inferences whose validity depends on certain arrangements of propositions which partake in these forms. Since Aristotle, inferences of this kind are called *syllogisms*. A syllogism is present, for example, when 'every δ is an α' is inferred from two premises of the form 'every δ is a β' and 'every β is an α'. Likewise, there is a syllogism when from two premises of the form 'if some α is an ε, then that α is a β' and 'some α is an ε', 'that α is a β' is inferred. The validity of syllogisms is independent of the conceptual content of the propositions that comprise them. That is, it is totally immaterial for the validity of syllogisms what names or nominal phrases appear (via concept variables) in the schemata of their premises and conclusion. Only the *logical form* of syllogisms is decisive for their validity. And logical form is represented by some arrangement of syllogistic propositional schemata.

That a syllogism possesses validity *on the basis of its logical form* alone implies that this validity can be made intelligible by explaining the meaning of the non-variable expressions which occur in the syllogistic schemata of the propositions that comprise it. Appropriate definitions which explain the meaning of these expressions will of course be needed to make intelligible the validity of rules which correspond to syllogistic inferences.

I will leave aside for now the question as to what precise content these definitions should have. For so far I have neither established a survey of what syllogistic propositional schemata there are, nor have I clarified the systematic relevance of these schemata for the theory of deductive inference. Hence it may suffice preliminarily to stipulate that the definitions we seek have the task of making explicit the

---

[20] Further below, I will come to speak about the fact that syllogistic propositional schemata can, in certain circumstances, result in truth-functional propositional schemata without themselves being truth-functional. Hence, one can read out not only syllogistic but also truth-functional propositional schemata from Figure 1.

* TN: The convention 'that . . .' is often used to represent the author's phrase "das in Rede stehende . . ." (lit. 'the . . . being discussed', or 'the . . . in question'). See below (§ 15) for further discussion of this phrase.

meaning tied to the expressions of syllogistic propositional schemata insofar as they are suited to represent conceptual hierarchies.

§ 2 In Search of a Universal Language of Deductive Logic

We can see that the task of the syllogistic consists in making intelligible, using definitions, the validity of rules according to which propositions conforming to propositional schemata follow from other such propositions. Provided it fulfills precisely this task, we can regard the syllogistic as a *subdomain of deductive logic*, namely, as a subdomain of the theory of valid deductive inference.

Yet we can also ask whether the syllogistic is an *irreducible, indispensable* subdomain of deductive logic.

Without doubt, deductive logic would get along without the syllogistic if it were possible to reduce all syllogistic rules of deductive inference to non-syllogistic rules. In that case, such *non-syllogistic rules* would be understood as forms of deductive inference which cannot be rendered by arranging syllogistic propositional schemata, or – to the extent that they could be rendered by such arrangements – whose validity does not depend on (or not only on) the meaning of the expressions that occur in syllogistic propositional schemata.

To be able to decide on the question whether syllogistic rules can be reduced to non-syllogistic rules, we must establish how far it is possible to translate the language of syllogistic propositional schemata into a language that can render both syllogistic as well as non-syllogistic forms of inference. If it should be possible to reduce all syllogistic rules to non-syllogistic rules, then it may also be possible to deal with a sphere of deductive logic in a uniform formal language, which encompasses the syllogistic and is thus greater than it. This language, if its sphere encompassed the whole of deductive logic, would be considered a universal language of deductive logic.

In the following sections I intend to test the pertinent possibilities of such a translation.

At the basis of this test, I will set a criterion by which the language of the syllogistic can be distinguished from non-syllogistic formal languages. This criterion consists in the fact that the only *object variables* which the syllogistic language requires are concept variables, so that all remaining expressions occurring in the language are used only to present relations between concepts as they belong to a hierarchical order as in the diagram in Figure 1. As for concept variables ('α', 'β', etc.), they are to be regarded as substitutes or placeholders for any *nomina apellativa*, or for nominal phrases of any complexity that can be prefixed by a definite or indefinite article. I call these expressions *concept expressions* or – if they are not composed of several words (like, e.g., 'horse') – *concept words*. When a concept expression is represented by a syllogistic concept variable, it is called a *term*.[21] Accordingly, a concept is to be regarded as *that for which a term stands*. Whatever else concepts may be does not need to be further explained for the purposes of the syllogistic. From the perspective of the syllogistic, concepts are what comprise the *conceptual content* or the *logical material* of a judgment. The remaining expressions belonging to the language of the syllogistic which occur in syllogistic propositional schemata make up the *logical vocabulary* of this language. From the standpoint of the syllogistic, the *logical form* of propositions or judgments depends on these, while their *conceptual content* depends on the interpretation conferred on the concept variables of each propositional schema that expresses their logical form.

For the moment, I do not need to make a final decision on the question as to which expressions can be counted among the logical vocabulary of syllogistic. No complete survey of this vocabulary is required at the outset of this investigation, since for the time being there is no telling how large the sphere of the syllogistic is. Rather, we must first know whether the syllogistic is possible as a systematically relevant, independent, irreducible sphere of deductive logic at all. This question can already be discussed to some extent with the logical vocabulary that occurs in propositional schemata (1) to (8), enumerated in § 1. Only when this vocabulary has proved to be dispensable or indispensable for deductive logic will we be able to deal with the question of how it relates to other parts of the syllogistic vocabulary.

§ 3 The Logical Vocabulary of the Assertoric Syllogistic

The logical vocabulary that occurs in the propositional schemata (1) to (8) consists in the following seven expressions:

'every . . .',
'. . . is a . . .',
'. . . is not a . . .',

---

[21] "Term" is a literal translation of the metaphor "ὅρος" used by Aristotle. John Stuart Mill, in his work *A System of Logic* (1843, Vol. 1, Ch. 1, § 3) called concept expressions "general names", in order to distinguish them from proper names and identifying labels, so-called "singular" or "individual" names. Following Mill, modern logicians sometimes call syllogistic terms *general terms* in order to distinguish them from *singular terms*. See Quine 1959, 65 (§ 12). The reasons for which I do not follow this custom will become clearer in what follows; see especially §§ 33–35 below.

'some . . .',
'if . . ., then . . .',
'that . . .',
'either . . ., or . . .'

It will be helpful to organize these seven expressions from a logico-semantic perspective.

As for the expressions 'every . . .', 'some . . .', 'that . . .', the traditional syllogistic literature uses them for what is called the *quantitative* determination – or simply the *quantity* – of a judgment.[22] These three expressions (or their equivalents) determine whether a given judgment is *universal, particular,* or *singular*.

The collocations '. . . is a . . .' and 'is not a . . .' establish a judgment as *affirmative* or *negative*. Affirmation and negation can be regarded as the logical forms of a judgement's *qualitative* determination – what is traditionally called the *logical quality* of a judgment.[23]

Finally, if a proposition contains the collocations 'if . . ., then . . .' or 'either . . ., or . . .', it is a *hypothetical* or *disjunctive* statement, respectively. The special role of these expressions is to indicate a *logical relation* between two or (as is possible in the case of the disjunctive statement) more than two parts of a statement.[24] The clauses of a hypothetical or distinctive judgment stand in a logically relevant relation to the extent that the truth or falsity of the judgment depends in a definite way on the truth or falsity of each of the relevant clauses. Thus, a hypothetical judgment says that it is impossible that the statement of its antecedent is true and the statement of its consequent false. That is, it says that there is a *consequence relation* between the statement of the antecedent and the consequent. A disjunctive judgment says, first, that no more than one of its sub-propositions can be true and, second, that it is impossible that one of its sub-propositions is false but none of the remaining sub-propositions true. In this way, it renders an *opposition within a totality of alternative* statements.[25]

---

22 Apuleius Madaurensis, "Peri hermeniae" (*Opera* 3, 1908, 177) is the *locus classicus* here.
23 This tradition goes back to Apuleius as well; see the passage just cited in note 22.
24 'Relation' as a name of a logical criterion for classifying judgments goes back to a terminology introduced by Kant; see *CPR*, § 9. It has sometimes been seen as appropriate from the standpoint of modern logic to polemicize with unnecessary sharpness against the classification of the forms of judgment which Kant carried out in his "arbitrarily compiled table of judgments" (Menne 1985, 11). We will deal with the question of the substantiality of this polemic in the course of the following investigation.
25 The words 'hypothetical' and 'disjunctive' are used in various ways in the literature on modern logic. I use them here and in what follows exclusively to designate syllogistic relations. I give a more precise explanation below in § 47. Already in the conception of the ancient Peripatetics

In this way, the logical vocabulary used in § 1 to formulate the syllogistic propositional schemata (1) to (8) can be divided, from a logico-semantic perspective, into three groups of expressions which we can take as the *logical constants* of the syllogistic.

§ 4 Additions to the Logical Vocabulary of the Assertoric Syllogistic

Given the criterion mentioned in § 2, according to which the language of the syllogistic is distinguished from non-syllogistic formal language in that its only object variables are concept variables, it is not hard to realize that a list of the logical constants of syllogistic would be incomplete if it contained only the seven expressions enumerated. This enumeration is indeed incomplete, since the propositional schemata (1) to (8) reflect only a special case of hierarchical conceptual arrangement. I had illustrated this arrangement in § 1 as a fragment of a pyramid in Figure 1.

---

and of Stoic logic, the junctor of the hypothetical proposition, 'if . . ., then . . .', portrays that a "consequence" (ἀκολουθία) obtains. Kant followed this conception as well (cf. *CPR*, § 9). The hypothetical 'if . . ., then . . .' should not, as often occurs in modern logic books, be confused with (truth-functional) subjunction (which is also sometimes called a conditional; in German it corresponds instead to the colloquial propositional connective 'nicht. . ., ohne daß. . .' ['not. . ., without. . .']) (See §§ 30 f.). It is hence unfounded when Günther Patzig, in his essay "Die logischen Formen praktischer Sätze in Kants Ethik" (1994, 212), writes that the truth value of 'if p, then q' depends "only on the truth value of the connected statements." Patzig adds as a comment: "A factual implication obtains between the statements p and q when the new statement produced by the 'if-then' junctor is *true*; logical implication obtains when this molecular statement is *logically true*. Only in this last case does it make unambiguous sense to speak of ground-consequence relations in terms of derivability. Kant did not see through the fuzziness of his contemporary logic, reflected in its fuzzy terminology; [. . .]." But this comment does not improve the matter. Rather, according to *modus ponendo ponens*, q is derivable from p if and only if 'if p, then q' is true. And 'if p, then q' is true if and only if q (factually or logically) follows from p. It is not necessary that 'if p, then q' is *logically* true for this consequence relation to obtain. Neither does the truth value of 'if p, then q' depend *only* on the truth values of p and q: if q is true or p false, q need not follow from p. Frege also made note of this situation in order to distinguish between the 'if-then' of the "hypothetical" judgment and that of the subjunction sign (i.e., his conditional stroke). See Frege 1879/1967, § 5; Frege 1882a, 102 (1968, 93). The terminological fuzziness of which Patzig here accuses Kant rests entirely on his own side, namely, in his confusion of subjunctive and hypothetical judgments. Incidentally, we can see here how much caution and restraint is needed in using the maxim which Patzig (1970, 85) recommends for the interpretation of philosophical texts, namely, the maxim: to assume that "wherever" it "is not possible" in such a text "to translate [its propositions and its context] into the Fregean concept-script or one of the later notations influenced by it," it "is not worth-while" to want "to proceed with the effort of philosophical interpretation, because the text is not sufficiently thought out."

There are, however, hierarchical conceptual relations which are not considered in this diagram. First of all, only *dichotomies* are considered in it, without allowing for conceptual divisions into three or more lower concepts.[26] Second, this diagram leaves out of consideration the case where the dichotomy consists in an *analytic concept division*. I speak of an analytic concept division in the following sense. Let α be a concept to which β is subordinated. Then every β is an α. And if, moreover, some α is not a β, but instead a γ, δ, or whatever else, then it belongs to some α not to be a β. Another way of saying this is that it falls under the concept not-β. Of two concepts which related to each other as β and not-β, I say that each is the *antonym* of the other. I call the division of a concept into a subordinate concept and its antonym *analytic*.[27] Every concept division into two or more lower concepts can be replaced by an analytic concept division without its validity being altered. Hence a propositional schema like (7) ('either some α is a β, or that α is a γ') can be replaced by:
(9) 'either some α is a β, or that α is a not-β'.

This can be illustrated by the following diagram:

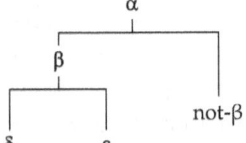

Figure 2

This diagram should not be misunderstood as if it said that the concept for which 'not-β' stands is *subordinated* to the concept for which 'α' stands in the same way as the concept for which 'β' stands is subordinated to it. That is, the scope of the concept not-β is too great on any interpretation of α and β to be contained in the scope of the concept α. Hence, Figure 2 should not be interpreted as always corresponding to a propositional schema of the form 'every not-β is an α'. Instead, Figure 2 should be interpreted so that it expresses a conceptual relationship that can be stated by the propositional schema
(10) 'some α is a not-β'.

---

26 The two-membered disjunctive judgment, as already indicated in § 3, is a special case.
27 As far as I know, it was Kant who introduced the expression 'analytic division' with the meaning just mentioned. Cf. Kant, *Critique of Judgment*, Ak. 5: 197.

Judgments conforming to (10) are distinguished from affirmative judgments in that they attribute a predicate to an object *by denying* another predicate of it at the same time. They are, however, also distinguished from negative particular judgments by the fact that they can be converted in the manner of affirmative particular judgments, so that from a judgment conforming to schema (10), we can derive a judgment that corresponds to the schema
(11) 'some not-β is an α'.

Judgments corresponding to schema (11) present a concept of the form not-β as satisfied (non-empty), since they affirm of an object (with the predicate α) the predicate not-β. In this way they attribute to the concept not-β a *scope* that is so large that, *with the exception of the conceptual scope of β*, the scope of every other concept is at least partially contained in it. I call this type of ascription of conceptual scope, following the nomenclature introduced by Kant, *limitation*.[28] Judgments which determine the scope of a concept through limitation can accordingly be called *limitative* judgments. There are not only particular limitative judgments, that is, judgments whose form correspond to the schema (10), but also universal and singular limitative judgments, i.e., judgments of the form 'every α is a not-β' or 'that α is a not-β'. Thus, a proposition corresponding to propositional schema (9) entails a singular limitative judgment of the form 'that α is a not-β' as a clause. Judgments of this form, as well as their corresponding universal limitative judgments, are like negative judgments in that they deny to objects a predicate β; but they are also like affirmative judgments in that convertible particular judgments are derivable from them.[29]

The form of the *limitative* judgment can be understood as a *logical quality*, and as such should be grouped together with the forms of the affirmative and negative judgment.

However, the limitative form plays only a subordinate role in the syllogistic, since limitative judgments can in many (or even most) cases be treated as special cases of affirmative judgments. Namely, the propositional schema of an affirmative judgment can be readily produced in all cases by transformation, simply by replacing the *concept expression schema* 'not-α' in the schema of the limitative judgment with a lower-case Greek letter, e.g., with 'β' here. After all, the expression schema 'not-α' stands merely for specific conceptual contents, which can also be represented by 'β'. Considered in this way, the schema of a limitative proposition contains a

---

[28] Schmid, "Limitation" (1798, 315). Cf. Sigwart 1889, 153.
[29] I will treat the relevant conversion rules systematically in the third section of Part III of this book.

schema for a concept expression instead of a concept variable. This schema does not represent any arbitrary term but can rather stand only for such concept expressions which designate the antonym of another concept *in terms of their content*. However, this way of considering them does not warrant us in regarding the linguistic expressions that can be used to represent antonyms as non-syllogistic vocabulary. For according to the criterion which I adduced above to distinguish syllogistic from non-syllogistic modes of expression, every limitative propositional schema can be considered as a syllogistic one, since they contain no object variables apart from concept variables and no expression occurs in them apart from what is necessary to represent conceptual hierarchies. Considered in this way, a limitative propositional schema is distinguished from other syllogistic propositional schemata only in that its logical vocabulary is suited to present conceptual relations that cannot be presented with the vocabulary of other syllogistic propositional schemata.[30]

Thus, the list of logical constants that syllogistic utilizes is to be expanded with the expression by which the propositional schemata (9) and (10) are distinguished from the schemata of affirmative and negative propositions, namely with the expression

'. . . is a not- . . .'.

If we pay attention to the *constellation of words* which occur in the logical constants used for affirmation, negation, and limitation, '. . . is a . . .', '. . . is not a . . .', '. . . is a not- . . .', then it is striking in comparing these constants that affirmation is expressed by the *lack* of a negating expression ('not') or by the *lack* of a privative prefix ('not-'). In colloquial contexts, there is no lack of words for expressing or emphasizing an affirmation or the affirmative character of a proposition. In German, for example, the word '*doch*' is available, a word which can be used syntactically just like 'not' and which serves to indicate a discrepancy between an affirmative statement and its previous denial or an expected denial. Even in symbolic logical languages, there is no lack of expressions which aid in making affirmations explicit. Thus, in traditional presentations of syllogistic since the Middle Ages the first two vowels *A* and *I* of the Latin verb *affirmo* are used to designate the affirmation of a universal or particular statement, while both vowels *E* and *O* of the verb *nego* serve to designate the negation of such statements.

---

30 Syllogistic rules which can be applied to affirmative judgments remain valid when these judgments are replaced by limitative judgments. This does not mean, however, that all valid syllogistic rules which hold for limitative judgments are reducible to other rules.

§ 5 Categorical Form

Just as the absence of 'not ...' and 'not- ...' can indicate an affirmation, so the absence of 'if ..., then ...' and 'either ..., or ...' in proposition schemata (1) to (4) ('every β is an α,' 'every γ is not a β,' 'some α is a γ,' 'some α is not a δ') can indicate the schemata of *categorical* propositions. However, since in accordance with § 2 concept variables can stand for nominal phrases of arbitrary complexity and can be composed of propositions of arbitrary complexity, it is possible that categorical propositions can consist of several sub-propositions, including hypothetical or disjunctive propositions. Thus, e.g., the following inference consists of nothing but categorical propositions:

> *Every dog who wags his tail when he approaches his master is a brave animal.*
> *No dog who is berated by his master is a brave animal.*
> *Therefore: No dog who is berated by his master is a dog who wags his tail when he approaches his master.*

This is a typical categorical inference, which is valid not according to the rules of hypothetical but of categorical inference. It is inessential for the form of the categorical judgment whether it is represented by a proposition composed of sub-propositions or not. What is essential for its form is rather that this proposition satisfies two conditions: first, that it is not part of a hypothetical or disjunctive proposition, but rather has *logical independence*; and second, that it renders a relationship between exactly two concepts which can be represented by logical constants such as, e.g., 'every ... is a ...', and in that way possesses *logical simplicity*.

In this connection, it is necessary to distinguish grammatically simple propositions from logically simple propositions. Propositions are *grammatically simple* when they are not composed of other propositions (with the help of relative pronouns or conjunctions); they thus neither consist of several main clauses nor are they propositions, which consist of a main clause and at least one subordinate clause. By contrast, propositions are *logically simple* only if they connect two concept expressions with the help of logical constants. The *logical* simplicity of propositions in no way precludes that they consist of several propositions *grammatically*.[31]

---

[31] The view espoused by Frege in § 4 of his *Begriffsschrift* that "The distinction of judgments into categorical, hypothetical, and disjunctive seems to me to have only grammatical significance," ultimately depends on a (unfortunately significant) confusion of grammatical and logical simplicity. For a more precise discussion, see M. Wolff 2006, 272–85.

In the syllogistic tradition of logic, the designation *categorical proposition* was introduced for logically simple propositions which are not part of a hypothetical or disjunctive proposition. Their syntactic position outside of a hypothetical or disjunctive proposition guarantees categorical propositions a certain type of *logical independence*, which in addition to logical simplicity is the second essential characteristic of categorical propositions. If one dispenses with this second characteristic and considers, as sometimes happens, logical simplicity as a sufficient mark of categorical propositions, then we get the view that hypothetical and disjunctive propositions can consist of categorical sub-propositions. However, with this view a characteristic property of categorical propositions is lost, namely that they do not, like hypothetical or disjunction propositions, attribute predicates to objects or say something of something *conditionally*, but rather *unconditionally*, indeed categorically (from the Greek κατηγορεῖν = to say something of something). Let p be a logically simple subject-predicate proposition and let it occur, e.g., in two places of a *modus ponendo ponens* inference, namely, as the antecedent of the first premise 'if p, then q' and as the second premise p, so that q is the conclusion. Then, *in terms of content*, the same proposition p may be present in two places, but what p says of objects unconditionally (categorically) in the second premise, p says only conditionally in the first premise (namely, only on the condition that q is not denied, but is a true proposition).[32] Hence, in terms of content, categorical judgments lie "at the basis of all other [judgments]," as Kant says in the *Prolegomena*, § 39 (Ak. 4: 325). For as *logically simple* subject-predicate-judgments they provide as it were the fabric for logically complex judgments. But they perform their function *as categorical judgments* only in virtue of the syntactic position they require as *logically independent* judgments.[33]

---

[32] Likewise, in 'if p, then q' q is stated on the condition that q. Incidentally, this also comports with Kant's conception of the hypothetical judgment. See his *Logic*, § 25, remark 2 (Ak. 9: 106). The view that Günther Patzig advances in his essay "Die logischen Formen praktischer Sätze in Kants Ethik" (1994, 214) that Kant's conception of the hypothetical judgment as a "conditional" mode of judgment is "incompatible" with Kant's "standard explanation," according to which the hypothetical judgment states a "consequence" of the statement of the consequent from that of the antecedent (*CPR*, § 9), is unfounded. Kant's standard explanation implies this conception, as one can easily make clear and as the ancient Peripatetics had already seen. For the relevant references to sources in the ancient literature, see Prantl (1855, vol. 1, 383–88).

[33] The marks of logical simplicity and logical independence can of course also be applied to hypothetical and disjunctive judgments. That is, there are logically simple and logically independent hypothetical and disjunctive propositions, namely, judgments in which the logical constants of the respective hypothetical or disjunctive proposition occur exactly once. But the marks of logical simplicity and logical independence are not constitutive for these judgments, since there can also be logically complex and thus logically dependent hypothetical and disjunctive judgments.

As the form of logically independent subject-predicate propositions, categorical form, much like the hypothetical or disjunctive form, has to do with a *logical relation*, yet it is one whose relata are not judgments, as with the hypothetical or disjunctive relation, but rather concepts. Every categorical judgment has to do with an ordered pair of concepts, one of which is to be regarded as the *subject concept*, the other as the *predicate concept* of the judgment. The logical distinction between the subject and predicate concept of a judgment corresponds to the grammatical subject-predicate distinction but does not coincide with it. *Grammatically*, every simple declarative proposition that is not composed of other propositions can be analyzed into subject and predicate. The *grammatical subject* of a proposition stands for that *about which* the proposition says something. The *grammatical predicate* stands for *what* it says about something. 'All humans are mortal', for example, is a declarative proposition which says of all humans that they are mortal. Hence, the component 'all humans' is its grammatical subject, while the remainder of the proposition, 'are mortal', is its grammatical predicate.[34] But the dissection of a proposition into grammatical subject and grammatical predicate does not coincide with the analysis of a logically simple proposition into its *logical subject*, its *logical predicate*, and its logical constants.[35] From a logical perspective, the proposition 'All humans are mortal' says the same thing as 'Every human is a mortal being'. In the conception of the syllogistic tradition, 'human' is here the logical subject, 'mortal being' the logical predicate. Accordingly, in the traditional conception the proposition has the logical form 'every S is a P'. Logical subject and logical predicate, whose positions are designated here with 'S' and 'P', have, *grammatically*, a common form: they are both expressions that can be preceded by a definite or indefinite article; and because of their common grammatical form their positions in the proposition can be interchanged. They are distinguished merely by this syntactic position. They are thus distinguished in that the logical subject is part of a grammatical subject, and the logical predicate is part of a grammatical predicate. Since the logical subject can

---

34 Traditional grammar, taking its orientation from Latin, counts not only auxiliary verbs and predicate names (predicatives) as belonging to the predicate, but also adverbs, object expressions, and any other expression that belongs to a subject-predicate proposition but not to its grammatical subject.

35 Frege pointed out in his 1879 *Begriffsschrift* that the subject-predicate distinction that is standard in the syllogistic is not directly applicable to functional expressions in quantificational logic. From this finding, he could have actually concluded that one should speak of *logical* subject and predicate only in the sense in which the syllogistic intends the distinction between subject and predicate. This would have been reasonable as well. In §§ 27–28 below, I will show how the traditional *grammatical* subject-predicate distinction can be applied to quantified functional expressions.

exchange its position in the proposition with that of the logical predicate, every subject concept of a categorical proposition is suited to act as predicate concept in other categorical propositions. This is why certain categorical judgments can be joined together in a *modus Barbara* inference and why it is permissible to pass immediately (by mere conversion) from 'no α is a β' to 'no β is an α'.

Unlike the forms of the hypothetical and disjunctive judgment, the categorical form presents no occasion to extend the list of logical constants assembled above. For this form is expressed not by using a certain logical vocabulary but only by the syntax according to which, within a logically simple proposition that is not part of a hypothetical or disjunctive proposition, pairs of expressions which are represented by concept variables are *ordered*.

The fact that categorical judgments are logically simple and logically independent subject-predicate propositions that do not occur as part of hypothetical or disjunctive propositions, does not preclude them from taking the position of a subordinate clause. For it changes nothing pertaining to logical form (i.e., the logical simplicity and independence of categorical propositions), when they are embedded in the expression 'it is true that . . .', 'it is possible that . . .', and 'it is necessary that . . .'. Nor does anything change in the logical form of hypothetical and disjunctive propositions through such an embedding.

2 The Language of the Modal Syllogistic

§ 6 The Logical Vocabulary of the Modal Syllogistic

One can understand the expressions

>'it is true that . . .',
>'it is possible that . . .',
>'it is necessary that . . .'

in such a way that they are equivalent to 'it is actually (in fact) true that. . .', 'it is possibly true that . . .', or 'it is necessarily true that . . .', respectively. Understood in this way, these logical constants express distinctions in *alethic modality*. Propositions which are introduced by one of the three enumerated modal expressions are called *assertoric*, *problematic*, and *apodictic*, respectively.[36]

---

[36] As such, these expressions must be distinguished from similar sounding expressions of *deontic* or *epistemic* modality, i.e., from expressions like 'it is permissible that . . .', 'it is forbidden that . . .' or 'it can be supposed that . . .', 'it is known that . . .', etc. See *Appendix 9*.

These expressions, which did not previously occur in my list of logical constants, can be counted among the syllogistic vocabulary for the following reasons. Concerning first the expression 'it is true that . . .', all previously enumerated propositional schemata ((1) to (11)) can be embedded in it. In this way they are converted (from being schemata of implicitly assertoric propositions) into schemata of (explicitly) assertoric propositions. Such a conversion changes nothing in the truth of the propositions corresponding to the logical form of schemata (1) to (11). Namely, every true non-modalized (i.e., not introduced by one of the three modal expressions) proposition A is an expression from which a proposition of the form 'it is true that A' logically follows.[37] For if A is true, the statement that A is true cannot be false. In addition, all valid inferences maintain their validity when one adds to their premises as well as to their conclusions (so long as they are not apodictic or problematic propositions) the prefix 'it is true that . . .'. For the same reason, the validity of all inferences is preserved if one sets aside this prefix in all places of its occurrence. Since this prefix only emphasizes a property which is presupposed anyway in every (including every non-modalized) premise of an inference, one often already designates non-modalized premises as assertoric. This is precisely the reason that the label 'assertoric syllogistic' has arisen for that part of the syllogistic which entirely disregards inferences from modalized, especially apodictic or problematic, premises. Connected with this is the fact that the expression 'it is true that . . .' (or an equivalent expression) has mostly not been treated as a logical constant in traditional treatments of the syllogistic at all. Even so, this does not speak against regarding it as a part of the logical vocabulary of the syllogistic.

There is a systematic reason for the adoption of the expressions 'it is necessary that . . .' and 'it is possible that . . .' in the list of logical constants as well. For just as the proposition 'it is true that p' can be directly deductively derived from p, so can the proposition 'it is possible that p', and p in turn can be

---

[37] If one takes only the propositional schemata (1) to (11) into consideration, one may say that this consequence relation also goes in the other direction. But this does not mean, strictly speaking, that the same holds for propositions of arbitrary content. Rather, whether a proposition of the form 'not p' follows logically from a proposition of the form 'it is true that p' depends on the meaning of the negation sign. As will emerge below (in § 10), there is a truth-ambivalent, paraconsistent use of negation which precludes the logical equivalence of 'A' and 'It is true that A'. Hence the expression 'it is true that . . .' is not, or at least not in all cases, simply redundant, as is often supposed. This issue can be set aside for the moment. However, it is not unimportant to take heed of it in a precise way. Alfred Tarski has shown that this equivalence is not applicable without contradiction to every colloquial statement. He thereby questioned "even the possibility of a consistent use of the expression 'true statement' that thereby agrees with the principles of logic and the spirit of common speech". See Tarski 1935, 458.

derived from the proposition 'it is necessary that *p*'. In other words: 'it is possible that *p*' is a logical weakening of the proposition *p* according to the scholastic rule *ab esse ad posse valet consequentia*, just as *p* is a logical weakening of the proposition 'it is necessary that *p*' according to the scholastic rule *a necesse esse ad esse valet consequentia*. Since these rules can be directly applied to every syllogistic propositional schema and remain valid in this application, it has not been merely convenient but also always standard to adopt the expressions 'it is possible that . . .' and 'it is necessary that . . .' into the logical vocabulary of the syllogistic.

Alethic modalities are called *de dicto* modalities because they state the actual, possible, or necessary truth of propositions (*dicta*). Yet statements about the possible or necessary truth of propositions can also be understood as statements about the possibility or necessity of the states of affairs these propositions are about. If the propositions are categorical propositions, the prefixes added to them 'it is possible that . . .' and 'it is necessary that . . .' can also be understood as dealing with *de re* possibility or *de re* necessity, respectively. Thus, a proposition of the form 'it is possible that every α is a β' can be understood such that it means the same thing as: 'for every α it is possible to be a β' or 'every α is possibly a β'. Quite generally, problematic categorical propositions can be understood as attributing to a thing (*res*) a possibility. Analogously, apodictic categorical propositions can be understood as saying of something (*de re*) that a predicate belongs to it necessarily.

Within the syllogistic, categorical modal statements are of interest to the same extent as it is of interest when we consider hierarchical conceptual arrangements to distinguish cases in which objects of a certain kind fall under a concept β *in all thinkable circumstances* (and thus necessarily) from cases in which this does *not* hold under all thinkable circumstances (thus not necessarily). For conceptual divisions cannot be conducted only on the basis of problematic categorical propositions without further ado. Thus, e.g., the proposition 'for every human it is possible to sleep' does not preclude this proposition from being true as well: 'for every human it is possible not to sleep'. If a stable classification system is to be rendered in a conceptual division, it is not enough to present conceptual relationships in non-modalized form according to the pattern of Figure 1 in § 1. For categorical statements whose logical form corresponds to one of syllogistic schemata (1) to (4) are as such only suited to classify objects through the subordination of concepts conditionally. Thus, a proposition of the form 'every α is a β' indeed subordinates the concept α under the concept β, but its form does not preclude that it is *possible* that objects that fall under the concept α do *not* fall under the concept β. In that way, it does not yet say anything at all about whether β is a stable superordinate concept of α and suited to classify the objects falling under α. It rather leaves it open whether β stands for a *contingent* property of the objects falling under α. Namely, non-modalized statements are not always statements which, if true, always follow from corresponding apodictic statements, so that they would be logical weakenings of such statements. Rather, if a non-modalized proposition (e.g., a proposition of the form 'every α is a β') is true and β stands for a *contingent* property of the objects falling under α, then a problematic proposition of the form 'for every α it is possible not to be β' is also true. And the latter proposition stands in contradiction to the apodictic strengthening of the first non-modalized proposition, i.e., to a corresponding proposition of the form 'for every α it is necessary to be a β'. In contrast, if a non-modalized proposition (e.g., a proposition of the form 'every α is a β') is true and β stands for a *necessary* (*non-contingent*) property of the objects falling under α, then there must be a corresponding apodictic proposition (namely, a proposition of the form 'for every α it is necessary to be a β') from which the non-modalized proposition follows as the latter's logical weakening.[38]

As these considerations show, the inclusion of the modal expressions 'it is necessary that . . .' and 'it is possible that . . .' as well as the inclusion of the *de re* variants of these expressions ('. . . necessarily . . .' or '. . . possibly . . .') in the logical vocabulary of the syllogistic is already demanded because we depend on the use of modal vocabulary to make explicit the just described double meaning of non-modalized syllogistic propositional schemata and to correct corresponding ambiguities in the use of non-modal logical constants. Once this modal vocabulary is introduced into the syllogistic, the question immediately arises about which deductive inferences depend for their validity on the meaning of the expressions of this vocabulary alone. The same question comes up with respect to the rest of the logical vocabulary of the syllogistic, and I will return to it in Part II of this book.

But are all modal expressions relevant for the syllogistic already captured in the logical vocabulary I have described so far? One could suppose that by forming antonyms of 'true', 'possible', and 'necessary' three further logical constants can be immediately produced, namely: 'it is non-true that . . .', 'it is impossible that . . .', and 'it is non-necessary that . . .'. These constants can be interpreted so that they are equivalent in sequence with the expressions

---

[38] Wolfgang Wieland (1966, 55) has argued that in the Aristotelian syllogistic the weakening rule, according to which a non-modalized proposition of the form A follows from an apodictic proposition of the form 'it is necessary that A', is invalid, since Aristotle always uses assertoric and non-modalized statements in his doctrine of necessary inferences "when he wants to assert the realization of one – among several – possibilities." Ulrich Nortmann has criticized this view with convincing arguments in Ebert & Nortmann 2007, 441–43. The validity of the mentioned weakening rule in no way precludes there being assertoric and non-modalized statements in which the realization of a possibility, which can also not be realized, is claimed.

'it is false that . . .',
'it is impossibly true that . . .', and
'it is contingent(ly true) that . . .'.

I would like to consider these somewhat more precisely one by one, in order to examine how much interest they may have for the syllogistic.

A proposition of the form 'it is false that p' is equivalent to 'it is not true that p', in any case so long as one assumes the validity of the bivalence principle, according to which there is no other truth value besides true or false. On this assumption, the expressions 'it is non-true that . . .', 'it is false that . . .', and 'it is not true that . . .' can be interchanged and are not to be regarded as special logical constants but simply as expressions of *de dicto* negation, i.e., negation of an explicitly assertoric proposition. I will get into the reasons for regarding the bivalence principle as valid in the syllogistic in § 8 below, as well as in *Appendix 8*. The use of a *de dicto* negation is dispensable in the syllogistic for the same reason that the use of 'it is true that . . .' is dispensable. Since 'it is true that p' follows logically from p, likewise 'not p' (i.e., the *de re* negation of p) follows from 'it is not true that p'. Nothing in the validity of syllogistic inferences alters when all *de dicto* negations that occur in their premises and conclusions are replaced with *de re* negations.[39]

Neither is a new logical constant introduced with the expression 'it is impossible that . . .'. After all, since a proposition is possibly true if and only if its truth is not impossible, this expression merely denies the possible truth of a proposition. It is thus equivalent to 'it is not possibly true that . . .'. Moreover, as an expression of the negation of a problematic proposition, it is equivalent to the apodictic expression 'it is necessarily true that not . . .'. For the impossibility of the truth of a proposition consists just in that its negation is necessarily true.

Accordingly, that the negation of a proposition is possibly true can be rendered by the negation of an apodictic proposition. The modal expression 'it is not necessarily true that . . .' is thus equivalent to 'it is possibly true that not . . .'.

The expression 'it is contingently true that . . .' is different from this in that it does not only negate the necessary truth of a proposition (and thereby immediately assert the possible truth of a negative proposition corresponding to it), but beyond this also negates the impossible truth of this proposition (and thereby immediately asserts the possible truth of the negative proposition corresponding to it). In this way, the expression 'it is contingently true that . . .' combines both problematic *de dicto* expressions, 'it is possible that . . .' and 'it is possible that

---

[39] The fact that *de re* and *de dicto* negations are not used equivalently in every respect and in all circumstances does not need to concern us further for now. I will return to this issue in §§ 8–10.

not . . .', and is thus logically stronger than either of these expressions on their own. Yet it should be noticed that this combination cannot pertain to every arbitrary pair of problematic propositions of which one is the contrary of the other. Rather, this combination pertains always only to such pairs of propositions in which *both* problematic propositions are *both* either universal or particular or singular. Thus, e.g., the (universal) propositional schema 'it is contingently true that every α is a β' combines the (universal) propositional schema 'it is possibly true that every α is a β' along with (likewise universal) propositional schema 'it is possibly true that *not every* α is a β', yet not the (particular) propositional schema 'it is possibly true that *not every* α is a β'. Similarly, the (particular) propositional schema 'it is contingently true that *some* α is a β' implies the (likewise particular) propositional schema 'it is possibly true that *some* α is *not* a β', but not the (universal) proposition schema 'it is possibly true that *not any* α is a β'. Only when the quantity of both propositional schemata agrees is the *de dicto* contingency (represented by 'it is contingent(ly true) that . . .') equivalent to a corresponding *de re* contingency, represented by '. . . is contingently a . . .'. For only in this case are both problematic *de re* expressions '. . . is possibly a . . .' and '. . . is possibly not a . . .' combined by the *de re* expression '. . . is contingently a . . .'. Accordingly, every proposition of the form 'it is contingent(ly true) that A', as well as every proposition which contains such a proposition as a clause, can be regarded as abbreviating a combination of a pair of propositions that are problematic or contain such propositions as clauses.[40]

From my analysis of the three expressions

'it is false that. . .',
'it is impossibly true that. . .', and
'it is contingent(ly true) that. . .',

---

[40] The fact that contingent propositions are equivalent to a pair of problematic propositions enables one to recognize that the modality of contingent propositions is a second kind of possibility. Along the same lines, Aristotle distinguishes in *An. pr.* 1. 13 two meanings of the word "possible." According to the first meaning, the possible is the contingent, namely, "[what] is not necessary but nothing impossible will result if it is put as being the case" (*An. pr.* 32 a 18–20 [1989, 18]). According to the second meaning, the possible is a logical weakening of the necessary; according to this meaning, one can say of the necessary "that it is possible" (32 a 20–21 [1989, 18]). In the literature on Aristotle, the modality of *contingent* propositions is called 'two-sided possibility', while the modality of *simple problematic* propositions is called 'one-sided possibility'. The kinds of possibility statement distinguished in this way can be regarded as logical weakenings of two kinds of assertoric statement: on the one hand, of statements which deal with the factual or actual, which is the realization of a possibility, but which might not have been realized; on the other hand, of statements which deal with the factual or actual but as itself a logical weakening of apodictic statements.

we find that, if one assumes the validity of the bivalence principle, they contain no logical vocabulary whose meaning could not be made explicit by means of the logical vocabulary I have already introduced. There is thus no compelling reason to add these expressions to the vocabulary that expresses the distinction between assertoric, problematic, and apodictic propositions.

There is, however, also no reason to reduce the modal vocabulary any further than this. It may be true that the expressions 'it is possible that not . . .' and 'it is not necessary that . . .' are equivalent, just as the expressions 'it is not possible that . . .' and 'it is necessary that not . . .' are equivalent, and thus that the expressions 'it is necessary that . . .' and 'it is not possible that not . . .' and likewise the expressions 'it is possible that . . .' and 'it is not necessary that not . . .' are pairwise equivalents. But since neither the expression 'it is possible that . . .' nor 'it is necessary that . . .' has a noticeable privilege over the other, they have equal interest for the syllogistic and hence should be adopted in its list of the logical constants.[41] Accordingly, if A is a syllogistic propositional schema, then the expressions 'it is necessary that A' and 'it is possible that A' can be regarded as equally legitimate propositional schemata.

Finally, concerning distinctions in the *de dicto* and *de re* use of modal expressions (e.g., the use of 'possibly' in 'it is possibly true that . . .' and '. . . is possibly a . . .'), it suffices to establish for the time being that though these distinctions may well concern grammar, they need not affect the meaning of these expressions

---

[41] The content of this list agrees with the content of the table of judgments with which Kant claimed to provide a systematic division and complete enumeration of elementary logical forms. This agreement is not accidental, but rather rests on the fact that Kant developed the content of the table of judgments on the basis of a description of what he called the 'logical use of the understanding' – the *usus logicus intellectus*. Kant understood this latter as consisting in the use of concepts in judging insofar as these concepts are related to each other in subordination relationships. See M. Wolff 1995, 192–94. The twelve forms of the table of judgments are in Kant's view *elementary* logical forms in the sense that they can be combined into more complex forms. Each of the proposition schemata (1) to (11) enumerated above represents a complex logical form; and if the issue is *the* logical form of a judgment, then we typically mean a form composed of several elementary forms. The fact that Kant's table of judgments is only supposed to contain *elementary forms* has sometimes been missed by logicians. Thus, Arthur N. Prior (1967b, 549) supposes that Kant's division according to quality is "absurd": "where would one put, for example, the forms 'X is-not not-Y' and 'Not-X is Y'?" If we interpret the examples of propositional schemata Prior brings in as schemata of predicative propositions (not as examples of schemata for identity propositions), then the first example (according to Kant's approach) pertains to assertoric, quantitatively indefinite, categorical propositions, in which the forms of negative and limitative judgments are combined. The second example pertains to assertoric, quantitatively indefinite, categorical, affirmative propositions, which result from infinite propositions through conversion, just as particular propositions result from universal propositions through conversion.

when they are applied to syllogistic propositional schemata. This holds in any case for the modal expressions of problematic, apodictic, and contingent propositions. *De dicto* and *de re* expressions of the same modality are to that extent equivalent. (See also *Appendix 7.*)

§ 7 The Indispensability of the Logical Vocabulary of the Modal Syllogistic

However, to pursue the question of whether the logical vocabulary of the syllogistic can be translated into a non-syllogistic formal language that is suitable for other parts of deductive logic, we do not need to draw attention to modal expressions, or at least not in the first instance. For even to make explicit the meaning of (non-modal) syllogistic vocabulary with the help of a non-syllogistic formal language, one will in no way be able to dispense with the use of the *modal* vocabulary of the syllogistic. We can preliminarily clarify this relative indispensability of the expressions of the modal syllogistic in the following way.

I already pointed out in § 3 that the 'if-then' connection of the hypothetical proposition expresses a consequence relation that obtains between a proposition p and a consequent q if and only if it is impossible that the statement of its antecedent is true and the statement of its consequent false. For this reason, we should understand a hypothetical proposition of the form 'if p, then q' as equivalent to a proposition of the form 'it is impossible that p and not q'. The propositional schema 'it is impossible that A and not B' is, as it seems, not a syllogistic propositional schema (even if A and B are themselves such schemata). For it contains at least one logical constant, namely '... and ...', which according to § 1 should not (or not without further ado) be assumed to belong to the logical vocabulary of the syllogistic. In this way, it does look as though one can translate the schema of a hypothetical proposition into a language which contains non-syllogistic vocabulary. But it is, at least so it seems, also unavoidable in this translation to make use of the vocabulary of the modal syllogistic. For though 'it is impossible that ...' can be replaced by a *different* modal expression, namely by 'it is necessary that not ...', it cannot (so it seems) be replaced by an expression in which no constant of the modal syllogistic occurs at all. This fact leads us to expect that at least hypothetical propositional schemata can be translated into a non-syllogistic language only if this language has adopted the *modal* vocabulary of the syllogistic.

Modern, *non-syllogistic modal logic* can be described such that it makes use of at least one of the syllogistic expressions of alethic modality, but it connects this usage with the use of a truth-functional vocabulary. It arose from the semantics of the hypothetical proposition and originated in the logical work of Clarence Irving Lewis as the logic of *strict implication*. Following Hugh MacColl, Lewis interpreted the form of the hypothetical proposition 'if A, then B' as equivalent to 'it is impossible that A is true and B false'.[42] He assumed (Lewis & Langford 1932, 123) that according to this interpretation the form could be presented in symbolic notation with an expression which corresponds to the following schema:

'∼ ◇ (A & ∼ B)'.

In this schema, '... & ...' stands for *logical conjunction* ('... and ...'), the tilde '∼ ...' expresses *negation*, and the diamond sign '◇ ...' can be considered an abbreviation for 'it is possible that ...'. The logical constants '... & ...' and '∼ ...' are used in this schema as *truth-functional* signs. That is, 'A & B' and '∼ A' are schemata for truth functions. Truth functions are to be understood as those functions whose values are truth values and whose arguments are statements which have a truth value. If *p*, *q*, and *r* are statements which are true or false, then *p* & *q* and ∼ *r* are functions whose truth value depends only on the truth values of *p*, *q*, and *r*. In contrast to '... & ...' and '∼ ...', however, neither '◇ ...' nor 'if ..., then ...' is a truth functional sign. Namely, if a proposition fills the empty place of '◇ ...', then its truth will be counted by the prefixed modal sign as possible truth, and its *possible* truth obviously does not depend on which truth value it *actually* has. Similarly, the truth of a hypothetical proposition does not depend on the truth values of its subpropositions alone. For such a proposition is true, as we have seen, only if it is not *possible* that its consequent is false and its antecedent true.

Lewis called the relation he accepted between the clauses of a hypothetical proposition of the form 'if A, then B' *strict implication*, and to abbreviate '∼ ◇ (A & ∼ B)' he introduced the expression

'A ⥽ B'.

Modern axiomatic modal logic has come about because Lewis, on the basis of the definition of strict implication, established various axiomatic systems whose basic formulas include the three logical constants '... & ...', '∼ ...', and '◇ ...' as the only as undefined signs.[43] 'It is necessary that ...' is replaced in this language by '∼ ◇ ∼ ...'; 'it is impossible that ...' is rendered in this language with '∼ ◇ ...'.

We must thus ask of the three signs '... & ...', '∼ ...', and '◇ ...' how they relate to the logical vocabulary of the syllogistic.

---

42 See MacColl 1903, 356. Cf. Hughes & Cresswell 1977, 214.
43 Kneale & Kneale 1975, 549–50. For details, see *Appendix* 5 below.

3 Analysis of Expressions of Negation

§ 8 The Bivalence Principle

At first glance, apparently only '... & ...' is a sign that cannot be read as an abbreviation for one of the constants of the syllogistic as enumerated above. As a *truth-functional* sign, it connects two propositions to each other so that the proposition which arises out of this connection is true if and only if the connected propositions are true, while it is false whenever one of its sub-propositions is false.

By contrast, the signs '~ ...', and '◇ ...' suggest a comparison with syllogistic vocabulary. If it is defined no further, '◇ ...' can simply mean the same thing as the expression of the modal syllogistic 'it is possible that ...'. In systems of modal logic which use the defined sign '□ ...' ('it is necessary that...') as an abbreviation of '~ ◇ ~ ...', however, it is standard to equate the meaning of '◇ ...' with the meaning of '~ □ ~ ...'.[44] Whether '◇ ...' and '□ ...' in these systems are equivalent to the modal expressions of the syllogistic depends partly on how '~ ...' as a sign for truth-functional negation relates to *syllogistic negation*, and partly on how '~ ◇ ...' and '~ □ ...' relate to the *syllogistic modal expressions* 'it is impossible that...' and 'it is not necessary that...'.

Regarding the relationship of the sign for *truth-functional* negation to *syllogistic negation*, we first need an answer to the question of whether 'not A' taken as a *syllogistic* schema of a negative proposition is a *truth-functional* expression or not.

One should not dismiss this question in the opinion that *every* negation of a proposition is a truth-functional negation.[45] For this opinion is not tenable without further justification. Consider, for example, the following propositions:

(a) 'the greatest number is not greater than a thousand' and
(b) 'the greatest number is greater than a thousand'.

Proposition (a) negates (the content of) proposition (b) in a certain respect. But proposition (a) does not contain a *de dicto* negation of proposition (b), and thus does not say explicitly *that* (b) is false; rather, proposition (a) contains only a *de re* negation regarding the greatest number.[46]

---

[44] The sign '□ ...' was introduced as an abbreviation for '~ ◇ ~ ...' by Ruth C. Barcan (1946, 12). Cf. Hughes & Cresswell 1977, 347.

[45] Very many logic books unfortunately do just this, as if there were only truth-functional negations. In those which do not do this, a systematic treatment of kinds of negation is for the most part lacking.

[46] The distinction encountered here between two kinds of negation is similar to the distinction Fred Sommers has introduced between "denying a predicate" and "negating a sentence", though not exactly. Predicate negation for Sommers consists in the use of terms of the form 'not-α'. See

To be able to analyze what it is to *negate* a proposition (or its content) without negating it in the sense of a *de dicto* negation, we first should know what it would be to say that proposition (b) is *false*. To say a proposition is false means at least: *saying it is not true*. Supposing the word 'false' is used as synonymous with 'not true', it *suffices* for the truth of a *de dicto* negation that the negated proposition is not true.

Of course, no one is prevented from using the word 'false' in a different way: one may treat both propositions (a) and (b) as if they were not *false* but rather *meaningless* – namely, *neither true nor false* – since they deal with something that does not exist. Yet then one assumes a usage in which 'false' and 'not true' are *not* synonyms. We should not attempt here to decide which usage is correct, since one can use words however one likes. But we can (and should) stick to a usage once we have chosen it (at least in a scientific treatment).

In the following, I will use 'false' and 'not true' as equivalent expressions and precisely for that reason will assume that a declarative proposition which is not true is false. I call this assumption, since it is fundamental, the *bivalence principle*. This principle should be considered a semantic principle: it stipulates the meaning of the word 'false', since it lets the falsity of a proposition *consist* in its not being true.

It follows from the bivalence principle that there is no truth value besides the true and the false.[47] This too follows from it: a proposition containing a *de dicto* negation of proposition (b) is for its part already true if (b) is not true. Even proposition (a) is true or false, according to the bivalence principle. As a *de re* negation, it does not need to be true if (b) is not true.[48]

§ 9 The Principle of Excluded Middle

The bivalence principle should not be confused with the *principle of excluded middle*.[49] The latter principle does not merely stipulate the meaning of a word and is thus not merely a semantic principle. It is also less fundamental than the bivalence

---

Sommers 1982, viii; 326–27; 340. *De re* negation is what Aristotle speaks about in *De Interpretatione* 17 a 26 (1984, 27), when he says: "[A] negation is a statement denying something of something."

47 To avoid misunderstandings, one should say more precisely: The bivalence principle says that *for expressions which are used as declarative propositions, i.e., as judgments*, there is no truth value apart from true and false and that they must have at least one of these two values. I provide a more extensive discussion of the bivalence principle below in *Appendix* 8. I will argue there that the formality of formal logic is incompatible with the invalidity of this principle.

48 It is a widespread error to think that even "purely formally" "the negation of a false proposition [must] be true." Patzig 1970, 83.

49 The confusion of the two principles can be found again and again, e.g., in Pirmin Stekeler-Weithofer's article "Satz vom ausgeschlossenen Dritten" (1992, 1198). By contrast, compare the

principle. It plays the role of a basic logical supposition, by which it is assumed that of two propositions of which one contradicts (or contradictorily negates) the other, exactly one is true; *tertium non datur* ['there is no third']. Whether this supposition is universally valid and thus holds for *all* negations depends on whether there are negations which are not truth-functional (or contradictory negations).[50]

For truth-functional negations the principle of excluded middle is universally valid and fundamental. This can be shown in the truth table for ~ A:

~A	A
F	T
T	F

De dicto negations as well, provided they explicitly state that an affirmative proposition is false, satisfy the principle of excluded middle and are contradictory or truth-functional negations. It is a sufficient and necessary condition of their truth that the negated proposition is not true. And it is false for its part if and only if the negated affirmative proposition is true.

However, one can illustrate the fact that there are non-contradictory (non-truth-functional) negations with the example of propositions (a) and (b) from § 8.

According to the bivalence principle both (a) and (b), as declarative propositions, have (at least) one of the two truth values. They also admit an interpretation which is incompatible with the principle of excluded middle, because they do not contradict each other but are contrary, i.e., they are *both* false, even though proposition (a) negates proposition (b). They are ostensibly to be taken as *singular* propositions, which as such can only be true when they refer to a definite singular object. Since there is no question of a greatest number – whether greater than a thousand or not – neither (a) nor (b) refers to a definite singular object. Hence it is neither true that the greatest number is greater than a thousand, nor is it true that the greatest number is *not* greater than a thousand.

What I have determined regarding the pair of propositions (a) and (b) holds quite generally for any pair of singular propositions of the form 'that α is a β' and

---

clear and distinct manner in which Richard Purtill distinguishes between the two principles in his articles "Principle of Bivalence" (1995a, 644) and "Principle of Excluded Middle" (1995b, 645).

50 Aristotle formulated the principle of excluded middle (without calling it thus) just so that it applies only to pairs of *contradictory* propositions: "But then neither is it possible for there to be anything in the middle between contradictories, but it is necessary either to affirm or to deny one thing, whatever it may be, of one thing" (*Metaphysics* 4. 7, 1011 b 24–25 [2016, 78]). Aristotle does not provide an independent criterion for contradictoriness. (Cf. also *Metaphysics* 10. 7, 1057 a 33 ff.)

'that α is not a β'. These pairs consist exclusively of false propositions if and only if (with the same interpretation of α and β) a universally negative proposition is true which states that no α is a β. The principle of excluded middle finds no application to these pairs of propositions taken in general.

Note well that the principle of excluded middle is applicable to *every* pair of propositions of which one *truth-functionally* or contradictorily negates the other. This holds even with a pair of propositions which relate to each other as A and ~ A, and A is the syllogistic schema of a singular affirmative proposition. In no interpretation of the concept variables occurring in A can both A and ~ A be false. If one replaces, e.g., the false proposition

(a) 'the greatest number is not greater than a thousand'

with the truth-functional expression

(a') '~ [the greatest number is greater than a thousand]',

then a true proposition takes the place of a false one. For the sub-proposition standing in the brackets of (a') is false, and consequently (a') is true according to the principle of excluded middle.

§ 10 Truth-Functional and Non-Truth-Functional Negation

In order to make it clear that proposition (a) – as a false proposition – is not supposed to be the translation of (a'), but rather a *non-contradictory* and *non-truth-functional negation* of (b), we require an unambiguous terminology. Let A be a formula which corresponds to the syllogistic schema of an affirmative or negative proposition. Then I will use the designation '*N* A' for the non-truth-functional negation of A. By '*N* A' it is asserted that A is false, *without also asserting*, were A equal to *N* B, *that B is true*. The meaning (or the use) of

'*N* . . .'

can be fixed by way of definition[51] so that, for every interpretation in which A and B are true or false proposition, the following holds:

---

[51] A definition as it is made here (and in what follows, for the use of logical constants other than *N*) I call a *use-definition*, where it is permitted to make use in the *definiens* of the sign whose use is the subject of the definition.

(1) *N* A is true if A is false or there is a false proposition B, with A = *N* B, and it is possible that *N* A and *N* B are both true;
(2) *N* A is false if A is true or there is a true proposition B, with A = *N* B, and it is possible that *N* A and *N* B are both false. (Cf. § 43, def. 2)

In distinction from ~ B, according to this definitional stipulation *N* B does *not* have the opposite truth value of B in every interpretation in which B is a false proposition. Let us assume an interpretation in which B is true or false, without a proposition C existing with B equivalent to *N* C. Then the truth table for *N* B shows that if B has the value F, it is *indeterminate* what value *N* B has.

N B	B
?	T
?	F

Since with the meaning I have given to the bivalence principle, it is strictly universally valid, this table does not mean that there is a third truth value of *N* B besides true and false, called '?'. It means rather only that the value assigned to *N* B, if B has the value F, is indeed, according to the bivalence principle, T or F, but it is not fixed by the value of B alone which value *N* B has. To be sure, the statement that *N* B is true, just like the statement that ~ B is true, entails the statement that B is false. But it is not at all the case that the statement that B is false would also preclude that *N* B is also false. *N* B and B could also both be true. Let 'B' abbreviate the proposition '*N* A'. Then, if A and *N* A are both false, A and *N* A should both be negated, so that, according to the bivalence principle, B and *N* B are mutually compatible and both true. Considered in this way, both lower rows of the columns for *N* B and B in the truth table above are integrated into the four lower rows of the columns for A (= *N* B) and B in the following table:

	NNN A	*NN* A	*N* A	A	B
. . .	F	T	F	T	T
. . .	T	F	T	F	T
. . .	F	T	F	T	F
. . .	T	F	T	F	F

Incidentally, this table (which could be continued to the left) displays how the truth value of *N* A, with A = *N* B, develops according to its definition. The case in which A and B both have the value T occurs precisely when there is a proposition C, with B = N C, and both C and N C are false. What this table does not capture is the fact that the value T for B in the first row and value F for A in the lowest row are definitionally compatible with their respective opposite values. Accordingly, a proposition of the form N B can, in precisely determined limit cases, be *truth-ambivalent*, i.e., both true and false. That is, the proposition is true in these cases insofar as it correctly negates a false proposition B, and false insofar as it is itself correctly negated by NN B. We call such attribution of opposite truth values to one and the same proposition 'paraconsistent' and a logic which in a restricted and regulated way admits such attribution a 'paraconsistent logic'.[52]

We can also indirectly extract the following from the last table: the truth values of ~ A and N A concur exclusively in cases in which A and N A have opposite truth values and there is no proposition B of which A is the negation. If A is true, then both N A and ~ A are false, and NN A and ~ ~ A are both true.[53] Yet an assessment in which NN A is true only says that N A is false, but *not* also that A is true. For A and N A could both be false. Hence, the true values of A and NN A could be different, while the true values of A and ~ ~ A are always the same.

Now it is of the greatest logical significance that the negation designated by 'N . . .' under a certain assumption turns into a truth-functional negation. Namely, '~ A' is ostensibly interchangeable with (or substitutable for) the expression

'N A'

if and only if in every interpretation in which A is true or false, the expression

'either A or N A'

is a true proposition. With 'either A or N A' it is supposed that not both A and N A are false. On this supposition, the meaning of 'N A' turns into the meaning of

---

[52] A paraconsistent logic in the strict sense explicitly annuls, in a restricted and regulated way, the *principle of the incompatibility of opposite truth values*, which is tacitly assumed as universally valid in truth-functional logics. Those logical systems which are at least compatible with the invalidity of this principle can be called paraconsistent in a broader sense. It should thus be kept in mind that the invalidity of this principle is compatible with the unrestricted validity both of the bivalence principle as well as of the principle of excluded middle for contradictory propositions. As will emerge in what follows, the "elementary" syllogistic (of § 15) can be understood as a paraconsistent logic. The Aristotelian syllogistic can also be presented as a paraconsistent system in the broader sense just now discussed. On the origin of the label 'paraconsistent logic' see *Appendix 6* below.

[53] When A is true and not equivalent to N B (for arbitrary B), it follows from A, according to the just established meaning of 'N A', that NN A is true.

'∼ A'. We can also carry out this transformation by replacing the expression 'either A or N A' with

$$\text{'if } NN \text{ A, then A'.}^{54}$$

That is, '∼ A' may be substituted for 'N A' if one assumes (in every interpretation in which A is true or false) that 'if NN A, then A' is a true proposition, hence, so that the principle *duplex negatio affirmat* ('double negation affirms') holds. In the following, this assumption is called *the principle of the affirmative use of double negation*.

We must now ask how the negation designated by 'N . . .' is related to that negation which is contained in my list of the logical constants of the syllogistic (see § 3).

Here our concern is the negation which appears in the syllogistic schemata of universal and particular negative propositions. This can be quite adequately rendered using the sign 'N . . .'. In line with the way we have fixed the meaning of the logical constants as they appear in particular and universal affirmative propositions (thus in the contradictory opposites of the just mentioned negative propositions), the rules for the use of 'N . . .' can also be fixed so that the syllogistic schemata of these propositions are each equivalent to their respective double non-truth-functional negations:

Thus, the schema of the *universal negative* proposition 'every α is not a β' is equivalent to 'no α is a β'. 'No α is a β' is the contradictory of 'some α is a β'. Two propositions are contradictories of each other when they can be neither both false nor both true. Hence, as the contradictory of 'no α is a β', 'some α is a β' is equivalent to the non-truth-functional negation of 'no α is a β', and thus equivalent to

$$\text{'}N \text{ [no α is a β]'.}$$

In contrast, 'no α is a β' is equivalent to the simple non-truth-functional negation of 'some α is a β', i.e., it is equivalent to

$$\text{'}N \text{ [some α is a β]'.}$$

The schema of the *particular affirmative* proposition 'some α is a β' is accordingly equivalent to '*NN* [some α is a β]'.

---

54 To be sure, this expression (which permits the interpretation that *NNN* B follows from *N* B) is not equivalent to the expression 'either A or *N* A'. For the latter also entails the supposition that *NN* A follows from A, if A is not equal to *N* B (for arbitrary B). But this supposition is already valid on logical grounds (see note 53 above and § 44, rule (I. 1)) and thus does not need to be cited explicitly.

As for the schema of the *particular negative* proposition 'some α is not a β', it is equivalent to 'not every α is a β' and is the contradictory opposite of 'every α is a β'. 'Every α is a β' is, as the contradictory opposite of 'not every α is a β', equivalent to the elementary negation of 'not every α is a β', and 'not every α is a β' is thus equivalent to the elementary negation of 'every α is a β', i.e., equivalent to

'N [every α is a β]'.

The schema of the *universal affirmative* proposition 'every α is a β' is accordingly equivalent to 'NN [every α is a β]'.

§ 11 The Strong Logical Square of Assertoric Opposition

In order to present the logical relations between the schemata of universal and particular propositions in a clear manner, I have followed the tradition in organizing these schemata in a square in such a way that the positional relations between them correspond directly to logical relations. In deference to the traditional nomenclature, I call these relations *the relations of the logical square of assertoric opposition*.

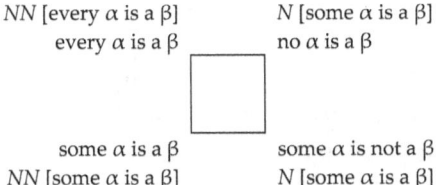

NN [every α is a β]	N [some α is a β]
every α is a β	no α is a β
some α is a β	some α is not a β
NN [some α is a β]	N [some α is a β]

Figure 3

The following relations are hereby intended:
1. Propositions are *equivalent* when they (with the same interpretation of the concept variables α and β) come from schemata which are assigned to the same corner of the square.[55]

---

[55] All propositional schemata which appear in Figure 3 can of course be replaced by other equivalent expressions. This is particularly relevant for expressions which are in the plural. These are expressions like 'all α are β', 'all β are not β', 'some [*einige*, rather than *irgendein*; WCW] α are β' and 'some α are not β'. For reasons of clarity, I will use the expressions appearing in Figure 3 as the standard expressions of the syllogistic propositional schemata.

2. Propositions are *contradictories* of each other when they (with the same interpretation of the concept variables α and β) come from schemata which are opposed diagonally to each other.
3. Propositions are *contraries* of each other when they (with the same interpretation of the concept variables α and β) come from schemata which are assigned to different upper corners of the square.
4. A proposition that comes from a schema (with any interpretation of the concept variables α and β) which is assigned to one of the lower corners of the square is *subaltern* to a proposition which (with the same interpretation) comes from a schema that is assigned to the corner of the square standing vertical to it.
5. Propositions are *subcontraries* of each other when they (with the same interpretation of the concept variables α and β) come from schemata which are assigned to different lower corners of the square.

That the first two relations enumerated here obtain stems directly from what was said already in § 10; the fact that the three remaining relations obtain of course also stems from what was said, though indirectly. This will emerge from the following considerations.

A *contrary* relation, as it is mentioned in the third point, obtains between two propositions if and only if they can both be false, but not both true. A universal affirmative proposition of the form 'every α is a β' is already false if not all objects that fall under α are a β, but only some. But this is precisely the condition on which a universal negative proposition of the form 'no α is a β' (with the same interpretation of the concept variables) is false as well.

A proposition is the *subaltern* of another if and only if the truth of the first follows from that of the second, but it does not follow from the fact that the first is true that the second is. Now a universal proposition cannot be true unless the proposition which is its contrary is false. Precisely for this reason the particular proposition which is the contradictory of the latter contrary proposition must be true. Conversely, though, a particular proposition cannot be true unless the universal proposition which is its contradictory is false. But precisely for this reason the universal proposition opposed to this contrary does not need to be true. Thus, the particular proposition stands in a subaltern relationship to the proposition which is the contrary of its contradictory opposite.

Finally, two propositions are *subcontraries* if and only if both can be true, but not both false, or when, in other words, one of the two propositions follows from the non-truth-functional negation of the other. Now the non-truth-functional negation of a particular proposition is equivalent to the proposition that is its contradictory, from which follows the particular proposition that is the subaltern of this universal proposition. Hence, the particular proposition which is the subaltern of this universal proposition follows from it immediately.

§ 12 The Weak Logical Square of Assertoric Opposition

With the exception of the contradictory relation, all relations of the logical square of assertoric opposition remain preserved when we replace the expressions for the schemata of universal propositions in Figure 3 with expressions for the schemata of singular propositions in the following way:[56]

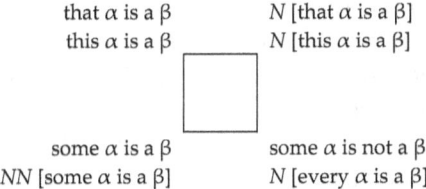

that α is a β   N [that α is a β]
this α is a β   N [this α is a β]

some α is a β   some α is not a β
NN [some α is a β]   N [every α is a β]

Figure 4

We have already seen in § 9 that the schemata of singular propositions which appear in Figure 4 are schemata of pairwise equivalent or pairwise contrary singular propositions.[57] Hence the upper horizontals in Figure 4 correspond to the same logical relation as the upper horizontals in Figure 3. The same holds for the

---

56 On the logical relationship between singular and universal propositions, see Leibniz (1840, IV. 17, § 8). On this, see Kneale & Kneale 1975, 323. – Kant alluded to this logical relationship with the remark, "that in the use of judgments in syllogisms singular judgments can be treated like universal ones" (*CPR*, A 71/B 96). Treating 'like' is of course not equating. It therefore rests on a confusion when Russell (1960, 40) claims of traditional logic, among whose representatives Kant is surely to be counted, "The first serious advance in real logic since the time of the Greeks was made independently by Peano and Frege – both mathematicians. Traditional logic regarded the two propositions 'Socrates is mortal' and 'All men are mortal' as being of the same form; Peano and Frege, who pointed out the error did so for technical reasons [. . .] but the philosophical importance of the advance which they made is impossible to exaggerate." Following Leibniz, Kant seems to have seen the distinction between the universal and singular forms of judgment in that with the latter the form of the particular judgment coincides with the universal.

57 Of course, each of these four expressions have other equivalents. Along the lines of *non-singular* propositions, I would also like to accept plural expressions like 'these α are (not) β' or 'those α are (not) β' as syllogistic schemata of *singular* propositions, assuming that plural expressions are also used for particular propositions. For reasons of clarity, I use the expressions appearing in Figure 4 as standard expressions.

lower horizontals, since the same schemata are assigned to them in both figures. Finally, both verticals in Figure 4 correspond to a subaltern relation. For when a singular affirmative proposition of the form 'this α is a β' is true, at least *some* α must be a β; just so, it must be that *not every* α is a β if a singular negative proposition of the form '*N* [this α is a β]' is true. Only the diagonals in Figure 4 stand for a different (and indeed weaker) logical relation than the diagonals in Figure 3. They do not correspond to contradictoriness, but subcontrariety. That is, they each connect schemata of two propositions which cannot both be false, but both can be true: from the non-truth-functional negation of one proposition it follows that the other proposition is true; yet from the truth of one of the two propositions the non-truth-functional negation of the other does not follow.

The system of logical relations which correspond to the positional relations in Figure 4 agree so much with the system depicted in Figure 3 that the designation 'logical square of assertoric opposition' could perhaps be used for both systems. But to avoid confusion, I will call the system illustrated by Figure 3 the *strong logical square of assertoric opposition*, while the system illustrated by Figure 4 should be called the *weak logical square of assertoric opposition*.

As the expressions assigned to the right verticals in Figures 3 and 4 show, all syllogistic schemata of negative propositions can be understood as expressing not truth-functional but rather non-truth-functional negation. That is, they show that 'not A', whenever A is a syllogistic schema, is equivalent to '*N* A', not to '~ A'.

§ 13 The Logical Square of Modal Opposition

As a result of what we have said, we should certainly not take syllogistic modal expressions like 'it is necessary that not A' and 'it is possible that not A' as if they were equivalent to '□ ~ A' and to '◇ ~ A', respectively. It would not even be correct to say that they are equivalent to '□ *N* A' and to '◇ *N* A'. For '□ . . .' and '◇ . . .' are used such that they are equivalent to '~ ◇ ~ . . .' and to '~ □ ~ . . .', respectively. In contrast, the expressions 'it is necessary that *N* A' and 'it is possible that *N* A' stand in relations that are precisely analogous to those of the square of assertoric opposition, and which I would like to call *relations of the logical square of modal opposition*:[58]

---

[58] These relations correspond to those Aristotle presents in *De Interpretatione* 13, 22 a 14 ff.

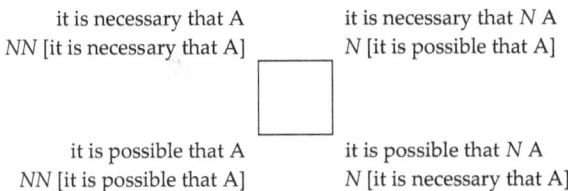

it is necessary that A
NN [it is necessary that A]

it is necessary that N A
N [it is possible that A]

it is possible that A
NN [it is possible that A]

it is possible that N A
N [it is necessary that A]

Figure 5

That is, for propositions which conform to the schemata in Figure 5, the following points also hold:

1. If schemata are assigned to the same corner of the square, they are *equivalent*. 2. If schemata are diagonal to each other, they are *contradictories*. 3. If schemata are assigned to different corners of the upper horizontals, they are *contraries*. 4. If schemata are assigned to different corners of the lower horizontals, they are *subcontraries*. 5. If schemata are assigned to lower horizontals, they are related as *subalterns* to the schemata standing vertically above them.

If we place the sign of non-truth-functional negation before every expression of the right side in Figure 5 (in order), then we get the following four propositional schemata:

'*N* [it is necessary that *N* A]',
'*NN* [it is possible that A]',
'*N* [it is possible that *N* A]',
'*NN* [it is necessary that A]',

of which the first and last schemata must again be equivalent expressions. Since moreover '*NN* [it is possible that A]' is equivalent to 'it is possible that A' and '*NN* [it is necessary that A]' is equivalent to 'it is necessary that A]' (as the left side of Figure 5 shows), then '*N* [it is necessary that *N* A]' is also equivalent to 'it is possible that A' and '*N* [it is possible that *N* A]' to 'it is necessary that A'.

To abbreviate 'it is necessary that . . .', when this expression should not be understood in the sense of '□ . . .', but rather in the sense of '*N* [it is possible that *N*. . .]', I use '*L* . . .'. Accordingly, '*NLN* . . .' is equivalent to '*N* [it is necessary that *N* . . .]' and will be abbreviated by '*M* . . .' ('it is possible that . . .') in what follows. In this notation, the syllogistic propositional schemata 'it is necessary that not A' and 'it is possible that not A' are rendered respectively with '*LN* A' and by '*MN* A'.

In this notation, '*NLN* . . .' and '~ □ ~ . . .' are different ways to understand and abbreviate one and the same expression, namely, 'it is not necessary that not . . .'. They are distinguished from each other simply because the word 'not' is understood differently. The same holds for '*NMN* . . .' and '~ ◇ ~. . .'; these, too, are abbreviations of one and the same expression, namely, 'it is not possible that not . . .', only the negation sign is understood differently in them.

4 Symbolic Abbreviations

§ 14 Syllogistic and Non-Syllogistic Modal Expressions

This notation makes it possible in certain circumstances to replace modal-logical expressions in which the signs '◇ . . .', '□ . . .' or '~ . . .' occur with expressions in which a certain configuration of '*M* . . .', '*L* . . .' and '*N* . . .' appear instead. Thus '◇ A' and '□ A' are in turn equivalent to

'*M* A' and
'*L* A',

assuming that the principle of the affirmative use of double negation holds for non-truth-functional negation, thus assuming that A follows from *NN* A. This equivalence in meaning can be easily made clear if one only considers that '~ A', under the just mentioned assumption, may be translated into '*N* A' and that '◇ ~ A' and '□ ~ A' are equivalent to '~ [it is necessary that A]' and '~ [it is possible that A]', respectively. When A follows from *NN* A, the just named expressions may be replaced with '*N* [it is necessary that A]' and '*N* [it is possible that A]', respectively, i.e., with expressions which according to § 13 are equivalent to '*MN* A' and '*LN* A'. These are thus expressions into which we may under the stated assumption convert '◇ ~ A' and '□ ~ A'; and we may under this assumption with equal right convert '*NMN* A' and '*NLN* A' into '~ ◇ ~ A' and '~ □ ~ A' respectively as well, and consequently '*L* A' and '*M* A' into '□ A' and '◇ A' respectively.

Even the expression for strict implication, 'A ⥽ B' can in certain circumstances be replaced by a configuration of signs in which, besides '. . . & . . .', only constants of the syllogistic occur. Since 'A ⥽ B' only abbreviates '~ ◇ (A & ~ B)', 'A ⥽ B' is equivalent to

'*NM* (A & *N* B)',

on the assumption that A follows from *NN* A for every interpretation of A. Namely, on this assumption non-truth-functional negation behaves like truth-functional negation.[59]

The assumption that A follows from *NN* A is the assumption that a hypothetical proposition of the form 'if *NN* A, then A' is true. Hence, the supposition discussed in § 7 that 'if . . ., then . . .' expresses *exactly the same thing* as '. . . ⊰ . . .' needs to be corrected. If both these expressions were really equivalent, then explaining strict implication by means of an expression in which 'if . . ., then . . .' occurs would be out of the question. This occurrence points to a *circulus vitiosus*. This circle is inevitable if one wants to interpret the hypothetical proposition 'if A, then B' as an expression which implicitly makes use of the signs '◇ . . .' and '~ . . .'. There are, to be sure, still good reasons to hold with Lewis that 'if A, then B' is equivalent to

'it is impossible that A and not B'.

But apparently this expression, insofar as it is supposed to represent the same thought as 'if A, then B', calls for a reading that is inevitably lacking in Lewis' formula '~ ◇ (A & ~ B)'. We find a better match for this reading by replacing the signs '◇ . . .' and '~ . . .' in this formula with logical constants of the syllogistic, namely with '*M* . . .' and '*N* . . .' respectively, though *without* assuming that a hypothetical proposition of the form 'if *NN* A, then A' is true.

But *which* logical vocabulary is best suited to represent the meaning of 'if . . ., then . . .'? This is a question which I cannot answer before answering the question whether dyadic truth functions – among which belongs the logical constant '. . . & . . .' – are elements of a language into which one can adequately translate the language of the syllogistic. (I will return to this question only in § 30.)

However, it has now already become clear that neither '◇ . . .', '□ . . .', nor '~ . . .' belong among these elements. Moreover, it has already become apparent that there are elements of the language of the syllogistic – namely '*M* . . .', '*L* . . .', and '*N* . . .' – which cannot without more ado be replaced by logical vocabulary of another language without loss, and in any case not by the logical vocabulary of a *truth-functional* language.

---

[59] A simple way of abbreviating ~ ◇ (A & ~ B) from *NM* (A & *N* B) will result from the relations between the forms of the hypothetical proposition and strict implication and will be considered below in the last paragraph of § 30. Further details are also in *Appendix* 5.

§ 15 Other Expressions in the Language of Elementary Syllogistic

Concerning the remaining elements of the syllogistic language, it will prove useful in what follows to introduce abbreviating expressions for them as well. I will use the following notation:

I use the relational constants with empty places 'A ( )', 'E ( )', 'I ( )', and 'O ( )' for the four forms of (in order) the universal affirmative, universal negative, particular affirmative, and particular negative statement.[60] I use these letters in deference to a traditional terminology (see § 4 above), which here is reshaped into a functional notation to enable combination with other functional expressions (which will prove to be useful in what follows). The empty places of these expressions are always to be filled with an ordered pair of concept expressions which can be represented by variables ('α', 'β', etc.). The sequence of concept expressions within the empty places is always ordered so that the expression of the predicate concept precedes the expression of the subject concept. Accordingly, 'A (α, β)' should be read as an abbreviation of 'α is a predicate of every β' (or for 'α is said of every β'); 'E (α, β)' stands for 'α is not a predicate of a β' ('α is said of no β'); 'I (α, β)' and 'O (α, β)' mean in turn 'α is a predicate of some β' ('α is said of some β') and 'α is not a predicate of every β' ('α is not said of some β'). Ordering the sequence of concept expressions in this way has the advantage of displaying the transitivity of the subordination relation in conceptual hierarchies.

To designate the forms of singular affirmative and singular negative statements, I propose the relational constants '$\dot{A}$ ( )' and '$\dot{E}$ ( )' respectively. The correspondence of the pointed capital letters with the constants for forms of universal statements is meant to suggest the logical affinity described in § 12 above: that $\dot{A}$ (α, β) and $\dot{E}$ (α, β) have a similar place in the logical square of assertoric opposition as A (α, β) and E (α, β).

Concerning the representation of $\dot{A}$ (α, β) and $\dot{E}$ (α, β) in normal language (read: 'α is a predicate of that β' or 'α is said of that β' and 'α is not a predicate of

---

60 These forms are sometimes equated with the forms of the *categorical* judgment. See, e.g., Mautner 1996, 66–67: "In aristotelian logic, a *categorical proposition* is a proposition of one of these four forms: *All S is P* / *Some S is P* / *No S is P* / *Some S is not P*. / Thus defined, every categorical proposition is either universal affirmative, or universal negative, or particular affirmative, or particular negative." Since Aristotle himself did not yet use 'categorical' as the designation of a judgment, it seems that "aristotelian logic" must here mean the logical tradition following Aristotle. – The equation of categorical statements with the four above-mentioned forms is nevertheless systematically misleading for two reasons. *First*, from a traditional perspective, of course, these forms also include non-categorical statements, namely the sub-statements of hypothetical and disjunctive judgments. *Second*, in the traditional conception there are besides the four mentioned forms also singular categorical statements.

that β' or 'α is not said of that β', respectively), one may for convenience replace the use of the phrase *'that . . .'** with the less cumbersome use of the demonstrative pronoun *'this . . .'*. Yet it should be made clear that the use of the demonstrative pronoun has the disadvantage of allowing two possible misunderstandings to arise which concern the formal semantics of the syllogistic vocabulary.

The first misunderstanding would be to suppose that it belongs to the form of singular statements to be able to treat only such objects which one can *show*; for demonstrative pronouns are often used in connection with pointing gestures. However, a meaningful statement can also be singular in its syllogistic form if it deals with an object which is neither showable nor perceptible but is rather an abstract *ens rationis* which may not even exist. This is the kind of object at issue in a singular statement like 'this number does not exist' – a statement which is true, for example, when it is about the greatest natural number. It corresponds to a statement of the form $E\,(\alpha, \beta)$, with 'number' in the place of β and 'exist' in the place of α.

The second misunderstanding would be to suppose that singular propositions of the form $A\,(. . ., \beta)$ and $E\,(. . ., \beta)$ have, as demonstratives, a changeable object-reference with repeated occurrence in the same context ('this flower is blue; this is red. . .'). But the expression 'that β . . .', as it is used in these propositions must be understood so that it always refers to the same object with repeated occurrence in the same context. It is used both *anaphorically* as well as *kataphorically*; i.e., it points back to places within an already given context when the same β is discussed in propositions of the form $I\,(. . ., \beta)$, $A\,(. . ., \beta)$, or $E\,(. . ., \beta)$, or it points forward to such a place within an (at least potentially) subsequent context. To that extent, the use of the expression 'that β . . .' resembles the use of a proper name.[61] For example, 'Socrates' in a proposition like 'Socrates is mortal' refers to *some* bearer of this name, namely, to precisely the bearer this proposition is discussing. *Which* bearer this is can of course depends on the context of this proposition – if there is such a context. Since the possibility of referring to a *certain* individual is presupposed by the use of a proper name, but the determinacy of the reference depends on the occurrence of the name in several places of a common context, the use of a proper name also has an anaphoric-kataphoric character.[62] This is seen in the fact that, if the same proper name occurs in different

---

* TN: the more "cumbersome" expression used in the original where I use "that . . ." is *"das in Rede stehende . . ."*.

[61] I will give more a precise account of the reason for this similarity in § 33.

[62] The view proposed here and in what follows about the use of proper names is close in some ways to conception developed by Fred Sommers (following W.V.O. Quine), according to which proper names and individual identifiers are anaphoric expressions which relate back to statements of the form 'some S is a P'. See Sommers 1982, 5.

places of a common context, e.g., in an inference chain, it refers to the same individual in all these places unless several bearers of this name are *explicitly* distinguished from each other in this context. In just the same way, *which* object the expression 'that β . . .' refers to in propositions of the form A (. . ., β) or E (. . ., β) depends on how the β in question is determined in other places in the context, to which the expression points anaphorically or kataphorically.

In place of the three negative expressions 'E ( )', 'O ( )', and 'E ( )' one may write '$N I$ ( )', '$N A$ ( )', and '$N A$ ( )' respectively; that is, the relations of the logical square of assertoric opposition admit a more parsimonious collection of basic signs.

So that we have a symbolic expression for the form of a limitative judgment, I replace 'not-α', 'not-β', etc. with '^{N}α', ^{N}β', etc.

Finally, the two-place relational constant 'H ( )' serves to abbreviate the hypothetical propositional connection 'if . . ., then . . . .'. Corresponding abbreviations for *n*-membered disjunctive propositional connections, i.e., for 'either . . ., or . . . .', 'either . . ., or . . . ., or . . . .', etc., are made possible by the use of the *n*-place relational constant 'D ( )', with $n \geq 2$. The formula 'H (A, B)' is accordingly a propositional schema which is equivalent to 'if A, then B', while 'D (A, B)' and 'D (A, B, C)' stand for 'either A, or B' and for 'either A, or B, or C' respectively.[63]

I use non-italicized Latin uppercase letters A, B, C, etc. here and in what follows as *meta-variables*. They represent a formula for which there is an interpretation as a true or false proposition. They can stand in just as much for categorical as well as hypothetical or disjunctive propositional schemata.

From now on I will call a formal language in which only concept variables occur as object variables and in which there are no constants other than the logical constants of the syllogistic previously enumerated the *elementary syllogistic language*. A language which is distinguished from the elementary syllogistic language only by replacing at least one concept variable with a special *interpretation* of this variable, I will call an *extended language of the syllogistic*. A logical system which makes do with the use of the elementary syllogistic language and in which the rules of the logical squares of §§ 11–13 are valid unrestrictedly, I will call the *elementary syllogistic*.

---

[63] Since 'D (A, B)' is equivalent to 'H (A, N B)' and H (N A, B)', the possibility – see § 6 above – of replacing 'D ( )' with a truth-functional expression without loss of meaning depends on the possibility of translating 'H ( )' into a truth-functional language. In any case, so long as we have not decided whether this possibility obtains, it is convenient to have a special notation to designate the syllogistic 'either . . ., or . . .'.

Section Two
The Language of the Calculus of Classes

1 A Translation Program

§ 16 The Vocabulary of the Calculus of Classes

The standard work *Principles of Mathematical Logic* by David Hilbert and Wilhelm Ackermann contains in its second chapter, "The Calculus of Classes," a paragraph with the heading "Systematic Derivation of the Traditional Aristotelian Inferences" (Hilbert & Ackermann 1967, 57–63 [1950, 48–54]). It is supposed to be shown here that all universally valid rules of the categorical syllogistic, so far as they apply to non-singular statements, can be reduced to non-syllogistic rules of inference belonging to the calculus of classes. This program, which in its outlines is committed to the model provided by Ernst Schröder in his three volume *Lectures on the Algebra of Logic* [*Vorlesungen über die Algebra der Logik*] of 1890–95 for the interpretation of syllogistic rules, is guided by the conviction that "the calculus of classes" makes possible "a more systematic treatment of logical questions than traditional logic" (Hilbert & Ackermann 1967, 65 [1950, 55, modified]) – whereby 'traditional logic' is here a name which has become standard for a deductive logic that uses the language of the *categorical* syllogistic. Carrying out Schröder's program assumes that the vocabulary of this language, so far as it applies to non-singular statements, can be replaced successfully and without loss by the vocabulary of the calculus of classes. I will now lay out what vocabulary that is supposed to be.

Yet before I do, I would like briefly to discuss the label 'calculus of classes'. Hilbert and Ackermann (1967, 42 [1950, 44]) use this term to designate a subsphere of mathematical logic which, along with set theory – of which it forms only "a relatively small excerpt" (Hilbert & Ackermann 1967, 153 [1950, 139]) – was developed out of Boolean algebra. The calculus of classes, like set theory, occupies itself with the investigation of set-theoretical operations, but limits itself to such operations in which only relations between *classes* are taken into consideration; relations between classes and *elements* of classes are thus disregarded. In other words, the calculus of classes is occupied with the relations of the *inclusion, intersection, union, identity*, and *complementarity* of classes, yet not with the relation of elementhood, which is the fundamental relation of set theory. Otherwise, *classes* are the same for the calculus of classes as *sets* are for set theory. That is, "class is just another expression for set" (Hilbert & Ackermann 1967, 153 [1950, 13]), and furthermore both expressions are widely held to be equivalent to what is called the *scope* (or *extension*) *of a concept* in the older logic literature.[64] A distinction between sets and classes, as it is sometimes made within presentations of set theory, is disregarded at least within the calculus of classes.[65]

Now, regarding the systematic derivation of syllogistic rules from relations of the calculus of classes, as well the translation of syllogistic expressions into the language of classes which is foundational for this derivation, Hilbert and Ackermann follow Ernst Schröder in his view that we can read A, E, I, and O propositions as dealing with *class inclusions*. This reading is suggested by the fact that the syllogistic schema '$A\,(\alpha, \beta)$' can be reasonably translated by the propositional schema 'the scope of the concept β is contained in the scope of the concept α'. If we replace here the expressions 'the scope of the concept α' and 'the scope of the concept β' with class variables, i.e., with the Latin lower-case letters '**a**' and '**b**' respectively, and further symbolize the relational expression '. . . is contained in . . .' with the inclusion sign '. . . $\subset$ . . .', we get the expression '**b** $\subset$ **a**'. This may be translated 'the class **b** is contained in the class **a**' (or '**b** is a subclass of **a**'). This schema is apparently equivalent to the propositional schema '$A\,(\alpha, \beta)$'.

Following Schröder, Hilbert and Ackermann suppose that not only the schema of A, but also those of E, I, and O propositions can be reasonably replaced by expressions dealing with class inclusions. Just as one replaces '$A\,(\alpha, \beta)$' with '**b** $\subset$ **a**', one can apparently with equal right replace '$O\,(\alpha, \beta)$' with the truth-functional negation of '**b** $\subset$ **a**', thus with the expression '$\sim$ (**b** $\subset$ **a**)', which means something like '**b** is not a subclass of **a**'. For, in the same way that '$O\,(\alpha, \beta)$' is the contradictory of '$A\,(\alpha, \beta)$', so every formula $\sim A$ is the contradictory of A. Concerning '$E\,(\alpha, \beta)$', this propositional schema means something like 'every β is not an α'. A proposition whose form corresponds to this schema is true when the scope of the concept β is contained in the scope of the antonym of α: if **a** is the scope of the concept α, then the scope of the concept not-α is the complementary class of **a**. If one designates this with '$\overline{\mathbf{a}}$', then one may represent the propositional schema 'the scope of the concept β is contained in the scope of the concept not-α' with '**b** $\subset$ $\overline{\mathbf{a}}$'. Finally, since '$I\,(\alpha, \beta)$' is the

---

[64] This holds in any case so long as we understand by scope of a concept *the objects that fall under this concept*, and not also, as in the logic of Port-Royal (e.g.), *the concepts which are subordinated to this concept*.

[65] Thus it is not unusual for the concept of a class to be defined by that of the set, by taking a class as the *scope* of a condition $S\,(x)$ of a subset $\{x \in A\colon S\,(x)\}$; see Halmos 1976, 22. There is also the opposite procedure of defining the concept of a set by the concept of a class; so that in some presentations of set theory a set is defined as that class which is the element of another class. On this conception of sets, the calculus of classes has to do essentially with classes, while according to the first mentioned conception this calculus could just as well be called the 'calculus of sets'.

contradictory of '$E\,(\alpha, \beta)$', and '$\sim (\mathbf{b} \subset \overline{\mathbf{a}})$' is the contradictory of '$\mathbf{b} \subset \overline{\mathbf{a}}$', '$\sim (\mathbf{b} \subset \overline{\mathbf{a}})$' relates to '$\mathbf{b} \subset \overline{\mathbf{a}}$' as '$I\,(\alpha, \beta)$' to '$E\,(\alpha, \beta)$'.

§ 17 The Strong Logical Square of Assertoric Opposition in the Language of the Calculus of Classes

Summarizing these considerations, Hilbert and Ackermann write:

> We provide [. . .] symbolic presentation of the four forms A, E, I, O of a judgment. [. . .] If a is the class corresponding to α and b to β, then the judgment ['All β are α'] is presented by '$\mathbf{b} \subset \mathbf{a}$'. We can also express the judgment 'Some β are α' as 'It is not true that all β are not α'. It is therefore presented symbolically with '$\sim (\mathbf{b} \subset \overline{\mathbf{a}})$'. For 'No β is α' we can also say that 'All β are not α' and represent it with '$\mathbf{b} \subset \overline{\mathbf{a}}$'. Finally, for 'Some β are not α' we can say 'It is not true that all β are α', which is represented by '$\sim (\mathbf{b} \subset \mathbf{a})$'.

And Hilbert and Ackermann add:

> From this notation result the traditional doctrines about *opposition and inversion* which concern these forms of judgment. Namely, from the four judgments, the last was expressed as the opposite [*Gegenteil*] of the first, the second as the opposite of the third. Furthermore, both middle judgments in β and α (**b** and **a**, for us), are symmetric. Namely, the judgments '$\sim (\mathbf{b} \subset \overline{\mathbf{a}})$' and '$(\mathbf{b} \subset \overline{\mathbf{a}})$ are equivalent to the judgments '$\sim (\mathbf{a} \subset \overline{\mathbf{b}})$' and '$\mathbf{a} \subset \overline{\mathbf{b}}$'. (Hilbert & Ackermann 1967, 59 [1950, 49–50])[66]

When the authors speak of the "traditional doctrines" of "*inversion*" in this quotation, they mean conversion rules according to which propositions of the form $E\,(\alpha, \beta)$ and of the form $I\,(\alpha, \beta)$ may be transformed into logically equivalent propositions of the form $E\,(\beta, \alpha)$ and $I\,(\beta, \alpha)$ respectively.[67] What Hilbert and Ackermann are referring to here is the fact that all syllogistic conversion rules remain in force when one replaces E and I propositions with expressions for class inclusions: the class variables may be interchanged in these expressions just as one can interchange concept variables in the corresponding syllogistic formulas.

And further: when Hilbert and Ackermann speak of "traditional doctrines of *opposition*" they mean everything the syllogistic teaches about the relations of the

---

[66] In this quotation, I have adapted the symbolic notation Hilbert and Ackermann use to the conventions I have introduced.

[67] What are meant are rules of *conversio simplex*, which are dealt with below in § 55 together with a further inversion rule, *conversio per accidens*, according to which one may move from $A\,(\alpha, \beta)$ to $I\,(\beta, \alpha)$. This rule shortens a procedure in which, on the basis of a further rule that results from one of the relations of the strong logical square (the subalternation rule), one first moves from $A\,(\alpha, \beta)$ to $I\,(\alpha, \beta)$ in order to then to apply *conversio simplex* to $I\,(\alpha, \beta)$.

strong logical square of assertoric opposition. With this they point to the following logical situation. According to Figure 6, it is possible to replace the four propositional schemata in Figure 3 (see § 11 above) with (moving clockwise) '**b** ⊂ **a**', '**b** ⊂ **ā**', '~ (**b** ⊂ **a**),' and '~ (**b** ⊂ **ā**)' (except here with '**a**' standing for the scope of β and '**b**' for the scope of α), without affecting anything in the logical relations which are expressed by the positional relationships in Figure 3.

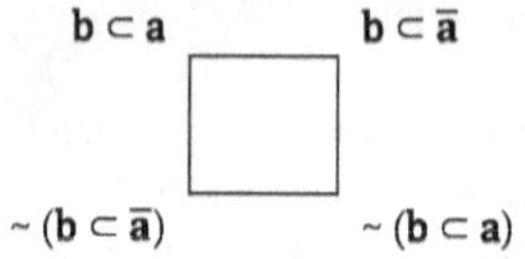

```
   b ⊂ a              b ⊂ ā
   ┌─────────────────┐
   │                 │
   └─────────────────┘
 ~ (b ⊂ ā)          ~ (b ⊂ a)
```

Figure 6

Now it must nevertheless be assumed here that there is no interpretation for '**a**' and '**b**' in which **b** stands for an *empty set* or the scope of an *empty concept* and that neither of the expressions '**b** ⊂ **a**' and '**b** ⊂ **ā**' stand for a false proposition. Otherwise, there would not be a contrary relationship between them; and, consequently, the contradictory opposites of these propositions, namely, propositions conforming to the schemata '~ (**b** ⊂ **a**)' and '~ (**b** ⊂ **ā**)', would be subcontraries nor subalterns of '**b** ⊂ **a**' and '**b** ⊂ **ā**' respectively. This would mean that the logical relations indicated in Figure 6 do not correspond to the logical relations expressed in Figure 3.

This assumption agrees, of course, with a supposition the syllogistic also already implicitly employs. Namely, the syllogistic also assumes in its use of the subaltern rules that result from the relations of the strong logical square that there is no interpretation of α and β in which A (α, β) is a true proposition but β occurs as an *empty concept*, i.e., has a scope of zero. Hilbert and Ackermann rightly point out this out when they write regarding Aristotle's syllogistic, "According to Aristotle, a statement 'All β are α' holds as correct only if there are objects which are β" (Hilbert & Ackermann 1967, 62 [1950, 53]). (This is something that needs more discussion and which I will return to in more detail in § 18 and § 19.)

The propositional schemata appearing in Figure 6, then, are only to be regarded as *adequate* translations of the syllogistic schemata of A, E, I, and O propositions if the logical relations that obtain between them correspond *exactly* to the relations of the logical square of assertoric opposition. Assuming that there is no interpretation of '**a**' and '**b**', where '**b** ⊂ **a**' and '**b** ⊂ **ā**' both express true propositions that deal with **b** as a null class, we find an exact correspondence between these relations. For, under this assumption, though two propositions of the form **b** ⊂ **a** and **b** ⊂ **ā** can both be false, they cannot both be true; they are therefore *contraries*. The truth-functional negations of both propositions, accordingly, are *subcontraries*, since though they are both true if their contradictories are both false, they cannot both be false, since it is not possible that their contradictories are both true. Finally, just for this reason they are *subalterns* to the expressions from Figure 6 standing above them vertically. For there is no interpretation of 'a' and 'b' in which one of these expressions stands for a true proposition unless the expression which is the contradictory of the (true) proposition's contrary is true as well.

Now, within the calculus of classes, one admittedly does *not* typically make use of the assumption that there is no interpretation for 'a' and 'b' in which either '**b** ⊂ **a**' or '**b** ⊂ **ā**' stands for a true proposition and yet **b** is the scope of an empty concept or an empty set. Rather, the inclusion relation is usually understood – as it was by Hilbert and Ackermann – so that interpretations of '**b** ⊂ **a**' and '**b** ⊂ **ā**' are permitted in which these schemata represent propositions which are both true and yet deal with the *null class*. I will call this understanding the *set-theoretical conception of class-inclusion*. On this conception, it is not only not a necessary condition for the truth of statements of the form **b** ⊂ **a** and **b** ⊂ **ā** that **b** is *not* the null class; on the contrary, the opposite condition, that **b** *is* the null class, is even sufficient for their truth.

I call this conception *set-theoretical* because a theorem of set theory underlies it. This theorem states that the null class is a sub-class of *every* class (or that the empty set is a sub-set of *every* set).[68] Expressed symbolically: ∅ ⊂ **a** (and ∅ ⊂ **ā**), for arbitrary **a**. If we assume the validity of this theorem, then it holds immediately for **b** = ∅ that **b** is a subset both of **a** as well as of **ā** (for arbitrary **a**). Expressed symbolically: **b** ⊂ **a** and **b** ⊂ **ā**.

Under the assumption of this theorem, it would be entirely inappropriate not to admit everywhere the interpretation of class variables in which **b** is the null class. Hilbert and Ackermann then write, "Our deviation from Aristotle on this point is justified by, e.g., the consideration for mathematical applications of the logic [of the calculus of classes], in which taking the Aristotelian conception as a basis would be inappropriate" (Hilbert & Ackermann 1967, 62 [1950, 53]). What is labeled here the 'Aristotelian conception' is the view that statements of the form **b** ⊂ **a** and **b** ⊂ **ā** are true only if **b** ≠ ∅. The latter view is opposed to the set-theoretical conception and states that the subject concept of propositions of the form $A(\alpha, \beta)$ and $E(\alpha, \beta)$ cannot, if true, be a concept whose scope is the null class.

Now given the assumption of the set-theoretical theorem that the null class is contained as a sub-class in *every* class, we can express *that* a given sub-class is not the null class by means of the truth-functional negation of a class-inclusion. For example, under this assumption the formulas which appear in Figure 6 '∼ (**b** ⊂ **ā**)'

---

[68] In Schröder (1890, Vol. I, 238), this theorem is worded: "the nothing" is "the subject to every predicate."

and '~ (b ⊂ a)' each express that **b** is not the null class. The language of the calculus of classes is capable, under this assumption, of making explicit those suppositions which are implicitly contained in expressions for class inclusions according to the so-called 'Aristotelian' conception. If we want to say that **b** is not the null class, we thus simply write: '~ (**b** ⊂ **b̄**)'. Then, if we add this formula to proposition schemata such as '**b** ⊂ **a**' or '**b** ⊂ **ā**', we can make explicit what, according to the "tacit Aristotelian assumption", is implicitly stated by a proposition of the form **b** ⊂ **a** or **b** ⊂ **ā** (Hilbert & Ackermann 1967, 63 [1950, 53]).[69]

Thus, to express that the concept β in '*A* (α, β)' and '*E* (α, β)' does not have a scope that coincides with the null class, one can replace '**b** ⊂ **a**' and '**b** ⊂ **ā**' with pairs of propositional schemata, namely with '~ (**b** ⊂ **b̄**)' and '**b** ⊂ **a**' and with '~ (**b** ⊂ **b̄**)' and '**b** ⊂ **ā**' respectively. The expressions in the following Figure 7 thus render in a precise way what was *actually* meant by the expressions in Figure 6.

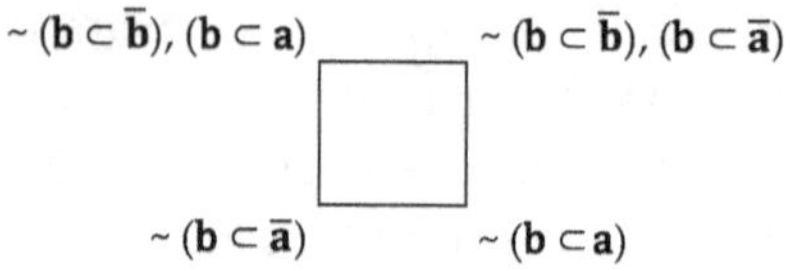

~ (**b** ⊂ **b̄**), (**b** ⊂ **a**)   ~ (**b** ⊂ **b̄**), (**b** ⊂ **ā**)

~ (**b** ⊂ **ā**)   ~ (**b** ⊂ **a**)

Figure 7

Of course, the relations of the logical square continue to obtain in Figure 7, just as in Figure 6, only if one assumes that there is no interpretation of the class variable '**b**' where **b** is the scope of an empty concept, in which '~ (**b** ⊂ **b̄**)' is thus a false proposition.

2 The Problem of Implicit Existence Assumptions

§ 18 The Problem of the Empty Class

At least at first glance, it looks as if the language into which Hilbert and Ackermann translate syllogistic expressions is in a completely advantageous position: it is

---

[69] Following Ernst Schröder (1890, Vol. II/1, 220), Hilbert and Ackermann (like Bertrand Russell; see § 56 below) maintain here (1967, 63 [1950, 53]) that it is impossible to correctly present the syllogistic modes *Darapti*, *Falapton*, *Bamalip*, and *Fesapo* in the language of syllogistic. They say that one cannot treat them like standard Aristotelian syllogisms as inferences with two premises; they require a third premise of the form ~ (**a** ⊂ **ā**) for their correct presentation. This additional premise is supposed to have the task of making explicit the existential implication which is contained in the remaining premises of each of these inferences on the view of the syllogistic.

apparently suited to make explicit class-logical assumptions which are implicitly contained in the syllogistic propositional schemata, but which cannot be expressed in the elementary language of the syllogistic itself. *If* it is the case that an *A* or *E* proposition is true only on the condition that the scope of its subject concept is not zero, then *A* or *E* propositions should in truth be understood as *complex* propositions; they then admit a *logical analysis* in which they are equivalent to pairs of (or to logical conjunctions of) propositional schemata as they occur in Figure 7. On this analysis, syllogistic conceptual relations are reducible to class-logical relations, which prove to be the more elementary.

In the elementary language of the syllogistic, by contrast, both *A* and *E* propositions appear to be simple and *elementary* propositions, which are not further reducible. There is no vocabulary in this language with which it would be possible to distinguish concept variables as signs for empty or non-empty concepts. At first glance, it may seem that this lacuna should be taken as a deficiency in the language.

Yet we must now examine whether it was correct after all to suppose with Hilbert and Ackermann (see § 17 above) that *not only A but also E* propositions should be understood such that they cannot be true when their subject concept has a null scope. For whether syllogistic expressions admit the analysis Hilbert and Ackermann proposed for them depends on this supposition.

As we have seen, they suppose that the "traditional theories of opposition" are tenable only on the condition that relations between *A, E, I,* or *O* propositions with non-empty subject concepts are considered; i.e., they suppose that on this condition do these relations correspond to the relations of the strong logical square, and only on this condition are the rules of the strong logical square, which depend on these relations, *valid.*

§ 19 Alternative Theories

The view held by Hilbert and Ackermann, following Ernst Schröder, about the presuppositions of the validity of the rules of the strong logical square corresponds to a version of the theory of the *existential import* of categorical statements which was developed in the logic books of the nineteenth century. In his book *Studies and Exercises in Formal Logic*, one of the last significant contributions to the syllogistic, John Neville Keynes gave the theory a comprehensive presentation (cf. Keynes 1928, 210–48). Keynes discusses various versions of this theory.

In his view, four alternative possibilities serve to interpret categorical propositions: *A, E, I,* and *O* statements, if they occur as categorical statements, can be interpreted so that they either

(i) all imply that their subject concept, the antonym of their subject concept, their predicate concept and the antonym of their predicate concept are non-empty concepts, or
(ii) all imply that their subject concept is a non-empty concept, or
(iii) all imply neither that their subject concept nor their predicate concept is a non-empty concept, or, finally,
(iv) imply, if they are particular, that their subject concept is a non-empty concept, but if they are universal, do not imply this.[70]

If, according to one of these four interpretations, the subject concept of a categorical statement must be a non-empty concept to be true, this means that it contains an implicit existence assumption with respect to the objects it deals with. One can then say that it has *existential import* in this respect.

Keynes (1928, 227–31) shows that none of the four alternative interpretations allow *all* relations of the strong logical square to be preserved:

Assuming interpretation (i), the relations of contradictoriness and subcontrariety fall away, so that only the relations of subalternation and contrariety remain in effect. That is, on this assumption, it is already enough for statements of the form $A\ (\alpha, \beta)$, $O\ (\alpha, \beta)$, $E\ (\alpha, \beta)$, and $I\ (\alpha, \beta)$ to be false that α is an empty concept. In that case, no two of these four statements can ever form a pair of subcontrary or contradictory statements.

For similar reasons, the same consequences result in the case of interpretation (ii). But while in the case of interpretation (i) a statement of the form 'either $O\ (\alpha, \beta)$, or there is no α, or no $^N\alpha$, or no β, or no $^N\beta$' is the contradictory of a statement of the form $A\ (\alpha, \beta)$, in the case of (ii), a statement of the form 'either $O\ (\alpha, \beta)$, or there is no β' constitutes the contradictory.

Assuming interpretation (iii), the subalternate and subcontrary relations remain intact, but the relations of contradictoriness and contrariety fall away. On this assumption, '$A\ (\alpha, \beta)$' says merely that there is no β that is not an α, without saying that a β exists. A statement of the form $O\ (\alpha, \beta)$ says on this assumption that some β is not an α, *if* there is a β. As a consequence, a statement of the form $A\ (\alpha, \beta)$ is not the contradictory of a statement of the form $O\ (\alpha, \beta)$. For if no α exists, it is not the case that one of the two statements is false. In this case, however, two statements of the form $A\ (\alpha, \beta)$ and $E\ (\alpha, \beta)$ are also compatible with each other and hence not contraries. For, if neither $A\ (\alpha, \beta)$ nor $E\ (\alpha, \beta)$ implies that there is a β, what is said with both

---

[70] As Keynes notes, interpretation (i) corresponds to the view maintained by William Stanley Jevons, (ii) to John Stuart Mill's view, and (iv) is the interpretation John Venn favored, since it was best suited within the framework of "symbolic logic." See Keynes 1928, 220.

statements taken together is merely that there is neither a β that is an α, nor a β that is not an α. And both of these taken together means only that there is no β at all.

In the fourth and last case (iv) it is supposed that particular but not universal categorical statements implicitly say that there is an object which falls under the subject concept of the statement. Under this supposition, the sub-alternate relationship dissolves. For here a particular statement is already false if the existential statement which it implies is false, and yet the universal statement from which the particular statement follows according to the rule of subalternation can be true in this case, since it implies no corresponding existence assumption. The relationship of contrariety dissolves under this supposition as well. For the supposition allows that two statements of the form $A\,(\alpha, \beta)$ and $E\,(\alpha, \beta)$ are compatible with each other. That is, if neither of the two statements implies an existence statement, each of them only denies that there are definite objects with the predicate β. And indeed the universal affirmative statement denies that there are β's which are *not* α, while the universal negative statement denies that there are β's which *are* an α. Finally, the relationship of subcontrariety is dissolved as well if it is supposed that particular statements imply that their subject concept is satisfied. For it suffices for statements of the form $I\,(\alpha, \beta)$ and $O\,(\alpha, \beta)$ to be false if their subject concepts are not satisfied.

Among the four alternatives considered, interpretation (iv) is the only one in which the contradictory relationship between $A\,(\alpha, \beta)$ and $O\,(\alpha, \beta)$ or between $E\,(\alpha, \beta)$ and $I\,(\alpha, \beta)$ remains intact. Keynes sees this relationship as the most important among all logical relations of opposition, and this assessment is the reason he gives preference to interpretation (iv) over the remaining three interpretations of categorical propositions: from his perspective it is best suited for what he calls "ordinary formal logic" (Keynes 1928, 220). It corresponds, as one easily recognizes, exactly to that interpretation in which A, E, I, and O propositions express *set-theoretically conceived class inclusions*, so that they correspond in turn to propositions of the form $\mathbf{b} \subset \mathbf{a}$, $\mathbf{b} \subset \bar{\mathbf{a}}$, $\sim (\mathbf{b} \subset \bar{\mathbf{a}})$ and $\sim (\mathbf{b} \subset \mathbf{a})$.

Now were one to suppose that the four alternatives considered exhausted *all* alternatives available for A, E, I, and O propositions, then one would have to conclude from the findings presented by Keynes that the relations of the strong logical square between propositions of the form $A\,(\alpha, \beta)$, $I\,(\alpha, \beta)$, $E\,(\alpha, \beta)$, and $O\,(\alpha, \beta)$ do not obtain in *all* circumstances, but rather only on the *specific* condition that these propositions contain implicit existence assumptions, and this such that the truth of these assumptions is beyond question. Since these assumptions can be explicitly made as referring to conceptual scopes, these propositions admit a logical analysis which corresponds exactly to the translation into the language of the calculus of classes carried out by Hilbert and Ackermann. This is the view that most modern logicians have followed.[71]

3 Limits of the Language of the Calculus of Classes

§ 20 Grounds for a Modification of the Translation Program

However, the enumeration of the four alternatives considered by Keynes is incomplete. A *fifth* interpretation of categorical propositions, which Keynes (1928, 219) mentions in a footnote[72] but otherwise did not consider further, says *that only affirmative but not negative categorical statements implicitly say that there is an object which falls under their subject concept.* Manley Thompson (1953) has argued at length that the relations between any *A*, *E*, *I*, and *O* propositions in the strong logical square obtain without exception if one takes the fifth alternative as a basis, thus if one assumes that not the *quantity* of a categorical statement (as in the case of interpretation (iv)), but only its *quality* decides whether an existential implication is present.[73] According to this assumption, the *existential import* of statements depends exclusively on their affirmative form. I would like to call this assumption the *principle of qualitative existential import.* – If this principle is assumed, we can show that the relations of the strong logical square are strictly and universally valid as follows:

First, the relation of *contradictoriness* remains preserved, since a negative proposition and a proposition it denies can neither be both true nor both false, so long as the negative proposition states nothing other than that the proposition it denies is false. But according to the principle of qualitative existential import, negative categorical propositions are to be understood such that they contain no other statement than that of the falsity of the statement they deny.

Second, the relation of *subalternation* remains preserved. For statements which stand in this relationship are of the same quality and, therefore, according to the

---

71 Peter F. Strawson is among the logicians who suppose that the syllogistic quite generally presupposes that concepts are *non-empty*, or that *A*, *E*, *I*, and *O* propositions imply that the objects of which they treat *exist*. He saw in the syllogistic a kind of 'logic of normal language' which is incommensurable with mathematical logic and maintained a doctrine which goes by the promising name of *free logic*. See Strawson 1952, 165–79; Lambert 1998; and Bencivenga 1998.
72 According to Keynes' note, this fifth interpretation is represented by Friedrich Ueberweg.
73 The assumption formulated by Ueberweg and Thompson corresponds to an old scholastic principle. Cf. Prior 1967a, 143. Thompson (1953, 61) also pointed out the recognition of this principle by Kant and Charles S. Peirce.

principle of qualitative existential import, they are not distinguished from each other with respect to their existence implications. Hence, universal statements cannot be true unless the statements which stand in a subalternate relationship to them are also true.

Third, the *relation of contrariety* holds as well: two universal statements which are distinguished from each other only by their quality cannot both be true, since each of them implies a subalternate statement which is the contradictory of the other; however, they can both be false if the subject concept is not empty, and they are both false if not everything that falls under the subject concept also falls under the predicate concept.

Fourth and finally, the *relation of subcontrariety* also remains preserved: two particular statements distinguished from each other only by their quality can both be true, but not both false. They are both true when they refer to different objects that fall under their subject concept. By contrast, both cannot be false. For if one of them is false, the statement which is its subaltern must also be false, so that the particular statement which is its contradictory counterpart must be true.

Thus, assuming the principle of qualitative existential import, the relations of the strong logical square between any A, E, I, and O propositions hold without exception.

Incidentally, this principle agrees in part – though *only* in part – with what Hilbert and Ackermann called the "tacit Aristotelian assumption."[74] This principle says that an (*affirmative*) statement 'all β are α' is only correct when there are objects which are β. It does *not* say, however, that this holds for either of the *negative* statements 'no β is an α' and 'not all β are an α'.

The principle of qualitative existential import really only expresses the fact that the *truth conditions* of categorical propositions are different in kind depending on whether they are affirmative or negative propositions. The truth of an *affirmative* categorical proposition consists in the *applying* of its predicate to the objects or object which it treats. By contrast, the truth of a *negative* categorical proposition, understood as the *non-truth-functional negation* of an affirmative categorical proposition, consists in the fact that this proposition, together with its double non-truth-functional negation, is false. If A is an affirmative categorical proposition, then the principle of qualitative existential import says merely that the truth of A depends on there being objects to which A applies, while by contrast the truth of N A does not assume the existence of such objects.

---

74 That Aristotle himself did not make use of the "tacit assumption" which is here imputed to him and that his syllogistic did not rely on it, I have shown in my 1998, 131–70.

Of course, 'existence' must be understood here in a very broad sense of the word, namely, such that existence coincides with belonging to the (non-empty) domain of individuals ("*universe of discourse*": Boole 1854, 166) to which the affirmative categorical proposition implicitly relates. A proposition like 'All Olympian gods are mentioned in the *Iliad*' can be true, even if Olympian gods do not belong to the domain of objects treated by the modern sciences or monotheistic religion, for example. It merely belongs to the necessary truth conditions of such a proposition that the objects it deals with occur among the objects mentioned in Homer's works. Likewise, a proposition like 'A regular ten-sided polyhedron is an empty chimera' does not assume that such figures occur, e.g., in physical space or among the objects of stereometry. For such a proposition to be true merely requires that its objects exist in that world to which it refers, namely in the world of chimeras.

Now, compare the following propositions with both propositions just mentioned: (1) 'All Olympian gods are gods' and (2) 'A regular ten-sided polyhedron has ten sides'. Whether they are true or false depends in each case on how they are to be understood. If what they say is that the predicate of being a god is *attributed* to all Olympian gods, or that the predicate of being ten-sided is *attributed* to a regular ten-sided polyhedron, then both propositions can be true, and this *due to the fact* that their objects belong to (non-empty) domains to which the propositions refer. These domains can in both cases be characterized as the *world of attributions*. – Yet both propositions could also be false.[75] If proposition (1) is supposed to say that Olympian gods *are* gods, then this proposition is false if the world of gods to which it refers is an empty domain or contains no Olympian gods. And if proposition (2) is supposed to say that a regular ten-sided polyhedron *has* the property of being ten-sided, then this proposition is false *if* the domain of objects which have ten sides is either empty or does not contain a regular polyhedron. However we understand these propositions and whatever domain of individuals they refer to – their truth depends, in *all* circumstances, on whether their respective domain is *non-empty*. Quite accordingly, the non-truth-functional negation of either proposition can be true *entirely independently* of whether the given domain is empty or not.

---

[75] It follows directly from the principle of qualitative existential import that affirmative propositions of the form $X(\alpha, \alpha)$, with $X = A$, $X = I$, or $X = A̱$, are false if instead of α the expression of an empty concept appears. If one calls propositions of this form 'analytic', then we must suppose that there are *false* analytic propositions. Analyticity and analytic truth, then, must be distinguished from each other. Analytic propositions which deal with objects that do not exist may only be taken as true in so far as they are reinterpreted as propositions which refer to the world of attributions. Analytic judgments are only true in all circumstances if they are understood as *judgments of attribution*. I will return to this point in § 21 and § 57.

3 Limits of the Language of the Calculus of Classes § 20 — 53

Now we can also formulate the principle of qualitative existential import without speaking of *existence* if we talk about *conceptual scopes* instead. In this manner of speaking, the principle says that an affirmative (in distinction to a negative) categorical statement is true only if its subject is not an *empty* concept, i.e., not a concept whose scope is zero.

If we suppose for the time being that the scope of an empty concept (= zero) is the same as the *null class*, and decide to present the relations of the strong logical square according to the principle of qualitative existential import in the language of the calculus of classes, then it proves necessary to subject Hilbert and Ackermann's translation of the schemata 'A (α, β)', 'I (α, β)', 'E (α, β)', and 'O (α, β)' to a *modification*. Since, according to the principle of qualitative existential import as well, a proposition of the form A (α, β) is true if and only if the scope of the concept β is not empty (thus not the null class) and is contained in the scope of α, it is equivalent to a proposition of the form **b** ⊂ **a** & ~ (**b** ⊂ **b̄**). But a proposition of the form E (α, β), unlike A (α, β), does *not* assume that the scope of β is greater than zero, such that ~ (**b** ⊂ **b̄**) holds. Hence it does *not* correspond to a proposition of the form **b** ⊂ **ā** & ~ (**b** ⊂ **b̄**), but rather to a proposition of the form **b** ⊂ **ā**. Finally, if we render I (α, β) and O (α, β) (as the contradictories of E (α, β) and A (α, β), respectively) with truth-functional negations as in Figure 7 of § 17, we can render the relations of the strong logical square with the diagram in Figure 8.[76]

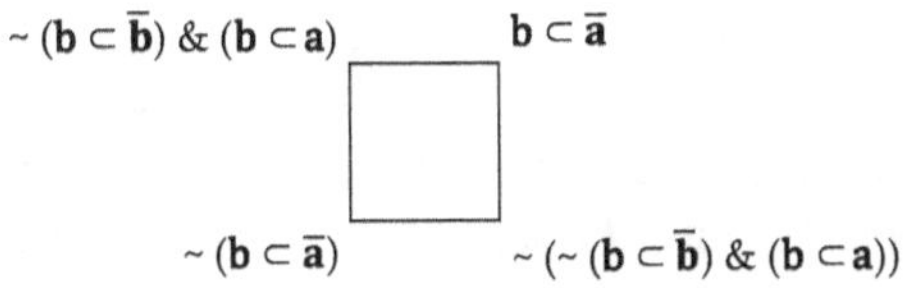

~ (**b** ⊂ **b̄**) & (**b** ⊂ **a**)   **b** ⊂ **ā**

~ (**b** ⊂ **ā**)   ~ (~ (**b** ⊂ **b̄**) & (**b** ⊂ **a**))

Figure 8

According to the way Figure 8 renders them, these relations remain in effect for *any* interpretation of the class variables **a** and **b**. Thus, a small modification of the translation program followed by Hilbert and Ackermann seems to have a chance of success.

---

[76] In this diagram, I needed to use the symbol for logical conjunction, although it does *not* belong to the language of the calculus of classes. The negation of a *pair* of propositional schemata, as occurred twice in Figure 7, can be presented only as the negation of a logical conjunction.

§ 21 The Null Class and Empty Conceptual Scopes

In fact, syllogistic propositional schemata can be translated perfectly into the language of the calculus of classes, according to the procedure presented at the end of § 20, *only if we assume that empty conceptual scopes are simply the same as the null class*. But this assumption is inadmissible. Strictly speaking, it is not at all possible in the language of the calculus of classes to express that a concept – understood as that for which a syllogistic concept variable stands – is not empty but rather satisfied. An expression of the form ~ (**b** ⊂ **b̄**), as it was used in Figure 8, states merely that **b** is not a subclass of every class, in particular that **b** is not the subclass of the complementary class of **b**. This implies that **b** is not the null class. But this in no way precludes that the concept whose scope is designated by 'b' is *empty* nonetheless. This can be clarified as follows.

As a set-theoretical *theorem*, the supposition that the null class is a subclass of every class follows from two set-theoretical axioms, the *axiom of choice* and the *axiom of extensionality*. In addition, it must be assumed that some set exists.

The axiom of choice states: *For any set* **a** *and for every condition S (x), there exists a set* **b**, *whose elements are exactly the x from* **a** *for which S (x) holds*. This axiom tacitly supposes that the condition $S(x)$ may be unsatisfiable. It follows from this that a proposition may be false which states of every x from **a** that $S(x)$ holds. For example, '$S(x)$' may stand for the condition that $x \neq x$; and it may be supposed that $x \neq x$ does not apply to the x from **a**.

From the axiom of choice, it follows that a set exists which has no elements. For given the assumption that some set exists (whatever it may be), it follows from the axiom of choice that there is a set, for example the set $\{x \in \mathbf{a} : x \neq x\}$, which has no elements.

In connection with this, the axiom of extensionality ensures that there is no *more* than one set which has no elements. For this axiom states: *sets are identical only if it holds for every object that it either belongs as an element to all or none of these sets*. It follows from the axiom of extensionality that empty sets are identical with each other, since there is no object that is an element of any of these sets. Hence they are also identical with the set $\{x \in \mathbf{a} : x \neq x\}$, which was already supposed to be empty and which was already shown to exist. It is called *the null set* or *the null class* and is designated by '∅'.

Now from the proposition that the null class exists, it can be derived that it is the subclass of every class or subset of every set, or symbolically: ∅ ⊂ **a**, for arbitrary **a**. In carrying out this derivation, one usually argues something like this (see Halmos 1976, 19): it cannot be false that the null class is a subclass of every class. For if ∅ ⊂ **a** were false, then an element must be contained in ∅ that does not belong to **a**. But since there is no element contained in ∅, neither can it contain an element that does not belong to **a**. Of course, this argumentation assumes that there could only be *one* reason that a proposition like 'Every element of the null class is an element of every class' (namely, an affirmative proposition of the form *A* (α, β)) is false, which is that a counterexample exists by which the proposition can be refuted. However, according to the principle of qualitative existential import, a quite different reason for the falsity of such a proposition can be given, namely, that what the proposition treats simply does not exist (so that a counterexample does exist either). According to this principle, the supposition that every element of the null class is an element of every class is simply false *prima facie*, *precisely because* elements of the null class do not exist.

However, seen in the light of day, the set-theoretical theorem that the null class is a subclass of every class is in no way incompatible with the principle of qualitative existential import. Rather, it even assumes this principle. It only requires for its derivation the use of an additional logical rule which is dispensable within the syllogistic, namely, the rule that from a *false* proposition any *arbitrary* proposition may be immediately derived (whether or not it is affirmative or negative): *ex falso quodlibet*.*

According to the principle of qualitative existential import, the following is already a false proposition: 'Some object has the predicate of being an element of the null class.' For the predicate of being an element of the null class is clearly incompatible with the implicit existence assumption of affirmative propositions. Thus, according to the rule *ex falso quodlibet*, any *arbitrary* proposition may be immediately derived from the supposition that an object is an element of the null class. Accordingly, it is true that *if* some object is an element of the null class, the predicate of being an element of an arbitrary class **a**, whatever may be meant by '**a**', may be attributed to this object. The set-theoretical theorem expresses precisely this situation: ∅ ⊂ **a**, for arbitrary **a**.[77]

We will see at a later point, in § 30, that it is not necessarily appropriate to regard the rule *ex falso quodlibet* as a strictly and universally valid logical rule. Actually, one can already recognize in its wording ('From the false anything regularly follows') that it should not be counted among the *rules of formal logic* (in the narrow sense of this term); that is, if we want to count among these rules only those whose validity depends only on the meaning of logical constants that occur in the expressions to which they are applied. As I said (and as we will see further

---

* TN: 'From the false anything follows'.
77 Usually, the same situation is portrayed something like this: the statement '*if* some object is an element of the null class, *then* it possesses the predicate of being the element of an arbitrary class' is true, assuming the *if-then*-relation in this statement is understood as *truth-functional*, i.e., assuming it is accepted as a sufficient truth-condition for this statement that its antecedent is false. Cf. J. Schmidt 1966, vol. 1, 61.

below, in Part II of this essay), we do not need to make use of this rule in the syllogistic. But when this rule is not enlisted, it is *not* the case that the scopes of empty concepts (as represented by variables in syllogistic propositional schemata) coincide with the null class as a subclass of every class. *Accordingly, empty conceptual scopes are simply not the same as the null class of axiomatic set theory.*

At this point, one could perhaps object that any difference between empty conceptual scopes and the null class had already precluded out by the axiom of extensionality. For it does indeed state that empty sets – and ultimately the scopes (or extensions) of empty concepts must be counted among them – are *identical*. But this objection rests on a misunderstanding. To prevent this misunderstanding from arising, the axiom of extensionality should be made more precise and formulated as follows: *sets are identical if and only if, for every element of the given non-empty domain of individuals, it is an element either of all or none of these sets*. In the axiomatic system to which the axiom of extensionality is supposed to belong, it does need to be specified which non-empty domain is given. For the axioms should hold *regardless of which* domain is given. But this obviously does not mean that the axiom of extensionality supposes the identity of *all* sets which are empty with reference to a certain non-empty domain. The axiom states nothing about how sets relate to each other insofar as they are empty *relative to different domains*. Suppose, for example, a pink Ferrari occurs only in the imaginary world of a certain crime novel; thus suppose things of our everyday world are contained in the set of pink Ferraris just as little as in the set of round squares; then, in relation to the everyday world, both sets are identical according to the axiom of extensionality. But it does not follow from the axiom that both sets are also identical with respect to the imaginary world of the crime novel. Otherwise, the commissar appearing in that world would have no chance from the outset of clearing up his case.

Accordingly, in axiomatic set theory as properly understood, there can be no talk of an *absolute* identity of empty sets at all. Consequently, neither can it claim the *absolute* but only *the relative uniqueness of empty sets*.[78] The supposition that empty conceptual scopes should not be identified with the empty set that is the subclass of every set is completely compatible with this claim.

Taken as a subclass of every class, an empty set is exactly the same as a set whose elements are objects to which only contradictory predicates apply. If **a** and **ā** are the scopes of the concept α and its antonym $^N α$, then the null class can be understood as the scope of a concept under which falls every object to which,

---

[78] Correspondingly, axiomatized set theory as properly understood does not claim that the complement class of the null class is an *absolute universal class*, i.e., the class of all objects. The so-called universal class is always only the class of all objects of a certain, given domain of individuals.

with an arbitrary interpretation of 'α', *both* the predicate α *and* the predicate ^{N}α apply.[79] Considered in this way, the null class is to be understood as the scope of a *certain* empty concept. This concept could be called the *concept of inconsistently determined objects*.

We can distinguish *other* empty concepts from this concept without difficulty. While the concept of inconsistently determined objects is empty simply because inconsistently determined objects are impossible on *logical* grounds, other concepts are empty without there being a logical reason for this. Non-existence can clearly also have contingent reasons, or at least reasons which lie outside of logic.

For example, suppose α stands for the concept expression 'present king of France' and β stands for the concept word 'bald'. Then, according to the principle of qualitative existential import, we must suppose, if α has a scope of zero, that the proposition 'that α is a β' is false. And according to the rules of the weak logical square it is to be supposed that the non-truth-functional negation of this proposition, namely the proposition 'that α is not a β' is likewise false. Both suppositions taken together are in no way equivalent to the supposition that, in the given interpretation, the α is *both* β *and* not β. This would be the case only if from the falsity of two propositions p and $N\,p$, both $N\,p$ and $NN\,p$ always followed, and thus both $N\,p$ and p. But p may not be inferred from $NN\,p$, since, as we have already seen in § 10, the principle of the affirmative use of double negation is not valid for *non-truth-functional negation*. For this reason, the scope of the concept of the present king of France can be empty without our having to suppose that there are objects that fall under it that are determined inconsistently.

To clarify with yet another, perhaps more difficult example, let us also consider the proposition 'An Olympian god is a god'. Let us assume that the concept of an Olympian god is empty. Then, according to the principle of qualitative existential import, this proposition is false. Nevertheless, according to the rules of the strong logical square, its negation, namely 'No Olympian god is a god', can be true. It may perhaps seem that this proposition makes use of an empty concept of inconsistently determined objects, since it speaks of a god which is not a god. But the truth of this proposition depends merely on the fact that even affirmative propositions which

---

79 If one *defines* the null class as the *intersection of a class and its complement class*, then it is trivial to assume that the null class is a subclass of every class. For it is trivial to assume that the intersection of two arbitrary classes is a subclass of each of these classes, from which it follows that the intersection of an arbitrary class **a** and its complement must be a subclass of **a**. – But the above definition itself would not be trivial if it were understood as saying *the scope of an empty concept* is the same as the intersection of a class and its complement class.

look like so-called analytic truths[80] can be false if the objects they deal with do not exist, as the principle of qualitative existential import allows. The proposition 'No Olympian god is a god' expresses the non-existence of Olympian gods, without implicitly assuming that Olympian gods are objects to which an *arbitrary* pair of contradictory predicates may be attributed.

Both examples we have considered should suffice to make clear that interpretations of concept variables in syllogistic propositional schemata are available in which they stand for expressions for concepts with a null scope, *without* this scope being understood as the subclass of every class. Strictly speaking, the scopes of empty concepts should not be equated with what is called the null class in set theory. Hence, an expression of the form ~ (**b** ⊂ **b̄**), as it is used in Figures 7 and 8, actually denies that **b** is the null class. However, it does not yet express that **b** is the scope of a *satisfied* concept. For even if **b** is not the null class, this is still far from ruling out that **b** is the scope of an empty concept.

For this reason, it is simply impossible to subject a syllogistic propositional schema to a logical analysis in which conceptual relations are reduced to class-logical relations and logical constants are translated into the language of the calculus of classes.

The tacit Aristotelian assumption that is tied to syllogistic expressions according to the principle of qualitative existential import, cannot be adequately represented in this language at all. Consequently, *neither* the translation of the syllogistic expressions carried out by Hilbert and Ackermann *nor* the modification of this translation considered above at the end of § 20, is able to make possible a "systematic derivation" of the modes of inference of the categorical syllogistic.

The translation program followed by Hilbert and Ackermann has thus failed definitively.

§ 22 Translation of Class-Logical Propositional Schemata into the Language of the Syllogistic

It is now relatively easy to convince oneself that it is, quite to the contrary, completely possible to represent, in a language that contains no logical constants

---

80 Already above in note 75 I have pointed out that analyticity and analytic truth should not be identified without further ado. In the recent philosophical literature, one becomes used to seeing this equation. It is noteworthy that Kant, from whom the modern distinction of analytic and non-analytic (synthetic) propositions derives, nowhere made such an identification – even if he is mostly interpreted as doing just this.

other than those of the elementary syllogistic, exactly what all the class-logical expressions mean that Hilbert and Ackermann used to derive the modes of inference of the categorical syllogistic within the calculus of classes.

To this end, consider in turn the expressions for inclusion relations as they appear above, for example in Figure 7, starting with the propositional schema '**b** ⊂ **a**'. According to the set-theoretical conception of the inclusion relation, this expression is further analyzable as a propositional schema which implicitly entails four more elementary propositional schemata, namely:

(1) Either **b** is the null class, or **b** is not the null class.
(2) If **b** is the null class, then **b** is a subclass of **a**.
(3) If **b** is the null class, then **b** is a subclass of **ā**.
(4) If **b** is not the null class, then **b** is a subclass of **a**.

Subschema (1) is equivalent to the statement that the class **b** is either the null class or not the null class. Understood in this way, it is a case of applying the principle of the affirmative use of double negation. That is, the disjunction in (1) precludes a case in which **b** is neither the null class nor not the null class. Concerning the sub-statements (2) and (3), together they express a consequence of the set-theoretical theorem that the null class is a subclass of every class. On the basis of this theorem, a sufficient condition for the truth of a statement of the form **b** ⊂ **a** is that **b** is the null class. Finally, concerning the sub-statement (4), it expresses the hypothetical weakening of a categorical proposition of the form A ($α$, $β$). That is, while this later type of proposition says that the scope of the (non-empty) concept $β$ is contained in the scope of the concept $α$, its hypothetical weakening simply says: *if* something is a $β$, then it is an $α$. (4) is a modification of this weakening and says: *if* not every object which belongs to the scope of the concept $β$ is an element of the null class, then every $β$ (i.e., every object belonging to the scope of the concept $β$) is an $α$.

The other propositional schemata as they occur above in Figure 7 can be analyzed in a similar way as well. Concerning the schema '**b** ⊂ **ā**', just like the schema '**b** ⊂ **a**' it is reducible to four propositional schemata, corresponding to schemata (1) to (4), if one exchanges the signs '**a**' and '**ā**' in all places of their occurrence. Concerning the truth-functional negation of '**b** ⊂ **ā**', according to the set-theoretical conception, it expresses two things; first:

(5) The class **b** is not the null class,

and second:

(6) The class **b** is not a subclass of $\bar{\mathbf{a}}$.

The propositional schema '~ (**b** ⊂ $\bar{\mathbf{b}}$)' can likewise be reduced to schemata (5) and (6) if one exchanges '$\bar{\mathbf{a}}$' in (6) with '$\bar{\mathbf{b}}$'.

We can readily render all of proposition schemata (1) to (6) in a formal language in which only the logical constants of syllogistic are used. Of course, to this end one must expand the language of the syllogistic, since one now requires in addition to concept variables also a conceptual constant which can represent the concrete conceptual content that occurs in each of proposition schemata (1) to (6). A propositional schema such as '**b** is the null class' is distinguished from a syllogistic propositional schema not only with respect to the type of variables that appear in it, but rather also by the occurrence of a specific conceptual content; that is, '**b** is the null class' is equivalent to the syllogistic propositional schema 'every element of **b** is an element of the null class'. We may here replace the concept expression 'element of **b**' with the concept variable 'β' if **b** is interpreted as the scope of the concept β. By contrast, the concept expression 'element of the null class' clearly stands for a concept with concrete content. We could also represent it with the concept expression 'inconsistently determined object' (see § 21). To abbreviate this or the expression 'element of the null class', I will use the conceptual constant 'ε_0'. Accordingly, we may abbreviate the propositional schema 'every element of **b** is an element of the null class' with '$A(\varepsilon_0, \beta)$'.

Concerning propositional schema (1), the thought contained in it that the class **b** is either the null class or not the null class can be rendered with the propositional schema 'either every β is an element of the null class, or not every β is an element of the null class'. We can abbreviate this schema with the syllogistic formula '$D(A(\varepsilon_0, \beta), N A(\varepsilon_0, \beta))$'.

Propositional schema (2) comes to 'If every β is an element of the null class, then every β is an α'. Written as a syllogistic formula, it is: '$H(A(\varepsilon_0, \beta), A(\alpha, \beta))$' (where **a** is interpreted as the scope of α).

Correspondingly, propositional schema (3) means 'If every β is an element of the null class, then every β is a $^N\alpha$'. Written as a syllogistic formula, it is: '$H(A(\varepsilon_0, \beta), A(^N\alpha, \beta))$'.

(4) should be translated as 'If not every β is an element of the null class, then every β is an α'; abbreviated: '$H(NA(\varepsilon_0, \beta), A(\alpha, \beta))$'.

(5) comes to 'Not every β is an element of the null class'; in symbolic notation, it says: '$NA(\varepsilon_0, \beta)$'.

Finally, (6) can be translated by 'Not every β is a $^N\alpha$', which says in symbolic notation: '$NA(^N\alpha, \beta)$'.

3 Limits of the Language of the Calculus of Classes § 22 — 61

According to this analysis, the expressions in the left column of the following Table 1 are reduced to expressions in the right column of this table. (I disregard the case (as a special case) in which **b** = **a**, and hence α = β.)

Table 1

b ⊂ a	$D(A(\varepsilon_0, \beta), NA(\varepsilon_0, \beta))$
	$H(A(\varepsilon_0, \beta), A(\alpha, \beta))$
	$H(A(\varepsilon_0, \beta), A(^N\alpha, \beta))$
	$H(NA(\varepsilon_0, \beta), A(\alpha, \beta))$
b ⊂ ā	$D(A(\varepsilon_0, \beta), NA(\varepsilon_0, \beta))$
	$H(A(\varepsilon_0, \beta), A(^N\alpha, \beta))$
	$H(A(\varepsilon_0, \beta), A(\alpha, \beta))$
	$H(NA(\varepsilon_0, \beta), A(^N\alpha, \beta))$
~ (**b ⊂ ā**)	$NA(\varepsilon_0, \beta)$
	$NA(^N\alpha, \beta)$
~ (**b ⊂ a**)	$NA(\varepsilon_0, \beta)$
	$NA(\alpha, \beta)$

One can see that this analysis is correct by assuming that ~ A designates the contradictory of A. Accordingly, the expressions of the first and fourth rows of the left column are contradictories of each other; the same holds for the expressions of the second and third rows of this column. The expressions appearing in the right column of the same rows stand in exactly corresponding relationships to each other. Consider first one of the sub-formulas which stand next to the schema '**b ⊂ a**' in the first of the four rows on the right, namely, '$H(NA(\varepsilon_0, \beta), A(\alpha, \beta))$'. A proposition of this form is false on the condition that its antecedent is true and its consequent false. Precisely this condition is expressed by both sub-formulas in the fourth row on the right. Conversely, two propositions of the form $NA(\varepsilon_0, \beta)$ and $NA(\alpha, \beta)$ cannot both be true if a proposition of the form $H(NA(\varepsilon_0, \beta), A(\alpha, \beta))$ is true. Thus, propositions whose formulas are expressed by the schemata of the first and fourth rows of Table 1 respectively cannot all be true at once. They can, however, all be false at once. For, assuming a proposition is false whose form corresponds to one of the two schemata of the fourth column on the right, one of the propositions whose form corresponds to the schemata of the first rows cannot be false as well. Three cases are thinkable here:

(a) Two propositions of the forms $NA(\varepsilon_0, \beta)$ and $NA(\alpha, \beta)$ are both false;
(b) only the first of these propositions is false;
(c) only the second of these propositions is false.

In case (a), the consequent of a proposition of the form $H(NA(\varepsilon_0, \beta), A(\alpha, \beta))$ is true, but its antecedent is false. But the hypothetical proposition as a whole must be true. For, on the basis of the principle of the affirmative use of double negation, whose validity is expressed by the first sub-formula of the first row on the right, that is by '$D(A(\varepsilon_0, \beta), NA(\varepsilon_0, \beta))$', a proposition of the form $A(\varepsilon_0, \beta)$ must be true. Now the null class is a subclass of every class, according to the set-theoretical theorem whose validity is expressed by the second and third sub-formulas of the first row on the right. From this it follows that, if a proposition of the form $NA(\varepsilon_0, \beta)$ is false, a proposition of the form $A(\alpha, \beta)$ must be true. Thus, in this case a proposition of the form $H(NA(\varepsilon_0, \beta), A(\alpha, \beta))$ is true. But every proposition whose form corresponds to one of the remaining sub-formulas in the first row on the right is true as well – at least assuming the validity of the principle of the affirmative use of double negation and the validity of the principle that the null class is a subclass of every class.

Consider now case (b). It is distinguished from case (a) only in that it supposes that a proposition of the form $NA(\alpha, \beta)$ is true. In this case, too, all propositions are true whose form corresponds respectively to one of the four schemata in the first row on the right. That a hypothetical proposition of the form $H(NA(\varepsilon_0, \beta), A(\alpha, \beta))$ is true when both of its sub-propositions are false holds if the principle of the affirmative use of double negation is valid and the null class is a subclass of every class.

Finally, in case (c) as well, all the propositions are true whose form corresponds to each of the four schemata in the first row on the right. In this case, it is supposed that a hypothetical proposition of the form $H(NA(\varepsilon_0, \beta), A(\alpha, \beta))$ consists only of true sub-propositions. In this case, too, the hypothetical proposition as a whole is true – assuming that the principle of the affirmative use of double negation is valid and the null class is a subclass of every class. On this assumption, all propositions are true whose form corresponds respectively to one of the remaining sub-formulas of the first row on the right.

In summary, one can thus establish that propositions whose forms are expressed respectively by the schemata of the first and fourth rows can be neither all true at once nor all false at once. There is thus a contradictory relationship between the formulas of the first row on the one hand and the formulas of the fourth row on the other, both in the right as well as the left column of Table 1. In just the same way, we can show that there is likewise a contradictory relationship between the formulas of the second and third rows of the right column.

There are therefore good reasons to suppose that the relations which correspond to the expressions in the left column of Table 1 are appropriately analyzed when they are reduced to syllogistic relations which correspond to the expression in the right column of this table.

§ 23 Reduction of Class-Logical Modes of Inference to Syllogistic Modes of Inference

At this point, we return again for a moment to the derivation attempted by Hilbert and Ackermann. They held that the class calculus makes possible "a more systematic treatment of logical questions than traditional logic" (Hilbert & Ackermann 1967, 65 [1950, 55]), by which they meant the syllogistic.

Underlying this view was the conviction that one could reasonably substitute every premise of a categorical syllogism with one or more premises, each of which is an expression from the calculus of classes, and that, on the basis of this substitution, it was to be possible to reduce all syllogistic rules to rules of the calculus of classes. This conviction has proved to be erroneous. By contrast, it is possible to properly substitute every premise which consists of an expression for a class inclusion by a series of syllogistic premises. It is therefore reasonable to suppose that a reduction of the modes of inference of the calculus of classes to the modes of inference of the categorical syllogistic is possible.

Accordingly, we should expect a more systematic treatment of logical questions from the framework of the syllogistic than from the framework of the calculus of classes.

In the attempt to derive class-logical rules from the syllogistic modes of inference, we have struck upon a path which is exactly the opposite of the one taken by Hilbert and Ackermann. For example, to derive the rule that from two premises of the form **b ⊂ a** and **c ⊂ b** a conclusion of the form **c ⊂ a** may be inferred, according to Table 1 (§ 22) the first premise schema ('**b ⊂ a**') should be replaced immediately by four premise schemata, namely by '$D(A(\varepsilon_0, \beta), NA(\varepsilon_0, \beta))$', '$H(A(\varepsilon_0, \beta), A(\alpha, \beta))$', $H(A(\varepsilon_0, \beta), A(^N\alpha, \beta))$', and '$H(NA(\varepsilon_0, \beta), A(\alpha, \beta))$'. Now the inference schema

$$\frac{D(A(\varepsilon_0, \beta), NA(\varepsilon_0, \beta))}{H(A(\varepsilon_0, \beta), A(\alpha, \beta))}$$
$$\frac{H(NA(\varepsilon_0, \beta), A(\alpha, \beta))}{A(\alpha, \beta)}$$

is a special application of the syllogistic rule of the constructive dilemma, whose general form can be represented with this schema:[81]

$$D (A, C)$$
$$H (A, B)$$
$$\underline{H (C, B)}$$
$$B.$$

The rule of the constructive dilemma may immediately be applied to three of the four premise schemata that take the place of '**b** ⊂ **a**' in Table 1. This means that the first premise schema '**b** ⊂ **a**' may be replaced by the schema '*A* (α, β)'. Analogously, the second premise schema '**c** ⊂ **b**' may be replaced by '*A* (β, γ)'.

Now according to the *modus Barbara* an inference of the form

$$A (α, β)$$
$$\underline{A (β, γ)}$$
$$A (α, γ)$$

is universally valid. From two premises of the form **b** ⊂ **a** and **c** ⊂ **b**, therefore, a proposition of the form *A* (α, γ) may be derived. For this reason, then, an inference of the form

$$\textbf{b} ⊂ \textbf{a}$$
$$\underline{\textbf{c} ⊂ \textbf{b}}$$
$$\textbf{c} ⊂ \textbf{a}$$

must also be valid. For a proposition of the form **c** ⊂ **a** – as we have already seen above, in § 16 – is directly derivable from a proposition of the form *A* (α, γ), so long as it is assumed that **a** is the scope of a concept α and **c** the scope of a concept γ. But this assumption would already be used in order to convert the two premise schemata '**b** ⊂ **a**' and '**c** ⊂ **b**' into syllogistic expressions. Accordingly, the validity of the rule according to which from **b** ⊂ **a** and **c** ⊂ **b**, we may infer **c** ⊂ **a**, relies on the

---

[81] For the proof of this rule's validity, see below in § 49. Note of course that the mode of inference (II. 24) there called the constructive dilemma only permits the inference to a conclusion of the form *NN* B. If it is assumed that the principle of the affirmative use of double negation is valid, so that *D* (B, *N* B) holds, (compare § 10) then from this conclusion we may immediately infer one of the form B.

validity of syllogistic modes of inference. It would be easy to show that the validity of all remaining rules of the calculus of classes, as they deal with inferences whose premises and conclusions involve only with negated or non-negated class inclusions, can be reduced to the validity of syllogistic rules in a similar way.

However, the attempt to reduce the modes of inference of the calculus of classes to the syllogistic modes of inference, which is indicated here only by way of example, quickly comes up against natural limits. I would like to point them out in the following paragraphs.

§ 24 Advantages of a Transformation of the Language of the Calculus of Classes into the Language of the Calculus of Functions

These limits begin to become apparent as soon as one draws attention to the fact that the language of the calculus of classes is richer than the language in which Hilbert and Ackermann attempted in vain to present syllogistic modes of inference. Indeed, this language contains still other logical constants than those I have taken into consideration up to now. There are thus modes of inference that can be fully treated within this language which cannot be presented in the language of syllogistic, or at least not without further explanation. While the symbols '... ⊂ ....', '$\overline{...}$', and '~ ...' correspond to syllogistic expressions, namely the logical constants 'A (..., ...)', '^{iN}...', and 'N ...', such equivalents are lacking for the remaining logical constants of the calculus of classes: the symbols '... = ...', '... ∩ ...', and '... ∪ ...', which are used as signs for the *identity, intersection,* and *union* of classes, respectively.

As to the meaning of '... = ...', it can admittedly be reduced to the meaning of the inclusion sign. For '**a** = **b**' combines the content of '**a** ⊂ **b**' and '**b** ⊂ **a**' in one expression. That is, **a** = **b** is equivalent to **a** ⊂ **b** & **b** ⊂ **a**, so that two statements of the form **a** ⊂ **b** and **b** ⊂ **a** can be abbreviated by '**a** = **b**'. An inference of the form

$$\frac{\begin{array}{c}a = b\\ b = c\end{array}}{a = c}$$

can to that extent be reduced to two inferences of the form

$$\frac{\begin{array}{c}a \subset b\\ b \subset c\end{array}}{a \subset c} \quad \text{and} \quad \frac{\begin{array}{c}b \subset a\\ c \subset b\end{array}}{c \subset a.}$$

As far as the connectors '... ∩ ...' and '... ∪ ...' are concerned, they join class variables together so that the schema of an expression that is itself a class designator arises. Thus, an expression of the form **a** ∩ **ā** designates the null class and an expression of the form **a** ∪ **ā** the complement of the null class, i.e., the entirety of individuals of the given domain (the 'universal class'). Stated generally, '**a** ∩ **b**' is the schema used to designate a class which consists of all elements which belong to both **a** and **b**; '**a** ∪ **b**' is the schema to designate a class which consists of all elements which belong to at least one of the classes **a** and **b**.

The signs of intersection and union are distinguished from the signs of inclusion and identity by the fact that they connect two class variables not to a *propositional schema*, but rather to a schema for a designator, i.e., a schema of an expression which itself stands for a class. Since classes are scopes of concepts, these signs serve (whether taken by themselves or in combination with each other or in combination with the complement sign) to designate scopes of *specific*, namely *complex* concepts and at the same time to indicate the *logical form of their composition*. The forms indicated by means of '... ∩ ...' or '... ∪ ...' can be called *logical* to the extent that they are relevant for the validity of inferences, as, e.g., in the following:

$$\frac{\begin{array}{c} a = b \cup \bar{b} \\ c = d \cup \bar{d} \end{array}}{a \cap c = d \cup \bar{d}.}$$

In the elementary language of the syllogistic, there seem to be no logical constants that can indicate the logical form of the composition of concepts, because concept variables are the only conceptual expressions which occur in it. In this language, concept variables represent not only every *conceptual content*, but they also occupy the syntactic places of a proposition, where the parts of a complex conceptual expression could be linked by logical constants. Already for this reason, we can hardly expect that the language of the syllogistic is rich enough to be able to represent all logical relations which can be presented in the language of the calculus of classes.

Of course, the position can also be taken that the logical form of the composition of concepts, as it is indicated by '... ∩ ...' or '... ∪ ...', does not yet find its most appropriate expression in the language of the calculus of classes either. Even if it is a question of explaining or defining the relations of the intersection and union of classes, we can hardly avoid using a vocabulary that brings explicitly into play *elements of classes* in addition to classes and *objects* or *individuals* in addition to conceptual scopes. Thus, the intersection of two classes **a** and **b** is to be seen as the set of objects x, for which it holds that $x \in$ **a** and $x \in$ **b**. Symbolically expressed:

$$\mathbf{a} \cap \mathbf{b} = \{x: x \in \mathbf{a} \ \& \ x \in \mathbf{b}\}.$$

Similarly, the union of two classes **a** and **b** can be conceived as the set of objects x for which it holds that $x \in \mathbf{a}$ *or* $x \in \mathbf{b}$. Symbolically expressed:

$$\mathbf{a} \cup \mathbf{b} = \{x: x \in \mathbf{a} \lor x \in \mathbf{b}\}.$$

These definitions bring a new type of variable into play, namely *individual variables* ('x', 'y', etc.), in addition to the elementhood designator ('... $\in$ ...') familiar from set theory, as well as the set designator '$\{x: \ldots\}$' as an abbreviation for the expression 'the set of all x such that: ...'. Moreover, they also make use of the truth-functional propositional connectives for *logical conjunction* ('... & ...') and *adjunction* ('... $\lor$ ...'). Neither of these logical constants belongs to the language of the calculus of classes. Neither do they belong to the traditional vocabulary of the syllogistic.

As for *logical conjunction*, I have indicated in § 7 that it was used by C.I. Lewis so that he could with its help read the hypothetical 'if ..., then ...' of the syllogistic as strict implication.

As for *adjunction*, it is to be clearly distinguished from syllogistic *disjunction*. If 'p' and 'q' stand for two statements which are true or false, then $D\,(p, q)$ is true only if exactly one of the two statements p and q is true, indeed such that: $H\,(p, N\,q)$ and $H\,(N\,p, q)$ (see above § 6). The adjunction $p \lor q$ states, by contrast, that *at least* one of the statements p and q is true and *at most* one of them is false. It is, like logical conjunction, a truth function. This can be gathered from the fact that the second of the two De Morgan's laws, $\mathbf{a} \cap \mathbf{b} = \overline{\mathbf{a}} \cup \overline{\mathbf{b}}$ and $\mathbf{a} \cup \mathbf{b} = \overline{\mathbf{a}} \cap \overline{\mathbf{b}}$, has a counterpart in the logical equivalence of $A \lor B$ and $\sim (\sim A \ \& \sim B)$. Hence, '... $\lor$ ...' can be taken as an abbreviation of '$\sim (\sim \ldots \ \& \sim \ldots)$'.

Now the translation of expressions from the calculus of classes into a language that makes use of individual variables and truth-functional propositional connectives can be both extended and completed if one also translates class-logical schemata, i.e., expressions containing an inclusion sign, into this language. This can be easily accomplished simply by saying that '$\mathbf{a} \subset \mathbf{b}$' is equivalent to

$$(\forall x)\,(x \in \mathbf{a} \supset x \in \mathbf{b}).$$

In this expression, too, a truth-functional propositional connective appears, namely the sign for *subjunction* ('... $\supset$ ...'). It works for the abbreviation because '$A \supset B$' is equivalent to '$\sim (A \ \& \sim B)$'. The connective used as a prefix, '$(\forall x) \ldots$', is the *universal quantifier* and serves to abbreviate the expression 'for every x such that: ...'.

We can translate arbitrarily complex expressions of the calculus of classes into a language containing individual variables, truth-functional propositional connectives, and quantifiers. For example, we can render '~ (a ∩ c ⊂ b)' with the expression

'(∃ x) ~ ((x ∈ a & x ∈ c) ⊃ x ∈ b)',

whereby the prefix '(∃ x) . . .' is to be treated as the *existential quantifier*, which is simply an abbreviation for '~ (∀ x) ~ . . .'.

The language in which individual variables, quantifiers, and truth-functional connectives are used can still be further improved in logical respects. To do so, we can not only make redundant the use of logical constants of the calculus of classes (except for the sign for truth-functional negation), but also the use of class variables, and thus replace connectives of the type 'x ∈ a' with other connectives. We can see the point of such a replacement by considering that the relation of elementhood, more precisely the relation between an individual x from a domain X and a class of which x is an element, is *also* to be taken as a relation between x in X and the set {T, F}, i.e., the set of truth values. Let a be a certain class, e.g., the set of square roots of 4. Then 'x ∈ a' stands for the propositional schema 'x is a square root of 4', in which 'x' is a placeholder for an expression which is suited to designate an individual from the given domain of individuals X, e.g., an element of the domain of natural numbers. For $x = 2$ and for $x = -2$, 'x is a square root of 4' has the truth value T; but for all other individuals of the given domain, the value F. Therefore, the expression 'x is a square root of 4' for every x in X takes one of the two truth values. The supposition that there is an interpretation of 'x' in which 'x is a square root of 4' is a true or false proposition hence assumes that there is a *relation F of X to Y* such that there is for every x in X exactly one y in Y, with Y = {T, F} and with (x, y) ∈ F.

A *function f*: X → Y (in words, a *function f from X to Y*) is defined as a relation f of X to Y such that there is for every x in X exactly one y in Y with (x, y) ∈ f. If Y = {T, F}, then the function of X to Y is called a *propositional function*, and we write 'F: X → T' and '(x, y) ∈ F' instead of 'f: X → Y' and '(x, y) ∈ f'. A propositional function F : X → Y is accordingly defined by the fact that its domain of values contains only the two truth values as elements. Instead of '(x, y) ∈ F', one can also write 'F (x) = y'. The first formula expresses that F is the set of the ordered pairs consisting of x and y. The second formula says that F, in the argument place x, takes the value y. Both formulas express that y is the value the function F takes depending on which individual of the given domain x is.

Since the interpretation by which the expression 'x is a square root of 4' is transformed into a true proposition corresponds to an operation on the basis of which the right side '= y' of the above equation 'F (x) = y' may be replaced by '= T', it is legitimate to regard 'x is a square root of 4' as equivalent to the functional expression

'$F(x)$' and thus to use the latter as an abbreviation of the former. If one puts another class designator than the set of the square roots of four in place of '**a**' in '$x \in$ **a**', then '$x \in$ **a**' accordingly turns into an expression that can be represented with functional expression '$G(x)$'. Since there are arbitrary many possibilities to substitute for '**a**', one needs correspondingly many functional expressions which can stand for '$x \in$ **a**'. To this end, I will avail myself of an index-notation and write $F_1(x)$ instead of $F(x)$, '$F_2(x)$' instead of $G(x)$, and so on. Nevertheless, I will for the sake of simplicity continue to use expressions '$F(x)$', '$G(x)$', etc. as well, so that they correspond not to *class variables* but rather *class constants*. If a functional expression is supposed to correspond to a *class variable*, then I will write '$F_i(x)$', '$F_j(x)$', etc., and add 'with $i \geq 1$' or 'with $i \neq j, j \geq 1$', etc., respectively; or I will replace '$F_i(x)$, with $i \geq 1$' with '$\Phi(x)$', and '$F_j(x)$, with $i \neq j, j \geq 1$' with '$\Psi(x)$', etc.

The advantage of replacing expressions of the type '$x \in$ **a**' with functional expressions of the type '$\Phi(x)$' stems from the fact that functional expressions can have more than one argument place. By replacing '4' in 'x is a square root of 4' with an individual variable, we get the expression 'x is a square root of y'. Corresponding to this expression is a functional expression of the form $F(x, y)$. For when there is an operation by which an expression is transformed into a true or false proposition, there is a function F from X to {T, F} such that for every ordered pair (x, y) in X there is exactly one element z in {T, F} with $F(x, y) = z$.

(Propositional) functions with more than one argument are called *polyadic functions*. We similarly distinguish between *monadic, dyadic, triadic*, etc. *propositional functions*. Polyadic functions can only be designated by functional expressions with two, three, or more than three argument places.

The admission of n-place functional expressions with $n > 1$ provides the logical advantage of enabling the presentation of modes of inference and types of consequence whose validity depends on one relation between objects following from another such relation.

If, e.g., from the proposition 'There is something of which everything consists' the proposition 'For everything there is something of which it consists' is derived, then this consequence (whose inversion is not valid without further addition) is to be seen as an application of a consequence rule that can be represented by means of a two-place functional expression, namely through the consequence schema

$$\frac{(\exists y)(\forall x)\,\Phi(x, y)}{(\forall x)(\exists y)\,\Phi(x, y).}$$

This schema merely expresses a rule according to which quantifiers, provided they appear in a certain order, may exchange their places. That this rule can be applied to the proposition 'There is something of which everything consists' rests simply on the fact that the functional expression that can render 'x consists of y', namely '$F(x, y)$', admits a two-fold quantification. Quite generally, the fact that n-place functional expressions can be quantified n-fold opens up a space for the presentation of logical rules of which there is no counterpart in the framework of the calculus of classes.

Finally, we can enhance still further the logical capability of using functional expressions by admitting *individual constants* in addition to individual variables. Individual constants – for which I use italicized lowercase Latin letters from the beginning of the alphabet in what follows – are to be seen as (abbreviations for) proper names or as (abbreviations for concrete) designators of certain individuals of the given domain. By this means, once again, the space for the formulation of logical rules is expanded in a manner for which there is no expression in the language of the calculus of classes. The simplest cases are the rules expressed by the following two schemata:

$$\frac{(\forall x)\, \Phi(x)}{\Phi(a)} \qquad \frac{\Phi(a)}{(\exists x)\, \Phi(x).}$$

The functional schema '$\Phi(x)$' here can stand both for polyadic propositional functions like $F(b, x)$ or $F(x, b, c)$ and for complex propositional functions like $F(x)\ \&\ G(x)$. Accordingly, in these cases, the functional schema '$\Phi(a)$' would stand for $F(b, a)$, $F(a, b, c)$, or $F(a)\ \&\ G(a)$.

I call the formal language one attains when one uses no other expressions than
(1) the truth-functional negation sign,
(2) truth-functional propositional connectives,
(3) individual variables and constants,
(4) quantifiers, and
(5) functional expressions,

the *language of the calculus of functions*.[82] This language is distinguished from the languages of the syllogistic and the calculus of classes mainly by the fact that its task

---

[82] Hilbert and Ackermann use the label 'calculus of functions' in the first two editions of their work *Principles of Mathematical Logic* [*Grundzüge der theoretischen Logik*]. Ackermann replaced it in all later editions with the designation 'predicate calculus'. I prefer 'calculus of functions', and indeed for reasons which should become clear in the following. Still more felicitous appears to me 'the logical calculus of functions', the designation used by Kurt Gödel (1933a, 433–43). By 'calculus of functions' here and in the following, I always mean the logical calculus of functions, i.e., the calculus of classical propositional and predicate logic.

is presenting truth functions and propositional functions. Propositional functions and truth functions deal with functions of a similar kind. Namely, every truth function is a function $f: X \to Y$ with $X = \{p_1, \ldots, p_n\}$ and $Y = \{T, F\}$. Here $\{p_1, \ldots, p_n\}$, with $n \geq 1$, is the set of statements, i.e., the set of everything that has one of the two truth values. Propositional and truth functions are thus distinguished from each other only in that their argument domains are different.

Section Three
The Language of the Logical Calculus of Functions

1 A Translation Program

§ 25 The Representation of Concept Expressions with Functional Expressions

The fact that the language of the calculus of functions is, considered logically, far superior to the language of the calculus of classes gives us reason to ask whether this superiority also includes the capacity to make the vocabulary of syllogistic at least partially redundant as the vocabulary of deductive logic. Is it possible to represent the conceptual relations with which the syllogistic is concerned with functional expressions? Can the vocabulary that appears within syllogistic propositional schemata be at least partially replaced by expressions that present propositional functions and truth functions?

It was Gottlob Frege who maintained that *all* conceptual relations dealt with in the syllogistic can be presented in the language of the calculus of functions and who developed this language as the core component of what he called a *concept-script*.

Frege believed that "all relations between concepts" – and by this he meant relations which can be represented by (non-modal) syllogistic propositional schemata like '$A\,(\alpha, \beta)$', '$N\,I\,(\alpha, \beta)$', etc. – "can be reduced" to a "fundamental logical relation," which he designated as the relation "of an object's falling under a concept" (Frege 1983, 128 [1979, 118]), by which he meant the relation between an individual of a given domain and a monadic propositional function. The logical relation between an individual a and a concept under which it falls is portrayed by an expression of the type '$F\,(a)$', which just means that 'a is an F' or 'a falls under the concept F'.

We can clarify provisionally what Frege intended with this reduction by keeping in view how, in § 12 of his 1879 *Begriffsschrift*, he interpreted the logical square that I presented in § 11 by means of Figure 3. Frege presents this square in the form of a diagram corresponding to the following arrangement:[83]

---

[83] The notation I use here and in what follows differs from the two-dimensional 'concept-script' notation used by Frege.

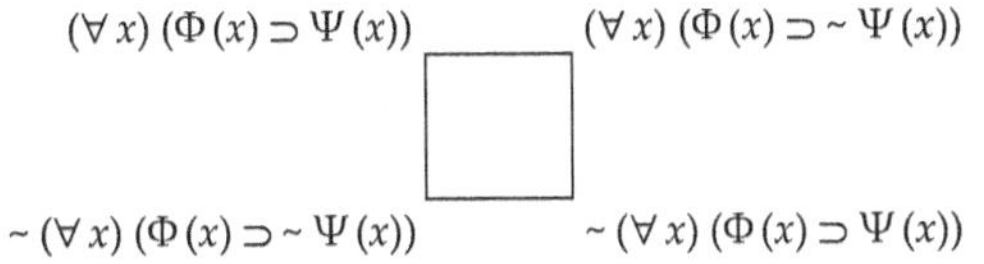

```
(∀x)(Φ(x) ⊃ Ψ(x))         (∀x)(Φ(x) ⊃ ~Ψ(x))

~(∀x)(Φ(x) ⊃ ~Ψ(x))       ~(∀x)(Φ(x) ⊃ Ψ(x))
```

Figure 9

In this diagram, four functional expressions are used which are supposed to present the syllogistic conceptual relations from the strong logical square of opposition. The two universally quantified subjunctions, which appear in the upper corners of the diagram, are thus supposed to present *A* and *E* relations, while the truth-functional negations, which stand opposite them in this diagram, are supposed to stand for *O* and *I* relations respectively.

As one can see, in Frege's diagram longer chains of signs stand in the place of simple triads of syllogistic letters, which already indicates that Frege takes the conceptual relations occurring in the *A*, *E*, *I*, and *O* expressions as complex structures, whose complexity cannot be recognized in the syllogistic expressions. In Frege's eyes, what are *logically fundamental* are apparently not the qualitative and quantitative moments of the four relevant syllogistic conceptual relations, but rather the relations which are designated by means of functional expressions of the form Φ(x) and Ψ(x). These take the place of the syllogistic concept variables. If the individual variable '*x*' in both functional expressions is replaced by an individual constant, or, as in Figure 9, bound by a quantifier, then 'Φ(x)' and 'Ψ(x)' become expressions indicating individuals of a given domain falling under a concept. Understood in this way, the expression '(∀ x)(F(x) ⊃ G(x))' states that for every individual of the given domain, x does not fall under *F* unless x falls under *G*. And understood in this way, the expression '(∀ x)(Φ(x) ⊃ Ψ(x))' should correspond exactly, according to Frege, to the syllogistic schema of a universally affirmative categorical proposition, namely the propositional schema 'every α is a β', – in which the concept variables 'α' and 'β' correspond to the functional expressions 'Φ(x)' and 'Ψ(x)' respectively.

I had said in § 1 that in a proposition of the form 'every α is a β' a *concept* α is *subordinated* to a concept β. Of propositions which state that an object falls under a concept, by contrast, I would like to say that in them an *object* is *subsumed* under a concept. Frege rightly attached great significance to carefully distinguishing the *subsumption* of an *object* under a concept from the *subordination* of a *concept* under *another* concept. Since '*a*' in '*F*(*a*)' stands not for a concept but rather an object, in '*F*(*a*)' an object is subsumed under a concept, apparently without at the same time a concept being subordinated to another concept. By contrast, the subordination of a concept under another concept, as it is expressed for Frege by '(∀ x)(F(x) ⊃ G(x))', apparently always presupposes a subsumption of an object under concepts. This circumstance is, as it seems, what convinced Frege that the subsumption of an object is a logically more fundamental operation than the subordination of concepts. Thus, an object's falling under a concept is a more basic logical relation than the relation which one concept can have to another.

Since it is always possible to represent the subsumption of an object under a concept with the connection of a function sign with an argument letter, it may seem reasonable to regard monadic propositional functions, with Frege, as logically more basic than conceptual relations which are rendered with syllogistic expressions. In the formal language of syllogistic there is, as it appears, no special expression for the subsumption of an object under a concept. This may suggest the conclusion that the formal language of syllogistic is inferior to the calculus of functions, which is the richer language: it thus may look as if one could indeed present in the latter all syllogistically relevant relations, while conversely it does not seem possible to render *even the logically fundamental relations* in the language of the syllogistic.

§ 26 The Function Theory of Concepts

But what exactly do concepts have to do with functions? For the purposes of a precise comparison of the two languages, we need to notice the specific assumptions on which Frege's equalization of function and concept relies. It is indeed relatively easy to see that this equalization does not concern concepts in the same sense in which syllogistic treats concepts and their relations. When Frege says of the 'concept F' that an object a falls under it if $F(a)$, then he apparently does not use the word 'concept' in exactly the same sense in which the concept expressions represented by 'α' and 'β' in '$A(\alpha, \beta)$' stand for concepts.

Frege himself emphasized that function variables should be clearly distinguished from concept variables as they are used in the syllogistic to represent subject-predicate relations.[84] Unlike concept variables, function variables stand for incomplete (syncategorematic) bearers of meaning, since they must carry with them at least one empty place. The variable 'x' appearing free in '$\Phi(x)$', as a non-quantified functional expression, always only designates an empty place. Its task is merely to indicate that the empty place it occupies is to be filled by an expression that designates an individual variable. Only when the empty place is

---

[84] Frege 1964a, xiii (1967, 7): "In particular, I believe that the replacement of the concepts *subject* and *predicate* by *argument* and *function*, respectively, will stand the test of time. It is easy to see how regarding a content as a function of an argument leads to the formation of concepts." – Here and in what follows I disregard the fact that Frege himself declined to make use of the expressions 'function variable', 'concept variable', 'individual variable', or 'quantifier'.

filled by an argument letter ('*a*', '*b*', . . .) or by a *bound* (i.e., not occurring free) individual variable does a complete bearer of meaning arise.

Thus, although that which a term stands for is not a function for Frege, he nevertheless curiously takes it to be appropriate to regard concepts as functions. Indeed, Frege is even prepared to develop something like a *theory* according to which a concept is nothing else than *just such* a function with exactly one argument and whose value is always a truth value.[85] Frege's theory of concepts undertakes a profound revision of the syllogistic concept of concepts. To begin with, we must ask ourselves whether this revision is truly necessary in order to give a reasonable sense to Frege's claim that all conceptual relations (as they occur in the non-modal syllogistic) could be reduced to what he called the basic logical relation, namely, to the relation of the type $F(a)$.

According to Frege's function theory of concepts, concepts are monadic propositional functions.[86] This definition requires an explanation, since it can easily be misunderstood. '$F(a)$' does not stand for a concept; it is rather a *closed proposition* – i.e., it contains no empty place. In Frege's view, a functional expression represents a concept only *insofar* as it contains (at least) one empty place, such as the incomplete expression '$F(\ )$'. Frege calls a function represented by a functional expression with at least one argument place "unsaturated."[87] His function theory of concepts is thus to be understood as saying that concepts are essentially the same as *unsaturated monadic propositional functions*.

In this conception, *neither* a (non-syncategorematic) expression like 'square root of four' *nor* a (syncategorematic) expression like 'square root of x' is a concept expression. The first expression is suited rather to play the role of a term; it is thus a concept expression only in the syllogistic sense of this word. Accordingly, we could call 'square root of x' an *open* syllogistic concept expression, since it is suited to play the role of a term so long as the empty place designated by 'x' in it is filled in such a way that it becomes a closed syllogistic expression. By contrast, in Frege's function

---

[85] See "[Comments on Sense and Meaning]" in Frege 1983, 129 (1979, 119), and "Funktion und Begriff" (1891) in Frege 1990, 133 (1960, 30).

[86] Frege does not use the words 'monadic' or 'propositional function'. One should also note that the designation 'propositional function' as I use it is not completely equivalent to what is called a propositional function following Bertrand Russell. The latter is usually understood as a function whose value is not T or F, but rather $F(a)$ or $F(b)$, etc.

[87] See the passages linked to the keyword "Funktion, – Ungesättigtheit (Ergänzungsbedürftigkeit)" ["Function, – unsaturatedness of a –"] in the index to Frege 1983, 318 (1979, 284). Here and in what follows, I adopt a simplified usage, according to which functions and concepts have empty places, although of course neither functions nor concepts can contain brackets or the like. What this usage intends is that functions and concepts are *designated* by expressions which contain freely occurring variables enclosed by brackets.

theory of concepts, the expression '$x^2 = 4$' stands for a concept, since it corresponds to a function $F(x)$ that takes the value T (*the True*) for $x = 2$ or $x = -2$ and the value F (*the False*) for all other arguments. Represented in words, the concept expression '$x^2 = 4$' is equivalent to the *open proposition* 'x is a square root of four'.

Now according to the function theory of concepts 'x is a square root of x' is also an expression of a concept. This expression corresponds to a function $F(x, y)$ with $x = y$. Its value is the truth value T for $x = 1$, and the truth value F for all other arguments. Though '$F(x, x)$' is a two-place functional expression, since it refers to a function with only one argument, it can be translated into an open proposition with only one empty place, namely '. . . is a square root of itself'.

Strictly speaking, according to the function theory of concepts 'x is a square root of y' can also be an expression for a concept, though if and only if 'x' and 'y' take the same argument. Indeed, taken on their own, individual variables have no distinct meaning, but designate only empty places; they are as it were placeholders for expressions that designate individuals. Hence one cannot simply see in a formula like '$F(x, y)$' whether it is supposed to be an expression for a monadic or a dyadic function. Neither the number of places nor the shape of individual variables decides whether a functional expression is suited to represent an unsaturated monadic propositional function – and thereby a concept.

Incidentally, we cannot even tell from an expression '$\Phi(x)$', as it occurred, e.g., in Figure 9, whether it is supposed to stand for a one- or many-place functional expression. '$\Phi(x)$', as an expression for a monadic propositional function, can stand for either '$F(x)$' and '$G(x, y)$', as well as for '$H(x, y, z)$', etc., so long as the individual variables other than 'x' are used in such a way that they either designate the same individual as 'x', are replaced by an individual constant, or are bound by a quantifier. In all these cases, it is possible to render '$\Phi(x)$' as an open proposition with exactly one empty place, in which this empty place is *the place of the grammatical subject*. In this way, e.g., the three-place functional expression (true for $x = 2$) 'x is a square root of the sum of x and x', is equivalent to the open proposition 'x is a square root of the sum of two summands, which are equal to the root of both'. This open proposition is also a concept in the sense of the function theory of concepts.

In the literature on Frege, the erroneous equation of being a monadic function and being represented by a one-place functional expression is completely widespread. Hence it is sometimes thought that concept expressions in Frege's sense would have to be functional expressions with exactly one empty place, as if a greater number of empty places could only occur in expressions of *polyadic* functions.[88] But

---

[88] Frege's stipulation that concepts are functions with exactly one argument, whose value is always a truth value, is often interpreted as if concepts could only be portrayed with *one-place*

Frege carefully considered the fact that the *number of places* in a functional expression need not correspond to the *number of arguments* of the given function and noticed exactly the distinction between the number of arguments and the number of empty places. He thus counted an expression like '*a* is not identical to itself' explicitly as a monadic propositional function, although it is rendered with '~ $F(a, a)$,' namely, '~ $(a = a)$' (see Frege 1986/1950, § 74).

Since in Frege's view a concept is an unsaturated function and can be presented with an expression with more than one empty place, expressions for what Frege calls a "relation concept," or "relation" for short, can be transformed into concept expressions. Frege uses "relation" or "relation concept" for propositional functions with more than one argument. For polyadic propositional functions with three or more than three arguments, Frege speaks of "relations" with three or more than three "fundaments" (Frege 1983, 270 [1979, 250, modified]). There is in his view an exact analogy between concepts and relation concepts: in a similar way as a singular object a falls under a concept F, in his view an ordered n-tuple of objects fall under a relation concept R, such that R is a relation in which one of the elements of the n-tuple stands to the remaining elements of this n-tuple.[89] A functional expression which represents a relation or a relation concept is accordingly transformed into a concept expression when all the available empty places in it are filled by the same individual signs, or by such individual signs as refer to one and the same argument (e.g., x, y, z ... with $x = y, y = z$ ...).

Concepts are at bottom to be regarded as *limit cases of relations*. That is, for every relation (in Frege's sense) there is always one concept which can be produced out of it through partial saturation as it were, so that all empty places in its

---

functional expressions. This is a misunderstanding which even Gottfried Gabriel, the editor of Frege's *Schriften zur Logik und Sprachphilosophie* (1971, 176 n. 13) has followed. We find the same misunderstanding on the part of the editors of Frege's scholarly correspondence; see Frege 1976, 202. As proof, they refer to Frege's *Grundgesetze der Arithmetik* (1893, 8 [2013, 8]). But here Frege, quite consistently, characterizes concepts not as one-place functions, but rather as functions "with only one argument". In the Frege literature, the talk of one-place functions as abbreviations for "functions which correspond to a functional expression with exactly one empty place, that is an expression of the type '$F(x)$'," has become normalized; it is often discussed as if one-place and monadic functions were the same.

89 Frege 1986/1950, § 70: "The singular pairs of ordered objects are related in a similar way – one could say as subjects – to the relation-concepts, as is the singular object to the concept under which it falls. The subject is here something composite. [. . .] Here the particular content of the relation is not under consideration, but rather only the logical form. [. . .] Just as '*a* falls under the concept F' is the general form of a judgeable content which deals with an object a, so can we take '*a* stands in the relation ϕ to *b*' as the general form for a judgeable content which deals with the object a and the object b."

expression but one are filled.[90] For example, the expression '... is a square root of ...', which is suited to present a relation, immediately becomes a Fregean concept expression when its second empty place is occupied by the name of an individual or by a bound variable, while its first argument place remains unoccupied. All relation expressions can be transformed into concept expressions through this procedure. By contrast, an (inverse) transformation of concept expressions into relation expressions is not always possible. For some concept expressions – like, e.g., '... is a horse' – are composed in such a way that no Fregean relation expression would arise by replacing one of its component expressions with a (second) argument place.

§ 27 Grammatical and Logical Predicates

Propositions which are true or false obviously contain no empty places. Hence, in cases in which a true or false proposition deals with a relation, it is *always* possible to understand the *relation expression* as a mere *component of a concept expression* in the function-theoretical sense of this word. Hence there is a respect in which concept expressions have a systematic priority to other propositional parts, not only from the standpoint of syllogistic, but also from the perspective of the function theory of concepts.

Taken on its own, a function-theoretical concept expression always has the form of an open proposition whose empty place is the place of the propositional subject and whose components always form a totality which stands in a predicative position to the propositional subject. Since in the function theory of concepts a concept expression is suited to play a predicative role in every proposition, Frege ascribes to concepts quite generally a "predicative nature."[91] "What in the case of a function we call unsaturatedness, we may, in the case of a concept, call its predicative nature" (Frege 1983, 129 [1979, 119]).

On this point as well, the function theory of concepts resonates with the syllogistic conception of concepts. For such concepts as can be represented through syllogistic concept expressions also have something like a *predicative* nature. Concepts for which a syllogistic term can stand are, namely, (as I have indicated in § 5) either predicate concepts or at least suited to adopt the role of a predicate concept. The same concept which appears as the *subject concept* in the context of one proposition can be the *predicate concept* in another proposition. For this reason, Kant could

---

[90] Compare "Logik in der Mathematik" in Frege 1983, 259 (1979, 240). See also Frege 1986, 79, § 70 (1950, 83): "The doctrine of relation concepts is thus ... a part of pure logic."
[91] See Frege 1983, 107–09; 120; 129–30; 133 (1979, 97–98; 110; 119–20; 122).

characterize concepts quite generally by the fact that they "are predicates of possible judgments" (see *CPR* A 69/B 94).

Yet from the traditional syllogistic perspective, *predicates*, provided they are concept expressions, are *logical*, not *grammatical* predicates. In the traditional syntax, which goes back to the Latin grammarians, a simple proposition consists of two parts, which are distinguished from each other as 'subject' and 'predicate'.[92] As related to parts of propositions, of course, this distinction is not a logical but merely grammatical distinction, so that the two distinct parts of the proposition are regarded as the *grammatical subject* or as the *grammatical predicate*. Nevertheless, the grammatical subject/predicate distinction is systematically connected with the logical subject/predicate distinction. For the grammatical subject stands for the *object of the proposition*, i.e., that which the proposition is about and of which the predicate is stated. In propositions like 'Theaetetus flies' or 'Every human flies', Theaetetus (or more precisely, the sole bearer of the name 'Theaetetus' who is being discussed) or every human are the *objects* to which the grammatical predicate in these propositions, '... flies', is related. From a *logical* point of view, the grammatical subjects 'Theaetetus ...' and 'every human ...' are distinguished by the fact that they are components of propositions of distinct quantity. Namely, 'Theaetetus flies' is equivalent to the singular proposition 'That bearer of the proper name "Theaetetus" flies'. From a *logical* point of view, the grammatical subject 'Theaetetus' is equivalent to a complex expression which on the one hand contains the concept expression 'bearer of the proper name "Theaetetus"', and on the other hand the logical constant characteristic of singular propositions, 'that ...', just as the grammatical subject 'Every human ...', apart from the concept word 'human' contains the logical constant characteristic of universal propositions, 'every ...'. In traditional syllogistic logic, the concept expression that appears in the grammatical subject of a proposition is called the *logical subject* of the proposition.[93] Just as in this conception the grammatical subject is, from a logical point of view, composed of the concept expression designated as logical subject and a logical constant, so too in this conception the grammatical predicate is to be understood as logically composite. Thus 'Theaetetus flies' and

---

92 See Martianus Capella, *De nuptiis Philologiae et Mercurii* (1983, IV, 361) and Apuleius, *Peri hermeniae* (1908, IV, 267). The grammatical doctrine of the bipartite character of simple propositions goes back ultimately to the thesis, developed in Plato's *Sophist* (261 c–263 a), that every simple proposition consists of noun (ὄνομα) and verb (ῥῆμα).

93 Unlike the syllogistic tradition, in the literature influenced by Frege, e.g., in Peter F. Strawson (1959, 12), the object of the proposition (designated by the *grammatical* subject of the proposition), namely, what Strawson calls the "object of reference," is equated with the *logical* subject of the proposition.

'Every human flies' are logically categorical propositions, each of which brings something under the concept of flying with the grammatical predicate '... flies'. Here the object of the proposition is subsumed under the concept of flying with '... flies'. But this does not mean that '... flies' is itself already a concept expression. As a verb, this part of the proposition only implicitly contains such an expression, namely, insofar as it is equivalent to an expression which can be reasonably analyzed into the *auxiliary word* 'is' and a *predicate noun* 'a flying thing'. The *nominal* component of the grammatical predicate contains the *logical predicate* of the proposition, 'flying thing', while '... is a ...' belongs among the logical constants of categorical propositions.[94]

Since the predicate noun, as the nominal component of the grammatical predicate, is representable by a concept variable, we can say that the expression

'... is an α'

is, from the syllogistic perspective, the basic form of a grammatical predicate in logical syntax. Considered in this way, it is essential to grammatical predicates to contain syllogistic concept expressions, i.e., expressions for logical predicates in the traditional meaning of this word.[95]

If one decides to maintain the traditional distinction between grammatical and logical predicates and grammatical and logical subjects, – and I see no substantial reason requiring us to abandon this distinction[96] – then it turns out that what Frege called the 'predicative nature' of unsaturated monadic propositional functions consists precisely in not being able to be designated by the *logical* but by the *grammatical* predicate of a proposition. While from the syllogistic perspective only the *nominal* component of the grammatical predicate '... is an α' – thus that for which 'α' stands – is the expression of a concept, it follows from the function theory

---

[94] I will go into the relationship between grammatical and logical subjects more extensively below, in §§ 33 and 65. The similarity with the relationship between grammatical and logical predicates will become clearer there.

[95] And, conversely, it is in the traditional conception characteristic of concept expressions that they are able to be syntactic components of grammatical predicates. For the syllogistic conversion rules depend on the fact that terms standing in the subject place of one proposition are suited to stand in the predicate place of other propositions.

[96] Since Frege it has become usual to distinguish between logical and grammatical predicates in a way that is almost exactly opposite to the traditional distinction. Occasionally Frege calls "grammatical predicate" the expression of what is traditionally taken as the *logical* predicate of a proposition; cf. Frege 1983, 106 (1979, 96). But the advantage that is gained from this terminological revolution seems, quite questionably, limited to depriving the basis for classifying functional expressions like '$F(\ )$' in '$F(a)$' and '... flies' in 'Theaetetus flies' as *grammatical* predicates.

of concepts that *the grammatical predicate itself* is a concept expression. As a grammatical predicate, it has the shape of an open proposition, whose argument place is the place of the grammatical subject.

It is the specific structure of the *grammatical* predicate, '... is an α', that makes it possible to represent *A*, *E*, *I*, and *O* statements with functional expressions. Consider the form *A* (α, β), which can be reasonably rendered by 'every β is an α'. According to the function theory of concepts, this form is reducible to the form $(\forall x)(\Phi(x) \supset \Psi(x))$. According to Frege, we can translate this expression with:

'For every *x*: if *x* falls under the concept Φ, then *x* falls under the concept Ψ',

or more briefly with:

'For every *x*: if *x* is a Φ, then *x* is a Ψ', or more briefly still with:
'Every Φ is a Ψ'. (Frege 1879/1967, § 12)

The last three translations are distinguished from 'Every β is an α' only by the shape of the variables used. All three translations rely on the assumption that one can represent the form Φ (*x*) with '*x* is a Φ'. For '*x* falls under the concept Φ' is supposed to say nothing else than that *x* is a Φ.

What is irritating in all three translations is that they involve a different use of 'Φ' and 'Ψ' than occurs in the formula to be translated, '$(\forall x)(\Phi(x) \supset \Psi(x))$'. For both letters are used in the translations as if they were not function signs bearing empty places, but syllogistic concept variables. Even the talk of a 'concept *F*' under which an object *x* falls, and turns of phrase like '... is an *F*', make it seem that '*F*' is only supposed to stand for a *nominal* expression, that it therefore stands not for an incomplete functional expression with an empty place. Of course, it would be no less irritating to translate '*F* (*x*)' with an expression like '*x* falls under the concept *F* ( )', or with '... is an *F* ...', namely with an expression with *more* than just one argument place; this expression would be completely unintelligible. Since '*F* ( )', as the expression of an unsaturated propositional function, is an indivisible expression, the use of the bare letter '*F*' for the schematic designation of a concept '*F* ( )' is in fact inadmissible.[97] For this reason it is, strictly speaking, not completely correct to say '*F*

---

[97] See Frege 1983, 131–32 (1979, 121): "Even if we only indicate concepts schematically by a function-letter, we must see to it that we give expression to their unsaturatedness by an accompanying empty place as in Φ ( ) and X ( ). In other words, we may only use the letters (Φ, X), which are meant to indicate or designate concepts, as function-letters, i.e. in such a way that they are accompanied by a place for the argument (the space between the following brackets). This being so, we may not write Φ = X, because here the letters Φ and X do not occur as function-letters. But nor may we write Φ ( ) = X ( ), because the argument-places have to be filled. But when they are filled, it is not the functions (concepts) themselves that are put equal to one another: in addition

'( )' is equivalent to the phrase '... falls under the concept F' or with the phrase '... is an F'. The letter 'F' is in all such expressions either meaningless, *or it is a syllogistic concept variable*, which like α, β, γ ... represents nothing else than a term.

The irritation can be most simply avoided if one adopts two measures which I would like to recommend in view of all that follows. They will be helpful for consistently observing the distinction between concepts in the syllogistic sense and unsaturated monadic propositional functions and for avoiding the confusion which rests on an ambiguous or unclear way of speaking.

The *first* measure which I recommend is technical and consist in a slight expansion of our logical vocabulary. This expansion should help us to avoid entirely Frege's pseudo-syllogistic use of letters in translations for functional expressions. If with the letter F or with 'concept F' a *predicate concept* is intended, namely something which can be represented only with the predicate noun contained in the *grammatical predicate '$F(x)$'*, then a special mode of notation is needed to make this *predicate concept* recognizable as such. For this purpose, I suggest we prefix the expression '$F(x)$' with the sign '(x)', and call this sign the *predicate prefix* or *predicator*.[98] In this notation, '$F(a)$' signifies that a falls under the concept '$(x) F(x)$'. And if one wants to say with Frege that in '$(\forall x)(x^3 = 8 \supset x^2 = 4)$' we have a subordination of the concept of 'the cube root of eight' under the concept 'the square root of four', one can designate these concepts conveniently with '$(x)(x^3 = 8)$' or with '$(x)(x^2 = 4)$'. The expressions '$(x)(x^3 = 8)$' and '$(x)(x^2 = 4)$' are nothing else than terms. In the same way as β is subordinated under α in '$A(α, β)$', a subordination of '$(x) \Phi(x)$' under '$(x) \Psi(x)$' occurs in '$(\forall x)(\Phi(x) \supset \Psi(x))$'. In the same way as the concept variables α and β are substitutes for terms, the concept expression schemata '$(x) \Phi(x)$' and '$(x) \Psi(x)$' are substitutes for terms.

The *second* measure I recommend is terminological and consists in reworking Frege's revision of the syllogistic conception of concepts. I simply prefer to preserve the traditional, syllogistic terminology and to make Frege's definition of concepts dispensable by simply speaking only of unsaturated monadic functions whenever con-

---

to the function-letter there will be something else on either side of the equality sign, something not belonging to the function." – Frege himself nevertheless sometimes uses '$F(x)$' as if this expression were the same sign (and capable of being supplemented in the same way) as '$F( )$'. See e.g., "Funktion und Begriff," Frege 1990, 128–27 (1950, 24). This usage is somewhat inconsistent.

98 On the mode of notation recommended here, cf. the symbolism discussed by Kneale & Kneale 1975, 587. – Rudolf Carnap introduced the coinage 'predicator' to designate (unsaturated) sentential functions. See Carnap 1947, 4; 6–7. Since 'predicator' is dispensable in this meaning, but coinages are needed for newly introduced symbols, I would like to deviate from Carnap's terminology.

cepts in Frege's sense of this word are meant. This terminological stipulation should serve to avoid misunderstandings which result from an ambiguous use of words.

Frege's idea that it is possible to translate conceptual relations into the language of the calculus of functions and to reduce them to logically more fundamental expressions, which render the falling of objects under concepts, is entirely independent of this definition. In any event, 'conceptual relations' means here, at least in the first instance, relations between concepts in the syllogistic sense.

I also suggest avoiding Frege's identification of relation *concepts* with *relations*. I would prefer to understand relation concepts as *concepts of a specific content*, and to distinguish them in this way from relations. I suggest calling multiply unsaturated polyadic propositional functions *relations* from now on. In this sense 'x is a square root of y', with $x \neq y$, is a *dyadic relation*. In distinction from this, the concept word 'square root' is the designation of a concept which, according to its content, can be understood as a relation concept, since square roots are always only square roots *of numbers*, just as mothers are always only mothers *of children* and sisters always only sisters *of siblings*.[99] Relation concepts, understood in this way, are neither relations in which several individual stand to each other, nor relations under which pairs, triples, or other n-tuples fall. Rather, singular objects can fall under these concepts in the same way as they fall under concepts in general.

It might be objected to my recommendation not to take up Frege's function theory of concepts – for my proposed measures ultimately amount to this recommendation – that Frege's had still another aim than to be able to introduce an abbreviated designation for unsaturated monadic functions. In fact, Frege was convinced that concepts *must* be considered as unsaturated functions, because he believed one *needs* the idea of unsaturatedness of concepts and the unsaturatedness or incompleteness of concept words in order to explain the unity of judgments in which concepts appear – a unity that does not allow propositions to be considered as mere series of words or names.[100] Frege did not pursue merely terminological goals with his revision of the syllogistic conception of concepts. Rather, he believed

---

99 Terms like 'square root', 'mother', or 'north' are designated in the logical tradition as *relative* terms, in order to distinguish them from *absolute* terms like 'horse', 'square root of four', 'mother of a daughter', or 'north of Boston'. This distinction is useful but from the standpoint of the syllogistic it concerns only the conceptual content of propositions. "Words capable of behaving as relative terms can regularly be used *also* as absolute terms, though what amounts to a tacit existential quantification in the context; thus we may say absolutely that Abraham is a father, meaning that there is something of which Abraham is a father." Quine 1959, 118 (§ 22). Relative terms admit an absolute use, while conversely absolute terms do not admit a relative use.
100 See Frege 1983, 193 and 207 (1979, 178 and 190).

that he possessed even a *judgment-theoretical* argument for this revision that equated concepts with unsaturated monadic propositional functions. However, it is easy to recognize that this argument was not actually a good one. It may suffice here very briefly to indicate two of its weaknesses.

First, all logical constants which occur in a syllogistic schema for universal, particular, or singular propositions can be regarded as incomplete expressions or, if one likes, as expressions for 'unsaturated' relations, and even as expressions which each have two argument places; one for the subject concept, the other for the predicate concept. In the traditional syllogistic, this was also expressly indicated by the grammatico-syntactic concept of the *copula*.[101] Hence if one really needs the saturation analogy to be able to explain the *unity of judgment*, then Frege's supposition that concepts are unsaturated *as such* would still be superfluous.

Second, in any case, chemical or mechanical *analogies*, as they are connected with logico-syntactic notions of saturation and binding, do not suffice to be able to explain something like the unity of the judgment in an appropriate way. Yet since in the framework of formal logic, no problem seems to arise which such an explanation would be needed to solve, neither does it need to be provided within this framework.[102]

§ 28 Remarks on the Function Theory of Concepts

In my estimation, Frege would have done better to stick consistently to the traditional use of the word 'concept' in order to avoid ambiguities. He often avails himself of a way of speaking according to which, for example, the equation $2^2 = 4$ says that two falls under the concept *square root of four*. This sounds as if he believes that the concept under which this number falls is designated by the syllogistic concept expression 'square root of four' (cf. Frege 1983, 17–18 [1979, 16]). But according to his own concept theory, this way of speaking is not correct. For as we have said concepts, which are functions in Frege's sense, cannot be designated by closed nominal phrases, but only by functional expressions of the form $\Phi(\ )$ that require supplementation. These are essentially indivisible expressions, whose empty places are supposed to indicate the "unsaturatedness" of concepts (Frege 1983, 131 [1979, 121]).

---

[101] Jonathan Barnes has extensively discussed this objection against Frege's argument in his 1996, 175–219.
[102] Frege seems not to have known or studied the more demanding explanations of the unity of the judgment as they were developed, e.g., in Kant's theory of apperception or in Hegel's doctrine of the concept.

When Frege speaks of an object falling under a 'concept F', this way of speaking clearly stems from an embarrassment. He thus writes:

> I use the word 'concept' in such a way that 'a falls under the concept F' is the general form of a judgeable content which deals with one object a and which remains judgeable whatever else one puts for a. And in this sense, 'a falls under the concept "unequal to itself"' is equivalent to 'a is unequal to itself' or 'a does not equal a'. (Frege 1986/1950, § 74)[103]

There are *three* things that Frege wants to note here. *First*, he wants to explain what "the general form" of singular statements is. *Second*, he wants to indicate the fact that the general form of singular statements should not be confused with the general form of statements which deal with pairs, triples, etc. *Third*, he wants to inform us about his use of words.

As for the *first* point, Frege designates the singular statement as a "judgeable content which deals with an object a and which remains judgeable whatever else one puts for a." He means that "the general form" of singular statements can be rendered with a functional expression of the form $\Phi(a)$. That is, all more specific forms of singular statements correspond to expressions which can arise in a twofold manner, namely: first, by replacing '$\Phi(\ )$' with an n-place functional expression with $n > 1$, whose empty places are without exception filled by 'a'; and second, by replacing the individual constant a in an expression of the form $\Phi(a)$ with a sign which is distinct from 'a' but which likewise stands for an individual object. Further below, in § 33, I will come back to the thesis contained in this point that 'a falls under the concept F' is the general form of singular statements.

Concerning the *second* point, Frege writes:

> Just as 'a falls under the concept F' is the general form of a judgeable content which deals with an object a, so can we take 'a stands in the relation ϕ to b' as the general form for a judgeable content which deals with the object a and the object b. (Frege 1986/1950, § 74)

Here one should take note of the fact that Frege does not really see the distinction between the general *form* of a statement dealing with an individual falling under a *concept* and the general *form* of a statement dealing with a *relation* between two (or more) individuals to consist in a distinction of *form* concerning the incomplete functional expressions as such. He rather sees it exclusively in a distinction of the *content* through which their argument places are filled. (Frege's talk of the "form" of a "content" can easily belie this fact.)

---

[103] In another place, Frege writes in a corresponding way: "If I say 'Plato is a human,' I am not as it were giving Plato a new name – the name 'human' – but I am saying that Plato falls under the concept *human*." Frege 1983, 231 (1979, 214). Cf. also the example in "Funktion und Begriff," Frege 1990, 133 (1960, 30).

As for the *third* point, it expresses a difficulty which is connected with the revision of the traditional conception of concepts. Frege wants to clarify his new, function-theoretical understanding of the word 'concept', but he does this as if a concept in this understanding were something which could stand in place of a syllogistic concept variable. That is, he does this as if the concept (in his *new* usage) under which *a* is supposed to fall is a concept (in the *old* usage) under which *a* is supposed to fall, when it falls under *F*. In order to explain the new usage of the word, he would have really needed to clearly distinguish it from the old usage, instead of confounding both usages together.[104]

Thus it would have ultimately been basically reasonable if, in place of his definition, Frege would have told us that the function theory of concepts uses the word 'concept' in such a way that a phrase like '*a* falls under the concept *F*' is actually *not* about a concept at all.[105] For according to this theory, when '*F* (*a*)' is true, it is not '*F*' but rather an open proposition of the form '. . . is an *a*' that is supposed to stand for the concept under which *a* falls. And this open proposition is not equivalent to '*F*' or '*a*', but rather to '. . . falls under the concept *F*' when '*F* (*a*)' is equivalent to '*a* falls under the concept *F*'.

Of course, Frege also has a systematic reason to sometimes use the function letter '*F*' as if it *did* stand for a closed expression, and to speak of a concept *square root of four*, a concept *horse*, or a concept *F*, as if the concepts designated in this way were *not* unsaturated propositional functions. Namely, in his system Frege wants to permit function signs to be replaced by *bound function variables*, so that the latter could occur in quantifiers (see *Begriffsschrift*, § 9).[106] This occurrence assumes that function letters may be treated as if they were object variables and as if they carried no empty places. Along these lines, Frege suggests that the function variable 'Φ' in an expression of the form (∀ Φ) (. . . Φ . . .) stands for 'the property Φ, whatever Φ may be' (Frege 1879, 61, § 26 [1967, 60]) among all possible properties, such as, for example, "the property of being a heap of beans" (Frege

---

104 Perhaps the fact that Frege's way of designating concepts and functions is fluctuating, as when he indicates sometimes '*F*', sometimes '*F* ( )', and sometimes '*F* (*x*)' as signs for functions, helps explain why Frege also wavers in his conception of what a concept word is: sometimes he supposes that the copula '. . . is . . .' belongs to it (see Frege 1983, 192 [1979, 178]), sometimes he supposes that concept words are those which can be preceded by the expressions 'all', 'some', etc. (See the letter to Heinrich Liebmann from August 25, 1900, in Frege 1976, 150 [1980, 92], and Frege 1983, 230 [1979, 213]).
105 In his article "Über Begriff und Gegenstand" of 1892, Frege (1990, 170) himself expressly indicated that in his theory a certain concept, like, e.g., the concept *horse*, is in truth *not* a concept.
106 "On the other hand, it may also be that the argument is determinate and the function indeterminate." Frege 1879, 17 (1967, 23). §§ 10 and 11 then elucidate how indeterminate functions are to be represented by the use of variables.

1879, 64 [1967, 62]). Such a property is strictly speaking not an unsaturated function, but rather something that corresponds to a syllogistic concept expression which carries no empty place.

The license to treat function variables as if they were object variables leads Frege to draw an analogy between the subsumption of an object under a concept and the subsumption of a *first-level concept* under a *second-level concept*. The proposition '($\exists\,\Phi$) ($\exists\,x$) $\Phi\,(x)$' states that there is a propositional function with the property of applying to an object. It is related to the proposition '($\exists\,x$) ($x^2 = 4$)' like the proposition '($\exists\,x$) $F\,(x)$' is related to the proposition '$F\,(a)$'. Now Frege supposes that, just as '$F\,(a)$' states that the object a falls under the concept F, so '($\exists\,x$) ($x^2 = 4$)' states that the concept *square root of four* falls *within* the concept "'there is'-existence" (Frege 1976, 151 [1980, 93]). Instead of speaking twice here of the relation of subsumption, Frege prefers to speak in the first case of falling *under* a concept, and in the second case of falling *within* a concept. This is just supposed to underscore that a concept such as *square root of four* is not an object but rather a "first-level concept," while the concept *within* which it falls, namely, the concept of "'there is'-existence" (i.e., the concept of being a satisfied concept) is a "second-level concept" (Frege 1976, 150–51 [1980, 93]). Now, '($\exists\,x$) ($x^2 = 4$)' can also be rendered with the words: 'some object is a square root of four,' or with the words: 'There is at least one square root of four'. These propositions correspond to the schemata 'Some object is an α' and 'There is at least one α', respectively. This circumstance finally prompts Frege to state explicitly:

> Concept words come with the indefinite article and with words like 'all', 'some', 'many', etc. (Frege 1976, 150 [1980, 92])

For what Frege calls a first-level concept can be subsumed under a second-level concept only if it is a concept which can be represented by a syllogistic concept variable. Open propositions, by contrast, which represent an unsaturated monadic propositional function, are meaningless expressions on their own and hence unsuited to designate concepts capable of being subsumed.

Hence, Frege is not at all in a position to maintain his function theory of concepts even somewhat consistently.

In his famous first letter to Frege from June 16, 1902, Russell, referring to the passage in § 9 of the *Begriffsschrift* we have just discussed, calls attention to the hazards connected to the use of the bound function variables, since he understood this as the source of the contradiction which later became known as 'Russell's paradox'. Russell writes:

> I have encountered a difficulty only on one point. You assert (p. 17) that a function could also constitute the undefined element. This is what I used to believe, but this view now

seems to me dubious because of the following contradiction: Let w be the predicate of being a predicate which cannot be predicated of itself. Can w be predicated of itself? From either answer follows its contradictory. We must therefore conclude that w is not a predicate. Likewise, there is no class (as a whole) of those classes which, as wholes, are not members of themselves. From this I conclude that under certain circumstances a definable set does not form a whole. (Frege 1976, 211 [1980, 130–31])

Russell here calls attention to the fact that an expression of the form $(\forall \Phi) (\ldots \Phi \ldots)$ refers to an argument domain which contains neither mere objects, to which bound individual variables refer, nor mere concepts, which are predicates of objects falling under them, but is populated by such suspicious entities as the predicates of predicates of which w is an example. Predicates of predicates are necessarily entities which are *neither* unsaturated monadic propositional functions *nor* first-level concepts in Frege's sense; they are rather concepts in the syllogistic sense. For a predicate *can* be predicated of itself only if it is a predicate concept, namely a *logical predicate* in the sense of this expression discussed above. Only in propositions like 'the w is a w' or 'a w is a w' – with a term w – can w be predicated of itself.[107] Predicates of which another predicate, or itself, can be predicated must also be suited to appear as the subject concept. Yet these must be precisely predicates of a specific *conceptual content*. That predicates of predicates can belong to the argument domain of a function of the form $(\forall \Phi) (\ldots \Phi \ldots)$ is due to the fact that, though this form admits unsaturated propositional functions as values of bound variables, it comes with no provisions prohibiting *concepts in the syllogistic sense of this word* from saturating these functions. Thus, through the saturation of $\Phi ( )$, a propositional function of the form $\Phi (\Psi ( ))$, with $\Phi = \Psi$ or with $\Phi \neq \Psi$, can arise, and then, through the tacit metamorphosis of $\Psi ( )$ into a concept of the form $('x) \Psi (x)$, a predicate of a predicate of the form $\Phi (('x) \Psi (x))$ is formed.

The letter in which Frege immediately reacted to Russell's note shows that Frege recognized at once the extensive consequences of this problem. The contradiction Russell discovered, he says, "has rocked the ground on which I meant to build arithmetic" (Frege 1976, 213 [1980, 132]). Frege recognized immediately that foundational assumptions of his work *Basic Laws of Arithmetic* had become frail, since their implicit reference to unrestricted argument domains of predicates of predicates makes it possible to derive contradictory consequences (see Frege 1976, 213–15 [1980, 132–35]).

---

[107] It should be mentioned here only in passing that no deeper logical problem arises when it happens that two propositions of the form 'the w is a w' and 'the w is not a w' are both false. For this problem immediately dissolves if one is only ready to treat these propositions as cases of the application of the weak logical square of assertoric opposition, as per § 12.

The heart of the problem that Frege here ran up against, and which made his project of grounding arithmetic on the basis of pure logic miscarry, was the fact that with the binding of variables for propositional functions by quantifiers, the given argument domain was expanded beyond its intended size. With this expansion, the saturation of unsaturated propositional functions by unsaturated propositional functions was tacitly permitted without restriction.

Frege's motive, already in the *Begriffsschrift* of 1879, for admitting the occurrence of function variables in quantifiers is connected with his project of deducing the principle of mathematical induction from the axioms of the *Begriffsschrift* with the help of the definitions from the third part of that work. For in the framework of this deduction he saw that it was necessary to quantify over function variables. This motive could have been omitted had Frege's notation as it concerned the inseparability of function letters and empty places been more consistent. Yet showing this would exceed the bounds of the present investigation.[108]

As for Frege's thesis of the reducibility of all conceptual relations to the basic logical relation of objects falling under concepts, it was in any case unnecessary to abandon for the sake of this thesis the terminology appropriate for the syllogistic, according to which concepts are subject concepts or predicate concepts and can be presented by terms. For even in a – from Frege's perspective – logically fundamental expression like '$F(a)$' a concept always occurs implicitly which can be understood as a predicate concept and designated with '$(x) F(x)$'. The fact that Frege could claim the "conceptual content" of a judgment should be regarded as a "function of this or that argument" substantially depends on this circumstance.[109] For something conceptual is a function of this or that argument only insofar as there is something in it under which an object is subsumable and which, as a *logical predicate*, can be represented by a syllogistic concept variable.

When Frege writes, "A distinction between *subject* and *predicate* does *not occur* in my way of representing a judgment,"[110] it would have been helpful if he

---

108 On the question of what shape a more consistent notation in connection with the deduction of the generalized principle of mathematical induction from the axioms of the *Begriffsschrift* could have taken, compare my sketch of a deduction below in Appendix 2. According to this sketch, there is no need to introduce a *higher-level* predicate logic (which makes possible Russell's Paradox).

109 Frege 1879, 17, § 9 (1967, 23): "For us the fact that there are various ways in which the same conceptual content can be regarded as a function of this or that argument has no importance so long as function and argument are completely determinate." – In the Preface to the *Begriffschrift*, Frege also used this explanation to justify the name 'concept-script'. See Frege 1879, iv (1967, 6).

110 Frege 1879, 3, § 3 (1967, 12): "A distinction between *subject* and *predicate* does *not occur* in my way of representing a judgment. In order to justify this I remark that the contents of two judgments may differ in two ways: either the consequences derivable from the first, when it is combined with certain other judgments, always follow also from the second, when it is combined

had here explicitly indicated that the *grammatical* distinction of subject and predicate – which must be carefully distinguished from the *logical* subject/predicate distinction – remains completely applicable to expressions of his concept-script. For though a function of this or that argument, provided its value is always a truth value, never plays the role of a *logical* predicate, it does always play the role of a grammatical predicate. And the empty place of an unsaturated monadic propositional function always corresponds to the place of a *grammatical* subject.

In the following, I will stick to the terminology in which a concept is understood as that for which a term (i.e., a nominal expression) can stand, whether this expression is a simple word or a nominal phrase of arbitrary complexity, and whether it is a substantival or adjectival expression. Accordingly, when the contrary is not explicitly mentioned, from here on out I will speak of an object's falling under a concept and of the subordination of one concept to another concept always only in such a way that a formula like '$F(a)$' should be read as equivalent to 'a falls under the concept ($'x$) $F(x)$', and a formula like '$(\forall x)(F(x) \supset G(x))$' should be understand as subordinating the concept ($'x$) $F(x)$ to the concept ($'x$) $G(x)$.

The notion that concepts are entities with a special kind of empty stomach and with a specific appetite for objects should perhaps best be treated as a mythical fable, which may have helped the calculus of functions and its language free itself from the syllogistic, but which is dispensable for logic and which – now that there is hardly anyone left who doubts the capability of this calculus and its language – creates more troubles than it brings advantages.

2 Examination of the Translation Program

§ 29 Subordination of Concepts in the Language of the Calculus of Functions

Since I have in the previous paragraphs (§§ 25–28) shown how Frege's thesis of the reducibility of all conceptual relations to relations of the form $F(a)$ needs to be understood more precisely, I would now like to turn to the question of whether this thesis is also substantially convincing. Is it right to assume that one could appropriately translate all syllogistic schemata for universal, particular, or singular propositions into the formal language of the calculus of functions? Can one represent the syllogistic in the language of a concept-script at all?

---

with these same judgments, [and conversely,] or this is not the case. The two propositions 'The Greeks defeated the Persians at Plataea' and 'The Persians were defeated by the Greeks at Plataea' differ in the first way. Even if one can detect a slight difference in meaning, the agreement outweighs it. Now I call that part of the content that is the *same* in both the *conceptual content*."

To be able to answer these questions precisely, we first must consider once again how universally quantified subjunctions should be properly understood, as they came up above in Figure 9 (see § 25) as translations of syllogistic propositional schemata.

In § 12 of his *Begriffsschrift*,[111] Frege (1879, 23 [1967, 27]) argues that the universally quantified subjunction

$$(\forall x)\,(\Phi(x) \supset \Psi(x))$$

may be translated *both* by the hypothetical expression, 'If something has the property Φ, then it also has the property Ψ', *and* the categorical expression, 'All Φ's are Ψ's'. Here, the Greek letters Frege uses in both these translations of his formula correspond to syllogistic concept variables. They may be appropriately replaced by '$(x)\,\Phi(x)$' or by '$(x)\,\Psi(x)$', respectively. Frege proposes analogous translations for the remaining formulae which occurred in Figure 9, which are distinguished from each other and from the formula of subjunction just discussed only because the sign for truth-functional negation occurs in different places in them.

Above, in §§ 1, 3, and 5, I had put forth the schemata of categorical and hypothetical propositions as schemata of propositions of distinct *logical* form. By contrast, Frege (1879/1967, § 4) attaches only "grammatical significance" to the distinction between categorical and hypothetical form. In his view, 'every α is a β' and 'if something is an α, then it is a β' are only *grammatically* different forms of the subordination of one concept to another concept. The common logical 'deep structure' of this operation is expressed in his view through a universally quantified subjunction.

Incidentally, the view that 'every α is a β' and 'if something is an α, then it is a β' are equivalent propositions was already held before Frege. One of the principles of the traditional syllogistic, the so-called *dictum de omni et nullo* was sometimes understood as saying that a categorical proposition of the form 'every α is a β' is true if and only if a hypothetical proposition of the form 'if something is an α, then it is a β' is true; and likewise that a categorical proposition of the form 'no α is a β' is true if and only if a hypothetical proposition of the form 'if something is an α, then it is not a β' is true. Even from the syllogistic perspective, both a universal affirmative proposition and hypothetical proposition that follows from it express the subordination of one concept to another. Because of this, Christian Wolff (1740, 229, § 226), for example, held that categorical propositions were in truth hypothetical propositions, and reducible to the latter. Of course, Frege's conception differs

---

[111] Frege maintained the conception developed there in his later logical writings; cf. Stuhlmann-Laeisz 1995, 182–91.

from this view in that it does not reduce categorical to hypothetical propositions, but rather reduces both categorical and hypothetical propositions equally to propositions which are *neither* categorical *nor* hypothetical.

I will here leave aside the question of what Frege meant when he says in § 4 of his *Begriffsschrift* that the distinction between categorical and hypothetical propositions has only grammatical significance. But we must examine whether the view is true on which this opinion of Frege's depends, namely: whether categorical propositions of the form 'every ('x) Φ (x) is a ('x) Ψ (x)' and hypothetical propositions of the form 'if something is a ('x) Φ (x), then it is a ('x) Ψ (x)' are reducible to universally quantified subjunctions of the form (∀ x) (Φ (x) ⊃ Ψ (x)).

First of all, I will turn to the question of how hypothetical propositions relate to universally quantified subjunctions.

§ 30 Truth Functions and their Reduction to Non-truth-functional Forms

The issue will depend on explaining how the meaning of the hypothetical 'if . . ., then . . .' relates to the meaning of the subjunction sign '. . . ⊃ . . .'. Above, in § 6 and § 7, we have already seen that these meanings do not coincide, since 'if . . ., then . . .' unlike '. . . ⊃ . . .' is not a truth-functional connective. The subjunction 'A ⊃ B' corresponds to a proposition of the form 'not A, unless B' rather than a proposition of the form 'if A, then B'. The proposition '3 × 7 does not equal 21, unless the sun shines' can be true, while the corresponding hypothetical proposition 'if 3 × 7 equals 21, then the sun shines' is false. The latter states that the content of the consequent *follows* from the content of the antecedent. Hence, its truth would be incompatible with the sun's not shining even once.

Frege himself clearly recognized the basic distinction between 'if . . ., then . . .' and '. . . ⊃ . . .' and correctly describes it in § 5 of his *Begriffsschrift* (see Frege 1879, 6, § 5 [1967, 14]). Yet he believed that the subjunction sign could adopt the meaning of the hypothetical 'if . . ., then . . .' so long as it stands within the scope of a universal quantifier. In that case, the "causal connection" that is represented by a hypothetical proposition could be represented by means of the subjunction sign (Frege 1879/1967, § 12). There is an essential distinction, in Frege's eyes,[112] between '*p* ⊃ *q*' and '(∀ x) ([x is an ('x) Φ (x)] ⊃ [x is a ('x) Ψ (x)])' due to the fact that in the first case,

---

[112] Frege held that "In the hypothetical propositional connection we have as a rule improper propositions of such a kind that neither the antecedent by itself nor the consequent by itself expresses a thought, but only the whole propositional complex." See "Frege to Husserl 30.10–1.11.1906," in Frege 1976, 103 (1980, 68). By a hypothetical propositional connection is meant here a complex corresponding to the propositional schema 'If something is an α, then it is a β'.

there are two standalone closed propositions p and q, independent of each other, which are connected by the subjunction sign, while in the second case an inner connection between the contents of two open propositions is represented by both propositions being joined together by means of a quantifier.

Of course, what Frege has overlooked here is the fact that the expression '($\forall$ x) ([x is an ('x) Φ (x)] $\supset$ [x is a ('x) Ψ (x)]' is not at all equivalent to the hypothetical expression '($\forall$ x) H ([x is a ('x) Φ (x)], [x is a ('x) Ψ (x)])'. Namely, while the hypothetical proposition 'if x, whatever x may be, is a ('x) Φ (x), then x is a ('x) Ψ (x)' is true if and only if the content of the consequent follows from the content of the antecedent, it already suffices for the truth of the subjunction '($\forall$ x) ([x is an ('x) Φ (x)] $\supset$ [x is a ('x) Ψ (x)]' that there is no x to which the antecedent applies.

That is, the inner connection between two states of affairs which can be represented by a universally quantified subjunction belongs to a quite different kind of connection than the one expressed by 'if . . ., then . . .'. Different *truth conditions* hold for hypothetical propositions than hold for subjunctive propositions.

The truth conditions of a proposition of the form ($\forall$ x) (F (x) $\supset$ G (x)) correspond exactly to the truth conditions of a proposition of the form **b** $\subset$ **a**. For a proposition of this form to be true, it suffices that the conceptual scope **b** is the null class. This follows from the set-theoretically justified theorem that says that the null class is a sub-class of every class. Consequently, as Table 2 shows,

Table 2

b $\subset$ **a**	($\forall$ x) (Φ (x) $\supset$ Ψ (x))
b $\subset$ **ā**	($\forall$ x) (Φ (x) $\supset$ ~ Ψ (x))
~ (**b** $\subset$ **ā**)	~ ($\forall$ x) (Φ (x) $\supset$ ~ Ψ (x))
~ (**b** $\subset$ **a**)	~ ($\forall$ x) (Φ (x) $\supset$ Ψ (x))

the formulas of the calculus of functions in Figure 9 (see § 25 above) can be collated with the formulas of the calculus of classes in Figure 6 (see above § 17) in such a way that for every interpretation in which **a** is the scope of the concept ('x) Ψ (x) and **b** the scope of the concept ('x) Φ (x), the formulas of the left column of this table are true if and only if the corresponding formulas on the right side are true. Yet none of the expressions on the right column correspond to a (non-negated or negated) hypothetical propositional connection.[113]

---

[113] Frege's error in thinking that hypothetical propositions that express a subordination of one concept to another are equivalent to definite universal affirmative categorical propositions can probably only be explained historically. Boole had already conceived propositions of the form A (α, β) such that they are true when there is no object with the property β. He saw them, namely,

Therefore, a careful investigation is needed in order to find out how propositions of the form (∀ x) ([x is an ('x) Φ (x)] ⊃ [x is a ('x) Ψ (x)] and (∀ x) H ([x is a ('x) Φ (x)], [x is a ('x) Ψ (x)]) are related to each other.

Above, in § 7, I had already discussed the view that a hypothetical proposition of the form H (A, B) is to be understood as an expression of strict implication. From this view it follows that the universally quantified hypothetical connection is to be understood as a universally quantified strict implication. '(∀ x) H ([x is a ('x) Φ (x)], [x is a ('x) Ψ (x)])' would then be equivalent to

'(∀ x) □ (Φ (x) ⊃ Ψ (x))'.

For the strict implication 'A ⊰ B' is equivalent to '□ (A ⊃ B)'. Namely, since 'A ⊃ B' is an abbreviation for '~ (A & ~ B)' and '□ . . .' an abbreviation for '~ ◇ ~ . . .', '~ (A & ~ B)' is equivalent to '□ (A ⊃ B)'. In conclusion, 'A ⊰ B' is *per definitionem* equivalent to '~ ◇ (A & ~ B)'.

However, I had already indicated in § 14 that strict implication, for its part, can be further analyzed as a relation which is presentable by means of logical constants of which none apart from '. . . & . . .' is a truth-functional expression. It was also already clear that since the hypothetical 'if . . ., then . . .' is found among these constants, it would amount to a circular explanation if we wanted to understand the form of the hypothetical proposition as a strict implication. Hence the first question that suggests itself is whether it might be possible to reduce strict implication *completely* to non-truth-functional relations, and whether it might be possible to avoid a circle in explaining the hypothetical propositional form.

To respond to this question, I would first like to turn to the question of whether the logical conjunction A & B might also be understood as a relation that can be presented with only non-truth-functional signs.

That such a presentation is possible can be relatively easily seen. We can assign logical conjunction as a truth function the following truth table.

---

as equivalent to 'primary propositions' of the form $A = A \cdot B$. For expressions of *this* form, '(∀ x) (A (x) ⊃ B (x))' was a completely appropriate translation. It can be called appropriate in any case if one ignores that 'A' and 'B' in Boole stand for conceptual scopes, while Frege interpreted these letters as functional expressions bearing empty argument places. That Frege was ready to equate Boole's 'primary propositions' with categorical propositions can be seen in his early essay, "Über den Zweck der Begriffsschrift" (1882), in Frege 1964a, 97–106 (1968, 89–97). On p. 101 (1968, 93), he explicitly equates the "Boolean conception" with the "Aristotelian."

A & B	A	B
T	T	T
F	T	F
F	F	T
F	F	F

What this table expresses can be portrayed in the following way. The first row under the double lines says: in an interpretation in which A and B are propositions which have one of the two truth values, it follows from the truth of A and B that A & B is true. Hence, inference rules according to the following schema are valid:

$$\frac{\begin{array}{c}A\\B\end{array}}{A \& B}$$

The three subsequent rows of the truth table say that in an interpretation such that at least one of A or B is false, A & B is false. In other words: if A & B is true, A is also true; and further, if A & B is true, B is also true. Hence the so-called simplification rules are valid, i.e., consequence rules according to these two schemata:

$$\frac{A \& B}{A} \qquad \frac{A \& B}{B.}$$

Now compare these two schemata with the following inference schemata:

$$\frac{\begin{array}{c}A\\B\end{array}}{A} \qquad \frac{\begin{array}{c}A\\B\end{array}}{B}$$

What essentially distinguishes these schemata from the two prior is that they *are not valid for the same reasons as the former*.[114] The reason why the two prior schemata are valid according to consequence rules can be called a *logical reason*. It lies *in the truth-functional meaning of* '. . . & . . .'. By contrast, neither in the premises nor in the conclusion of an inference corresponding to the latter two schemata does a logical sign occur whose meaning underwrites the *logically* validity of such an inference.

---

[114] In a somewhat simplified manner of speaking, I call here and in what follows the schema of valid rules a valid schema.

Let '*p*' stand for a proposition which is true or false. Then an inference from *p* to *p* is valid if and only if the *content* – or the *meaning* – of '*p*' is everywhere (i.e., both in the premise and the conclusion) *identical*. The supposition that a conclusion *follows* from a premise when it has the same *content* as the latter suggests that there is a *content-related reason* – which as such need be no merely *logical reason* –, on which the supposed consequence depends. I will here and in what follows designate a rule as *logically valid* or *valid for a logical reason* only if its validity depends on the meaning of a logical constant which occurs in one of the premises or in the conclusion of the consequence to which the rule refers. Accordingly, the schema, e.g.,

$$\frac{A}{A}$$

may be valid, but it is so in any case not *for a logical reason* (in the just mentioned sense). It is valid at best for a content-related reason: only because the formulas for which the letter A stands above and below the conclusion line can be interpreted as propositions of the same content are they suited to be regarded as propositions of a valid inference of the indicated form.[115]

Were the rule according to which one may infer a premise from itself *valid for a logical reason*, then the rule *ex falso quodlibet* would be a universally valid logical rule. This rule says that from two premises of which one negates the other, an arbitrary conclusion may be drawn. We arrive at this rule by transforming an inference of the form

$$\frac{\begin{array}{c}A\\B\end{array}}{A}$$

so that

$$\frac{\begin{array}{c}A\\N\,A\end{array}}{N\,B.}$$

---

[115] As it happens, we find in Sextus Empiricus the argument that it cannot be proved that a hypothetical proposition like 'If it is day, then it is day' is true and a proposition can follow from itself or be implicitly contained in itself. For this already presupposes that a proof is valid if its conclusion follows from the conjunction of its premises. See *Outlines of Pyrrhonism* II, 111–15.

results.[116] With B = N C and assuming the principle of the affirmative use of double negation, which allows passing from NN C to C, we then have N B = C.

Now there is no *logical* reason to accept the rule *ex falso quodlibet* as a universally valid rule. For there is no logical reason, but only a content-related reason to accept inferences as valid whose conclusion is identical with one of their premises. And in no way can we find a logical reason for the validity of the rule *ex falso quodlibet* because it may seem as if an arbitrary pair of premises were equivalent to the connection of both premises by '. . . & . . .'. That this is only a logical illusion (which was nevertheless as good as universally accepted in the logic of the twentieth century) which incidentally can easily be dissolved, can be shown as soon as one has only made it clear that it is completely permissible, logically speaking, to accept all the modes of inference and consequence which depend on the truth table for A & B as logical rules *and yet at the same time to refuse the logical validity of any inference whose conclusion A is equivalent to one of its premises and in which no premise of the form H (A, H (B, A)) appears.*[117]

The supposition that an inference from two premises p and q is valid whose conclusion coincides with one of its premises, for example with p, is equivalent to the supposition that p follows from p and q. This supposition is in turn equivalent to the supposition that p follows from q, if p. This supposition can be rendered symbolically as '$H (p, H (q, p))$'. It is an application of what I would henceforth like to call the *principle of the arbitrary sufficient reason*. For this is what will I call the supposition that in every interpretation in which A and B are true or false propositions, the proposition $H (A, H (B, A))$ is true. This principle says that, so long as A is true, the truth of an arbitrary proposition B is the sufficient condition for the truth of A. Now, the premise 'p & q' apparently admits an analysis in which it combines not *two* but *three* premises in total, namely, 'p', 'q', and '$H (p, H (q, p))$'. The rule according to which A arises out of A & B hence corresponds to this mode of inference:

$$\frac{A \\ B \\ H (A, H (B, A))}{A}$$

---

116 The right to this transformation rests on the validity of a metarule, which is traditionally called *reductio ad absurdum* and will be more precisely discussed in § 44 of Part II of this essay.

117 For Paul Hoyningen-Huene (1998, 124), there is an insoluble connection here; he writes "the validity of this inference [from A & B to A] has up to now never yet been doubted." And he adds with a rhetorical question: "How should one even attack this: if the truth of A *and* of B is admitted, then one may of course infer to the truth of A (or that of B)."

The logical validity of this mode of inference depends on supposing that A can be logically derived on the basis of a twice-over application of *modus ponendo ponens* from A and B, *so long as* a proposition of the form H (A, H (B, A)) is true (thus so long as the principle of the arbitrary sufficient reason is a valid principle).

Hence, the logical conjunction A & B is not equivalent *in all cases* to a pair of formulas consisting only of A and B. *Only on the assumption* that the principle of the arbitrary sufficient reason is valid may the logical conjunction of A and B and the truth function A & B be interchanged.

This of course does not mean that one could not still supply the connective '... and ...' with a *second* meaning that deviates from '... & ...': rather, 'p and q' can also stand for 'both p and q' and be understood as an expression which arranges p and q as a pair of compatible propositions, *without* stating that one of the sub-propositions is true taken on its own. 'Both ... and ...' can be introduced as a special logical constant. I will use the abbreviation '(..., ...)' for it. '(A, B)' is not a truth-functional expression. The meaning of

$$(\ldots, \ldots)$$

can rather be fixed by way of definition so that for every interpretation in which A and B are true or false propositions,
(1) (A, B) is true if A and B are both true or N (A, B) is false;
(2) (A, B) is false if it is possible that A or B is false and therefore N A or N B true.

With the definition we have established, the meaning of '(A, B)' is fixed in such a way that this expression contains no truth-functional connective. Because of this, in the main column of the truth table for (A, B), there is a question mark in all the places in which the analogous column of the truth table for A & B contains the value F. Only in the first row do the two truth tables agree:

(A, B)	A	B
T	T	T
?	T	F
?	F	T
?	F	F

The question marks express the fact that, in interpretations in which two formulas A and B have one of the two truth values, the value F for A or B does not sufficiently determine that (A, B) has the value F.

In no interpretation in which A and B are true or false, does A or B follow logically from (A, B). Consequently, it does not follow logically from the falsity of A or from the falsity of B that (A, B) is false. That is, an inference according to the schema

$$\frac{\begin{array}{c}A\\B\end{array}}{(A,\ B)}$$

is indeed valid for a logical reason. But neither

$$\frac{(A,\ B)}{A}$$

nor

$$\frac{N\,A}{N\,(A,\ B)}$$

holds for a logical reason. '(A, B)' is therefore an expression with which a conjunction of premises, namely, a pair of premises A and B, can be represented without its being implicitly supposed that from A and B follows A, or that so long as A and B stand for true or false propositions, '$H\,(A,\,H\,(B,\,A))$' is a true proposition.

Since the logical relation which '(. . ., . . .)' stands for is not a truth function, in what follows I will call it *non-truth-functional (logical) conjunction*; it can also be called *elementary conjunction*. It is elementary insofar as the meaning of '. . . & . . .' can be reduced to the meaning of '(. . ., . . .)'. This results from the following consideration. The conjunction of premises '(A, B)' according to the just stated definition is true if both premises A and B are true. Now we have just seen that the meaning of '(A, B)' as it were turns into the meaning of 'A & B' when, for every interpretation in which A and B are true or false propositions, not only A and B but also $H\,(A,\,H\,(B,\,A))$ is true. Given the latter's truth, an inference from A and B to A is valid. Such an inference can be reduced to a pair of inferences of which the first is logically valid and infers from A and B to (A, B), while the second contains the *non*-logically valid conclusion of A from (A, B). The supposition that both A and B follow from (A, B) is thus based on the premise that $H\,(A,\,H\,(B,\,A))$ is true. That is, one may substitute the expression 'A & B' for the expression

'(A, B)'

if and only if '(A, B)' is used on the assumption that the principle of the arbitrary sufficient reason is valid.

This situation can be portrayed in still another way. Namely, since a use of propositions of the form (A, B) under the assumption that the principle of the arbitrary sufficient reason is valid occurs if and only if it is supposed that conjunctions of the form ((A, B), (H (A, B), A), H ((A, B), B))) are true, it is correct to say that 'A & B' is equivalent to

$$'((A, B), (H (A, B), A), H ((A, B), B)))'.$$

Strictly speaking, this expression renders the meaning of 'A & B' even more precisely than the truth table for A & B. For in the truth table, the case in which an expression of the form N C occurs in A or in B (or in both) remains unconsidered. But such is exactly the case in which it is apparent that 'A & B' becomes a truth function only when the validity of the principle of the arbitrary sufficient reason is tacitly assumed. For only on this assumption does it hold quite generally that the truth value of A & B is fixed truth-functionally, i.e., through the truth values of A and B alone. On the same assumption, the expression '((A, B), (H (A, B), A), H ((A, B), B)))' also becomes a truth function. For on this assumption, its subexpression '(H (A, B), A), H ((A, B), B))' becomes (in every interpretation in which A and B are true or false propositions) a true proposition. Assuming the truth of the latter, '(A, B)' is a proposition which, like 'A & B', is true if and only if its subpropositions are true, and false if and only if they are not.[118]

Hence, 'A & B' is at bottom only an abbreviation for a more complex expression which lets its logical structure be more clearly recognized. Accordingly, the meaning of '... & ...' can be definitionally reduced to the meanings of '(..., ...)' and 'H ( )', whereas an inverse reduction of the meaning of '(..., ...)' to the meanings of '... & ...' or other (truth-functional or non-truth-functional) expressions cannot be accomplished. Non-truth-functional logical conjunction is to that extent more elementary than the truth-functional one.

We may now also regard non-truth-functional *negation* as *elementary*, namely, as elementary in relation to truth-functional negation, for the same reason we regard the conjunction represented by '(..., ...)' as elementary. Above, in § 10, it had turned out that '~ A' is substitutable for 'N A' if and only if 'N A' is used on the assumption that the principle of the affirmative use of double negation is valid for pairs of propositions of the form A and N A. Now, this expression is used in this

---

118 A more exact exposition of this idea can be found in Appendix 3.

way if and only if it is supposed that both N A and H (NN A, A) hold. We may now abbreviate the expression 'both N A and H (NN A, A)' with:

'(N A, H (NN A, A))'.

'~ A' is thus equivalent to this expression. It represents the meaning of '~ A' even more exactly than the truth table (depicted in § 9) for ~ A. For this table disregards the case in which an expression of the form N B is contained in A. Though the truth table is supposed to be universally valid, it is only so if we implicitly suppose in using it that the principle of the affirmative use of double negation also holds for pairs of propositions of the form A and N A. Precisely this supposition is made explicit with the expression '(N A, H (NN A, A))'. It, too, becomes an expression for a truth function only if the validity of H (NN A, A) is assumed. Assuming this validity, N A is true if and only if A is false, and false if and only if A is true.

'~ A' is thus at bottom only an abbreviation for a more complex expression which lets its logical structure be more clearly recognized. Accordingly, the meaning of '~ ...' can be definitionally reduced to the meaning of 'N ...', 'H ( )' and '(..., ...)'. By contrast, there is no question of a reducibility of the meaning of 'N ...' to the meaning of '~ ...' or of other (truth-functional or non-truth-functional) expressions. For this reason, non-truth-functional negation is more elementary than truth-functional negation.

Let us consider the following situation as well: all dyadic truth functions can be presented by means of the signs '... & ...' and '~ ...'.[119] Therefore, since *both* truth-functional negation *and* truth-functional conjunction may be replaced by expressions containing exclusively non-truth-functional signs, *all* truth functions can be rendered with non-truth-functional signs. (See Appendix 3.)

Even strict implication can now be completely reduced to non-truth-functional relations. Namely, if we replace one of the formulas which according to § 14 renders the meaning of 'A ⥽ B', that is, the formula '~ ◇ (... & ~ ...)', with 'NM (..., N ...)', then

'NM (A, N B)'

results. 'A ⥽ B' may be used as a substitute for this formula if and only if the new formula is used on the assumption that the principles of the affirmative use of

---

[119] There can be no more than 16 different value distributions which are presentable in the main column of truth tables for dyadic truth functions. As can be seen from Table 4 in Appendix 3, for each of the 16 possible value distributions there corresponds a negated or non-negated logical conjunction.

double negation and arbitrary sufficient reason are valid. Or, put differently, 'A ⥽ B' is equivalent to a conjunction which connects the expression '*NM* (A, *N* B)' with formulas which result from the application of these two principles to it. Let *H* (*NN* C, C) and *H* ((D, E), D) be valid for arbitrary formulae C, D, and E. Then 'A ⥽ B' is equivalent to:

'(*NM* (A, *N* B), (*H* (*NN* C, C), *H* ((D, E), D)))'.[120]

In this formula the hypothetical propositional connective occurs (twice). Hence, we are precluded from regarding the hypothetical connective ('if . . ., then . . .') as equivalent to the expression for the relation of strict implication. But we can now explain the hypothetical propositional connective non-circularly. It should be interpreted (according to § 3) like Lewis interpreted strict implication, namely, so that (see § 7 above) '*H* (A, B)' states: *it is impossible that A is true and B is false.* Only one should no longer render this interpretation, as Lewis attempted, with truth-functional signs; nor should one assume that with the use of the hypothetical propositional connective, as with the use of strict implication, the validity of the principles of the affirmative use of double negation and arbitrary sufficient reason is tacitly assumed. Rather we may proceed henceforth on the assumption that '*H* (A, B)' is simply equivalent to the expression we just discovered,

'*NM* (A, *N* B)'.

Since '*NM* (A, *N* B)' expresses, for its part, that A and *N* B are incompatible with each other, we can also say that the hypothetical propositional connective '*H* (A, B)' not only expresses that B follows from A, but also that A is incompatible with the elementary negation of B.[121]

§ 31 An Extension of the Language of the Syllogistic

In § 30 it was shown that the meaning of all truth-functional signs can be explained without difficulty by completely reducing them to the meaning of non-truth-functional-signs, which (except for the sign for elementary conjunction) belong to the elementary language of the syllogistic. A comparable reduction in the opposite

---

[120] This formula serves here merely to abbreviate a much more complex formula in which no metavariables for formulae occur apart from the letters A and B.
[121] I give an extensive explanation of the concepts of compatibility and incompatibility in Appendix 4.

direction has proved to be impossible. Thus the view that non-truth-functional syllogistic propositional connections can be adequately rendered in the calculus of functions has turned out to be an error: *the syllogistic propositional connectives have for their part proved to be elementary expressions.* It is thus the case – quite contrary to that view – *that we can render all of what we can express with truth-functional connectives in a language whose vocabulary – apart from the sign for elementary conjunction – belongs exclusively to the elementary language of the syllogistic.*

For this reason, it is not possible in particular to reduce hypothetical expressions to subjunctive expressions. Above, in § 30, I had raised the question of how two propositions of the form '($\forall$ x) ([x is a ('x) Φ (x)] ⊃ [x is a ('x) Ψ (x)])' and '($\forall$ x) H ([x is a ('x) Φ (x)], [x is a ('x) Ψ (x)])' are related. We can now answer this question if we, first, explain how '... ⊃ ...' and 'H (..., ...)' are logically related and, second, explain how the inner connection between the open sub-propositions 'x is a ('x) Φ (x)' and 'x is a ('x) Ψ (x)' is to be understood so that it expresses that the individual variables that occur free in them are bound together by means of a universal quantifier.

Concerning the first question, we can immediately establish a similarity between the relations A ⊃ B and H (A, B) merely by bearing in mind that 'A ⊃ B' is an abbreviation of '~ (A & ~ B)', and 'H (A, B),' according to § 30, may be replaced by 'NM (A, N B)'. The expression for strict implication, '~ ◇ (A & ~ B)', which is analogous to the latter one, is distinguished from '~ (A & ~ B)' only by the appearance of the modal sign '◇'. The expression '~ ◇ ...' is simply a modal strengthening of '~ ...', just as 'NM ...' is a modal strengthening of 'N ...'. That is, ~ A is derivable from ~ ◇ A, just as N A is from NM A. For, according to the principle *ab esse ad posse valet consequentia,* ◇ A follows from A, or M A from A. Hence, just as A ⊃ B follows from A ⥛ B, N (A, N B) also follows from NM (A, N B). The logical relationship between A ⊃ B and H (A, B) can hence be precisely described in the following way:

It resulted from § 30 that, when the expressions 'N C' and '(D, E)' are used on the assumption that the principles of the affirmative use of double negation and the arbitrary sufficient reason are valid, then '~ C' or 'D & E' may be substituted by 'N C' and '(D, E)' respectively. Hence, on the same assumption, '~ (A & B)' (and consequently also 'A ⊃ B') are substitutable by 'N (A, N B)'. Since according to § 30, on the same assumption 'A ⥛ B' may be substituted by 'H (A, B)', and A ⊃ B follows from A ⥛ B, A ⊃ B follows from H (A, B) on this assumption. Hence, on this assumption, the move from H (A, B) to A ⊃ B can be carried out by a merely syntactic transformation of the formulas.

As for the other question, which pertains to the peculiarity of *quantified* subjunctions and which concerns the inner connection between the open sub-propositions of such subjunctions, the universal quantifier occurring in both expressions '($\forall$ x) ([x is a ('x) Φ (x)] ⊃ [x is a ('x) Ψ (x)])' and '($\forall$ x) H ([x is a ('x) Φ (x)], [x is a ('x) Ψ (x)])' does not bring it about that, say, the open sub-propositions within its scope should both be expanded into universal propositions. Rather, the universal quantifier expresses that for every individual of the given domain, namely, for every individual x, what the expression within its scope states applies to the domain *as a whole*. In this way, the universal quantifier brings it about that the individual variables it binds refer to the same individual in all places of their occurrence. The subjunctive expression

$$(\forall x) ([x \text{ is a } ('x) \, \Phi \, (x)] \supset [x \text{ is a } ('x) \, \Psi \, (x)])$$

is thus equivalent to the following propositional schema:

'some x, whatever individual of the given domain x may be, is not a $('x) \, \Phi \, (x)$ unless *it* (namely, that x) is a $('x) \, \Psi \, (x)$.'

The corresponding hypothetical structure is the propositional schema

'if some x, whatever individual of the given domain x may be, is a $('x) \, \Phi \, (x)$, then *it* (namely, that x) is a $('x) \, \Psi \, (x)$.'

It can be recognized relatively easily that the antecedent in both cases is a particular proposition, while the second proposition in both cases is a singular proposition. For in the sub-expression that appears in both antecedents, 'x, whatever individual of the given domain x may be' can be appropriately replaced by a conceptual constant, e.g., by a nominal phrase 'individual of the domain given with x'. The pronoun 'it' in both consequents refers to the same object treated in the antecedents and is therefore equivalent to 'that individual of the domain given with x'. It can therefore appropriately be replaced by an expression which is composed, in logico-syntactic terms, of the logical constant for singular propositions, 'that . . .', and the logical subject 'individual of the domain given with x'. We can in this way render both the universally quantified expression and the universally quantified hypothetical expression with equivalent propositional schemata, each of which are composed of schemata of particular and singular propositions, respectively. Let 'ξ' be an abbreviation for the conceptual constant 'object', or, more precisely, for the conceptual constant 'individual of the non-empty domain of individuals which are designated by an individual variable v'. The above mentioned universally quantified subjunction is then equivalent to the propositional schema

$$I \, (('v) \, \Phi \, (v), \xi) \supset A \, (('v) \, \Psi \, (v), \xi).$$

Likewise, the above mentioned universally quantified hypothetical expression is equivalent to the propositional schema

$$`H (I ((`v) \Phi (v), \xi), A ((`v) \Psi (v), \xi))`.$$

Since the expressions '('v) Φ (v)' and '('v) Ψ (v)' play the same role as concept variables, namely they only designate those empty places which are filled by terms, we may say that the second (hypothetical) propositional schema belongs to an *extended* syllogistic language (in the sense of § 15), which is distinguished essentially from the language of the *elementary* syllogistic only by the use of the conceptual constant ξ. The first (subjunctive) propositional schema can be transformed into the language of the syllogistic, as extended in the same way, so long as one includes the logical constant for elementary conjunction in this language. Furthermore, the translation here of '... ⊃ ...' with 'N (..., N...)' assumes the validity of the principles of the affirmative use of double negation and the arbitrary sufficient reason.

One can likewise translate the negations of universally quantified subjunctions, as they appeared above in Figure 9 (see § 25), in a non-truth-functional language; they are equivalent to existentially quantified conjunctions of the forms (∃ v) (Φ (v)) & Ψ (v)) and (∃ v) (Φ (v)) & ~ Ψ (v)), respectively. We can appropriately render these with expressions of the form A & B, in which $I (('v) \Phi (v), \xi)$ is put in place of A and $A (('v) \Psi (v), \xi)$ is put in place of B.

§ 32 The Categorical Form in the Language of the Calculus of Functions

After showing in § 31 that Frege's view that it is possible to represent hypothetical propositions with universally quantified subjunctions is untenable, I would now like to examine whether his view that it is possible to render categorical propositions with universally quantified subjunctions is tenable. He thought we could in this way "reduce all conceptual relations" to the "basic logical relation" of "an object's falling under a concept."

There is an immediate reason to doubt the tenability of this view. We have already seen in the beginning of § 30 that Frege's interpretation of the strong logical square, as expressed in Figure 9 (see § 25), is *incompatible* with the rules of the logical square *in precisely the same way* as it is in the class-logical interpretation espoused by Hilbert and Ackermann (see Table 2 in § 30). Now, it is of course not difficult to modify Frege's interpretation so that all relations of the strong logical square remain preserved. This can happen in a way that is closely analogous to the modification which I have carried out with Figure 8 (see § 20) in the interpretation of Hilbert and Ackermann. We must therefore ask whether Frege's thesis that categorical propositions have the logical 'deep structure' of universally quantified subjunctions can be rescued in this way.

In order to maintain the relations of the strong logical square, we could attempt to explain A, E, I, and O forms through the definitions as they are summarized in the following Table 3.

Table 3

	Defining Expression	
A (('x) Ψ (x), ('x) Φ (x))	(∀ x) (Φ (x) ⊃ Ψ (x)) & (∃ x) Φ (x)	Def. 1
E (('x) Ψ (x), ('x) Φ (x))	(∀ x) (Φ (x) ⊃ ~ Ψ (x))	Def. 2
I (('x) Ψ (x), ('x) Φ (x))	~ (∀ x) (Φ (x) ⊃ ~ Ψ (x))	Def. 3
O (('x) Ψ (x), ('x) Φ (x))	~ (∀ x) (Φ (x) ⊃ Ψ (x)) ∨ ~ (∃ x) Φ (x)	Def. 4

Only two of the four definitions here involve an adjustment to Frege's reading of the strong logical square. *Definition 1* explains the A form with the help of a supplementary addition, namely, with the help of the second member of its conjunction. *Definition 4* involves a corresponding adjustment in the explanation of the O form. For the O form corresponds to the truth-functional negation of an A form proposition. Both adjustments successfully adhere to the principle of qualitative existential import, so that the affirmative propositions, but not the negative propositions, contain existence assumptions. Hence, with these definitions, all rules of the strong logical square remain in force.[122]

Now, I have shown in § 31 that universally quantified subjunctions, as they occur in all four definitions in Table 3, must be treated from a logical point of view as if they were expressions of the form A ⊃ B. However, even if the rules of the strong logical square are valid for functional expressions as they appear in the middle column of this table, this need not suggest that these expressions represent the sense of A, E, I, and O propositions. Rather, the fact that these rules are valid can be explained simply by the fact that the logical relations of the strong logical square are all preserved when one replaces A, E, I, and O propositions with the truth functions which are introduced in Figure 10, as follows:

---

[122] Strawson believed that the (strong) logical square of assertoric opposition could not be translated into the language of mathematical logic at all. Of course, the translation suggested above did not figure among those he considered, which is curious given the fact that he did consider translations with *more complex* predicate-logical structure. I have commented on his reading of the square in my essay, "Freges Kritik an der Kantischen Urteilstafel in seiner *Begriffsschrift* von 1879" in my 1995, 281–95.

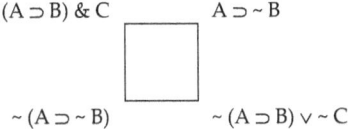

Figure 10

If one replaces the sub-expression appearing in Table 3, '(∀ x) (Φ (x) ⊃ Ψ (x))' everywhere with 'A ⊃ B', and also '(∀ x) (Φ (x) ⊃ ~ Ψ (x))' everywhere with 'A ⊃ ~ B', and finally the sub-expression '(∃ x) Φ (x)' everywhere with 'C', then four expressions result from the four rows of Table 3 which correspond exactly to the four expressions in Figure 10 and for which all rules of the strong logical square are valid.

The truth functions appearing in this figure have nothing at all to do with conceptual relationships as they concern the strong logical square, which are relations between concepts. Indeed, in these truth-functional expressions there are no letters other than metavariables which represent arbitrary propositional variables. Hence, the logical relations which obtain between the four expressions in Figure 10 clearly do not at all depend on conceptual relations as they occur in categorical propositions.

The fact that the validity of the rules of the strong logical square remain in effect for the definitional expressions in Table 3 may thus not be taken as a *sufficient* reason for letting these expressions pass as schemata of *categorical* propositions.

Of course, we are free to use the designation 'categorical proposition' as we please. One may even, if one so wishes, designate the definitional expressions in Table 3 as categorical propositions. But one should bear in mind that Frege's claim that it is possible to reduce a categorical proposition to a subjunctive expression was not supposed simply to introduce a new use of words – in which case one would no longer need to dispute about it. Rather, his claim was supposed to attack the view that the categorical form of propositions is logically fundamental and elementary and that the conceptual relations appearing in a categorical proposition are not reducible to logically more fundamental relations. Indeed, in *this* view categorical propositions are essentially *logically simple* and *logically independent* propositions, in which exactly two concepts, namely a subject concept and a predicate concept, are related *directly* to each other by one of the logical constants 'A ( )', 'E ( )', 'I ( )', 'O ( )', 'A ( )', and 'E ( )' (see § 5 above).

Now the latter view would be without doubt untenable, as Frege saw, if it could be demonstrated that categorical propositions are genuinely equivalent to propositions which are, like these, not further analyzable into other propositions, but are distinguished formally from categorical propositions by the fact that in them two concepts are related to each other *not directly, but indirectly*, namely, by the fact that objects are subsumed under each of these concepts. Demonstrating this point would comport with Frege's thesis that all conceptual relations can be reduced to the falling of objects under concepts, and that every subordination of concepts presupposes a subsumption of objects under concepts. But to be able to achieve this demonstration, Frege would have to try to prove *two* things: *first*, that categorical propositions are equivalent to propositions of a more complex structure, as is characteristic of subjunctive and hypothetical propositions; *second*, that propositions of this more complex structure are likewise unanalyzable into propositions which, as simple propositions, have in turn a categorical form. Hence, Frege would not only have to demonstrate that the same subordination which is expressed by a proposition of the form 'every α is a β' can also be expressed by a proposition of the form 'if something is an α, then it is a β' (and by the universally quantified subjunction corresponding to it). Rather, he would also have to hold that a proposition of the form 'if something is an α, then it is a β' *is not analyzable into simpler propositions*; "only the whole complex proposition" expresses a "thought", while "neither the conditional proposition on its own nor the consequent on its own [expresses] a thought"; these clauses are "improper propositions".[123] This view precludes supposing that ('improper') propositions of the form 'something is an α' or of the form 'it is a β' are to be understood as if each of them could also appear as an independent, categorical proposition.

Now, I have already shown in § 31 above that nothing at all prevents us from understanding the words 'something' and 'it' in the context of a proposition of the form 'if something is an α, then it is a β' so that they are equivalent to 'some ξ' or to 'that ξ', respectively, whereby 'ξ' is an abbreviation for the term 'object' (whereby 'object' means more precisely an object of the domain of individuals given with *x*). On the contrary, it is not to be seen how *else* the words 'something' and 'it' can be meaningfully interpreted in this context. Hence, it is immediately established that the main clauses of propositions of the form 'if something is an α, then it is a β' are in turn *I* and *A* propositions. And as such they are readily suited to occur as independent, categorical propositions.

Incidentally, we can already be seen that the clauses in 'if something is an α, then it is a β' are suited to occur as independent, categorical propositions from the fact that an inference according to *modus ponendo ponens* is meaningful and universally valid when it has the following content:

> If something is an α, then it is a β.
> Something is an α.
> Therefore, it is a β.

---

[123] Thus says Frege (1976, 103 [1980, 68]) in a letter to Husserl.

The same holds for an inference of the form:

> If something is an α, then it is a β.
> Nothing is a β.
> Therefore, nothing is an α.

This is a mode of inference which can be reduced to *modus tollendo tollens* when the second premise and the conclusion are taken as negations of 'something is a β' and 'something is an α', respectively. Since the negation of a particular affirmative proposition is a universal negative, and since from a universal negative proposition the negation of a singular proposition of the same conceptual content follows, we can infer from this latter negation in conjunction with the major premise the negation of its antecedent.

Since Frege's thesis of the 'impropriety' of the clauses of a proposition of the form 'if something is an α, then it is a β' is thus untenable, and these clauses can rather be stated independently, it is not acceptable to ignore the logical distinction between the independent and the dependent form in which one and the same proposition can occur, in one case as a categorical proposition and in another as part of a hypothetical proposition.

It is also in light of this distinction that we can see that *two different kinds of subordination* should not be confounded with each other. I will call the subordination of a concept under a concept as carried out by a categorical proposition *original* or *primary subordination*. By contrast, I will call subordination *derived* or *secondary* when it takes place in a hypothetical proposition. This distinction is supposed to indicate that though from a categorical proposition of the form $A\,(\alpha, \beta)$ a hypothetical proposition of the form $H\,(I\,(\beta, \xi), A\,(\alpha, \xi))$ is derivable, conversely, the latter is not derivable from the former. The *dictum de omni et nullo* states (1) that, if a proposition of the form $A\,(\alpha, \beta)$ is true, a concept γ can always be formed such that it holds that if some γ is a β, then it (i.e., that γ) is also an α, and (2) that, if a proposition of the form $E\,(\alpha, \beta)$ is true, a concept γ can always be formed such that it holds that if some γ is a β, then it (i.e., that γ) is not an α. (See below, Part II, Section 3, rules (III. 1) and (III. 2).)

Given what has been said, it should be clear that propositions of the form $(\forall\,v)\,\Phi\,(v)$ and $(\exists\,v)\,\Phi\,(v)$ are quite typical categorical propositions. We can translate both formulas into the extended language of the syllogistic, since they are equivalent in sequence to the propositional schemata '$A\,(('v)\,\Phi\,(v), \xi)$' and '$I\,(('v)\,\Phi\,(v), \xi)$'. Accordingly, all rules of the strong logical square remain in effect when one replaces the formulas in Figure 3 (see § 11 above) so that the following Figure 11 arises:

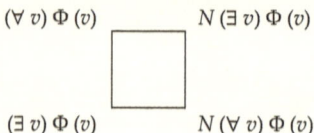

Figure 11

§ 33 The Logical Form of Singular Propositions

But what about expressions of the type 'F (a)', that is, 'a falls under the concept F', and thus what Frege called "the general form of a judgeable content which deals with one object a and which remains judgeable whatever else one puts for a" (Frege 1986/1950, § 74; see § 28 above)? As we have seen (see § 25), in 'F (a)' a *concept* is not *subordinated* to a concept, but rather an *object* is *subsumed* under a concept. Thus, it looks as if 'F (a)' does not express a relation *between* concepts and as if it is *not categorical* in the sense of the discussion given above in § 5.

Frege occasionally uses the term "indefinitely indicating" for 'a' and for other individual constants which can stand in the place of 'a' in a proposition. According to Frege, these constants differ from proper or singular names such as 'two', 'the highest mountain,' or 'Julius Caesar', which are "definitely designating" parts of a proposition. But the former have in common with the latter that, unlike a functional expression, they do not have an empty place, but (like 'something') designate an individual (Frege 1983, 280 [1979, 260]).[124]

Now, the question we have before us at this point is this:

Is there a fundamental distinction between the independent meaning of a singular name and the independent meaning of expressions which we have already become acquainted with, e.g., of the type 'that object'? For such an expression has a definite conceptual content insofar as it is composed of a concept word ('object') and an expression suited to play the role of a logical constant: 'that . . .'. Do singular names have a conceptual content as well?

To be able to answer this question it is useful first to distinguish between *two kinds of singular names*. Among the first kind I count designations which are

---

[124] Frege uses the designations 'singular name' and 'proper name' synonymously (cf. Frege 1983, 128 [1979, 118]), and indeed such that *all* object designations, as long as they are "definitely designating" names, are proper names. Since it is usual to use the word 'proper name' in a narrower sense, I will not follow Frege's use of the word, but rather only use the expression 'singular name' as a unified term for designations of individuals or individual objects.

called, following John Stuart Mill, *singular names* or *singular terms*.[125] Among the second I count *proper names* in the stricter sense. The latter are distinguished from singular terms in that they designate definite singular objects without ascribing any (descriptive) attribute to them. Thus, for example, 'Julius Caesar' or 'two' are proper names, while 'the even prime number', 'this mountain', or 'Charles the Fifth' are singular terms. Of course, singular terms can be complex enough that they also contain proper names, as for example 'the mother of Julius Caesar' or 'Charles the Fifth'.

Let's turn first to singular terms and suppose that the letter 'a' in '$F(a)$' stands for *this kind* of term. In this case, 'a' clearly carries with it a conceptual content. Singular terms can be recognized in that they, just like 'that object', are two-part expressions, where the first part (a definite article or demonstrative pronoun) can play the role of a logical constant and the second part is a concept expression. The general structure of a singular term is: 'that α'.

That singular terms have the standard form 'that α' shows that calling them singular terms is basically misleading and so actually quite inappropriate. For as expressions of the form just discussed, they do not at all belong among the kind of expression for which I have introduced the designation 'term' in § 2, for which it is characteristic that it can play the role of a subject concept or a predicate concept. Simply because of its form, a so-called singular term cannot take the place of a subject or predicate concept, but always only the place of a *grammatical* subject (cf. § 27). To that extent, it belongs neither (as its designation 'singular term' would suggest) to a subclass of terms nor to the class of terms at all.[126]

Incidentally, it would also be inappropriate to designate those expressions which I have up to now designated as terms (and will continue to do so) as *general* terms, to distinguish them from singular terms. For this, too, would be misleading. This designation could be understood as if it ruled out that only one singular object might fall under the concept for which a term stands. In truth, the number of

---

125 Mill distinguishes between singular and general terms, which he calls "singular names" and "general names" respectively: "A general name is [. . .] a name which is capable of being truely affirmed [. . .] of each of an indefinite number of things. An individual or singular name is a name which is only capable of being truely affirmed [. . .] of one thing." See Mill (1843, Vol. I, Ch. 1, §3). Statements ('propositions') are singular for Mill "when the subject is an individual name." 'Subject' means here not the logical but the grammatical subject of a statement. Mill's explanation of singular statements does not capture statements of the form $A\,(α, β)$ or $F\,(α, β)$.

126 For this reason, I do not wish to follow the widespread view adopted by, e.g., Tugendhat & Wolf (1983, 94–95) when they treat expressions of the type 'this horse' as singular terms yet classificatory expressions of the type 'horse' as general terms. Whether these expressions refer to a singular object or a totality of objects depends on whether they belong to a singular or universal proposition, respectively.

objects each subject or predicate concept applies to (provided they are not empty concepts) depends always only on its *conceptual content*. Thus, e.g., under the concept designated by the term 'even prime number' exactly one object falls, namely the number *two* – just as under the concept *apostle* exactly twelve individuals fall and under the concept *element of the null class* no object falls at all. Yet 'even prime number' should not be regarded as a singular term. This is simply because this term, like any other, can stand both in the place of the subject concept as well as in the place of the predicate concept of a (true or false) proposition ('three is (not) an even prime number').

For this reason, it is actually quite unsuitable to speak of singular and general terms as it is still standard in the literature influenced by Mill, as if there were two sub-classes of the class of all terms.[127] To avoid terminological confusion, I will in the following no longer speak of singular terms, but instead only of *individual identifiers* when I mean expressions of the standard form 'that α'.[128]

The specific conceptual content of a term which is nested in an individual identifier can be rendered with functional expressions. If it contains one or more proper names, like 'Caesar's mother' or 'city between Köln and Bonn', then we have individual identifiers of the form 'that ('x) $R(x, a)$', 'that ('x) $P(x, a, b)$', etc. If it contains no proper names, like 'that object', then the individual identifier consists in an expression of the form 'that ('x) $F(x)$'.

If 'a' is an individual identifier, then '$\Phi(a)$' can be consistently rendered by expressions of the form

---

[127] It is, accordingly, unsuitable to designate propositions of the form $A(\alpha, \beta)$, $E(\alpha, \beta)$, $I(\alpha, \beta)$ and $O(\alpha, \beta)$ as *general* propositions as has become standard in many cases in the literature on logical semantics. See, e.g., Tugendhat & Wolf 1983, 79–103. By *general propositions* are understood propositions in which only general terms occur. If α and β are general terms, and if 'that β' is a singular term, the propositions of the form $A(\alpha, \beta)$ and $E(\alpha, \beta)$ would have to be both general as well as not general.

[128] This designation does not allow the misunderstanding to arise, as does Mill's talk of singular terms, that the capacity of a term (which can always be only a part of statement or a judgment) to refer to a definite singular object depends on something other than the context of the judgment in which the term stands. No term can refer to an object on its own. Its relation to objects can only be mediated *by the logical form of the judgment.* – I would like to be spared here from going into the massive and still growing literature in the philosophy of language that busies itself with how the 'reference' of singular terms to objects can be explained. An engagement with this literature would not be very fruitful because, as far as I can see, the participants in that literature spare themselves from entertaining the view (not discovered by me, but extensively justified by Kant, Hegel, and others) that the objective reference ('objectivity') of a judgment depends on its logical form.

$$A\,(('x)\,\Phi\,(x), ('x)\,F\,(x)),$$
$$A\,(('x)\,\Phi\,(x), ('x)\,R\,(x, b)),$$
$$A\,(('x)\,\Phi\,(x), ('x)\,P\,(x, b, c)),$$
etc.,

whether the term which is nested in the individual identifier contains proper names or not. It can be easily seen that the more general form $A\,(\alpha, \beta)$ is common to the form of all these expressions.

We now must ask how 'a' in '$\Phi\,(a)$' is to be understood in case 'a' itself is a *proper name*.

One might think that in this case 'a' bears no conceptual content, since proper names *qua* proper names contain no descriptive expression. For it may seem that it is only if individual identifiers contain descriptive expressions that they have a conceptual content. In truth, however, even proper names can play their role as proper names only if they are implicitly tied to conceptual content. That is, proper names on their own are just as little in a position to designate a definite singular object as are indexical expressions (e.g., 'this here') – unless the context in which they are used already contains a response to the question *which* individual is meant by them. In no case do context-free proper names designate something definite. The use of a proper name always admits the further inquiry: who or what is intended? 'This here' – even connected with a clear corresponding point of the finger – can, without comment, signify the shelf, but also the stain on the shelf or the point in the stain on the shelf or the color of this point, and still more. In a similar way, 'Julius Caesar', just like any other peculiar proper name that seems to refer in a definite way, can always be transferred to a new bearer, entirely at will. This of course holds for the names of numbers as well: with numerals various arbitrary objects can always be named.

This well-known situation (not only familiar to ship owners and pet lovers, but to us all) shows at once that a proper name 'N' can only be a singular name if it is equivalent to a complex expression of the form 'that bearer of the name "N"'. Accordingly, the argument letter t in '$\Phi\,(t)$' is equivalent to 'that bearer of the name t'. As an argument letter, t plays the same role in '$\Phi\,(t)$' which the grammatical subject plays in the propositional schema 'that bearer of the name t is a ('v') $\Phi\,(v)$'. If we replace the term 'bearer of the name t' in this schema with an abbreviation, namely, with the conceptual constant 'ζ', e.g., we can say that '$\Phi\,(t)$' is equivalent to the expression '$A\,(('v)\,\Phi\,(v), \zeta)$'. Ultimately, even '$\Phi\,(t)$' expresses a conceptual relation, namely, a designation of the form $A\,(\alpha, \beta)$.[129]

---

[129] Since proper names and individual identifiers are disguised expressions of the form 'that α ...', I do not share the conception maintained by Fred Sommers (1982, 5; 252–81) according to

This result rests on an analysis of the character of proper names as singular names which, incidentally, Frege already undertook in a similar way.

In Frege's view, proper names, as "definitely designating" names, (thus proper names in a stricter sense as well) are essentially bipartite. They consist first of a demonstrative pronoun or definite article and secondly of a "concept word", as – surprisingly – Frege himself explicitly maintains when he writes, "With the help of the definite article or demonstrative pronoun, language forms proper names out of concept-words" (Frege 1983, 193 [1979, 178]). In another context, he explicitly points out that there are concept words which serve to designate an object: "the same word is used to symbolize both a concept and an object falling under that concept," for "there is no sharp distinction made between concept and individual" in language (Frege 1882b, 108 [1964b, 156]). "Yet in language the sharpness of the distinction [sc. between proper names and concept words] is somewhat blurred, in that what were originally proper names (e.g., 'moon') can become concept words and what were originally concept words (e.g., 'god') can become proper names" (Frege 1976, 150 [1980, 92]).

It should be sufficiently clear that in these quotations Frege never means by "concept" an unsaturated monadic propositional function, as one should rightly expect from his function theory of concepts. Rather, in these quotations he apparently understands a concept word as an expression which can be prefixed by an indefinite or definite article, consequently an expression which is capable of being used as a term.[130] In addition, these quotations also seem to deal with proper names in the broader sense of this word, thus with singular names, among which, besides singular names in the stricter sense, individual identifiers belong as well.

Since Frege himself, as one can see here, saw with great clarity that 'a' in '$F(a)$' is equivalent to a bipartite expression of the form 'that α', there is good reason to raise the question: why then could he have been so firmly convinced that '$F(a)$' expresses merely the subsumption of an object under a concept, *but not at the same time a conceptual relation*, i.e., why could he think that '$F(a)$' does not have the totally standard form of a singular categorical proposition?

To be able to give this question an answer, I must go a bit further afield.

---

which they are anaphoric expressions. It would be more correct to say that singular propositions in which they appear are '*phoric*' expressions, namely, expressions which refer anaphorically *or* kataphorically to other propositions, and indeed to propositions which are particular or singular.

130 On Frege's use of the designation 'concept word' see above § 28, note 104.

§ 34 Quantifier Rules and the Weak Logical Square

The use of individual constants, through which the language of the calculus of functions is distinguished essentially from the language of the syllogistic, makes one logical constant characteristic of the syllogistic superfluous: an expression that can present the singular form of a proposition. While the universal quantifier and the existential quantifier ensure that the forms of universal and particular propositions are presentable in the language of the calculus of functions as well, a quantifier specifically designed to present singular propositions is lacking. Just because such a quantifier is dispensable does not mean, however, that it could not be introduced in a sensible way, e.g., as a combination of signs like '(∇ x) . . .', meaning '(∇ v) F (v)': 'for that individual designated by v in the given non-empty domain, it holds that v is a ('v) F (v)'. This expression is equivalent to 'A (('v) F (v), ξ)'.

For every expression of this form, of course, the rules of the weak logical square remain in effect. With corresponding insertions into Figure 4 (see § 12 above), the following diagram results, in which the verticals and horizontals correspond exactly to the logical relations which hold according to the rules of the weak logical square.

(∇v) $\Phi (v)$ N (∇v) $\Phi (v)$

($\exists v$) $\Phi (v)$ N ($\forall v$) $\Phi (v)$

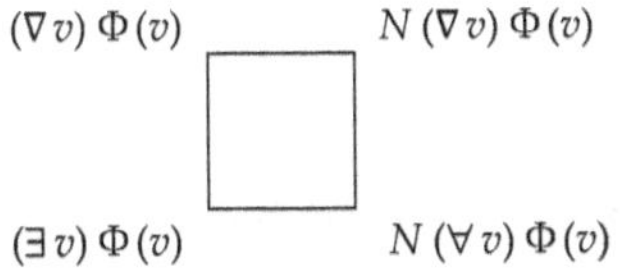

Figure 12

Since one may always abbreviate the grammatical subject of the proposition 'that individual designated by v in the given non-empty domain is a ('v) F (v)' *ad hoc* and replace it with an argument letter t, so that '(∇ v) Φ (v)' is equivalent to 'Φ (t)', the language of the calculus of functions can be considerably simplified, since (as indeed it is standard in this language) the use of a third quantifier can be dispensed with and individual constants can regularly take the place of individual variables bound by this quantifier.

Of course, in this way the subalternation rules of the weak logical square also immediately transform into *quantifier rules*, namely, into rules which establish the circumstances in which a universal or existential quantifier may be *introduced* or *eliminated* and, by the same token, when a free individual variable may be replaced by an individual constant or when such a constant may be replaced by a bound variable.

The subalternation relation which corresponds to the left vertical in Figure 12 immediately becomes the *introduction rule of the existential quantifier* (which is also called *rule of existential generalization*). It permits the passage from Φ (*t*) to (∃ *v*) Φ (*v*) at any time, so that this pattern results:

$$\frac{\Phi\ (t)}{(\exists\ v)\ \Phi\ (v)}.$$

A second quantifier rule, namely the *elimination rule of the universal quantifier* (which also goes by the title *rule of universal instantiation*) corresponds to the right vertical in Figure 12. Yet it does not arise directly from the latter, but rather assumes the validity of the principle of the affirmative use of double negation for all types of negation. According to Figure 12, *N* (∀ *v*) Φ (*v*) initially follows from *N* Φ (*t*), so that according to the meta-rule of *reductio ad absurdum*, *NN* Φ (*t*) can be derived directly from (∀ *v*) Φ (*v*). However, according to the principle of the affirmative use of double negation, not only does *NN* A follow from A, but A follows from *NN* A as well, so that ultimately Φ (*t*) follows from (∀ *v*) Φ (*v*):[131]

$$\frac{(\forall\ v)\ \Phi\ (v)}{\Phi\ (t)}.$$

Assuming the validity of the principle of the affirmative use of double negation, all elementary negations which occur in Figure 12 as it were tacitly transform into truth-functional negations. On this assumption, the subalternation relation which is portrayed by the right vertical in Figure 12 turns into a relation in which rules conforming to the following schema hold as well:

$$\frac{\sim \Phi\ (t)}{\sim (\forall\ v)\ \Phi\ (v)}.$$

If we replace the formulas in Figure 12 with the expressions with which the subalternation relations can be presented as quantifier rules, then we get the following diagram:

---

[131] In § 22 of his *Begriffsschrift* (Frege 1879/1967), Frege gave this rule the form of an axiom which corresponds to the formula '(∀ *x*) *F* (*x*) ⊃ *F* (*y*)', in which arbitrary function letters may be substituted for '*F*'.

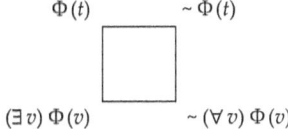

Figure 13

One can immediately notice in this diagram that, after replacing 'N...' with '~...', the *rule of contrariety* – according to which two propositions of the same conceptual content, where one is a negated and the other a non-negated singular proposition, can both be false but not both true – *is no longer in effect*. For according to § 9, the use of '~...' is fixed so that two propositions which are related as A and ~ A can neither both be true nor both false; and the validity of the quantifier rules entails that two singular propositions of the same conceptual content, where one negates the other, relate as A to ~ A.

This is a logical situation which threatens the consistent use of the truth-functional negation sign, so long as no adequate supplementary provisions are made. For F (a) and ~ F (a) *can* both be *false*, namely, when there is no object designated by 'a'. Let us suppose that 'a' is an abbreviation for 'present king of France' and there is no present king of France; i.e., the concept designated by 'present king of France' is empty. Then, whatever the predicate '(x) F (x)' may have for a content, both F (a) and ~ F (a) are false. In this case, the quantifier rule of universal instantiation becomes invalid. For insofar as there can be no interpretation for Φ (x) in which (∀ x) Φ (x) is true, then the proposition Φ (a) that follows from it becomes false in this interpretation. For the same reason, the instantiation rule for the existential quantifier becomes invalid in this case as well. For there can likewise be no interpretation for Φ (x) in which ~ Φ (a) is true, since a does not exist, so that (∃ x) ~ Φ (x) is false in this interpretation.

There are also circumstances in which F (a) and ~ F (a) are both true, namely when 'a' in both propositions refer to *different* objects. Let 'a', for example, be equivalent to 'two'. But 'F (a)' states that two is an even prime number, while '~ F (a)' is a proposition about a train-line. Then both propositions may be considered as true, although they are related as A to ~ A.

Now, if it is supposed to be guaranteed that there is in all circumstances a contradictory relationship between A and ~ A, then special provisions must be made for this guarantee. –

Frege did make special provisions in this connection. On the one hand, he stipulated that 'a' in 'F (a)' should be interpreted as a latently bipartite expression containing a concept word; yet, on the other hand, he insisted at the same time that the concept whose designation is used to form the name 'a' must satisfy specific demands in order to contribute to the formation of a *legitimately formed* singular name. Frege writes:

> With the help of the definite article or demonstrative pronoun, language forms proper names out of concept-words. [. . .] If forming a proper name in this way is to be legitimate, the concept whose designation is used in its formation must satisfy two conditions: 1. It may not be empty. / 2. Only one object may fall under it. (Frege 1983, 193 [1979, 178])

The satisfaction of the first condition that Frege mentions here would guarantee that there is no interpretation of $\Phi(x)$ in which $\Phi(a)$ and $\sim \Phi(a)$ are two false propositions. The satisfaction of the second condition is supposed to guarantee that two such propositions cannot both be true.

Before I go on to examine what can be said for the two demands which Frege thinks should be placed on the legitimate formation of singular names, I would first like to return to the question of why Frege saw it necessary to believe that the proposition $F(a)$ expresses *not a relation between concepts*, but rather only the falling of an object under a concept. An answer to this question is now possible. For connected with the postulate that a concept may not be empty if it is supposed to contribute to the formation of a singular name is the view that 'a' in 'F (a)' is a mere *pseudo proper name* if there is no a, and consequently that in this case 'F (a)' is not a true or false proposition at all. Frege is thus prepared to abandon the universal validity of the bivalence principle with respect to singular propositions. After abandoning this principle it follows at once that the proposition 'F (a)' expresses a relation between *empty* concepts if there is no a. But since in this case 'F (a)' is not a true or false proposition at all, and only true or false propositions are logically relevant, the conceptual relation expressed is logically irrelevant. Rather, in order for 'F (a)' to be a logically relevant expression, it is necessary that a is an object which falls under the concept designated by 'F ( )'. Thus, whether (as according to Frege) propositions of the type 'F (a)' are logically relevant at all depends not on the presence of a conceptual relation, but rather on whether an object falls under a concept.

§ 35 The Assumption of Non-Empty Domains

But we now must ask whether it is at all reasonable to suppose with Frege that the formation of a singular name is only legitimate if the concept designated in its use satisfies the following two conditions: first, that it is not empty, and second, that only one unique object falls under it.

Let us begin with the second mentioned condition.

The satisfaction of this condition is supposed to guarantee that there is no interpretation of $\Phi(x)$ in which both $\Phi(a)$ and $\sim \Phi(a)$ are true propositions. Suppose 'a' stands for a singular name which uses the concept of the even prime number in its formation. This is a concept under which exactly one object falls, namely the number *two*. Let 'a' thus abbreviate the expression 'the even prime number'. Does the fact that *two* is the only even prime number guarantee that two propositions of the form Φ (a) and ~ Φ (a) are not both true? Clearly not. Concept expressions on their own never indicate how many objects fall under the concept which they designate. Even a concept expression like 'even prime number' can at any time be used as a name which does not refer to the number two: why should one not be *legitimately* permitted, e.g., to give his favorite teacher the nickname 'Even Prime Number'? It is not concept expressions as such – or their contents – which are in a position to ensure that a definite singular name is legitimately formed. Rather, it is always only the *context* in which a concept expression occurs that can guarantee it is a component of an *unambiguously* used singular name.[132] First and foremost, this context includes the proposition itself in which the concept expression occurs. For it is first and foremost the *logical form* of the proposition, more precisely *its singular form*, which *makes* the concept expression part of a singular name. Secondarily, how it is *determinate* that the proposition is about *one and only one* object this depends essentially on the context of the singular proposition *as a whole*. The problem of the *determinacy* of a proposition 'F (a)' can in general only be solved if a sufficiently large number of propositions, including 'F (a)', are consulted to establish that there is *exactly one* object to which 'F (a)' refers (see Marciszewski 1981, 109).

In addition, the following should be noted: in formal-language contexts, e.g., in the context of a series of lines which represents an inference chain in the language of the calculus of functions, a mere stipulation suffices to ensure that one and the same individual constant always refers to the same object in all places of its occurrence in the context. In the same way, a mere convention suffices to ensure that expressions of the form A (. . ., β) or E (. . ., β), which appear in a series of lines which can present an inference chain in the elementary language of the syllogistic can always refer to the same object in all places of their occurrence. Thus, from a logical point of view, the guarantee of the unambiguity of singular names presents no problem that would require special provisions for its solution.

However, Frege's other prescription that a concept may *not* be *empty* if it is supposed to contribute to the legitimate formation of a singular name at least seems to be targeted at a serious logical problem. For this prescription is supposed to exclude at once the cases in which the quantifier rules become invalid. These are precisely

---

[132] Frege himself set store by the declaration, "[I]t is only in the context of a proposition that words have any meaning." Frege 1986/1950, § 62. This declaration tends to be called Frege's 'context principle'.

the cases in which two expression of the form Φ (*a*) and ~ Φ (*a*) are both false. I would like now to ask whether this prescription is genuinely reasonable. In particular, it should be asked whether it is really necessary to follow Frege in abandoning the universal validity of the bivalence principle.

This abandonment as such already causes difficulties. Above, in § 8, I had introduced the bivalence principle as a strictly universally valid semantic principle. Thus, its universal validity depends merely on fixing the meaning of the word 'false'. Truth can be explained by means of a mere nominal definition as the correspondence of a proposition with the object or objects it deals with. According to the semantic bivalence principle, falsity consists in the respective non-correspondence. Now if one abandons the universal validity and the semantic character of the bivalence principle, then one burdens oneself with the semantic problem of having to give a new explanation for the truth and falsity of a proposition, and especially to explain what it means to say of a proposition which does not correspond to the object it is about that it is not false.

Without doubt, one should be prepared to take on this semantic problem if it appeared compellingly necessary to reject the bivalence principle as a universally valid semantic principle. But of this there can be no question at all.

For to sustain the validity of the quantifier rules, it is not necessary to abandon the bivalence principle. Rather it is enough to be aware of a condition on which the use of the language of the calculus of functions depends, namely, that the principle of the affirmative use of double negation is valid. For whether two propositions of the form A and ~ A are contradictory, so that there is no 'third' apart from A and ~ A, and not both A as well as ~ A can be false, does by no means depend on an implicit presupposition only in cases where A is a *singular* proposition.

Rather, this presupposition is also in play with universal and particular propositions. Pairs of propositions related as '(∃ v) Φ (v)' and '~ (∃ v) Φ (v)' are contradictory propositions only *if there are elements of the domain* to which the bound variable 'v' tacitly refers. According to the principle of qualitative existential import, (affirmative) propositions of the form A (('v) Φ (v), ξ) and I (('v) Φ (v), ξ), for which '(∀ v) Φ (v)' and '(∃ v) Φ (v)' are only translations, are true only if the concept ξ is satisfied. Likewise, the truth-functional negations of propositions of the form (∀ v) Φ (v) and (∃ v) Φ (v) assume a non-empty domain. This is due to the way the quantifiers are used. According to the rules of the strong logical square, the expressions '~ (∀ v) Φ (v)' and '~ (∃ v) Φ (v)' correspond initially only to the expressions '*E* (('v) Φ (v), ξ)' and '*O* (('v) Φ (v), ξ)', and the latter (as non-truth-functional expressions) *in no way* assume that the concept ξ is a non-empty concept. (For according to the principle of qualitative existential import, '*E* (('v) Φ (v), ξ)' and '*O* (('v) Φ (v), ξ)' are to be understood as implying neither an affirmative nor a limitative proposition. Nor, then, do they entail an existential proposition in some indirect way.) But the quantifier '(∃ v) . . .' is used as an abbreviation of '~ (∀ v) ~ . . .'. Even Frege, who entirely dispensed with the use of an existential quantifier, explains in § 12 of the *Begriffsschrift* that the expression '~ (∀ v) Φ (v)' means "that we could find some object, say Δ, such that Φ (Δ) would be denied. We can therefore translate it as 'There are some objects which do not have the property Φ'" (Frege 1879, 23, § 12 [1967, 27]). Quite in accord with this, '(∀ v) ~ Φ (v)' means that "There does not exist anything having property Φ" (Frege 1879, 23, § 12 [1967, 27]). Here it is almost stipulated purely by definition first that '~ (∀ v) Φ (v)' is equivalent to '(∃ v) ~ Φ (v)' and second that '~ (∃ v) Φ (v)' is equivalent to '(∀ v) ~ Φ (v)'. In this way, however, it is just stipulated not only that '(∀ v) Φ (v)' and '(∃ v) Φ (v)' but also their truth-functional negations have *existential implications*; namely, they implicitly assume that the domains to which they refer are not empty, so that there *is* at least one object that falls under the concept ξ.

That is: if A is a quantified formula, there is no interpretation in which A or ~ A is a true or false proposition unless the domain given with A is not empty. *The validity of the principle of the affirmative use of double negation is clearly paired in these cases with the assumption that the domain implicitly given with the quantified formulas is non-empty.*

Now the language the calculus of functions involves the same pairing for singular propositions as well: if A is a formula which contains an individual constant 'a', then there is no interpretation in which A or ~ A is a true or false proposition unless *a* is an element of the given non-empty domain. Frege's supposition that *a* must exist if F (a) and ~ F (a) stand in a contradictory relationship is thus entirely correct. But it is not at all necessary to deny the validity of the bivalence principle. It is rather enough to suppose that the validity of the principle of the affirmative use of double negation for pairs of propositions of the form A and ~ A is *universally* tied to the assumption that *all* individual signs (including individual constants) refer to elements of non-empty domains. In the language of the calculus of functions, individual constants are used in such a way that they are always equivalent to singular names of the form 'that ζ'. Here, ζ is either the same concept as ξ or not the same, and if not the same, then it is a sub-concept of ξ. Every object that falls under ζ, is thus to be regarded as an object which, whatever content ζ has, falls under the concept ξ. That is, every object discussed is regarded as an object which falls under the concept *object that is an element of the given domain*. Along with the supposition that the domain is not empty, it is directly supposed here that all individual constants are singular names which use a concept in their formation which is either the concept ξ or is subordinated to it.

It is for this reason surely correct that a concept used to form a singular name must satisfy the condition of not being empty, so that a consistent use of the truth-functional negation sign is assured. *However, within formal-language contexts no special provisions need to be made to satisfy this condition.* It is enough to assume what must be assumed in the calculus of functions anyway: that the domain to which *any* designation for individuals refers is not empty; it is indifferent here whether such a designation is a bound variable or an individual constant.

It can be seen here that there is no reasonable ground for calling into question the validity of the bivalence principle. It is enough rather to suppose (what I have already supposed anyway) that the principle of the affirmative use of double negation is *not* valid *for every kind of negation*. So far as its validity is connected to the exclusive use of the language of the calculus of functions, especially to the use of '~ . . .', its validity (and precisely therewith the consistent use of the language of the calculus of functions as well) depends on the implicit assumption of non-empty domains. In other words, the validity of this principle and the use of this language depends on the implicit supposition that certain concepts, specifically the concepts ξ and ζ, are singled out as non-empty concepts. –

This may be the place for a *short excursus* on Bertrand Russell's attempt to read the form Φ (a) as merely the apparent, surface form of singular propositions and, by reducing this form to a more complex form, to defend against Frege the universal validity of the bivalence principle.

This attempt is based on the introduction of the iota operator. Russell's analysis of propositions of the form Φ (a), put briefly, consisted in making explicit the conceptual (or descriptive) content of 'a' – insofar as there is such.[133] He thus interpreted 'a' as abbreviating a functional expression of the form '(ι x) G (x)' (read: 'that x for which G (x) holds'). In this interpretation, '(ι x) G (x)' involves the supposition that there is exactly one object x to which G (x) applies; symbolically expressed: (∃ x) G (x) & (∀ x) (∀ y) ((G (x) & G (y)) ⊃ (x = y)). '(ι x) G (x)' stands for this expression as an abbreviation, so that 'F (a)' is equivalent to '(ι x) G (x) & F (x))' (read: 'There is exactly one x for which G (x) and F (x) hold').

In this analysis, the bivalence principle remains in effect, since, in case the concept contained in 'G (x)' is empty, – in case there thus is no bearer for 'a' – both '(ι x) G (x) & F (x))' as well as '(ι x) G (x) & ~ F (x))' have a truth value, namely, F. Hence, in this analysis 'F (a)' and '~ F (a)' can *both* be *false*. Both the singular propositions 'the king of France reigning in 1905 is bald' and 'the king of France reigning in 1905 is not bald' are, if there is no reigning king of France in 1905, both false, since they are not in Russell's analysis related as '*p*' and '~ *p*', but rather as two complex propositions, where the first component in both is the

---

[133] Russell distinguished cases in which 'a' has a descriptive content from cases in which 'a' stands for a 'logically proper name'. He supposed – unjustifiably of course – that such proper names, including demonstratives like 'this' as they refer to sense-data, cannot fail in any case to refer to exactly one object.

same false existential proposition ('There is exactly one x such that x is a king of France reigning in 1905') and the second component is the open proposition 'x is bald' and the open proposition 'x is not bald', respectively.

Russell's analysis and the connected theory of *definite descriptions* – as he designated expressions of the form $(\iota\, x)\, \Psi\, (x)$ – has not found many supporters, but it has provoked a flood of ambitious reactions in the philosophy of language. Some, like Strawson, were not inclined to recognize the bivalence principle and preferred to accept as logically relevant the *ordinary usage* of the words 'true' and 'false', where this principle does not hold, or at least not always.[134] Others took exception to the assumption that ordinary proper names are connected to a descriptive meaning and that their "reference" depends on this connectedness.

Concerning the descriptive meaning and the reference of proper names, Russell's theory certainly contains – at least as Saul A. Kripke understood it[135] – the assailable supposition that ordinary and correctly used proper names are always abbreviated or disguised individual identifiers. According to this supposition, 'Scott' and 'the author of *Waverly*', e.g., are used as synonyms, so that 'the author of *Waverly*' is equivalent to 'Scott' and a proposition like 'Scott is the author of *Waverly*' would be understood as an analytically true proposition – which is not very plausible.

To avoid this consequence, several loopholes have been considered. Among them, the following three have become the most well-known: (1) the *'bundle theory'*, according to which proper names have descriptive meanings, but which only can be rendered by a *bundle* of individual identifiers, among which most or at least the most important apply to bearer of the name; (2) the *'causal theory'*, according to which there is no descriptive meaning of proper names, and their significance depends merely on a baptism which establishes their reference and on which all naming (passed down in a chain of communication) of the name's bearer causally depends; (3) the *'use theory'*, according to which proper names have meaning, not in the sense of descriptive meaning, but rather in the sense of a certain use or habit in which the name points to individual identifiers of the name's bearer. In none of these theories is it systematically considered that (*a*) any reference of proper names and individual identifiers only occurs in propositions (a salutation, too, is a proposition, namely a proposition of request or invitation), that (*b*) in declarative propositions there is a bipartite expression corresponding to every proper name and every individual identifier, where the first part expresses a term, while the other part expresses the logical form of the declarative proposition, here its singularity, and that

---

[134] The criticism which Strawson (1950) passed on Russell in his essay "On Referring" was rightly rebutted in Russell's (1957) rejoinder, "Mr. Strawson on Referring."

[135] See Kripke 1980, 27–31; 53–60.

(c) it is the logical form which establishes the reference, first of the proposition itself, but then indirectly of all the expressions occurring in it as well.

It would bring us too far afield to follow up on the loopholes just described. It may instead suffice to recall once again the starting point of all these attempts, namely, the task of Russell's theory of definite descriptions to defend the bivalence principle by reducing the forms Φ (a) and ~ Φ (a) to forms which do not relate as A and ~ A. This theory, just like those of its critics, rested on the assumption that the form of truth-functional negation is the only form of negation. That is, Russell and his critics did not see that there is no need to interpret pairs of singular propositions from ordinary language which relate as 'p' and 'not p' as if their surface form were 'p' and '~ p'. When interpreted according to the latter form, they are coupled first to the validity of the principle of the affirmative use of double negation and second to the assumption that the singular names occurring in them always have existing bearers.[136]

Now if, with Russell and in contrast to Frege, one wants to let the bivalence principle hold unrestrictedly, without having to make use of auxiliary assumptions from the philosophy of language or logic about the reference and meaning of singular names, then, according to the analysis of singular propositions I have carried out above, the following consequences result, which are of interest both with respect to logic and the philosophy of language:

First, all reasons fall away for maintaining Frege's view that the falling of an object under a concept is the basic logical relation to which all relations of concepts to concepts can be reduced. Rather, all affirmative propositions have equally to do – even if not manifest in the same way – with subsuming objects under concepts just as they have to do with relating concepts to other concepts.

Second, the view that it is possible to translate at least in part the elementary syllogistic language into the language of the calculus of functions should be abandoned; on the contrary, it should rather be recognized that the language of the calculus of functions can be translated into a language that dispenses with a truth-functional vocabulary and does not differ at all from the elementary syllogistic language,[137] or only by making use of elementary conjunction and using expressions of the form ('v) Φ (v) instead of concept variables.

Finally, *third*, it should be recognized that the use of the logical vocabulary of the calculus of functions is tied to specific *suppositions* or *assumptions* which are not needed for the use of the syllogistic vocabulary. For the truth-functional signs that

---

[136] Compare this excursus to the comments of Fred Sommers (1982, 208–26; 327), with which I partly agree.
[137] See § 40 below and Appendix 1.

are essential for the calculus of functions do not only entail, as I have already shown in § 30, that the validity of the *principle of the affirmative use of double negation* and the validity of the *principle of the arbitrary sufficient reason* are tacitly in effect. Rather, as has emerged in these paragraphs, the use of this calculus, when it is tied to the use of quantifiers and individual signs, also entails the invalidity of the principle of qualitative existential import, so that it is instead assumed that from the negation of an arbitrary (universal, particular, or singular) statement it follows that there *is* something (to which the predicate of the negated statement does not apply) – and this no matter what the negated statement is about. In other words, the use of quantifiers and individual signs in conjunction with truth-functional signs is tied to the assumption that *there are objects* to which individual constants and bound individual variables refer. I will call this assumption the *principle of non-empty domains*.

3 Limits of the Language of the Logical Calculus of Functions

§ 36 A Formal Language of Non-Pure Thinking

In the preceding paragraphs, it has turned out that Frege's thesis that all conceptual relations are reducible to relations of objects falling under concepts is untenable. Every expression Φ (*t*) which presents the relation of an object falling under a concept should be understood rather as the expression of a conceptual relation. Moreover, it has been shown that the language of the calculus of functions can be completely translated into a formal language whose vocabulary is distinguished from the elementary language of syllogistic in three ways: first, it contains the propositional connective of elementary conjunction as an additional logical constant; second, it uses expressions of the form ('v) Φ (v) in place of concept variables; and finally, third, by using the conceptual constants ξ and ζ, it brings abbreviations for specific concepts into play.[138]

---

[138] Incidentally, the point of view we have arrived at here is distinguished in at least one important respect from that which Fred Sommers and his followers of the so-called 'new syllogistic' have adopted. Sommers, too, ties his 'logic of natural language' to the pre-Fregean tradition of logical theory, for which it was beyond doubt that propositions of natural language (so far as they are subject to deductive inference) needed an analysis for logical purposes which is oriented to subject-predicate (or nominal-verbal phrase) syntax. Noam Chomsky also pays respect to this need with his generative transformation grammar, according to which 'a human being', 'some human being', 'Socrates', 'every human being', and 'the snowman' are all expressions which belong to one and the same substitution class. But the syllogistic system developed by Sommers, which claims to be as capable as modern (Fregean) quantified logic, is even still a truth-functional system. For this reason,

This finding requires us to take leave of firmly held convictions concerning the systematic relationship between the syllogistic and the calculus of functions (classical predicate logic), which have been ever more widespread as the systems of syllogistic logic have been displaced, while mathematical logic has been further established and ramified. Among these convictions belongs not least a view which has been typical of the Fregean point of view and which has been adopted (or at least tolerated) by most of his followers without much reservation: namely, the conviction that the language of the calculus of functions, or what Frege called a "concept-script," is something like a "formal language [. . .] of pure thought."[139]

It can now be seen relatively easily that this conviction, too, is ultimately untenable, if we only consider its content somewhat more closely. Frege was convinced that his concept-script language would be restricted to "expressing relations that are independent of the particular characteristics of objects" (Frege 1879, iv [1967, 6]). Accordingly, by a "purely logical" procedure, he understood one "that disregards the particular characteristics of objects," in which "nothing intuitive [may] intrude" (Frege 1879, iii–iv [1967, 5]).

In his characterization of the "pure logical" and in his talk of the "intuitive" it becomes clear that Frege takes up conceptions that were characteristic of Kant's point of view. Disregarding all particular characteristics of things and omitting all intuitive content was also from *Kant's* perspective an essential mark of pure thinking and for the purity of what Kant called *formal logic* (see M. Wolff 2007, 53–70). For Kant, the syllogistic provided the paradigm of formal logic precisely because it has to do only with conceptual relations and thus abstracts from all content of concepts and from all relations to objects.[140] This Kantian point of view comports with the description I gave above in §§ 1–15 of the basic features of the elementary syllogistic.

---

the objections which Peter F. Strawson (1982) raised against its claim to the title of a 'logic of natural language' are not unjustified, though this does not call into question the capability of this system.

139 Frege's *Begriffsschrift* (1879/1967) bears the subtitle "A Formal Language, Modelled on that of Arithmetic, of Pure Thought."

140 See *CPR* A 130–31/B 169, in connection with A 266/B 322, A 132–33/B 171–72, and A 55/B 79. Cf. also M. Wolff 1995, 120–24. In this earlier book, I show that for Kant formal logic is that subdomain of logic which distinguishes itself by its universality and purity and whose formality consists in abstracting from the "logical material" of judgments, i.e., from the content of the concepts occurring in them. John MacFarlane (2000) has in his dissertation, *What Does it Mean to Say that Logic is Formal*, and in his essay, "Kant, Frege, and the Logic of Logicism" (2002), argued that in Kant's view the formality of logic is a consequence of its universality. MacFarlane's view that universal logic is universal in exactly the same sense from both Kant's and Frege's perspective (MacFarlane 2002, 60) is untenable because Frege does not share Kant's view that universal and pure logic must, as formal logic, abstract completely from the logical material of judgments, i.e., from the content of concepts.

We can see the specifically formal, pure character of the syllogistic precisely in that its rules concern operations between concepts alone. In their essentials, these operations (which I have already pointed out in § 1) involve nothing else than the relating of concepts to concepts, whether in subordinating or coordinating them.[141] Accordingly, apart from propositional variables, concept variables are the only variables in the syllogistic elementary language. The syllogistic is *formal* and thereby *pure logic* precisely in the sense that it neither makes use of conceptual *constants* nor takes into consideration other interpretations for concept variables (so that it totally disregards the *content* of concepts). It therefore makes use neither of *individual* variables nor of *individual* constants and hence disregards everything *intuitive* and *non-conceptual*, consequently all relations of concepts to *objects*. The subsuming of objects under concepts is considered in the syllogistic only *insofar as it already belongs to the logical form of judgments to refer to objects in such and such a way*, even if this comes about only in a totally *abstract form*.[142]

Unlike the expressions of the syllogistic, expressions for propositional functions do *not* refer to *purely* logical operations, at least not to purely logical operations in the sense just described. Though propositional functions can likewise be considered as operations whose field consists of concepts, yet already their form, which essentially involves being equipped with empty places that are meant for *individual variables*, indicates that in propositional functions concepts are given consideration *only to the extent that* they refer directly to objects, and not to concepts. Insofar as individual signs are partly bound variables and partly constants, what is explicitly given consideration here are partly objects in general (as elements of the given domain) and partly objects in particular (as bearers of specific designations or proper names).[143] *In this respect*, the logic of the calculus of functions is precisely not a *formal logic*. Since with concepts like ξ and ζ it implicitly takes specific conceptual contents into consideration, it is in any case not a formal logic *in the precise and radical sense in which the syllogistic is formal.* Nor is the logic of the calculus of

---

141 Kant summarizes these operations, accordingly, under the concept of the logical use of the understanding, the *usus logicus intellectus*. See *CPR* A 67/B 92, and the 1771 *Dissertation*, § 5 (Ak. 2: 393–94).
142 After what has been said, it may perhaps not be superfluous to declare explicitly that, not only in singular but also in particular and universal judgments, objects are subsumed under concepts. The *grammatical subject* of particular or universal propositions, whose standard form can be portrayed by 'some α' and 'every α' respectively, like 'a' in 'F (a)', stands for exactly the object which is subsumed under a concept by means of these propositions, respectively.
143 Here I disregard entirely the fact that the calculus of functions also takes characteristics of objects into consideration insofar as belonging to an n-tupel, (reflexive) self-relation, and other properties of an object can be determined more precisely by the number and type of the empty places in a functional expression.

functions *pure in the precise and radical sense in which syllogistic is pure*. Since the logic of the calculus of functions allows as one of its assumptions that concepts like ξ and ζ *neither* have the same content *nor* are empty, it is *neither* fitting to say with Frege that the procedure of the calculus of functions disregards "the particular characteristics of objects," *nor* is it correct to suppose that nothing "intuitive" intrudes in this procedure.

As far as disregarding the particular characteristics of things is concerned, it should not be overlooked that already features like *belonging to a definite domain which is tacitly assumed as non-empty* and the *property of being the bearer of a certain name* or the *bearer of a certain identifier* are particular characteristics, through which objects can be distinguished from each other and which the calculus of functions does not disregard.

As for the intrusion of intuitive representations, it should not go unnoticed that already the definite (if also relatively abstract) representation of a non-empty domain is an *intuitive* representation in Kant's sense. According to *Kant's* terminology – which Frege picks up with his talk of the intuitive – *all* representations insofar as they represent something singular are *intuitions*.[144] Whether the singular that is represented is something spatial, something temporal, something spatio-temporal, or even something intuitive in a non-*sensory* way, is a completely secondary question. The representation of a non-empty domain of individuals is *eo ipso* the representation of something singular, namely: the representation of a singular, even if indefinitely large number of singular objects. A given domain is non-empty if and only if it contains at least *one* element – however else this singular object may be more precisely determined. The supposition that there is a definite (even if not more precisely designated) domain which is non-empty but contains at least *one* singular element is – at least according to Kant's understanding of 'intuitive' – *intuitive to exactly the same degree* as, e.g., the geometrical supposition that there is a space (namely, a domain of spatial objects) which contains points, lines, surfaces, etc., as its elements. The distinction between the two suppositions does not lie in the first's being non-

---

[144] Cf. Hintikka 1992, 23: "According to his [i.e. Kant's] definition, presented in the first paragraph of his lectures on logic, every particular idea as distinguished from general concepts is an intuition. Everything, in other words which in the human mind represents an individual is an intuition. There is, we may say, nothing 'intuitive' about intuitions so defined. Intuitivity simply means individuality." Hintikka 1992, 26–27: "If we can assume that the symbols we use in algebra stand for individual numbers, then it becomes trivially true to say that algebra is based on the use of intuitions, i.e., on the use of representations of individuals as distinguished from general concepts."

intuitive; it lies only in the fact that this supposition leaves indefinite *the kind of intuition* that can represent the elements of that domain.[145]

To be sure, the language of the calculus of functions is able to leave open *which* kind of intuition that can represent the singular object that encompasses any given domain. But already with the assumption that a given domain is not empty, something intuitive intrudes into the use of this language. In this respect, it cannot be employed as a language "of pure thought."

For this reason, the language of the calculus of functions is not correctly described when classified as a "formal language of pure thought", as Frege did. For the same reason, it is inappropriate to characterize the calculus of functions as a 'pure logic'.

§ 37 Reference to Intuition and Symbolic Construction

Instead of speaking of pure thought in this connection, it would be more appropriate, if we wanted to maintain Kant's terminology, to speak of a language of *symbolic construction*. I would like to explain this idea somewhat more precisely.

Kant uses '*construction*' to name the relating, especially the *subsuming*, of particular objects or particular intuitions under concepts. He also designates this relating as a 'presenting' of concepts 'in' intuitions. Kant uses '*symbolic*' to name such a construction when substitutive symbols (or 'characters', i.e., signs) are put in place of *particular* intuitions in which a concept is supposed to be presented. These symbols leave it totally indefinite what type (or types) of intuition the presentation can occur in. We have such substitutes in, e.g., analytic geometry. There letters take the place of spatial objects like line-segments. With this kind of substitute, it remains completely indefinite what kind of (pure or empirical) intuition it is that represents those objects to which the substitutive signs can be related.[146]

Kant related the designation 'symbolic construction' specifically to *algebraic* operations as they occur in analytic geometry and elsewhere. A letter like 'a' in '$a^3 = 8$' admits various interpretations: it is interpretable as a line-segment, as a unit of time, as a section which can be plotted both on an abscissa and on a coordinate, etc.; in

---

[145] According to § 2 of the *Critique of Pure Reason*, everything which determines "inner sense" is the content of inner intuition. Accordingly, even (e.g.) thoughts, insofar as they are enumerable in a series, – thus insofar as they can 'affect' inner sense in a series – are of course *something intuitive*.

[146] Even a numeric formula like '7 + 5 = 12' can be regarded as a symbolic construction in Kant's sense. Here numerals are the symbols which stand as substitutes for intuitive magnitudes. They stand for magnitudes of a number of empirical objects, magnitudes of spatial extensions, magnitudes of time periods, etc.

this way, '*a*' admits intuitive interpretations of various kinds. But the symbolic construction of a concept concerns none of these specific interpretations. In the formula '$a^3 = 8$' only the abstract concept of the cube root of eight is constructed. With '$a^3 = b$' it can be replaced by the still more abstract concept of the cube root of *b*. Once such a concept is constructed, we can pose algebraic problems, e.g., the problem of finding out what *a*, the square of *a*, the quintuple of *a*, etc. are identical to. A specific domain can, but need not, be assumed with such problems, e.g., the domain of the natural numbers. The solution to such problems can be presented as a chain of informal conclusions, as in the following manner:

$$\frac{a^3 = 8}{a = 2}$$
$$a^2 = 4$$
$$\vdots$$

With each conclusion here, there is always only an inference from one symbolic construction to another. There are, however, also logical operations within algebra by which *algebraic laws* are inferred. Inferences drawn from symbolic constructions can form the basis of these operations, which occur according to the rule of complete induction. Since $a^2 = 4$ follows from $a^3 = 8$, a hypothetical and thus also subjunctive proposition of the same content as the first premise of the inference of the form

$$\frac{F(a)}{F(n) \supset F(n+1)}$$
$$F(n)$$

can be formulated, so that the following results:

$$\frac{(a^3 = 8) \supset (a^2 = 4)}{((n^3 = 8) \supset (n^2 = 4)) \supset (((n+1)^3 = 8) \supset ((n+1)^2 = 4))}$$
$$(n^3 = 8) \supset (n^2 = 4).$$

The letter '*n*' is used here, as is still generally standard in the older algebra, as a substitute for an *arbitrary natural number*, and indeed so that '*n*' is equivalent to '($\forall x$) ... *x* ...', with $x \in \mathbb{N}$, where all occurrences of *x* in each line lie within the scope of the universal quantifier. In this way, the conclusion comes to express an algebraic law valid for all natural numbers.

The inference just described also remains valid if an *arbitrary non-empty domain* is assumed and if both the second premise as well as the conclusion are *explicitly* tied to the instruction that n is an element from the set of natural numbers. The inference then says:

$$\frac{(a^3 = 8) \supset (a^2 = 4)}{(\forall\, n)\,(((n^3 = 8) \supset (n^2 = 4)) \supset (((n+1)^3 = 8) \supset ((n+1)^2 = 4)))}$$
$$(\forall\, n)\,(n \in \mathbb{N} \supset ((n^3 = 8) \supset (n^2 = 4))).$$

'$(\forall\, n)\ldots n\ldots$' does not only refer to all natural numbers. Rather, an arbitrary individual variable may be put in place of 'n', so that the conclusion of the inference is a statement of a law in which 'n' refers to "everything thinkable" (cf. Frege 1990, 103 [1984, 112]).

Although the inference just described refers, with its universally quantified propositions, to everything thinkable, it still deals with something intuitive. For even if thinking and intuiting are opposed activities, with the mention of *the* thinkable in the present context something intuitive is meant. *Something* thinkable, as an element of a non-empty domain, is some singular individual, however else it may be more precisely determined; *to the extent* that this individual remains completely indeterminate, it is represented as something that, though it *can* be subsumed under concepts, is not *yet* determined by a concept. To that extent, it is *not conceptually* represented but is rather *without conceptual mediation*. Such a *representation of something singular that takes place without conceptual mediation* is precisely what Kant calls an *intuition*.[147]

Hence, algebraic inferences (provided they proceed according to the rule of complete induction like the inference just described) consist of propositions which refer essentially to intuition or something intuitive; and this reference can take place because of the way these propositions make use of a language of symbolic construction.

Frege correctly saw that one basically does not leave the sphere of algebra or the sphere of arithmetic if one advances from algebraic inferences like those I have just described to the rules according to which these inferences are made. In any case, one still remains entirely within the sphere of algebra if in the propositions of the last inference above one puts abbreviating expressions like '$F(x)$' and '$G(x)$' in place of the equations '$n^2 = 4$' and '$n^3 = 8$'. Nor does anything change in essentials when, in addition, function variables are put in place of function constants and more general expressions replace specific propositional connectives, so that for example '$F(x) \supset G(x)$' is replaced by '$\Phi(x)$'. We then obtain (through a corresponding transformation of the mode of inference described above with $a = 0$) the schema for a universal rule, namely, the schema for the rule of complete induction:

---

147 See above in § 36, especially p. 190 and note 144.

$$\frac{\Phi(0)}{(\forall x)(\Phi(x) \supset \Phi(x+1))}$$
$$(\forall x)(x \in \mathbb{N} \supset \Phi(x)).$$

However, with the sign for zero, with '$x + 1$', and with '$x \in \mathbb{N}$' included, a specifically arithmetical vocabulary is still in play, with which the given domain is restricted to the domain of the natural numbers.

It was Frege's great discovery that the concepts whose symbolic constructions we can view as '$x + 1$' and '$x \in \mathbb{N}$' can be defined almost exclusively with expressions that belong to the vocabulary of the calculus of functions.[148] The concept which is symbolically constructed with '$a = b + 1$', is the predicate concept in 'a is the successor of b in the series beginning with zero'. Frege could show of this concept that it is the sub-concept of a more abstract concept which no longer makes reference to the number zero. This concept is the predicate concept in the expression 'b bequeaths the property ($'x$) $\Phi(x)$ to a in the ψ-series', and this expression can, by means of a definition, be completely rendered in the language of the calculus of functions. Finally, as for the concept which is symbolically constructed with '$a \in \mathbb{N}$', it corresponds to the logical predicate in the expression 'a equals zero or follows the successor of zero in the series beginning with zero'. And Frege could also show of this concept that it is a sub-concept of a more abstract concept which can likewise, by means of a definition, be rendered entirely in the language of the concept-script, so that there is no longer any mention of zero in it either. This concept corresponds to the logical predicate in 'a follows b in the ψ-series'. It was one of Frege's main aims in his *Begriffsschrift* to show that the inference schema of complete induction introduced above is valid because a still more abstract inference schema is valid, namely, the schema:

$$\frac{\Phi(x)}{\Phi \text{ is hereditary in the } \Psi\text{-series from } x \text{ to } y}$$
$$[y \text{ follows } x \text{ in the } \Psi\text{-series}] \supset \Phi(y).$$

Frege could show that schema can be rendered entirely in the language of the calculus of functions.[149]

---

[148] On this, see Appendix 2.
[149] On this, see Appendix 2.

Frege correctly concluded from his discovery that there is not a very great difference between the mathematical rule of complete induction and the comparatively more general rule of inference in the concept-script. The difference between them can be reduced in its essentials to the fact that to formulate the inference rule purely in the concept-script one needs neither an algebraic sign (like the sign for zero) nor the identity sign ('... = ...'). For this reason, Frege believed that arithmetic and logic are ultimately the same.[150] 'Logic' meant here the logic of the calculus of functions, and to the extent that *only* this logic was meant, it is difficult to see what convincing objection would speak against Frege's conclusion.

However, mathematical and pure logic – the logic of the calculus of functions and the syllogistic – can be clearly distinguished from each other. What Frege did not notice is first the fact that expressions of the type 'b bequeaths the property ('x) Φ (x) to a in the ψ-series' and 'a follows b in the ψ-series' involve concepts being symbolically constructed in intuition, just as '$x + 1$' and '$x \in \mathbb{N}$' do. Thus, he could take the language in which they are formulable as a language of *pure* (i.e., abstracting entirely from intuition) *thought*. Second, Frege was erroneously convinced that the rules of the syllogistic can be reduced to the rules of the calculus of functions. He believed syllogistic propositional schemata could be rendered in the language of the calculus of functions. He could therefore suppose that the validity of syllogistic rules were provable within the logical system of the *Begriffsschrift* (see Frege 1879, 9–10, § 6 [1967, 17]).

§ 38 The Problem of Synthetic Propositions A Priori in Arithmetic

The founding father of the logical analysis of language did not base his conviction that the calculus of functions belongs to or coincides with the sphere of what Kant called '*pure* logic' on an analysis of the languages which are utilized *within* logic. Instead, what was decisive for his conviction was the speculative, philosophical aim of casting doubt on Kant's view of the synthetic character of arithmetic. To achieve this aim, Frege had to assume that no suppositions that depend on intuition are tied to the use of the calculus of functions, that this language is rather a formal language of pure thought – an assumption which cannot stand, as I established in §§ 36–37.

---

[150] I here set aside the fact that Frege in *The Foundations of Arithmetic* went a step further still when he wanted to show there that even numeric concepts like the concept of zero and the concept of the successor of zero can be defined in a language of the calculus of functions which is only marginally extended.

The speculative, philosophical aim Frege pursued was already clearly expressed in his *Begriffsschrift* and indeed in the context of the "General Theory of Sequences," which is developed in the third part of that work. In this part, the principle of complete induction is supposed to be derived from the basic formulas of the logical system of the *Begriffsschrift*. Frege explicitly assumes that the above-mentioned definition (from § 37), which he establishes in this part of the *Begriffsschrift*, is *not* a synthetic judgment; and Frege does not fail to add immediately here:

> I point this out because Kant considers all judgments of mathematics to be synthetic. (Frege 1879, 56, § 24 [1967, 55])

Frege thus seems to assume of the basic formulas of his logical system that their universal validity follows from the mere meaning of the logical constants that appear in them;[151] they are consequently analytically true expressions.

As Frege already says in the Preface to the *Begriffsschrift*, it was his main aim to demonstrate that *arithmetical* judgments can be proven "purely by means of logic" (Frege 1879, iii [1967, 5]) and indeed "by means of inference alone", without reliance on intuition, but "with the sole support of those laws of thought which transcend all particulars" (Frege 1879, iv [1967, 5]). With the derivation of the principle of complete induction, which is fundamental for arithmetic, it is supposed to be shown "how pure thought, irrespective of any content given by the senses or even by an intuition *a priori*, can, solely from the content that results from its own constitution, bring forth judgments that at first sight appear to be possible only on the basis of some intuition" (Frege 1879, 55, § 23 [1967, 55]).

To dispel at once the astonishment that "pure logic" and "pure thought" are in a position to "bring forth judgments that at first sight appear to be possible only on the basis of some intuition," Frege compares – not without pride – the success of his undertaking with a progress in the experimental science of nature. He says this result

> can be compared with condensation, through which it is possible to transform the air that to a child's consciousness appears as nothing into a visible fluid that forms drops. (Frege 1879, 55, § 23 [1967, 55])

The scientific "consciousness" to which the process of condensation appears not as *creatio ex nihilo* but rather a mere transformation of available materials, should, if Frege is correct, also be prepared to regard the derivation of the generalized principle of induction as a mere *transformation of a content*, which is already given with

---

[151] For example, Frege traces the validity of the basic formula A ⊃ (B ⊃ A) in § 14 of the *Begriffsschrift* immediately back to the meaning of '... ⊃ ...' explained in § 5.

the basic formulas and definitions from which the derivation follows.[152] To provide the demonstration that "arithmetical modes of inference" have "a purely logical nature" (Frege 1990, 103 [1984, 112]) and do not *already implicitly* make use of synthetic propositions, Frege would thus have had to demonstrate that among the basic assumptions from which they are derivable, *no* synthetic assumptions can be found. But such a demonstration, as far as I know, he did not carry out.

At the end of § 35 I had already pointed out in summary that *three* basic assumptions are connected to the use of the language of the calculus of functions, *none* of which is beyond suspicion of being a non-analytic, *synthetic* assumption. They are the following three basic assumptions:

– first, the *principle of the affirmative use of double negation*,
– second, the *principle of the arbitrary sufficient reason*,
– third, the *principle of non-empty domains*.

At this point, it is not clear, even in outline, how it could really be denied that these basic assumptions are synthetic.

4 The Vocabulary of the Universal Language of Deductive Logic

§ 39 Non-Syllogistic Basic Rules in the Language of Syllogistic

The foregoing analysis of logical languages has shown that the language of the syllogistic can be suitably translated neither into the language of the calculus of classes nor into the language of the calculus of functions without loss. Conversely, however, the language of the calculus of functions – and *a fortiori* the language of the calculus of classes as well – can be thoroughly translated into a language that is distinguished from the language of syllogistic only in that it makes use of elementary conjunction and uses instead of concept variables expressions of the form $('v)\ \Phi\ (v)$.[153]

---

[152] On the question of what it means that the *Begriffsschrift* claims to derive the *generalized* principle of mathematical induction, see M. Wolff 2000, 87–96.
[153] For this reason, it would not be correct to suppose that inferences involving many-place propositional functions (i.e., inferences like the example I gave at the end of § 24 [see above p. 69]) could not be presented and proved in their validity in the language of the syllogistic. On this, see the examples of rules which are treated below (in §§ 66 and 76).

Now the supposition that the language of the calculus of functions is 'reducible' to a non-truth-functional formal language[154] should not be misunderstood, however. It does not mean that it would be possible to reduce the validity of the logical rules and laws of the calculus of functions completely to the validity of principles which hold within the syllogistic or within a non-truth-functional logic. Rather, the use of the language of the calculus of functions is tied to principles which are not (or at least not without further ado) valid within the syllogistic or a non-truth-functional logic. Among these principles are the three basic principles recounted at the end of §§ 35 and 38, namely:
- the *principle of the affirmative use of double negation,*
- the *principle of the arbitrary sufficient reason,* and
- the *principle of non-empty domains.*

I have still not shown how the syllogistic can be presented as a system of rules which makes *no* use of these three basic principles. This presentation will require setting up an effective system of the rules characteristic of the syllogistic and then tracing them back to principles whose validity consists exclusively in the meaning of the logical vocabulary used within the rules, i.e., to principles which do not include those three just enumerated. This presentation belongs among the tasks of Part II of this essay. Yet one may already expect this much: even if the three basic principles just enumerated do *not* belong among the principles to which the rules of the syllogistic can be traced back, i.e., even if these three basic principles have *no* validity within the syllogistic, this does not mean that these basic rules are not *completely formulable in the syllogistic language. Rather, this language proves to be the universal language of deductive logic.*

Concerning the principle of the affirmative use of double negation, I had already said in § 10 that it assumes that the double elementary negation of A is equivalent to A. It says thus that not only rules which correspond to the schema

$$\frac{A}{NN\ A}$$

---

154 Since the non-truth-functional language of the syllogistic can also be considered a *non-extensional* language, the result that the truth-functional language of the calculus of functions is reducible to it is opposed to the extensionalism temporarily advocated by Rudolf Carnap and other philosophers.

are valid (for purely logical reasons, namely due to the meaning of 'N A'), but also rules which correspond to the converse schema (*duplex negatio affirmat*), i.e., the schema

$$\frac{NN\ A}{A.}$$

I will in what follows call the prescription to consider as valid rules that follow this schema the *postulate of the affirmative use of double negation.*

It is also possible to give the principle of the arbitrary sufficient reason (introduced in § 30) the shape of an inference schema without having to make use of non-syllogistic vocabulary. This schema is:

$$\frac{\begin{array}{c}A\\B\end{array}}{A,}$$

for an inference of this form is valid if and only if a proposition of the form H (A, H (B, A)) or a proposition of the form H ((A, B), A) is true. In what follows, I will designate the prescription to consider rules as valid if they correspond to this schema the *postulate of the arbitrary sufficient reason.*

Finally, the principle of non-empty domains, introduced at the end of § 35, i.e., the supposition that there are objects which are elements of the domain to which a saturated propositional function refers, can also be rendered in the syllogistic language. Since this supposition in particular assumes that negations of universally affirmative propositions always have existential implications (see § 35), it can be represented as the prescription to consider both the following schemata valid:

$$\frac{N\,A\,(\alpha,\,\beta)}{I\,(^{N}\!\alpha,\,\beta)} \quad \text{and} \quad \frac{N\,A\,(^{N}\!\alpha,\,\beta)}{I\,(\alpha,\,\beta).}$$

If we replace 'α' here with '('v') Φ (v)', then we get these schemata:

$$\frac{N\,A\,(('v)\,\Phi\,(v),\,\beta)}{I\,(('v)\,N\,\Phi\,(v),\,\beta)} \quad \text{and} \quad \frac{N\,A\,(('v)\,N\,\Phi\,(v),\,\beta)}{I\,(('v)\,\Phi\,(v),\,\beta).}$$

If we further replace 'β' with the conceptual constant 'ξ', then the two schemata turn into expressions of consequence rules which differ from quantifier rules only in that elementary negation appears in them instead of truth-functional negation. They correspond to the following schemata:

$$\frac{N\,(\forall\,v)\,\Phi\,(v)}{(\exists\,v)\,N\,\Phi\,(v).} \quad \text{and} \quad \frac{N\,(\forall\,v)\,N\,\Phi\,(v)}{(\exists\,v)\,\Phi\,(v).}$$

The equation of '~ (∀ v) Φ (v)' and '(∃ v) ~ Φ (v)' mentioned in § 35, which is fundamental for the use of quantifier rules, assumes the validity of both of these consequence schemata. I will designate the prescription to consider as valid the rules which are at the basis of these schemata, which can be formulated in the language of the elementary syllogistic, the *postulate of non-empty domains*. Clearly, this postulate annuls the principle of qualitative existential import, which is valid in the syllogistic. For as a prescription it ensures that negations, whether they are negations of universal, particular, or singular propositions, are bound to an existence assumption for the objects they treat. For negations of singular or particular propositions each imply the negation of a universal proposition with the same conceptual content. This principle thus guarantees that the concepts for which the variables α and β stand are not empty.

I speak of mere *postulates* with respect to the three principles mentioned here because they are principles whose validity does not depend on the meaning of the logical constants that are needed for their formulation. Precisely in this are these postulates distinguished from other principles of deductive logic (as will be shown still more clearly in Part II of this essay).

If we transform (through conditionalization[155]) the three postulates (formulated as schemata of rules) into schemata of hypothetical propositions, then, for every interpretation in which a true or false proposition is formed from any of these schemata, we get laws whose validity is assumed by the rules and laws of the calculus of functions and which *to that extent* can be regarded as *logical* laws. But these are *not at all laws which are true or valid on purely logical grounds*.

Thus, with the *principle of the affirmative use of double negation* it is assumed that '*H* (*NN* A, A)' is a valid schema of a law. But that a proposition of the form *H* (*NN* A, A) is true depends not at all on logical, but at best on grounds pertaining

---

[155] The transformation (of the schema) of a consequence rule into a hypothetical expression is permitted because every hypothetical proposition basically only states that a rule is valid according to which its consequent follows from its antecedent. On this and on the rules of transformation through conditionalization, see §§ 48 and 50.

to its content. The negation of such a proposition would not necessarily entail a contradiction or some other kind of inconsistency.

To the *principle of the arbitrary sufficient reason* correspond propositions of the form $H\,((A, B), A)$ or propositions of the form $H\,(A, H\,(B, A))$.[156] Such propositions cannot be assumed to be true on purely logical grounds either. The truth of propositions of such a form is based on supposing not only that (A, B) but also that A follows from a pair of premises A and B. Now this supposition of course entails that the truth of an arbitrary proposition of the form $H\,(B, A)$ follows from A. But here again no contradiction or some other kind of inconsistency results from *denying* that a proposition of the form $H\,(B, A)$ follows from a proposition of the form A. It would thus be mistaken to think that '$H\,((A, B), A)$' and '$H\,(A, H\,(B, A))$' are schemata for laws which are valid on purely logical grounds.

Finally, the *principle of non-empty domains* does not yield a universally valid schema for a law either. To this principle correspond both the schemata '$H\,(N\,A\,(\alpha, \beta), I\,(^{N}\alpha, \beta))$' and '$H\,(N\,A\,(^{N}\alpha, \beta), I\,(\alpha, \beta))$'. That propositions corresponding to these schemata are not necessarily true on purely logical grounds can be seen already from the fact that the existence of objects is not something which could have a purely logical ground. Nothing contradictory or inconsistent follows from assuming an empty domain.

Because none of these three principles is valid on the basis of experience, and yet each can be negated without contradiction, they may be called non-analytic (or synthetic) principles a priori. If one presupposes their validity and postulates the validity of rules of inference which correspond to them in the way indicated, then the syllogistic signs '$N \ldots$' and '$H\,(\ldots, \ldots)$' take on a truth-functional meaning and the rules of the logical square turn into rules of the quantifier usage.

The following Part II will show, first, that the syllogistic, as it is understood in this essay, is completely independent of the assumption that one of the three principles just mentioned is valid. Secondly, it will show that the logical calculus of functions can be derived from basic assumptions of the syllogistic only by means of these three principles.

§ 40 The Dispensability of an Expression for Logical Conjunction in the Elementary Language of Syllogistic

I have shown in the last paragraphs that the use of the language of the calculus of functions is tied to the recognition of three non-syllogistic principles. It will be the

---

[156] We have seen these already above in § 30.

task of Part II of this essay to display how the rules and laws of the calculus of functions assume the validity of these three principles. I will show in Part II that, besides these three principles, the structure of the calculus of functions need only assume as valid those principles which the syllogistic assumes as valid.

Precisely *which* principles must be counted as belonging to the syllogistic depends of course on the language which is definitively set apart as the language of the syllogistic. *Conceptual* constants will certainly not be needed in this language, since the syllogistic is distinguished in its *formal* character from the calculus of functions by abstracting completely from conceptual contents, so that its language contains only (apart from propositional variables) conceptual variables.

But the question arises: can we get by in this language with the *logical* constants which according to § 15 belong to the elementary language of the syllogistic, or do we need to extend this language with the logical constant of elementary conjunction introduced in § 30?

If we do without elementary conjunction in this language, we will get a system of rules which, as shown below, has a similarity with (or coincides with) the *Aristotelian syllogistic*; otherwise, we get a system of rules that contains an element of the *Stoic syllogistic*. The Aristotelian variant can only result if it is possible to reduce all expressions in which elementary conjunction occurs to equivalent syllogistic expressions in which elementary conjunction does not occur. In order to establish whether such a reduction is possible, the following facts must be made clear.

The elementary conjunction of A and B is *defined* to be equivalent to the pair premises consisting of A and B (see § 30 above). An inference of the form

$$\frac{\begin{array}{c} A \\ B \end{array}}{(A, B)}$$

is thus universally valid. According to the rule of *reductio ad absurdum* this mode of inference can be converted into this one:

$$\frac{\begin{array}{c} N\,(A, B) \\ A \end{array}}{N\,B.}$$

The first of these two modes of inference merely says that any premise of the form (A, B) can be replaced by a pair of premises A and B. Expressions of the form (A, B) are therefore dispensable as expressions for premises. By contrast, the second of these modes of inference was regarded by Chrysippus and other representatives of Stoic logic as a mode in which the premise expression is not replaceable by other expressions. Yet Chrysippus and other Stoics did not clearly distinguish between a truth-functional and non-truth-functional negation. The Greek Aristotle-commentator Alexander of Aphrodisias rejected the Stoic view that the expression N (A, B) is logically indispensable. He claimed that a negated conjunctive statement consisting of two sub-statements p and q is equivalent to a hypothetical statement whose antecedent is p and whose consequent is the negation of q.[157] Galen held a similar view as well.[158]

In fact, propositions of the form N (A, B) and H (A, N B) are interchangeable because of two things: first, a proposition of the form H (A, N B) follows logically from a proposition of the form N (A, B); and, second, conversely a proposition of the form N (A, B) follows logically from a proposition of the form H (A, N B).

We can see that a proposition of the form H (A, N B) follows logically from N (A, B) by recognizing a principle which was also recognized by the representatives of Stoic logic.[159] I call this principle (which corresponds to rule (II. 1), which will be presented below in § 48) the *conditionalization principle*. According to this principle one may, from an inference of two premises, proceed to infer from the first premise of this inference a hypothetical proposition whose antecedent is drawn from the second premise of the inference and whose consequent is drawn from its conclusion. From Chrysippus' rule, according to which from a first premise of the form N (A, B) and a second premise of the form A, a conclusion of the form N B follows, one may, according to the conditionalization principle, immediately proceed to a consequence of the form

$$\frac{N\,(A,\,B)}{H\,(A,\,N\,B)}.$$

Hence a proposition of the form H (A, N B) follows purely logically from a proposition of the form N (A, B).

But, conversely, a proposition of the form N (A, B) follows purely logically from a proposition of the form H (A, N B) as well. For 'H (A, N B)' means that A and B are incompatible. Therefore, NM (A, B) logically follows from H (A, N B). Now 'not possible' is equivalent to 'necessarily not' ('LN'), and from the logically stronger formula LN (A, B) follows the logically weaker formula N (A, B). So also holds:

---

[157] Alexander, *In An. pr.* 264, lines 14–17 and 264, line 33. Cf. Frede 1974, 151–52.
[158] See Galen, *Institutio logica*, 32, lines 17–21; 34, lines 9–10. On this, see Frede 1987, 118.
[159] See Sextus Empiricus, *Adv. Math.* VIII, 415–23. Mates 1973, 74–77, and Appendix A, 106–8.

$$\frac{H\,(A,\,N\,B)}{N\,(A,\,B).^{160}}$$

Hence, '*N* (A, B)' *may be replaced everywhere with* the equivalent expression '*H* (A, *N* B)'.[161]

Finally, the schema of a proposition in which a conjunctive expression is nested is replaceable by a conjunction-free schema as well. Two cases are thinkable. Either the proposition is hypothetical, or it is disjunctive. If disjunctive, it is equivalent to a conjunction of hypothetical components. (See § 47, def. 3.) If the compound is hypothetical, either the antecedent or the consequent can contain a conjunction. In the first case it has the form *H* ((A, B), C) and is, according to § 30, replaceable with the equivalent expression *H* (A, *H* (B, C)). In the second case, it has the form *H* (A, (B, C)) and is replaceable with *H* (A, *NH* (B, *N* C)). This replaceability rests on the general replaceability of conjunctive expressions of the form (A, B) with negated hypothetical expressions. (For the extensive proof of this replaceability, see Appendix 1.)

It follows from these considerations that *elementary conjunction is dispensable as a logical constant of the syllogistic.*

As a result, the principles of the syllogistic can be formulated completely in a vocabulary which contains neither elementary nor truth-functional logical conjunction. The three non-syllogistic principles which the calculus of functions rests on can and indeed must be formulated in this vocabulary as well. The elementary language of the syllogistic suffices to present them.[162] The principles of the syllogistic thus coincide with the principles of the elementary syllogistic (in the sense of § 15).

---

[160] For the relations between elementary conjunction and 'if . . ., then . . .' see the more detailed Appendix 1 below.
[161] At the end of § 30, it had turned out that '*H* (A, B)' is equivalent to '*NM* (A, *N* B)'. Now, it turns out in addition that '*N* (A, B)' is equivalent to '*H* (A, *N* B)'.
[162] To this extent, Galen and Alexander of Aphrodisias were correct in their objections to Chrysippus. For the same reason, Kant's claim for the completeness of his table of judgment can be upheld.

II Synthetic Part: Construction of the Logical Calculus of Functions from the Elements of the Syllogistic

§ 41 General Preliminary Remark

The part of the present essay that begins here is arranged so that its first five sections concern only *syllogistic* rules and principles. Only in the sixth and seventh section will *non-syllogistic* rules and principles be treated. By *syllogistic rules* I mean here only such rules which can be formulated in a language which I designated above – at the end of § 15 – as the elementary language of the syllogistic, the validity of which rests solely on the meaning of the logical constants that occur in it. Simply formulating non-syllogistic rules requires no other logical constants besides those of the elementary syllogistic. But the validity of these rules does not rest on the meaning of these constants. I would like to show that all logical rules which can be expressed in the language of the calculus of functions are reducible to syllogistic rules, *provided* that we grant validity to the three principles that are not strictly universally valid, since this validity is implicitly assumed in the calculus of functions: these are the principles of the affirmative use of double negation (for pairs of propositions of the form A and *N* A), arbitrary sufficient reason, and non-empty domains (see § 39 above).[163] Within the elementary syllogistic they are not valid, but they can nevertheless be formulated in its language (and actually only in its language).

To show that the validity of syllogistic rules rests only on the meaning of logical constants which occur in the expressions of these rules, it is first necessary to fix this meaning explicitly through *definitions*. Rules whose validity can be supported directly by definitions I call *principles*. They should merely bring to expression in a different form what the definitions already express. Their content rests essentially on the analysis of logical vocabulary carried out in Part I of this essay.

Yet I do not wish to impose on *all* the definitions which will be established in what follows the task of making intelligible and explaining the validity of principles. As I have shown in Part I of this essay, the vocabulary of the calculus of functions, insofar as it consists of non-syllogistic logical constants and quantifiers, can be explained as serving to abbreviate complex expressions, and indeed such expressions as can be completely represented in a language which I designated at the end of § 15 as the elementary language of the syllogistic. Thus, no new basic rules will result from the discussion of the use of quantifiers (in § 65) or from the

---

[163] The calculus of functions of the second level and higher, the language of which unjustifiably (see § 28 and § 37) permits quantifying over function variables as well, is not considered in what follows. In *Appendix 2*, I show that the step into predicate logic of the second level, which Frege carried out to derive the generalized principle of mathematical induction from the basic propositions of his *Begriffsschrift* (see Frege 1879/1967, § 26), can be avoided.

explanation of the meaning of truth-functional constants (in § 71), but rather only rules for abbreviating expressions.

The syllogistic and non-syllogistic principles will be established in what follows neither as propositions nor as propositional schemata. Instead, they will exclusively take the form of rules and be expressed in inference schemata. Even if it is always possible to render rules and inference schemata in the form of 'if-then' expressions, I will entirely forgo this mode of presentation. I will explain the meaning of 'if . . ., then . . .' by means of a definition in which the concept of the *regular consequence* of propositions from other propositions is assumed (see § 47, def. 2). This definition comes down to the same as the explanation given at the end of § 30, according to which 'if . . ., then . . .' is equivalent to 'it is impossible that both: . . . and not . . . .'. What it means for a proposition to follow regularly from other propositions will be explained in § 43 with just this expression.

Definition 3 in § 43 belongs among the few fundamental definitions on which depends the validity of those *special basic rules* which must be made use of to be able to derive rules from other rules at all. These basic rules are *metalogical* rules. They must be established first of all, since the synthetic derivation procedure in its entirety, which makes up the whole of Part II of this book, depends on them.

Given the metalogical character of this procedure, it would not be correct to call it *deductive* or *axiomatic* – although there are some respects in which it is similar to a deductive-axiomatic procedure. Typically, a deductive-axiomatic method already makes use of rules of deductive inference, even applying them to principles which are *not* in the form of rules, but rather in the form of propositions. A deductive-axiomatic method is synthetic in the sense that it ties together given principles or already derived theorems as premises or premise schemata in such a way that, according to a given basic rule, a conclusion or conclusion schema results. Each theorem derived according to the deductive-axiomatic method is derived as a conclusion or as a conclusion schema. By contrast, the synthetic method which I make use of in what follows consists in joining principles (which for their part only render rules) and theorems (which likewise express only rules), not to inferences or inference schemata, but rather to *schemata of inference chains*. Metalogical rules are here needed to reduce schemata of inferences and of inference chains to other schemata and to abbreviate inference chains.

In their essentials, all metalogical rules which I make use of can be traced back to *three metalogical basic rules*, the validity of which depends on definitions of logical constants and metalogical signs (namely, the signs of regular and logical consequence). One of these three rules specifies how one may abbreviate inference chains. This rule was already known in the school of Aristotle, and this under the name "synthetic theorem," and will be rendered below (in § 44) by rule (I. 3).

The second basic rule (see § 44, rule (I. 2)) specifies merely how one may, assuming the validity of just one inference, proceed to another inference. This rule likewise corresponds to an ancient rule of argumentation, known already even in the pre-Aristotelian era, which I, following the traditional nomenclature, call '*reductio ad absurdum*' and which appears in the Aristotelian syllogistic as *reductio ad impossibile*. As a metalogical rule, it should of course not be confused with the rule that is likewise called *reductio ad absurdum*, which in the method of so-called natural deduction is used for the introduction of the sign for truth-functional negation.

Finally, the third metalogical basic rule (see § 48, rule (II. 1)) is also one that was already familiar to ancient logicians. According to this rule, it is permitted to proceed from an inference whose validity is already granted, to a second inference, whose premises are the same as the first with one exception, and whose conclusion is a hypothetical proposition whose antecedent is the exceptional premise and whose consequent is the conclusion of the first inference. I call this basic rule the *principle of conditionalization*.

The *synthetic* character of the derivation procedure which I use here, in line with the just given description, rests essentially on the application of the metalogical basic rule I mentioned first, namely, the synthetic principle of the ancient Peripatetics. For this reason, one could designate the method I take up to derive logical rules the *method of inference chain abbreviation*. I will call it the *syllogistic method of derivation*, thanks to its provenance in the ancient syllogistic.[164]

---

[164] In the following reconstruction of the validity proofs of the Aristotelian syllogistic, I assume that Aristotle was familiar with this method *in its essentials*. No direct evidence for or against Aristotle's familiarity (or the probability of his familiarity) with rules (I. 3) and (II. 1) have been offered up to this point, as far as I know. My supposition that he made use not only of rule (I. 2) but also of these other rules, however, can already be seen to be not implausible by the fact that the syllogistic method demonstrably goes back to the school of Aristotle, and other methods for proving the validity of syllogisms have not survived from antiquity. In addition, carrying out proofs according to the syllogistic method is so simple, clear, convenient, and brief that it is in no way inferior, but rather much superior, in 'naturalness' to the method of so-called natural deduction (despite its name), which Aristotle certainly could not have known (since it was developed by Gerhard Gentzen only in the last century), which some of Aristotle's modern commentators and interpreters (e.g., Ebert & Nortmann 2007) have used to reconstruct Aristotelian proofs nevertheless.

Section One
Rules for Deriving Rules

1 Principles

§ 42 Notation

The language of the elementary syllogistic will be gradually constructed in this and in the following four sections. In the next three paragraphs we are concerned only with a few signs, namely, only those allotted to this language to present the derivation of rules from other rules. They are the following:

(1) Descriptive symbols: I use 'p_1', 'p_2', ..., 'p_n' as signs for propositions. Each of these signs stands for a certain declarative proposition and can be regarded as an abbreviation for such a proposition. I use 'p', 'q', and 'r' to abbreviate the first three signs 'p_1', 'p_2', and 'p_3'.

(2) Logical constants: Of the logical signs which can appear within a proposition, in this section the only one that occurs is '$N\ldots$', the sign for elementary negation. Its meaning will be explained in § 43, definition 2.

(3) Metalogical signs: More than one kind of sign will be needed to be able to speak about the logical properties of propositions and about the relations between propositions rendered with logical constants. As names (or metavariables) for formulas that stand for declarative propositions, such as, e.g., 'p_1', '$N\, p_2$', or '$NN\, p_3$', I use a non-cursive capital letter, e.g., A, with a subscripted index number: 'A_1', 'A_2', 'A_3', ..., 'A_n'. To abbreviate, I also write instead of the first five of these signs 'A', 'B', 'C', 'D', and 'E'.

To express that a proposition B *regularly follows* from a set of propositions A_1, ..., A_n, I write '$A_1, \ldots, A_n \prec B$'. To express that a proposition follows from others *logically*, I write '$A_1, \ldots, A_n \therefore B$'. Definitions 3 and 4 in § 43 will explain the distinction between regular and logical consequence.

To express that a rule of inference σ_{n+1} can be *reduced* to a rule of inference σ_n or to several rules of inference $\sigma_1, \ldots, \sigma_n$, I write '$\sigma_1, \ldots, \sigma_n / \sigma_{n+1}$'. The relation between inferences expressed by '$\ldots / \ldots$' will be explained in § 43, definition 5.

(4) Punctuation signs:
(a) Comma: To save space, the first premises of an inference will not be written one below the other, as in this example

$$\frac{\begin{array}{c}A\\B\end{array}}{C,}$$

but beside each other, separated by a comma, as in the example A, B ∴ C or A, B ≺ C. Secondly, 'A₁, ..., Aₙ ≺ B, C' and 'A₁, ..., Aₙ ∴ B, C' express that each B and C follow from the same premises.

(b) Brackets: The binding strength of expressions of the form 'N...', '...,...', '... ≺ ...' (or '...∴...'), and '.../...' decrease in this order. When an expression that contains a logical constant or a metalogical sign is enclosed in round brackets, '(...' and '...)', the parts of this expression are bound more strongly together than with expressions outside the brackets.

(5) Simplification rules:
(a) The outermost brackets of a formula may be omitted.
(b) Two expressions 'A₁, ..., Aₙ ∴ B' and 'A₁, ..., Aₙ ∴ C' may be combined into the expression 'A₁, ..., Aₙ ∴ B, C'. Likewise, two expressions 'A₁, ..., Aⱼ ∴ B' and 'Aₖ, ..., Aₙ ∴ B' may be combined into the expression 'A₁, ..., Aⱼ, Aₖ, ..., Aₙ ∴ B'.
(c) Two expressions 'A₁, ..., Aₙ ∴ B₁, ..., Bₙ' and 'B₁, ..., Bₙ ∴ A₁, ..., Aₙ' may be combined into the expression 'A₁, ..., Aₙ ∷ B₁, ..., Bₙ'. Likewise, two expressions 'A₁, ..., Aₙ ≺ B₁, ..., Bₙ' and 'B₁, ..., Bₙ ≺ A₁, ..., Aₙ' may be combined into the expression 'A₁, ..., Aₙ ≻≺ B₁, ..., Bₙ'.
(d) The order of propositional formulas A₁, A₂, ..., B, C, etc. may be arbitrarily interchanged if they are separated by no other signs than commas and are the only expressions that appear before or after the signs ≺ or ∴. Thus, 'A₁, ..., Aₙ, B ∴ C, D' may be replaced by 'B, A₁, ..., Aₙ ∴ D, C'.

§ 43 Definitions

1. A is a *negatable expression* if and only if one of the two following conditions is satisfied: (a) A is a substitute for one of the propositional letters $p_1, \ldots, p_n$, i.e., there is an interpretation in which A is a true or false proposition, or (b) A equals N B and B is in turn a negatable expression.

2. A is an *elementary negation*, that is, A equals N B (in words: *not* B), if and only if, for every interpretation in which B and C are true or false: (1) A is true if B is false or there is a false proposition C, with B = N C, and it is possible that N B and N C are both true; (2) A is false if B is true or there is a true proposition C, with B = N C, and it is possible that N B and N C are both false.

Scholium: 'False' should here mean simply 'not true'. Propositions are in this usage true or false (therefore bivalent).[165]

Elementary negation, as it is defined here, is not a truth function; i.e., the possible truth values of the elementary negation are not sufficiently determined by the truth value of the negated proposition. One could also say: there is no two-column truth table for N B – unless one assumes for such a table that there is no C such that B equals N C. But even in this case, the main column of the table contains a row which may not be filled in with T or F, since it can happen that B and N B are *both* false.[166]

N B	B
?	T
?	F

The question marks in this table are each supposed to express that the truth or falsity of B is, in certain circumstances, compatible with the falsity or truth of N B. The falsity of B is not a sufficient condition for the truth of N B. In case B and N B are both false, N B is *ambivalent* with respect to its truth value, i.e., it is *also* true. Namely, in this case N B is true insofar as N B rightly denies a false proposition, and at the same time false, insofar as N B is rightly negated by NN B. Because of the possible truth-ambivalence of expressions of the form N C, the case can arise in which N C and NN C are both true. This case is accounted for in the table. It is the case in which B = N C and C as well as N C are both false. Only the case in which B is a true proposition and there is *no* false proposition C with B = N C is a case in which NN B is also true at the same time.

3. If $A_1, \ldots, A_n$ (with $n \geq 1$) and B are formulas which admit an interpretation as true or false propositions, then with this interpretation B *follows regularly* from $A_1, \ldots, A_n$ (symbolically expressed: $A_1, \ldots, A_n \prec B$) if and only if it is impossible that each of the premises $A_1, \ldots, A_n$ as well as N B is true, and it is impossible, if B is a negated proposition of the form N C, that each of the premises $A_1, \ldots, A_n$ as well as C is true.[167]

---

[165] A proposition like "Ten is not a wicked number" – which one might treat as meaningless and thus as *neither* true *nor* false – is false in all circumstances if one takes it as the elementary negation of the proposition 'Ten is a wicked number'. That it is false does not mean, however, that the negated proposition is true. Compare my comments above in § 10.

[166] See above, §§ 8 to 10.

[167] In his 1936 work, Alfred Tarski has defined the concept of *logical* consequence in a similar way as I have here defined the (broader) concept of *regular* consequence, namely thus: "The statement form B is a logical consequence of the statement forms $A_1, \ldots, A_n$, if any interpretation of the propositional, predicate, and individual variables appearing in $A_1, \ldots, A_n$ and B which turns all of $A_1, \ldots,$

Scholium: This definition agrees in essentials with the four principles established by Aristotle in *An. pr.* B 1–4 in order to isolate the concept of consequence. These principles say roughly: (1) From the true, only the true follows; (2) from the false, the true or false can follow; (3) the false can follow only if at least one premise is false; and (4) the true can follow from premises which are true or false.

The modality expressed in the above definition and in the Aristotelian principle (1) can be understood in such a way that it says that *at no time* and *in no thinkable circumstances* is a proposition true whose consequent is nevertheless false. Accordingly, a proposition q follows *regularly* from a proposition p if and only if – on any grounds whatever – it holds at no time and in no thinkable circumstances that p and the negation of q are true. In this sense, one can say for example that it follows regularly – say, on grounds pertaining to geometrical optics – that the moon appears as a half-circle from the fact that it stands at quadrature. In the same sense one can say that the diagnosis of a sickness follows – on medical grounds – from the determination of all unambiguous symptoms of this sickness. Valid rules, according to which such consequences occur and make possible contentful inference, can be rules of *arbitrary* content, e.g., conventions, natural laws, or mathematical theorems; they need not be *logical* rules: not all grounds on which it is *impossible* or *necessary* that different propositions have different or the same truth values are logical grounds.

Equivalent to the proposition 'B follows regularly from $A_1, \ldots, A_n$' is the proposition: 'B (the consequent) may be concluded from $A_1, \ldots, A_n$ (the premises)'. The *consequence* which is here being discussed need not be a consequence valid on formal grounds or according to logical rules. If n is greater than 1, then the consequence is called an inference and the consequent a *concluding proposition* or simply a *conclusion*.

4. If $A_1, \ldots, A_n$ (with $n \geq 1$) and B are formulas which admit an interpretation as true or false propositions, then B *follows logically* from $A_1, \ldots, A_n$ (symbolically expressed: $A_1, \ldots, A_n \therefore B$) if and only if the proposition B follows regularly from $A_1, \ldots, A_n$ and this consequence depends only on the definition of the logical constants which occur in B and $A_1, \ldots, A_n$ respectively.

Scholium: Logical consequence is a special case of regular consequence; it is namely just that form of consequence based on the meaning of logical constants which occur in those propositions between which the consequence relation obtains.

I call an inference from two premises whose conclusion follows logically from them a *formal inference* or *syllogism*.

A_n into true statements, also turns B into a true statement." In §§ 80–81, I will go more precisely into the relationship between the now standard ('semantic') concept of *logical consequence*, which goes back to Tarski, and the here defined concept of *regular consequence*.

5. If $\sigma_1, \ldots, \sigma_n$ and σ_{n+1} are rules according to which propositions follow from other propositions regularly, then σ_{n+1} is *reducible* to $\sigma_1, \ldots, \sigma_n$ (symbolically expressed: $\sigma_1, \ldots, \sigma_n /\sigma_{n+1}$) if and only if, on that assumption that $\sigma_1, \ldots, \sigma_n$ are valid rules, σ_{n+1} cannot be an invalid rule.

§ 44 Basic Rules

By *basic rules* I understand here and in what follows only those rules whose validity depends exclusively and immediately on the meaning of the logical and meta-logical signs which are used in their formulation. To see their validity, it suffices to consider the definitions which underlie the signs used in them. Denying their validity results in a contradiction with the respective definitions.

If $A, A_i, \ldots, A_k, B, C_m, \ldots, C_n$ and D are formulas which admit an interpretation which has one of the two truth values, then there are valid rules which correspond to schemata (I. 1) to (I. 3):

1. Double negation as a result of an affirmation:

$$A \therefore NN\,A \text{ (with } A \neq N\,B, \text{ for arbitrary } B)\,^{168} \tag{I. 1}$$

2. Reduction rules:

Reduction rules are metalogical rules, i.e., rules for the derivation of logical rules.

Reductio ad absurdum (or rule for inference conversion):

$$(A_1, \ldots, A_n \therefore A) / (N\,A, A_2, \ldots, A_n \therefore N\,A_1), \ldots, (N\,A, A_1, \ldots, A_{n-1} \therefore N\,A_n) \text{ (with } n \geq 1) \tag{I. 2}$$

Scholium: The schema (I. 2) corresponds to a metalogical basic rule of the Aristotelian syllogistic.[169] Apuleius formulates it in this way: "*If a third [proposition] is collected [i.e., is inferred] from two, either of them together with the opposite of the conclusion collects [i.e., entails] the opposite of the remaining one*" (Apuleius, *De int.*

---

[168] The converse counterpart to (I. 1), that is: $NN\,A \therefore A$, is not valid, since $NN\,A$ does not state that A is true, but rather only that $N\,A$ is false, and it is not ruled out that A and $N\,A$ are *both* false. The medieval doctrine "*duplicata negatio efficit affirmatio*" – which, based on Diogenes Laertius, *Vitae*, VII. 89, is sometimes attributed already to Chrysippus – holds only for $A = N\,B$, with $B \neq N\,C$ (for arbitrary C), or in the form (VI. 4) $NN\,A \prec A$; see § 72 below.
[169] See Aristotle, *Sophistici Elenchi* 163 a 32 and *An. pr.* 59 b 1 ff.; cf. Alexander, *In an. pr.* 29, 7 ff., *In top.* 582, 23 ff. and Philoponus, *In an. pr.* 423, 4 ff. On these passages, see Frede 1974, 172. – The rule also plays a fundamental role in Stoic logic under the name "first directive" (πρῶτον θέμα). See Frede 1974, 172–73, and Mates 1973, 77.

191, 5 ff. [1987, 101]).[170] The index signs specify no fixed order of premise formulas. Rather, this order may be arbitrarily altered in a derivation.

> Peripatetic inference chain rule:
> $(A_b, \ldots, A_k \therefore B), (B, C_m, \ldots, C_n \therefore D) / (A_b, \ldots, A_k, B, C_m, \ldots, C_n \therefore D)$
> $(i \geq 0, k \geq i, m \geq 0 \text{ and } n \geq m)$ (I. 3)

Scholium: The inference chain schema (I. 3) corresponds to the so-called synthetic theorem of the Peripatetic syllogistic.[171] Its validity results from the transitivity of the relation of logical consequence, which is why B may be omitted in the third position. Here as well, the index signs do not specify a fixed order of premise formulas. This order may be arbitrary altered in a derivation (according to § 42 (5) (*d*)).

2 Derived Rules

§ 45 Rules Derived From the Basic Rules

If A, $A_b, \ldots, A_k,$ B, $C_m, \ldots, C_n$ and D are formulas which admit an interpretation as propositions that are true or false, then the following rules (I. 4) to (I. 8) are valid:

1. Metalogical rules:[172]

> Simple transitivity in the inference chain:[173]
> $(A_b, \ldots, A_k \therefore B), (B, C \therefore D) / A_b, \ldots, A_k, C \therefore D$ (with $i \geq 0, k \geq i$) (I. 4)

> *Derivation:*
> [1] $(A_b, \ldots, A_k \therefore B), (B, C_m, \ldots, C_n \therefore D) / A_b, \ldots, A_k, C_m, \ldots, C_n \therefore D$
> [2] $(A_b, \ldots, A_k \therefore B), (B, C \therefore D) / A_b, \ldots, A_k, C \therefore D$

---

[170] Compare here Frede 1974, 173.
[171] See Alexander of Aphrodisias, *In an. pr.* 384, 13–15; cf. Frede 1974, 173; Frede has represented the synthetic theorem in a form which substantially corresponds to schema (I. 3).
[172] Rules (I. 4), (I. 5), and (II. 6) correspond to the three metalogical rules – so-called directives (θέματα) – in Stoic logic. They go by the designations "second," "third," and "fourth directive," respectively. According to Alexander of Aphrodisias, the Stoics developed these three rules from the synthetic theorem of Peripatetic logic. See Alexander, *In an. pr.* 284, 13–15. The way in which I present these rules here corresponds to the reconstruction of these rules by Frede; compare his 1974, 178–80. Instead of letters as metavariables, the Stoics use designations for numbers of order: "the first," "the second," etc.
[173] Rule (I. 4) agrees with the third directive of the Stoic syllogistic; cf. Frede's 1974, 192–93, reconstruction.

The reduction formula in line [1] of this derivation is identical to (I. 3). The move from [1] to [2] results from the stipulation of $m = 1$ and $C_n = C_m$.

Complex transitivity in the inference chain:[174]
$(A_i, \ldots, A_k \therefore A), (A_{k+1}, \ldots, A_n \therefore B_1), (A, B_1 \therefore D) / A_1, \ldots, A_n \therefore D$
(with $i \geq 0, k \geq i, n \geq k + 1$) (I. 5)

Derivation:
[1] $(A_i, \ldots, A_k \therefore B), (B, C \therefore D) / (A_i, \ldots, A_k, C \therefore D)$
[2] $(A_i, \ldots, A_k \therefore B), (B, C_m, \ldots, C_n \therefore D)$
   $/ (A_i, \ldots, A_k, C_m, \ldots, C_n \therefore D)$
[3] $(A_{k+1}, \ldots, A_n \therefore C), (A_i, \ldots, A_k, C \therefore D)$
   $/ (A_i, \ldots, A_k, A_{k+1}, \ldots, A_n \therefore D)$
[4] $(A_i, \ldots, A_k \therefore B), (A_{k+1}, \ldots, A_n \therefore C), (B, C \therefore D)$
   $/ (A_i, \ldots, A_n \therefore D)$

The reduction formula in line [1] corresponds to rule (I. 4), the reduction formula in line [2] corresponds to basic rule (I. 3). The move from [2] to [3] depends merely on substitutions, namely on the substitution (1) of C for B, (2) of $A_{k+1}, \ldots, A_n$ (with $n \geq k + 1$) for $A_i, \ldots, A_k$, and (3) of $A_i, \ldots, A_k$ (with $i \geq 0$ and $k \geq 1$) for $C_m, \ldots, C_n$. The move to [4] is possible for the following reason: the same expression, '$A_i, \ldots, A_k, C \therefore D$', stands *behind* the sign '/' in line [1], while it stands *before* that sign in line [3]. This means that the expression may be replaced in [3] by the whole expression which stands *before* the sign '/' in [1]. The license for this replacement rests on the transitivity of the relation of reducibility. The reduction formula is in this respect a combination of the reduction formulas of lines [1] and [3].

2. Negation rules

$NNN A \therefore N A$ (with $A \neq N B$, for arbitrary B) (I. 6)

Proof:[175]
[1] $A \therefore NN A$ (I. 1)
[2] $NNN A \therefore N A$ (I. 2) [1]

---

174 Schema (I. 5) corresponds to the fourth Stoic directive; cf. Frede 1974, 193–94.
175 Here and in the following, I call 'proof' applications of metalogical rules to basic logical rules and to logical rules derived from them.

General notice on notation:

I use the following abbreviations in proofs for the validity of rules which are not metalogical rules:

All lines of the proof are designated with numerals in square brackets on the left side. To the right of this designation, there is a symbolic expression which indicates the schema either of a basic rule, a rule already proven as valid, or a provable rule. If it is a basic rule or an already proven rule, then on the right side of the line there is only the designation of its schema (e.g., '(I. 1)', as in line [1] in the proof above for (I. 6)). If it is a provable rule (or the rule to be proved), then on the right side of the column there are two references. The first reference is the designation of a rule, according to which the expression standing in the same line has been derived (e.g., (I. 2) as in line [2] of the above proof). The second reference, placed to the right, indicates in square brackets either one or more of the preceding lines to whose formula the mentioned rule has been applied. If more than one line is referenced, the line numbers are placed together in square brackets.

NN A $\therefore$ $NNNN$ A (with A ≠ N B, for arbitrary B)   (I. 7)

Proof:
[1] NNN A $\therefore$ N A   (I. 6)
[2] NN A $\therefore$ $NNNN$ A   (I. 2) [1]

A $\therefore$ $NNNN$ A (with A ≠ N B, for arbitrary B)   (I. 8)

Proof:
[1]   A $\therefore$ NN A   (I. 1)
[2] NN A $\therefore$ $NNNN$ A   (I. 7)
[3]   A $\therefore$ $NNNN$ A   (I. 4) [1, 2]

Scholium: The addition "(with A ≠ N B, for arbitrary B)" appearing in (I. 1), (I. 6), (I. 7), and (I. 8) prohibits erroneous substitutions. Thus a rule would be clearly invalid which corresponded to the schema N B $\therefore$ NNN B (with B ≠ N C for an arbitrary C) and was gained from (I. 1) by substitution. Consider the case in which there is an interpretation in which both B and N B are false. In this case, N B is compatible with NN B. It is thus not impossible that N B is true but NNN B false. Accordingly, NNN B does not follow logically from N B – assuming that "logical consequence" is understood in the sense of § 43, def. 4.

If N B $\therefore$ NNN B yielded a valid rule, then on the basis of (I. 6) – as well as (I. 4) – the validity of N B $\therefore$ N B would be provable. It is conceivable, however, as in the case we have considered, that N B is compatible with NN B. Hence, it cannot be true that N B follows logically from N B.

Since a rule of the form N B $\therefore$ N B is obviously invalid, it is also obvious that a rule of the form A $\therefore$ A is invalid. In order to see this, we do not have to take the indirect route of seeing the invalidity of N B $\therefore$ N B. Rather, we can see that the expression 'A $\therefore$ A' is not a valid rule already from the fact that in this expression there appear no logical constants on whose meaning could rest the logical consequence (as according to § 43, def. 4) of A from A.

The reason why it is impossible that A is true as a premise but false as a conclusion can only consist in the fact that A *gets an interpretation* in the places of its occurrence according to which A is incompatible with N A. However, nothing forces us to regard this reason as a *logical* one, especially since it is already established that there *is* an interpretation for A in which A equals N B and N B is compatible with NN B.

If there is a valid rule according to which a proposition follows from itself, then it cannot express a *logical* but at best a *regular* consequence and take the form: 'A $\prec$ A'. Such a rule will be discussed further below (see § 72, scholium to rule (VI. 3)).

Section Two
Hypothetical and Disjunctive Syllogistic

1 Preliminary Remark

By *hypothetical syllogistic* I understand the theory of valid inferences which can be drawn from one or more 'if-then' propositions in conjunction with other premises. I designate as *disjunctive syllogistic* a theory which pertains correspondingly to 'either-or' propositions. In these theories, the meanings of 'if . . ., then . . .' and 'either . . ., or . . .' will be fixed with definitions which will be established below in § 47 for hypothetical and disjunctive propositions. We could call both theories taken together – the hypothetical and disjunctive syllogistic – the *logic of conditional statements*, since hypothetical and disjunctive propositions can be understood as propositions that ascribe only conditional truth to statements of the clauses they consist of.

Contrary to a widespread opinion according to which Aristotle was only familiar with a categorical syllogistic, the basics of the hypothetical and disjunctive syllogistic go back to Aristotle and his school. In that school, hypothetical and disjunctive syllogisms were treated under the common designation for syllogisms ἐξ ὑποθέσεως ['from a presupposition']. Aristotle mentions the theory which is meant to deal systematically with such modes of inference in *Analytica priora* 1. 44, 50 b 1–2, though only as program yet to be carried out. He insists in 1. 44, 50 a 16 f. that these modes of inference are not reducible to the categorical. In 1. 45 b 19 f., he even announces a systematic treatment of the non-categorical syllogistic which is to investigate how many types of inference ἐξ ὑποθέσεως there are. According to Alexander of Aphrodisias, *In An. pr.* 390, 1 ff., Aristotle's system of presuppositional inferences depends on the supposition of a total of four elementary rules of inference, presumably including *modus ponendo ponens* (see rule (II. 2) below). According to Alexander, the students of Aristotle Theophrastus of Eresos and Eudemus of Rhodes were supposed to have made the Aristotelian presuppositional inferences into the subject of systematic logical investigations.[176]

Niko Strobach and Theodor Ebert have argued that the inferences Aristotle designates as syllogisms ἐξ ὑποθέσεως are not syllogisms in the sense of the relevant definition of syllogism in *An. pr.* 1. 1, 24 b 18–22, where "Aristotle has fixed the concept of syllogism so that only inferences which deduce a predicative statement from

---

[176] For more details, see Frede 1974, 17–18.

predicative statements can count as syllogisms"; this "fixing" is supposed to be seen in a "determination" within the definitional formula used by Aristotle, according to which syllogisms "'[need] no further term from outside in order for the necessity to come about (24 b 21 f.)'" (Ebert & Nortmann 2007, 859).[177] With this determination, Aristotle "blocked the path to accepting in his logical theory inferences in which conditional statements play a role", as are characteristic of presuppositional inferences, e.g., for inferences of *modus ponendo ponens* (Ebert & Nortmann 2007, 859).[178] – What is overlooked here is the fact that Aristotle also explicitly supposes of presuppositional inferences that they are inferences from predicative statements to predicative statements. He says, namely, that "every syllogism must prove something either to belong or not to belong, and this either universally or particularly, and in addition either probatively or from a presupposition [ἐξ ὑποθέσεως]" (Aristotle, *An. pr.* 1. 23, 40 b 23–25 [1989, 3, slightly modified]). Accordingly, *all* syllogisms, including syllogisms ἐξ ὑποθέσεως, are regarded as inferences whose premises and conclusions are predicative propositions or contain predicative propositions, even if this fact does not have to play any role in the logical form of these inferences. Hence, even presuppositional inferences need nothing "further", nothing to be added "from outside" (ἔξωθεν), i.e., a "term" (ὅρος) contained in an additional premise, in order to be a compelling consequence. Incidentally, in his commentary on the passage in question, 24 b 18–22, Ebert himself points out that Aristotle's word ὅρος is not only used in the sense of "term": rather Aristotle "here and also elsewhere in the *Analytics* often speaks of a term but means a statement in which this term occurs" (Ebert & Nortmann 2007, 227). It is thus not at all inconsistent when Aristotle designates presuppositional inferences (and thus what I treat here and in what follows as hypothetical syllogisms) as syllogisms without any reservation.

2 Principles

§ 46 Notation

In addition to the signs introduced in § 42, in this section two further signs will be needed. They are the logical constants 'H (. . ., . . .)' and 'D ( )' (with at least two empty places). A two-place relational expression of the form H (A, B) stands for the *hypothetical proposition* in the sense of § 47, def. 2. The n-place relational

---

[177] English translation from Aristotle 1991, 2.
[178] A similar view is held in Strobach 2001, 248–57.

expression $D(A_1, \ldots, A_n)$ with $n \geq 2$, stands for the *disjunctive proposition* in the sense of § 47, def. 3.

§ 47 Definitions

1. A is a *formula of the hypothetical and disjunctive syllogistic* if and only if A satisfies one of the following conditions: (*a*) A is a negatable expression (in the sense of § 43, def. 1), or (*b*) A is a hypothetical or disjunctive proposition.

2. A is a *hypothetical proposition,* i.e., A equals $H(B, C)$ (in words: *if* B, *then* C), if and only if, if B, C, and D are formulas of the hypothetical and disjunctive syllogistic, and for any interpretation in which B, C, and D, are propositions which have one of the two truth values, then the following holds: A is true if and only if C follows regularly from B (according to § 43, def. 3), so that B is incompatible with N C and, in case C has the form N D, also incompatible with D.

Scholium: Hypothetical propositions can be rendered with 'if-then'- *propositions*. They are, according to the definitions just given, not truth functions; i.e., the truth value of a hypothetical proposition does not depend exclusively on the truth value of its clauses. To be sure, it is only true if these values are distributed in a certain way among its clauses. But this distribution is not sufficient to make it true. Nor does it suffice that its antecedent is false. Only in one of the four rows of the main column of the truth table for $H(A, B)$ is a definite value (namely, the value F) fixed by the truth values of both clauses; for the remaining three rows, no such value exists. The question marks in these rows do not stand for a third truth value – say, the value *indefinite* –, but merely indicate that the truth value in the three cases is not sufficiently determined by the truth values of the clauses:

$H(A, B)$	A	B
?	T	T
F	T	F
?	F	T
?	F	F

The view that only the occurrence of a *consequence* (ἀκολουθία, *consequentia*) can make a hypothetical proposition true corresponds to a doctrine widespread since antiquity, according to which the meaning of an 'if-then' proposition must be made explicit with the aid of the concept of *consequence*. Sextus Empiricus reports:

> Now all the dialecticians agree in asserting that a conditional holds whenever its consequent follows from its antecedent; but as to when and how it follows, they disagree with one another and set forth conflicting criteria for this 'following'. (Sextus Empiricus, *Adv. Math.* VIII, 112 [Mates 1973, 97])[179]

The Stoic Chrysippus seems to have been the logician among those Sextus Empiricus reports on who held the view that 'if p, then q' means that the negation of q "conflicts" with the antecedent p (Sextus Empiricus, *Outlines of Pyrronhism* II, 112). Accordingly, Chrysippus explained the consequence found in a hypothetical proposition in a similar way as Lewis and Langford (1932, 154) explained the relation they called 'strict implication': "That p strictly implies q means that p is inconsistent with the denial of q." The distinction between Chrysippus' conception and that of Langford and Lewis lies merely in that Chrysippus seems not to have made explicit what he called negation and conflict by means of unambiguously truth-functional expressions. If we replace all truth-functional signs which occur in the expression '$\sim \Diamond\, (p\, \&\, \sim q)$' (which for Lewis and Langford renders the strict implication of q by p) with non-truth-functional signs, as per § 30, then we get an expression – '$NM\,(p, N\,q)$' –, which according to my definition of the hypothetical proposition is equivalent to 'if p, then q' and is suited to explicate Chrysippus' explanation of the hypothetical proposition at least no less than the definition of strict implication.

While in the above definition the meaning of 'if . . ., then . . .' is traced back to the meaning of the concept of regular consequence, it seems to have been an interest of Stoic logic to be able to explain, conversely, the meaning of the concept of consequence with the aid of the truth conditions of the hypothetical proposition. They apparently wanted to determine what a demonstrative consequence is by means of the concept of a true hypothetical proposition:

> [Inferences] are valid whenever the conditional whose antecedent is the conjunction of the premises and whose consequent is the conclusion, is sound. (Sextus, *Outlines of Pyrhhonism* II, 137 [Mates 1996, 147])[180]

Accordingly, the idea that the meaning of 'if . . ., then . . .' can be fixed with the aid of the concept of regular consequence cannot have been completely foreign even to

---

179 Sextus Empiricus reports on the various approaches which especially in Stoic and Megarian logic were made to more precisely specify the truth conditions of the hypothetical proposition in his *Outlines of Pyrrhonism*, II, 110–11. According to this report, Philo of Megara held a truth-functional reading of the hypothetical proposition: "For Philo says that a true conditional is one which does not have a true antecedent and a false consequent; for example, when it is day and I am conversing, 'If it is day, then I am conversing'" (Mates 1973, 109). – Cf. Ebert 1991, 84–130; 319.
180 Cf. also *Outlines* II, 113, 138, 145 and 249; *Adv. Math.* VIII, 304, 415 and 417; Diogenes Laertius, *Vitae* VII, 77. For criticism of the Stoic criterion of validity for inferences, see Frede 1974, 120.

the Stoics. Namely, they maintained[181] that it results from the meaning of 'if . . ., then . . .' that both the hypothetical syllogisms they took to be elementary, *modus ponendo ponens* and *modus tollendo tollens*, are valid syllogisms. They thus maintained that anyone who assumes a proposition of the form $H(A, B)$ as true immediately also assumes that B follows from A (so that once A or N B is a second premise, then B or N A, respectively, is regarded as the conclusion of a valid inference). – According to Michael Frede's account, the Stoics took their departure from the fact that a hypothetical proposition is always "the expression of a supposition that can possibly be demonstrated about the connection of states of affairs," while conversely logicians like Aristotle and Theophrastus tended to regard hypothetical propositions as "the expression of an understanding that something should be treated as demonstrated or refuted *if* something else has been demonstrated or refuted" (Frede 1974, 16).[182] – The definition I have adopted corresponds more to the Aristotelian than to the Stoic conception of the hypothetical proposition. What a hypothetical proposition is can be explained by what it means for a proposition that is to be proved to *follow* from an already accepted proposition, or by what it means for a proposition that is to be disproved to *follow* from another, already disproved proposition.

3. A is a *disjunctive proposition*, i.e., A equals $D(A_1, \ldots, A_n)$, with $n > 1$ (in words: *either* A_1, *or* . . ., *or* A_n), if and only if, for any interpretation in which $A_1, \ldots, A_n$ are true or false propositions, the following condition is satisfied: A is true if and only if from one of the propositions $A_1, \ldots, A_n$ the negation of each of the remaining propositions regularly follows (i.e., when from A_i, with $n \geq i \geq 1$, $N A_k$, with $n \geq k \geq i$, regularly follows), and if from the negation of one of the propositions $A_1, \ldots, A_n$, exactly one of the remaining propositions regularly follows (i.e., when from $N A_i$, with $n \geq i \geq 1$, exactly one of the propositions A_k, with $n \geq k \neq i$, regularly follows).

Scholium: The disjunctive proposition is not a truth function either. It is not sufficient for the truth of a disjunctive proposition that exactly one of its clauses is true. Hence, the truth table for the disjunctive compound is necessarily gappy, and its main column contains only the value F when the truth values of the clauses are clearly determined. For example, the table for the three-member disjunctive compound looks like this:

---

[181] See the scholium to (II. 7) below.
[182] As evidence for the Aristotelian view, Frede refers to Aristotle *An. pr.* 40 b 23–25; 41 a 40; 50 a 18; 50 a 25.

D (A, B, C)	A	B	C
F	T	T	T
F	T	T	F
F	T	F	T
?	T	F	F
F	F	T	T
?	F	T	F
?	F	F	T
F	F	F	F

In order to make clear the distinction between a truth-functional and non-truth-functional disjunctive compound, consider an example which was discussed in ancient logic:[183]

The proposition 'Either now is day, or now is night' is on a truth-functionally understood 'either . . ., or . . .' already true when it is now (let's say at noon on January 30, 2009) day and not night. Whether there is a point in time apart from day and night, whether there is even a division of the totality of alternatives, is irrelevant according to this understanding of the truth of the proposition. As a truth function, the same proposition would also be true if its second part would have stated: '. . ., or triangles have only two corners'. But as a complete enumeration of alternatives, the proposition is not at all true, and thus, as a disjunctive proposition in the sense of the definition established above, is false. Otherwise, the second premise in the following inference should not be true and the conclusion should not be false (see Alexander, *In an. pr.* 374, 25 ff.):

> Either now is night or now is day.
> If nothing exists now [that would bring about the distinction of day and night], now is not night.
> Thus: if nothing exists now [that would bring about the distinction of day and night], now is day.

---

183 On the meaning of '(either) . . . or . . .' there was a discussion in ancient logic which mirrors quite exactly the one concerning the meaning of 'if . . ., then . . .'. According to Mates (1973, 51), two types of disjunction were distinguished by the Stoics, the exclusive and the inclusive. Inclusive disjunction corresponds to modern (truth-functional) adjunction ('p or q, or both p and q'). Yet some Stoics demand incompatibility for disjunctive members (1973, 52–53), and thus exclusivity. This reading seems to correspond to modern (truth-functional) bisubtraction – 'p or q, but not both' –, as long as only two-membered disjunctions are considered. However, Frede (1974, 96) mentions Plutarch's statement (*De Sollertia Animalium* 969 A) that a many-membered disjunction must be "complete" "if it is possible neither that the members are true together, nor that they are false together." This statement belongs to a tradition which Kant (see *CPR* § 9) was part of as well.

Since the concluding proposition is clearly false, and since the second premise is undeniably true, the first premise cannot be true. But since it is a disjunctive proposition, and since it is now day and not night, it can be a false proposition only in terms of the definition of a disjunction, i.e., not as a truth function.

§ 48 Basic Rules

If A, $A_1, \ldots, A_n$, B, and C are formulas which admit an interpretation as propositions which have one of the two truth values, then the following rules (II. 1) to (II. 4) are valid:

1. Extension of the system of metalogical reduction rules:

   Principle of conditionalization:[184]
   $A_i, \ldots, A_k, B \therefore C / A_i, \ldots, A_k \therefore H (B, C)$ (with $i \geq 0$ and $k \geq i$) (II. 1)

The validity of this basic rule rests on the definitions of the hypothetical proposition and of logical consequence. By the sign '$\therefore$' on the left side of '/' in (II. 1) it is expressed that C follows logically from the premises $A_i, \ldots A_k$ and therefore cannot be false, *if* (in addition to these premises) B is also true. This means that, as per § 43, def. 4, '$H (B, C)$' follows logically from the same premises.

2. Basic rule of the hypothetical and disjunctive syllogistic:

   Modus ponendo ponens:
   $H (A, B), A \therefore B$ (II. 2)

Scholium: There is evidence that Aristotle and his students, as well as the Megarian logicians, regarded *modus ponendo ponens* as not further reduceable. (See my preliminary remark to this Section and Frede 1974, p. 15–18)

3. Reduction of disjunctions to hypothetical propositions:

   Reduction of two-membered disjunctions:
   $D (A_1, A_2) :: H (A_1, N A_2), H (N A_1, A_2), H (N A_2, A_1), H (A_2, N A_1)$ (II. 3)

   Reduction of three-membered disjunctions:
   $D (A_1, A_2, A_3) :: H (D (A_1, A_2), N A_3),$
   $ H (D (A_1, A_3), N A_2),$
   $ H (D (A_2, A_3), N A_1),$

---

[184] For discussion on the designation 'principle of conditionalization', compare the scholium to (II. 29); see § 50 below.

$H\ (N\ A_1,\ D\ (A_2,\ A_3))$,
$H\ (N\ A_2,\ D\ (A_1,\ A_3))$,
$H\ (N\ A_3,\ D\ (A_1,\ A_2))$ (II. 4)

3 Derivation of Formulas of the Hypothetical and Disjunctive Syllogistic

§ 49 Derived Rules

If $A, A_1, \ldots, A_n, B$, and C are formulas which admit an interpretation as propositions which have one of the two truth values, then the following rules (II. 5) to (II. 27), for example, are valid:

1. Metalogical rules:

Deconditionalization of a conclusion:
$A_i, \ldots, A_k \therefore H\ (B, C)\ /\ A_i, \ldots, A_k, B \therefore C$ (with $i \geqq 0$ and $k \geqq 0$) (II. 5)

Derivation:
[1] $(A_i, \ldots, A_k \therefore H\ (C, D)), (H\ (C, D), C \therefore D)\ /$
    $(A_i, \ldots, A_k, C \therefore D)$
[2] $A_i, \ldots, A_k \therefore H\ (C, D)\ /\ A_i, \ldots, A_k, C \therefore D$

Line [1] is an application case of the metalogical basic rule (I. 3), with $H\ (C, D)$ for B and with C for $C_m, \ldots, C_n$. Line [2] indicates that in line [1] the inference formula $H\ (C, D), C \therefore D$ may be omitted for the sake of abbreviation, since it renders *modus ponendo ponens* (II. 2) and thus an already universally valid rule.

Scholium: The metalogical rules rendered by (II. 1) and (II. 5) stand together at the basis of a rule that was used in Stoic logic (see below the scholium to (II. 29)).

Idempotency rule:[185]
$A_i, \ldots, A_k, A_1, A_1 \therefore D\ /\ A_1, A_i, \ldots, A_k \therefore D$ (with $i \geqq 0, k \geqq i$) (II. 6)

According to definition 4 in § 43, the proposition D logically follows from two identical propositions A_1 and A_1 in conjunction with other propositions if and only if D follows regularly from all these propositions and this consequence depends only on the definition of the logical constants that occur in these propositions or in D. Whether A_1 occurs more than once among the premises of D is thus

---

[185] Schema (II. 6) corresponds to the second Stoic directive according to Frede's (1974, 185–90) reconstruction.

irrelevant to whether D follows from A_1. In other words: basic rules remain valid if their antecedents are duplicated, as, e.g., with these transformations of (II. 2):

H (A, B), A, A ∴ B,
H (A, B), H (A, B), A ∴ B.

2. Rules of hypothetical inference:

Modus tollendo tollens:
N B, H (A, B) ∴ N A (II. 7)

Proof:
[1] A, H (A, B) ∴ B (II. 2)
[2] N B, H (A, B) ∴ N A (I. 2) [1]

Scholium: The Stoics counted inferences according to *modus tollendo tollens* among elementary inferences, i.e., those which are valid, but 'unprovable' and not further reducible. The validity of these inferences, as well as the validity of the inferences of *modus ponendo ponens*, depends in their view directly on the meaning of the logical constants which occur in their hypothetical premises (see Frede 1974, 199). It is suspected – even if we lack unambiguous evidence for it – that Aristotle and his students, as well as the Megarian logicians, regarded *modus tollendo tollens* as an elementary rule, i.e., as not further reducible (compare Frede 1974, 16–18).

Contraposition:
H (A, B) ∴ H (N B, N A) (II. 8)

Proof:
[1] H (A, B), N B ∴ N A (II. 7)
[2] H (A, B) ∴ H (N B, N A) (II. 1) [1]

Scholium: Aristotle mentions this mode of inference in *Analytica priora* 2. 2, 53 b 12 f. (1989, 66) with the words: "For if it is necessary for B to be when A is, then when B is not it is necessary for A not to be." It is worth mentioning that Aristotle here uses letter symbols not as concept variables, but rather as place-holders for something that is true or false.

Peritrope:[186]
H (A, N A) ∴ N A (with A ≠ N B, for arbitrary B) (II. 9)

---

[186] A different traditional designation for the consequence mode corresponding to schema (II. 9) is *Consequentia mirabilis* or *Lex Clavii*.

Proof:
[1]	$H(A, NA), A \therefore NA$	(II. 2)
[2]	$NNA, A \therefore NH(A, NA)$	(I. 2) [1]
[3]	$A \therefore NNA$	(I. 1)
[4]	$A, A \therefore NH(A, NA)$	(I. 4) [2, 3]
[5]	$A \therefore NH(A, NA)$	(II. 6) [4]
[6]	$NNH(A, NA) \therefore NA$	(I. 2) [5]
[7]	$H(A, NA) \therefore NNH(A, NA)$	(I. 1)
[8]	$H(A, NA) \therefore NA$	(I. 4) [6, 7]

Scholium: (II. 9) corresponds to a rule which was passed down in Sextus Empiricus, *Adv. Math.* VII, 389–90, under the designation περιτροπή. One can find early examples of its application in the Presocratics (see Barnes 1982, 279), in Plato, *Theaetetus* 169 A – 171 E and *Euthydemus* 286 B–C, as well as in Euclid's *Elements*, Book IX, prop. 12. It was treated as logical rule by Christian Wolff (1740, § 558. 9), Johann Heinrich Lambert (1764, § 383), and Bernard Bolzano (1829–31, vol. IV § 530, Rem. 3).

Inverse of *peritrope*:
$H(NA, A) \therefore NNA$ **(II. 10)**

Proof:
[1]	$H(NA, A), NA \therefore A$	(II. 2)
[2]	$NA, NA \therefore NH(NA, A)$	(I. 2) [1]
[3]	$NA \therefore NH(NA, A)$	(II. 6) [2]
[4]	$NNH(NA, A) \therefore NNA$	(I. 2) [3]
[5]	$H(NA, A) \therefore NNH(NA, A)$	(I. 1)
[6]	$H(NA, A) \therefore NNA$	(I. 4) [5, 4]

Exchange of the antecedents of a nested hypothetical proposition:
$H(A, H(B, C)) \therefore H(B, H(A, C))$ **(II. 11)**

Proof:
[1]	$H(A, H(B, C)), A \therefore H(B, C)$	(II. 2)
[2]	$H(B, C), B \therefore C$	(II. 2)
[3]	$H(A, H(B, C)), B, A \therefore C$	(I. 4) [1, 2]
[4]	$H(A, H(B, C)), B \therefore H(A, C)$	(II. 1) [3]
[5]	$H(A, H(B, C)) \therefore H(B, H(A, C))$	(II. 1) [4]

Elimination of an antecedent in a nested hypothetical proposition:
$H(A, H(A, B)) \therefore H(A, B)$ **(II. 12)**

Proof:
[1]	$H(A, H(A, B)), A \therefore H(A, B)$	(II. 2)
[2]	$H(A, B), A \therefore B$	(II. 2)

[3] $H(A, H(A, B)), A, A \therefore B$	(I. 4) [1, 2]
[4] $H(A, H(A, B)), A \therefore B$	(II. 6) [3]
[5] $H(A, H(A, B)) \therefore H(A, B)$	(II. 1) [4]

Basic form of a purely hypothetical syllogism:
$H(A, B), H(B, C) \therefore H(A, C)$ **(II. 13)**

Proof:

[1] $H(A, B), A \therefore B$	(II. 2)
[2] $H(B, C), B \therefore C$	(II. 2)
[3] $H(A, B), H(B, C), A \therefore C$	(I. 4) [1, 2]
[4] $H(A, B), H(B, C) \therefore H(A, C)$	(II. 1) [3]

Scholium: By negating A, B, or C and by exchanging their places as antecedents or consequents of hypothetical propositions, many types of hypothetical syllogisms can be produced. Theophrastus is supposed to have systematically organized these types, after the example of Aristotle's division of categorical syllogisms, according to three 'figures' of purely *hypothetical syllogisms*. See Kneale & Kneale (1975, 110). According to their account, which is based on Alexander of Aphrodisias' commentary on Aristotle's *Prior Analytics* (*Commentaria in Aristotelem Graeca* II. 1, 326), Aristotle provides an instance of the basic form (II. 13) of the purely hypothetical syllogism with the following inference: "[I]f it is necessary for an animal to be if a man is, and a substance if an animal is, then it is necessary for a substance to be if a man is [. . .]" (cf. *An. pr.* 1. 32, 47 a 28–30 [1989, 51]). Within Stoic logic, apparently none of the types of purely hypothetical syllogisms found consideration, although these types can, as the proof we just carried out for their basic form shows, be reduced to the syllogisms that the Stoics regarded as elementary. In Frede's view (1974, 183 and 197), Stoic logic was systematically incomplete, since it did not permit such a reduction. (See, by contrast, the above proof.)

Inference to a non-hypothetical conclusion:
$H(A, B), H(A, NB) \therefore NA$ (with $B \neq NC$, for arbitrary C) **(II. 14)**

Proof:

[1] $H(A, NB) \therefore NNH(A, NB)$	(I. 1)
[2] $A, H(A, NB) \therefore NB$	(II. 2)
[3] $A, H(A, B) \therefore B$	(II. 2)
[4] $B \therefore NNB$	(I. 1)
[5] $NNB, A \therefore NH(A, NB)$	(I. 2) [2]
[6] $A, A, H(A, B) \therefore NH(A, NB)$	(I. 4) [3, 4, 5]
[7] $A, H(A, B) \therefore NH(A, NB)$	(II. 6) [6]

[8] H (A, B), NNH (A, N B) ∴ N A	(I. 2) [7]
[9] H (A, B), H (A, N B) ∴ N A	(I. 4) [1, 8]

Scholium: Aristotle discusses a variant of (II. 14), namely the inference from two premises of the form (1) H (p, q) and (2) H (N p, q), in *An. pr.* 2. 4, 57 a 36–b 17. He seems here to want to reject the inference to p. According to William & Martha Kneale (1975, 97), Aristotle argues roughly as follows: by contraposition on (1) (i.e., on the basis of (II. 8)) we get: (3) H (N q, N p). From (3) and (2), following the rule of the completely hypothetical syllogism (II. 13), we get the further consequence: (4) H (N q, q). The Kneales suppose that Aristotle should infer from here to q, since the inverse of *peritrope* (II. 10) is applicable. But they hereby tacitly assume that the inverse of *peritrope*, as well as *peritrope* itself, permit not only the inference to NN p, but also the inference to p.

Inferring from a nested hypothetical premise:	
H (A, H (A, B)), A ∴ B	**(II. 15)**

Proof:	
[1] H (A, B), A ∴ B	(II. 2)
[2] H (A, H (A, B)), A ∴ H (A, B)	(II. 2)
[3] H (A, H (A, B)), A, A ∴ B	(I. 4) [2, 1]
[4] H (A, H (A, B)), A ∴ B	(II. 6) [3]

Scholium: In Stoic logic, syllogisms with nested hypothetical premises are classified under the name ἄπειρος ὕλη. (See Frede 1974, 186)

Purely hypothetical inferences from a nested hypothetical premise:	
H (H (A, C), H (B, C)), H (D, C), H (C, D) ∴ H (H (A, D), H (B, D))	**(II. 16)**

Proof:	
[1] H (A, D), H (D, C) ∴ H (A, C)	(II. 13)
[2] H (H (A, C), H (B, C)), H (A, C) ∴ H (B, C)	(II. 2)
[3] H (H (A, C), H (B, C)), H (A, D), H (D, C) ∴ H (B, C)	(I. 4) [1, 2]
[4] H (B, C), H (C, D) ∴ H (B, D)	(II. 13)
[5] H (H (A, C), H (B, C)), H (A, D), H (D, C), H (C, D) ∴ H (B, D)	(I. 4) [3, 4]
[6] H (H (A, C), H (B, C)), H (D, C), H (C, D) ∴ H (H (A, D), H (B, D))	(II. 1) [5]

H (H (A, C), H (B, C)), H (D, H (A, C)) ∴ H (D, H (B, C))	**(II. 17)**

Proof:
[1]	$H(H(A, C), H(B, C)), H(A, C) \therefore H(B, C)$	(II. 2)
[2]	$H(D, H(A, C)), D \therefore H(A, C)$	(II. 2)
[3]	$H(H(A, C), H(B, C)), H(D, H(A, C)), D \therefore H(B, C)$	(I. 4) [2, 1]
[4]	$H(H(A, C), H(B, C)), H(D, H(A, C))$	
	$\therefore H(D, H(B, C))$	(II. 1) [3]

$H(H(A, C), H(B, C)), H(A, D) \therefore H(H(D, C), H(B, C))$ **(II. 18)**

Proof:
[1]	$H(A, D), H(D, C) \therefore H(A, C)$	(II. 13)
[2]	$H(H(A, C), H(B, C)), H(A, C) \therefore H(B, C)$	(II. 2)
[3]	$H(H(A, C), H(B, C)), H(A, D), H(D, C) \therefore H(B, C)$	(I. 4) [1, 2]
[4]	$H(H(A, C), H(B, C)), H(A, D)$	
	$\therefore H(H(D, C), H(B, C))$	(II. 1) [3]

$H(H(A, C), H(B, C)), H(D, B) \therefore H(H(A, C), H(D, C))$ **(II. 19)**

Proof:
[1]	$H(H(A, C), H(B, C)), H(A, C) \therefore H(B, C)$	(II. 2)
[2]	$H(D, B), H(B, C) \therefore H(D, C)$	(II. 13)
[3]	$H(H(A, C), H(B, C)), H(A, C), H(D, B) \therefore H(D, C)$	(I. 4) [1, 2]
[4]	$H(H(A, C), H(B, C)), H(D, B)$	
	$\therefore H(H(A, C), H(D, C))$	(II. 1) [3]

$H(A, NB) \therefore H(B, NA)$ (with $B \neq NC$, for arbitrary C)   **(II. 20)**

Proof:
[1]	$H(A, NB), A \therefore NB$	(II. 2)
[2]	$H(A, NB), NNB \therefore NA$	(I. 2) [1]
[3]	$B \therefore NNB$	(I. 1)
[4]	$H(A, NB), B \therefore NA$	(I. 4) [3, 2]
[5]	$H(A, NB) \therefore H(B, NA)$	(II. 1) [4]

3. Rules of disjunctive and disjunctive-hypothetical inference:[187]

Modus ponendo tollens:
$D(A, B), A \therefore NB$ **(II. 21)**

---

[187] According to the system of Stoic logic, the mixed inferences in which a non-composite or simple statement is inferred exclusively from two or three hypothetical premises belong among syllogisms διὰ δύο τροπικῶν or syllogisms διὰ τριῶν τροπικῶν, respectively.

3 Derivation of Formulas of the Hypothetical and Disjunctive Syllogistic § 49 — 171

Proof:
[1] $D(A, B) \therefore H(A, NB)$ (II. 3)
[2] $H(A, NB), A \therefore NB$ (II. 2)
[3] $D(A, B), A \therefore NB$ (I. 4) [2, 3]

Modus tollendo ponens:
$D(A, B), NA \therefore B$ **(II. 22)**

Proof:
[1] $D(A, B) \therefore H(NA, B)$ (II. 3)
[2] $H(NA, B), NA \therefore B$ (II. 2)
[3] $D(A, B), NA \therefore B$ (I. 4) [1, 2]

Scholium: Among the five syllogisms which the Stoics took to be elementary (i.e., valid but 'unprovable') are two rules which correspond to (II. 21) and (II. 22). On the Stoic view, they are valid on the basis of the meaning of the logical constants which occur in the major premise of the disjunctive syllogism (see Frede 1974, 199). It is suspected (though we lack unambiguous evidence for it) that the Stoics were not alone in this view, but that Aristotle and the Megarians also recognized elementary disjunctive syllogisms (cf. Frede 1974, 16–18).

Destructive dilemma:
$D(NB, NC), H(A, B), H(A, C) \therefore NA$
(with $B \neq ND$ and $C \neq NE$, for arbitrary D and E) **(II. 23)**

Proof:
[1] $D(NB, NC), NNC \therefore NB$ (II. 22)
[2] $NNC, NNB \therefore ND(NB, NC)$ (I. 2) [1]
[3] $H(A, B), A \therefore B$ (II. 2)
[4] $B \therefore NNB$ (I. 1)
[5] $H(A, B), A \therefore NNB$ (I. 4) [3, 4]
[6] $H(A, C), A \therefore C$ (II. 2)
[7] $C \therefore NNC$ (I. 1)
[8] $H(A, C), A \therefore NNC$ (I. 4) [6, 7]
[9] $H(A, B), H(A, C), A, A \therefore ND(NB, NC)$ (I. 5) [5, 8, 2]
[10] $H(A, B), H(A, C), A \therefore ND(NB, NC)$ (II. 6) [9]
[11] $H(A, B), H(A, C), NND(NB, NC) \therefore NA$ (I. 2) [10]
[12] $D(NB, NC) \therefore NND(NB, NC)$ (I. 1)
[13] $D(NB, NC), H(A, B), H(A, C) \therefore NA$ (I. 4) [12, 11]

Weak constructive dilemma:
$H(A, B), H(C, B), D(A, C) \therefore NNB$ **(II. 24)**

Proof:

[1]	$D(A, C), NC \therefore A$	(II. 22)
[2]	$NA, NC \therefore ND(A, C)$	(I. 2) [1]
[3]	$H(C, B), NB \therefore NC$	(II. 7)
[4]	$H(A, B), NB \therefore NA$	(II. 7)
[5]	$H(C, B), NB, H(A, B), NB \therefore ND(A, C)$	(I. 5) [3, 4, 2]
[6]	$H(C, B), NB, H(A, B) \therefore ND(A, C)$	(II. 6) [5]
[7]	$H(C, B), NND(A, C), H(A, B) \therefore NNB$	(I. 2) [6]
[8]	$D(A, C) \therefore NND(A, C)$	(I. 1)
[9]	$H(C, B), H(A, B), D(A, C) \therefore NNB$	(I. 4) [8, 7]

Constructive dilemma:
$H(NA, A), H(A, A), D(NA, A) \therefore A$ **(II. 25)**

Proof:

[1]	$H(NA, A), NA \therefore A$	(II. 2)
[2]	$NA, NA \therefore NH(NA, A)$	(I. 2) [1]
[3]	$H(A, A), NA \therefore NA$	(II. 7)
[4]	$H(A, A), NA, NA \therefore NH(NA, A)$	(I. 4) [3, 2]
[5]	$H(A, A), NA \therefore NH(NA, A)$	(II. 6) [4]
[6]	$H(A, A), NNH(NA, A) \therefore NNA$	(I. 2) [5]
[7]	$D(A, NA), NNA \therefore A$	(II. 22)
[8]	$NNH(NA, A), H(A, A), D(NA, A) \therefore A$	(I. 4) [6, 7]
[9]	$H(NA, A) \therefore NNH(NA, A)$	(I. 1)
[10]	$H(NA, A), H(A, A), D(NA, A) \therefore A$	(I. 4) [9, 8]

Scholium: One can find a case of the application of (II. 25) in Aristotle; see Aristotle (1886, fragment 51): "Either we should philosophize, or we should not. If we should, then we should. If we should not, then we likewise should [namely, because otherwise we could not justify that we should not do it]. Thus, we should philosophize in any case."

Simple disjunctive conversion:
$D(A, B) \therefore D(B, A)$ **(II. 26)**

Proof:

[1]	$D(A, B) \therefore H(A, NB), H(NA, B), H(NB, A), H(B, NA)$	(II. 3)
[2]	$H(B, NA), H(NB, A), H(NA, B), H(A, NB) \therefore D(B, A)$	(II. 3)
[3]	$D(A, B) \therefore D(B, A)$	(I. 4) [1, 2]

Complex disjunctive conversion:
$D(D(A, B), NH(A, NB))$
$\therefore D(D(B, A), NH(B, NA)))$ (with $B \neq NC$, for arbitrary C)   **(II. 27)**

Proof:

[1] $D(D(A, B), NH(A, NB))$
 $\therefore H(D(A, B), NNH(A, NB))$ (II. 3)

[2] $D(D(A, B), NH(A, NB)), D(A, B) \therefore NNH(A, NB)$ (II. 5) [1]

[3] $D(D(A, B), NH(A, NB))$
 $\therefore H(ND(A, B), NH(A, NB))$ (II. 3)

[4] $D(D(A, B), NH(A, NB)), ND(A, B) \therefore NH(A, NB)$ (II. 5) [3]

[5] $D(D(A, B), NH(A, NB))$
 $\therefore H(NNH(A, NB), D(A, B))$ (II. 3)

[6] $D(D(A, B), NH(A, NB)), NNH(A, NB) \therefore D(A, B)$ (II. 5) [5]

[7] $D(B, A) \therefore D(A, B)$ (II. 26)

[8] $D(D(A, B), NH(A, NB)); D(B, A) \therefore NNH(A, NB)$ (I. 4) [7, 2]

[9] $D(A, B) \therefore D(B, A)$ (II. 26)

[10] $ND(B, A) \therefore ND(A, B)$ (I. 2) [9]

[11] $H(A, NB) \therefore H(B, NA)$ (II. 20)

[12] $NH(B, NA) \therefore H(A, NB)$ (I. 2) [11]

[13] $NNH(A, NB) \therefore NNH(B, NA)$ (I. 2) [12]

[14] $D(D(A, B), NH(A, NB)), D(B, A) \therefore NNH(B, NA)$ (I. 4) [8, 13]

[15] $D(D(A, B), NH(A, NB)) \therefore H(D(B, A), NNH(B, NA))$ (II. 1) [14]

[16] $D(D(A, B), NH(A, NB)), ND(B, A) \therefore NH(A, NB)$ (I. 4) [10, 4]

[17] $D(D(A, B), NH(A, NB)) \therefore H(ND(B, A), NH(A, NB))$ (II. 1) [16]

[18] $D(D(A, B), NH(A, NB)), NNH(A, NB) \therefore D(B, A)$ (I. 4) [6, 9]

[19] $D(D(A, B), NH(A, NB)) \therefore H(NNH(A, NB), D(B, A))$ (II. 1) [18]

[20] $D(D(A, B), NH(A, NB))$
 $\therefore H(NH(A, NB), ND(A, B))$ (II. 3)

[21] $D(D(A, B), NH(A, NB)), NH(A, NB) \therefore ND(A, B)$ (II. 5) [20]

[22] $ND(A, B) \therefore ND(B, A)$ (I. 2) [7]

[23] $D(D(A, B), NH(A, NB)), NH(A, NB) \therefore ND(B, A)$ (I. 4) [21, 22]

[24] $D(D(A, B), NH(A, NB)) \therefore H(NH(A, NB), ND(B, A))$ (II. 1) [23]

[25] $H(D(B, A), NNH(B, NA)),$
 $H(ND(B, A), NH(A, NB)),$
 $H(NNH(A, NB), D(B, A)),$
 $H(NH(A, NB), ND(B, A))$
 $\therefore D(D(B, A), NH(B, NA))$ (II. 3)

[26] $D(D(A, B), NH(A, NB)),$
 $D(D(A, B), NH(A, NB)),$
 $D(D(A, B), NH(A, NB)),$
 $D(D(A, B), NH(A, NB))$
 $\therefore D(D(B, A), NH(B, NA))$ (I. 4) [1, 3, 5, 24, 25]

[27] $D(D(A, B), NH(A, NB)),$
 $\therefore D(D(B, A), NH(B, NA))$ (II. 6) [26]

§ 50 Conditionalization

1. Derivation of metalogical rules

If A, B, and C are formulas of deductive logic, then a metalogical rule is valid which corresponds to the following schema:

Rule of conditionalization:
$*, B \therefore C / * \therefore H (B, C)$ (II. 28)

Derivation:
[1] $A_i, \ldots, A_k, B \therefore C / A_i, \ldots, A_k \therefore H (B, C)$ (II. 1)
[2] $*, B \therefore C / * \therefore H (B, C)$

Line [2] results from the substitution of the empty premise set (which here and in what follows is designated with the asterisk '*') for $A_i, \ldots, A_k$.[188] This substitution is permitted since the regular consequence of C from B rendered by '$H (B, C)$', according to § 43, def. 3, is a necessary condition for the logical consequence of C from B, even if this consequence is independent of other premises.

Scholium: The supposition that a statement follows logically from the empty premise set is equivalent to the supposition that this statement is logically valid. Hence, one may, in case C follows logically from B, proceed to '$* \therefore H (B, C)$' and from there to '$H (B, C)$'.

Generalized rule of conditionalization:
$A_1, A_i, \ldots, A_n \therefore B / * \therefore H (A_1, H (A_i, H (\ldots, H (A_n, B))) \ldots)$
(with $i \geq 1, n \geq i$) (II. 29)

Derivation:
[1] $A_1, A_i, \ldots, A_n \therefore B / A_1, \ldots A_{n-1} \therefore H (A_n, B)$ (II. 1)
[2] $A_1, \ldots, A_{n-1} \therefore H (A_n, B) /$
  $A_1, \ldots, A_{n-2}, H (A_{n-1}, H (A_n, B))$ (II. 1)
⋮

---

[188] In the use of this notation here and in what follows, I follow Carnap (1934, § 31 and § 47). The talk of an empty premise set is perhaps easily misunderstood. The little star * is meant to indicate that the full transformation of an inference schema into a propositional schema through conditionalization has come to completion. Such a completion comes about as soon as all premise schema which belonged to the conditionalized inference schema have been converted into (more or less nested) 'if'-propositions. In other words, 'A follows logically from the empty premise set' basically means: 'A is valid because the consequent C of A (= $H (B, C)$) logically follows from the antecedent B of A.'

3 Derivation of Formulas of the Hypothetical and Disjunctive Syllogistic § 50

[n] $A_1 \therefore H(A_i, H(\ldots, H(A_n, B))\ldots)$ /
      $^* \therefore H(A_1, H(A_i, H(\ldots, H(A_n, B)))\ldots)$ (II. 1)
[n + 1] $A_1, A_i, \ldots, A_n \therefore B$ / $^* \therefore H(A_1, H(A_i, H(\ldots, H(A_n, B)))\ldots)$

Line [n + 1] may be added here because of the transitivity of the relation of reducibility.

Scholium: The generalized conditionalization rule corresponds to a metalogical basic rule which, according to Jan Łukasiewicz (1935, 115), was already a Stoic principle. However, that principle must have been stronger than (II. 29), since it was supposed to have said that an inference is valid *if and only if* a hypothetical statement is true whose antecedent consists in a conjunction of premises and whose consequent is identical with the conclusion. That is, the Stoics must have recognized the inverse counterpart of the generalized rule of conditionalization as well, i.e., (II. 30). Compare on this the account in Sextus Empiricus, *Adv. Math.*, VIII, 415–23. In his book *Stoic Logic* (1973, 74–77, and Appendix A, 106–8), Benson Mates has compared the Stoic principle highlighted by Łukasiewicz with the one he himself calls 'principle of conditionalization'. This principle says: "If a conclusion β is validly derivable from the premises $α_1, α_2, \ldots, α_n$, then the conditional proposition '$(α_1, α_2, \ldots, α_n) \supset β$' is logically true" (Mates 1973, 74–75). Mates certainly emphasizes: (1) the Stoics formulated their principle always as an equivalence claim, not merely as a conditional proposition; (2) the contexts in which the Stoic principle appears are always those in which Sextus interprets the Stoics as attempting to give a criterion for the validity of inferences; (3) 'logically true' should be replaced with another expression – Mates himself proposes replacing it with "Diodorian-true"; and (4) there is no evidence available showing the Stoics using their principle as a rule of inference. It would be appropriate to add a fifth point, namely: (5) the Stoics understood 'if . . ., then . . .' not in the sense of '. . . ⊃ . . .', i.e., not in the Philonic sense.[189] – On the question of whether and in which way the Stoics used what Mates has called a conditionalization principle, compare Frede (1974, 105–6).

I have taken up the word 'conditionalization principle' to label something else than Mates does, namely the rule represented by (II. 1). Because the remaining conditionalization rules (II. 5) and (II. 28) to (II. 30) depend on this latter rule, I consider the deviation from Mates' way of designating appropriate.

Deconditionalization (the converse counterpart to the generalized rule of conditionalization):
$^* \therefore H(A_1, H(A_i, H(\ldots, H(A_n, B)))\ldots)$ / $^*, A_1, A_i, \ldots, A_n \therefore B$
(with $i \geq 1, n \geq i$) (II. 30)

---

[189] See above, Scholium to § 47, Definition 2.

Derivation:

[1] $*\therefore H(A_1, H(A_i, H(\ldots, H(A_n, B)))\ldots)\,/$
       $A_1 \therefore H(A_i, H(\ldots, H(A_n, B))\ldots)$ **(II. 5)**

[2] $A_1 \therefore H(A_i, H(\ldots, H(A_n, B))\ldots)\,/$
       $A_1, A_i \therefore H(A_{i+1}, H(\ldots, H(A_n, B))\ldots)$ **(II. 5)**

⋮

[n] $A_1, A_i \ldots A_{n-1} \therefore H(A_n, B)\,/$
       $A_1, A_i \ldots A_n \therefore B$ **(II. 5)**

[n + 1] $*\therefore H(A_1, H(A_i, H(\ldots, H(A_n, B)))\ldots)\,/$
          $*, A_1, A_i \ldots A_n \therefore B$

Line [n + 1] may be added because of the transitivity of the relation of reducibility.

2. Derived universally valid propositional schemata

By conditionalization according to (II. 28), any universally valid rule of deductive logic can be transformed into a formula which in the appropriate interpretation becomes a nested hypothetical proposition which is logically valid. In what follows, I will call such a formula a 'universally valid propositional schema'.

If A, B, and C are formulas of deductive logic, then the expressions (II. 31) to (II. 33) are universally valid propositional schemata.

     $*\therefore H(A, NN\,A)$ (with $A \neq N\,B$, for arbitrary B)   **(II. 31)**

Proof:

[1] $A \therefore NN\,A$ **(I. 1)**

[2] $*, A \therefore NN\,A\,/\,*\therefore H(A, NN\,A)$ **(II. 28)**

[3] $*\therefore H(A, NN\,A)$ **[2] [1]**

From *modus ponendo ponens*, we can get the following universally valid propositional schema:

     $*\therefore H(A, H(H(A, B), B\,A))$ **(II. 32)**

Proof:

[1] $A, H(A, B) \therefore B$ **(II. 2)**

[2] $A \therefore H(H(A, B), B)$ **(I. 2)**

[3] $*\therefore H(A, H(H(A, B), B))$ **(II. 28) [2]**

Much more complicated universally valid propositional schemata can be derived from *modus ponendo ponens* as well, e.g., the following:

*∴ $H(H(A, H(B, C)), H(H(A, B), H(A, C)))$ (II. 33)

Proof:

[1]	$H(A, B), A \therefore B$	(II. 2)
[2]	$B, H(B, C) \therefore C$	(II. 2)
[3]	$H(A, H(B, C)), A \therefore H(B, C)$	(II. 2)
[4]	$H(A, B), H(B, C), A \therefore C$	(I. 4) [1, 2]
[5]	$H(A, H(B, C)), H(A, B), A, A \therefore C$	(I. 4) [3, 4]
[6]	$H(A, H(B, C)), H(A, B), A \therefore C$	(II. 6) [5]
[7]	$H(A, H(B, C)), H(A, B) \therefore H(A, C)$	(II. 1) [6]
[8]	$H(A, H(B, C)) \therefore H(H(A, B), H(A, C))$	(II. 1) [7]
[9]	*∴ $H(H(A, H(B, C)), H(H(A, B), H(A, C)))$	(II. 28) [8]

Scholium: In light of the formulas which can be gained from universally valid rules, an interesting distinction arises between forms of nested hypothetical propositions on the one hand and forms of similarly nested subjunctions and forms of likewise nested 'strict implications', as they were introduced by Wilhelm Ackermann.[190]

Compare, e.g., with formula (II. 32) the two following, similarly nested expressions in which the arrow, '... → ...', indicates the relation of strict implication:

$$A \rightarrow ((A \rightarrow B) \rightarrow B),$$
$$A \rightarrow (B \rightarrow A).$$

According to Wilhelm Ackermann, *neither* of these two formulas are universally valid. If '... → ...' were read as subjunction, then *both* formulas would be universally valid. If '... → ...' were taken as the hypothetical propositional connective, then the first formula would be valid, but not the second.

---

[190] See Ackermann 1956, 113–28, and Hilbert & Ackermann 1967, 36–40.

Section Three
Categorical Syllogistic

1 Preliminary Remark

In contrast to the hypothetical and disjunctive syllogistic, the categorical syllogistic has to do with rules of inferring from propositions that are not logically composite. The rules of the categorical syllogistic depend therefore not on definitions which fix the meaning of propositional connectives, but rather on definitions which fix the meaning of expressions used to logically connect concept expressions.

2 Principles

§ 51 Notation

In this section the signs which were introduced in § 42 and § 46 will be put to further use, as well as the following signs being added:
(1) Letter symbols: '$\alpha_1, \ldots, \alpha_n$' as concept variables (i.e., as substitutes for terms). I abbreviate by replacing the first four concept variables 'α_1', 'α_2', 'α_3', and 'α_4' with 'α', 'β', 'γ', and 'δ'.
(2) Logical constants: '$A\,(\ldots, \ldots)$', '$I\,(\ldots, \ldots)$', and '$\underline{A}\,(\ldots, \ldots)$' for two-place relations in which the concept variables appear in the empty places, as well as '$N \ldots$' to designate antonyms.

§ 52 Definitions

1. A is a *formula of the categorical syllogistic* if and only if A satisfies one of the following conditions: (*a*) A takes the form of a universal, particular, or singular affirmative proposition, or (*b*) A is a negatable expression (in the sense of § 43) and equals N B or NN C, and B and C each take the form of a universal, particular, or singular affirmative proposition.

Scholium: Categorical propositions are not truth functions, because they cannot be reduced to simpler propositions, and if they are propositions of the form N A, they do not contain a truth-functional negation. The truth of affirmative categorical propositions consists in their correspondence with the objects they deal with. This correspondence presupposes that these objects exist, or in any case belong to the 'world of attributions' in the sense of § 20. The truth of negative categorical propositions is independent of such a presupposition.[191]

2. A is a *universally affirmative proposition*, i.e., a proposition of the form $A\ (α, β)$ (in words: *every β is an α*), if and only if, for every interpretation of α and β in which A is a true or false proposition, the following holds: (1) A is true if and only if β is not an empty concept (thus, some object which falls under the concept β is a β after all) and moreover, if any object – whether it falls under an arbitrary concept γ or δ or whatever other concept – falls under the concept β, this very object γ also falls under the concept α; (2) A is false if and only if $N\ A\ (= O\ (α, β))$ is true and $NN\ A = N\ O\ (α, β)$ is false (so that an arbitrary concept – call it γ or δ or whatever else – can be formed for which it holds that: no object that falls under it falls under the concept α, but there is an object that falls under it, and the latter falls under the concept β if there is in that case some object at all that falls under the concept β).

Corollary to definition 2: If a proposition of the form $A\ (α, β)$ is false, so that $N\ A\ (α, β)$ is true, according to definition 2 this means that β is an empty concept or it is not true that, if some object which falls under an arbitrary concept γ also falls under the concept β, this object γ falls under the concept α. This means: if $N\ A\ (α, β)$ is true, then a concept γ – e.g., the concept of a β that is not an α – can be formed for which it holds that: there is, in case β is not an empty concept (so that some object that falls under the concept β is a β), an object that falls under the concept γ, and this same object γ also then falls under the concept β, but no object that falls under the concept γ falls under the concept α.

---

[191] I here make use of one of the ideas which I developed in Section Three of Part I (especially in § 32), namely the idea that the universal form of the categorical proposition cannot be rendered in the language of the calculus of functions, and that it must be characterized by what I called 'qualitative existential import'. This idea also seems to me to be compatible with the conception of the categorical proposition in Aristotle. By contrast, Günther Patzig (1969, 47–48) cannot find support in the text of Aristotle when he writes: "The form of the proposition '*A* belongs to all *B*' is in mathematical logic $(x)\ (Bx \supset Ax)$. For Aristotle, the subject of this proposition is not the universal class of individuals, but rather the class of individuals of which *B* holds, thus in short the class *B*. And the predicate of the proposition is the predicate *A*. Aristotle's conception thus differs from the conception of mathematical logic in that in Aristotle the 'universe of discourse' is restricted to the objects of which *B* holds. This restriction has the consequence that, though the Aristotelian proposition is not true in any case in which the proposition in mathematical logic is false, in some cases the proposition of Aristotle is neither true nor false, but rather meaningless while in the interpretation of mathematical logic it is true: this occurs in all the cases in which an individual is substituted for *x* which does not belong to the class *B*. The Aristotelian proposition says nothing at all about this; yet the proposition in mathematical logic remains true in that case: it claims only that the predicate *A* applies to *x*, *if* the predicate *B* applies to it."

Scholium: Definition 2 determines the meaning of both the logical constant A (..., ...) as well as the logical constant O (..., ...). This determination corresponds to how Aristotle understands their meaning. He fixes the meaning of the constant A (..., ...) with the following words (see *An. pr.* 1. 1, 24 b 28–30 [1989, 2]): "We use the expression '[α is] predicated of every [β]', whenever none (μηδὲν)[192] of the things [e.g., γ] which fall under the subject-term [β] can be taken (λαβεῖν) of which the other term [α] cannot be said. And we use '[α is] predicated of none [no β]' likewise [that is, no β can be taken of which α can be said]." As for the constant O (..., ...), Michael Wedin (1990, 134–35) has pointed out the interesting fact that Aristotle does not choose 'Some S is not P' as the canonical form of the O proposition, but rather 'Not every S is P', and that this choice apparently expresses the view that O propositions can be true without 'existential import'. That Aristotle has an additional motive for this choice can be seen in the fact that he explicitly takes the form 'Some S is not P' as the form of a (quantitively) indefinite (ἀδιόριστος) proposition (*An. pr.* 1. 4, 26 b 14–19), i.e., as the form of a proposition which can be understood both as an O and as an E proposition (namely, as a negated I proposition). In fact, Aristotle seems to use the form 'Some S is not P' as the form of a (quantitatively definite) O proposition only in cases where, on the basis of the context, the quantity of the proposition is not only determined, but it is also determined that S exists.[193]

3. A is a *particular affirmative proposition*, i.e., a proposition of the form I (α, β) (in words: *some β is an α*) if and only if, for every interpretation of α and β in which A is a true or false proposition, the following holds: (1) A is true if and only if some concept (e.g., the concept of an α that is a β) – call it γ or δ or whatever – can be formed for which it holds that: there is an object that falls under it, and it is the case both that this object falls under the concepts α and β, as well as that every

---

[192] In the MSS, the readings μηδὲν τοῦ ὑποκειμένου and μηδὲν τῶν τοῦ ὑποκειμένου have been passed down. In his edition, Ross follows, against all MSS, Alexander of Aphrodisias, who brings to the text an older manuscript which omits these genitives. They are to be understood as commentarial additions to the original.

[193] The view of Hermann Weidemann (see the remarks in his edition of Aristotle's writing *Peri Hermeneias*: Aristotle 2002, 208) that Aristotle supposes a statement of the form 'not every S is P' implies a statement 'some S is not P', which is incompatible with the above observation, relies on a translation which seems to me to incompletely render and thus to distort the sense of *An. pr.* 1. 4, 26 b 15–16. That passage is not concerned with such an implication, but rather with the fact that if there is a quantitatively indefinite negative premise ('B does not belong to some C'), it is true in both meanings (both in the particular as well as in the universal meaning), so that it is thus true "both if B belongs to no C, as well as if it does not belong to every C," and indeed "*because B does not belong to some C*" (ὅτι τινὶ οὐχ ὑπάρχει). With Weidemann's translation, which represents the ὅτι-clause as a 'that'-clause, it becomes redundant, as he concedes. As a 'that'-clause, it states what is already stated in a previous part of the sentence, namely in the nominal expression 'τὸ [. . .] ὑπάρχειν'.

object which falls under this concept falls under the concepts α and β; (2) A is false if and only if N A (= E (α, β)) is true and NN A is false (so that, if some object which falls under the concept γ or δ or whatever other concept falls under one of the concepts α and β, this object does not fall under the other of these concepts).

Corollary to definition 3: If a proposition of the form I (α, β) is true, then a concept γ – for example, the concept of a β that is an α – can be formed[194] such that the following holds: some individual falls under the concept γ, and this individual with predicate γ is a β, and there is no γ that does not fall under the concept α. If by contrast a proposition of the form I (α, β) is false, this means, according to definition 3, that a proposition of the form $N I$ (α, β) is true and that, if some individual which falls under an arbitrary concept γ also falls under one of the two concepts α and β, this individual γ then does not fall under the other of these two concepts.

Scholium: The last sentence of the corollary to definition 3 determines the meaning of the logical constant E (. . ., . . .). This determination corresponds to the discussion in which Aristotle explains this meaning. (See *An. pr.* 1. 1, 24 b 28–30.)

4. A is a *singular affirmative proposition*, i.e., a proposition of the form $\underline{A}$ (α, β) (in words: *that β is an α*) if and only if, for any interpretation of α and β in which A is a true or false proposition, the following holds: (1) A is true if and only if there is some object β to which the predicate α belongs, and this object is the same as that object β which is discussed in $\underline{A}$ (α, β) and in the context of $\underline{A}$ (α, β) (in case there is such a context); (2) A is false if and only if N A (= $\underline{E}$ (α, β)) is true or β is an empty concept.

Scholium: Impredicative propositions like 'It is raining' are usually understood as non-categorical propositions, but they can as a rule be understood as propositions which are singular categorical propositions in disguise. Thus, the proposition 'It is raining' is about the weather and states roughly: 'This weather – the weather being discussed or that is supposed to be discussed – is rainy weather.'

5. A is a *limitative proposition*, i.e., a proposition of the form Y (^{N}α, β), with Y = A, Y = I, or Y = $\underline{A}$, (in words: *every* or *some* or *that β is a not-α*) if and only if, for any interpretation of the concept variables α and β in which A is a true or false proposition, the following holds: (1) A is true if and only if the predicate β is not an empty concept and N Z (α, β), with Z = I, Z = A, or Z = $\underline{A}$, is a true proposition whose quantity is the same as that of the proposition Y (^{N}α, β), and (2) A is false if and only if N A is true or β is an empty concept.

---

[194] For illustration by way of example, one can insert for α, β, and γ in sequence the concept words 'white', 'horse', and 'white horse [*Schimmel*]'.

§ 53 Basic Rules

The basic rules from which all the rules of the categorical syllogistic are derived, and which are treated in these paragraphs, rest on the meanings of the logical constants $A(\ )$, $I(\ )$, $A(\ )$, and $^N(\ )$, which are determined in the definitions established in § 52. More precisely, rule (III. 1) corresponds to definition 2 (1). Rules (III. 2) and (III. 3) correspond to the second and first sentences, respectively, in the corollary to definition 3. Rule (III. 4) corresponds to the corollary to definition 2. Rule (III. 5) corresponds to definition 1 (2), rule (III. 6) to definition 3 (2). The validity of (III. 7) arises from definition 4, while the validity of rules (III. 8) to (III. 10) results from definition 5.

If α, β, and γ are concept variables, then rules (III. 1) and (III. 2) are valid (cf. Aristotle, *An. pr.* 1. 1, 24 b 28–30):

Dictum de omni:
$A\,(α, β) :: I\,(β, β), H\,(I\,(β, γ), A\,(α, γ))$ \hfill (III. 1)

Dictum de nullo:
$N\,I\,(α, β) :: H\,(I\,(β, γ), N\,A\,(α, γ))$ \hfill (III. 2)

Rules (III. 1) and (III. 2) also remain valid if the concept variable γ is replaced in all places of its occurrence in the formulas which render these rules.

Let γ be a variable which occurs in no premise formula of the lines of a proof which proceed the line in which one of the two following formulas (III. 3) and (III. 4) stands. Then and only then does this formula express a valid rule:

First exposition rule:
$I\,(α, β) \therefore A\,(α, γ), A\,(β, γ)$ \hfill (III. 3)

Second exposition rule:
$N\,A\,(α, β) \therefore N\,I\,(α, γ), H\,(I\,(β, β), A\,(β, γ))$ \hfill (III. 4)

Scholium: Similarities may be noticed between the way Aristotle describes the operation he designate as ἔκθεσις ("exposition") and the way he expresses, in *An. pr.* 1. 1, 24 b 28–30 (1989, 2), what the logical constants 'predicated of every' and 'predicated of none' mean. Namely, to explain this meaning he uses the same Greek word for "can be taken" (λαβεῖν) that he also uses for the expository procedure. He writes in *An. pr.* 1. 1, 24 b 28–30: "We use the expression '[α is] predicated of every [β]', whenever none of the things [e.g., γ] which fall under the subject-term [β] (μηδὲν τῶν τοῦ ὑποκειμένου)[195] can be taken (λαβεῖν) of which the other term [α] cannot be said. And we use '[α is] predicated of none [no β]' likewise [that is, when no γ can be

---

195 Compare note 192.

taken of which α can be said]." What is meant here should be more clear from *An. pr.* 1. 41. There (49 b 14–32 [1989, 57]), he says something more about the meaning of 'α is predicated of all β'. He says that '*A* (α, β)' means: "α belongs to everything to which all β belongs."[196] This statement can be paraphrased in the following way: if one only finds *some* example of those objects to which the predicate β belongs, and designate it, e.g., as γ (so that *I* (β, γ) holds), then on the assumption that *A* (α, β) is the case it also immediately holds that *this* γ is an α. That is, '*A* (α, β)' means that no concept, e.g., no concept γ, can be formed for which it would not at once also hold that if *some* γ is a β, then *this* γ is an α; symbolically expressed: *A* (α, β) ∴ *H* (*I* (β, γ), *A* (α, γ)). This corresponds to the *dictum de omni* in its above formulation (III. 1).

> Contradiction rules of the logical square:
> *NN A* (α, β) ∴ *A* (α, β)   (III. 5)
> *NN I* (α, β) ∴ *I* (α, β)   (III. 6)

I call rules (III. 5) and (III. 6) contradiction rules, since they are equivalent to rules which, together with certain other rules, express that two propositions of the form *N A* (α, β) and *A* (α, β) or two propositions of the form *N I* (α, β) and *I* (α, β) are contradictory to each other, respectively. These other rules do not need to be introduced explicitly as basic rules, since their validity results from the validity of the more general basic rules. These rules are the converse counterparts to (III. 5) and (III. 6), namely,

> (1) *A* (α, β) ∴ *NN A* (α, β) and
> (2) *I* (α, β) ∴ *NN I* (α, β),

thus cases of the direct application of rule (I. 1), from which – on the basis of (I. 4) – in conjunction with (III. 5) or (III. 6) the rules *A* (α, β) ∴ *A* (α, β) and *I* (α, β) ∴ *I* (α, β), respectively, are immediately derivable. From which in turn result – on the basis of (I. 2) – the two following rules:

> (3) *N A* (α, β) ∴ *N A* (α, β) and
> (4) *N I* (α, β) ∴ *N I* (α, β).

If one takes '*E* (α, β)' and '*O* (α, β)' as abbreviations for '*N I* (α, β)' and '*N A* (α, β)', respectively, then (3) and (4) can be understood as expressions that summarize the four contradiction rules of the logical square; to them the following formulas correspond:

> *N A* (α, β) :: *O* (α, β) and
> *N I* (α, β) :: *E* (α, β).

---

[196] As according to Günther Patzig's (1963, 43, n. 1) translation of this passage in the second edition of his book *Die aristotelische Syllogistik*.

The remaining contradiction rules of the logical square, i.e.,

$N O (\alpha, \beta) :: A (\alpha, \beta)$ and
$N E (\alpha, \beta) :: I (\alpha, \beta)$,

are only transformations of rules (III. 5) and (III. 6), respectively, or the inverse counterparts of (1) and (2).

Subalternation in the weak logical square:
$A (\alpha, \beta) \therefore I (\alpha, \beta)$ (III. 7)

As for the remaining rules of the logical square, they can all be taken as derived rules of the categorical syllogistic (see § 54 below).

Basic rules of the limitative proposition:
$A (^N\alpha, \beta) \therefore N I (\alpha, \beta)$ (III. 8)
$I (^N\alpha, \beta) \therefore N A (\alpha, \beta)$ (III. 9)
$A (^N\alpha, \beta) \therefore N A (\alpha, \beta)$ (III. 10)

According to these rules, a negative proposition follows logically from a limitative proposition of the same quantity if the subject concepts of both propositions concur and the predicate concept of the limitative proposition is the antonym of the predicate concept of the negative proposition (see also Aristotle, *An. pr.* 1. 46, 51 b 41–52 a 5). Incidentally, the validity of an inference does not change at all when a positive concept expression is replaced in all places of its occurrence with a negative concept expression of the form $^N\alpha$.

3 Derived Rules

§ 54 Rules of the Strong and Weak Logical Squares

With the division of the rules of the logical square which Aristotle treats in *De interpretatione* 7 and *An. pr.* 2. 15 into basic rules ((III. 5) to (III. 7)) and derived rules ((III. 11) to (III. 16)), I do not claim to be presenting an Aristotelian division. Yet it can be supposed that Aristotle was familiar with the six rules which I will use here to derive rules (III. 11) to (III. 16). These are the rules (I. 1), (I. 2), (I. 4), (I. 5), (II. 2), and (II. 6). As for rule (I. 1), it is in substance simply a summary of rules of the logical square. Concerning Aristotle's acquaintance with the rule of *modus ponendo ponens*

(II. 2), I refer the reader to my remark on this rule in § 48.[197] Concerning his acquaintance with the four metalogical rules (I. 2), (I. 4), (I. 5), and (II. 6), though the observance of the syllogistic method of proof, and with this the general use of the metalogical rules in the school of Aristotle, is well-documented (see § 41 above), there is a lack of investigation into the manner and extent to which Aristotle's *Prior Analytics* show clear traces of the application of these rules. This is especially true of the application of rules (I. 4) and (I. 5), which follow from the synthetic theorem, i.e., the Peripatetic inference chain rule (I. 3), as well as the idempotency rule (II. 6). Rule (I. 2) is used explicitly by Aristotle under the name of ἀπαγωγὴ εἰς τὸ ἀδύνατον.

1. Subordination rule:

$A(\alpha, \beta) \therefore \underline{A}(\alpha, \beta)$ (III. 11)

Proof:
[1] $A(\alpha, \beta) \therefore I(\beta, \beta)$ (III. 1)
[2] $A(\alpha, \beta) \therefore H(I(\beta, \beta), \underline{A}(\alpha, \beta))$ (III. 1)
[3] $H(I(\beta, \beta), \underline{A}(\alpha, \beta)), I(\beta, \beta) \therefore \underline{A}(\alpha, \beta)$ (II. 2)
[4] $A(\alpha, \beta), A(\alpha, \beta) \therefore \underline{A}(\alpha, \beta)$ (I. 6) [1, 2, 3]
[5] $A(\alpha, \beta) \therefore \underline{A}(\alpha, \beta)$ (II. 6) [4]

2. Derived rules of the weak logical square:

Subalternation:
$N\underline{A}(\alpha, \beta) \therefore NA(\alpha, \beta)$ (III. 12)

Proof:
[1] $A(\alpha, \beta) \therefore \underline{A}(\alpha, \beta)$ (III. 11)
[2] $N\underline{A}(\alpha, \beta) \therefore NA(\alpha, \beta)$ (I. 2) [1]

(III. 12) is the negative counterpart to subalternation rule (III. 7). Assuming that '$N\underline{A}(\alpha, \beta)$' can be abbreviated by '$\underline{E}(\alpha, \beta)$' and '$NA(\alpha, \beta)$' by '$O(\alpha, \beta)$', rule (III. 12) expresses that a proposition of the form $O(\alpha, \beta)$ is related as subaltern to a proposition of the form $\underline{E}(\alpha, \beta)$.

---

[197] Although Theodor Ebert believes that *modus ponendo ponens* is for Aristotle "not a valid syllogistic mode" (Ebert & Nortmann 2007, 329), he also supposes that Aristotle makes use of this inference form in his syllogistic. He attributes the fact that Aristotle does not explicitly draw attention to this use to the "self-evident character of this form of consequence" (Ebert & Nortmann 2007, 329).

Contrariety:
The fact that there is a contrary relation between $A\,(\alpha,\,\beta)$ and $N\,A\,(\alpha,\,\beta)$, so that two propositions of these forms can both be false but not both true, is the direct result of the fact that, as per rule (I. 1), $NN\,A\,(\alpha,\,\beta)$ follows logically from $A\,(\alpha,\,\beta)$ and that, as per § 53, def. 4 (2), $A\,(\alpha,\,\beta)$ is false when $N\,A\,(\alpha,\,\beta)$ is true, but both $A\,(\alpha,\,\beta)$ and $N\,A\,(\alpha,\,\beta)$ are false in case β is an empty concept.

2. Derived rules of the strong logical square:

Subalternation:
$A\,(\alpha,\,\beta) \therefore I\,(\alpha,\,\beta)$ **(III. 13)**

Proof:
[1] $A\,(\alpha,\,\beta) \therefore A\,(\alpha,\,\beta)$ (III. 11)
[2] $A\,(\alpha,\,\beta) \therefore I\,(\alpha,\,\beta)$ (III. 7)
[3] $A\,(\alpha,\,\beta) \therefore I\,(\alpha,\,\beta)$ (I. 4) [1, 2]

$N\,I\,(\alpha,\,\beta) \therefore N\,A\,(\alpha,\,\beta)$ **(III. 14)**

Proof:
[1] $A\,(\alpha,\,\beta) \therefore I\,(\alpha,\,\beta)$ (III. 13)
[2] $N\,I\,(\alpha,\,\beta) \therefore N\,A\,(\alpha,\,\beta)$ (I. 2) [1]

In (III. 14) are compressed three further rules of the logical square, which can be immediately distinguished from each other if we replace '$N\,I\,(\alpha,\,\beta)$' with '$E\,(\alpha,\,\beta)$' and '$N\,A\,(\alpha,\,\beta)$' with '$O\,(\alpha,\,\beta)$'. These rules are:

$E\,(\alpha,\,\beta) \therefore O\,(\alpha,\,\beta)$,
$N\,I\,(\alpha,\,\beta) \therefore O\,(\alpha,\,\beta)$, and
$E\,(\alpha,\,\beta) \therefore N\,A\,(\alpha,\,\beta)$.

The first of these three rules is another subalternation rule. The second along with (III. 15) indicates the subcontrariety between $I\,(\alpha,\,\beta)$ and $O\,(\alpha,\,\beta)$, the third along with (III. 16) indicates the contrariety between $E\,(\alpha,\,\beta)$ and $A\,(\alpha,\,\beta)$.

Subcontrariety:
$NN\,A\,(\alpha,\,\beta) \therefore I\,(\alpha,\,\beta)$ **(III. 15)**

Proof:
[1] $N\,I\,(\alpha,\,\beta) \therefore N\,A\,(\alpha,\,\beta)$ (III. 14)
[2] $NN\,A\,(\alpha,\,\beta) \therefore NN\,I\,(\alpha,\,\beta)$ (I. 2) [1]
[3] $NN\,I\,(\alpha,\,\beta) \therefore I\,(\alpha,\,\beta)$ (III. 6)
[4] $NN\,A\,(\alpha,\,\beta) \therefore I\,(\alpha,\,\beta)$ (I. 4) [2, 3]

Contrariety:
$A(α, β) ∴ NN I(α, β)$ (III. 16)

Proof:
[1] $A(α, β) ∴ NN A(α, β)$ (I. 1)
[2] $N I(α, β) ∴ N A(α, β)$ (III. 14)
[3] $NN A(α, β) ∴ NN I(α, β)$ (I. 2) [2]
[4] $A(α, β) ∴ NN I(α, β)$ (I. 4) [1, 3]

Scholium: The rule indicating the contrariety of $A(α, β)$ and $N A(α, β)$, namely:

$A(α, β) ∴ NN A(α, β)$,

does not need a derivation, since it depends on the immediate application of (I. 1). The fact that the relationship between $A(α, β)$ and $N A(α, β)$ is not contradictory is a result of the invalidity of the rule $NN A(α, β) ∴ A(α, β)$.

§ 55 Conversion Rules

1. Simple conversion (*conversio simplex*):

Conversion of E propositions (with $E = N I$):
$N I(α, β) ∴ N I(β, α)$ (III. 17)

Proof:
[1] $I(β, α) ∴ A(α, γ), A(β, γ)$ (III. 3)
[2] $A(β, γ) ∴ I(β, γ)$ (III. 13)
[3] $I(β, α) ∴ I(β, γ)$ (I. 4) [1, 2]
[4] $N A(α, γ) ∴ N I(β, α)$ (I. 2) [1]
[5] $N I(α, β) ∴ H(I(β, γ), N A(α, γ))$ (III. 2)
[6] $N I(α, β), I(β, γ) ∴ N A(α, γ)$ (II. 5) [5]
[7] $N I(α, β), I(β, γ) ∴ N I(β, α)$ (I. 4) [6, 4]
[8] $N I(α, β), I(β, α) ∴ N I(β, α)$ (I. 4) [3, 7]
[9] $N I(α, β) ∴ H(I(β, α), N I(β, α))$ (II. 1) [8]
[10] $H(I(β, α), N I(β, α)) ∴ N I(β, α)$ (II. 9)
[11] $N I(α, β) ∴ N I(β, α)$ (I. 4) [9, 10]

This is an (indirect) proof by *reductio ad impossibile* (as per rule (I. 2)) and by *peritrope* (II. 9). Aristotle likewise supposes (*An. pr.* 1. 2, 25 a 15–17) that (III. 17) must be proved indirectly, and indeed by exposition (as in line [1], as per (III. 3)), and that this proof does not already assume the validity of (III. 18), as does the following shorter proof.

[1] $I(β, α) ∴ I(α, β)$ (III. 18)
[2] $N I(α, β) ∴ N I(β, α)$ (I. 2) [1]

Conversion of *I* propositions:
$I(\beta, \alpha) \therefore I(\alpha, \beta)$ (III. 18)

Proof:
[1]	$I(\beta, \alpha) \therefore A(\alpha, \gamma), A(\beta, \gamma)$	(III. 3)
[2]	$N I(\alpha, \beta) \therefore H(I(\beta, \gamma), N A(\alpha, \gamma))$	(III. 2)
[3]	$N I(\alpha, \beta), I(\beta, \gamma) \therefore N A(\alpha, \gamma)$	(II. 5) [2]
[4]	$A(\beta, \gamma) \therefore I(\beta, \gamma)$	(III. 13)
[5]	$N I(\alpha, \beta), A(\beta, \gamma) \therefore N A(\alpha, \gamma)$	(I. 4) [3, 4]
[6]	$NN A(\alpha, \gamma), A(\beta, \gamma) \therefore NN I(\alpha, \beta)$	(I. 2) [5]
[7]	$A(\alpha, \gamma) \therefore NN A(\alpha, \gamma)$	(I. 1)
[8]	$A(\alpha, \gamma), A(\beta, \gamma) \therefore NN I(\alpha, \beta)$	(I. 4) [6, 7]
[9]	$NN I(\alpha, \beta) \therefore I(\alpha, \beta)$	(III. 6)
[10]	$A(\alpha, \gamma), A(\beta, \gamma) \therefore I(\alpha, \beta)$	(I. 4) [8, 9]
[11]	$I(\beta, \alpha) \therefore I(\alpha, \beta)$	(I. 4) [1, 10]

The rule derived in line [10] is different from *modus Darapti* (III. 30) in that it does not bring only universal premises into play. The validity of (III. 17) thus does not presuppose, as is sometimes supposed, the validity of *Darapti*.

Theodor Ebert, in his reconstruction of the Aristotelian proof of the validity of *I*-conversion, assumes the convertibility of *E* propositions. In his reconstruction of the (indirect) proof of the convertibility of *E* propositions, however, he carries out an *I*-conversion on the basis of the supposition that *I* propositions have the form ($\exists$ x) (A x & B x) and, because of the commutativity of the &-relation, are convertible (see Ebert & Nortmann 2007, 235–38). According to this reconstruction, Aristotle avoids a circle in the validity proof of *E*-conversion only because he (unlike how it appears in his text) carries out two different proofs for the validity of *I*-conversion and further helps himself to a theory (namely, modern quantification theory) which he could not have known. The indirect proof for the validity of *I*-conversion appears, according to this reconstruction, as an unnecessary detour.

2. Conversion of *A* propositions *per accidens*

$A(\alpha, \beta) \therefore I(\beta, \alpha)$ (III. 19)

Proof:
[1]	$A(\alpha, \beta) \therefore I(\alpha, \beta)$	(III. 13)
[2]	$N I(\beta, \alpha) \therefore N I(\alpha, \beta)$	(III. 17)
[3]	$NN I(\alpha, \beta) \therefore NN I(\beta, \alpha)$	(I. 2) [2]
[4]	$I(\alpha, \beta) \therefore NN I(\alpha, \beta)$	(I. 1)
[5]	$NN I(\beta, \alpha) \therefore I(\beta, \alpha)$	(III. 6)
[6]	$I(\alpha, \beta) \therefore I(\beta, \alpha)$	(I. 4) [4, 3, 5]
[7]	$A(\alpha, \beta) \therefore I(\beta, \alpha)$	(I. 4) [1, 6]

Scholium: The three conversion rules were proven by Aristotle in the same order as above and in the same way, namely, indirectly.[198]

Since universally negative propositions are convertible, it can be proven simply through *subalternation* that the rule $N\,I\,(\alpha, \beta) \therefore N\,A\,(\beta, \alpha)$ is valid as well. But this of course does not allow us to say that also *particular* negative propositions are also convertible. Rather, only *E*, *I* and *A* propositions are convertible, and the latter only *per accidens*. This may be the simple reason why Aristotle only considers *three* rules as conversion rules. Ebert, by contrast, sees the reason for this in the fact that Aristotle did not need "the convertibility of *BeA* to *AoB*" for the validity proofs of valid modes in the second and third figures (Ebert & Nortmann 2007, 238–39). It would be more appropriate to say: Aristotle did not need the simple conversion of negative universal propositions (with a subsequent subalternation) for these validity proofs.

§ 56 Categorical Syllogisms

1. Perfect syllogisms

The label 'perfect syllogisms' corresponds to a classification of inference rules which goes back to Aristotle.[199] Among modern interpreters, the reigning opinion is that the perfection of syllogisms consists for Aristotle in their 'self-evidence', and this self-evidence makes a derivation from more basic principles (like the *dictum de omni* (III. 1) and the *dictum de nullo* (III. 2)) neither necessary nor possible. For Robin Smith Aristotle's distinction between perfect and imperfect syllogisms concerns nothing but "the difference between a valid and an *evidently* valid argument" (Aristotle 1989, 110). Günther Patzig (1969, 51–93) has also attempted to offer justification for this interpretation. He summarizes what a perfect syllogism is for Aristotle with the following words:

> [A] perfect inference is an inference in which the defined necessity is not only present but rather '*appears*' or becomes clear, while an imperfect inference may have this necessity as well but still requires certain operations in order to make this necessity 'appear' or become clear. In a word: perfect inferences are *self-evident* inferences. Accordingly, Aristotle also calls 'perfect' syllogisms 'apparent' inferences. (Patzig 1969, 54)

Yet this opinion cannot be supported by Aristotle's texts. According to the relevant definition of the perfect syllogism in 1. 1, 24 b 22–26, perfect syllogisms are not

---

[198] For the reconstruction of the proof, see M. Wolff 1998, 131–70.
[199] Even though Aristotle often renders syllogisms with 'if-then'-propositions, the view that for Aristotle syllogisms are not propositions but rules can be defended on good grounds, though it is disputed by Łukasiewicz and others. On this see, Ebert & Nortmann 2007, 220–25.

distinguished from imperfect syllogisms by their self-evidence, nor by a higher degree of self-evidence, but rather only in that "in order to be evident" (πρὸς τὸ φανῆναι) they "require nothing else beyond what already has been supposed [with their premises]" (παρὰ τὰ εἰλημμένα).[200] In other words: a syllogism is perfect when its validity (i.e., when the necessity with which its conclusion follows from its premises) can be made clear without (as is necessary with imperfect syllogisms) taking into consideration *more* than what is present with the premises which are assumed to be true and their meaning.

This explanation of the perfect syllogism of course does not only exclude but precisely assumes that the validity even of perfect syllogisms can be proved on the basis of deeper principles. But such proof of validity must be distinguished essentially from that of an imperfect syllogism. Imperfect syllogisms are proved by Aristotle with *reductio ad impossibile* (according to rule (I. 2)), with exposition (according to rule (III. 3) or (III. 4)) or with conversion (according to one of rules (III. 17) to (III. 19)). All these proofs rely on using a supposition which does *not* belong among the premises of the syllogism that is to be proved. For: in order to carry out a proof with *reductio ad impossibile*, one must bring into play a supposition which does not belong to the syllogism to be proved; rather, it is the contradictory of the conclusion of the syllogism to be proved, from which, in conjunction with one of its premises, the precise contradictory of the other premise follows. Exposition proofs as well can only be carried out with the introduction of an additional supposition, for the application of one of the exposition rules (III. 3) and (III. 4) is tied to the introduction of a concept variable which does not occur anywhere among the variables of the inference rule to be proved itself. Finally, conversions also rely on the introduction of an additional supposition. As the above proofs for the validity of the conversion rules (III. 17) to (III. 19) show, any application of one of these rules consists in the abbreviation of a procedure in which, through exposition, an additional concept variable which does not already occur in the formula to be converted is introduced, and then a *reductio ad impossibile* still comes into play. By contrast, the validity proofs for perfect syllogisms are carried out directly and exclusively from the premises that occur in them. Namely, in order to see the validity of a perfect syllogism, it suffices to pay attention to the meanings (as fixed by their definitions) of the logical constants which occur in the premises of the syllogism. That is, it suffices here to make use of *dictum de omni et nullo*, namely of basic rules (III. 1) and (III. 2), which in accordance with definitions

---

200 Aristotle, *An. pr.* 1. 1, 24 b 22–26 (1984, 40): "I call perfect a deduction which needs nothing other than what has been stated to make the necessity evident (πρὸς τὸ φανῆναι τὸ ἀναγκαῖον); a deduction is imperfect if it needs [in addition] either one or more things [suppositions], which are indeed the necessary consequences of the terms set down, but have not been [explicitly] assumed in the propositions."

2 and 3 in § 52 (or in accordance with the definitions which Aristotle introduced in connection with his explanation of the perfect syllogism at the end of chapter 1 of the first book of *Analytica priora* (24 b 28–30)) make explicit what it means for premises of the form $A\,(α, β)$ or $N\,I\,(α, β)$ to be true.

The distinction between perfect and imperfect syllogisms thus depends on an underlying structural distinction in the validity proofs of perfect and imperfect syllogisms. One can only see this structural distinction if one grasps what conversion proofs depend on for Aristotle. If one believes with Ebert and other Aristotle interpreters that *I*-conversion can only be explained on the basis of a modern quantification theory (see my comment above to (III. 18)), one is blocked from understanding the distinction Aristotle describes between the perfection and imperfection of syllogisms.

Ebert supposes with Günther Patzig that perfect syllogisms distinguish themselves as self-evidently valid modes of inference through the *"formulation* of their premises" and "the *position of the middle term* between the two extremes."[201] Yet Aristotle nowhere explains the perfection of syllogisms through peculiarities of their inner structure. Rather, he traces their perfection quite expressly back to the way their validity is proved. Thus he says that syllogisms are perfect because they are "at once" (εὐθύς (*An. pr.* 1. 16, 36 a 6–7 [1989, 26])) "brought to completion [. . .] by means of the initial premises" (*An. pr.* 1. 4, 26 b. 30)). In other places, he says of perfect syllogisms that their validity is "evident from the definition" (φανερὸν ἐκ τοῦ ὁρισμοῦ (14, 32 b 40 and 14, 33 a 24–25 [1989, 19–20])), namely from the definition of the logical constants that occur in the premises; and he designates the derivation of their validity "from the definition" explicitly as "proof" (ἀπόδειξις (14, 33 a 27 and 15, 35 a 35)). By contrast, he says of an imperfect syllogism "that it is imperfect is clear from the proof" (16, 36 a 1). Syllogisms are imperfect because "the necessary result is brought to completion not from the initial premises alone, but from others in addition" (1. 5, 27 a 16–17 [1989, 7]; cf. 28 a 5–7).

For this reason, treating perfect syllogisms as modes of inference whose validity requires no proof, as is typical in the recent Aristotle literature, does not conform to the views of Aristotle.

Modus Barbara:
$A\,(α, β), A\,(β, γ) \therefore A\,(α, γ)$ (III. 20)

Proof:
[1] $A\,(α, β) \therefore H\,(I\,(β, γ), A\,(α, γ))$ (III. 1)
[2] $A\,(β, γ) \therefore I\,(γ, γ)$ (III. 13)
[3] $A\,(β, γ) \therefore H\,(I\,(γ, γ), A\,(β, γ))$ (III. 1)

---

201 Ebert & Nortmann 2007, 296.

[4] $A(\beta, \gamma) \therefore I(\beta, \gamma)$ (III. 7)
[5] $* \therefore H(A(\beta, \gamma), I(\beta, \gamma))$ (II. 28) [4]
[6] $H(I(\gamma, \gamma), A(\beta, \gamma)), H(A(\beta, \gamma), I(\beta, \gamma))$
      $\therefore H(I(\gamma, \gamma), I(\beta, \gamma))$ (II. 13)
[7] $*, A(\beta, \gamma) \therefore H(I(\gamma, \gamma), I(\beta, \gamma))$ (I. 5) [3, 5, 6]
[8] $H(I(\gamma, \gamma), I(\beta, \gamma)), H(I(\beta, \gamma), A(\alpha, \gamma))$
      $\therefore H(I(\gamma, \gamma), A(\alpha, \gamma))$ (II. 13)
[9] $*, A(\beta, \gamma), A(\alpha, \beta) \therefore H(I(\gamma, \gamma), A(\alpha, \gamma))$ (I. 5) [7, 1, 8]
[10] $I(\gamma, \gamma), H(I(\gamma, \gamma), A(\alpha, \gamma)) \therefore A(\alpha, \gamma)$ (III. 1)
[11] $*, A(\beta, \gamma), A(\beta, \gamma), A(\alpha, \beta) \therefore A(\alpha, \gamma)$ (I. 5) [2, 9, 10]
[12] $*, A(\alpha, \beta), A(\beta, \gamma) \therefore A(\alpha, \gamma)$ (II. 6) [11]

This derivation of *Barbara* from basic rule (III. 1) corresponds to the justification which Aristotle indicates in *An. pr.* 1. 4, 25 b 37–40 for his supposition of the validity of *Barbara*: this supposition relies on the meaning of the expression (i.e., the logical constant) '... is said of every ...'. He gives an analogous justification in 25 b 40–26 a 2 for the supposition of the validity of *Celarent*. Accordingly, the following proof proceeds analogously to the proof for *Barbara*.

Modus Celarent:
$NI(\alpha, \beta), A(\beta, \gamma) \therefore NI(\alpha, \gamma)$ **(III. 21)**

Proof:
[1] $NI(\alpha, \beta) \therefore H(I(\beta, \gamma), NA(\alpha, \gamma))$ (III. 2)
[2] $A(\beta, \gamma) \therefore H(I(\gamma, \gamma), A(\beta, \gamma))$ (III. 1)
[3] $A(\beta, \gamma) \therefore I(\beta, \gamma)$ (III. 7)
[4] $* \therefore H(A(\beta, \gamma), I(\beta, \gamma))$ (II. 28) [3]
[5] $H(I(\gamma, \gamma), A(\beta, \gamma)), H(A(\beta, \gamma), I(\beta, \gamma))$
      $\therefore H(I(\gamma, \gamma), I(\beta, \gamma))$ (II. 13)
[6] $*, A(\beta, \gamma) \therefore H(I(\gamma, \gamma), I(\beta, \gamma))$ (I. 5) [2, 4, 5]
[7] $H(I(\gamma, \gamma), I(\beta, \gamma)), H(I(\beta, \gamma), NA(\alpha, \gamma))$
      $\therefore H(I(\gamma, \gamma), NA(\alpha, \gamma))$ (II. 13)
[8] $*, A(\beta, \gamma), NI(\alpha, \beta) \therefore H(I(\gamma, \gamma), NA(\alpha, \gamma))$ (I. 5) [6, 1, 7]
[9] $H(I(\gamma, \gamma), NA(\alpha, \gamma)) \therefore NI(\alpha, \gamma)$ (III. 2)
[10] $*, A(\beta, \gamma), NI(\alpha, \beta) \therefore NI(\alpha, \gamma)$ (I. 4) [8, 9]

From *Barbara* and *Celarent*, syllogisms of the modes *Barbari* and *Celaront* can be derived by weakening the respective conclusion according to subalternation rules (III. 13) and (III. 14). The same holds for all syllogisms with universal conclusions that are derived in what follows.

Although the following two modes (III. 22) and (III. 23), i.e., *Darii* and *Ferio*, can be derived from modes of the second figure, namely from *Camestres* (III. 25) and *Cesare* (III. 24) respectively (see (III. 28) and (III. 29)), they can also count as perfect syllogisms, since like *Barbara* and *Celarent* they can be derived directly from basic rules (III. 1) and (III. 2), respectively (cf. *An. pr.* 1. 4, 26 a 17–23). This happens in the following way:

Modus Darii:
A (α, β), I (β, γ) ∴ I (α, γ) (III. 22)

Proof:
[1] A (α, β) ∴ H (I (β, γ), A (α, γ)) (III. 1)
[2] A (α, β), I (β, γ) ∴ A (α, γ) (II. 5) [1]
[3] A (α, γ) ∴ I (α, γ) (III. 7)
[4] A (α, β), I (β, γ) ∴ I (α, γ) (I. 4) [2, 3]

Modus Ferio:
N I (α, β), I (β, γ) ∴ N A (α, γ) (III. 23)

Proof:
[1] N I (α, β) ∴ H (I (β, γ), N A (α, γ)) (III. 2)
[2] N I (α, β), I (β, γ) ∴ N A (α, γ) (II. 5) [1]
[3] N A (α, γ) ∴ N A (α, γ) (III. 12)
[4] N I (α, β), I (β, γ) ∴ N A (α, γ) (I. 4) [2, 3]

Unlike the conclusion of *Ferio*, the conclusions of *Barbara*, *Celarent*, and *Darii* can each be converted according to one of the rules (III. 17) to (III. 19). This is something that Aristotle points out in *An. pr.* 3. 1, 53 a 3–14. Each of the modes of the traditionally titled 'fourth figure', namely, *Bamalip*, *Calemes*, and *Dimatis* in turn, result from these conversions. Modes of the fourth figure in which the conclusion is a particular negative proposition, namely, *Fesapo* and *Fresison*, can be derived directly through the conversion of the universal negative premise of a mode of the third figure.[202] (See my remarks to (III. 31) and (III. 35) below.)

2. Imperfect syllogisms

Imperfect syllogisms are reduced in the Aristotelian syllogism to perfect syllogisms through one of the three following operations: (1) by conversion (as per (III. 17), (III. 18), or (III. 19)), with transposition of the terms that occur in them, (2) by exposition (as per (III. 3), or (III. 4)), or (3) by indirect proof (that is, through *reductio ad absurdum* as per (I. 2)).

(1) Conversion proofs all rely on rules whose validity depends on the validity of exposition rule (III. 3) (see the proof of (III. 18)). Proofs by conversion – including those by *conversio per accidens* – are to that extent indirectly proofs by exposition.

---

[202] It is not the case, as Theodor Ebert believes, that through the premise conversion that Aristotle describes in *An. pr.* 1. 7, 29 a 21–27, "new" syllogisms "never" result from modes of the second and third figure, but rather always only syllogisms already proven from the second and third figure. See his commentary on *An. pr.* 1. 7, 29 a 21–27 in Ebert & Nortmann 2007, 347.

(2) Proofs by exposition, as the rules (III. 3) and (III. 4) show, rely essentially on the introduction of a term which does not occur at all in the premises of the syllogism whose validity is to be proved by exposition. (3) The third kind of proof, *reductio ad absurdum*, belongs to the type of indirect proofs; these can only be carried out by introducing an additional premise in the argumentation, namely, the negation of the conclusion. – Since no other than these three kinds of proof must be brought into play, it is entirely appropriate and understandable when Aristotle defines syllogisms called 'imperfect' as deductions which are distinguished from perfect syllogisms not, say, by a lack of self-evidence, but rather because in order to be self-evident this kind of syllogism "needs [in addition] either one or more things [suppositions], which are indeed the necessary consequences of the terms set down, but have not been [explicitly] assumed in the propositions" (I. 1, 24 b. 24–26 [1984, 40]).

a. The categorical syllogisms of the second figure:

Cesare:
$NI(\beta, \alpha), A(\beta, \gamma) \therefore NI(\alpha, \gamma)$ (III. 24)

Proof:
[1] $NI(\alpha, \beta), A(\beta, \gamma) \therefore NI(\alpha, \gamma)$ (III. 21)
[2] $NI(\beta, \alpha) \therefore NI(\alpha, \beta)$ (III. 17)
[3] $NI(\beta, \alpha), A(\beta, \gamma) \therefore NI(\alpha, \gamma)$ (I. 4) [2, 1]

This conversion proof corresponds to the proof sketched by Aristotle in *An. pr.* 1. 5, 27 a 5–9.

Camestres:
$A(\beta, \alpha), NI(\alpha, \gamma) \therefore NI(\alpha, \gamma)$ (III. 25)

Proof:
[1] $NI(\gamma, \beta), A(\beta, \alpha) \therefore NI(\gamma, \alpha)$ (III. 21)
[2] $NI(\gamma, \alpha) \therefore NI(\alpha, \gamma)$ (III. 17)
[3] $NI(\gamma, \beta), A(\beta, \alpha) \therefore NI(\alpha, \gamma)$ (I. 4) [1, 2]
[4] $NI(\beta, \gamma) \therefore NI(\gamma, \beta)$ (III. 17)
[5] $A(\beta, \alpha), NI(\beta, \gamma) \therefore NI(\alpha, \gamma)$ (I. 4) [4, 3]

Cf. the corresponding conversion proof in Aristotle, *An. pr.* 1. 5, 27 a 9–14. The validity of *Camestres* can also – as Aristotle indicates in *An. pr.* 1. 5, 27 a 14 f. – be proved indirectly, by *reductio ad absurdum*, by applying rule (I. 2) to *Darii* thus:

[1] $A(\beta, \alpha), I(\alpha, \gamma) \therefore I(\beta, \gamma)$ (III. 22)
[2] $NI(\beta, \gamma), A(\beta, \alpha) \therefore NI(\alpha, \gamma)$ (I. 2) [1]

Festino:
$NI(\beta, \alpha), I(\beta, \gamma) \therefore NA(\alpha, \gamma)$ (III. 26)

Proof:

[1]	$NI(α, β), I(β, γ) \therefore NA(α, γ)$	(III. 23)
[2]	$NI(β, α) \therefore NI(α, β)$	(III. 17)
[3]	$NI(β, α), I(β, γ) \therefore NA(α, γ)$	(I. 4) [1, 2]

This conversion proof, which Aristotle sketches in *An. pr.* 1. 5, 73 a 32, can be replaced by an indirect proof, namely this one:

[1]	$NI(β, α), A(α, γ) \therefore NI(β, γ)$	(III. 21)
[2]	$NI(β, α), NNI(β, γ) \therefore NA(α, γ)$	(I. 2) [1]
[3]	$I(β, γ) \therefore NNI(β, γ)$	(I. 1)
[4]	$NI(β, α), I(β, γ) \therefore NA(α, γ)$	(I. 4) [2, 3]

Baroco:
$A(β, α), NA(β, γ) \therefore NA(α, γ)$ **(III. 27)**

Proof:

[1]	$A(β, α), A(α, γ) \therefore A(β, γ)$	(III. 20)
[2]	$A(β, α), NA(β, γ) \therefore NA(α, γ)$	(I. 2) [1]

This indirect proof corresponds to Aristotle's sketch of a proof in *An. pr.* 1. 5, 27 a 36 ff.

b. The categorical syllogisms of the first figure that are reducible to *Celarent*:

Darii:
$A(α, β), I(β, γ) \therefore I(α, γ)$ **(III. 28)**

Proof:

[1]	$A(α, β), NI(α, γ) \therefore NI(β, γ)$	(III. 25)
[2]	$A(α, β), NNI(β, γ) \therefore NNI(α, γ)$	(I. 2) [1]
[3]	$NNI(α, γ) \therefore I(α, γ)$	(III. 6)
[4]	$A(α, β), NNI(β, γ) \therefore I(α, γ)$	(I. 4) [2, 3]
[5]	$I(β, γ) \therefore NNI(β, γ)$	(I. 1)
[6]	$A(α, β), I(β, γ) \therefore I(α, γ)$	(I. 4) [4, 5]

Ferio:
$NI(α, β), I(β, γ) \therefore NA(α, γ)$ **(III. 29)**

Proof:

[1]	$NI(α, β), A(α, γ) \therefore NI(β, γ)$	(III. 24)
[2]	$NI(α, β), NNI(β, γ) \therefore NA(α, γ)$	(I. 2) [1]
[3]	$I(β, γ) \therefore NNI(β, γ)$	(I. 1)
[4]	$NI(α, β), I(β, γ) \therefore NA(α, γ)$	(I. 4) [2, 3]

The fact already remarked by Aristotle (*An. pr.* 1. 7, 29 b 6–15) that *Darii* and *Ferio* can both be derived from modes of the second figure, namely from *Camestres* and *Cesare* respectively, whose validity in each case depends on the validity of

Celarent, shows that imperfect syllogisms which are reducible to *Darii* or *Ferio* are further reducible to *Celarent*.

c. The categorical syllogisms of the third figure:

Darapti:
$A(\alpha, \beta), A(\gamma, \beta) \therefore I(\alpha, \gamma)$ **(III. 30)**

Proof:
[1] $A(\alpha, \beta), I(\beta, \gamma) \therefore I(\alpha, \gamma)$ (III. 22)
[2] $A(\gamma, \beta) \therefore I(\beta, \gamma)$ (III. 19)
[3] $A(\alpha, \beta), A(\gamma, \beta) \therefore I(\alpha, \gamma)$ (I. 4) [1, 2]

Darapti can be derived not only, as here, by conversion from *Darii*, but also by *reductio ad impossibile* from *Celarent*, namely thus:

[1] $NI(\alpha, \gamma), A(\gamma, \beta) \therefore NI(\alpha, \beta)$ (III. 21)
[2] $NNI(\alpha, \beta), A(\gamma, \beta) \therefore NNI(\alpha, \gamma)$ (I. 2) [1]
[3] $A(\alpha, \beta) \therefore NNI(\alpha, \beta)$ (III. 16)
[4] $NNI(\alpha, \gamma) \therefore I(\alpha, \gamma)$ (III. 6)
[5] $A(\alpha, \beta), A(\gamma, \beta) \therefore I(\alpha, \gamma)$ (I. 4) [3, 2, 4]

A proof by *ekthesis* is also possible. It looks like this:

[1] $I(\alpha, \beta) \therefore A(\beta, \delta)$ (III. 3)
[2] $A(\beta, \delta) \therefore I(\beta, \delta)$ (III. 7)
[3] $A(\alpha, \beta) \therefore I(\alpha, \beta)$ (III. 13)
[4] $A(\alpha, \beta) \therefore I(\beta, \delta)$ (I. 4) [3, 1, 2]
[5] $I(\alpha, \beta) \therefore A(\alpha, \delta)$ (III. 3)
[6] $A(\alpha, \beta) \therefore A(\alpha, \delta)$ (I. 4) [3, 5]
[7] $A(\gamma, \beta), I(\beta, \delta) \therefore I(\gamma, \delta)$ (III. 22)
[8] $A(\gamma, \beta), A(\alpha, \beta) \therefore I(\gamma, \delta)$ (I. 4) [4, 7]
[9] $I(\gamma, \delta) \therefore I(\delta, \gamma)$ (III. 18)
[10] $A(\gamma, \beta), A(\alpha, \beta) \therefore I(\delta, \gamma)$ (I. 4) [8, 9]
[11] $A(\alpha, \delta), I(\delta, \gamma) \therefore I(\alpha, \gamma)$ (III. 22)
[12] $A(\alpha, \beta), A(\alpha, \beta), A(\gamma, \beta) \therefore I(\alpha, \gamma)$ (I. 5) [6, 10, 11]
[13] $A(\alpha, \beta), A(\gamma, \beta) \therefore I(\alpha, \gamma)$ (II. 6) [12]

For the three kinds of proof that Aristotle mentions for the validity of *Darapti*, see *An. pr.* 1. 6, a 28–25. But he sketches there only the proofs by conversion and exposition. That there is a proof by *reductio ad impossibile* he only claims.

Scholium: Since these proofs are valid, the criticism put forth by Hilbert and Ackermann on the syllogistic treatment of *Darapti* (see § 17 above) comes to nought. The evidence offered by Bertrand Russell in his essay "The Philosophy of Logical Atomism" is unable to support the (certainly correct) claim in the last sentence of the following quotation, when he writes:

I want to say emphatically that general propositions are to be interpreted as not involving existence. [. . .] This notion, of course, of general propositions not involving existence is one which is not in the traditional doctrine of the syllogism. In the traditional doctrine of the syllogism it was assumed that when you have such a statement as "All Greeks are men," that implies that there are Greeks, and this produced fallacies. For instance, "All chimeras are animals, and all chimeras breath flame, therefore some animals breathe flame." This is a syllogism in *Darapti*, but that mood of the syllogism is fallacious, as this instance shows. That was a point, by the way, which had a certain historical interest, because it impeded Leibniz in his attempts to construct a mathematical logic. He [. . .] was always failing because of his respect for Aristotle. Whenever he invented a really good system, as he did several times, it always brought out that such moods as *Darapti* are fallacious. If you say "All A is B and all A is C, therefore some B is C" – if you say this you incur a fallacy, but he could not bring himself to believe that it was fallacious, so he began again. *That shows you should not have too much respect for distinguished men.* (Russell, 1919a, 190–91, my emphasis)

Felapton:
$NI(α, β), A(γ, β) ∴ NA(α, γ)$ (III. 31)

Proof:
[1] $NI(α, β), I(β, γ) ∴ NA(α, γ)$ (III. 23)
[2] $A(γ, β) ∴ I(β, γ)$ (III. 19)
[3] $NI(α, β), A(γ, β) ∴ NA(α, γ)$ (I. 4) [1, 2]

Aristotle mentions this proof by conversion in *An. pr.* 1. 6, 28 a 26–30; he mentions in addition a proof *per impossibile*, which could proceed as follows:

[1] $A(α, γ), A(γ, β) ∴ A(α, β)$ (III. 20)
[2] $NA(α, β), A(γ, β) ∴ NA(α, γ)$ (I. 2) [1]
[3] $NI(α, β) ∴ NA(α, β)$ (III. 14)
[4] $NI(α, β), A(γ, β) ∴ NA(α, γ)$ (I. 4) [3, 2]

The first two lines already present an indirect proof for *Bocardo* (III. 34), which is described by Aristotle as a proof *per impossibile* in *An. pr.* 1. 6, 28 b 17–20. *Disamis* and *Datisi* can be proved in a similar way. In these cases, however, *Celarent* (III. 21) rather than *Barbara* (III. 20) is the point of departure. Aristotle points out in *An. pr.* 1. 6, 28 b 7–25 that *Disamis* and *Datisi* are to be proved by conversion or *ekthesis* as well. This can be done as follows.

By conversion of the first premise according to rule (III. 17) a mode of the so-called fourth figure (traditionally called *Fesapo*) can be derived from *Felapton*, which Aristotle points out in *An. pr.* 1. 7, 29 a 21–27.

Disamis:
$I(\alpha, \beta), A(\gamma, \beta) \therefore I(\alpha, \gamma)$ **(III. 32)**

Proof:
[1] $A(\gamma, \beta), I(\beta, \alpha) \therefore I(\gamma, \alpha)$ (III. 28)
[2] $I(\beta, \alpha) \therefore I(\alpha, \beta)$ (III. 18)
[3] $I(\gamma, \alpha) \therefore I(\alpha, \gamma)$ (III. 18)
[4] $I(\alpha, \beta), A(\gamma, \beta) \therefore I(\alpha, \gamma)$ (I. 4) [2, 1, 3]

An exposition proof for *Disamis* can be carried out in the following way:

[1] $I(\alpha, \beta) \therefore A(\alpha, \delta)$ (III. 3)
[2] $I(\alpha, \beta) \therefore A(\beta, \delta)$ (III. 3)
[3] $A(\beta, \delta) \therefore I(\beta, \delta)$ (III. 7)
[4] $I(\alpha, \beta) \therefore I(\beta, \delta)$ (I. 4) [2, 3]
[5] $A(\gamma, \beta), I(\beta, \delta) \therefore I(\gamma, \delta)$ (III. 22)
[6] $A(\gamma, \beta), I(\alpha, \beta) \therefore I(\gamma, \delta)$ (I. 4) [4, 5]
[7] $I(\gamma, \delta) \therefore I(\delta, \gamma)$ (III. 18)
[8] $A(\gamma, \beta), I(\alpha, \beta) \therefore I(\delta, \gamma)$ (I. 4) [6, 7]
[9] $A(\alpha, \delta), I(\delta, \gamma) \therefore (\alpha, \gamma)$ (III. 22)
[10] $I(\alpha, \beta), A(\gamma, \beta), I(\alpha, \beta) \therefore I(\alpha, \gamma)$ (I. 5) [1, 8, 9]
[11] $I(\alpha, \beta), A(\gamma, \beta) \therefore I(\alpha, \gamma)$ (II. 6) [10]

Datisi:
$A(\alpha, \beta), I(\gamma, \beta) \therefore I(\alpha, \gamma)$ **(III. 33)**

Proof:
[1] $A(\alpha, \beta), I(\beta, \gamma) \therefore I(\alpha, \gamma)$ (III. 28)
[2] $I(\gamma, \beta) \therefore I(\beta, \gamma)$ (III. 18)
[3] $A(\alpha, \beta), I(\gamma, \beta) \therefore I(\alpha, \gamma)$ (I. 4) [1, 2]

An exposition proof for *Datisi* proceeds in just the same way as the exposition proof for *Disamis*, namely:

[1] $I(\gamma, \beta) \therefore A(\gamma, \delta)$ (III. 3)
[2] $I(\gamma, \beta) \therefore A(\beta, \delta)$ (III. 3)
[3] $A(\beta, \delta) \therefore I(\beta, \delta)$ (III. 7)
[4] $I(\gamma, \beta) \therefore I(\beta, \delta)$ (I. 4) [2, 3]
[5] $A(\alpha, \beta), I(\beta, \delta) \therefore I(\alpha, \delta)$ (III. 22)
[6] $A(\alpha, \beta), I(\gamma, \beta) \therefore I(\alpha, \delta)$ (I. 4) [4, 5]
[7] $I(\alpha, \delta) \therefore I(\delta, \alpha)$ (III. 18)
[8] $A(\alpha, \beta), I(\gamma, \beta) \therefore I(\delta, \alpha)$ (I. 4) [6, 7]
[9] $A(\gamma, \delta), I(\delta, \alpha) \therefore I(\gamma, \alpha)$ (III. 22)
[10] $I(\gamma, \alpha) \therefore I(\alpha, \gamma)$ (III. 18)
[11] $A(\gamma, \delta), I(\delta, \alpha) \therefore I(\alpha, \gamma)$ (I. 4) [9, 10]
[12] $I(\gamma, \beta), A(\alpha, \beta), I(\gamma, \beta) \therefore I(\alpha, \gamma)$ (I. 5) [1, 8, 11]
[13] $A(\alpha, \beta), I(\gamma, \beta) \therefore I(\alpha, \gamma)$ (II. 6) [12]

Bocardo:
$NA(\alpha, \beta), A(\gamma, \beta) \therefore NA(\alpha, \gamma)$ **(III. 34)**

Proof:
[1]	$NA(\alpha, \beta) \therefore NI(\alpha, \delta)$	(III. 4)
[2]	$NA(\alpha, \beta) \therefore H(I(\beta, \beta), A(\beta, \delta))$	(III. 4)
[3]	$NA(\alpha, \beta), I(\beta, \beta) \therefore A(\beta, \delta)$	(II. 5) [2]
[4]	$A(\gamma, \beta) \therefore I(\beta, \beta)$	(III. 1)
[5]	$NA(\alpha, \beta), A(\gamma, \beta) \therefore A(\beta, \delta)$	(I. 4) [4, 3]
[6]	$A(\gamma, \beta) \therefore H(I(\beta, \delta), A(\gamma, \delta))$	(III. 1)
[7]	$A(\gamma, \beta), I(\beta, \delta) \therefore A(\gamma, \delta)$	(II. 5) [6]
[8]	$A(\gamma, \delta) \therefore I(\gamma, \delta)$	(III. 7)
[9]	$I(\gamma, \delta) \therefore (\delta, \gamma)$	(III. 18)
[10]	$A(\gamma, \beta), I(\beta, \delta) \therefore I(\delta, \gamma)$	(I. 4) [7, 8, 9]
[11]	$NI(\alpha, \delta), I(\delta, \gamma) \therefore NA(\alpha, \gamma)$	(III. 29)
[12]	$NA(\alpha, \beta), A(\gamma, \beta), I(\beta, \delta) \therefore NA(\alpha, \gamma)$	(I. 5) [1, 10, 11]
[13]	$A(\beta, \delta) \therefore I(\beta, \delta)$	(III. 13)
[14]	$NA(\alpha, \beta), A(\gamma, \beta), A(\beta, \delta) \therefore NA(\alpha, \gamma)$	(I. 4) [13, 12]
[15]	$NA(\alpha, \beta), A(\gamma, \beta), NA(\alpha, \beta), A(\gamma, \beta)$ $\therefore NA(\alpha, \gamma$	(I. 4) [5, 14]
[16]	$NA(\alpha, \beta), A(\gamma, \beta) \therefore NA(\alpha, \gamma)$	(II. 6) [15]

As lines [1] and [2] show, this proof depends on exposition. Aristotle claims that such a proof for *Bocardo* is possible in *An. pr.* 1. 6, 28 b 17–21. However, he does not give a more precise description of this proof. Instead, he only sketches there the proof *per impossibile*, which was already contained in the indirect proof for *Felapton*. (See my remarks to (III. 31) above.)

Ferison:
$NI(\alpha, \beta), I(\gamma, \beta) \therefore NA(\alpha, \gamma)$ **(III. 35)**

Proof:
[1]	$NI(\alpha, \beta), I(\beta, \gamma) \therefore NA(\alpha, \gamma)$	(III. 29)
[2]	$I(\gamma, \beta) \therefore I(\beta, \gamma)$	(III. 18)
[3]	$NI(\alpha, \beta), I(\gamma, \beta) \therefore NA(\alpha, \gamma)$	(I. 4) [1, 2]

This proof by conversion corresponds to the proof sketched by Aristotle in *An. pr.* 1. 6, 28 b 33–35.

By conversion of the first premise, according to rule (III. 17), a mode of the so-called fourth figure, traditionally called *Fresison*, can be derived from *Ferison*, as Aristotle indicates in *An. pr.* 1. 7, 29 a 21–27.

However, Aristotle speaks neither of a fourth figure nor of modes, since the order of premises is irrelevant for his system.

3. Singular syllogisms:

Syllogisms of the first and second figure with two universal premises remain valid when the minor premise and the conclusion are replaced by singular expressions. Syllogisms of the third figure with two universal premises remain valid when they are replaced by singular premises.

a. First figure:

Barbara modified:
$A(\alpha, \beta), A(\beta, \gamma) \therefore A(\alpha, \gamma)$ **(III. 36)**

Proof:
[1]	$A(\alpha, \beta) \therefore H(I(\beta, \gamma), A(\alpha, \gamma))$	(III. 2)
[2]	$A(\alpha, \beta), I(\beta, \gamma) \therefore A(\alpha, \gamma)$	(II. 5) [1]
[3]	$A(\beta, \gamma) \therefore I(\beta, \gamma)$	(III. 7)
[4]	$A(\alpha, \beta), A(\beta, \gamma) \therefore A(\alpha, \gamma)$	(I. 4) [3, 2]

In Sextus Empiricus (*Outlines of Pyrrhonism* II, 163–66 [2000, 11–12]) a syllogism is discussed as an example of the "categorical syllogisms" which "were especially used by the Peripatetics," which corresponds to rule (III. 36):

> "Socrates is a human being;
> All human beings are animals;
> So Socrates is an animal."

Syllogisms of this type, which Aristotle did not yet explicitly address, were treated in more detail by medieval logicians, e.g., by William of Ockham. He discusses the syllogism mentioned by Sextus in *Summa Logicae* (1957, III 1. 20; 41 rb).

Celarent modified:
$NI(\alpha, \beta), A(\beta, \gamma) \therefore NA(\alpha, \gamma)$ **(III. 37)**

Proof:
[1]	$NI(\alpha, \beta) \therefore H(I(\beta, \gamma), NA(\alpha, \gamma))$	(III. 2)
[2]	$NI(\alpha, \beta), I(\beta, \gamma) \therefore A(\alpha, \gamma)$	(II. 5) [1]
[3]	$A(\beta, \gamma) \therefore I(\beta, \gamma)$	(III. 7)
[4]	$NI(\alpha, \beta), A(\beta, \gamma) \therefore NA(\alpha, \gamma)$	(I. 4) [3, 2]

b. Second figure:

Cesare modified:
$NI(\beta, \alpha), A(\beta, \gamma) \therefore NA(\alpha, \gamma)$ **(III. 38)**

Proof:
[1]	$NI(\alpha, \beta), A(\beta, \gamma) \therefore NA(\alpha, \gamma)$	(III. 37)
[2]	$NI(\beta, \alpha) \therefore NI(\alpha, \beta)$	(III. 17)
[3]	$A(\beta, \gamma), NI(\beta, \alpha) \therefore NA(\alpha, \gamma)$	(I. 4) [1, 2]

Camestres modified:
$A(β, α), NA(β, γ) ∴ NA(α, γ)$ **(III. 39)**

Proof:
[1] $A(β, α), A(α, γ) ∴ A(β, γ)$ (III. 36)
[2] $A(β, α), NA(β, γ) ∴ NA(α, γ)$ (I. 2) [1]

c. Third figure:

Darapti modified:
$A(α, β), A(γ, β) ∴ I(α, γ)$ **(III. 40)**

Proof:
[1] $NI(α, γ), A(α, β) ∴ NA(γ, β)$ (III. 38)
[2] $NNA(γ, β), A(α, β) ∴ NNI(α, γ)$ (I. 2) [1]
[3] $A(γ, β) ∴ NNA(γ, β)$ (I. 1)
[4] $NNI(α, γ) ∴ I(α, γ)$ (III. 6)
[5] $A(α, β), A(γ, β) ∴ I(α, γ)$ (I. 4) [3, 2, 4]

Felapton modified:
$NA(α, β), A(γ, β) ∴ NA(α, γ)$ **(III. 41)**

Proof:
[1] $A(α, γ), A(γ, β) ∴ A(α, β)$ (III. 36)
[2] $NA(α, β), A(γ, β) ∴ NA(α, γ)$ (I. 2) [1]

§ 57 Universally Valid Propositional Schemata

Through conditionalization, according to (II. 28), all universally valid rules of categorical inference can be transformed into universally valid propositional schemata. Thus, e.g., from (III. 18) the schema

$*∴ H(I(α, β), I(β, α))$ **(III. 42)**

or from (III. 20) the schema

$*∴ H(A(α, β), H(A(β, γ), A(α, γ)))$ **(III. 43)**

can be derived. I will spare myself the simple proofs for the universal validity of these two propositional schemata.

By contrast, formulas like

$*∴ I(β, β), *∴ A(β, β)$ or $*∴ A(β, β)$

are neither derivable from the principles established above, nor do such formulas for their part express principles which would have to be assumed as valid within the categorical syllogistic. At best, formulas are derivable in which a tautological expression occurs as a sub-formula, for example:

$\ast\therefore H(I(\alpha, \beta), A(\beta, \beta))$. (III. 44)

This formula is derivable, because the following rule is derivable.

$I(\alpha, \beta) \therefore A(\beta, \beta)$ (III. 45)

Proof:
[1] $N A(\beta, \beta) \therefore N I(\beta, \alpha)$ (III. 4)
[2] $N I(\beta, \alpha) \therefore N I(\alpha, \beta)$ (III. 17)
[3] $N A(\beta, \beta) \therefore N I(\alpha, \beta)$ (I. 4) [1, 2]
[4] $N N I(\alpha, \beta) \therefore N N A(\beta, \beta)$ (I. 2) [3]
[5] $I(\alpha, \beta) \therefore N N I(\alpha, \beta)$ (I. 1)
[6] $N N A(\beta, \beta) \therefore A(\beta, \beta)$ (III. 5)
[7] $I(\alpha, \beta) \therefore A(\beta, \beta)$ (I. 4) [5, 4, 6]

On the basis of (III. 45) the following formulas are derivable as well, as can be easily understood:

$\ast\therefore H(A(\alpha, \beta), A(\beta, \beta))$, (III. 46)
$\ast\therefore H(A(\alpha, \beta), A(\beta, \beta))$, (III. 47)
$\ast\therefore H(I(\alpha, \beta), I(\beta, \beta))$, (III. 48)
$\ast\therefore H(A(\alpha, \beta), I(\beta, \beta))$, (III. 49)
$\ast\therefore H(A(\alpha, \beta), I(\beta, \beta))$, (III. 50)
$\ast\therefore H(A(\alpha, \beta), A(\beta, \beta))$, (III. 51)
$\ast\therefore H(I(\alpha, \beta), A(\beta, \beta))$ and (III. 52)
$\ast\therefore H(A(\alpha, \beta), A(\beta, \beta))$. (III. 53)

The fact that tautological propositions of the *categorical* form A (α, α), I (α, α) or A (α, α) do not need to be assumed as true within the elementary syllogistic is to be construed as the expression of a deeper-seated logical sitation. Namely, the truth of an affirmative categorical proposition depends on whether the concepts to which its terms relate are satisfied or empty (see § 53, scholium to def. 1). Thus, for any interpretation one gives to expressions of the form A (α, α), I (α, α) or A (α, α), it depends on the content of the concept for which the concept variable α stands whether it is a true or false. A proposition of the form A (α, α) can accordingly be false, if the concept α is empty. If one supposes that a proposition of this form is analytic, there are – against a widespread conviction – analytic propositions which are false.

Section Four
Modal Syllogistic

1 Preliminary Remark

In view of the main aim of Part II of this essay, namely in view of the reduction of the calculus of functions to syllogistic principles and to a triad of postulates that are not strictly universally valid, this section is superfluous, since that calculus contains no modal expressions. Nevertheless, I would like to show in this section how the method pursued above for deriving syllogistic rules can be consistently and successfully maintained in the modal syllogistic; and that the basic rules on which the modal syllogistic relies agree with a common use of the relevant modal expressions and can be rendered in the language of the elementary syllogistic, i.e., in a language which, on the one hand, is restricted to the use of the syllogistic vocabulary standardized above, but, on the other hand, is suitable and rich enough to render universally valid rules of modal logic, which are also used implicitly in the modern modal-logical systems developed in the framework of the calculus of functions (as shown in *Appendix 5*).

Concerning the syllogistic vocabulary, in order to make Aristotle's validity claims verifiable and his argumentation replicable, I need no other logical constants to render *de re* modalities (as per § 6) than those that represent *de dicto* modalities. It will also turn out to be unnecessary to distinguish modalities of various strengths (as they occur, e.g., in $\exists x (A\ x\ \&\ \Box B\ x)$ and $\exists x \Box (A\ x\ \&\ \Box B\ x)$). In this way, the Aristotelian modal logic is shown to be a system of rules of greater unity and uniformity than all the modern presentations and reconstruction attempts known to me concede to it.[203]

The definitions established in § 59 give the modal expressions appearing in this system ('necessarily', 'possibly', etc.) a uniform formal semantics, which agrees with their natural usage but also comes at least very close to the semantics of modal expressions suggested by Aristotle. In § 60, basic rules which result from these definitions are established. On the basis of these rules, as well as the rules derived from them in § 61, I will in § 62 carry out a detailed reconstruction of the proofs which Aristotle has provided in chapters 8 to 22 of his *Prior Analytics* for

---

[203] Ulrich Nortmann (in Ebert & Nortmann 2007, 242–66 and 365–73) gives a very good systematic description both of the problems that stem from rendering Aristotelian modal expressions with modalized expressions of quantificational logic, and of the strategies that have been taken since Albrecht Becker to solve these problems.

the validity of modal syllogisms, which he did almost only suggestively yet nevertheless with admirable soundness and systematicity.[204]

2 Principles

§ 58 Notation

In this section, I will continue to use the signs which I introduced in § 42, § 46, and § 51; new logical constants will be added as well: '$L\ldots$', '$M\ldots$', and '$K\ldots$' (as in § 13 and § 14). Their meaning will be fixed in the definitions of the following paragraphs.

§ 59 Definitions

1. A is a *formula of the modal syllogistic* if and only if A satisfies one of the following conditions: (*a*) A is a formula of the categorical, hypothetical, or disjunctive syllogistic (in the sense of § 47 or § 52), or (*b*) A renders the form of an apodictic, problematic, or contingent proposition.

2. A is an *apodictic proposition*, i.e., a proposition of the form L B (in words: *necessarily (it is true that)* B), if and only if, for every interpretation in which B and C are true or false, the following holds: (1) A is true if and only if, firstly, B is not false in any thinkable circumstances, but rather true in all thinkable circumstances; secondly, any proposition C which follows regularly from B is likewise not false in any thinkable circumstances, but rather true in all thinkable circumstances; and, thirdly, if B is a categorical proposition, A satisfies the truth conditions as per one of the following definitions 5, 6, and 7; (2) A is false if and only if there is some thinkable circumstance in which B is false, thus if it is possibly true that N B.

3. A is a *problematic proposition*, i.e., a proposition of the form M B (in words: *possibly (it is true that)* B), if and only if, for every interpretation in which B is a true or false proposition, the following holds: (1) A is true if and only if, firstly, B is not necessarily false and, secondly, if B is a categorical proposition, A satisfies

---

[204] In the space of this essay, I can engage only very limitedly with the extensive interpretive literature on Aristotle. Hence, as much as possible, I leave philological questions out of consideration. In addition, I largely restrict myself to the reconstruction of Aristotelian validity proofs; I delve into the invalidity proofs, carried out in the *Analytics* using sample propositions, only insofar as their demonstrative force is contested in the literature.

the truth conditions as per one of the following definitions 8, 9, and 10; (2) A is false if and only if N B is necessarily true.

4. A is a *contingent proposition*, i.e., A is equivalent to K B (in words: *contingently (it is true that)* B), if and only if, for every interpretation in which B is true or false, the following holds: A is true if and only if, firstly, B is a categorical proposition of the form Y (α, β), with Y equivalent to A, I, or $Ą$, or a categorical proposition of the form Z (α, β), with Z equivalent to N Y; secondly, Y (α, β) satisfies the truth conditions as per one of definitions 11, 12, and 13; and thirdly, it is both possibly true that Y (α, β) as well as possibly true that Z (α, β), so that if Y = A, then Z = I, if Y = I, then Z = A, and if Y = $Ą$, then Z = $Ą$.

Scholium: According to this definition, K B is not equivalent to the truth of both M B and MN B. According to definition 4, contingency is defined only for categorical propositions and such that K B is equivalent to the truth of both M B and MN B, *and both* B *as well as* N B *are categorical propositions of the same quantity*. The statement in which Aristotle defines contingency (see *An. pr.* 1. 13, 32 a 18–20 [1989, 17–18]; compare § 6, footnote 40) can be understood in a similar way. To be sure, this definition is often taken as if Aristotle equates the contingent *in general* with that which is neither necessary nor impossible. But this conception is not quite correct. Instead, Aristotle says that he uses "to be contingent" and "what is contingent" for that which is not necessary, but when "nothing impossible will result if it is put as being the case." For "put as being the case" Aristotle uses a word (ὑπάρχειν) here which he typically pertains to predicates. Accordingly, he can be understood as saying that it is really predicates to which the property of being contingent would be attributed, and that propositions are only contingent insomuch as contingent predicates are stated in them. He seems to treat a predicate as contingent if and only if it is a predicate that either both possibly applies as well as possibly does not apply to every or to some or to one specific exemplar of a certain kind.[205]

Aristotle pointed out that the logical form of contingent negative propositions, i.e., the form KN B, deviates from the logical form of typical negative propositions, i.e., of the form N B, and from the form of problematic negative propositions, i.e., of the form MN B, insofar as it actually is an "affirmative form" (*An. pr.* 1. 3, 25 b 20–21 [1989, 4]); it basically expresses an affirmation as in "is not-good" (*An. pr.* 1. 3, 25 b

---

[205] Patzig (1969, 71) thus misunderstands the meaning of 'K . . .' when he takes the proposition 'K [all women are taller than 1.9 m]' as true and consequently *Barbara XKM* (see rule (IV. 90) below) as invalid.

21–14 [1989, 4]).²⁰⁶ An example can make clear what is meant here: the proposition *'It holds contingently of every mammal that it does not sleep'* and the equivalent proposition *'Every mammal contingently does not sleep'* mean that every mammal can both sleep and not sleep. That every mammal can not sleep in this context means precisely not that no mammal can sleep, but rather only that every mammal is capable of not sleeping, or is just as capable of not-sleeping as of sleeping. Hence, just like affirmative and limitative propositions, i.e., propositions of the form Y (ᴺα, β), contingent negative propositions have a qualitative existential import.

5. A is an *apodictic universal affirmative proposition*, i.e., a proposition of the form L A (α, β) (in words: *necessarily (it is true that) every β is an α*), if and only if, for every interpretation of α and β in which A is true or false, the following holds: A is true if and only if β is a non-empty concept (so that some object which falls under the concept β is a β) and it is the case that if some object – whether it falls under an arbitrary concept γ or δ or whatever other concept – falls under the concept β, this object necessarily falls under the concept α.

Comment: Definition 5 is distinguished, as are the following definitions 6 to 13, from all the definitions up to this point by not introducing any new logical constant. The reason for this is a merely technical one, pertaining to the presentation. I didn't want to impede the comprehension of definitions 2 to 4 with the nesting of additional sub-clauses. Such a nesting would have been necessary wherever reference was made to definitions 5 to 13 in these earlier definitions.

The fact that definition 5 does not introduce any new logical constant means that the logical form of apodictic universal affirmative propositions is not distinguished from the logical form of other apodictic affirmative propositions inasmuch as the truth conditions specified in definition 2 hold for all apodictic propositions. Special truth conditions for universal affirmative propositions must thus be specified only inasmuch as the definition of universal affirmative propositions, as they are found above in § 52, does not yet explain how modalization affects these propositions. That is, definition 2 in § 52 does not explain by itself what it means for the expression it defines, 'A (α, β)', to be connected to the logical constant 'L . . .'. The following definitions 6 to 13 are required for the construction of a modal categorical syllogistic for exactly the same kind of reason.

The fact that in definitions 5 to 13 no new logical constant is introduced also means that, logically speaking, it makes no difference whether expressions of necessity, possibility and contingency are used *de dicto* or *de re*. That is, logically speaking there is no difference between expressions of the form 'it is necessarily

---

206 For another reading of this passage, compare the commentary in Ebert & Nortmann 2007, 282–86).

true that … β is an α' and sentences of the form '… β is necessarily an α', and likewise there is no difference between analogously formed expressions in which an expression such as 'possibly' or 'contingently' is substituted for 'necessarily'.

6. A is an *apodictic particular affirmative proposition*, i.e., a proposition of the form L I (α, β) (in words: *necessarily (it is true that) some β is an α*), if and only if, for every interpretation of α and β in which A is a true or false proposition, the following holds: (1) A is true if and only if some concept (e.g., the concept of a β that is an α) – call it γ or δ or whatever else – can be formed for which it holds that: there is an object that falls under this concept, such that this object necessarily falls under the concept α or necessarily under the concept β; (2) A is false if and only if it holds that, if some object – whether it falls under an arbitrary concept γ or δ or whatever else – possibly falls under one of the two concepts α and β, then this object possibly does not fall under the other of these two concepts α and β.

7. A is an *apodictic singular affirmative proposition*, i.e., a proposition of the form L A̱ (α, β) (in words: *necessarily (it is true that) that β is an α*), if and only if, for every interpretation of α and β in which A is true or false, the following holds: (1) A is true if and only if some β is necessarily an α and this very β is identical with that object β which is discussed in A and in the context of A (in case there is such a context); (2) A is false if and only if a concept (e.g., the concept of a β that is an α) – call it γ or δ or whatever else – can be formed for which it holds that: either there is no object which falls under the concepts γ and δ, or there is such an object, and this object is identical with the one discussed in A and (where applicable) the context of A, but it possibly does not fall under the concept α.

8. A is a *problematic universal affirmative proposition*, i.e., a proposition of the form M A (α, β) (in words: *possibly (it is true that) every β is an α*), if and only if, for every interpretation of α and β in which A is true or false, the following holds: (1) A is true if and only if α and β are non-empty concepts (so that some object that falls under the concept α is an α, and some object that falls under the concept β is a β) and it holds that, if some object – whether it falls under an arbitrary concept γ or δ or whatever else – possibly falls under the concept β, this object also possibly falls under the concept α; (2) A is false if and only if some concept (e.g., the concept of a β that is not an α) – call it γ or δ or whatever else – can be formed for which it holds that: there is an object that falls under it such that this object falls under the concept β, and necessarily none of the objects which likewise falls under it fall under the concept α.

9. A is a *problematic particular affirmative proposition*, i.e., a proposition of the form M I (α, β) (in words: *possibly (it is true that) some β is an α*), if and only if, for every interpretation of α and β in which A is a true or false proposition, the following holds: (1) A is true if and only if α and β are non-empty concepts (so that some

object that falls under the concept α is an α, and some object that falls under the concept β is a β), and some concept – call it γ or δ or whatever else – can be formed for which it holds that: there is some object that falls under it, such that this object both possibly falls under the concept α and possible falls under the concept β; (2) A is false if and only if, if some object – whether it falls under an arbitrary concept γ or δ or whatever else – possibly falls under one of the two concepts α and β, then this object necessarily does not also fall under the other of these two concepts.

10. A is a *problematic singular affirmative proposition*, i.e., a proposition of the form $M\underline{A}$ (α, β) (in words: *possibly (it is true that) that β is an α*), if and only if, for every interpretation of α and β in which A is true or false, the following holds: (1) A is true if and only if some β is possibly an α and this very α is identical with the object β which is discussed in A and in the context of A (if there is such a context); (2) A is false if and only if an arbitrary concept – call it γ or δ or whatever else – can be formed for which it holds that: either there is no object that falls under the concepts β and γ, or there is such an object, and this very object is identical to that object β discussed in A and (if applicable) the context of A, but it necessarily does not fall under the concept α.

11. A is a *contingent universal proposition*, i.e., a proposition of the form KX (α, β), with X equal to A or NI (in words: *contingently (it is true that) every β is (not) an α*), if and only if, for every interpretation of α and β in which A is true or false, the following holds: A is true if and only if α and β are non-empty concepts (so that some object that falls under the concept α is an α, and some object that falls under the concept β is a β), and it holds that, if some object – whether it falls under the concept γ or δ or whatever else – falls under the concept β, this object also contingently falls under the concept α.

12. A is a *contingent particular proposition*, i.e., a proposition of the form KX (α, β), with X equal to I or NA (in words: *contingently (it is true that) some β is (not) an α*), if and only if, for every interpretation of α and β in which A is a true or false proposition, the following holds: A is true if and only if some concept – call it γ or δ or whatever else – can be formed for which it holds that: there is some object that falls under it, and it is true both that this very object possibly falls under the concept α and possibly falls under the concept β, and that it possibly does not fall under the concept α and possibly does not fall under the concept β.

13. A is a *contingent singular proposition*, i.e., a proposition of the form KX (α, β), with X equal to $\underline{A}$ or $N\underline{A}$ (in words: *contingently (it is true that) that β is an α*), if and only if, for every interpretation of α and β in which A is true or false, the following holds: A is true if and only if some concept – call it γ or δ or whatever else – can be formed, for which it holds that: there is an object that falls under it

and under the concept β and which is identical to that object which is discussed in A and in the context of A, and it is true that this very object possibly falls under the concept α, but also possibly does not fall under the concept α. –

– *General Comment on These Definitions*: Aristotle assumes in his modal syllogistic as well as in his assertoric syllogistic that there are definitions (ὁρισμοί) for the logical constants which appear in the relevant syllogisms. For without such definitions there are, in his view, no perfect syllogisms (see my preliminary comment to § 56, Section I, and § 63, Section II). Of course, we find at best hints at the content of these definitions in the *Analytica priora*. This is even more true of the modal syllogistic than of the assertoric, where at least the meanings of '*A* . . . .' And '*E* . . .' are explained clearly enough (see above § 52, scholium to def. 2). Sufficiently clear elucidations are absent for '*L* . . .', '*M* . . .', and '*K* . . .'. We must thus decipher the meaning that Aristotle wants to give these expressions largely from their use. Aristotle's neglect in this matter as well as the sketchiness of his presentation in many details can probably only be explained by the fact that the text of Book I of the *Analytica priora* "according to all we know" belongs to the kind of lecture manuscript which was intended as a "sourcebook for teaching" in which "much could be made up for with oral elucidations" (Ebert & Nortmann 2007, 419). Precisely in the case of the definitions a corresponding approach may have suggested itself. For in the framework of a lecture it is much less helpful to read out an exact, complete definition from the manuscript than, on a case-by-case basis, to give short relevant hints for grasping certain aspects of a word's meaning. Concerning the meaning of '*L* . . .', we find such a hint, e.g., in *An. pr.* 1. 8, 30 a 2–3 (1989, 13), where Aristotle suggests that the logical vocabulary in assertoric and apodictic universal propositions can be interpreted "in a similar way." At the same time, Aristotle warns of failing to notice that analogies between assertoric and apodictic propositions do not hold completely exactly but rather only "approximately" (σχεδόν) (8, 29 b 36–37). We find a somewhat more extensive hint regarding the meanings of '*M* . . .' and '*K* . . .' at the beginning of *An. pr.* 1. 13, 32 a 18–21 (1989, 17–18). He states: "I use the expressions 'to be possible' (ἐνδέχεσθαι) and 'what is possible' (ἐνδεχόμενον) in application to something if it is not necessary (ἀναγκαῖον) but nothing impossible (ἀδύνατον) will result if it is put as being the case (ὑπάρχειν) (for it is only equivocally that we say that what is necessary (ἀναγκαῖον) is possible (ἐνδέχεσθαι)." It is here indicated that *M* A follows logically from *L* A (see the following rule (IV. 1)), but only if '*M* . . .' is not used in the sense of '*K* . . .'. Accordingly, after this indication Aristotle gives a series of more concrete hints on the distinct applications of '*M* . . .' and '*K* . . .' to affirmative and negative statements and on the application of the negation sign to '*M* . . .' and '*K* . . .' (*An. pr.* 1. 13, 32 a 21–b 3). Hints on the modes of conversion for propositions which deal with what is "said to be possible" (ἐνδέχεσθαι) (and indeed "the way that we define what is possible" (καθ' ὂν τρόπον διορίζομεν τὸ ἐνδεχόμενον)), are anticipated by Aristotle already in *An. pr.* 1. 3, 25 b 14 ff. (1989, 3–4).

§ 60 Basic Rules

1. Universally valid rules which rely on definition 2 in § 59:

   A necesse esse ad esse valet consequentia:

L B ∴ B	(IV. 1)
L B, H (B, C) ∴ L C	(IV. 2)

2. Universally valid intermodal rules which rely on definitions 2 and 3 in § 59:

M B : : NLN B	(IV. 3)
NM B : : LN B	(IV. 4)
L B : : NMN B	(IV. 5)
NL B : : MN B	(IV. 6)

Aristotle points to rules (IV. 3) and (IV. 4) in *An. pr.* 1. 13, 32 a 25–27 and 22–24, respectively. He formulates a rule corresponding to (IV. 5) in *An. pr.* 1. 16, 37 a 9 ff.

3. Universally valid rules which rely on definition 4 in § 59:

Let Y be a sign which in all places of its occurrence within one of the formulas (IV. 7) and (IV. 8) is replaced by one of the signs A, I, or $A̲$, and Z be a sign which in all places of its occurrence within these formulas is replaced by $N I$, $N A$, or $N A̲$, so that in this formula Z = $N I$ if Y = A, and Z = $N A$ if Y = I, and finally Z = $N A̲$ if Y = $A̲$; then these formulas each represent a valid rule:

K Y (α, β) : : M Y (α, β), M Z (α, β)	(IV. 7)
K Z (α, β) : : M Y (α, β), M Z (α, β)	(IV. 8)

We can render $K A$ (α, β) and $KN I$ (α, β) according to rules (IV. 7) and (IV. 8) with 'for every β it is possible both to be an α and not to be an α'. Similarly, $K I$ (α, β) and KN (α, β) can be rendered with 'for some β it is possible both to be an α and not to be an α'.

Often, the meaning of $K A$ is equated with the meaning of the conjunction of M A and MN A. But this equation does not comport in all circumstances with the use, within and outside of logic, of expressions like 'It is contingently true that . . .' and 'contingently'. Nor does it comport exactly with the Aristotelian use (see § 59, def. 4, scholium). The meaning of K A coincides with the conjunction of premises M A and MN A only if both A and N A stand for expressions of categorical propositions of the same quantity (with qualitative existential import). Moreover, the grammatical form of these propositions in some languages (e.g, in German) must be standardized in an appropriate way (see § 6 above). For example, if A represents a universal proposition of the form 'every β is an α', N A must stand for a proposition of the grammatically homogenous form 'every β is not an α'. The negation of A is in this case neither the (particular) proposition 'not every β is an α', nor the (universal) proposition 'no β is an α'. Otherwise, K A and the conjunction of M A and MN A are not equivalent. The same holds for the case in which K A is a particular proposition. In this case, it is equivalent to the conjunction of 'M [some β is an α]' and 'M [some β is not an α]'. That is, MN A stands here neither for 'M [no β is an α]' nor for 'M [not every β is an α]'. The simple equation of K A and the conjunction of M A and MN A, as one can see, assumes a specific grammar and is logically misleading.

4. Modal-syllogistic versions of the *dictum de omni* which depend in turn on the definitions 5, 8, 11, and 13 in § 59:

The following rules (IV. 9) to (IV. 11) are valid for arbitrary γ and also remain valid if the concept variable γ is replaced by an arbitrary concept variable in all places of its occurrence in the formula which expresses one of these rules:

$L A (α, β) :: I (β, β), H (I (β, γ), L A (α, γ))$ (IV. 9)
$M A (α, β) :: I (α, α), I (β, β), H (M I (β, γ), M A (α, γ))$ (IV. 10)
$K A (α, β) :: I (α, α), I (β, β), H (I (β, γ), M A (α, γ)),$
$H (I (β, γ), MN A (α, γ))$ (IV. 11)

5. Modal-syllogistic versions of the *dictum de nullo* which depend on the definitions 6 and 9 in § 59:

The following rules (IV. 12) to (IV. 14) are valid for arbitrary γ and also remain valid if the concept variable γ is replaced by an arbitrary concept variable in all places of its occurrence in the formula which expresses one of these rules:

$NL I (α, β) :: H (M I (β, γ), MN A (α, γ))$ (IV. 12)
$NM I (α, β) :: H (M I (β, γ), LN A (α, γ))$ (IV. 13)
$NM I (α, β) :: H (M I (β, β), LN A (α, β))$ (IV. 14)

6. Modal syllogistic exposition rules which depend in turn on definitions 6, 8, 9, and 12 in § 59:

Let γ be a variable which occurs in no premise formula in the lines of proof preceding the line in which one of the formulas (IV. 15) to (IV. 18) stand; then this formula expresses a valid rule (otherwise, the rule is only valid if the variable γ is replaced by another concept variable in all places of its occurrence in the formula expressed by one of these rules):

$L I (\alpha, \beta) :: D (D (L \underline{A} (\beta, \gamma), L \underline{A} (\alpha, \gamma)), NH (L \underline{A} (\alpha, \gamma), NL \underline{A} (\beta, \gamma))),$
$\quad H (L \underline{A} (\beta, \gamma), H (L \underline{A} (\alpha, \gamma), L \underline{A} (\beta, \gamma))),$
$\quad H (L \underline{A} (\alpha, \gamma), H (L \underline{A} (\beta, \gamma), L \underline{A} (\alpha, \gamma)))$ (IV. 15)

$NM A (\alpha, \beta) \therefore LN I (\alpha, \gamma), \underline{A} (\beta, \gamma))$ (IV. 16)

$M I (\alpha, \beta) \therefore M \underline{A} (\alpha, \gamma), M \underline{A} (\beta, \gamma), I (\alpha, \alpha), I (\beta, \beta)$ (IV. 17)

$K I (\alpha, \beta) :: M \underline{A} (\alpha, \gamma), MN \underline{A} (\alpha, \gamma), M \underline{A} (\beta, \gamma), MN \underline{A} (\beta, \gamma)$ (IV. 18)

None of the rules (IV. 7) to (IV. 18) is explicitly assumed by Aristotle; but in *An. pr.* 1. 9, 30 1 21–13, he argues in a way that can be read as if he assumes at least the validity of rules (IV. 9) and (IV. 12). With regard to the rules (IV. 11), (IV. 13), and (IV. 14), the corresponding implicit suppositions can be found in *An. pr.* 1. 13, 32 b 31–37.

3 Derived Rules

§ 61 Modal Consequence Rules

1. Consequence rules for apodictic propositions:

$H (A, B) \therefore H (L A, L B)$ (IV. 19)

Proof:
[1] $L A, H (A, B) \therefore L B$ (IV. 2)
[2] $H (A, B) \therefore H (L A, L B)$ (II. 1) [1]

Aristotle assumes the validity of rule (IV. 19) in *An. pr.* 1. 15, 34 a 22–24. He claims that, if one labels the premises of an inference with A and its conclusion with B, then with the assumed necessity of A, B is also necessary.

$L A \therefore LNN A$ (IV. 20)

Proof:
[1] $NMN A \therefore LNN A$ (IV. 4)
[2] $L A \therefore NMN A$ (IV. 5)
[3] $L A \therefore LNN A$ (III) [2, 1]

$LNN A \therefore L A$ (IV. 21)

Proof:
[1] $LNN A \therefore NMN A$ (IV. 4)
[2] $NMN A \therefore L A$ (IV. 5)
[3] $LNN A \therefore L A$ (III) [1, 2]

$L\,A \therefore NNL\,A$	**(IV. 22)**

Proof:
[1]	$L\,A \therefore LNN\,A$	(IV. 20)
[2]	$LNN\,A \therefore NMN\,A$	(IV. 4)
[3]	$NL\,A \therefore MN\,A$	(IV. 6)
[4]	$NMN\,A \therefore NNL\,A$	(I) [3]
[5]	$L\,A \therefore NNL\,A$	(III) [1, 2, 4]

As this proof shows, rule (IV. 22) is also valid independently of the validity of basic rule (I. 1).

$NNL\,A \therefore L\,A$	**(IV. 23)**

Proof:
[1]	$MN\,A \therefore NL\,A$	(IV. 6)
[2]	$NNL\,A \therefore NMN\,A$	(I. 1) [1]
[3]	$NMN\,A \therefore LNN\,A$	(IV. 4)
[4]	$LNN\,A \therefore L\,A$	(IV. 21)
[5]	$NNL\,A \therefore L\,A$	(III) [2, 3, 4]

$L\,A\,(\alpha, \beta) \therefore L\,I\,(\beta, \alpha)$	**(IV. 24)**

Proof:
[1]	$A\,(\alpha, \beta) \therefore I\,(\alpha, \beta)$	(III. 13)
[2]	$* \therefore H\,(A\,(\alpha, \beta), I\,(\alpha, \beta))$	(II. 28) [1]
[3]	$H\,(A\,(\alpha, \beta), I\,(\alpha, \beta)), L\,A\,(\alpha, \beta) \therefore L\,I\,(\alpha, \beta)$	(IV. 2)
[4]	$*, L\,A\,(\alpha, \beta) \therefore L\,I\,(\alpha, \beta)$	(I. 4) [2, 3]

2. Consequence rules for problematic propositions:

Ab esse ad posse valet consequentia:

$A \therefore M\,A$	**(IV. 25)**

Proof:
[1]	$LN\,A \therefore N\,A$	(IV. 1)
[2]	$NN\,A \therefore NLN\,A$	(I. 2) [1]
[3]	$A \therefore NN\,A$	(I. 1)
[4]	$NLN\,A \therefore M\,A$	(IV. 3)
[5]	$A \therefore M\,A$	(III) [3, 2, 4]

A necesse esse ad posse valet consequentia:

$L\,A \therefore M\,A$	**(IV. 26)**

Proof:
[1]	$L\,A \therefore A$	(IV. 1)
[2]	$A \therefore M\,A$	(IV. 25)
[3]	$L\,A \therefore M\,A$	(I. 4) [1, 2]

Compare Aristotle, *De Interpretatione* 23 a 17.

$MA \therefore NNMA$ (IV. 27)

Proof:
[1] $MA \therefore NLNA$ (IV. 3)
[2] $NMA \therefore LNA$ (IV. 4)
[3] $NLNA \therefore NNMA$ (I) [2]
[4] $MA \therefore NNMA$ (III) [1, 3]

As this proof shows, rule (IV. 27) is also valid independently of the validity of basic rule (I. 1).

$NNMA \therefore MA$ (IV. 28)

Proof:
[1] $LNA \therefore NMA$ (IV. 4)
[2] $NNMA \therefore NLNA$ (I. 1) [1]
[3] $NLNA \therefore MA$ (IV. 3)
[4] $NNMA \therefore MA$ (III) [2, 3]

$H(A, B) \therefore H(MA, MB)$ (IV. 29)

Proof:
[1] $H(A, B) \therefore H(NB, NA)$ (II. 8)
[2] $H(NB, NA) \therefore H(LNB, LNA)$ (IV. 19)
[3] $H(LNB, LNA) \therefore H(NLNA, NLNB)$ (II. 8)
[4] $H(NLNA, NLNB), H(NLNB, MB) \therefore H(NLNA, MB)$ (II. 13)
[5] $NLNB \therefore MB$ (IV. 3)
[6] $* \therefore H(NLNB, MB)$ (II. 28) [5]
[7] $*, H(NLNA, NLNB) \therefore H(NLNA, MB)$ (I. 4) [6, 4]
[8] $*, H(A, B) \therefore H(NLNA, MB)$ (I. 4) [1, 2, 3, 7]
[9] $*, H(A, B), NLNA \therefore MB$ (II. 5) [8]
[10] $MA \therefore NLNA$ (IV. 3)
[11] $*, H(A, B), MA \therefore MB$ (I. 4) [10, 9]
[12] $*, H(A, B) \therefore H(MA, MB)$ (II. 1) [11]

In *An. pr.* 1. 15, 34 a 22–24, Aristotle assumes the validity of rule (IV. 29) without restriction. He claims there that, if one labels the premises of an inference A and the conclusion B, it holds that if A is possible, then B is possible as well.

$MA \therefore MNNA$ (IV. 30)

Proof:
[1] $NLNA \therefore MNNA$ (IV. 6)
[2] $MA \therefore NLNA$ (IV. 3)
[3] $MA \therefore MNNA$ (III) [2, 1]

$MNN\,A \therefore M\,A$ (IV. 31)

Proof:
[1] $MNN\,A \therefore NLN\,A$ (IV. 6)
[2] $NLN\,A \therefore M\,A$ (IV. 3)
[3] $MNN\,A \therefore M\,A$ (III) [1, 2]

$M\,A\,(\alpha, \beta) \therefore M\,I\,(\alpha, \beta)$ (IV. 32)

Proof:
[1] $A\,(\alpha, \beta) \therefore I\,(\alpha, \beta)$ (III. 13)
[2] $^* \therefore H\,(A\,(\alpha, \beta), I\,(\alpha, \beta))$ (II. 28) [1]
[3] $H\,(A\,(\alpha, \beta), I\,(\alpha, \beta)) \therefore H\,(M\,A\,(\alpha, \beta), M\,I\,(\alpha, \beta))$ (IV. 29)
[4] $^* \therefore H\,(M\,A\,(\alpha, \beta), M\,I\,(\alpha, \beta))$ (I. 4) [2, 3]
[5] $^*, M\,A\,(\alpha, \beta) \therefore M\,I\,(\alpha, \beta)$ (II. 30) [4]

$MN\,\underline{A}\,(\alpha, \gamma) \therefore MN\,A\,(\alpha, \gamma)$ (IV. 33)

Proof:
[1] $N\,\underline{A}\,(\alpha, \gamma) \therefore N\,A\,(\alpha, \gamma)$ (III. 12)
[2] $^* \therefore H\,(N\,\underline{A}\,(\alpha, \gamma), N\,A\,(\alpha, \gamma))$ (II. 28) [1]
[3] $H\,(N\,\underline{A}\,(\alpha, \gamma), MN\,A\,(\alpha, \gamma))$
 $\therefore H\,(MN\,\underline{A}\,(\alpha, \gamma), MN\,A\,(\alpha, \gamma))$ (IV. 29)
[4] $^* \therefore H\,(MN\,\underline{A}\,(\alpha, \gamma), MN\,A\,(\alpha, \gamma))$ (I. 4) [2, 3]
[5] $^*, MN\,\underline{A}\,(\alpha, \gamma) \therefore MN\,A\,(\alpha, \gamma)$ (II. 30) [4]

$M\,\underline{A}\,(\alpha, \gamma) \therefore M\,I\,(\alpha, \gamma)$ (IV. 34)

Proof:
[1] $\underline{A}\,(\alpha, \gamma) \therefore I\,(\alpha, \gamma)$ (III. 7)
[2] $^* \therefore H\,(\underline{A}\,(\alpha, \gamma), I\,(\alpha, \gamma))$ (II. 28) [1]
[3] $H\,(\underline{A}\,(\alpha, \gamma), I\,(\alpha, \gamma)) \therefore H\,(M\,\underline{A}\,(\alpha, \gamma), M\,I\,(\alpha, \gamma))$ (IV. 29)
[4] $^* \therefore H\,(M\,\underline{A}\,(\alpha, \gamma), M\,I\,(\alpha, \gamma))$ (I. 4) [2, 3]
[5] $^*, M\,\underline{A}\,(\alpha, \gamma) \therefore M\,I\,(\alpha, \gamma)$ (II. 30) [14]

$MN\,I\,(\alpha, \beta) \therefore MN\,A\,(\alpha, \beta)$ (IV. 35)

Proof:
[1] $A\,(\alpha, \beta) \therefore I\,(\alpha, \beta)$ (III. 13)
[2] $^* \therefore H\,(A\,(\alpha, \beta), I\,(\alpha, \beta))$ (II. 28) [1]
[3] $H\,(A\,(\alpha, \beta), I\,(\alpha, \beta)), L\,A\,(\alpha, \beta) \therefore L\,I\,(\alpha, \beta)$ (IV. 2)
[4] $^*, L\,A\,(\alpha, \beta) \therefore L\,I\,(\alpha, \beta)$ (I. 4) [2, 3]
[5] $^*, NL\,I\,(\alpha, \beta) \therefore NL\,A\,(\alpha, \beta)$ (I. 2) [4]
[6] $MN\,I\,(\alpha, \beta) \therefore NL\,I\,(\alpha, \beta)$ (IV. 6)
[7] $NL\,A\,(\alpha, \beta) \therefore MN\,A\,(\alpha, \beta)$ (IV. 6)
[8] $^*, MN\,I\,(\alpha, \beta) \therefore MN\,A\,(\alpha, \beta)$ (I. 4) [6, 5, 7]

3. Consequence rules for contingent propositions:

$K\,A\,(\alpha, \beta) \therefore H\,(M\,I\,(\beta, \gamma), M\,\underline{A}\,(\alpha, \gamma))$ (IV. 36)

Proof:

[1]	$M A (\alpha, \beta) \therefore H (M I (\beta, \gamma), M \underline{A} (\alpha, \gamma))$	(IV. 10)
[2]	$K A (\alpha, \beta) \therefore M A (\alpha, \beta)$	(IV. 7)
[3]	$K A (\alpha, \beta) \therefore H (M I (\beta, \gamma), M \underline{A} (\alpha, \gamma))$	(I. 4) [1, 2]

$K A (\alpha, \beta) \therefore H (M I (\beta, \gamma), MN \underline{A} (\alpha, \gamma))$ **(IV. 37)**

Proof:

[1]	$MN I (\alpha, \beta) \therefore NL I (\alpha, \beta)$	(IV. 6)
[2]	$NL I (\alpha, \beta) \therefore H (M I (\beta, \gamma), MN \underline{A} (\alpha, \gamma))$	(IV. 12)
[3]	$MN I (\alpha, \beta) \therefore H (M I (\beta, \gamma), MN \underline{A} (\alpha, \gamma))$	(I. 4) [1, 2]
[4]	$K A (\alpha, \beta) \therefore MN I (\alpha, \beta)$	(IV. 7)
[5]	$K A (\alpha, \beta) \therefore H (M I (\beta, \gamma), MN \underline{A} (\alpha, \gamma))$	(I. 4) [3, 4]

$KN I (\alpha, \beta) \therefore H (M I (\beta, \gamma), M \underline{A} (\alpha, \gamma))$ **(IV. 38)**

Proof:

[1]	$M A (\alpha, \beta) \therefore H (M I (\beta, \gamma), M \underline{A} (\alpha, \gamma))$	(IV. 10)
[2]	$KN I (\alpha, \beta) \therefore M A (\alpha, \beta)$	(IV. 8)
[3]	$KN I (\alpha, \beta) \therefore H (M I (\beta, \gamma), M \underline{A} (\alpha, \gamma))$	(I. 4) [1, 2]

$KN I (\alpha, \beta) \therefore H (M I (\beta, \gamma), MN \underline{A} (\alpha, \gamma))$ **(IV. 39)**

Proof:

[1]	$MN I (\alpha, \beta) \therefore NL I (\alpha, \beta)$	(IV. 6)
[2]	$NL I (\alpha, \beta) \therefore H (M I (\beta, \gamma), MN \underline{A} (\alpha, \gamma))$	(IV. 12)
[3]	$MN I (\alpha, \beta) \therefore H (M I (\beta, \gamma), MN \underline{A} (\alpha, \gamma))$	(I. 4) [1, 2]
[4]	$KN I (\alpha, \beta) \therefore MN I (\alpha, \beta)$	(IV. 8)
[5]	$KN I (\alpha, \beta) \therefore H (M I (\beta, \gamma), MN \underline{A} (\alpha, \gamma))$	(I. 4) [3, 4]

$H (M I (\beta, \gamma), M \underline{A} (\alpha, \gamma)), H (M I (\beta, \gamma), MN \underline{A} (\alpha, \gamma)), I (\alpha, \alpha), I (\beta, \beta)$
$\therefore KN I (\alpha, \beta)$ **(IV. 40)**

Proof:

[1]	$H (M I (\beta, \gamma), M \underline{A} (\alpha, \gamma)), I (\alpha, \alpha), I (\beta, \beta) \therefore M A (\alpha, \beta)$	(IV. 10)
[2]	$H (M I (\beta, \gamma), MN \underline{A} (\alpha, \gamma)) \therefore NL I (\alpha, \beta)$	(IV. 12)
[3]	$NL I (\alpha, \beta) \therefore MN I (\alpha, \beta)$	(IV. 6)
[4]	$H (M I (\beta, \gamma), MN \underline{A} (\alpha, \gamma)) \therefore MN I (\alpha, \beta)$	(I. 4) [2, 3]
[5]	$M A (\alpha, \beta), MN I (\alpha, \beta) \therefore KN I (\alpha, \beta)$	(IV. 8)
[6]	$H (M I (\beta, \gamma), M \underline{A} (\alpha, \gamma)), H (M I (\beta, \gamma),$	
	$MN \underline{A} (\alpha, \gamma)), I (\alpha, \alpha), I (\beta, \beta) \therefore KN I (\alpha, \beta)$	(I. 5) [1, 4, 5]

$H (M I (\beta, \gamma), M \underline{A} (\alpha, \gamma)), H (M I (\beta, \gamma), MN \underline{A} (\alpha, \gamma)), I (\alpha, \alpha), I (\beta, \beta)$
$\therefore K A (\alpha, \beta)$ **(IV. 41)**

Proof:

[1]	$H (M I (\beta, \gamma), M \underline{A} (\alpha, \gamma)), I (\alpha, \alpha), I (\beta, \beta) \therefore M A (\alpha, \beta)$	(IV. 10)
[2]	$H (M I (\beta, \gamma), MN \underline{A} (\alpha, \gamma)) \therefore NL I (\alpha, \beta)$	(IV. 12)
[3]	$NL I (\alpha, \beta) \therefore MN I (\alpha, \beta)$	(IV. 6)

[4]	$H\,(M\,I\,(\beta, \gamma), MN\,A\,(\alpha, \gamma)) \therefore MN\,I\,(\alpha, \beta)$	(I. 4) [2, 3]
[5]	$M\,A\,(\alpha, \beta), MN\,I\,(\alpha, \beta) \therefore K\,A\,(\alpha, \beta)$	(IV. 7)
[6]	$H\,(M\,I\,(\beta, \gamma), M\,A\,(\alpha, \gamma)), H\,(M\,I\,(\beta, \gamma),$	
	$MN\,A\,(\alpha, \gamma)), I\,(\alpha, \alpha), I\,(\beta, \beta) \therefore K\,A\,(\alpha, \beta)$	(I. 5) [1, 4, 5]

Aristotle indicates in *An. pr.* 1. 13, 32 b 23–37 that universal contingent propositions admit a distinction in meaning. According to one meaning, a proposition of the form 'every α is contingently (not) a β' entails the statement 'if something (e.g., a γ) is *possibly* a β, then it is contingently (not) an α'. According to the other meaning, by contrast, it entails the statement 'if something (e.g., a γ) (*in fact*) is a β, then it is contingently (not) an α'. According to the first meaning, one must understand it so that rules (IV. 36) to (IV. 41) hold, which depend only on basic rules (IV. 7) and (IV. 8). In contrast, according to the second meaning, a universal contingent proposition is to be understood so that basic rule (IV. 11) and rule (IV. 42), which is derived from (IV. 11) (in conjunction with rules (IV. 43) to (IV. 46)), hold. In *An. pr.* 1. 13, 32 b 23–37, Aristotle indicates that the perfect *KKK*-syllogisms (see (IV. 73) and (IV. 74)) presuppose the first meaning, while for perfect syllogisms with only *one* contingent premise (see (IV. 75) and (IV. 76)) the second meaning can *also* be assumed.

This clue from Aristotle is of special interest inasmuch as it shows that one could also construct the whole contingency syllogistic while entirely forgoing the expression 'contingently (it is true that) (not) . . .' as an extra *logical constant*, along with the definitions 11 to 13 that pertain to this constant. In that case, definition 4 in § 59 and basic rules (IV. 7) and (IV. 8) would be understood only as conventions which stipulate how certain pairs of problematic propositions can be combined into a single proposition. Even these conventions could be forgone in the construction of the whole contingency syllogistic. In place of pairs of combined problematic propositions in syllogisms within the contingency syllogistic, there would in each case only be problematic propositions. More precisely, in place of *K*-premises and *K*-conclusions there would always be *M*-propositions of the same quality and quantity. Of course, in the relevant validity proofs, the *MN*-propositions which are involved in the respective *K*-propositions of the same quantity would also occur. In this way, *M*-premises and *K*-conclusions would take on a special connotation for contingent propositions, so that 'possibly (it is true that) . . .' simultaneously implies 'possibly (it is true that) not . . .' as well, and conversely 'possibly (it is true that) not . . .' simultaneously implies 'possibly (it is true that) . . .'. This situation may explain the fact that Aristotle himself does not yet use any special expression for contingency, but rather only speaks of a 'to be possible' or a 'can'.

$H\,(I\,(\beta, \gamma), M\,A\,(\alpha, \gamma)), H\,(I\,(\beta, \gamma), MN\,A\,(\alpha, \gamma)), I\,(\alpha, \alpha), I\,(\beta, \beta)$
$\therefore KN\,I\,(\alpha, \beta)$ (IV. 42)

Proof:

[1]	$H(I(\beta, \gamma), MA(\alpha, \gamma)), H(I(\beta, \gamma), MA(\alpha, \gamma)),$	
	$I(\alpha, \alpha), I(\beta, \beta) \therefore KA(\alpha, \beta)$	(IV. 11)
[2]	$KA(\alpha, \beta) \therefore MA(\alpha, \beta)$	(IV. 7)
[3]	$KA(\alpha, \beta) \therefore MNI(\alpha, \beta)$	(IV. 7)
[4]	$MA(\alpha, \beta), MNI(\alpha, \beta) \therefore KNI(\alpha, \beta)$	(IV. 8)
[5]	$H(I(\beta, \gamma), MA(\alpha, \gamma)), H(I(\beta, \gamma), MA(\alpha, \gamma)),$	
	$I(\alpha, \alpha), I(\beta, \beta) \therefore KNI(\alpha, \beta)$	(I. 5) [1, 2, 3, 4]

$KA(\alpha, \beta) \therefore H(I(\beta, \gamma), MA(\alpha, \gamma))$ **(IV. 43)**

Proof:

[1]	$KA(\alpha, \beta) \therefore H(MI(\beta, \gamma), MA(\alpha, \gamma))$	(IV. 36)
[2]	$KA(\alpha, \beta), MI(\beta, \gamma) \therefore MA(\alpha, \gamma)$	(II. 5) [1]
[3]	$I(\beta, \gamma) \therefore MI(\beta, \gamma)$	(IV. 25)
[4]	$KA(\alpha, \beta), I(\beta, \gamma) \therefore MA(\alpha, \gamma)$	(I. 4) [2, 3]
[5]	$KA(\alpha, \beta) \therefore H(I(\beta, \gamma), MA(\alpha, \gamma))$	(II. 1) [4]

$KA(\alpha, \beta) \therefore H(I(\beta, \gamma), MNA(\alpha, \gamma))$ **(IV. 44)**

Proof:

[1]	$KA(\alpha, \beta) \therefore H(MI(\beta, \gamma), MNA(\alpha, \gamma))$	(IV. 37)
[2]	$KA(\alpha, \beta), MI(\beta, \gamma) \therefore MNA(\alpha, \gamma)$	(II. 5) [1]
[3]	$I(\beta, \gamma) \therefore MI(\beta, \gamma)$	(IV. 25)
[4]	$KA(\alpha, \beta), I(\beta, \gamma) \therefore MNA(\alpha, \gamma)$	(I. 4) [2, 3]
[5]	$KA(\alpha, \beta) \therefore H(I(\beta, \gamma), MNA(\alpha, \gamma))$	(II. 1) [4]

$KNI(\alpha, \beta) \therefore H(I(\beta, \gamma), MNA(\alpha, \gamma))$ **(IV. 45)**

Proof:

[1]	$KNI(\alpha, \beta) \therefore H(MI(\beta, \gamma), MNA(\alpha, \gamma))$	(IV. 39)
[2]	$KA(\alpha, \beta), MI(\beta, \gamma) \therefore MNA(\alpha, \gamma)$	(II. 5) [1]
[3]	$I(\beta, \gamma) \therefore MI(\beta, \gamma)$	(IV. 25)
[4]	$KNI(\alpha, \beta), I(\beta, \gamma) \therefore MNA(\alpha, \gamma)$	(I. 4) [2, 3]
[5]	$KNI(\alpha, \beta) \therefore H(I(\beta, \gamma), MNA(\alpha, \gamma))$	(II. 1) [4]

$KNI(\alpha, \beta) \therefore H(I(\beta, \gamma), MA(\alpha, \gamma))$ **(IV. 46)**

Proof:

[1]	$KNI(\alpha, \beta) \therefore H(MI(\beta, \gamma), MA(\alpha, \gamma))$	(IV. 38)
[2]	$KA(\alpha, \beta), MI(\beta, \gamma) \therefore KA(\alpha, \gamma)$	(II. 5) [1]
[3]	$I(\beta, \gamma) \therefore MI(\beta, \gamma)$	(IV. 25)
[4]	$KNI(\alpha, \beta), I(\beta, \gamma) \therefore MA(\alpha, \gamma)$	(I. 4) [2, 3]
[5]	$KNI(\alpha, \beta) \therefore H(I(\beta, \gamma), MA(\alpha, \gamma))$	(II. 1) [4]

$KA(\alpha, \beta) \therefore KNI(\alpha, \beta)$ (IV. 47)

Proof:
[1] $KA(\alpha, \beta) \therefore MA(\alpha, \beta)$ (IV. 7)
[2] $KA(\alpha, \beta) \therefore MNI(\alpha, \beta)$ (IV. 7)
[3] $MA(\alpha, \beta), MNI(\alpha, \beta) \therefore KNI(\alpha, \beta)$ (IV. 8)
[4] $KA(\alpha, \beta), KA(\alpha, \beta) \therefore KNI(\alpha, \beta)$ (I. 5) [1, 2, 3]
[5] $KA(\alpha, \beta) \therefore KNI(\alpha, \beta)$ (II. 6) [4]

Compare *An. pr.* 1. 13, 32 a 35 ff. – William David Ross has introduced the designation "complementary conversion" for the rules (IV. 47) to (IV. 50). (See his edition of Aristotle 1949, 298.) Of course, these rules, unlike rules (IV. 51) to (IV. 60), have nothing to do with conversions in the proper sense.

$KNI(\alpha, \beta) \therefore KA(\alpha, \beta)$ (IV. 48)

Proof:
[1] $KNI(\alpha, \beta) \therefore MA(\alpha, \beta)$ (IV. 8)
[2] $KNI(\alpha, \beta) \therefore MNI(\alpha, \beta)$ (IV. 8)
[3] $MA(\alpha, \beta), MNI(\alpha, \beta) \therefore KA(\alpha, \beta)$ (IV. 7)
[4] $KNI(\alpha, \beta), KNI(\alpha, \beta) \therefore KA(\alpha, \beta)$ (I. 5) [1, 2, 3]
[5] $KNI(\alpha, \beta) \therefore KA(\alpha, \beta)$ (II. 6) [4]

$KI(\alpha, \beta) \therefore KNA(\alpha, \beta)$ (IV. 49)

Proof:
[1] $KI(\alpha, \beta) \therefore MI(\alpha, \beta)$ (IV. 7)
[2] $KI(\alpha, \beta) \therefore MNA(\alpha, \beta)$ (IV. 7)
[3] $MI(\alpha, \beta), MNA(\alpha, \beta) \therefore KNA(\alpha, \beta)$ (IV. 8)
[4] $KI(\alpha, \beta), KI(\alpha, \beta) \therefore KNA(\alpha, \beta)$ (I. 5) [1, 2, 3]
[5] $KI(\alpha, \beta) \therefore KNA(\alpha, \beta)$ (II. 6) [4]

$KNA(\alpha, \beta) \therefore KI(\alpha, \beta)$ (IV. 50)

Proof:
[1] $KNA(\alpha, \beta) \therefore MI(\alpha, \beta)$ (IV. 8)
[2] $KNA(\alpha, \beta) \therefore MNA(\alpha, \beta)$ (IV. 8)
[3] $MI(\alpha, \beta), MNA(\alpha, \beta) \therefore KI(\alpha, \beta)$ (IV. 7)
[4] $KNA(\alpha, \beta), KNA(\alpha, \beta) \therefore KI(\alpha, \beta)$ (I. 5) [1, 2, 3]
[5] $KNA(\alpha, \beta) \therefore KI(\alpha, \beta)$ (II. 6) [4]

§ 62 Modal Conversion Rules[207]

1. Conversion of apodictic propositions:

---

[207] Aristotle discusses these rules especially in *An. pr.* 1. 3 and 1. 13.

$LN\,I\,(\alpha, \beta) \therefore LN\,I\,(\beta, \alpha)$ **(IV. 51)**

Proof:
- [1] $M\,I\,(\beta, \alpha) \therefore M\,A\,(\alpha, \gamma), M\,A\,(\beta, \gamma)$ (IV. 17)
- [2] $NM\,A\,(\alpha, \gamma) \therefore NM\,I\,(\beta, \alpha)$ (I. 2) [1]
- [3] $LN\,A\,(\alpha, \gamma) \therefore NM\,A\,(\alpha, \gamma)$ (IV. 4)
- [4] $LN\,A\,(\alpha, \gamma) \therefore NM\,I\,(\beta, \alpha)$ (I. 4) [2, 3]
- [5] $M\,A\,(\beta, \gamma) \therefore M\,I\,(\beta, \gamma)$ (IV. 34)
- [6] $M\,I\,(\beta, \alpha) \therefore M\,I\,(\beta, \gamma)$ (I. 4) [1, 5]
- [7] $NM\,I\,(\alpha, \beta) \therefore H\,(M\,I\,(\beta, \gamma), LN\,A\,(\alpha, \gamma))$ (IV. 13)
- [8] $NM\,I\,(\alpha, \beta), M\,I\,(\beta, \gamma) \therefore LN\,A\,(\alpha, \gamma)$ (II. 5) [7]
- [9] $NM\,I\,(\alpha, \beta), M\,I\,(\beta, \gamma) \therefore NM\,I\,(\beta, \alpha)$ (I. 4) [4, 8]
- [10] $NM\,I\,(\alpha, \beta), M\,I\,(\beta, \alpha) \therefore NM\,I\,(\beta, \alpha)$ (I. 4) [6, 9]
- [11] $NM\,I\,(\alpha, \beta) \therefore H\,(M\,I\,(\beta, \alpha), NM\,I\,(\beta, \alpha))$ (II. 1) [10]
- [12] $H\,(M\,I\,(\beta, \alpha), NM\,I\,(\beta, \alpha)) \therefore NM\,I\,(\beta, \alpha)$ (II. 9)
- [13] $NM\,I\,(\alpha, \beta) \therefore NM\,I\,(\beta, \alpha)$ (I. 4) [11, 12]
- [14] $LN\,I\,(\alpha, \beta) \therefore NM\,I\,(\alpha, \beta)$ (IV. 4)
- [15] $NM\,I\,(\beta, \alpha) \therefore LN\,I\,(\beta, \alpha)$ (IV. 4)
- [16] $LN\,I\,(\alpha, \beta) \therefore LN\,I\,(\beta, \alpha)$ (I. 4) [14, 13, 15]

It follows from line [2] that we have here an indirect proof, i.e., a proof by *reductio ad impossibile* (according to rule (I. 2)). This form of the proof corresponds to the short description that Aristotle gives of it in *An. pr.* 1. 3, 25 a 27 ff. It is noteworthy that in line [12], as in the proof of *N I*-convertibility (III. 17), a *peritrope* (II. 9) is used. – I point to an alternative proof below in my remark to (IV. 52) (which however is not sufficiently conclusive, since it does not consider the full meaning of '*L* . . .' as per definition 2 in § 59).

The present proof for the validity of (IV. 51) does not, of course, refute Nortmann's claim that it must hold "with complete generality" that "there can be no modal logic which contains a corresponding equivalence theorem [meaning the theorem that $\forall x\,(B\,x \supset \Box \sim A\,x)$ is equivalent to $\forall x\,(A\,x \supset \Box \sim B\,x)$] and yet would still preserve the distinction between necessity and actuality" (Ebert & Nortmann 2007, 370; cf. Nortmann 1996, 56–57). Instead, the proof shows only that the convertibility of apodictic negative propositions does not need to rely on supposing that the logical form of these propositions can be represented by formulas of the type $\forall x\,(B\,x \supset \Box \sim A\,x)$. Nortmann has shown that these propositions are convertible if they have a structure that can be represented by a formula like $\forall x\,(B\,x \supset \Box \sim A\,x)$ and if one assumes that the modal-logical system S5 holds in the Aristotelian syllogistic. This assumption, however, as Nortmann himself concedes, can meet with "grave concerns," since it allows "for a series of modal-syllogistic premise combinations that are stronger than the conclusions that Aristotle claims are possible" (Ebert & Nortmann 2007, 519). Nortmann has also drawn on the system S5 to reconstruct the proof of the validity of *Darii KKK*, and this procedure is defended by supposing that it was "Aristotle himself who always, when he converted an e_N-statement [meaning (in my terminology) a *LN I*-statement], in effect used S5-logical means – even if he did not suspect this and could not at all have in mind the conception used today" (Ebert & Nortmann 2007, 530–31). The proof I have offered makes superfluous the hypothesis underlying Nortmann's argumentation that the structure of *LN I*-propositions is captured in formulas like $\forall x \Box (B x \supset \Box \sim A x)$ and, because of this structure, that *LN I*-propositions are convertible only on the assumption of an S5-logic.[208]

$L I (\alpha, \beta) \therefore L I (\beta, \alpha)$ (IV. 52)

Proof:
[1] $D (D (L A (\alpha, \gamma), L A (\beta, \gamma)), NH (L A (\beta, \gamma), NL A (\alpha, \gamma))) \therefore$
     $D (D (L A (\beta, \gamma), L A (\alpha, \gamma)), NH (L A (\alpha, \gamma), NL A (\beta, \gamma)))$ (II. 30)
[2] $L I (\alpha, \beta) \therefore (D (L A (\alpha, \gamma), L A (\beta, \gamma)), NH (L A (\beta, \gamma), NL A (\alpha, \gamma))),$
     $H (L A (\alpha, \gamma), (H L A (\beta, \gamma), L A (\alpha, \gamma))),$
     $H (L A (\beta, \gamma), H (L A (\alpha, \gamma), L A (\beta, \gamma)))$ (IV. 15)
[3] $D (D (L A (\beta, \gamma), L A (\alpha, \gamma)), NH (L A (\alpha, \gamma), NL A (\beta, \gamma))),$
     $H (L A (\beta, \gamma), H (L A (\alpha, \gamma), L A (\beta, \gamma)),$
     $H (L A (\alpha, \gamma), H (L A (\beta, \gamma), L A (\alpha, \gamma))) \therefore L I (\beta, \alpha)$ (IV. 15)
[4] $L I (\alpha, \beta) \therefore L I (\beta, \alpha)$ (I. 4) [24, 23, 25]

The exposition rule (IV. 15), which is applied twice here, is easier to understand once one has recognized that it corresponds to the rule

$L I (\alpha, \beta) :: L A (\alpha, \gamma) \vee L A (\beta, \gamma)$

(in which '∨', stands for logical adjunction, i.e., for the non-exclusive '. . . or . . .').

It is indicated in *An. pr.* 1. 3, 25 a 33–34 that there is an indirect proof for (IV. 52) and (IV. 53). The proof carried out here as well as for (IV. 53), by contrast, is direct.

An indirect proof for (IV. 52) would be possible if, instead of definition 6 in § 59, the apodictic particular proposition were defined in such a way that for every true proposition of the form $L I (\alpha, \beta)$, it would be possible to form a concept γ for which an object falls under it to which *both* concepts α and β necessarily apply. In this case, it would be possible to apply a rule instead of (IV. 15) (as in the previous proof), which is used in line [1] of the following proof:

[1] $L I (\alpha, \beta) \therefore L A (\beta, \gamma), L A (\alpha, \gamma)$
[2] $NL A (\beta, \gamma) \therefore NL I (\alpha, \beta)$ (I. 2) [1]
[3] $MN A (\beta, \gamma) \therefore NL A (\beta, \gamma)$ (IV. 6)
[4] $MN A (\beta, \gamma) \therefore NL I (\alpha, \beta)$ (I. 4) [2, 3]

---

[208] On the relationship between the modal syllogistic and S5-logic, see *Appendix 5*.

[5]	$NL\,I\,(\beta, \alpha) \therefore H\,(M\,I\,(\alpha, \gamma), MN\,A\,(\beta, \gamma))$	(IV. 12)
[6]	$NL\,I\,(\beta, \alpha), M\,I\,(\alpha, \gamma) \therefore MN\,A\,(\beta, \gamma)$	(II. 5) [5]
[7]	$NL\,I\,(\beta, \alpha), M\,I\,(\alpha, \gamma) \therefore NL\,I\,(\alpha, \beta)$	(I. 4) [4, 6]
[8]	$M\,A\,(\alpha, \gamma) \therefore M\,I\,(\alpha, \gamma)$	(IV. 34)
[9]	$L\,A\,(\alpha, \gamma) \therefore M\,A\,(\alpha, \gamma)$	(IV. 26)
[10]	$L\,I\,(\alpha, \beta) \therefore M\,I\,(\alpha, \gamma)$	(I. 4) [1, 9, 8]
[11]	$NL\,I\,(\beta, \alpha), L\,I\,(\alpha, \beta) \therefore NL\,I\,(\alpha, \beta)$	(I. 4) [10, 7]
[12]	$NNL\,I\,(\alpha, \beta), L\,I\,(\alpha, \beta) \therefore NNL\,I\,(\beta, \alpha)$	(I. 2) [11]
[13]	$L\,I\,(\alpha, \beta) \therefore NNL\,I\,(\alpha, \beta)$	(IV. 22)
[14]	$NNL\,I\,(\beta, \alpha) \therefore L\,I\,(\beta, \alpha)$	(IV. 23)
[15]	$L\,I\,(\alpha, \beta), L\,I\,(\alpha, \beta) \therefore L\,I\,(\beta, \alpha)$	(I. 4) [13, 12, 14]
[16]	$L\,I\,(\alpha, \beta) \therefore L\,I\,(\beta, \alpha)$	(I. 6) [15]

But the definition of $L\,I$ assumed by this proof is not only incompatible with some cases in which Aristotle needs a $L\,I$-conversion (see my remarks to (IV. 88) and (IV. 89) below), but also it does not correspond to the ordinary use of $L\,I$. So it is hardly plausible to take this proof to be Aristotelian.

It is more likely that Aristotle assumed that $L\,I$-convertibility is directly provable because it can be derived in the following way from the indirectly provable I-convertibility:

[1]	$I\,(\alpha, \beta) \therefore I\,(\beta, \alpha)$	(III. 18)
[2]	$* \therefore H\,(I\,(\alpha, \beta), I\,(\beta, \alpha))$	(II. 28) [1]
[3]	$H\,(I\,(\alpha, \beta), I\,(\beta, \alpha)) \therefore H\,(L\,I\,(\alpha, \beta), L\,I\,(\beta, \alpha))$	(IV. 19)
[4]	$H\,(I\,(\alpha, \beta), I\,(\beta, \alpha)), L\,I\,(\alpha, \beta) \therefore L\,I\,(\beta, \alpha)$	(II. 30) [3]
[5]	$*, L\,I\,(\alpha, \beta) \therefore L\,I\,(\beta, \alpha)$	(I. 4) [2, 4]

That Aristotle could have had such a derivation in mind is perhaps supported by his remark in *An. pr.* 1. 8, 30 a 1–3 (1989, 13), saying that with statements of necessity "the [universal] negative premise converts in the same way" as assertoric statements, and that the logical constants of the assertoric syllogistic, namely, "being in as a whole" as well as "predicated of all" are to be "interpret[ed] [. . .] in the same way" in the case of both apodictic and assertoric statements. Aristotle could be thinking here of a similarity as expressed in rule (IV. 19), just applied in line [3], which bears not only on the convertibility of apodictic universal negative statements but also on the convertibility of apodictic particular affirmative statements. Indeed, a proof for apodictic universal negative propositions would be possible in just the same way as the one just carried out. It would differ from the latter only by using (III. 17) instead of (III. 18) in line [1].

$L\,A\,(α, β) ∴ L\,I\,(β, α)$ (IV. 53)

Proof:
[1] $L\,A\,(α, β) ∴ L\,I\,(α, β)$ (IV. 24)
[2] $L\,I\,(α, β) ∴ L\,I\,(β, α)$ (IV. 52)
[3] $L\,A\,(α, β) ∴ L\,I\,(β, α)$ (I. 4) [1, 2]

Compare *An. pr.* 1. 3, 25 a 40–25 b 3.

2. Conversion of problematic propositions:

$MN\,I\,(α, β) ∴ MN\,I\,(β, α)$ (IV. 54)

Proof:
[1] $L\,I\,(β, α) ∴ L\,I\,(α, β)$ (IV. 52)
[2] $NL\,I\,(α, β) ∴ NL\,I\,(β, α)$ (I. 2) [1]
[3] $MN\,I\,(α, β) ∴ NL\,I\,(α, β)$ (IV. 6)
[4] $NL\,I\,(β, α) ∴ MN\,I\,(β, α)$ (IV. 6)
[5] $MN\,I\,(α, β) ∴ MN\,I\,(β, α)$ (I. 4) [2, 3, 4]

The commentary by Ebert & Nortmann (2007, 273) points out that the argument produced in *An. pr.* 1. 3, 25 b 11 for the validity of (IV. 54) assumes the validity of *L I*-conversion (IV. 52), as is also the case in the present proof. But this does not mean that there is a circular proof here, since the proof for (IV. 52) can be carried out directly and was carried out directly here above. (On the "general reservation about circularity" [Ebert & Nortmann 2007, 273] that exists in the Aristotle literature regarding the conversion proofs in *An. pr.* 1. 3, see the discussion in this commentary [Ebert & Nortmann 2007, 266].)

$M\,I\,(α, β) ∴ M\,I\,(β, α)$ (IV. 55)

Proof:
[1] $LN\,I\,(β, α) ∴ LN\,I\,(α, β)$ (IV. 51)
[2] $NLN\,I\,(α, β) ∴ NLN\,I\,(β, α)$ (I. 2) [1]
[3] $M\,I\,(α, β) ∴ NLN\,I\,(α, β)$ (IV. 3)
[4] $NLN\,I\,(β, α) ∴ M\,I\,(β, α)$ (IV. 3)
[5] $M\,I\,(α, β) ∴ M\,I\,(β, α)$ (I. 4) [3, 2, 4]

The convertibility of $M\,I\,(α, β)$ is here proven indirectly. This corresponds to the sparse description of the proof for the validity of (IV. 55) in *An. pr.* 1. 3, 25 a 40–25 b 2. Although this proof assumes the validity of *LN I*-conversion (IV. 51), and the latter is also proven indirectly according to Aristotle's line of argumentation, there is no circular proof here, since the validity of (IV. 55) is not assumed in the proof for the validity of (IV. 51).

$MA(\alpha, \beta) \therefore MI(\beta, \alpha)$ **(IV. 56)**

Proof:
[1]	$MA(\alpha, \beta) \therefore MI(\alpha, \beta)$	(IV. 32)
[2]	$MI(\alpha, \beta) \therefore MI(\beta, \alpha)$	(IV. 55)
[3]	$MA(\alpha, \beta) \therefore MI(\beta, \alpha)$	(I. 4) [1, 2]

Compare *An. pr.* 1. 3, 25 a 40–25 b 2.

3. Conversion of contingent propositions:

$KI(\alpha, \beta) \therefore KI(\beta, \alpha)$ **(IV. 57)**

Proof:
[1]	$KI(\alpha, \beta)$ $\therefore M\underset{\sim}{A}(\alpha, \gamma), MN\underset{\sim}{A}(\alpha, \gamma), M\underset{\sim}{A}(\beta, \gamma), MN\underset{\sim}{A}(\beta, \gamma)$	(IV. 18)
[2]	$M\underset{\sim}{A}(\beta, \gamma), MN\underset{\sim}{A}(\beta, \gamma), M\underset{\sim}{A}(\alpha, \gamma), MN\underset{\sim}{A}(\alpha, \gamma)$ $\therefore KI(\beta, \alpha)$	(IV. 18)
[3]	$KI(\alpha, \beta) \therefore KI(\beta, \alpha)$	(I. 4) [1, 2]

Compare *An. pr.* 1. 3, 25 a 40–25 b 2.

$KA(\alpha, \beta) \therefore KI(\beta, \alpha)$ **(IV. 58)**

Proof:
[1]	$KA(\alpha, \beta) \therefore MA(\alpha, \beta)$	(IV. 7)
[2]	$MA(\alpha, \beta) \therefore MI(\alpha, \beta)$	(IV. 32)
[3]	$KA(\alpha, \beta) \therefore MI(\alpha, \beta)$	(I. 4) [1, 2]
[4]	$KA(\alpha, \beta) \therefore MNI(\alpha, \beta)$	(IV. 7)
[5]	$MNI(\alpha, \beta) \therefore MNA(\alpha, \beta)$	(IV. 35)
[6]	$KA(\alpha, \beta) \therefore MNA(\alpha, \beta)$	(I. 4) [4, 5]
[7]	$MI(\alpha, \beta), MNA(\alpha, \beta) \therefore KI(\alpha, \beta)$	(IV. 7)
[8]	$KA(\alpha, \beta), KA(\alpha, \beta) \therefore KI(\alpha, \beta)$	(I. 5) [3, 6, 7]
[9]	$KA(\alpha, \beta) \therefore KI(\alpha, \beta)$	(II. 6) [8]
[10]	$KI(\alpha, \beta) \therefore KI(\beta, \alpha)$	(IV. 57)
[11]	$KA(\alpha, \beta) \therefore KI(\beta, \alpha)$	(I. 4) [9, 10]

Compare *An. pr.* 1. 3, 25 a 40–25 b 2.

$KNA(\alpha, \beta) \therefore KNA(\beta, \alpha)$ **(IV. 59)**

Proof:
[1]	$KNA(\alpha, \beta) \therefore KI(\alpha, \beta)$	(IV. 50)
[2]	$KI(\alpha, \beta) \therefore KI(\beta, \alpha)$	(IV. 57)
[3]	$KI(\beta, \alpha) \therefore KNA(\beta, \alpha)$	(IV. 49)
[4]	$KNA(\alpha, \beta) \therefore KNA(\beta, \alpha)$	(I. 4) [1, 2, 3]

Compare *An. pr.* 1. 3, 25 b 17–18.

$KA(\alpha, \beta) \therefore KNA(\beta, \alpha)$ (IV. 60)

Proof:
[1] $KA(\alpha, \beta) \therefore KI(\beta, \alpha)$ (IV. 58)
[2] $KI(\beta, \alpha) \therefore KNA(\beta, \alpha)$ (IV. 49)
[3] $KA(\alpha, \beta) \therefore KNA(\beta, \alpha)$ (I. 4) [1, 2]

§ 63 Modal Syllogisms

I. Perfect modal syllogisms
Aristotle calls the syllogisms to be derived in what follows "perfect" in the sense that their validity can be proven without having to make use of conversion rules, exposition rules, or of a *reductio ad impossibile*, i.e., rule (I. 2). In this, these syllogisms are in accord with the perfect assertoric syllogisms of the previous section (see § 56). The fact that a perfect modal syllogism is provable without having to carry out a conversion, exposition, or *reductio ad impossibile* means that no further suppositions are needed for the proof of such a syllogism besides its two premises (or besides the suppositions explicitly contained in these premises). A *reductio ad absurdum* makes such a supposition, since it uses a proposition that does not belong to the premises of the syllogism that is to be proven, but which rather expresses the negation of the conclusion that follows from these premises. Conversion also brings a further supposition into play. This is true for conversions of *M*-, *L*-, or *K*-propositions as well, as emerges from the proofs of the relevant conversion rules (IV. 51) to (IV. 60). Indeed, these proofs each rely on concept expressions (or concept variables) being introduced which are not contained in the propositions (or formulas) to be converted. This can be seen in the validity proofs for rules (IV. 51), (IV. 52), and (IV. 57), on which the remaining modal conversion rules rely.

With reference to singular modal perfect syllogisms, Aristotle says explicitly that their validity us "apparent from the definition" (φανερὸν ἐκ τοῦ ὁρισμοῦ) of the modal-logical constants that occur in their premises (14, 32 b 40 and 14, 33 a 24–25). In doing so, he explicitly attributes the apparentness of their validity to their "proof" (ἀπόδειξις) (14, 33 a 27 and 15, 35 a 35). Accordingly, he claims of "imperfect" syllogisms that it "is clear (δῆλον) from [their] proof" that they are imperfect (16, 36 a 1 [1984, 57]). From these hints we can see that treating the modal perfect syllogisms as it has become usual in the recent literature on Aristotle, i.e., regarding them as "syllogistic implication relations" that have "a self-evident character" (Ebert & Nortmann 2007, 398), does not conform to Aristotle's views. Instead, they should be treated as modes of inference whose validity requires a proof which is essentially distinct in its structure from proofs of the validity of imperfect syllogisms.

1. Two apodictic premises in the first figure (*An. pr.* 1. 8):

Barbara LLL:
$L\,A\,(\alpha, \beta), L\,A\,(\beta, \gamma) \therefore L\,A\,(\alpha, \gamma)$ (IV. 61)

Proof:
[1]	$L\,A\,(\alpha, \beta) \therefore H\,(I\,(\beta, \gamma), L\,A\,(\alpha, \gamma))$	(IV. 9)
[2]	$L\,A\,(\beta, \gamma) \therefore I\,(\gamma, \gamma)$	(IV. 9)
[3]	$L\,A\,(\beta, \gamma) \therefore H\,(I\,(\gamma, \gamma), L\,A\,(\beta, \gamma))$	(IV. 9)
[4]	$L\,A\,(\beta, \gamma) \therefore A\,(\beta, \gamma)$	(IV. 1)
[5]	$A\,(\beta, \gamma) \therefore I\,(\beta, \gamma)$	(III. 7)
[6]	$L\,A\,(\beta, \gamma) \therefore I\,(\beta, \gamma)$	(I. 4) [4, 5]
[7]	$^{*} \therefore H\,(L\,A\,(\beta, \gamma), I\,(\beta, \gamma))$	(II. 28) [6]
[8]	$H\,(I\,(\gamma, \gamma), L\,A\,(\beta, \gamma)), H\,(L\,A\,(\beta, \gamma), I\,(\beta, \gamma))$ $\therefore H\,(I\,(\gamma, \gamma), I\,(\beta, \gamma))$	(II. 13)
[9]	$^{*}, L\,A\,(\beta, \gamma) \therefore H\,(I\,(\gamma, \gamma), I\,(\beta, \gamma))$	(I. 5) [3, 7, 8]
[10]	$H\,(I\,(\gamma, \gamma), I\,(\beta, \gamma)), H\,(I\,(\beta, \gamma), L\,A\,(\alpha, \gamma))$ $\therefore H\,(I\,(\gamma, \gamma), L\,A\,(\alpha, \gamma))$	(II. 13)
[11]	$^{*}, L\,A\,(\beta, \gamma), L\,A\,(\alpha, \beta) \therefore H\,(I\,(\gamma, \gamma), L\,A\,(\alpha, \gamma))$	(I. 5) [9, 1, 10]
[12]	$I\,(\gamma, \gamma), H\,(I\,(\gamma, \gamma), L\,A\,(\alpha, \gamma)) \therefore L\,A\,(\alpha, \gamma)$	(IV. 9)
[13]	$^{*}, L\,A\,(\beta, \gamma), L\,A\,(\beta, \gamma), L\,A\,(\alpha, \beta) \therefore L\,A\,(\alpha, \gamma)$	(I. 5) [2, 11, 12]
[14]	$^{*}, L\,A\,(\alpha, \beta), L\,A\,(\beta, \gamma) \therefore L\,A\,(\alpha, \gamma)$	(II. 6) [13]

In broad outlines, this proof proceeds similarly to the proof for *Barbara* (III. 20). This conforms to the way Aristotle in *An. pr.* 1. 8, 29 b 36 ff., regarding the question of the validity of perfect syllogisms with only apodictic premises, is content with the general explanation that syllogisms of necessity behave "much the same" (σχεδὸν ὁμοίως) as the assertoric. "In the case of what is necessary, things are pretty much the same as in the case of what belongs; for when the terms are put in the same way, then, whether something belongs or necessarily belongs (or does not belong), a deduction will or will not result alike in both cases, the only difference being the addition of the expression 'with necessity' to the terms" (29 b 37–30 a 2 [1984, 48]). It fits with this remark that the following proofs for *Celarent LLL*, *Darii LLL*, and *Ferio LLL* also proceed largely similarly to the proofs for *Celarent* (III. 21), *Darii* (III. 22) and *Ferio* (III. 23), respectively.

Celarent LLL:
$L\,N\,I\,(\alpha, \beta), L\,A\,(\beta, \gamma) \therefore L\,N\,I\,(\alpha, \gamma)$ (IV. 62)

Proof:
[1]	$L\,N\,I\,(\alpha, \beta) \therefore N\,M\,I\,(\alpha, \beta)$	(IV. 4)
[2]	$N\,M\,I\,(\alpha, \beta) \therefore H\,(M\,I\,(\beta, \gamma), L\,N\,A\,(\alpha, \gamma))$	(IV. 13)
[3]	$L\,N\,I\,(\alpha, \beta) \therefore H\,(M\,I\,(\beta, \gamma), L\,N\,A\,(\alpha, \gamma))$	(I. 4) [1, 2]
[4]	$L\,A\,(\beta, \gamma) \therefore H\,(I\,(\gamma, \gamma), L\,A\,(\beta, \gamma))$	(IV. 9)
[5]	$L\,A\,(\beta, \gamma) \therefore A\,(\beta, \gamma)$	(IV. 1)
[6]	$A\,(\beta, \gamma) \therefore I\,(\beta, \gamma)$	(III. 7)

[7]	$L\, \underset{\cdot}{A}\, (\beta, \gamma) \therefore I\, (\beta, \gamma)$	(I. 4) [5, 6]
[8]	$* \therefore H\, (L\, \underset{\cdot}{A}\, (\beta, \gamma), I\, (\beta, \gamma))$	(II. 28) [7]
[9]	$H\, (I\, (\gamma, \gamma), L\, \underset{\cdot}{A}\, (\beta, \gamma)), H\, (L\, \underset{\cdot}{A}\, (\beta, \gamma), I\, (\beta, \gamma))$	
	$\therefore H\, (I\, (\gamma, \gamma), I\, (\beta, \gamma))$	(II. 13)
[10]	$*, L\, A\, (\beta, \gamma) \therefore H\, (I\, (\gamma, \gamma), I\, (\beta, \gamma))$	(I. 5) [4, 8, 9]
[11]	$H\, (I\, (\gamma, \gamma), I\, (\beta, \gamma)) \therefore H\, (M\, I\, (\gamma, \gamma), M\, I\, (\beta, \gamma))$	(IV. 29)
[12]	$*, L\, A\, (\beta, \gamma) \therefore H\, (M\, I\, (\gamma, \gamma), M\, I\, (\beta, \gamma))$	(I. 4) [10, 11]
[13]	$H\, (M\, I\, (\gamma, \gamma), M\, I\, (\beta, \gamma)), H\, (M\, I\, (\beta, \gamma), LN\, \underset{\cdot}{A}\, (\alpha, \gamma))$	
	$\therefore H\, (M\, I\, (\gamma, \gamma), LN\, \underset{\cdot}{A}\, (\alpha, \gamma))$	(II. 13)
[14]	$*, L\, A\, (\beta, \gamma), LN\, I\, (\alpha, \beta)$	
	$\therefore H\, (I\, (\gamma, \gamma), LN\, \underset{\cdot}{A}\, (\alpha, \gamma))$	(I. 5) [10, 3, 13]
[15]	$H\, (M\, I\, (\gamma, \gamma), LN\, \underset{\cdot}{A}\, (\alpha, \gamma)) \therefore NM\, I\, (\alpha, \gamma)$	(IV. 14)
[16]	$NM\, I\, (\alpha, \gamma) \therefore LN\, I\, (\alpha, \gamma)$	(IV. 4)
[17]	$*, LN\, I\, (\alpha, \beta), L\, A\, (\beta, \gamma) \therefore LN\, I\, (\alpha, \gamma)$	(I. 4) [14, 15, 16]

Darii LLL:
$L\, A\, (\alpha, \beta), L\, I\, (\beta, \gamma) \therefore L\, I\, (\alpha, \gamma)$ **(IV. 63)**

Proof:

[1]	$L\, A\, (\alpha, \beta) \therefore H\, (I\, (\beta, \gamma), L\, \underset{\cdot}{A}\, (\alpha, \gamma))$	(IV. 9)
[2]	$L\, A\, (\alpha, \beta), I\, (\beta, \gamma) \therefore L\, \underset{\cdot}{A}\, (\alpha, \gamma)$	(II. 5) [1]
[3]	$L\, I\, (\beta, \gamma) \therefore I\, (\beta, \gamma)$	(IV. 1)
[4]	$L\, A\, (\alpha, \beta), L\, I\, (\beta, \gamma) \therefore L\, \underset{\cdot}{A}\, (\alpha, \gamma)$	(I. 4) [3, 2]
[5]	$\underset{\cdot}{A}\, (\alpha, \gamma) \therefore I\, (\alpha, \gamma)$	(III. 7)
[6]	$* \therefore H\, (\underset{\cdot}{A}\, (\alpha, \gamma), I\, (\alpha, \gamma))$	(II. 28) [5]
[7]	$H\, (\underset{\cdot}{A}\, (\alpha, \gamma), I\, (\alpha, \gamma)), L\, \underset{\cdot}{A}\, (\alpha, \gamma) \therefore L\, I\, (\alpha, \gamma)$	(IV. 2)
[8]	$*, L\, \underset{\cdot}{A}\, (\alpha, \gamma) \therefore L\, I\, (\alpha, \gamma)$	(I. 4) [6, 7]
[9]	$*, L\, A\, (\alpha, \beta), L\, I\, (\beta, \gamma) \therefore L\, I\, (\alpha, \gamma)$	(I. 4) [4, 8]

Ferio LLL:
$LN\, I\, (\alpha, \beta), L\, I\, (\beta, \gamma) \therefore LN\, A\, (\alpha, \gamma)$ **(IV. 64)**

Proof:

[1]	$LN\, I\, (\alpha, \beta) \therefore NM\, I\, (\alpha, \beta)$	(IV. 4)
[2]	$NM\, I\, (\alpha, \beta) \therefore H\, (M\, I\, (\beta, \gamma), LN\, \underset{\cdot}{A}\, (\alpha, \gamma))$	(IV. 13)
[3]	$LN\, I\, (\alpha, \beta) \therefore H\, (M\, I\, (\beta, \gamma), LN\, \underset{\cdot}{A}\, (\alpha, \gamma))$	(I. 4) [1, 2]
[4]	$LN\, I\, (\alpha, \beta), M\, I\, (\beta, \gamma) \therefore LN\, \underset{\cdot}{A}\, (\alpha, \gamma)$	(II. 5) [3]
[5]	$L\, I\, (\beta, \gamma) \therefore M\, I\, (\beta, \gamma)$	(IV. 26)
[6]	$LN\, I\, (\alpha, \beta), L\, I\, (\beta, \gamma) \therefore LN\, \underset{\cdot}{A}\, (\alpha, \gamma)$	(I. 4) [5, 4]
[7]	$N\, \underset{\cdot}{A}\, (\alpha, \gamma) \therefore N\, A\, (\alpha, \gamma)$	(III. 12)
[8]	$* \therefore H\, (N\, \underset{\cdot}{A}\, (\alpha, \gamma), N\, A\, (\alpha, \gamma))$	(II. 28) [7]
[9]	$H\, (N\, \underset{\cdot}{A}\, (\alpha, \gamma), N\, A\, (\alpha, \gamma)), LN\, \underset{\cdot}{A}\, (\alpha, \gamma) \therefore LN\, A\, (\alpha, \gamma)$	(IV. 2)
[10]	$*, LN\, \underset{\cdot}{A}\, (\alpha, \gamma) \therefore LN\, A\, (\alpha, \gamma)$	(I. 4) [8, 9]
[11]	$*, LN\, I\, (\alpha, \beta), L\, I\, (\beta, \gamma) \therefore LN\, A\, (\alpha, \gamma)$	(I. 4) [6, 10]

2. One assertoric and one apodictic premise in the first figure:

Barbara LXL:
$L\,A\,(α, β), A\,(β, γ) \therefore L\,A\,(α, γ)$ (IV. 65)

Proof:
[1]	$L\,A\,(α, β) \therefore H\,(I\,(β, γ), L\,A\,(α, γ))$	(IV. 9)
[2]	$A\,(β, γ) \therefore I\,(γ, γ)$	(III. 1)
[3]	$A\,(β, γ) \therefore H\,(I\,(γ, γ), A\,(β, γ))$	(III. 1)
[4]	$A\,(β, γ) \therefore I\,(β, γ)$	(III. 7)
[5]	$* \therefore H\,(A\,(β, γ), I\,(β, γ))$	(II. 28) [4]
[6]	$H\,(I\,(γ, γ), A\,(β, γ)), H\,(A\,(β, γ), I\,(β, γ))$ $\therefore H\,(I\,(γ, γ), I\,(β, γ))$	(II. 13)
[7]	$*, A\,(β, γ) \therefore H\,(I\,(γ, γ), I\,(β, γ))$	(I. 5) [3, 5, 6]
[8]	$H\,(I\,(γ, γ), I\,(β, γ)), H\,(I\,(β, γ), L\,A\,(α, γ))$ $\therefore H\,(I\,(γ, γ), L\,A\,(α, γ))$	(II. 13)
[9]	$*, A\,(β, γ), L\,A\,(α, β) \therefore H\,(I\,(γ, γ), L\,A\,(α, γ))$	(I. 5) [7, 1, 8]
[10]	$I\,(γ, γ), H\,(I\,(γ, γ), L\,A\,(α, γ)) \therefore L\,A\,(α, γ)$	(IV. 9)
[11]	$*, A\,(β, γ), A\,(β, γ), L\,A\,(α, β) \therefore L\,A\,(α, γ)$	(I. 5) [2, 9, 10]
[12]	$*, L\,A\,(α, β), A\,(β, γ) \therefore L\,A\,(α, γ)$	(II. 6) [11]

Compare *An. pr.* 1. 9, 30 a 15–23. According to Nortmann, we have in *Barbara LXL* a combination of premises which is best rendered as $∀x\,□\,(B\,x ⊃ □\,A\,x)\,\&\,∀x\,(C\,x ⊃ B\,x)$. However, he himself points out that from this combination only a weakened statement of necessity would follow, namely a statement of the form $∀x\,(C\,x ⊃ □\,A\,x)$ (Ebert & Nortmann 2007, 386–93).[209] Since *Barbara LXL* belongs among perfect syllogisms, whose validity according to Aristotle depends only on the definitions of the logical constants that occur in them, it certainly cannot be supposed that Aristotle could allow that the same logical vocabulary could, if it appears in different places of a perfect syllogism, be used with a different meaning.

Nortmann, however, is of the opinion that "the pure *de dicto* reading of necessity statements" – which is how he designates the depiction of these statements with expressions (which I use as well) of the type '$L\,A\,(α, β)$' – "must be given up if claims like that of the validity of *Barbara NXN* [meaning *Barbara LXL* in the notation I use] are supposed to be capable of verification" (Ebert & Nortmann 2007, 384). As his reason for this opinion, Nortmann states that with the "pure *de dicto* reading" of necessity statements, the move carried out in *Barbara LXL* from $L\,A\,(α, β)$ and $A\,(β, γ)$ to $L\,A\,(α, γ)$ would only be justified if one could move from $L\,A\,(α, β)\,\&\,A\,(β, γ)$ to $L\,(A\,(α, β)\,\&\,A\,(β, γ))$ (Ebert & Nortmann 2007, 383–84). He points out that this move is impermissible because, since $L\,(A\,(α, β)\,\&\,A\,(β, γ))$ is equivalent to $L\,A\,(α, β)\,\&\,L\,A$

---

[209] Here and in what follows I use a different notation than Nortmann.

(β, γ)), the move in question includes a move from A (β, γ) to $L\ A$ (β, γ), and this would conform to no reasonable use of the concept of necessity (Ebert & Nortmann 2007, 383–84). I do not want to call this point into question. But I see no grounds for Nortmann's tacit supposition that there is no *other* justification for the move in *Barbara LXL* from $L\ A$ (α, β) and A (β, γ) to $L\ A$ (α, γ) than the one he considers to be impermissible. That there is indeed such a justification can be seen in the proof for (IV. 65) that I have presented above. Yet it is immediately clear from the rules that come to application in this proof that it would be improper to designate my rendering of statements of necessity using expressions of the type '$L\ A$ (α, β)' as the 'pure *de dicto* reading' of such statements. To be sure, the expression '$L\ A$ . . .' does correspond to the *de dicto* use of 'necessary', since this expression is equivalent to 'it is necessar(ily true) that . . .'. But $L\ A$ (α, β) immediately implies, according to § 59, def. 6, and according to rule (IV. 9), 'If some γ is a β, then this γ is necessarily an α'. In this way, $L\ A$ (α, β) immediately entails a statement about a *de re* necessity.

Celarent LXL:
$LN\ I$ (α, β), A (β, γ) ∴ $LN\ I$ (α, γ) (IV. 66)

Proof:

[1]	$LN\ I$ (α, β) ∴ $NM\ I$ (α, β)	(IV. 4)
[2]	$NM\ I$ (α, β) ∴ H ($M\ I$ (β, γ), $LN\ A$ (α, γ))	(IV. 13)
[3]	$LN\ I$ (α, β) ∴ H ($M\ I$ (β, γ), $LN\ A$ (α, γ))	(I. 4) [1, 2]
[4]	A (β, γ) ∴ H (I (γ, γ), A (β, γ))	(III. 1)
[5]	A (β, γ) ∴ I (β, γ)	(III. 7)
[6]	*∴ H (A (β, γ), I (β, γ))	(II. 28) [5]
[7]	H (I (γ, γ), A (β, γ)), H (A (β, γ), I (β, γ)) ∴ H (I (γ, γ), I (β, γ))	(II. 13)
[8]	*, A (β, γ) ∴ H (I (γ, γ), I (β, γ))	(I. 5) [4, 6, 7]
[9]	H (I (γ, γ), I (β, γ)) ∴ H ($M\ I$ (γ, γ), $M\ I$ (β, γ))	(IV. 29)
[10]	*, A (β, γ) ∴ H ($M\ I$ (γ, γ), $M\ I$ (β, γ))	(I. 4) [8, 9]
[11]	H ($M\ I$ (γ, γ), $M\ I$ (β, γ)), H ($M\ I$ (β, γ), $LN\ A$ (α, γ)) ∴ H ($M\ I$ (γ, γ), $LN\ A$ (α, γ))	(II. 13)
[12]	*, A (β, γ), $LN\ I$ (α, β) ∴ H ($M\ I$ (γ, γ), $LN\ A$ (α, γ))	(I. 5) [10, 3, 11]
[13]	H ($M\ I$ (γ, γ), $LN\ A$ (α, γ)) ∴ $NM\ I$ (α, γ)	(IV. 14)
[14]	*, A (β, γ), $LN\ I$ (α, β) ∴ $NM\ I$ (α, γ)	(I. 4) [12, 13]
[15]	$NM\ I$ (α, γ) ∴ $LN\ I$ (α, γ)	(IV. 4)
[16]	*, $LN\ I$ (α, β), A (β, γ) ∴ $LN\ I$ (α, γ)	(I. 4) [14, 15]

Compare *An. pr.* 1. 9, 30 a 15–23.

According to Nortmann's interpretation, similarly to *Barbara LXL* a conclusion results for *Celarent LXL* whose logical form deviates from the form of the major premise. While the form of the major premise in this interpretation would be rendered with $\forall x\ \Box\ (B\ x \supset \Box \sim A\ x)$, the corresponding form of the conclusion would have to be $\forall x (B x \supset \Box \sim A x)$. Yet Nortmann himself has pointed out that a conclusion of this form is not convertible. This result is not compatible with Aristotle's supposition that the validity of *Camestres XLL*, *Darapti XLL*, and *Disamis XLL* is provable by the conversion of the conclusion of *Celarent LXL*. Accordingly, Nortmann takes Aristotle's claim for the validity of *Camestres XLL*, *Darapti XLL*, and *Disamis XLL* to be one of his logical errors. (See Ebert & Nortmann 2007, 388; 419; 456.)

In the modal predicate-logical reading of Klaus J. Schmidt as well, *Celarent LXL* is a mode of inference which is only valid if the statements of necessity in its conclusion position have a different structure than in the premise position. In his view, the one structure is rendered by the formula $\forall x \Box (\Diamond B x \supset \Box A x)$, the other by the formula $\forall x (C x \supset \Box A x)$. Furthermore, Schmidt points out that this formula is derivable from the premise formulas only on the assumption of a B-logic.[210]

Darii LXL:
$L A (\alpha, \beta), I (\beta, \gamma) \therefore L I (\alpha, \gamma)$ (IV. 67)

Proof:
[1] $L A (\alpha, \beta) \therefore H (I (\beta, \gamma), L A (\alpha, \gamma))$ (IV. 9)
[2] $L A (\alpha, \beta), I (\beta, \gamma) \therefore L A (\alpha, \gamma)$ (II. 5) [1]
[3] $A (\alpha, \gamma) \therefore I (\alpha, \gamma)$ (III. 7)
[4] $^* \therefore H (A (\alpha, \gamma), I (\alpha, \gamma))$ (II. 28) [3]
[5] $H (A (\alpha, \gamma), I (\alpha, \gamma)) \therefore H (L A (\alpha, \gamma), L I (\alpha, \gamma))$ (II. 13)
[6] $^* \therefore H (L A (\alpha, \gamma), L I (\alpha, \gamma))$ (I. 4) [4, 5]
[7] $^*, L A (\alpha, \gamma) \therefore L I (\alpha, \gamma)$ (II. 30) [6]
[8] $^*, L A (\alpha, \beta), I (\beta, \gamma) \therefore L I (\alpha, \gamma)$ (I. 4) [2, 7]

Compare *Analytica priora* 1. 9, 30 a 33–40.

Ferio LXL:
$LN I (\alpha, \beta), I (\beta, \gamma) \therefore LN A (\alpha, \gamma)$ (IV. 68)

Proof:
[1] $NM I (\alpha, \beta) \therefore LN I (\alpha, \beta)$ (IV. 4)
[2] $NM I (\alpha, \beta) \therefore H (M I (\beta, \gamma), LN A (\alpha, \gamma))$ (IV. 13)
[3] $LN I (\alpha, \beta) \therefore H (M I (\beta, \gamma), LN A (\alpha, \gamma))$ (I. 4) [1, 2]
[4] $LN I (\alpha, \beta), M I (\beta, \gamma) \therefore LN A (\alpha, \gamma)$ (II. 5) [3]
[5] $I (\beta, \gamma) \therefore M I (\beta, \gamma)$ (IV. 25)
[6] $LN I (\alpha, \beta), I (\beta, \gamma) \therefore LN A (\alpha, \gamma)$ (I. 4) [4, 5]
[7] $N A (\alpha, \gamma) \therefore N A (\alpha, \gamma)$ (III. 12)
[8] $^* \therefore H (N A (\alpha, \gamma), N A (\alpha, \gamma))$ (II. 28) [7]
[9] $H (N A (\alpha, \gamma), N A (\alpha, \gamma)) \therefore H (LN A (\alpha, \gamma), LN A (\alpha, \gamma))$ (II. 13)

---

[210] Schmidt 2000, 44. I use a different notation than Schmidt here and in what follows. On the relationship between B-logic and modal syllogistic, see *Appendix 5*.

[10]	*∴ H (LN A (α, γ), LN A (α, γ))	(I. 4) [8, 9]
[11]	*, LN A (α, γ) ∴ LN A (α, γ)	(II. 30) [10]
[12]	*, LN I (α, β), I (β, γ) ∴ LN A (α, γ)	(I. 4) [6, 11]

Compare *Analytica priora* 1. 9, 30 b 1 f.

3. One apodictic and one assertoric premise in the first figure:

Barbara XLX:
A(α, β), L A (β, γ) ∴ A (α, γ)   **(IV. 69)**

Proof:
[1]	A (α, β) ∴ H (I (β, γ), A (α, γ))	(III. 1)
[2]	L A (β, γ) ∴ A (β, γ)	(IV. 1)
[3]	A (β, γ) ∴ I (γ, γ)	(III. 1)
[4]	L A (β, γ) ∴ I (γ, γ)	(I. 4) [2, 3]
[5]	L A (β, γ) ∴ H (I (γ, γ), L A (β, γ))	(IV. 9)
[6]	L A (β, γ) ∴ A (β, γ)	(IV. 1)
[7]	A (β, γ) ∴ I (β, γ)	(III. 7)
[8]	L A (β, γ) ∴ I (β, γ)	(I. 4) [6, 7]
[9]	*∴ H (L A (β, γ), I (β, γ))	(II. 28) [8]
[10]	H (I (γ, γ), L A (β, γ)), H (L A (β, γ), I (β, γ)) ∴ H (I (γ, γ), I (β, γ))	(II. 13)
[11]	*, L A (β, γ) ∴ H (I (γ, γ), I (β, γ))	(I. 5) [5, 9, 10]
[12]	H (I (γ, γ), I (β, γ)), H (I (β, γ), A (α, γ)) ∴ H (I (γ, γ), A (α, γ))	(II. 13)
[13]	*, L A (β, γ), A (α, β) ∴ H (I (γ, γ), A (α, γ))	(I. 5) [11, 1, 12]
[14]	I (γ, γ), H (I (γ, γ), A (α, γ)) ∴ A (α, γ)	(III. 1)
[15]	*, L A (β, γ), L A (β, γ), A (α, β) ∴ A (α, γ)	(I. 5) [4, 13, 14]
[16]	*, A (α, β), L A (β, γ) ∴ A (α, γ)	(II. 6) [15]

Compare *An. pr.* 1. 9, 30 a 23–32.

Celarent XLX:
N I (α, β), L A (β, γ) ∴ N I (α, γ)   **(IV. 70)**

Proof:
[1]	N I (α, β) ∴ H (I (β, γ), N A (α, γ))	(III. 2)
[2]	L A (β, γ) ∴ H (I (γ, γ), L A (β, γ))	(IV. 9)
[3]	L A (β, γ) ∴ A (β, γ)	(IV. 1)
[4]	A (β, γ) ∴ I (β, γ)	(III. 7)
[5]	L A (β, γ) ∴ I (β, γ)	(I. 4) [3, 4]
[6]	*∴ H (L A (β, γ), I (β, γ))	(II. 28) [5]
[7]	H (I (γ, γ), L A (β, γ)), H (L A (β, γ), I (β, γ)) ∴ H (I (γ, γ), I (β, γ))	(II. 13)
[8]	*, L A (β, γ) ∴ H (I (γ, γ), I (β, γ))	(I. 5) [2, 6, 7]

[9] $H(I(\gamma, \gamma), I(\beta, \gamma)), H(I(\beta, \gamma), N\underset{\sim}{A}(\alpha, \gamma))$
      $\therefore H(I(\gamma, \gamma), N\underset{\sim}{A}(\alpha, \gamma))$ (II. 13)
[10] $*, LA(\beta, \gamma), NI(\alpha, \beta) \therefore H(I(\gamma, \gamma), N\underset{\sim}{A}(\alpha, \gamma))$ (I. 5) [8, 1, 9]
[11] $H(I(\gamma, \gamma), N\underset{\sim}{A}(\alpha, \gamma)) \therefore NI(\alpha, \gamma)$ (III. 2)
[12] $*, LA(\beta, \gamma), NI(\alpha, \beta) \therefore NI(\alpha, \gamma)$ (I. 5) [10, 11]

Compare *An. pr.* 1. 9, 30 a 32–33.

Darii XLX:
$A(\alpha, \beta), LI(\beta, \gamma) \therefore I(\alpha, \gamma)$ **(IV. 71)**

Proof:
[1] $A(\alpha, \beta) \therefore H(I(\beta, \gamma), \underset{\sim}{A}(\alpha, \gamma))$ (III. 1)
[2] $A(\alpha, \beta), I(\beta, \gamma) \therefore \underset{\sim}{A}(\alpha, \gamma)$ (II. 5) [1]
[3] $LI(\beta, \gamma) \therefore I(\beta, \gamma)$ (IV. 1)
[4] $A(\alpha, \beta), LI(\beta, \gamma) \therefore \underset{\sim}{A}(\alpha, \gamma)$ (I. 4) [3, 2]
[5] $\underset{\sim}{A}(\alpha, \gamma) \therefore I(\alpha, \gamma)$ (III. 7)
[6] $A(\alpha, \beta), LI(\beta, \gamma) \therefore I(\alpha, \gamma)$ (I. 4) [4, 5]

Compare *An. pr.* 1. 9, 30 b 2–6.

Ferio XLX:
$NI(\alpha, \beta), LI(\beta, \gamma) \therefore NA(\alpha, \gamma)$ **(IV. 72)**

Proof:
[1] $NI(\alpha, \beta) \therefore H(I(\beta, \gamma), N\underset{\sim}{A}(\alpha, \gamma))$ (III. 1)
[2] $NI(\alpha, \beta), I(\beta, \gamma) \therefore N\underset{\sim}{A}(\alpha, \gamma)$ (II. 5) [1]
[3] $LI(\beta, \gamma) \therefore I(\beta, \gamma)$ (IV. 1)
[4] $NI(\alpha, \beta), LI(\beta, \gamma) \therefore N\underset{\sim}{A}(\alpha, \gamma)$ (I. 4) [3, 2]
[5] $N\underset{\sim}{A}(\alpha, \gamma) \therefore NA(\alpha, \gamma)$ (III. 13)
[6] $NI(\alpha, \beta), LI(\beta, \gamma) \therefore NA(\alpha, \gamma)$ (I. 4) [4, 5]

Compare *An. pr.* 1.9, 30 2–6.

4. Two contingent premises in the first figure:

Barbara KKK:
$KA(\alpha, \beta), KA(\beta, \gamma) \therefore KA(\alpha, \gamma)$ **(IV. 73)**

Proof:
[1] $KA(\alpha, \beta) \therefore H(MI(\beta, \gamma), M\underset{\sim}{A}(\alpha, \gamma))$ (IV. 36)
[2] $KA(\beta, \gamma) \therefore MA(\alpha, \gamma)$ (IV. 7)
[3] $MA(\alpha, \gamma) \therefore I(\alpha, \alpha), I(\gamma, \gamma)$ (IV. 10)
[4] $KA(\beta, \gamma) \therefore I(\alpha, \alpha), I(\gamma, \gamma)$ (I. 4) [2, 3]
[5] $KA(\beta, \gamma) \therefore H(MI(\gamma, \gamma), M\underset{\sim}{A}(\beta, \gamma))$ (IV. 36)
[6] $KA(\beta, \gamma) \therefore H(MI(\gamma, \gamma), MN\underset{\sim}{A}(\beta, \gamma))$ (IV. 37)
[7] $\underset{\sim}{A}(\beta, \gamma) \therefore I(\beta, \gamma)$ (III. 7)
[8] $* \therefore H(\underset{\sim}{A}(\beta, \gamma), I(\beta, \gamma))$ (II. 28) [7]
[9] $H(\underset{\sim}{A}(\beta, \gamma), I(\beta, \gamma)) \therefore H(M\underset{\sim}{A}(\beta, \gamma), MI(\beta, \gamma))$ (IV. 29)

[10]	$*\therefore H(M\,A\,(\beta,\gamma), M\,I\,(\beta,\gamma))$	(I. 4) [8, 9]
[11]	$H(M\,I\,(\gamma,\gamma), M\,A\,(\beta,\gamma)), H(M\,A\,(\beta,\gamma), M\,I\,(\beta,\gamma))$	
	$\therefore H(M\,I\,(\gamma,\gamma), M\,I\,(\beta,\gamma))$	(II. 13)
[12]	$*, K\,A\,(\beta,\gamma) \therefore H(M\,I\,(\gamma,\gamma), M\,I\,(\beta,\gamma))$	(I. 5) [5, 10, 11]
[13]	$H(M\,I\,(\gamma,\gamma), M\,I\,(\beta,\gamma)), H(M\,I\,(\beta,\gamma), M\,A\,(\alpha,\gamma))$	
	$\therefore H(M\,I\,(\gamma,\gamma), M\,A\,(\alpha,\gamma))$	(II. 13)
[14]	$*, K\,A\,(\beta,\gamma), K\,A\,(\alpha,\beta)$	
	$\therefore H(M\,I\,(\gamma,\gamma), M\,A\,(\alpha,\gamma))$	(I. 5) [12, 1, 13]
[15]	$H(M\,I\,(\gamma,\gamma), M\,A\,(\alpha,\gamma)), H(M\,I\,(\gamma,\gamma), MN\,A\,(\alpha,\gamma)), I\,(\alpha,\alpha), I\,(\gamma,\gamma) \therefore$	
	$K\,A\,(\alpha,\gamma)$	(IV. 41)
[16]	$*, K\,A\,(\alpha,\beta), K\,A\,(\beta,\gamma), K\,A\,(\beta,\gamma), K\,A\,(\beta,\gamma)$	
	$\therefore K\,A\,(\alpha,\gamma)$	(I. 5) [4, 14, 6, 15]
[17]	$*, K\,A\,(\alpha,\beta), K\,A\,(\beta,\gamma) \therefore K\,A\,(\alpha,\gamma)$	(II. 6) [16]

Compare *An. pr.* 1.14, 32 b 38–33 a 1.

The proof for *Celarent KKK*, which Aristotle presents in *An. pr.* 1. 14, 33 a 1–5, proceeds in just the same way as the proof for *Barbara KKK*. There is likewise a similarity between the proof for (IV. 73) and *Celarent KKK*. The latter differs from (IV. 73) only in that in line [1] the rule (IV. 38) is applied, and in line [17] the rule (IV. 40) is applied.

Darii KKK
$K\,A\,(\alpha,\beta), K\,I\,(\beta,\gamma) \therefore K\,I\,(\alpha,\gamma)$ **(IV. 74)**

Proof:

[1]	$K\,A\,(\alpha,\beta) \therefore H(M\,I\,(\beta,\gamma), M\,A\,(\alpha,\gamma))$	(IV. 36)
[2]	$K\,A\,(\alpha,\beta) \therefore H(M\,I\,(\beta,\gamma), MN\,A\,(\alpha,\gamma))$	(IV. 37)
[3]	$K\,A\,(\alpha,\beta), M\,I\,(\beta,\gamma) \therefore M\,A\,(\alpha,\gamma)$	(II. 5) [1]
[4]	$K\,A\,(\alpha,\beta), M\,I\,(\beta,\gamma) \therefore MN\,A\,(\alpha,\gamma)$	(II. 5) [2]
[5]	$K\,I\,(\beta,\gamma) \therefore M\,I\,(\beta,\gamma)$	(IV. 7)
[6]	$K\,A\,(\alpha,\beta), K\,I\,(\beta,\gamma) \therefore MN\,A\,(\alpha,\gamma)$	(I. 4) [5, 3]
[7]	$K\,A\,(\alpha,\beta), K\,I\,(\beta,\gamma) \therefore M\,A\,(\alpha,\gamma)$	(I. 4) [5, 4]
[8]	$MN\,A\,(\alpha,\gamma) \therefore MN\,A\,(\alpha,\gamma)$	(IV. 33)
[9]	$M\,A\,(\alpha,\gamma) \therefore M\,I\,(\alpha,\gamma)$	(IV. 34)
[10]	$K\,A\,(\alpha,\beta), K\,I\,(\beta,\gamma) \therefore MN\,A\,(\alpha,\gamma)$	(I. 4) [6, 8]
[11]	$K\,A\,(\alpha,\beta), K\,I\,(\beta,\gamma) \therefore M\,I\,(\alpha,\gamma)$	(I. 4) [7, 9]
[12]	$MN\,A\,(\alpha,\gamma), M\,I\,(\alpha,\gamma) \therefore K\,I\,(\alpha,\gamma)$	(IV. 7)
[13]	$K\,A\,(\alpha,\beta), K\,I\,(\beta,\gamma), K\,A\,(\alpha,\beta), K\,I\,(\beta,\gamma)$	
	$\therefore K\,I\,(\alpha,\gamma)$	(I. 5) [10, 11, 12]
[14]	$K\,A\,(\alpha,\beta), K\,I\,(\beta,\gamma) \therefore K\,I\,(\alpha,\gamma)$	(II. 6) [13]

Compare *An. pr.* 1. 14, 33 a 23–25.

The proof for *Ferio KKK*, which Aristotle treats in *An. pr.* 1. 14, 33 a 25–27, differs from the one for (IV. 74) only in that in line [1] the rule (IV. 38) is applied, and in line [2] the rule (IV. 39) is applied, and in line [9] the rule (IV. 8) is applied.

Authors who give *Darii KKK* a modal predicate-logical interpretation concede no validity to this inference form unless they suppose that the logical structure of both the *K*-premises that occur here and thus the meaning of 'contingently (it is true that) …' is different in the two premises. According to K.J. Schmidt (2000, 121), in *Darii KKK* there are premises of the form $\forall x (\Diamond B x \supset \circ A x)$ and $\exists x (\circ C x \& \circ B x)$, (with $\circ A = \Diamond A \& \Diamond \sim A$). Nortmann puts at the basis of his interpretation the premise formulas $\forall x \Box (B x \supset \circ A x)$ and $\exists x \circ (C x \& \circ B x)$. He shows that, assuming an S5-logic, which admits the law of possibility simplification ($\Diamond \Diamond A \supset \Diamond A$), a valid inference to $\exists x \circ (C x \& \circ A x)$ comes about (Ebert & Nortmann 2007, 516–18).[211] Since Aristotle counts *Darii KKK* among perfect syllogism, i.e., among modes of inference whose validity depends only on the meaning of the logical constants that occur in them, the reconstruction proposals of Schmidt and Nortmann are rather to be rejected.

4. One contingent premise and one assertoric premise in the first figure:

Barbara KXK:
$K A (α, β), A (β, γ) \therefore K A (α, γ)$ (IV. 75)

Proof:

[1]	$K A (α, β) \therefore H (M I (β, γ), M A (α, γ))$	(IV. 36)
[2]	$K A (α, β) \therefore H (M I (β, γ), MN A (α, γ))$	(IV. 37)
[3]	$K A (α, β) \therefore M A (α, β)$	(IV. 7)
[4]	$M A (α, β) \therefore I (α, α)$	(IV. 10)
[5]	$K A (α, β) \therefore I (α, α)$	(I. 4) [3, 4]
[6]	$A (β, γ) \therefore I (γ, γ)$	(III. 1)
[7]	$A (β, γ) \therefore H (I (γ, γ), A (β, γ))$	(III. 1)
[8]	$A (β, γ) \therefore I (β, γ)$	(III. 7)
[9]	$* \therefore H (A (β, γ), I (β, γ))$	(II. 28) [8]
[10]	$H (I (γ, γ), A (β, γ)), H (A (β, γ), I (β, γ))$ $\therefore H (I (γ, γ), I (β, γ))$	(II. 13)
[11]	$*, A (β, γ) \therefore H (I (γ, γ), I (β, γ))$	(I. 5) [7, 9, 10]
[12]	$H (I (γ, γ), I (β, γ)) \therefore H (M I (γ, γ), M I (β, γ))$	(IV. 29)
[13]	$*, A (β, γ) \therefore H (M I (γ, γ), M I (β, γ))$	(I. 4) [11, 12]
[14]	$H (M I (γ, γ), M I (β, γ)), H (M I (β, γ), M A (α, γ))$ $\therefore H (M I (γ, γ), M A (α, γ))$	(II. 13)
[15]	$*, A (β, γ), K A (α, β)$ $\therefore H (M I (γ, γ), M A (α, γ))$	(I. 5) [13, 1, 14]

---

211 On the relationship between the modal syllogistic and S5-logic, see *Appendix 5*.

[16] $H(MI(\gamma, \gamma), M \underset{\sim}{A}(\alpha, \gamma)), H(MI(\gamma, \gamma), MN \underset{\sim}{A}(\alpha, \gamma)), I(\alpha, \alpha), I(\gamma, \gamma)$
 $\therefore KA(\alpha, \gamma)$ (IV. 41)
[17] $*, A(\beta, \gamma), A(\beta, \gamma), KA(\alpha, \beta), KA(\alpha, \beta), KA(\alpha, \beta) \therefore KA(\alpha, \gamma)$ (I. 5) [5, 6, 15, 2, 16]
[18] $*, KA(\alpha, \beta), A(\beta, \gamma) \therefore KA(\alpha, \gamma)$ (II. 6) [17]

Compare *Analytica priora* 1. 15, 33 b 33–36.

For *Celarent KXK* a proof can be given which is analogous to the proof for rule (VI. 75). It differs from the proof for (IV. 75) only in that in lines [1] and [2] the rules (IV. 38) and (IV. 39) are applied and in line [16] the rule (IV. 40) is used. According to Aristotle, this proof proceeds analogously to the proof for *Barbara KXK* (see *An. pr.* 1. 15, 33 b 36–40).

Darii KXK:
$KA(\alpha, \beta), I(\beta, \gamma) \therefore KI(\alpha, \gamma)$ **(IV. 76)**

Proof:
[1] $KA(\alpha, \beta) \therefore H(I(\beta, \gamma), M \underset{\sim}{A}(\alpha, \gamma))$ (IV. 43)
[2] $KA(\alpha, \beta) \therefore H(I(\beta, \gamma), MN \underset{\sim}{A}(\alpha, \gamma))$ (IV. 44)
[3] $KA(\alpha, \beta), I(\beta, \gamma) \therefore M \underset{\sim}{A}(\alpha, \gamma)$ (II. 5) [1]
[4] $KA(\alpha, \beta), I(\beta, \gamma) \therefore MN \underset{\sim}{A}(\alpha, \gamma)$ (II. 5) [2]
[5] $MN \underset{\sim}{A}(\alpha, \gamma) \therefore MN A(\alpha, \gamma)$ (IV. 33)
[6] $M \underset{\sim}{A}(\alpha, \gamma) \therefore MI(\alpha, \gamma)$ (IV. 34)
[7] $MN A(\alpha, \gamma), MI(\alpha, \gamma) \therefore KI(\alpha, \gamma)$ (IV. 7)
[8] $KA(\alpha, \beta), I(\beta, \gamma) \therefore KI(\alpha, \gamma)$ (I. 4) [3, 6, 4, 5, 7]

Compare *Analytica priora* 1. 15, 35 a 30–35.

The analogous proof for *Ferio KXK* can be carried out in such a way that in line [1] it is concluded according to rule (IV. 46), in line [2] according to rule (IV. 45), and in line [7] according to rule (IV. 8). Aristotle, who discusses *Ferio KXK* in *An. pr.* 1. 15, 35 a 30–35, indicates the analogy in its proof.

6. One contingent premise and one apodictic premise in the first figure:

Barbara KLK:
$KA(\alpha, \beta), LA(\beta, \gamma) \therefore KA(\alpha, \gamma)$ **(IV. 77)**

Proof:
[1] $KA(\alpha, \beta), A(\beta, \gamma) \therefore KA(\alpha, \gamma)$ (IV. 75)
[2] $LA(\beta, \gamma) \therefore A(\beta, \gamma)$ (IV. 1)
[3] $KA(\alpha, \beta), LA(\beta, \gamma) \therefore KA(\alpha, \gamma)$ (I. 4) [2, 1]

Compare *An. pr.* 1. 16, 35 b 23 ff. According to Klaus J. Schmidt (2000, 146–49), the necessity premise of *Barbara KLK* has the form $\forall x\ (C\ x \supset \Box\ B\ x)$, which deviates from *modus Barbara LKM* (IV. 94), where this premise is supposed to have the form $\Box \forall x (B x \supset A x)$. A uniform formalization of the modal syllogistic is thus not possible on this reading. According to Nortmann (1996, 115), the necessity premise of *Barbara KLK* has the form $\Box \forall x (C x \supset \Box B x)$. Schmidt and Nortmann agree in that they believe to have discerned the 'perfection' of *modus Barbara KLK* in its inner structure. Nortmann thinks that on the basis of this structure this mode has "the simplicity" of a "easily manageable transitivity inference" (Ebert & Nortmann 2007, 602).

The proof for *Celarent KLK* which Aristotle treats in *An. pr.* 1. 16, 36 a 17–21 differs from the one for (IV. 77) by starting in line [1] from *Celarent KXK*, rather than from *Barbara KXK*. In just the same way, *Darii KLK* and *Ferio KLK* can be derived from *Darii KXK* and *Ferio KXK*, respectively. Incidentally, these forms do not occur in Aristotle, but they are compatible with his suppositions. He merely rules out, in *An. pr.* 1. 16, 36 a 39–36 b 2, that an assertoric conclusion can be inferred from the premises which are assumed in accordance with these rules.

II. Imperfect modal syllogisms

1. Unmixed apodictic syllogisms of the second and third figure:

Cesare LLL
$LN I (\beta, \alpha), L A (\beta, \gamma) \therefore LN I (\alpha, \gamma)$ (IV. 78)

Proof:
[1] $LN I (\alpha, \beta), L A (\beta, \gamma) \therefore LN I (\alpha, \gamma)$ (IV. 62)
[2] $LN I (\beta, \alpha) \therefore LN I (\alpha, \beta)$ (IV. 51)
[3] $LN I (\beta, \alpha), L A (\beta, \gamma) \therefore LN I (\alpha, \gamma)$ (I. 4) [2, 1]

Compare *An. pr.* 1. 8.

Camestres LLL:
$L A (\beta, \alpha), LN I (\beta, \gamma) \therefore LN I (\alpha, \gamma)$ (IV. 79)

Proof:
[1] $LN I (\gamma, \beta), L A (\beta, \alpha) \therefore LN I (\gamma, \alpha)$ (IV. 62)
[2] $LN I (\beta, \gamma) \therefore LN I (\gamma, \beta)$ (IV. 51)
[3] $L A (\beta, \alpha), LN I (\beta, \gamma) \therefore LN I (\gamma, \alpha)$ (I. 4) [1, 2]
[4] $LN I (\gamma, \alpha) \therefore LN I (\alpha, \gamma)$ (IV. 51)
[5] $L A (\beta, \alpha), LN I (\beta, \gamma) \therefore LN I (\alpha, \gamma)$ (I. 4) [3, 4]

Compare *An. pr.* 1. 8.

Festino LLL:
$LN I (\beta, \alpha), L I (\beta, \gamma) \therefore LN A (\alpha, \gamma)$ (IV. 80)

3 Derived Rules § 63 — 237

Proof:

[1]	$LN\,I\,(\alpha,\beta), L\,I\,(\beta,\gamma) \therefore LN\,A\,(\alpha,\gamma)$	(IV. 64)
[2]	$LN\,I\,(\beta,\alpha) \therefore LN\,I\,(\alpha,\beta)$	(IV. 51)
[3]	$LN\,I\,(\beta,\alpha), L\,I\,(\beta,\gamma) \therefore LN\,A\,(\alpha,\gamma)$	(I. 4) [1, 2]

Baroco LLL:

$L\,A\,(\beta,\alpha), LN\,A\,(\beta,\gamma) \therefore LN\,A\,(\alpha,\gamma)$ **(IV. 81)**

Proof:

[1]	$LN\,A\,(\beta,\gamma) \therefore NM\,A\,(\beta,\gamma)$	(IV. 4)
[2]	$NM\,A\,(\beta,\gamma) \therefore LN\,I\,(\beta,\delta)$	(IV. 16)
[3]	$LN\,A\,(\beta,\gamma) \therefore LN\,I\,(\beta,\delta)$	(I. 4) [1, 2]
[4]	$NM\,A\,(\beta,\gamma) \therefore \underline{A}\,(\gamma,\delta)$	(IV. 16)
[5]	$LN\,A\,(\beta,\gamma) \therefore \underline{A}\,(\gamma,\delta)$	(I. 4) [1, 4]
[6]	$\underline{A}\,(\gamma,\delta) \therefore I\,(\gamma,\delta)$	(III. 7)
[7]	$I\,(\gamma,\delta) \therefore M\,I\,(\gamma,\delta)$	(IV. 25)
[8]	$M\,I\,(\gamma,\delta) \therefore M\,I\,(\delta,\gamma)$	(IV. 55)
[9]	$\underline{A}\,(\gamma,\delta) \therefore M\,I\,(\delta,\gamma)$	(I. 4) [6, 7, 8]
[10]	$L\,A\,(\beta,\alpha), LN\,I\,(\beta,\delta) \therefore LN\,I\,(\alpha,\delta)$	(IV. 79)
[11]	$NM\,I\,(\alpha,\delta) \therefore H\,(M\,I\,(\delta,\gamma), LN\,\underline{A}\,(\alpha,\gamma))$	(IV. 13)
[12]	$LN\,I\,(\alpha,\delta) \therefore NM\,I\,(\alpha,\delta)$	(IV. 4)
[13]	$LN\,I\,(\alpha,\delta) \therefore H\,(M\,I\,(\delta,\gamma), LN\,\underline{A}\,(\alpha,\gamma))$	(I. 4) [11, 12]
[14]	$LN\,I\,(\alpha,\delta), M\,I\,(\delta,\gamma) \therefore LN\,\underline{A}\,(\alpha,\gamma)$	(II. 5) [13]
[15]	$L\,A\,(\beta,\alpha), LN\,I\,(\beta,\delta), M\,I\,(\delta,\gamma) \therefore LN\,\underline{A}\,(\alpha,\gamma)$	(I. 4) [10, 1, 14]
[16]	$LN\,I\,(\beta,\delta), L\,A\,(\beta,\alpha), \underline{A}\,(\gamma,\delta) \therefore LN\,\underline{A}\,(\alpha,\gamma)$	(I. 4) [9, 15]
[17]	$L\,A\,(\beta,\alpha), LN\,A\,(\beta,\gamma), LN\,A\,(\beta,\gamma) \therefore LN\,\underline{A}\,(\alpha,\gamma)$	(I. 4) [3, 5, 16]
[18]	$L\,A\,(\beta,\alpha), LN\,A\,(\beta,\gamma) \therefore LN\,\underline{A}\,(\alpha,\gamma)$	(II. 6) [17]
[19]	$N\,\underline{A}\,(\alpha,\gamma) \therefore N\,A\,(\alpha,\gamma)$	(III. 12)
[20]	$* \therefore H\,(N\,\underline{A}\,(\alpha,\gamma), N\,A\,(\alpha,\gamma))$	(II. 28) [19]
[21]	$H\,(N\,\underline{A}\,(\alpha,\gamma), N\,A\,(\alpha,\gamma)), LN\,\underline{A}\,(\alpha,\gamma) \therefore LN\,A\,(\alpha,\gamma)$	(IV. 2)
[22]	$*, LN\,\underline{A}\,(\alpha,\gamma) \therefore LN\,A\,(\alpha,\gamma)$	(I. 4) [20, 21]
[23]	$*, L\,A\,(\beta,\alpha), LN\,A\,(\beta,\gamma) \therefore LN\,A\,(\alpha,\gamma)$	(I. 4) [18, 22]

This complicated proof, with exposition in lines [2] and [4], corresponds to Aristotle's hints in *An. pr* 1. 8, 30 a 9–10.

Disamis LLL:

$L\,I\,(\alpha,\gamma), L\,A\,(\beta,\gamma) \therefore L\,I\,(\alpha,\beta)$ **(IV. 82)**

Proof:

[1]	$L\,A\,(\beta,\gamma), L\,I\,(\gamma,\alpha) \therefore L\,I\,(\beta,\alpha)$	(IV. 63)
[2]	$L\,I\,(\alpha,\gamma) \therefore L\,I\,(\gamma,\alpha)$	(IV. 52)
[3]	$L\,I\,(\beta,\alpha) \therefore L\,I\,(\alpha,\beta)$	(IV. 52)
[4]	$L\,I\,(\alpha,\gamma), L\,A\,(\beta,\gamma) \therefore L\,I\,(\alpha,\beta)$	(I. 4) [2, 1, 3]

Datisi LLL:

$L\,A\,(\alpha,\gamma), L\,I\,(\beta,\gamma) \therefore L\,I\,(\alpha,\beta)$ **(IV. 83)**

Proof:

[1]	$L\,A\,(\alpha,\gamma), L\,I\,(\gamma,\beta) \therefore L\,I\,(\alpha,\beta)$	(IV. 63)
[2]	$L\,I\,(\beta,\gamma) \therefore L\,I\,(\gamma,\beta)$	(IV. 52)
[3]	$L\,A\,(\alpha,\gamma), L\,I\,(\beta,\gamma) \therefore L\,I\,(\alpha,\beta)$	(I. 4) [2, 1]

Ferison LLL:
$LN\,I\,(\alpha,\gamma), L\,I\,(\beta,\gamma) \therefore LN\,A\,(\alpha,\beta)$ **(IV. 84)**

Proof:

[1]	$LN\,I\,(\alpha,\gamma), L\,I\,(\gamma,\beta) \therefore LN\,A\,(\alpha,\beta)$	(IV. 64)
[2]	$L\,I\,(\gamma,\beta) \therefore L\,I\,(\beta,\gamma)$	(IV. 52)
[3]	$LN\,I\,(\alpha,\gamma), L\,I\,(\beta,\gamma) \therefore LN\,A\,(\alpha,\beta)$	(I. 4) [2, 1]

Bocardo LLL:
$LN\,A\,(\alpha,\gamma), L\,A\,(\beta,\gamma) \therefore LN\,A\,(\alpha,\beta)$ **(IV. 85)**

Proof:

[1]	$LN\,A\,(\alpha,\gamma) \therefore NM\,A\,(\alpha,\gamma)$	(IV. 4)
[2]	$NM\,A\,(\alpha,\gamma) \therefore LN\,I\,(\alpha,\delta)$	(IV. 16)
[3]	$LN\,A\,(\alpha,\gamma) \therefore LN\,I\,(\alpha,\delta)$	(I. 4) [1, 2]
[4]	$NM\,A\,(\alpha,\gamma) \therefore A\,(\gamma,\delta)$	(IV. 16)
[5]	$A\,(\gamma,\delta) \therefore I\,(\gamma,\delta)$	(III. 7)
[6]	$I\,(\gamma,\delta) \therefore I\,(\delta,\gamma)$	(III. 18)
[7]	$LN\,A\,(\alpha,\gamma) \therefore I\,(\delta,\gamma)$	(I. 4) [1, 4, 5, 6]
[8]	$L\,A\,(\beta,\gamma) \therefore H\,(I\,(\delta,\gamma), L\,A\,(\beta,\delta))$	(IV. 9)
[9]	$L\,A\,(\beta,\gamma), I\,(\delta,\gamma) \therefore L\,A\,(\beta,\delta)$	(II. 5) [8]
[10]	$A\,(\beta,\delta) \therefore I\,(\beta,\delta)$	(III. 7)
[11]	*$\therefore H\,(A\,(\beta,\delta), I\,(\beta,\delta))$	(II. 28) [10]
[12]	$H\,(A\,(\beta,\delta), I\,(\beta,\delta)), L\,A\,(\beta,\delta) \therefore L\,I\,(\beta,\delta)$	(IV. 2)
[13]	*, $L\,A\,(\beta,\delta) \therefore L\,I\,(\beta,\delta)$	(I. 4) [11, 12]
[14]	*, $L\,A\,(\beta,\gamma), I\,(\delta,\gamma) \therefore L\,I\,(\beta,\delta)$	(I. 4) [9, 13]
[15]	$LN\,I\,(\alpha,\delta), L\,I\,(\beta,\delta) \therefore LN\,A\,(\alpha,\beta)$	(IV. 84)
[16]	*, $LN\,I\,(\alpha,\delta), L\,A\,(\beta,\gamma), I\,(\delta,\gamma) \therefore LN\,A\,(\alpha,\beta)$	(I. 4) [14, 15]
[17]	*, $LN\,A\,(\alpha,\gamma), L\,A\,(\beta,\gamma), LN\,A\,(\alpha,\gamma)$ $\therefore LN\,A\,(\alpha,\beta)$	(I. 4) [3, 7, 16]
[18]	*, $LN\,A\,(\alpha,\gamma), L\,A\,(\beta,\gamma) \therefore LN\,A\,(\alpha,\beta)$	(II. 6) [17]

This proof by exposition in lines [2] and [4] corresponds to Aristotle's description in *An. pr.* 1. 8, 30 a 9 f.

2. Syllogisms of the second and third figure with one assertoric and one apodictic premise:

Cesare LXL:
$LN\,I\,(\alpha,\beta), A\,(\alpha,\gamma) \therefore LN\,I\,(\beta,\gamma)$ **(IV. 86)**

Proof:

[1]	$LN\,I\,(\beta,\alpha),\,A\,(\alpha,\gamma) \therefore LN\,I\,(\beta,\gamma)$	(IV. 66)
[2]	$LN\,I\,(\alpha,\beta) \therefore LN\,I\,(\beta,\alpha)$	(IV. 51)
[3]	$LN\,I\,(\alpha,\beta),\,A\,(\alpha,\gamma) \therefore LN\,I\,(\beta,\gamma)$	(I. 4) [2, 1]

Compare *An. pr.* 1. 10, 30 b 7–13.

General Comment on Section 2 ((IV. 86) – (IV. 89)):

For all syllogisms with the premise combination *LX* or *XL* in the second and third figure, apart from *Baroco* and *Bocardo*, validity proofs can be carried out with conversion, just as they can be carried out for syllogisms of these figures with the premise combination *LL* (see above (IV. 78) to (IV. 85)). In these proofs it is assumed that the syllogisms of the first figure with the corresponding combinations of premises are valid. A premise combination of *LX* or *XL* yields apodictic conclusions in the second figure only with *Camestres XLL* and *Festino LXL*, in the third figure only with *Darapti LXL* and *XLL*, *Felapton LXL*, *Disamis XLL*, *Datisi LXL*, and *Ferison LXL*. *Baroco* and *Bocardo*, with only one apodictic and only one assertoric premise, do not have an apodictic conclusion. That these, as with some of the remaining syllogisms with the premise combination *LX* or *XL*, do not have apodictic conclusions is proven by Aristotle in the manner typical of him elsewhere, with the aid of example substitutions for α, β, and γ.

The relevant invalidity proofs can be easily carried out, just like the validity proofs by conversion. They follow in general the pattern according to which *Cesare LXL* (IV. 86) is proven. It may thus suffice here to consider objections have been raised against the demonstrative force of some of these proofs.

Thus, against the invalidity proof for *Bocardo LXL* (*An. pr.* 1. 11, 32, a 4–5), i.e., for

$$LN\,A\,(\alpha,\gamma),\,A\,(\beta,\gamma) \therefore LN\,A\,(\alpha,\beta),$$

it has been objected that a *weakly* apodictic conclusion cannot be ruled out by the proof. Aristotle substitutes for α, β, and γ the terms 'bipedal', 'in motion', and 'animal' in turn. His argument can be understood as saying that the supposition that necessarily not every animal (e.g., no horse) is bipedal and that (in fact) every animal is in motion is compatible with the supposition that it is possible that everything that is in motion is bipedal (while everything else, including non-bipedal animals, are not in motion). According to this argument, *Bocardo LXL* is not a universally valid inference form. To see the demonstrative force of this argumentation, it suffices, on the one hand, to accept that animals are both capable of being in motion as well as capable of not being in motion, and, on the other hand, tacitly to assume a restricted set of objects as the relevant domain. For example, if one assumes that by 'animals' is meant the pets of Athens, and by 'objects in motion' is meant the objects which are on their feet in Athens, then the case in which everything is bipedal that is in Athens and on its feet is hardly less possible as the case in which all Athenian pets are without exception in motion. If thus the case in which all Athenian pets are in motion, even despite its improbability, is assumed as actually true (as here in the second premise), then indeed at least the bare possibility of the case cannot be ruled out that everything that moves in Athens is bipedal, even if one admits, with the first premise, that necessarily not every animal (and not even every Athenian pet) is bipedal.

Now, the objection to this argumentation does not involve, say, the suggestion that Aristotle's selection of example terms is unsuited for his invalidity proof, but rather the thesis that *Bocardo LXL* is valid and hence that an invalidity proof for it is impossible. Of course, this thesis rests on the assumption that the *L*-premise in *Bocardo LXL* has either (according to Nortmann) the form $\exists x \Box (C x \,\&\, \Box \sim A x)$ or (according to Schmidt) the weaker form $\exists x (C x \,\&\, \Box \sim A x)$, while the *X*-premise has the form $\forall x (C x \supset B x)$. On this assumption, *Bocardo LXL* has, relative to $\exists x \Box (B x \,\&\, \Box \sim A x)$, a *weakly* apodictic conclusion of the form $\exists x (B x \,\&\, \Box \sim A x)$.[212] It can be seen here that the objection brought forth is only convincing if one supposes that the Aristotelian syllogistic admits a variability in the meaning of logical constants. For even Schmidt assumes here such variability, since he supposes for the structure of the apodictic particular negative proposition that, though it does not (as according to Nortmann) vary within one and the same syllogism, it does vary within the system of the Aristotelian modal syllogistic, so that it must be represented sometimes by formulas of the type $\exists x (B x \,\&\, \Box \sim A x)$ but other times by formulas of the type $\exists x \Box (B x \,\&\, \sim A x)$ (see Schmidt 2000, 36 and 43). Such variability jars with Aristotle's basic suppositions.

In Nortmann's view, the proof that Aristotle sketches for the validity of *Camestres XLL* is also mistaken. This proof can be depicted as follows:

Camestres XLL:
$A (\alpha, \beta), LN I (\alpha, \gamma) \therefore LN I (\beta, \gamma)$ (IV. 87)

Proof
[1] $LN I (\gamma, \alpha), A (\alpha, \beta) \therefore LN I (\gamma, \beta)$ (IV. 66)
[2] $LN I (\alpha, \gamma) \therefore LN I (\gamma, \alpha)$ (IV. 51)
[3] $LN I (\gamma, \beta) \therefore LN I (\beta, \gamma)$ (IV. 51)
[4] $LN I (\alpha, \beta), A (\alpha, \beta) \therefore LN I (\beta, \gamma)$ (I. 4) [2, 1, 3]

Compare *An. pr.* 1. 10, 30 b 14–18.

According to Nortmann, the mistake in such a demonstration, in his view, is that the logical form of the conclusion of *Celarent LXL* (IV. 66), whose conversion is carried

---

[212] Ebert & Nortmann 2007, 461; Schmidt 2000, 59.

out in line [3] according to rule (IV. 51), should only be rendered by the formula ∀ x (B x ⊃ □ ~ C x), yet the latter does not imply the formula ∀ x (C x ⊃ □ ~ B x). The conversion in line [3] is thus not permitted. The exposure of the supposed logical error here, with the aid of modal quantificational logic, is in Nortmann's eyes so significant that he states: "One sees in cases like this that the standard schematic presentation of syllogistic reductions in the modal-logical domain which limit themselves to the traditional notation often turn out to be too undifferentiated to be able to guarantee a reliable estimation of the respective logical relationships" (Ebert & Nortmann 2007, 419). Yet Nortmann starts out from assumptions which in my view are not at all borne out. For, first of all, his objection to the proof for *Camestres XLL* assumes that the conclusion of *Celarent LXL* (see my remarks to (IV. 66)), deviates in its logical form from the logical form of the major premise of this mode. Of course, such variability jars with the basic suppositions of Aristotle, and especially not with the fact that *Celarent LXL* belongs among the perfect syllogisms, whose validity rest only on the definition of the logical constants that occur in them. This is already reason enough not to suppose that, if the same bit of logical vocabulary (here the expression '*LN I . . .*') occurs twice in a perfect syllogism, it is used with a different meaning each time. Secondly, Nortmann assumes that apodictic universal negative propositions are only convertible if they have a structure as in the premise position of *Celarent LXL*, namely, a structure which can be rendered by an (S5-logically convertible) formula of the type ∀ x □ (A x ⊃ □ ~ B x). This assumption too is not borne out (see § 59, def. 9) in connection with rule (IV. 13) and the proof of (IV. 51).[213]

Nortmann raises similar objections against the proofs Aristotle carries out for the validity of *Darapti XLL* and *Disamis XLL* as against *Camestres XLL*. These proofs can be presented as follows:

Darapti XLL:
A (α, γ), L A (β, γ) ∴ L I (α, β)   (IV. 88)

Proof:
[1] L A (β, γ), I (γ, α) ∴ L I (β, α)   (IV. 67)
[2] A (α, γ) ∴ I (γ, α)   (III. 19)
[3] L I (β, α) ∴ L I (α, β)   (IV. 52)
[4] A (α, γ), L A (β, γ) ∴ L I (α, β)   (I. 4) [2, 1, 3]

Compare *An. pr.* 1. 11, 31 a 31–33.

---

[213] K.J. Schmidt takes *Camestres XLL* to be valid, but he likewise supposes that the apodictic form in the premise position deviates from the apodictic form in the conclusion position. The latter can be portrayed with the formula ∀x □ (C x ⊃◇ ~ B x), the former with the formula ∀x □ (◇ C x ⊃~ A x). See Schmidt 2000, 51.

Disamis XLL:
$I(\alpha, \gamma), L A (\beta, \gamma) \therefore L I (\alpha, \beta)$ (IV. 89)

Proof:
[1] $L A (\beta, \gamma), I (\gamma, \alpha) \therefore L I (\beta, \alpha)$ (IV. 67)
[2] $I (\alpha, \gamma) \therefore I (\gamma, \alpha)$ (III. 18)
[3] $L I (\beta, \alpha) \therefore L I (\alpha, \beta)$ (IV. 52)
[4] $I (\alpha, \gamma), L A (\beta, \gamma) \therefore L I (\alpha, \beta)$ (I. 4) [2, 1, 3]

Compare *An. pr.* 1. 11, 31 b 16–20.

The conversion carried out in line [3] of both these proofs, of the *L I*-conclusion of the *modus Darii LXL* (IV. 67) used in line [1] of each, is in Nortmann's view illegitimate, since the logical form of this conclusion can in his opinion only be suitably rendered by the formula $\exists x (A x \& \Box \sim B x)$, but this (only *weakly* apodictic) formula does not imply the formula $\exists x (B x \& \Box \sim A x)$. (See Ebert & Nortmann 2007, 445–46 and 456.) It is doubtless true that the *L I*-conclusion that is to be converted in the first line of both proofs should only be understood as stating in each case the necessary pertaining of a predicate β to an object, but not also the necessary pertaining of α. For according to the expression of the second premise in this line, i.e., according to '*I* (γ, α)' and according to the conversion of *I* (γ, α) carried out in line [2], the predicate α pertains to an object γ, which falls under the concepts α and β, only actually or in fact. Hence α does not need to pertain to it necessarily. Yet it is incorrect to suppose that for this reason the *L I*-conclusion that is to be converted can only be suitably rendered by the formula $\exists x (A x \& \Box \sim B x)$. Rather, this conclusion admits a reading in the sense of definition 7 in § 59 and accordingly also admits a conversion according to rule (IV. 51).

3. Imperfect modal syllogisms of the first figure:

Barbara XKM:
$A (\alpha, \beta), K A (\beta, \gamma) \therefore M A (\alpha, \gamma)$ (IV. 90)

Proof:
[1] $N A (\alpha, \gamma), A (\beta, \gamma) \therefore N A (\alpha, \beta)$ (III. 34)
[2] $NN A (\alpha, \beta), A (\beta, \gamma) \therefore NN A (\alpha, \gamma)$ (I. 2) [1]
[3] $NN A (\alpha, \beta) \therefore H (A (\beta, \gamma), NN A (\alpha, \gamma))$ (II. 1) [2]
[4] $H (A (\beta, \gamma), NN A (\alpha, \gamma))$
    $\therefore H (M A (\beta, \gamma), MNN A (\alpha, \gamma))$ (IV. 29)
[5] $NN A (\alpha, \beta) \therefore H (M A (\beta, \gamma), MNN A (\alpha, \gamma))$ (I. 4) [3, 4]
[6] $NN A (\alpha, \beta), M A (\beta, \gamma) \therefore MNN A (\alpha, \gamma)$ (II. 5) [5]
[7] $A (\alpha, \beta) \therefore NN A (\alpha, \beta)$ (I. 1)
[8] $K A (\beta, \gamma) \therefore M A (\beta, \gamma)$ (IV. 7)

[9]	MNN A (α, γ) ∴ NLN A (α, γ)	(IV. 6)
[10]	NLN A (α, γ) ∴ M A (α, γ)	(IV. 3)
[11]	MNN A (α, γ) ∴ M A (α, γ)	(I. 4) [9, 10]
[12]	A (α, β), K A (β, γ) ∴ M A (α, γ)	(I. 4) [7, 8, 6, 11]

Aristotle proves the validity of rule (IV. 90) in *An. pr.* 1. 15, 34 a 34–b 2 likewise with *reductio ad impossibile*, i.e., by means of (I. 2). As the starting point for his proof, he selects a rule of the third figure and indicates that it is *modus Bocardo* (III. 34), as in line [1] above. The procedure in this proof of first replacing the *K*-premise with a non-modalized premise is designated by Alexander of Aphrodisias as metalepsis (*In de An. pr.* 217, 10). – According to K.J. Schmidt, *Barbara XKM* is not universally valid (see Schmidt 2000, 128–38). According to Nortmann, in the framework of an S4-logic, *Barbara XKM* can be justified as an inference from the premise $\forall x \Box (B x \supset A x)$, which here (despite the '$\Box$') is supposed to hold as assertoric, and the premise $\forall x \Box (C x \supset (\Diamond B x \& \Diamond \sim B x))$, to $\forall x \Box (C x \supset \Diamond A x)$ (see Ebert & Nortmann 2007, 557).[214]

Nortmann justifies rendering an assertoric premise with $\forall x \Box (B x \supset A x)$ by referencing 34 b 7 ff., where Aristotle says that in the present case the *A* premise should not be regarded as a statement about a temporally restricted, contingent fact, or else an invalidity proof for *Barbara XKM* could result. Aristotle may be thinking here of a kind of invalidity proof like the one he previously carried out for *Bocardo LXL* in *An. pr.* 1. 11, 32 a 4 f. (see my *General Comment* to section 2, (VI. 86) to (VI. 89)) (p. ff.)). The distinction which Aristotle here suggests for the assertoric statements corresponds to the distinction between two kinds of the 'factual' or actual, which I have pointed out above in § 6, note 40. According to Nortmann, we would have to suppose that this distinction corresponds to the distinction between the formulas $\forall x \Box (B x \supset A x)$ and $\forall x (B x \supset A x)$. But this should by no means be accepted. For a statement of the form $\forall x (B x \supset A x)$ is already true if there is no *x* at all to which *B x* would apply. Accordingly, the proposition, e.g., $\forall x$ ([now moves on this table] $x \supset$ [is an ant] x) is already true when there is nothing that now moves on this table. By contrast, in this case one would have to regard the proposition 'Everything that now moves on this table is an ant' as false if it is to be understood as a proposition that says something about a contingent fact. –

Aristotle describes the proof for *Celarent XKM* in *An. pr.* 1. 15, 34 b 19–16 as proceeding similarly to the proof for *Barbara XKM*, which takes *modus Disamis* as its starting point. Rule (IV. 29), which is used in both proofs, is briefly introduced by Aristotle in *An. pr.* 1. 15, 34 a 20–25, before he sketches both proofs.

---

[214] On the relationship between the modal syllogistic and S4-logic, see *Appendix 5*.

Celarent XKM:
$NI(\alpha, \beta), KA(\beta, \gamma) \therefore MNI(\alpha, \gamma)$ (IV. 91)

Proof:
[1]	$I(\alpha, \gamma), A(\beta, \gamma) \therefore I(\alpha, \beta)$	(III. 32)
[2]	$NI(\alpha, \beta), A(\beta, \gamma) \therefore NI(\alpha, \gamma)$	(I. 2) [1]
[3]	$NI(\alpha, \beta) \therefore H(A(\beta, \gamma), NI(\alpha, \gamma))$	(II. 1) [2]
[4]	$H(A(\beta, \gamma), NI(\alpha, \gamma)) \therefore H(MA(\beta, \gamma), MNI(\alpha, \gamma))$	(IV. 29)
[5]	$NI(\alpha, \beta) \therefore H(MA(\beta, \gamma), MNI(\alpha, \gamma))$	(I. 4) [3, 4]
[6]	$NI(\alpha, \beta), MA(\beta, \gamma) \therefore MNI(\alpha, \gamma)$	(II. 5) [5]
[7]	$KA(\beta, \gamma) \therefore MA(\beta, \gamma)$	(IV. 7)
[8]	$NI(\alpha, \beta), KA(\beta, \gamma) \therefore MNI(\alpha, \gamma)$	(I. 4) [7, 6]

In *An. pr.* 1. 15, 35 a 3–20, Aristotle points out that due to the 'complementary convertibility' of propositions of the form $KNI(\beta, \gamma)$ to $KA(\beta, \gamma)$ according to rule (IV. 48), the second premise in syllogisms of the form *Barbara XKM* and *Celarent XKM* is exchangeable for $KNI(\beta, \gamma)$.

Darii XKM:
$A(\alpha, \beta), KI(\beta, \gamma) \therefore MI(\alpha, \gamma)$ (IV. 92)

Proof:
[1]	$NI(\alpha, \gamma), I(\beta, \gamma) \therefore NA(\alpha, \beta)$	(III. 35)
[2]	$NNA(\alpha, \beta), I(\beta, \gamma) \therefore NNI(\alpha, \gamma)$	(I. 2) [1]
[3]	$NNA(\alpha, \beta) \therefore H(I(\beta, \gamma), NNI(\alpha, \gamma))$	(II. 1) [2]
[4]	$H(I(\beta, \gamma), NNI(\alpha, \gamma)) \therefore H(MI(\beta, \gamma), MNNI(\alpha, \gamma))$	(IV. 29)
[5]	$NNA(\alpha, \beta) \therefore H(MI(\beta, \gamma), MNNI(\alpha, \gamma))$	(I. 4) [3, 4]
[6]	$NNA(\alpha, \beta), MI(\beta, \gamma) \therefore MNNI(\alpha, \gamma)$	(II. 5) [5]
[7]	$A(\alpha, \beta) \therefore NNA(\alpha, \beta)$	(I. 1)
[8]	$KI(\beta, \gamma) \therefore MI(\beta, \gamma)$	(IV. 7)
[9]	$MNNI(\alpha, \gamma) \therefore NLNI(\alpha, \gamma)$	(IV. 6)
[10]	$NLNI(\alpha, \gamma) \therefore MI(\alpha, \gamma)$	(IV. 3)
[11]	$MNNI(\alpha, \gamma) \therefore MI(\alpha, \gamma)$	(I. 4) [9, 10]
[12]	$A(\alpha, \beta), KI(\beta, \gamma) \therefore MI(\alpha, \gamma)$	(I. 4) [7, 8, 6, 11]

Aristotle points out in *An. pr.* 1. 15, 35 a 35–40 that the proofs for the validity of *Darii XKM* and *Ferio XKM* are carried out in just the same way as the proofs for *Barbara XKM* and *Celarent XKM*, respectively. Following this (15, 35 b 2–8), Aristotle points out in addition that due to the 'complementary convertibility' of propositions of the form $KNA(\beta, \gamma)$ to $KI(\beta, \gamma)$ according to rule (IV. 50), the second premise in syllogisms of the form *Darii XKM* and *Ferio XKM* is exchangeable with $KNA(\beta, \gamma)$. – According to Nortmann, *Darii XKM* is valid if one supposes that it deals with the consequence of $\exists x (\Diamond Bx \& \Diamond Ax)$ from $\forall x \Box (Cx \supset Ax)$ and $\exists x (\circ Bx \& \circ Cx)$ (with $\circ A = \Diamond A \& \Diamond \sim A$). In that case, $\forall x \Box (Cx \supset Ax)$ is supposed to be taken as an assertoric formula, despite the appearance of $\Box$ (Ebert & Nortmann 2007, 696).

Ferio XKM:
$NI(\alpha, \beta), KI(\beta, \gamma) \therefore MNA(\alpha, \gamma)$ **(IV. 93)**

Proof:
[1] $A(\alpha, \gamma), I(\beta, \gamma) \therefore I(\alpha, \beta)$ (III. 33)
[2] $NI(\alpha, \beta), I(\beta, \gamma) \therefore NA(\alpha, \gamma)$ (I. 2) [1]
[3] $NI(\alpha, \beta) \therefore H(I(\beta, \gamma), NA(\alpha, \gamma))$ (II. 1) [2]
[4] $H(I(\beta, \gamma), NA(\alpha, \gamma)) \therefore H(MI(\beta, \gamma), MNA(\alpha, \gamma))$ (IV. 29)
[5] $NI(\alpha, \beta) \therefore H(MI(\beta, \gamma), MNA(\alpha, \gamma))$ (I. 4) [3, 4]
[6] $NI(\alpha, \beta), MI(\beta, \gamma) \therefore MNA(\alpha, \gamma)$ (II. 5) [5]
[7] $KI(\beta, \gamma) \therefore MI(\beta, \gamma)$ (IV. 7)
[8] $NI(\alpha, \beta), KI(\beta, \gamma) \therefore MNA(\alpha, \gamma)$ (I. 4) [7, 6]

Barbara LKM:
$LA(\alpha, \beta), KA(\beta, \gamma) \therefore MA(\alpha, \gamma)$ **(IV. 94)**

Proof:
[1] $LA(\alpha, \beta), LNA(\alpha, \gamma) \therefore LNA(\beta, \gamma)$ (IV. 81)
[2] $LA(\alpha, \beta), NLNA(\beta, \gamma) \therefore NLNA(\alpha, \gamma)$ (I. 2) [1]
[3] $NLNA(\alpha, \gamma) \therefore MA(\alpha, \gamma)$ (IV. 3)
[4] $MA(\beta, \gamma) \therefore NLNA(\beta, \gamma)$ (IV. 3)
[5] $KA(\beta, \gamma) \therefore MA(\beta, \gamma)$ (IV. 7)
[6] $LA(\alpha, \beta), KA(\beta, \gamma) \therefore MA(\alpha, \gamma)$ (I. 4) [4, 5, 2, 3]

Aristotle proves the validity of *Barbara LKM* in *An. pr.* 1. 16, 36 b 38–26 a 1.

Celarent LKX:
$LNI(\alpha, \beta), KA(\beta, \gamma) \therefore NI(\alpha, \gamma)$ **(IV. 95)**

Proof:
[1] $LNI(\beta, \alpha), I(\alpha, \gamma) \therefore LNA(\beta, \gamma)$ (IV. 68)
[2] $LNI(\beta, \alpha), NLNA(\beta, \gamma) \therefore NI(\alpha, \gamma)$ (I. 2) [1]
[3] $MA(\beta, \gamma) \therefore NLNA(\beta, \gamma)$ (IV. 3)
[4] $KA(\beta, \gamma) \therefore MA(\beta, \gamma)$ (IV. 7)
[5] $LNI(\beta, \alpha), KA(\beta, \gamma) \therefore NI(\alpha, \gamma)$ (I. 4) [4, 3, 2]
[6] $LNI(\alpha, \beta) \therefore LNI(\beta, \alpha)$ (IV. 51)
[7] $LNI(\alpha, \beta), KA(\beta, \gamma) \therefore NI(\alpha, \gamma)$ (I. 4) [6, 5]

Compare *An. pr.* 1. 16, 36 a 8–10.

Ferio LKX:
$LNI(\alpha, \beta), KI(\beta, \gamma) \therefore NA(\alpha, \gamma)$ **(IV. 96)**

Proof:
[1] $LNI(\beta, \alpha), A(\alpha, \gamma) \therefore LNI(\beta, \gamma)$ (IV. 66)
[2] $LNI(\beta, \alpha), NLNI(\beta, \gamma) \therefore NA(\alpha, \gamma)$ (I. 2) [1]
[3] $MI(\beta, \gamma) \therefore NLNI(\beta, \gamma)$ (IV. 3)
[4] $KI(\beta, \gamma) \therefore MI(\beta, \gamma)$ (IV. 7)

[5]	$LNI(\beta, \alpha), KI(\beta, \gamma) \therefore NA(\alpha, \gamma)$	(I. 4) [4, 3, 2]
[6]	$LNI(\alpha, \beta) \therefore LNI(\beta, \alpha)$	(IV. 51)
[7]	$LNI(\alpha, \beta), KI(\beta, \gamma) \therefore NA(\alpha, \gamma)$	(I. 4) [6, 5]

Compare *An. pr.* 1. 16, 36 a 34–36.

Darii LKM:
$LA(\alpha, \beta), KI(\beta, \gamma) \therefore MI(\alpha, \gamma)$ **(IV. 97)**

Proof:
[1]	$LA(\alpha, \beta), LNI(\alpha, \gamma) \therefore LNI(\beta, \gamma)$	(IV. 79)
[2]	$LA(\alpha, \beta), NLNI(\beta, \gamma) \therefore NLNI(\alpha, \gamma)$	(I. 2) [1]
[3]	$NLNI(\alpha, \gamma) \therefore MI(\alpha, \gamma)$	(IV. 3)
[4]	$MI(\beta, \gamma) \therefore NLNI(\beta, \gamma)$	(IV. 3)
[5]	$KI(\beta, \gamma) \therefore MI(\beta, \gamma)$	(IV. 7)
[6]	$LA(\alpha, \beta), KI(\beta, \gamma) \therefore MI(\alpha, \gamma)$	(I. 4) [4, 5, 2, 3]

Celarent LKM:
$LNI(\alpha, \beta), KA(\beta, \gamma) \therefore MNI(\alpha, \gamma)$ **(IV. 98)**

Proof:
[1]	$LNI(\alpha, \beta), KA(\beta, \gamma) \therefore NI(\alpha, \gamma)$	IV. 95)
[2]	$NI(\alpha, \gamma) \therefore MNI(\alpha, \gamma)$	(IV. 25)
[3]	$LNI(\alpha, \beta), KA(\beta, \gamma) \therefore MNI(\alpha, \gamma)$	(I. 4) [1, 2]

Compare *An. pr.* 1. 16, 36 a 15–17. Similarly to the proof for the validity of *Celarent LKM*, on the assumption of (IV. 96), the validity of *Ferio LKM* can also be proven. Compare *An. pr.* 1. 16, 36 a 32–33.

4. Syllogisms of the second figure, one premise assertoric, the other contingent:

Cesare XKM
$NI(\alpha, \beta), KA(\alpha, \gamma) \therefore MNI(\beta, \gamma)$ **(IV. 99)**

Proof:
[1]	$NI(\beta, \alpha), KA(\alpha, \gamma) \therefore MNI(\beta, \gamma)$	(IV. 91)
[2]	$NI(\alpha, \beta) \therefore NI(\beta, \alpha)$	(III. 17)
[3]	$NI(\alpha, \beta), KA(\alpha, \gamma) \therefore MNI(\beta, \gamma)$	(I. 4) [2, 1]

Compare *An. pr.* 1. 18, 37 b 23–28. An exactly similar proof can be run for *Festino XKM*, if one starts in line [1] from *Ferio XKM* (IV. 93) rather than from *Celarent XKM*. Compare Aristotle, *An. pr.* 1. 18, 38 a 3 f.

Camestres KXM:
$KA(α, β), NI(α, γ) ∴ MNI(β, γ)$ (IV. 100)

Proof:
[1] $NI(γ, α), KA(α, β) ∴ MNI(γ, β)$ (IV. 91)
[2] $NI(α, γ) ∴ NI(γ, α)$ (III. 17)
[3] $MNI(γ, β) ∴ MNI(β, γ)$ (IV. 54)
[4] $KA(α, β), NI(α, γ) ∴ MNI(β, γ)$ (I. 4) [2, 1, 3]

Compare *An. pr.* 1. 18, 37 b 29.

5. Syllogisms of the second figure, one premise apodictic, the other contingent:

Cesare LKM
$LNI(α, β), KA(α, γ) ∴ MNI(β, γ)$ (IV. 101)

Proof:
[1] $NI(β, α), KA(α, γ) ∴ MNI(β, γ)$ (IV. 91)
[2] $LNI(α, β) ∴ LNI(β, α)$ (IV. 51)
[3] $LNI(β, α) ∴ NI(β, α)$ (IV. 1)
[4] $LNI(α, β) ∴ NI(β, α)$ (I. 4) [2, 3]
[5] $LNI(α, β), KA(α, γ) ∴ MNI(β, γ)$ (I. 4) [4, 1]

Compare *An. pr.* 1. 19, 38 a 16–21. The proof could also be carried out by weaking the conclusion in (IV. 102) to an *M*-conclusion according to rule (IV. 25). In the same way, *Camestres LKM* and *Festino LKM* can be derived from *Camestres KLX* (IV. 103) and *Festino LKX* (IV. 104), respectively.

Cesare LKX
$LNI(α, β), KA(α, γ) ∴ NI(β, γ)$ (IV. 102)

Proof:
[1] $LNI(α, β), I(β, γ) ∴ LNA(α, γ)$ (IV. 68)
[2] $LNI(α, β), NLNA(α, γ) ∴ NI(β, γ)$ (I. 2) [1]
[3] $MA(α, γ) ∴ NLNA(α, γ)$ (IV. 3)
[4] $KA(α, γ) ∴ MA(α, γ)$ (IV. 7)
[5] $LNI(α, β), KA(α, γ) ∴ NI(β, γ)$ (I. 4) [4, 3, 2]

Compare *An. pr.* 1.19, 38 a 21–25.

Camestres KLX:
$KA(α, β), LNI(α, γ) ∴ NI(β, γ)$ (IV. 103)

Proof:
[1] $LNI(α, γ), I(γ, β) ∴ LNA(α, β)$ (IV. 68)
[2] $NLNA(α, β), LNI(α, γ) ∴ NI(γ, β)$ (I. 2) [1]

[3]	$MA(α, β) \therefore NLNA(α, β)$	(IV. 3)
[4]	$KA(α, β) \therefore MA(α, β)$	(IV. 7)
[5]	$KA(α, β), LNI(α, γ) \therefore NI(β, γ)$	(I. 4) [4, 3, 2]

Compare *An. pr.* 1. 19, 38 a 25 f.

Festino LKX:

$LNI(α, β), KI(α, γ) \therefore NA(β, γ)$	**(IV. 104)**

Proof:

[1]	$LNI(β, α), KI(α, γ) \therefore NA(β, γ)$	IV. 96)
[2]	$LNI(α, β) \therefore LNI(β, α)$	(IV. 51)
[3]	$LNI(α, β), KI(α, γ) \therefore NA(β, γ)$	(I. 4) [1, 2]

Compare *An. pr.* 1. 19, 38 a 25–27.

The non-canonical syllogism $LNI(α, β), KNA(α, γ) \therefore NA(β, γ)$ can be derived from *Festino LKX* by 'complementary conversion' according to rule (IV. 50). Further non-canonical syllogisms of the second figure can be similarly derived by 'complementary conversion' according to rules (IV. 47) to (IV. 50), from valid syllogisms of the first figure with a *K*-premise, e.g., syllogisms each with three propositions of the form *LNI*, *KNI*, and *MNI* (19, 38 b 6–12), or *LNI*, *KNI*, and *MNA* (19, 38 b 31–35), or *KNI*, *LNI*, and *MNI* (19, 38 b 12).

General Comment on Section 5 ((IV. 101) – (IV. 104)):

Concerning syllogisms in the second figure with one apodictic premise and the other contingent, the modern literature has contested not so much the relevant validity proofs of Aristotle as his proofs for the invalidity of singular modes of inference with the premise combinations *KL* and *LK*. However, it seems to me that there are opportunities to object only inasmuch as one starts from an understanding of the logical constants occurring in these modes of inference that does not correspond to the understanding expressed in the definitions of § 59. It should suffice here to comment on this issue with the help of an example. Thus, Nortmann views Aristotle's proof for the invalidity of *Cesare KLX*, i.e., for the inference form

$$KNI(α, β), LA(α, γ) \therefore NI(β, γ),$$

as erroneous. Aristotle runs the proof (see *An. pr.* 1. 19, 38 a 38–42) by substituting the terms 'in motion', 'animal', and 'in a waking state' for α, β, and γ, in sequence. Accordingly, he supposes that the inference:

> *Every animal is contingently at one time not in motion,*
> *Every being which is in a waking state is necessarily in motion,*
> *Therefore: no being which is in a waking state is an animal,*

is invalid because its conclusion is false. Aristotle even supposes that not only the contradictory of this conclusion (namely, 'Some being which is in a waking state is a living being'), but also the stronger statement 'Every being which is in a waking state is an animal' (38 b 1–2), is true. This supposition needs a comment, for apparently Aristotle assumes along with it – as happens occasionally elsewhere in his invalidity proofs (e.g., in the invalidity proof for *Bocardo LXL* (see above p. 340–41)) – a restricted domain of individuals. According to the views Aristotle holds elsewhere, there are animate beings (e.g., plants) to which something like a waking state can hardly be ascribed. Accordingly, one must presume that Aristotle supposes a restricted domain, so that by 'animal' in the conclusion (but then also already in its first premise) only, e.g., beasts or mammals are meant. The two remaining terms require an interpretation as well if both premises (by Aristotle's own standards) are supposed to be taken as true. At best, they are true if by 'motion' – Aristotle speaks even more generally in the present context of "change" (κίνησις, 38 a 42) – *particular* motions or changes are meant. For (in Aristotle's view as well) it should hold for all animals without exception that they necessarily have (*some* kind of) motion or change. The second premise suggests the presumption that Aristotle is thinking in both premises of a kind of motion which necessarily occurs in animals in a waking state. According to this presumption, 'motion' would be understood as something like the active intake of sensory stimuli.[215] On this reading, the first premise would be replaced by the surely true proposition 'Every mammal is contingently not in a condition of the active intake of sensory stimuli'; the second premise would be replaced by the likewise true proposition 'Everything that is in a waking state is necessarily in a condition of the active intake of sensory stimuli'. In this way, Aristotle's argumentation can admit a reading which shows it to present an example of the invalidity of inferences according to *modus Cesare KLX*, namely an example in which the premises are true and the conclusion false. The invalidity proof is thus unobjectionable.

---

215 That Aristotle is thinking of motions or changes which are necessarily, i.e., in all circumstances, connected to being awake is ultimately suggested by the fact that he makes formulaic use of his supposition that being in motion belongs to all that is awake in other invalidity proofs as well. See, e.g., 38 b 35–37 or 40 a 36–38. Consider especially that in *Parva Naturalia* 454 b 24–27 (1984, 723) "animal" or "beast" (ζῷον) is *defined* by "possessing sense-perception" (αἴσθησις); sleep is "as it were, a motionless bond, imposed on sense-perception (ἀκινησία)"; being awake is the "loosening or remission [of this bond]."

In Nortmann's view, by contrast, this proof is not unobjectionable.[216] His objection is to supposing the truth of the second premise, i.e., the proposition

Every being which is in a waking state is necessarily in motion.

For Nortmann, this proposition can be understood either as a statement about a pure *de dicto* necessity, i.e., as a statement of the form

(1) $\Box \forall x$ ([is awake] $x \supset$ [is in motion] x),

or as a statement of one of the following forms (if not as a statement that at least comes close to one of these forms):

(2) $\forall x$ ([is awake] $x \supset \Box$ [is in motion] x),
    $\forall x$ ($\Box$ [is awake] $x \supset \Box$ [is in motion] x),
    $\forall x$ ($\Diamond$ [is awake] $x \supset \Box$ [is in motion] x).

As a statement of the form (1), the premise could, Nortmann believes, indeed appear to be "plausible," but it would then have a logical form that necessity statements precisely cannot have in the framework of Aristotle's modal syllogistic. For it can be regarded as "sufficiently secure" that the Aristotelian modal syllogistic does not treat necessity statements like propositions of the form (1). However, as a statement of one of the forms under (2), the premise in question would have "no doubt [to be] taken as false". "Since for every awake animal, there is a possibility (to fall into sleep and then) not to be in motion."

Of course, this objection is only convincing if it may be assumed that the alternative of forms (1) and (2) is complete. But this assumption is not borne out. For this alternative leaves out of consideration the form

(3) *L A (in motion, awake)*,

which according to § 59, definition 6, and according to rule (IV. 9) implies the expression 'If something (e.g., a ξ) is awake, then it (this ξ) is necessarily in motion', whose logical form is represented by

(3') *H (I (awake, ξ), L A (in motion, ξ))*.

To be sure, (3) (just like (1)) can be considered as a form of a statement about a *de dicto* necessity. For (3) can be rendered by the proposition 'It is necessarily true that everything awake is in motion'. But since (3) implies the form (3'), (3) can just as well

---

216 See for the following Ebert & Nortmann 2007, 662–64 and 672.

(in a similar way as (2)) be understood as a form of a statement about a *de re* necessity. To that extent, (3) is a necessity statement neither "of a pure *de dicto* type", nor (like $\forall x (A x \supset \Box B x)$) "of a pure *de re* type" (to use Nortmann's phraseology). This is because (3') is equivalent to the *de dicto* necessity statement

(3″) *LH* (*I* (*awake*, ξ), *A* (*in motion*, ξ)).

One can therefore regard (3') as a necessity statement of a latent *de dicto* type, just as one can regard (3) as a necessity statement of a latent *de re* type. (3) and (3') are expressions that are not supposed to render different kinds of necessity, but rather one and the same kind of necessary truth, i.e., a kind of truth which is distinct from mere actual truth, e.g., the truth of the proposition 'Everything that is awake is less than 500 years old' (whether this should be true at once time or over larger periods of time). Since the term 'moves' in the context of the invalidity proof we have just considered must mean (as already mentioned) a state which is necessarily involved in waking states, (3') should be taken as a proposition which cannot be false. The possibility of being able to sleep (which is mentioned by Nortmann) and then no longer being in motion, which holds for any animal that is awake, does not stand in logical conflict with the statement of the second premise that if something (e.g., an animal) is awake, it is also necessarily in motion. The necessity of the truth of this statement rests simply on the fact that the concept of the state of motion involved in the waking state is subordinate to the concept of the waking state, so that the concept of the object which moves in a specific way due to its waking state is also subordinate to the concept of waking (just as the concept of the human being is subordinate to that of the animal); while, on the other hand, the concept of the object which is in a state of motion contingent for animals is not subordinate to the concept of the animal.

6. Syllogisms of the third figure, both premises contingent:

Darapti KKK:
$K A (α, γ), K A (β, γ) \therefore K I (α, β)$ **(IV. 105)**

Proof:
[1] $K A (α, γ), K I (γ, β) \therefore K I (α, β)$ (IV. 74)
[2] $K A (β, γ) \therefore K I (γ, β)$ (IV. 58)
[3] $K A (α, γ), K A (β, γ) \therefore K I (α, β)$ (I. 4) [2, 1]

Compare *An. pr.* 1. 20, 39 a 14–19. *Felapton KKK* can likewise be derived in three lines, starting from *Ferio KKK* rather than from *Darii KKK* (IV. 74). Compare *An. pr.* 1. 19, 39 a 19–23.

Datisi KKK:
$K A (\alpha, \gamma), K I (\beta, \gamma) \therefore K I (\alpha, \beta)$ (IV. 106)

Proof:
[1] $K A (\alpha, \gamma), K I (\gamma, \beta) \therefore K I (\alpha, \beta)$ (IV. 74)
[2] $K I (\beta, \gamma) \therefore K I (\gamma, \beta)$ (IV. 57)
[3] $K A (\alpha, \gamma), K I (\beta, \gamma) \therefore K I (\alpha, \beta)$ (I. 4) [2, 1]

Compare *An. pr.* 1. 20, 39 a 31–35.

Disamis KKK:
$K I (\alpha, \gamma), K A (\beta, \gamma) \therefore K I (\alpha, \beta)$ (IV. 107)

Proof:
[1] $K A (\beta, \gamma), K I (\gamma, \alpha) \therefore K I (\beta, \alpha)$ (IV. 74)
[2] $K I (\alpha, \gamma) \therefore K I (\gamma, \alpha)$ (IV. 57)
[3] $K I (\beta, \alpha) \therefore K I (\alpha, \beta)$ (IV. 57)
[4] $K I (\alpha, \gamma), K A (\beta, \gamma) \therefore K I (\alpha, \beta)$ (I. 4) [2, 1, 3]

Compare *An. pr.* 1. 20, 39 a 35–36.

Bocardo KKK:
$KN A (\alpha, \gamma), K A (\beta, \gamma) \therefore KN A (\alpha, \beta)$ (IV. 108)

Proof:
[1] $KN I (\beta, \gamma), K I (\gamma, \alpha) \therefore KN A (\beta, \alpha)$ Ferio KKK
[2] $KN A (\alpha, \gamma) \therefore K I (\alpha, \gamma)$ (IV. 50)
[3] $K I (\alpha, \gamma) \therefore K I (\gamma, \alpha)$ (IV. 57)
[4] $KN A (\alpha, \gamma) \therefore K I (\gamma, \alpha)$ (I. 4) [2, 3]
[5] $K A (\beta, \gamma) \therefore KN I (\beta, \gamma)$ (IV. 47)
[6] $KN A (\beta, \alpha) \therefore KN A (\alpha, \beta)$ (IV. 59)
[7] $KN A (\alpha, \gamma), K A (\beta, \gamma) \therefore KN A (\alpha, \beta)$ (I. 4) [4, 5, 1, 6]

Compare *An. pr.* 1. 20, 39 a 36–37.

Ferison KKK:
$KN I (\alpha, \gamma), K I (\beta, \gamma) \therefore KN A (\alpha, \beta)$ (IV. 109)

Proof:
[1] $KN I (\alpha, \gamma), K I (\gamma, \beta) \therefore KN A (\alpha, \beta)$ Ferio KKK
[2] $K I (\beta, \gamma) \therefore K I (\gamma, \beta)$ (IV. 57)
[3] $KN I (\alpha, \gamma), K I (\beta, \gamma) \therefore KN A (\alpha, \beta)$ (I. 4) [2, 1]

Compare *An. pr.* 1. 20, 39 a 36–37.

Through 'complementary conversion' according to rules (IV. 47) to (IV. 50), additional modes of the third figure with two contingent premises can be derived from canonical modes that have already been proven valid. Aristotle explicitly points out the following three non-canonical modes (IV. 107) to (IV. 112):

$KNI(α, γ), KNI(β, γ) ∴ KI(α, β)$ **(IV. 110)**

Proof:
[1] $KA(α, γ), KA(β, γ) ∴ KI(α, β)$ IV. 105)
[2] $KNI(α, γ) ∴ KA(α, γ)$ (IV. 48)
[3] $KNI(β, γ) ∴ KA(β, γ)$ (IV. 48)
[4] $KNI(α, γ), KNI(β, γ) ∴ KI(α, β)$ (I. 4) [3, 2, 1]

Compare *An. pr.* 1. 20, 39 a 26–28.

$KNI(α, γ), KNA(β, γ) ∴ KNA(α, β)$ **(IV. 111)**

Proof:
[1] $KA(α, γ), KI(β, γ) ∴ KI(α, β)$ IV. 106)
[2] $KNI(α, γ) ∴ KA(α, γ)$ (IV. 48)
[3] $KNA(β, γ) ∴ KI(β, γ)$ (IV. 50)
[4] $KI(α, β) ∴ KNA(α, β)$ (IV. 49)
[5] $KNI(α, γ), KNA(β, γ) ∴ KNA(α, β)$ (I. 4) [3, 2, 1, 4]

Compare *An. pr.* 1. 20, 39 a 26–28.

$KNI(α, γ), KNA(β, γ) ∴ KI(α, β)$ **(IV. 112)**

Proof:
[1] $KNI(α, γ), KI(β, γ) ∴ KNA(α, β)$ IV. 109)
[2] $KNA(β, γ) ∴ KI(β, γ)$ (IV. 50)
[3] $KNA(α, β) ∴ KI(α, β)$ (IV. 50)
[3] $KNI(α, γ), KNA(β, γ) ∴ KI(α, β)$ (I. 4) [2, 1, 3]

Compare *An. pr.* 1. 20, 39 a 38–b 2. According to the same pattern, Aristotle was able derive still further non-canonical modes, such as, e.g., the following:

$KA(α, γ), KNI(β, γ) ∴ KI(α, β)$ **(IV. 113)**

Proof:
[1] $KA(α, γ), KA(β, γ) ∴ KI(α, β)$ IV. 105)
[2] $KA(β, γ) ∴ KNI(β, γ)$ (IV. 47)
[3] $KA(α, γ), KNI(β, γ) ∴ KI(α, β)$ (I. 4) [2, 1]

7. Syllogisms of the third figure, one premise assertoric, the other contingent:

Darapti XKM:
$A(α, γ), KA(β, γ) ∴ MI(α, β)$ **(IV. 114)**

Proof:
[1] $A(α, γ), KI(γ, β) ∴ MI(α, γ)$ IV. 92)
[2] $KA(β, γ) ∴ KI(γ, β)$ (IV. 58)
[3] $A(α, γ), KA(β, γ) ∴ MI(α, β)$ (I. 4) [2, 1]

Compare *An. pr.* 1. 21, 39 b 10–14.

If rule (IV. 57) is applied in line [2], according to which one may move from KI (β, γ) to KI (γ, β), then *Datisi XKM* results (*An. pr.* 1. 21, 39 a 39 b 26–31). By contrast, *Felapton XKM* results if one begins in line [1] from *Ferio XKM* instead of *Darii XKM* (IV. 92) (compare *An. pr.* 1. 21, 39 b 17–19). To derive *Ferison XKM*, one can likewise begin in line [1] with *Ferio XKM*, but one then has to start with KI (β, γ) for the conversion in line [2], thus applying rule (IV. 57). Compare *An. pr.* 1. 21, 39 b 26–31.

Syllogisms of the third figure can be derived from *Darapti XKM* and *Felapton XKM* by 'complementary conversion' according to rule (IV. 48), which are each formed from three propositions of the form *A, KNI,* and *MI* and *NI, KNI,* and *MNA*, respectively (39 b 22–25).

According to Nortmann, *Darapti XKM* should be regarded as an S4-logical consequence of $\exists x (\Diamond Bx \,\&\, \Diamond Ax)$ from $\forall x \Box (Cx \supset Ax)$ and $\forall x \Box (Cx \supset \circ Bx) \,\&\, \exists x \Diamond Cx$ (with $\circ A = \Diamond A \,\&\, \Diamond {\sim} A$) (see Ebert & Nortmann 2007, 698).[217]

Darapti KXK:
KA (α, γ), A (β, γ) ∴ KI (α, β)   (IV. 115)

Proof:
[1] KA (α, β), I (β, γ) ∴ KI (α, γ)   (IV. 76)
[2] A (β, γ) ∴ I (γ, β)   (III. 19)
[3] KA (α, γ), A (β, γ) ∴ KI (α, β)   (I. 4) [2, 1]

Compare *An. pr.* 1. 21, 39 b 16–20. *Felapton KXK* can be derived according to the same rule, if one replaces rule (IV. 76) in line [1], i.e., *Darii KXK*, with *Ferio KXK* (*An. pr.* 1. 21, 39 b 17–19). By contrast, *Datisi KXK* results by applying the rule of particular *I*-conversion (III. 18) to *Darii KXK*. Compare *An. pr.* 1. 21, 39 b 26–31.

Disamis XKK:
I (α, γ), KA (β, γ) ∴ KI (α, β)   (IV. 116)

Proof:
[1] KA (β, γ), I (γ, α) ∴ KI (β, α)   (IV. 76)
[2] I (α, γ) ∴ I (γ, α)   (III. 18)
[3] KI (β, α) ∴ KI (α, β)   (IV. 57)
[4] I (α, γ), KA (β, γ) ∴ KI (α, β)   (I. 4) [2, 1, 3]

Whether Aristotle has rule (IV. 116) in mind when he mentions, in *An. pr.* 1. 21, 39 b 26–31, a combination of premises characteristic of *Disamis XKK* with an inference to a "being possible" (Ebert & Nortmann 2007, 57) is questionable.

---

[217] On the relationship between S4-logic and the modal syllogistic, see *Appendix 5*.

3 Derived Rules § 63 — 255

Disamis KXM:
$K I (α, γ), A (β, γ) ∴ M I (α, β)$ (IV. 117)

Proof:
[1] $A (β, γ), K I (γ, α) ∴ M I (β, α)$ IV. 92)
[2] $K I (α, γ) ∴ K I (γ, α)$ (IV. 57)
[3] $M I (β, α) ∴ M I (α, β)$ (IV. 55)
[4] $K I (α, γ), A (β, γ) ∴ M I (α, β)$ (I. 4) [2, 1, 3]

Compare *An. pr.* 1. 21, 39 b 26–31.

Bocardo KXM:
$KN A (α, γ), A (β, γ) ∴ MN A (α, β)$ (IV. 118)

Proof:
[1] $L A (α, β), A (β, γ) ∴ L A (α, γ)$ (IV. 65)
[2] $NL A (α, γ), A (β, γ) ∴ NL A (α, β)$ (I. 2) [1]
[3] $NL A (α, β) ∴ MN A (α, β)$ (IV. 6)
[4] $MN A (α, γ) ∴ NL A (α, γ)$ (IV. 6)
[5] $KN A (α, γ) ∴ MN A (α, γ)$ (IV. 8)
[6] $KN A (α, γ) ∴ NL A (α, γ)$ (I. 4) [5, 4]
[7] $KN A (α, γ), A (β, γ) ∴ MN A (α, β)$ (I. 4) [6, 3, 2]

Compare *An. pr.* 1. 21, 39 b 31–39. – Since according to rules (IV. 49) and (IV. 50), $K I$ propositions and $KN A$ propositions may be converted into each other, additional modes can be derived from (IV. 114) to (IV. 118).

Nortmann bases his reconstruction of the validity proof for *Bocardo KXM* (IV. 118) on the supposition that the formula of the conclusion of *Barbara LXL* (IV. 65) (i.e., the formula $L A (α, β)$ (see line [1]) may be translated into the formula $\forall x \Box (C x \supset \Box A x)$, so that the proof is led to its end successfully from this point, though only in the framework of an S4-logic (Ebert & Nortmann 2007, 706–12). Yet in his reconstruction of the validity proof for *Barbara LXL*, he had supposed that for this mode of inference only a weakened conclusion was possible, namely, $\forall x (C x \supset \Box A x)$. (See my remarks to (IV. 65) above.)

8. Syllogisms of the third figure, one premise apodictic, the other contingent:

Darapti LKM:
$L A (α, γ), K A (β, γ) ∴ M I (α, β)$ (IV. 119)

Proof:
[1] $L A (α, γ), K I (γ, β) ∴ M I (α, β)$ IV. 97)
[2] $K A (β, γ) ∴ K I (γ, β)$ (IV. 58)
[3] $L A (α, γ), K A (β, γ) ∴ M I (α, β)$ (I. 4) [2, 1]

Compare *An. pr.* 1. 21, 40 a 11–15.

Darapti KLK:
$KA(\alpha, \gamma), LA(\beta, \gamma) \therefore KI(\alpha, \beta)$ (IV. 120)

Proof:
[1]	$KA(\alpha, \gamma), LI(\gamma, \beta) \therefore KI(\alpha, \beta)$	Darii KLK
[2]	$LA(\beta, \gamma) \therefore LI(\gamma, \beta)$	(IV. 53)
[3]	$KA(\alpha, \gamma), LA(\beta, \gamma) \therefore KI(\alpha, \beta)$	(I. 4) [2, 1]

Compare *An. pr.* 1. 21, 40 a 16–18.

Felapton KLK:
$KNI(\alpha, \gamma), LA(\beta, \gamma) \therefore KNA(\alpha, \beta)$ (IV. 121)

Proof:
[1]	$KNI(\alpha, \gamma), LI(\gamma, \beta) \therefore KNA(\alpha, \beta)$	Ferio KLK
[2]	$LA(\beta, \gamma) \therefore LI(\gamma, \beta)$	(IV. 53)
[3]	$KNI(\alpha, \gamma), LA(\beta, \gamma) \therefore KNA(\alpha, \beta)$	(I. 4) [2, 1]

Compare *An. pr.* 1. 21, 40 a 18–23.

Felapton LKX:
$LNI(\alpha, \gamma), KA(\beta, \gamma) \therefore NA(\alpha, \beta)$ (IV. 122)

Proof:
[1]	$LNI(\alpha, \gamma), KI(\gamma, \beta) \therefore NA(\alpha, \beta)$	IV. 96)
[2]	$KA(\beta, \gamma) \therefore KI(\gamma, \beta)$	(IV. 58)
[3]	$LNI(\alpha, \gamma), KA(\beta, \gamma) \therefore NA(\alpha, \beta)$	(I. 4) [2, 1]

Compare *An. pr.* 1. 21, 40 a 25–32.

Further modes can be derived from *Darpapti LKM, Darapti KLK, Felapton KLK,* and *Felapton LKX* through 'complementary conversion' according to one of the rules (IV. 47) to (IV. 50).

Datisi LKM
$LA(\alpha, \gamma), KI(\beta, \gamma) \therefore MI(\alpha, \beta)$ (IV. 123)

Proof:
[1]	$LA(\alpha, \gamma), KI(\gamma, \beta) \therefore MI(\alpha, \beta)$	IV. 97)
[2]	$KI(\beta, \gamma) \therefore KI(\gamma, \beta)$	(IV. 57)
[3]	$LA(\alpha, \gamma), KI(\beta, \gamma) \therefore MI(\alpha, \beta)$	(I. 4) [2, 1, 3]

Compare *An. pr.* 1. 22, 40 a 40–40 b 2. A mode of the third figure with a combination of an *L A* and *KN A* premise can be derived from *Datisi* LKM through 'complementary conversion' according to rule (IV. 50).

Datisi KLK
$KA(\alpha, \gamma), LI(\beta, \gamma) \therefore KI(\alpha, \beta)$ **(IV. 124)**

Proof:
[1] $KA(\alpha, \gamma), LI(\gamma, \beta) \therefore KI(\alpha, \beta)$ *Darii KLK*
[2] $LI(\beta, \gamma) \therefore LI(\gamma, \beta)$ (IV. 52)
[3] $KA(\alpha, \gamma), LI(\beta, \gamma) \therefore KI(\alpha, \beta)$ (I. 4) [2, 1]

Compare *An. pr.* 1. 22, 40 a 40–40 b 2.

Disamis LKK
$LI(\alpha, \gamma), KA(\beta, \gamma) \therefore KI(\alpha, \beta)$ **(IV. 125)**

Proof:
[1] $KA(\beta, \gamma), LI(\gamma, \alpha) \therefore KI(\beta, \alpha)$ *Darii KLK*
[2] $LI(\alpha, \gamma) \therefore LI(\gamma, \alpha)$ (IV. 52)
[3] $KI(\beta, \alpha) \therefore KI(\alpha, \beta)$ (IV. 57)
[4] $LI(\alpha, \gamma), KA(\beta, \gamma) \therefore KI(\alpha, \beta)$ (I. 4) [2, 1, 3]

Compare *An. pr.* 1. 22, 40 a 40–40 b 2. Since a conversion is possible in line [3] according to rule (IV. 57), and it is not necessary to assign modal predicate-logical formulas to the premises in line [1], we do not need to suppose with Nortmann that only a weaker *M* conclusion is thinkable for *Disamis* with an *L* major premise and a *K* minor premise. (See the commentary on this passage in Ebert & Nortmann 2007, 730–31.)

Through 'complementary conversion' according to rule (IV. 48) and (IV. 49), modes of the third figure with a *KN I*-premise or with a *KN A* conclusion can be derived from *Disamis LKK*.

Something similar holds for the application of 'complementary conversion' to *Disamis KLK* according to rules (IV. 50) and (IV. 49). Compare *An. pr.* 1. 22, 40 b 8–10.

Disamis KLK
$LI(\alpha, \gamma), KA(\beta, \gamma) \therefore KI(\alpha, \beta)$ **(IV. 126)**

Proof:
[1] $KA(\beta, \gamma), LI(\gamma, \alpha) \therefore KI(\beta, \alpha)$ *Darii KLK*
[2] $LI(\alpha, \gamma) \therefore LI(\gamma, \alpha)$ (IV. 52)
[3] $LI(\alpha, \gamma), KA(\beta, \gamma) \therefore KI(\alpha, \beta)$ (I. 4) [2, 1]

Compare *An. pr.* 1. 22, 40 a 40–40 b 2.

Ferison KLK
$KNI(\alpha, \gamma), LI(\beta, \gamma) \therefore KNA(\alpha, \beta)$ **(IV. 127)**

Proof:
[1] $KNI(\alpha, \gamma), LI(\gamma, \beta) \therefore KNA(\alpha, \beta)$ *Ferio KLK*

[2] $L\,I\,(\beta, \gamma) \therefore L\,I\,(\gamma, \beta)$ (IV. 52)
[3] $KN\,I\,(\alpha, \gamma), L\,I\,(\beta, \gamma) \therefore KN\,A\,(\alpha, \beta)$ (I. 4) [2, 1]

Compare *An. pr.* 1. 22, 40 b 2–3.

Ferison LKX
$LN\,I\,(\alpha, \gamma), K\,I\,(\beta, \gamma) \therefore N\,A\,(\alpha, \beta)$ **(IV. 128)**

Proof:
[1] $LN\,I\,(\alpha, \gamma), K\,I\,(\gamma, \beta) \therefore N\,A\,(\alpha, \beta)$ IV. 96)
[2] $K\,I\,(\beta, \gamma) \therefore K\,I\,(\gamma, \beta)$ (IV. 57)
[3] $LN\,I\,(\alpha, \gamma), K\,I\,(\beta, \gamma) \therefore N\,A\,(\alpha, \beta)$ (I. 4) [2, 1]

Compare *An. pr.* 1. 22, 40 b 3–4.

Bocardo KLM
$KN\,A\,(\alpha, \gamma), L\,A\,(\beta, \gamma) \therefore MN\,A\,(\alpha, \beta)$ **(IV. 129)**

Proof:
[1] $L\,A\,(\beta, \gamma), K\,I\,(\gamma, \alpha) \therefore M\,I\,(\beta, \alpha)$ Darii LKM
[2] $KN\,A\,(\alpha, \gamma) \therefore K\,I\,(\alpha, \gamma)$ (IV. 50)
[3] $K\,I\,(\alpha, \gamma) \therefore K\,I\,(\gamma, \alpha)$ (IV. 57)
[4] $KN\,A\,(\alpha, \gamma) \therefore K\,I\,(\gamma, \alpha)$ (I. 4) [2, 3]
[5] $M\,I\,(\beta, \alpha) \therefore M\,I\,(\alpha, \beta)$ (IV. 55)
[6] $KN\,A\,(\alpha, \gamma), L\,A\,(\beta, \gamma) \therefore MN\,A\,(\alpha, \beta)$ (I. 4) [4, 1, 5]

Compare *An. pr.* 1. 22, 40 b 2–3.

Bocardo LKX
$LN\,A\,(\alpha, \gamma), K\,A\,(\beta, \gamma) \therefore N\,A\,(\alpha, \beta)$ **(IV. 130)**

Proof:
[1] $A\,(\alpha, \beta), K\,A\,(\beta, \gamma) \therefore M\,A\,(\alpha, \gamma)$ IV. 90)
[2] $NM\,A\,(\alpha, \gamma), K\,A\,(\beta, \gamma) \therefore N\,A\,(\alpha, \beta)$ (I. 2) [1]
[3] $LN\,A\,(\alpha, \gamma) \therefore NM\,A\,(\alpha, \gamma)$ (IV. 4)
[4] $LN\,A\,(\alpha, \gamma), K\,A\,(\beta, \gamma) \therefore N\,A\,(\alpha, \beta)$ (I. 4) [2, 1, 3]

Compare *An. pr.* 1. 22, 40 b 3–6. Aristotle points out in *An. pr.* 1. 22, 40 b 8–10 that further, non-canonical modes can be derived from modes that have already been proven as valid through 'complementary conversion' according to one of the rules (IV. 47) to (IV. 50), such as, e.g., the following mode:

$L\,I\,(\alpha, \gamma), KN\,I\,(\beta, \gamma) \therefore K\,I\,(\alpha, \beta)$ **(IV. 131)**

Proof:
[1] $L\,I\,(\alpha, \gamma), K\,A\,(\beta, \gamma) \therefore K\,I\,(\alpha, \beta)$ IV. 126)
[2] $KN\,I\,(\beta, \gamma) \therefore K\,A\,(\beta, \gamma)$ (IV. 48)
[3] $L\,I\,(\alpha, \gamma), KN\,I\,(\beta, \gamma) \therefore K\,I\,(\alpha, \beta)$ (I. 4) [2, 1]

III. Concluding Remarks to Section Four of Part II, 'Modal Syllogistic'

The reconstruction carried out in this Section, both of proofs of the validity of Aristotelian modal syllogisms as well as the invalidity of certain modal-logical modes of inference that Aristotle held to be invalid, shows that the Aristotelian modal syllogistic is a unified and internally coherent and consistent system of rules. In this reconstruction, I have, just like Ulrich Nortmann, let myself be guided by the "interesting question, which also corresponds to a well-established research tradition," of "how far one can do justice to the modal-logical chapters in their entirety with uniform presentations of the relevant types of statement" (Ebert & Nortmann 2007, 451). The interpretive maxims that Nortmann sets up turn out to be helpful: on the one hand, to admit the hypothesis that "Aristotle could here and there let logical mistakes creep in", but, on the other hand, to accept that "every interpretation of the modal syllogistic [must] have the aim of neither imputing too many errors to Aristotle, nor charging him with too trivial errors" (Ebert & Nortmann 2007, 277). As Nortmann is inclined to think, "One will hardly expect otherwise than that for each of Aristotle's validity claims that one encounters in the modal part of his syllogistic, some modal predicate-logical presentation of the thematized syllogistic statements can be found which allows the claim to be verified – so that with a corresponding variation of the presentations, the number of mistakes diagnosed in Aristotle can be easily minimized" (Ebert & Nortmann 2007, 451). An undertaking that would save as many parts of the Aristotelian modal syllogistic as possible at the cost of its coherence and systematic unity seems to me (as to Nortmann) to be a much less interesting and productive one than the attempt to stuck to a single (and as simple as possible) interpretive approach in the reconstruction of this system from start to finish.

It seems to me that such an attempt has been successfully carried out with the interpretative approach I have adopted in the present Section, even if I concede that in many details more precise textual analyses would be needed to verify that this approach nowhere comes into conflict with Aristotle's basic suppositions and the argumentative steps. This is a task to which, in my opinion, future investigations should be devoted. It could be that, when this task is achieved, here and there modifications of my interpretive approach will be required. Yet the suppositions I have formulated in § 59 regarding the meaning of the logical constants accepted by Aristotle and the basic rules of § 60, corresponding to these suppositions, have proven their worth in making demonstrable the throughgoing conclusiveness of the proofs in different parts of Aristotle's modal-logical system; and this seems to me to speak in favor of these suppositions' being essentially in agreement with the basic suppositions of Aristotle. To be sure, the definitions of § 59 may in some details be different than the definitions Aristotle explicitly mentions and which can be supposed to lay at the basis of his proofs for perfect syllogisms. They are surely different in their form. But in their content, they may largely agree with the Aristotelian definitions. If one pays attention to the precise content of these definitions, it should be seen that the logical constants whose meanings they determine at least approximate a natural and ordinary use of the expressions of the modal-syllogistic vocabulary.

In this way, the present reconstruction also shows that the undertaking to render rules of the Aristotelian syllogistic in a language I have called the elementary language of the syllogistic in Part I of this book is clearly superior to the attempt to translate these rules into the language of the calculus of functions, enriched with the vocabulary of modal logic. Until now, as far as I know, no one has been able to show that a modal predicate-logical interpretation of the Aristotelian modal syllogistic is possible as a uniform, coherent, and consistent system of rules that rests on precise and gapless proofs. By contrast, as has been shown here, it is completely possible to present the Aristotelian modal syllogistic as a system that exemplifies such qualities if it occurs in a notation which is the language of the elementary syllogistic.

Finally, it has also been shown in this way that, if one adds the results of the first three Sections of Part II of this book, it is possible to present the *entire* Aristotelian syllogistic as a uniform, coherent, and consistent system that rests on unobjectionable proofs. In this presentation, the logic of Aristotle can be recognized as a permanent scientific achievement, of which Hegel (1816, 21–22) has rightly said that it "must fill us with greatest admiration for the strength of this mind." To be sure, this achievement concerns, from a contemporary point of view, a relatively small sphere of logic as a whole. But since it would be inappropriate to regard the Aristotelian syllogistic with Günther Patzig (1969, 198) only as "the theory of a specific sphere of logic for two-place relations", which as a "specific theory" could not be "general", it is instead appropriate to say that its rules, because of their general validity, are foundational for logic in its entirety, so that Aristotle can be regarded, with greater right than any other logician, as the founder of *general* logic. That this is so will be seen even more clearly in what follows.

Section Five
Contentful Syllogistic Inference

Contentful syllogistic inference consists simply in putting in contentfully determinate propositions or concept expressions (i.e., propositions like 'Socrates is mortal' or concept expressions like 'mortal' and 'human being') in place of propositional or conceptual variables in the schemata for syllogistic inferences and consequences. However, in the present Section I will consider contentful syllogistic inferences only insofar as they contain contentfully determinate concept expressions which implicitly occur in the calculus of functions as well and play a foundational role in it. To this extent, this Section has only a preparatory character with respect to the sixth and seventh Sections. It shows that the language of the calculus of functions differs from the language of the syllogistic mainly in that the former involves complex conceptual contents and logically relevant structures of such contents. This Section also shows that this involvement entails a linguistic transformation of the logical rules of the syllogistic, without in any way affecting the validity of these rules. It shows, finally, that contrary to a widespread opinion, the syllogistic is completely capable of explaining the logical validity of inferences that seem to obey no rules other than those peculiar to the calculus of functions.

§ 64 Notation

To be able to present some concrete conceptual contents which may occur in premises and conclusions of syllogistic inferences, I will substitute for some concept variables certain conceptual constants and for others certain constellations of logical and descriptive signs of the following kind.

(1) I use as logical signs:
(a) the three quantifier prefixes '($\forall\ x_i$) ...' (as the prefix for the universal quantifier), '($\exists\ x_i$) ...' (as the prefix for the existential quantified) and '($\nabla\ x_i$) ...' (as the quantifier prefix for a singular proposition) (each with $i \geq 1$),
(b) the predicator prefix '($'x_i$) ...' (with $i \geq 1$).

(2) As descriptive signs I use:
(a) Individual constants 'a_1', 'a_2', 'a_3', etc.;
(b) Functional expressions

'$F_1(x_1)$', '$F_2(x_1)$', '$F_3(x_1)$', etc.,
'$F_1(x_1, x_2)$', '$F_2(x_1, x_2)$', '$F_3(x_1, x_2)$', etc.,
⋮
'$F_1(x_1, \ldots, x_n)$', '$F_2(x_1, \ldots, x_n)$', '$F_3(x_1, \ldots, x_n)$', (with $n > 2$) etc.;

in these expressions the different argument places (in which the individual variables 'x_1', 'x_2', ..., 'x_n' appear) can be fully or partly occupied by individual constants; they can also be occupied, fully or partly, by one and the same individual constant or by one and the same individual variable;

(c) Conceptual constants 'ξ_1', 'ξ_2', 'ξ_3' etc., and 'ζ_1', 'ζ_2', 'ζ_3', etc.

(3) Metalinguistic designations:

(a) As a substitute for an individual variable 'x_1' or 'x_2' or 'x_3' etc., I use the italicized lower-case letter '*v*'.

(b) As a substitute for an individual constant 'a_1' or 'a_2' or 'a_3' etc., I use the italicized lower-case letter '*t*'.

(c) As a substitute for an arbitrary (and arbitrarily complex) functional expression, but which contains only one freely occurring variable '*v*', I use one of the expressions 'A (*v*)', 'B (*v*)', 'C (*v*)', etc.

(d) As a substitute for a conceptual constant 'ξ_1' or ξ_2' or 'ξ_3', etc., I use 'ξ' (without an index numeral) and likewise for a conceptual constant 'ζ_1', or 'ζ_2' or 'ζ_3', etc., I use 'ζ' (without an index numeral).

(4) Abbreviations:

(a) 'F_1', 'F_2', and 'F_3' may be abbreviated by '*F*', '*G*', and '*K*', 'x_1', 'x_2', and 'x_3' by '*x*', '*y*', and '*z*', and finally 'a_1', 'a_2', and 'a_3' by '*a*', '*b*', and '*c*'.

(b) 'A ((*v*) A (*v*), ζ)' is abbreviated by '[A (*t*)]',
'A ((*v*) A (*v*), ξ)' by '($\forall$ *v*) A (*v*)',
'I ((*v*) A (*v*), ξ)' by '($\exists$ *v*) A (*v*)' and finally
'A ((*v*) A (*v*), ξ)' by '(∇ *v*) A (*v*)'.

The square brackets in '[A (*t*)]' deserve special notice, since they may not be set aside without further ado. Namely, if A equals *N* B, then '[A (*t*)]' abbreviates the expression 'A ((*v*) *N* B (*v*), ζ)', which, it should be noted, is not equivalent to '*N* A ((*v*) B (*v*), ζ)'. Hence, '[*N* B (*t*)]' and '*N* [B (*t*)]' are not equivalent either. The square brackets may be omitted only if it is provable that two formulas, which differ from each other only by the occurrence of one of these two expressions in each, render equally valid rules.

§ 65 Comments on the Notation

With the signs and sign connectors I have introduced in § 64 and which I will discuss more precisely in what follows, expressions are introduced which stand for concept words or components of certain concept expressions. Among such components, I also count the expressions which are called quantifiers in modern logic books. These are abbreviations for expressions which take the place of the *grammatical* subject in categorical propositions, but they can also appear as components of concept words.

1. The conceptual constant ξ abbreviates the specific concept expression 'object which is a member of the non-empty domain of the objects designated by "v". This constant can take the place of a concept variable in a syllogistic expression.

2. The conceptual constant ζ abbreviates the specific concept expression 'bearer of the proper name t'. This constant can also take the place of a concept variable in a syllogistic expression.

3. The predicator ($'v$) always appears as a prefix, and always in connection with a functional expression which by itself contains a freely occurring individual variable v. This prefix transforms an open proposition of the form A (v) into a concept expression, so that '($'v$) A (v)' is equivalent to the concept expression 'object which is designated by "v" in A (v) and for which A (v) holds'.

4. The universal quantifier ($\forall\ v$) always appears as a prefix, and always in connection with a functional expression which by itself contains a freely occurring individual variable v. This prefix transforms an open proposition of the form A (v) into a universal affirmative categorical proposition, so that '($\forall\ v$) A (v)' is equivalent to the syllogistic expression A (($'v$) A (v), ξ).

5. The existential quantifier ($\exists\ v$) always appears as a prefix, and always in connection with a functional expression which by itself contains a freely occurring individual variable v. This prefix transforms an open proposition of the form A (v) into a particular affirmative categorical proposition, so that '($\exists\ v$) A (v)' is equivalent to the syllogistic expression I (($'v$) A (v), ξ).

6. The quantifier ($\nabla\ v$) always appears as a prefix, and always in connection with a functional expression which by itself contains a freely occurring individual variable v. This prefix transforms an open proposition of the form A (v) into a singular affirmative categorical proposition, so that '($\nabla\ v$) A (v)' is equivalent to the syllogistic expression '$\underline{A}$ (($'v$) A (v), ξ)'.

Remark: The relationship between an open proposition A (v) and one of the expressions which transforms this proposition into a closed proposition, i.e., the relationship between A (*v*) and one of the expressions *t*, (∀ *v*), (∃ *v*) and (∇ *v*), corresponds to the relationship between the *grammatical* predicate and a *grammatical* subject of a categorical proposition. The grammatical subject is, namely, that part of the proposition which specifies or names that about which a categorical proposition deals. By contrast, the grammatical predicate is that part of the proposition which contains what the categorical proposition states about what it deals with (cf. § 27). Thus, *t*, (∀ *v*), (∃ *v*) or (∇ *v*) name or specify that about which a certain categorical proposition deals, namely, taken in sequence: the individual *t*, every individual *v*, some individual *v*, or precisely the individual *v*. By contrast, A (*v*) contains precisely that which is categorically stated about these subjects, namely: that A (*v*). ('A (*v*)' here means the same as '*v* is an A', where '*v*' only designates an empty place.)

Hence, the prefix ('*v*) can be taken as an operator which transforms a grammatical predicate A (*v*) into a logical predicate, i.e., into a concept expression (a so-called term). Namely, '('*x*) A *x*', '('*y*) B (*y*)', etc. are to be regarded as expressions which can stand for concept expressions of an *arbitrary* content, in the same way as 'α', 'β', etc. can. In other words, they fulfill the same task as concept variables. Unlike them, '('*x*) F *x*', '('*y*) G (*y*)', etc. always stand for concept expressions of a specific content. Namely, these expressions indicate that they correspond exclusively to *one-place* (monadic) functional expressions '*F* (*x*)', '*G* (*y*)', etc.

Frege noticed that functions have something to do with concepts and objects have something to do with arguments of functions. Yet since he confused the grammatical predicate with the logical predicate and the grammatical subject with the logical subject, he erroneously believed he could equate concepts with functions and that '*F* (*a*)' expresses not a relation between concepts, but rather stands for a "logically basic relation" (see §§ 25–28 and §§ 32–35 above).

§ 66 Examples of Contentful Syllogistic Inference

The language of signs discussed in § 65 can be employed directly for the sake of presenting concrete contentful inferences (not only modes of inference or inference rules). It goes without saying that all valid rules and modes of inference from §§ 53–63 remain valid when concept expressions of the form ('*v*) A (*v*), with an arbitrary interpretation for A, are substituted for a concept variable (α, β, . . .) in all places of its occurrence. But there is also a kind of contentful inference whose validity, though it is based on universally valid basic syllogistic rules, is not derivable from these as before. Consider as illustration the following inference.

Example:

> All circles are figures.
> Thus: if someone draws something that is not a figure, then someone draws something that is not a circle.

This inference can be presented symbolically in such a way that one makes use only of syllogistic formulas, but in that case a notation like the one discussed in § 65 must be used.

To this end, we can introduce the following conventions for the translation of the terms 'circle' and 'figure'. The functional sign '$C(x_1)$' abbreviates the open proposition (or the grammatical predicate) '... is a circle'. Then the formula '$('x_1) C(x_1)$' stands for the specific term 'circle'. In the same way, '$F(x_1)$' serves to abbreviate the grammatical predicate '... is a figure', so that '$('x_1) F(x_1)$' stands for the specific term 'figure'. On the basis of these two stipulations, we may render the premise of the above inference: 'All circles are figures' with the formula

$$'A (('x_1) F(x_1), ('x_1) C(x_1))'.$$

In addition, we can render the proposition 'this object is a circle' with the formula

$$'\underline{A} (('x_1) C(x_1), \xi_1)',$$

and, similarly, the proposition 'if something is a circle, then it is a figure' with the formula

$$'H (I (('x_1) C(x_1), \xi_1), \underline{A} (('x_1) F(x_1), \xi_1)'.$$

Now let the functional sign '$D(x_2, x_1)$' abbreviate 'x_2 draws x_1'. The expression '$('x_2) (\exists x_1) D(x_2, x_1)$' is then equivalent to the term 'drawer of something', whereby 'something' means a member of the domain which is referenced in the x_2-position of the functional sign that appears in the present context. On the basis of this further stipulation, we may write for 'someone draws an object':

$$'I (('x_2) (\exists x_1) D(x_2, x_1), \xi_2))'.$$

The proposition 'If someone draws something, then this is not a figure' can be expressed by the formula

$$'H (I (('x_2) (\exists x_1) D(x_2, x_1), \xi_2)), N \underline{A} (('x_1) F(x_1), \xi_1))',$$

so that the proposition, 'If someone draws something that is not a figure, then someone draws something that is not a circle' takes the following shape:

$$H\,(H\,(I\,((`x_2)\,(\exists\,x_1)\,D\,(x_2, x_1),\,\xi_2),\,N\,A\,((`x_1)\,F\,(x_1),\,\xi_1)),$$
$$H\,(A\,((`x_2)\,(\exists\,x_1)\,D\,(x_2, x_1),\,\xi_2),\,N\,A\,((`x_1)\,C\,(x_1),\,\xi_1))).$$

The following proof shows that exclusively syllogistic rules can be brought into play to make clear the validity of this inference.

Proof:

[1] $A\,((`x_1)\,F\,(x_1),\,(`x_1)\,C\,(x_1))$
$\therefore H\,(I\,((`x_1)\,C\,(x_1),\,\xi_1),\,A\,((`x_1)\,F\,(x_1),\,\xi_1))$ (III. 1)

[2] $A\,((`x_1)\,F\,(x_1),\,(`x_1)\,C\,(x_1)),\,I\,((`x_1)\,C\,(x_1),\,\xi_1)$
$\therefore A\,((`x_1)\,F\,(x_1),\,\xi_1)$ (II. 5) [1]

[3] $A\,((`x_1)\,C\,(x_1),\,\xi_1)\,\therefore I\,((`x_1)\,C\,(x_1),\,\xi_1)$ (III. 7)

[4] $A\,((`x_1)\,F\,(x_1),\,(`x_1)\,C\,(x_1)),\,A\,((`x_1)\,C\,(x_1),\,\xi_1)$
$\therefore A\,((`x_1)\,F\,(x_1),\,\xi_1)$ (I. 4) [2, 3]

[5] $A\,((`x_1)\,F\,(x_1),\,(`x_1)\,C\,(x_1)),\,N\,A\,((`x_1)\,F\,(x_1),\,\xi_1)$
$\therefore N\,A\,((`x_1)\,C\,(x_1),\,\xi_1))$ (I. 2) [4]

[6] $A\,((`x_1)\,F\,(x_1),\,(`x_1)\,C\,(x_1))$
$\therefore H\,(N\,A\,((`x_1)\,F\,(x_1),\,\xi_1),\,N\,A\,((`x_1)\,C\,(x_1),\,\xi_1))$ (II. 1) [5]

[7] $H\,(I\,((`x_2)\,(\exists\,x_1)\,D\,(x_2, x_1),\,\xi_2),\,N\,A\,((`x_1)\,F\,(x_1),\,\xi_1)),$
$H\,(N\,A\,((`x_1)\,F\,(x_1),\,\xi_1),\,N\,A\,((`x_1)\,C\,(x_1),\,\xi_1))$
$\therefore H\,(I\,((`x_2)\,(\exists\,x_1)\,D\,(x_2, x_1),\,\xi_2),\,N\,A\,((`x_1)\,C\,(x_1),\,\xi_1))$ (II. 13)

[8] $A\,((`x_1)\,F\,(x_1),\,(`x_1)\,C\,(x_1)),$
$H\,(I\,((`x_2)\,(\exists\,x_1)\,D\,(x_2, x_1),\,\xi_2),\,N\,A\,((`x_1)\,F\,(x_1),\,\xi_1))$
$\therefore H\,(I\,((`x_2)\,(\exists\,x_1)\,D\,(x_2, x_1),\,\xi_2),\,N\,A\,((`x_1)\,C\,(x_1),\,\xi_1))$ (I. 4) [6, 7]

[9] $A\,((`x_1)\,F\,(x_1),\,(`x_1)\,C\,(x_1))\,\therefore$
$H\,((H\,(I\,((`x_2)\,(\exists\,x_1)\,D\,(x_2, x_1),\,\xi_2),\,N\,A\,((`x_1)\,F\,(x_1),\,\xi_1)),$
$H\,(I\,((`x_2)\,(\exists\,x_1)\,D\,(x_2, x_1),\,\xi_2),\,N\,A\,((`x_1)\,C\,(x_1),\,\xi_1)))$ (II. 1) [8]

Second example:

All circles are figures.
Thus: if, when something is a figure a has not drawn it, then, when something is a circle, a has not drawn it.

Symbolically:

$$A\,((`x)\,F\,(x),\,(`x)\,C\,(x))$$
$$\therefore H\,(H\,(I\,((`x)\,F\,(x),\,\xi_1),\,N\,A\,((`x)\,D\,(a, x),\,\xi_1)),$$
$$H\,(I\,((`x)\,C\,(x),\,\xi_1),\,N\,A\,((`x)\,D\,(a, x),\,\xi_1))).$$

Proof:

[1] $H(I(('x) C(x), \xi_1), I(('x) F(x), \xi_1))$,
$H(I(('x) F(x), \xi_1), N A(('x) D(a, x), \xi_1))$
$\therefore H(I(('x) C(x), \xi_1), N A(('x) D(a, x), \xi_1))$ (II. 13)

[2] $H(I(('x) C(x), \xi_1), I(('x) F(x), \xi_1))$
$\therefore H(H(I(('x) F(x), \xi_1), N A(('x) D(a, x), \xi_1))$,
$H(I(('x) C(x), \xi_1), N A(('x) D(a, x), \xi_1))$ (II. 1) [1]

[3] $A(('x) F(x), ('x) C(x))$
$\therefore H(I(('x) C(x), \xi_1), A(('x) F(x), \xi_1))$ (III. 1)

[4] $H(I(('x) C(x), \xi_1), A(('x) F(x), \xi_1))$,
$H(A(('x) F(x), \xi_1), I(('x) F(x), \xi_1))$
$\therefore H(I(('x) C(x), \xi_1), I(('x) F(x), \xi_1))$ (II. 13)

[5] $A(('x) F(x), \xi_1) \therefore I(('x) F(x), \xi_1)$ (III. 7)

[6] $*\therefore H(A(('x) F(x), \xi_1), I(('x) F(x), \xi_1))$ (II. 30) [5]

[7] $*, H(I(('x) C(x), \xi_1), A(('x) F(x), \xi_1))$
$\therefore H(I(('x) C(x), \xi_1), I(('x) F(x), \xi_1))$ (I. 4) [6, 4]

[8] $A(('x) F(x), ('x) C(x))$
$\therefore H(I(('x) C(x), \xi_1), A(('x) F(x), \xi_1))$ (I. 4) [3, 7]

[9] $A(('x) F(x), ('x) C(x)) \therefore$
$H(H(I(('x) F(x), \xi_1), N A(('x) D(a, x), \xi_1))$,
$H(I(('x) C(x), \xi_1), N A(('x) D(a, x), \xi_1)))$ (I. 4) [8, 2]

As the example just discussed shows, it is not yet the mere use of functional signs which leads to an expansion of the domain of deductive logic that breaks open the limits of the syllogistic. As will be seen further below, and especially after § 72, we overstep these limits only when we abandon our practice up to now of only accepting such rules which are valid on the basis of definitions alone.

§ 67 Abbreviation Rules

If one assumes the conventions recommended in §§ 64 and 65, syllogistic expressions can be transformed according to the following rules in such a way that, both concept variables and conceptual constants become superfluous as required descriptive signs and the signs for conceptual relations are dispensable as logical constants:

1. Abbreviation for a formula for a singular categorical proposition:

$A(('v) A(v), \zeta) \mathrel{>\!\!<} [A(t)]$ (V. 1)

2. Abbreviation for a formula for a universal categorical proposition:

$A(('v) A(v), \xi) \mathrel{>\!\!<} (\forall v) A(v)$ (V. 2)

3. Abbreviation for a formula for a particular categorical proposition:

$$I\,((\!{'}v)\,A\,(v),\,\xi) \mathrel{>\!\!<} (\exists\,v)\,A\,(v) \tag{V. 3}$$

4. Abbreviation for a formula for a singular categorical proposition:

$$\underline{A}\,((\!{'}v)\,A\,(v),\,\xi) \mathrel{>\!\!<} (\nabla\,v)\,A\,(v) \tag{V. 4}$$

The validity of these eight rules follows directly from the comments given in § 65 and the notation introduced in § 64. Since, according to these comments, quantifiers are not truly logical constants, but rather only signs that abbreviate syllogistic expressions of a certain quantity, these rules should not be regarded as principles, but rather as transformation rules, which serve merely to abbreviate syllogistic expressions for certain categorical propositions with complex predicate expressions.

§ 68 Examples of Contentful Syllogistic Inference (Continued)

We have seen in § 66 that the validity of the inference

> All circles are figures.
> Thus: if someone draws something that is not a figure, then someone draws something that is not a circle.

is provable according to syllogistic rules, if one presents it in the following form:

$$A\,((\!{'}x_1)\,F\,(x_1),\,(\!{'}x_1)\,C\,(x_1))$$
$$\therefore H\,(H\,(I\,((\!{'}x_1)\,(\exists\,x_2)\,D\,(x_2,\,x_1),\,\xi_1),\,N\,\underline{A}\,((\!{'}x_1)\,F\,(x_1),\,\xi_1)),$$
$$H\,(\underline{A}\,((\!{'}x_1)\,(\exists\,x_2)\,D\,(x_2,\,x_1),\,\xi_1),\,N\,\underline{A}\,((\!{'}x_1)\,C\,(x_1),\,\xi_1))).$$

According to the transformation rules listed in § 67, the conclusion of this inference can now be transformed and abbreviated, and this in such a way that all the concept variables, conceptual constants, and expressions for conceptual relations that appear in it disappear. For the expression '$I\,((\!{'}x_1)\,(\exists\,x_2)\,D\,(x_2,\,x_1),\,\xi_1)$' we may substitute '$(\exists\,x)\,(\exists\,y)\,D\,(y,\,x)$'. For '$\underline{A}\,((\!{'}x_1)\,C\,(x_1),\,\xi_1)$' and '$\underline{A}\,((\!{'}x_1)\,F\,(x_1),\,\xi_1)$', we can insert the expressions '$(\nabla\,x)\,C\,(x)$' and '$(\nabla\,x)\,F\,(x)$'. We then get:

$$H\,(H\,((\exists\,x)\,(\exists\,y)\,D\,(y,\,x),\,N\,(\nabla\,x)\,F\,(x)),\,H\,((\exists\,x)\,(\exists\,y)\,D\,(y,\,x),\,N\,(\nabla\,x)\,C\,(x)).$$

One can also arrive at this formula by applying rules (V. 3) and (V. 4) to the last line of the derivation from § 66.

In just the same way, we can now also present the inference

All circles are figures.
Thus: if, when something is a figure a has not drawn it, then, when something is a circle, a has not drawn it.

by writing:

$$A\,(('x)\,F\,(x),\,('x)\,C\,(x))$$
$$\therefore H\,(H\,((\exists\,x)\,F\,(x),\,N\,(\nabla\,x)\,D\,(a,\,x)),$$
$$H\,((\exists\,x)\,C\,(x),\,N\,(\nabla\,x)\,D\,(a,\,x))).$$

If in addition we want to avoid the use of the signs '$(\nabla x)\ldots$' and '$('x)\ldots$', then we must, with the example inferences considered here, alter both the logical form of the premises as well as the logical form of the conclusions. This can be done, for example, first by weakening the categorical form as it appears in the premises to a hypothetical form and, second, by replacing the bound variables as they appear in the conclusions in all places with the same individual constant. In this way, the inference just considered becomes this one:

If something is a circle, then it is a figure;
Therefore: if a, when b is a figure, has not drawn b, then a, when b is a circle, has not drawn b.

or into the inference:

If b is a circle, then b is a figure;
Therefore: if a, when b is a figure, has not drawn b, then a, when b is a circle, has not drawn b.

An inference of this form can also be proven with the syllogistic method of derivation. It has the symbolic form:

$$H\,([C\,(b)],\,[F\,(b)])$$
$$\therefore H\,(H\,([F\,(b)],\,N\,[D\,(a,\,b)]),\,H\,([C\,(b)],\,N\,[D\,(a,\,b)])).$$

Its validity can be proven as follows:

Proof:
[1] $H\,(A\,(('x)\,C\,(x),\,\zeta_2),\,A\,(('x)\,F\,(x),\,\zeta_2)),$
     $H\,(A\,(('x)\,F\,(x),\,\zeta_2),\,N\,A\,(('x)\,D\,(a,\,x),\,\zeta_2))$
     $\therefore H\,(A\,(('x)\,C\,(x),\,\zeta_2),\,N\,A\,(('x)\,D\,(a,\,x),\,\zeta_2))$ (II. 13)
[2] $H\,(A\,(('x)\,C\,(x),\,\zeta_2),\,A\,(('x)\,F\,(x),\,\zeta_2))$
     $\therefore H\,(H\,(A\,(('x)\,F\,(x),\,\zeta_2),\,N\,A\,(('x)\,D\,(a,\,x),\,\zeta_2)),$
     $H\,(A\,(('x)\,C\,(x),\,\zeta_2),\,N\,A\,(('x)\,D\,(a,\,x),\,\zeta_2)))$ (II. 1) [1]

By substituting '[D (a, b)]', '[K (b)]', and '[F (b)]' for 'A (('x) D (a, x), ζ₂)', 'A (('x) C (x), ζ₂)', and 'A (('x) F (x), ζ₂)' in line [2] of this derivation, we get the following formula

$$H ([C (b)], [F (b)])$$
$$\therefore H (H ([F (b)], N [D (a, b)], H ([C (b)], N [D (a, b)])).$$

We get this formula by applying the transformation rule (V. 1) from § 67 to line [2].

§ 69 Further Abbreviation Rules

We can gain more than the transformation rules of § 67 from the conventions of § 65. They govern the manner of notation for syllogistic expressions in such a way that further derivation rules can be formulated with them. According to the explanation of the concept expression '('v) A (v)' in § 65 (3) and the comment on § 65, concept expressions of the type '('x) A (x)' are, unlike expressions of the type '('x) F (x)', indeterminate in such a way that they can play the same role as concept variables α, β, etc. We can thus say that α, β, etc. can *substantially* play the role of abbreviating expressions of the type '('v) A (v)', '('v) B (v)', etc. In just the same way, the concept expressions '('v) N A (v)', '('v) N B (v)', etc. can be represented by the equivalent briefer concept expressions $^N\alpha$, $^N\beta$, etc. Hence, the expressions Y (('v) A (v), β) and Y (('v) N A (v), β), with Y equal to A, I, or A̱, differ only by their manner of notation from the expressions Y (α, β) und Y ($^N\alpha$, β). Because of this equivalence in meaning, the following rules hold:

Y (('v) A (v), β) >< Y (α, β) (with Y = A, I, or A̱)   (V. 5)
Y (('v) N A (v), β) >< Y ($^N\alpha$, β) (with Y = A, I, or A̱)   (V. 6)

These rules are to be considered as abbreviation rules as well.

According to § 53, the rules (III. 8) to (III. 10) hold for expressions of the form A ($^N\alpha$, β), I ($^N\alpha$, β), and A̱ ($^N\alpha$, β), in sequence. From the application of rules (V. 5) and (V. 6) to these three rules, rules (V. 7) to (V. 9) result:

A (('v) N A (v), β) < N I (('v) A (v), β)   (V. 7)
I (('v) N A (v), β) < N A (('v) A (v), β)   (V. 8)
A̱ (('v) N A (v), β) < N A̱ (('v) A (v), β)   (V. 9)

Section Six
Derivation of Formulas within the Framework of a System Extended Beyond the Limits of Elementary Deductive Logic

1 Principles and Metalogical Rules

§ 70 Notation

The language of the extended deductive logic, as it will be used in what follows, differs from the extended language of the syllogistic in § 64, as it has been developed in the preceding five sections, merely by the use of
(a) the sign of truth functional negation: '~ . . .', and
(b) the subjunction sign: '. . . ⊃ . . .'.

The formulas A and ~ A may stand in the place of *NN* A and of *N* A if *H* (*NN* A, A) is a valid formula (see § 10, § 31, and § 71, definition 4).
    The formula A ⊃ B may stand in the place of *H* (A, B) if *H* (B, *H* (A, B)) and *H* (*NN* A, A) are valid formulas (see § 31 and § 71, definition 3).
    As for the use of square brackets as per § 64 (4), *N* A (*t*) (without square brackets) may replace both *N* [A (*t*)], as an abbreviation of *N A̱* (('v) A (v), ζ̱), and [*N* A (*t*)], as an abbreviation of A̱ (('v) *N* A (v), ζ̱), if *N* [A (*t*)] occurs in a valid formula and a second formula is valid which differs from the first only by replacing the sub-formula *N* [A (*t*)] in all places of its occurrence in the first formula with [*N* A (*t*)].

§ 71 Definitions

With the following definitions, the meaning of the signs newly introduced in § 70, '~ . . .' and '. . . ⊃ . . .', will be reduced to the meaning of the logical constants '*N* . . .' and '*H* (. . ., . . .)'.

1. A is a *formula of the extended deductive logic* if and only if B and C are also formulas of the extended deductive logic, i.e., they consist of signs which I have introduced in § 42, § 46, § 51, and § 64, and at least one of the following four conditions is satisfied: (*a*) A is a formula of the categorical, hypothetical, or disjunctive syllogistic, or

(b) A is a logical functional expression, or (c) A is a subjunction of the form B ⊃ C, or (d) A is a truth-functional negation of the form ~ B.

2. A is a *logical functional expression* if and only if A is a formula which corresponds to one of the expressions B *(t)*, [B *(t)*], (∀ v) B (v), (∃ v) B (v), or (∇ v) B (v) introduced in § 64.

3. A is a *subjunction*, i.e., an expression of the form B ⊃ C, if for every interpretation in which B and C are true or false propositions, the following condition is satisfied: A is true if and only if *H* (B, C) is true and, as per § 72, the postulates of the arbitrary sufficient reason (i.e., rule (IV. 3)) and the affirmative use of double negation (i.e., rule (IV. 4)) are valid.

Corollary to Definition 3:
If A and B are formulas of the extended deductive logic and if both A, B ≺ A, according to (VI. 3), as well as *NN* A ≺ A, according to (VI. 4), are valid rules, then according to this definition (and because of the equivalence in meaning of '*H* A, B)' and '*N* (A, *N* B)' (see § 40)), the following rule is valid:

$$H (A, B) \succ\!\!\prec A \supset B. \tag{VI. 1}$$

4. A is a *truth-functional negation*, i.e., an expression of the form ~ B, if for every interpretation in which B is a true or false proposition, the following holds: A is true if and only if *N* B is true and, as per § 72, the postulate of the affirmative use of double negation for pairs of propositions of the form B and *N* B (i.e., rule (IV. 4)) is valid.

Corollary to Definition 4:
If A is a formula of the extended deductive logic, and if *NN* A ≺ A, according to (VI. 4), is a valid rule, so that – on the basis of (II. 29)^w (see § 73 below) – *H* (*NN* A, A) is a valid propositional schema, then according to this definition (and according to § 30), the following rule is valid:

$$N A \succ\!\!\prec\, \sim A \tag{VI. 2}$$

§ 72 Postulates

1. The postulate of the arbitrary sufficient reason:
   Let it hold that:

$$A, B \prec A \tag{VI. 3}$$

Scholium: The validity of (VI. 3) does not rest on the validity of a logical constant, but rather on a mere supposition or on the content of the propositions that A and B stand for. If A, B ∴ A were a valid rule, then also the rules *ex quolibet verum* and *ex falso quodlibet* would be valid. For both A ∴ H (B, A) (according to (II. 1)) and A, N A ∴ B (according to (I. 2)) would be derivable (see § 30).[218]

If B stands for the empty premise set, then (VI. 3) turns into the rule A ≺ A. It says that it is impossible that A is true and N A is false. The reason for this impossibility cannot be a logical one. Otherwise, the expression A ≺ A would have to contain a logical constant on whose meaning the impossibility is supposed to depend. (cf. § 45, scholium).

2. The postulate of the affirmative use of double negation for A and N A:
Let NN A be equivalent with A. That is, let not only (I. 1), but in addition:

NN A ≺ A (VI. 4)

3. The postulate of non-empty domains:
Let it hold both that:

$N A (\alpha, \beta) \prec I (^N\alpha, \beta)$, and that: (VI. 5)
$N A (^N\alpha, \beta) \prec I (\alpha, \beta)$ (VI. 6)

Remark: According to rules (V. 5) and (V. 6) (see § 69), in formulas (VI. 5) and (VI. 6) the variable 'α' may be replaced everywhere by '(v) A (v)', and the expression '$^N\alpha$' by '(v) N A (v)'.

Scholium: When the validity of (VI. 5) and (VI. 6) is accepted, it is supposed that the domain of individuals to which propositions of the form $N A (\alpha, \beta)$ and $N A (^N\alpha, \beta)$ refer is not empty (see § 35 above). Namely, the validity of (VI. 5) permits passing from $N A (\alpha, \beta)$, $N I (\alpha, \beta)$, α), or $N A (\alpha, \beta)$ to $I (^N\alpha, \beta)$ according to the rules of the logical square; and *a fortiori* it permits passing from $N (\forall v) A (v)$, $N (\exists v) A (v)$, or from $(\forall v) A (v)$ to $(\exists v) N A (v)$. Similarly for (VI. 6). Accordingly, only on the assumption of the validity of (VI. 5) and (VI. 6) is it possible to derive a non-negative existential proposition from the negation of an affirmative proposition. It ultimately

---

[218] Also Paul Hoyningen-Huene (1998, 124) seems not to want to acknowledge the general validity of the rule according to which A follows from A and B; in his view, it is enough rather "to restrict its applicability to those cases in which B is different from ~ A", and then to "justify" that "nothing" (not even A or ~ A) "follows from A & ~ A". Since this view is excluded by the truth table for A & ~ A, it seems that Hoyningen hereby tacitly agrees to the assumption that there must be a non-truth-functional logical conjunction of premises.

rests on this fact that valid existential formulas, i.e., formulas of the type (∃ v) A (v), can be derived within the extended deductive logic.[219]

Only postulates (VI. 3) and (VI. 4) guarantee that every formula of the system of the extended deductive logic, provided they contain no free individual variables, can be given a gapless truth table.

The postulate of non-empty domains, which is expressed in rules (VI. 5) and (VI. 6), guarantees that all descriptive signs of the extended deductive logic have a definite semantic value, so that individual symbols always refer to objects of a satisfied domain. By contrast, a similar semantic value is not fixed for the descriptive signs of the elementary syllogistic. Nothing guarantees that syllogistic concept expressions stand for satisfiable, not to mention satisfied, concepts.

The fact that basic rules (VI. 3) to (VI. 6) are mere postulates means that propositions correspond to them from whose negation no inconsistency is derivable. Such propositions can be generated from them through conditionalization (according to (II. 29)^{W}) (see § 73) and subsequent interpretation. Proposition from whose negation no inconsistency is derivable are, according to § 39, to be regarded as non-analytic (i.e., as synthetic) propositions, and, so long they are not empirical propositions, as non-analytic propositions *a priori*.

One can raise the question of under which circumstances it is really *appropriate* to accept the rules (VI. 3) to (VI. 6) as valid postulates. The answer is: when it may be assumed that the domain to which individual constants and quantified individual variables refers is not empty, it may be postulated that these basic rules are valid. This assumption may be made, e.g., in the application of the logical calculus of functions in arithmetic and geometry, namely, when in this application individual signs become signs for objects whose existence or givenness (as numbers, quantities, line segments, etc.) is assumed. In this application, basic rules (VI. 3) to (VI. 6) turn into mathematical postulates whose validity neither needs nor is capable of proof. This holds directly for (VI. 5) and (VI. 6), but indirectly for rules (VI. 3) and (VI. 4) as well. For if it is ruled out that singular propositions have no existential presuppositions, then it is also ruled out that propositions of the form A (α, β) do not follow from propositions of the form NN A (α, β), and hence that propositions of the form A do not follow from propositions of the form NN A. Thus, in that case (VI. 4) holds. But then (VI. 3) holds as well, for if it is supposed to hold always that A follows from NN A, then it should also hold that there is no pair of propositions which are related as A and NN A and yet at the same time *both* negate a false proposition, so that as such they are both true. With this it is postulated that

---

[219] Examples of such existential formulas are (∃ y) (F (y) ⊃ (∀ x) F (x)), (∃ y) ((∃ x) F (x) ⊃ F (y)), or (∃ y) ((∀ x) F (x) ⊃ F (y)). See on this § 80, theorem (*15*). Cf. Quine 1963, 160–67.

there is no proposition which is true in one respect (insofar as it negates a false proposition), while it is false in another respect (insofar as it is negated by a true proposition). According to this postulate, there should only be propositions of which it may also be supposed that they (either alone or in conjunction with other propositions) follow from themselves.[220]

§ 73 Metalogical Rules

According to § 72, the extended deductive logic, in contrast to the syllogistic, makes use of rules whose validity does not rest on definitions, but is only postulated. These rules thus deal not with relations of logical consequence, but rather only with relations of regular consequence (see § 43, definitions 3 and 4). Hence, to derive rules from these postulates one needs metalogical rules which can be regarded for the most part as analogous variants of the metalogical rules I introduced above, in §§ 44 to 50, which are applicable to relations of *logical* consequence. Precisely analogous rules hold for relations of *regular* consequence, since logical consequence is only a special case of regular consequence (see § 43, definition 4). To be able to reduce relations of regular consequence to other relations of regular consequence, it suffices to reformulate the metalogical basic rules (I. 2) (*reductio ad absurdum*), (I. 3) (Peripatetic inference chain rule), and (II. 1) (principle of conditionalization) so that the sign '∴' is replaced in all places of its occurrence with the sign '≺'. We then get three new expressions that stand for reduction rules, for $(I.\ 2)^w$, $(I.\ 3)^w$, and $(II.\ 1)^w$, to which finally the weakening rule (VI. 7) is added:

1. Metalogical basic rules

   Reductio ad absurdum – variant on (I. 2):
   $(A_1, \ldots, A_n \prec A) / (N\,A, A_1, \ldots, A_{n-1} \prec N\,A_n), \ldots,$
   $(N\,A, A_2, \ldots, A_n \prec N\,A_1)$ (with $n \geq 1$) $(I.\ 2)^{w[221]}$

   Peripatetic inference chain rule – variant on (I. 3):
   $(A_k, \ldots, A_n \prec A), (A, B_1, \ldots, B_m \prec B) / (A_k, \ldots, A_n, B_1, \ldots, B_m \prec B)$
   (with $k \geq 0$, $n \geq k$ and $m \geq 1$) $(I.\ 3)^w$

---

[220] Basic rules (VI. 3) to (VI. 6), as postulates, regulate the mathematical use of letters as such, and, like the so-called postulates of Euclidean geometry, they have to guarantee that their concepts are satisfied.
[221] The superscripted lowercase letter w stands here and in what follows for 'weakened'. The weakening of rule $(I.\ 2)^w$ vis-à-vis the analogous rule (I. 2) consists in replacing the sign for logical consequence in all places of its occurrence with that of regular consequence.

Principle of conditionalization – variant on (II. 1):
$A_1, \ldots, A_n, B \prec C / A_1, \ldots, A_n \prec H(B, C)$ (II. 1)^w

Scholium: The reasons these three rules are valid are not different from the reasons the rules (I. 2), (I. 3), and (II. 1) are valid. For (I. 2)^w is valid because it is true *per definitionem* of regular consequence just as of logical consequence that the consequent cannot be false unless at least one of the premises is false; (I. 3)^w is valid because both the regular as well as the logical consequence relations are transitive; and (II. 1)^w is valid because the definition of the hypothetical proposition (see § 47, definition 2 above) refers to the relation of regular consequence of which the relation of logical consequence is only a special case (see § 42, definitions 3 and 4).

Weakening of logical consequence:
$A_1, \ldots, A_n \therefore B / A_1, \ldots, A_n \prec B$ (with $n \geq 1$) (VI. 7)

The validity of (VI. 7) rests on the fact that logical consequence, according to § 43, definitions 3 and 4, is a special case of regular consequence.

Note on Notation:
To abbreviate, in what the following derivations (as also up to now) I will add the superscripted lowercase letter w (as an abbreviation for '*weakened*') in the right column of a line, after the designation of a rule. This letter is placed here to indicate that two lines of a derivation, of which the second relies on the application of (VI. 7), have been combined into one line. For example, the two lines

$[n]$ $A \therefore NN\,A$ (I. 1)
$[n + m]$ $A \prec NN\,A$ (with $m \geq 1$) (VI. 7) [1]

may be replaced by the following line:

$[n]$ $A \prec NN\,A$ (I. 1)^w

2. Derivable metalogical rules

From the metalogical basic rules (I. 2)^w, (I. 3)^w, and (II. 1)^w rules can be derived which are precisely analogous to the metalogical rules (I. 4), (I. 5), (II. 5), and (II. 6) as well as rules (II. 29) and (II. 30), and which differ from them only by the appearance of '$\prec$' in place of '$\therefore$'. They are the following:

Simple transitivity in an inference chain – variant on (I. 4):
$(A_i, \ldots, A_k \prec B), (B, C \prec D) / A_i, \ldots, A_k, C \prec D$ (with $i \geq 0, k \geq i$) (I. 4)^w

Complex transitivity in an inference chain – variant on (I. 5):
$(A_i, \ldots, A_k \therefore A), (A_{k+1}, \ldots, A_n \prec B_1), (A, B_1 \prec D) / A_1, \ldots, A_n \prec D$
(with $i \geq 0, k \geq i, n \geq k + 1$) (I. 5)^w

Deconditionalization of a conclusion – variant on (II. 5):
$A_i, \ldots, A_k \prec H(B, C) / A_i, \ldots, A_k, B \prec C$ (with $i \geq 0$ and $k \geq 0$) (II. 5)^w

Idempotency rule – variant on (II. 6):
$A_i \ldots, A_k, A_1, A_1 \prec D / A_1, A_i \ldots, A_k \prec D$ (with $i \geq 0, k \geq i$) (II. 6)^w

Conditionalization rule – variant on (II. 29):
$A_1, A_i, \ldots, A_n \prec B / {}^* \prec H(A_1, H(A_i, H(\ldots, H(A_n, B))) \ldots)$
(with $i \geq 1, n \geq i$) (II. 29)^w

Deconditionalization – variant on (II. 30):
${}^* \prec H(A_1, H(A_i, H(\ldots, H(A_n, B))) \ldots) / {}^*, A_1, A_i, \ldots, A_n \prec B$
(with $i \geq 1, n \geq i$) (II. 30)^w

The derivations which can be carried out for (I. 4)^w, (I. 5)^w, (II. 5)^w, (II. 6)^w, (II. 29)^w, and (II. 30)^w are precisely analogous to the proofs which have been carried out above in § 45, § 49, and § 50 for the validity of rules (I. 4), (I. 5), (II. 6), (II. 29), and (II. 30), respectively.

2 Derived Formulas

§ 74 Derivation of Truth-Functional Rules

If A, B, and C are formulas of the extended deductive logic in the sense of § 71, definition 1, then the following rules (VI. 8) to (VI. 16) are derivable from the principles established above:

Simple detachment rule:
$A \supset B, A \prec B$ (VI. 8)[222]

Proof:
[1] $H(A, B), A \prec B$ (II. 2)^w
[2] $A \supset B, A \prec B$ (VI. 1) [1]

Complex detachment rule:
$(A \supset B), (B \supset C), A \prec C$ (VI. 9)

---

[222] In logic books, A, $A \supset B \therefore B$ and A, $A \supset B \prec B$ are not usually distinguished, and thus it is not noticed that, taken strictly, A, $A \supset B \therefore B$ is not a valid rule. There is also the habit of confusing A, $A \supset B \therefore B$ or A, $A \supset B \prec B$ with *modus ponendo ponens* (II. 2). In this way, the distinction between $H(A, B)$ and $A \supset B$ is overlooked. Frege (1879/1967, § 6) goes as far as designating his derivation rule, which likewise resembles expression (VI. 8), as "modus ponens," as if ultimately even the distinction between *modus ponendo ponens* and *modus tollendo ponens* should remain unnoticed.

Proof:

[1]	(A ⊃ B), A ≺ B	(VI. 8)
[2]	(B ⊃ C), B ≺ C	(VI. 8)
[3]	(A ⊃ B), (B ⊃ C), A ≺ C	(I. 4)^w [1, 2]

Generalization rule:
In case *t* occurs only in the argument places of A (*t*), then:
A (*t*) ≺ (∀ *v*) A (*v*)   **(VI. 10)**

Proof:

[1]	*A* (('*v*) A (*v*), ζ) ≺ *I* (('*v*) A (*v*), ζ)	(III. 7)^a
[2]	*I* (('*v*) A (*v*), ζ) ≺ *A* (('*v*) A (*v*), ξ)	(III. 3)^w
[3]	*A* (('*v*) A (*v*), ζ) ≺ *A* (('*v*) A (*v*), ξ)	(I. 4)^w [1, 2]
[4]	[A (*t*)] ≺ *A* (('*v*) A (*v*), ζ)	(V. 1)
[5]	*A* (('*v*) A (*v*), ξ) ≺ (∀ *v*) A (*v*)	(V. 2)
[6]	[A (*t*)] ≺ (∀ *v*) A (*v*)	(I. 4)^w [3, 4, 5]

The proof is not yet completed here, since the square brackets in line [6] must still disappear. Indeed, 'A (*t*)' and '[A (*t*)]' are not equivalent, according to § 64 (4). If A equals *N* B, then it is not proven with line [6] that (∀ *v*) *N* B (*v*) follows from *N* [B (*t*)]. At that point, it is only proven that (∀ *v*) *N* B (*v*) follows regularly from [*N* B (*t*)]. Hence, the proof for (VI. 10) is only completed when the formula *N* [B (*t*)] ≺ (∀ *v*) *N* B (*v*) is derived as well. This derivation can be performed in the following way:

[1']	*A* (('*v*) B (*v*), ζ) ≺ [B (*t*)]	(V. 1)
[2']	*N* [B (*t*)] ≺ *N A* (('*v*) B (*v*), ζ)	(I. 2)^w [1']
[3']	*A* (('*v*) B (*v*), ζ) ≺ *A* (('*v*) B (*v*), ζ)	(III. 11)^w
[4']	*N A* (('*v*) B (*v*), ζ) ≺ *N A* (('*v*) B (*v*), ζ)	(I. 2)^w [3']
[5']	*N A* (('*v*) B (*v*), ζ) ≺ *I* (('*v*) *N* B (*v*), ζ)	(VI. 5)
[6']	*I* (('*v*) *N* B (*v*), ζ) ≺ *A* (('*v*) *N* B (*v*), ξ)	(III. 3)^w
[7']	*A* (('*v*) *N* B (*v*), ξ) ≺ (∀ *v*) *N* B (*v*)	(V. 2)
[8']	*N* [B (*t*)] ≺ (∀ *v*) *N* B (*v*)	(I. 4)^w [2', 4', 5', 6', 7']

The (not unrestrictedly admissible) application of (III. 3), i.e., the first exposition rule, is permitted in lines [2] and [6'], since 'ξ' occurs in the place of a concept variable neither in the premise expression of line [1], nor in one of the premise expressions of lines [1'] to [5']. This can be made clear from the formulas abbreviated by A (*t*) and (∀ *v*) A (*v*), namely the formulas *A* (('*v*) B (*v*), ζ) and *N A* (('*v*) B (*v*), ζ) and the formulas *A* (('*v*) A (*v*), ξ) and *A* (('*v*) *N* B (*v*), ξ), respectively, between which takes place the transition made possible by (III. 3). In this way, these formulas differ from the expressions that abbreviate them, namely the expressions A (*t*) and (∀ *v*) A (*v*), which occur in the formula for rule (VI. 10). With reference to these expressions, if rule (VI. 10) is supposed to be valid, it must be stipulated that the letter *t* – and with that implicitly the concept expression ζ as well – does not occur even once in the functional expression A (*t*) other than in its argument places (which are designated by '*v*' in '(∀ *v*) A (*v*)'). This stipulation guarantees that '*t*' in the transition from A (*t*) to '(∀ *v*) A (*v*)' is replaced by '*v*', just as '*ζ*' is by '*ξ*'.

Rule of posterior generalization:
In case *t* occurs only in the argument places of B (*t*), then:
(A ⊃ B (*t*)) ≺ (A ⊃ (∀ *v*) B (*v*)) (VI. 11)

Proof:
[1] (A ⊃ B (*t*)), A ≺ B (*t*) (VI. 8)
[2] B (*t*) ≺ (∀ *v*) B (*v*) (VI. 10)
[3] (A ⊃ B (*t*)), A ≺ (∀ *v*) B (*v*) (I. 4)^W [1, 2]
[4] (A ⊃ B (*t*)) ≺ H (A, (∀ *v*) B (*v*)) (II. 1)^W [3]
[5] H (A, (∀ *v*) B (*v*)) ≺ (A ⊃ (∀ *v*) B (*v*)) (VI. 1)
[6] (A ⊃ B (*t*)) ≺ (A ⊃ (∀ *v*) B (*v*)) (I. 4)^W [4, 5]

Since in line [2] the restrictedly valid rule (VI. 10) is applied, there is the same restriction on the validity of rule derived in line [6] as for the validity of rule (VI. 10).

(∀ *v*) B (*v*) ≺ A (('*v*) NN B (*v*), *ξ*) (VI. 12)

Proof:
[1] N A (('*v*) NN B (*v*), *ξ*) ≺ I (('*v*) N B (*v*), *ξ*) (VI. 6)
[2] I (('*v*) N B (*v*), *ξ*) ≺ N A (('*v*) B (*v*), *ξ*) (V. 8)
[3] N A (('*v*) NN B (*v*), *ξ*) ≺ N A (('*v*) B (*v*), *ξ*) (I. 4)^W [1, 2]
[4] NN A (('*v*) B (*v*), *ξ*) ≺ NN A (('*v*) NN B (*v*), *ξ*) (I. 2)^W [3]
[5] A (('*v*) B (*v*), *ξ*) ≺ NN A (('*v*) B (*v*), *ξ*) (I. 1)^W
[6] NN A (('*v*) NN B (*v*), *ξ*) ≺ A (('*v*) NN B (*v*), *ξ*) (VI. 4)
[7] A (('*v*) B (*v*), *ξ*) ≺ A (('*v*) NN B (*v*), *ξ*) (I. 4)^W [5, 4, 6]
[8] (∀ *v*) B (*v*) ≺ A (('*v*) B (*v*), *ξ*) (V. 2)
[9] (∀ *v*) B (*v*) ≺ A (('*v*) NN B (*v*), *ξ*) (I. 4)^W [7, 8]

Particularization rule:
B (*t*) ≺ (∃ *v*) B (*v*) (VI. 13)

Proof:
[1]   A (('*v*) N B (*v*), *ζ*) ≺ N A (('*v*) B (*v*), *ζ*) (V. 9)
[2]   NN A (('*v*) B (*v*), *ζ*) ≺ N A (('*v*) N B (*v*), *ζ*) (I. 2)^W [1]
[3]   A (('*v*) B (*v*), *ζ*) ≺ NN A (('*v*) B (*v*), *ζ*) (I. 1)^W
[4]   A (('*v*) B (*v*), *ζ*) ≺ N A (('*v*) N B (*v*), *ζ*) (I. 4)^W [3, 2]
[5]   A (('*v*) N B (*v*), *ζ*) ≺ A (('*v*) N B (*v*), *ζ*) (III. 11)^W
[6]   N A (('*v*) N B (*v*), *ζ*) ≺ N A (('*v*) N B (*v*), *ζ*) (I. 2)^W [5]
[7]   N A (('*v*) N B (*v*), *ζ*) ≺ I (('*v*) B (*v*), *ζ*) (VI. 6)
[8]   I (('*v*) B (*v*), *ζ*) ≺ A (('*v*) B (*v*), *ξ*) (III. 3)^W
[9]   A (('*v*) B (*v*), *ξ*) ≺ I (('*v*) B (*v*), *ξ*) (III. 14)^W
[10] A (('*v*) B (*v*), *ζ*) ≺ I (('*v*) B (*v*), *ξ*) (I. 4)^W [4, 6, 7, 8, 9]
[11] [B (*t*)] ≺ A (('*v*) B (*v*), *ζ*) (V. 1)

[12] $I\,(('v)\,B\,(v),\,\xi) \prec (\exists\,v)\,B\,(v)$ (V. 3)
[13] $[B\,(t)] \prec (\exists\,v)\,B\,(v)$ (I. 4)^w [11, 10, 12]

To eliminate the square brackets in line [13], the proof according to § 64 (4) for the case in which B equals N B must be completed by deriving the formula $N\,[C\,(t)] \prec (\exists\,v)\,N\,C\,(v)$. This happens through the proof of rule (VI. 14):

Particularization rule with square brackets:
$N\,[C\,(t)] \prec (\exists\,v)\,N\,C\,(v)$ (VI. 14)

Proof:
[1'] $A\,(('v)\,C\,(v),\,\zeta) \prec A\,(('v)\,C\,(v),\,\zeta)$ (III. 11)^w
[2'] $N\,A\,(('v)\,C\,(v),\,\zeta) \prec N\,A\,(('v)\,C\,(v),\,\zeta)$ (I. 2)^w [1']
[3'] $N\,A\,(('v)\,C\,(v),\,\zeta) \prec I\,(('v)\,N\,C\,(v),\,\zeta)$ (VI. 5)
[4'] $I\,(('v)\,N\,C\,(v),\,\zeta) \prec A\,(('v)\,N\,C\,(v),\,\xi)$ (III. 3)^w
[5'] $A\,(('v)\,N\,C\,(v),\,\xi) \prec I\,(('v)\,N\,C\,(v),\,\xi)$ (III. 14)^a
[6'] $N\,A\,(('v)\,C\,(v),\,\zeta) \prec I\,(('v)\,N\,C\,(v),\,\xi)$ (I. 4)^w [2', 3', 4', 5']
[7'] $A\,(('v)\,C\,(v),\,\zeta) \prec [C\,(t)]$ (V. 1)
[8'] $N\,[C\,(t)] \prec N\,A\,(('v)\,C\,(v),\,\zeta)$ (I. 2)^w [7']
[9'] $I\,(('v)\,N\,C\,(v),\,\xi) \prec (\exists\,v)\,N\,C\,(v)$ (V. 3)
[10'] $N\,[C\,(t)] \prec (\exists\,v)\,N\,C\,(v)$ (I. 4)^w [8', 6', 9']

Singularization rule:
$(\forall\,v)\,B\,(v) \prec B\,(t)$ (VI. 15)

Proof:
[1] $N\,[B\,(t)] \prec (\exists\,v)\,N\,B\,(v)$ (VI. 14)
[2] $(\exists\,v)\,N\,B\,(v) \prec I\,(('v)\,N\,B\,(v),\,\xi)$ (V. 3)
[3] $N\,[B\,(t)] \prec I\,(('v)\,N\,B\,(v),\,\xi)$ (I. 4)^w [1, 2]
[4] $N\,I\,(('v)\,N\,B\,(v),\,\xi) \prec NN\,[B\,(t)]$ (I. 2)^w [3]
[5] $NN\,[B\,(t)] \prec [B\,(t)]$ (VI. 4)^w
[6] $A\,(('v)\,NN\,B\,(v),\,\xi) \prec N\,I\,(('v)\,N\,B\,(v),\,\xi)$ (V. 7)
[7] $(\forall\,v)\,B\,(v) \prec A\,(('v)\,NN\,B\,(v),\,\xi)$ (VI. 12)
[8] $(\forall\,v)\,B\,(v) \prec [B\,(t)]$ (I. 4)^w [7, 6, 4, 5]

Here, too, for the elimination of the square brackets that appear in line [10], the proof must be completed according to § 64 (4). This happens through the proof of rule (VI. 16), which makes possible, for the case where B equals N C, the regular transition from $(\forall\,v)\,N\,C\,(v)$ to $N\,[C\,(t)]$, and thus not only (like rule (VI. 15)) to $[N\,C\,(t)]$:

Singularization rule with square brackets:
$(\forall\,v)\,N\,C\,(v) \prec N\,[C\,(t)]$ (VI. 16)

Proof:

[1]	$[C(t)] \prec (\exists v) C(v)$	(VI. 13)
[2]	$(\exists v) C(v) \prec I(('v) C(v), \xi)$	(V. 3)
[3]	$N I(('x) C(x), \xi) \prec N [C(t)]$	(I. 2)^W [2]
[4]	$A(('v) N C(v), \xi) \prec N I(('v) C(v), \xi)$	(V. 7)
[5]	$(\forall v) A(v) \prec A(('v) N C(v), \xi)$	(V. 2)
[6]	$(\forall v) A(v) \prec N [C(t)]$	(I. 4)^W [5, 4, 3]

§ 75 Derivation of Truth-Functional Laws

If A, B, and C are formulas of the extended deductive logic in the sense of § 73, definition 1, then the following truth-functions (VI. 17) to (VI. 27), for example, are derivable from the principles established above. The expressions (VI. 17) to (VI. 24) – apart from (VI. 23) – correspond to seven of the nine "fundamental principles" which Frege established in Part II of his *Begriffsschrift* as axioms of his system of "laws of thought" and which he called its "core."[223] The two axioms which I leave aside here differ from the others in that they contain the sign of "identity of content" ('≡'), which Frege replaced in later writings by the ordinary identity sign ('='). They are rendered by the formulas '⊢ (c = d) ⊃ (A (c) ⊃ A (d)' and '⊢ c = d' in §§ 20 and 21 of the *Begriffsschrift*.

$$^* \prec A \supset (B \supset A) \qquad \text{(VI. 17)}$$

Proof:

[1]	$A, B \prec A$	(VI. 3)
[2]	$A \prec H(B, A)$	(II. 1)^W [1]
[3]	$H(B, A) \prec B \supset A$	(VI. 1)
[4]	$A \prec B \supset A$	(I. 4)^W [2, 3]
[5]	$^* \prec H(A, (B \supset A)$	(II. 29)^W [4]
[6]	$H(A, (B \supset A) \prec (A \supset (B \supset A))$	(VI. 1)
[7]	$^* \prec A \supset (B \supset A)$	(I. 4)^W [5, 6]

$$^* \prec (A \supset (B \supset C)) \supset ((A \supset B) \supset (A \supset C)) \qquad \text{(VI. 18)}$$

Proof:

[1]	$(A \supset B), (B \supset C), A \prec C$	(VI. 9)
[2]	$(A \supset (B \supset C)), A \prec (B \supset C)$	(VI. 8)
[3]	$(A \supset (B \supset C)), (A \supset B), A, A \prec C$	(I. 4)^W [2, 1]
[4]	$(A \supset (B \supset C)), (A \supset B), A \prec C$	(II. 6)^W [3]
[5]	$(A \supset (B \supset C)), (A \supset B) \prec H(A, C)$	(II. 1)^W [4]
[6]	$H(A, C) \prec (A \supset C)$	(VI. 1)
[7]	$(A \supset (B \supset C)), (A \supset B) \prec (A \supset C)$	(I. 4)^W [5, 6]

---

[223] Frege 1879, 25–26, § 13 (1967, 29).

[8]	$(A \supset (B \supset C)) \prec H((A \supset B), (A \supset C))$	(II. 1)^w [7]
[9]	$H((A \supset B), (A \supset C)) \prec ((A \supset B) \supset (A \supset C))$	(VI. 1)
[10]	$(A \supset (B \supset C)) \prec ((A \supset B) \supset (A \supset C))$	(I. 4)^w [8, 9]
[11]	$*\prec H(A \supset (B \supset C)), ((A \supset B) \supset (A \supset C)))$	(II. 29)^w [10]
[12]	$H(A \supset (B \supset C)), ((A \supset B) \supset (A \supset C)))$	
	$\prec (A \supset (B \supset C)) \supset ((A \supset B) \supset (A \supset C)))$	(VI. 1)
[13]	$*\prec (A \supset (B \supset C)) \supset ((A \supset B) \supset (A \supset C))$	(I. 4)^w [11, 12]

$*\prec (A \supset (B \supset C)) \supset (B \supset (A \supset C))$ **(VI. 19)**

Proof:

[1]	$H(A, H(B, C)), A \prec H(B, C)$	(II. 2)^w
[2]	$H(A, H(B, C)), A, B \prec C$	(II. 5)^w [1]
[3]	$H(A, H(B, C)), B \prec H(A, C)$	(II. 1)^w [2]
[4]	$H(A, C) \prec (A \supset C)$	(VI. 1)
[5]	$H(A, H(B, C)), B \prec (A \supset C)$	(I. 4)^w [3, 4]
[6]	$H(A, H(B, C)) \prec H(B, (A \supset C))$	(II. 1)^w [5]
[7]	$H(B, (A \supset C)) \prec (B \supset (A \supset C))$	(VI. 1)
[8]	$H(A, H(B, C)) \prec (B \supset (A \supset C))$	(I. 4)^w [6, 7]
[9]	$(A \supset (B \supset C)), A \prec (B \supset C)$	(VI. 8)
[10]	$(B \supset C), B \prec C$	(VI. 8)
[11]	$(B \supset C) \prec H(B, C)$	(II. 1)^w [10]
[12]	$(A \supset (B \supset C)), A \prec H(B, C)$	(I. 4)^w [9, 11]
[13]	$(A \supset (B \supset C)) \prec H(A, H(B\ C))$	(II. 1)^w [12]
[14]	$(A \supset (B \supset C)) \prec (B \supset (A \supset C))$	(I. 4)^w [13, 8]
[15]	$*\prec H((A \supset (B \supset C)), (B \supset (A \supset C)))$	(II. 29)^w [14]
[16]	$H((A \supset (B \supset C)), (B \supset (A \supset C)))$	
	$\prec ((A \supset (B \supset C)) \supset (B \supset (A \supset C)))$	(VI. 1)
[17]	$*\prec (A \supset (B \supset C)) \supset (B \supset (A \supset C))$	(I. 4)^w [15, 16]

The expressions (VI. 17) to (VI. 19) correspond to the three basic laws of "conditionality" (Frege 1879, 26, § 13 [1967, 29]) which Frege established as axioms in §§ 14 and 16 of his *Begriffsschrift*.

Truth-functional contraposition:
$*\prec (A \supset B) \supset (\sim B \supset \sim A)$ **(VI. 20)**

Proof:

[1]	$H(A, B), NB \prec NA$	(II. 7)^w
[2]	$NA \prec \sim A$	(VI. 2)
[3]	$H(A, B), NB \prec \sim A$	(I. 4)^w [1, 2]
[4]	$\sim B \prec NB$	(VI. 2)
[5]	$H(A, B), \sim B \prec \sim A$	(I. 4)^w [4, 3]
[6]	$H(A, B) \prec H(\sim B, \sim A)$	(II. 1)^w [5]
[7]	$H(\sim B, \sim A) \prec (\sim B \supset \sim A)$	(VI. 1)
[8]	$H(A, B) \prec (\sim B \supset \sim A)$	(I. 4)^w [6, 7]
[9]	$(A \supset B), A \prec B$	(VI. 8)

[10]	(A ⊃ B) ≺ H (A, B)	(II. 1)^W [9]
[11]	(A ⊃ B) ≺ (∼ B ⊃ ∼ A)	(I. 4)^W [10, 8]
[12]	*≺ H ((A ⊃ B), (∼ B ⊃ ∼ A))	(II. 29)^W [11]
[13]	H ((A ⊃ B), (∼ B ⊃ ∼ A)) ≺ ((A ⊃ B) ⊃ (∼ B ⊃ ∼ A))	(VI. 1)
[14]	*≺ (A ⊃ B) ⊃ (∼ B ⊃ ∼ A)	(I. 4)^W [12, 13]

Truth-functional variant on (I. 1):
*≺ A ⊃ ∼ ∼ A   (VI. 21)^{224}

Proof:
[1]	∼ A ≺ N A	(VI. 2)
[2]	NN A ≺ N ∼ A	(I. 2)^W [1]
[3]	A ≺ NN A	(I. 1)^W
[4]	A ≺ N ∼ A	(I. 4)^W [3, 2]
[5]	N ∼ A ≺ ∼ ∼ A	(VI. 2)
[6]	A ≺ ∼ ∼ A	(I. 4)^W [4, 5]
[7]	*≺ H (A, ∼ ∼ A)	(II. 29)^W [6]
[8]	H (A, ∼ ∼ A) ≺ (A ⊃ ∼ ∼ A)	(VI. 1)
[9]	*≺ (A ⊃ ∼ ∼ A)	(I. 4)^W [7,8]

Inverse of this variant:
*≺ ∼ ∼ A ⊃ A   (VI. 22)

Proof:
[1]	N A ≺ ∼ A	(VI. 2)
[2]	N ∼ A ≺ NN A	(I. 2)^W [1]
[3]	∼ ∼ A ≺ N ∼ A	(VI. 2)
[4]	∼ ∼ A ≺ NN A	(I. 4)^W [3, 2]
[5]	NN A ≺ A	(VI. 4)
[6]	∼ ∼ A ≺ A	(I. 4)^W [4, 5]
[7]	*≺ H (∼ ∼ A, A)	(II. 29)^W [6]
[8]	H (∼ ∼ A, A) ≺ (∼ ∼ A ⊃ A)	(VI. 1)
[9]	*≺ ∼ ∼ A ⊃ A	(I. 4)^W [7, 8]

The expressions (VI. 20) to (VI. 22) correspond to the three basic laws of "negation" (Frege 1879, 26, § 13 [1967, 29]) which Frege established as axioms in §§ 17 to 19 of his *Begriffsschrift*.

Inverse of truth-functional contraposition:
*≺ (∼ B ⊃ ∼ A) ⊃ (A ⊃ B)   (VI. 23)

---

224 (VI. 21) and (VI. 23) are here strictly speaking only proven for A ≠ N B (for arbitrary B). But the generalization is admissible in both cases, since N B ≺ NNN B is directly derivable from (VI. 4) with the help of (I. 2)^W, so that N A may be substituted for A in every line of both proofs.

Proof:

[1]	$H(NB, NA), NNA \prec NNB$	(II. 7)^W
[2]	$NNB \prec B$	(VI. 4)
[3]	$A \prec NNA$	(I. 1)^W
[4]	$H(NB, NA), A \prec B$	(I. 4)^W [3, 1, 2]
[5]	$H(NB, NA) \prec H(A, B)$	(II. 1)^W [4]
[6]	$H(A, B) \prec (A \supset B)$	(VI. 1)
[7]	$H(NB, NA) \prec (A \supset B)$	(I. 4)^W [5, 6]
[8]	$\sim A \prec NA$	(VI. 2)
[9]	$* \prec H(\sim A, NA)$	(II. 29)^W [8]
[10]	$H(NB, \sim A), H(\sim A, NA) \prec H(NB, NA)$	(II. 13)^W
[11]	$*, H(NB, \sim A) \prec H(NB, NA)$	(I. 4)^W [9, 10]
[12]	$NB \prec \sim B$	(VI. 2)
[13]	$* \prec H(NB, \sim B)$	(II. 29)^W [12]
[14]	$H(NB, \sim B), H(\sim B, \sim A) \prec H(NB, \sim A)$	(II. 13)^W
[15]	$*, H(\sim B, \sim A) \prec H(NB, \sim A)$	(I. 4)^W [13, 14]
[16]	$*, *, H(\sim B, \sim A) \prec H(NB, NA)$	(I. 4)^W [15, 11]
[17]	$*, *, H(\sim B, \sim A) \prec (A \supset B)$	(I. 4)^W [16, 7]
[18]	$(\sim B \supset \sim A), \sim B \prec \sim A$	(VI. 8)
[19]	$(\sim B \supset \sim A) \prec H(\sim B, \sim A)$	(II. 1)^W [18]
[20]	$*, *, (\sim B \supset \sim A) \prec (A \supset B)$	(I. 4)^W [19, 17]
[21]	$*, *, * \prec H((\sim B \supset \sim A), (A \supset B))$	(II. 29)^W [20]
[22]	$H((\sim B \supset \sim A), (A \supset B)) \prec ((\sim B \supset \sim A) \supset (A \supset B))$	(VI. 1)
[23]	$*, *, * \prec ((\sim B \supset \sim A) \supset (A \supset B))$	(I. 4)^W [21, 22]
[24]	$* \prec (\sim B \supset \sim A) \supset (A \supset B)$	(II. 6)^W [23]

Law of singularization:

$* \prec (\forall v) A(v) \supset A(t)$ **(VI. 24)**

Proof:

[1]	$(\forall v) A(v) \prec A(t)$	(VI. 15)
[2]	$* \prec H((\forall v) A(v), A(t))$	(II. 29)^W [1]
[3]	$H((\forall v) A(v), A(t)) \prec ((\forall v) A(v) \supset A(t))$	(VI. 1)
[4]	$* \prec (\forall v) A(v) \supset A(t)$	(I. 4)^W [2, 3]

The expression (VI. 24) corresponds to the ninth axiom in § 22 of Frege's *Begriffsschrift*. Instead of '$* \prec$' Frege uses the sign '⊢'. But that sign means something else, namely: that the expression standing to the right of it renders a truth (Frege 1879, 2, § 1 [1967, 11]) or corresponds to a 'fact' (Frege 1879, 4, § 3 [1967, 13]). Thus, it designates a property of all formulas which render a truth-functional law. This property is the result of the fact that it is impossible for each of these formulas according to (VI. 24) to contain an empty term, and it is guaranteed for each of these formulas according to (VI. 17) to (VI. 22) that it cannot have any other value (as a functional value) than the value T under any distribution of the truth-values T and F on A, B or C.

2 Derived Formulas § 75 — 285

Law of particularization:
$*\prec B(t) \supset (\exists v) B(v)$ **(VI. 25)**

Proof:
[1]	$B(t) \prec (\exists v) B(v)$	(VI. 13)
[2]	$*\prec H(B(t), (\exists v) B(v))$	$(II. 29)^w$ [1]
[3]	$H(B(t), (\exists v) B(v)) \prec (B(v) \supset (\exists v) B(v))$	(VI. 1)
[4]	$*\prec B(t) \supset (\exists v) B(v)$	$(I. 4)^w$ [2, 3]

$*\prec \sim (\forall v) \sim A(v) \supset (\exists v) A(v)$ **(VI. 26)**

Proof:
[1]	$*\prec A(t) \supset (\exists v) A(v)$	(VI. 25)
[2]	$*\prec (A(t) \supset (\exists v) A(v)) \supset (\sim (\exists v) A(v) \supset \sim A(t))$	(VI. 20)
[3]	$((A(t) \supset (\exists v) A(v)) \supset (\sim (\exists v) A(v) \supset \sim A(t))$, $(A(t) \supset (\exists v) A(v)) \prec (\sim (\exists v) A(v) \supset \sim A(t))$	(VI. 8)
[4]	$*, *\prec \sim (\exists v) A(v) \supset \sim A(t)$	$(I. 5)^w$ [1, 2, 3]
[5]	$\sim A(t) \prec (\forall v) \sim A(v)$	(VI. 10)
[6]	$*\prec H(\sim A(t), (\forall v) \sim A(v))$	$(II. 29)^w$ [5]
[7]	$H(\sim A(t), (\forall v) \sim A(v)) \prec (\sim A(t) \supset (\forall v) \sim A(v))$	(VI. 1)
[8]	$*\prec \sim A(t) \supset (\forall v) \sim A(v)$	$(I. 4)^w$ [6, 7]
[9]	$(\sim (\exists v) A(v) \supset \sim A(t)), (\sim A(t) \supset (\forall v) \sim A(v))$, $\sim (\exists v) A(v) \prec (\forall v) \sim A(v)$	(VI. 9)
[10]	$*, *, *, \sim (\exists v) A(v) \prec (\forall v) \sim A(v)$	$(I. 5)^w$ [4, 8, 9]
[11]	$N(\exists v) A(v) \prec \sim (\exists v) A(v)$	(VI. 2)
[12]	$*, *, *, N(\exists v) A(v) \prec (\forall v) \sim A(v)$	$(I. 4)^w$ [11, 10]
[13]	$*, *, *, N(\forall v) \sim A(v) \prec NN(\exists v) A(v)$	$(I. 2)^w$ [12]
[14]	$\sim (\forall v) \sim A(v) \prec N(\forall v) \sim A(v)$	(VI. 2)
[15]	$NN(\exists v) A(v) \prec (\exists v) A(v)$	(VI. 4)
[16]	$*, *, *, \sim (\forall v) \sim A(v) \prec (\exists v) A(v)$	$(I. 4)^w$ [14, 13, 15]
[17]	$*, \sim (\forall v) \sim A(v) \prec (\exists v) A(v)$	$(II. 6)^w$ [16]
[18]	$*\prec H(\sim (\forall v) \sim A(v), (\exists v) A(v))$	$(II. 29)^w$ [17]
[19]	$H(\sim (\forall v) \sim A(v), (\exists v) A(v))$ $\prec (\sim (\forall v) \sim A(v) \supset (\exists v) A(v))$	(VI. 1)
[20]	$*\prec \sim (\forall v) \sim A(v) \supset (\exists v) A(v)$	$(I. 4)^w$ [18, 19]

$*\prec (\exists v) A(v) \supset \sim (\forall v) \sim A(v)$ **(VI. 27)**

Proof:
[1]	$A(('v) N A(v), \xi) \prec N I(('v) A(v), \xi)$	(V. 7)
[2]	$NN I(('v) A(v), \xi) \prec N A(('v) N A(v), \xi)$	$(I. 2)^w$ [1]
[3]	$I(('v) A(v), \xi) \prec NN I(('v) A(v), \xi)$	$(I. 1)^w$
[4]	$(\exists v) A(v) \prec I(('v) A(v), \xi)$	(V. 3)
[5]	$(\exists v) A(v) \prec N A(('v) N A(v), \xi)$	$(I. 4)^w$ [4, 3, 2]
[6]	$(\forall v) N A(v) \prec A(('v) N A(v), \xi)$	(V. 2)
[7]	$N A(('v) N A(v), \xi) \prec N(\forall v) N A(v)$	$(I. 2)^w$ [6]
[8]	$N A(t) \prec (\forall v) N A(v)$	(VI. 10)
[9]	$N(\forall v) N A(v) \prec NN A(t)$	$(I. 2)^w$ [8]

[10]	$NN\ A\ (t) \prec A\ (t)$	(VI. 4)
[11]	$* \prec A\ (t) \supset {\sim}{\sim} A\ (t)$	(VI. 21)
[12]	$* \prec ((\forall\ v) \sim A\ (v) \supset \sim A\ (t))$	(VI. 24)
[13]	$* \prec (((\forall\ v) \sim A\ (v) \supset \sim A\ (t))$	
	$\supset ({\sim}{\sim} A\ (t) \supset \sim (\forall\ v) \sim A\ (v)))$	(VI. 20)
[14]	$(((\forall\ v) \sim A\ (v) \supset \sim A\ (t)) \supset ({\sim}{\sim} A\ (t) \supset \sim (\forall\ v) \sim A\ (v))),$	
	$((\forall\ v) \sim A\ (v) \supset \sim A\ (t))$	
	$\prec ({\sim}{\sim} A\ (t) \supset \sim (\forall\ v) \sim A\ (v))$	(VI. 8)
[15]	$*, *, * \prec ({\sim}{\sim} A\ (t) \supset \sim (\forall\ v) \sim A\ (v))$	(I. 5)^W [12, 13, 14]
[16]	$(A\ (t) \supset {\sim}{\sim} A\ (t)), ({\sim}{\sim} A\ (t) \supset \sim (\forall\ v) \sim A\ (v)), A\ (t)$	
	$\prec \sim (\forall\ v) \sim A\ (v)$	(VI. 9)
[17]	$*, *, A\ (t) \prec \sim (\forall\ v) \sim A\ (v)$	(I. 5)^W [11, 15, 16]
[18]	$*, *, (\exists\ v) A\ (v) \prec \sim (\forall\ v) \sim A\ (v)$	(I. 4)^W [5, 7, 9, 10, 17]
[19]	$*, (\exists\ v) A\ (v) \prec \sim (\forall\ v) \sim A\ (v)$	(II. 6)^W [18]
[20]	$* \prec H ((\exists\ v) A\ (v), \sim (\forall\ v) \sim A\ (v))$	(II. 29)^W [19]
[21]	$H ((\exists\ v) A\ (v), \sim (\forall\ v) \sim A\ (v)) \prec (\exists\ v) A\ (v) \supset \sim (\forall\ v) \sim A\ (v)$	(IV. 1)
[22]	$* \prec (\exists\ v) A\ (v) \supset \sim (\forall\ v) \sim A\ (v)$	(I. 4)^W [20, 21]

§ 76 Contentful Inference

First example:

We have seen above, in § 68, that the validity of the inference

> If b is a circle, then b is a figure;
> Therefore: if a, when b is a figure, has not drawn b, then a, when b is a circle, has not drawn b.

is valid and that it corresponds to the form

> $H ([C\ (b)], [F\ (b)])$
> $\therefore H (H ([F\ (b)], N [D\ (a, b)], H ([C\ (b)], N [D\ (a, b)]))$.

Neither an inference of this form, nor an inference from categorical propositions, as, e.g., the inference treated in § 66:

> All circles are figures.
> Thus: if, when something is a figure a has not drawn it, then, when something is a circle, a has not drawn it, –

can be expressed in the language of the calculus of functions, since categorical or hypothetical propositional forms cannot be presented in this language.

However, it is certainly possible to present sound inferences in this language that are quite similar. If, e.g., we replace in the just described inferences the logical constants '$H (\ldots, \ldots)$' and '$N \ldots$' everywhere with '$\ldots \supset \ldots$' and '$\sim \ldots$', and we replace the sign for logical consequence with the sign for regular consequence, then we get from the inference mentioned first the following one:

$[C(b)] \supset [F(b)])$
$\prec ([F(b)] \supset \sim D(a, b)) \supset ([C(b)] \supset \sim D(a, b))$.

Or in words:

> b is not a circle unless b is a figure;
> therefore: it is not the case that b is not a figure unless a has not drawn b, unless it is the case that b is not a circle unless a has not drawn b.

By generalization, this inference can be additionally transformed into the inference:

$[K(b)] \supset [F(b)])$
$\prec ([F(b)] \supset \sim G(a, b)) \supset ([K(b)] \supset \sim G(a, b))$.

In words:

> For all x: x is not a circle unless x is a figure;
> therefore: for all y: there is an x such that x is a circle and y has drawn x not unless there is an x such that x is a figure and y has drawn x.

However, it is worth mentioning that such an inference which relies on truth functions is only valid if one understands the little word 'therefore' as expression of *regular* consequence, rather than *logical* consequence (in the sense of § 44, definitions 3 and 4), and thus does not replace the sign '$\prec$' with '$\therefore$'. We can see this by paying attention to the rules according to which the inference considered in § 68

$H([C(b)], [F(b)])$
$\therefore (H([F(b)], N[D(a, b)], H([C(b)], N[D(a, b)]))$

can be transformed into the inference

$(\forall x)(C(x) \supset F(x))$
$\prec (\forall y)((\exists x)(C(x) \& D(y, x)) \supset (\exists x)(F(x) \& D(y, x)))$.

Essential among these rules are rules whose validity is postulated according to § 72 or which depends on the postulates of § 72 (according to § 74 and § 75). Let us consider this transformation, in which the rules (VI. 1), (VI. 2), (VI. 8), and (VI. 15) are applied, step by step. To make for an easier overview, I replace the expressions '$[C(b)]$', '$[F(b)]$', and '$[D(a, b)]$' from line [2] with the letters 'c', 'f', 'd', in sequence:

[1] $H(c, f)$
       $\prec H(H(f, N d), H(c, N d))$
[2] $(c \supset f), c \prec f$ (VI. 8)
[3] $(c \supset f) \prec H(c, f)$ (II. 1)^W [2]

[4] $(c \supset f)$
     $\prec H(H(f, Nd), H(c, Nd))$ (I. 4)^w [3, 1]

Following this, the premise in line [4] can be generalized:

[5] $(\forall x)(C(x) \supset F(x)) \prec (c \supset f)$ (VI. 15)
[6] $(\forall x)(C(x) \supset F(x))$
     $\prec H(H(f, Nd), H(c, Nd))$ (I. 4)^w [5, 4]

Then the two hypothetical clauses of the conclusion are to be replaced by truth functions, namely by $f \supset \sim d$ or by $c \supset \sim d$:

[7] $Nd \prec \sim d$ (VI. 2)
[8] $\ast \prec H(Nd, \sim d)$ (II. 29)^w [7]
[9] $\sim d \prec Nd$ (VI. 2)
[10] $\ast \prec H(\sim d, Nd)$ (II. 29)^w [9]
[11] $H(H(f, Nd), H(c, Nd)),$
      $H(\sim d, Nd), H(Nd, \sim d)$
      $\prec H(H(f, \sim d), H(c, \sim d))$ (II. 16)^w
[12] $\ast, \ast, H(H(f, Nd), H(c, Nd))$
      $\prec H(H(f, \sim d), H(c, \sim d))$ (I. 5)^w [8, 10, 11]
[13] $\ast, \ast, (\forall x)(C(x) \supset F(x))$
      $\prec H(H(f, \sim d), H(c, \sim d))$ (I. 4)^w [6, 12]
[14] $H(H(f, \sim d), H(c, \sim d)),$
      $H((f \supset \sim d), H(f, \sim d))$
      $\prec H((f \supset \sim d), H(c, \sim d))$ (II. 17)^w
[15] $(f \supset \sim d), f \prec \sim d)$ (VI. 8)
[16] $(f \supset \sim d) \prec H(f, \sim d)$ (II. 1)^w [15]
[17] $\ast \prec H((f \supset \sim d), H(f, \sim d))$ (II. 29)^w [16]
[18] $\ast, H(H(f, \sim d), H(c, \sim d))$
      $\prec H(f \supset \sim d), H(c, \sim g)$ (I. 4)^w [17, 14]
[19] $\ast, \ast, \ast, (\forall x)(C(x) \supset F(x))$
      $\prec H((f \supset \sim d), H(c, \sim d))$ (I. 4)^w [13, 18]
[20] $H(c, \sim d) \prec (c \supset \sim d)$ (VI. 1)
[21] $\ast \prec H(H(c, \sim d), (c \supset \sim d))$ (II. 29)^w [20]
[22] $H((f \supset \sim d), H(c, \sim d)),$
      $H(H(c, \sim d), (c \supset \sim d))$
      $\prec H((f \supset \sim d), (c \supset \sim d))$ (II. 13)^w
[23] $\ast, H((f \supset \sim d), H(c, \sim d))$
      $\prec H((f \supset \sim d), (c \supset \sim d))$ (I. 4)^w [21, 22]
[24] $\ast, \ast, \ast, \ast, (\forall x)(C(x) \supset F(x))$
      $\prec H((f \supset \sim d), (c \supset \sim d))$ (I. 4)^w [19, 23]

2 Derived Formulas § 76 — 289

Next, the two truth-functional sub-propositions of the conclusion can be generalized:

[25] $(\forall x)(F(x) \supset \sim [D(a, x)]) \prec (f \supset \sim d)$ (VI. 15)
[26] $* \prec H(((\forall x)(F(x) \supset \sim [D(a, x)])), (f \supset \sim [D(a, x)]))$ (II. 29)^w [25]
[27] $H(((\forall x)(F(x) \supset \sim [D(a, x)])), (f \supset \sim d)),$
$H((f \supset \sim d), (c \supset \sim d))$
$\prec H((\forall x)(F(x) \supset \sim [D(a, x)]), (c \supset \sim d))$ (II. 13)^w
[28] $*, H((f \supset \sim d), (c \supset \sim d))$
$\prec H((\forall x)(F(x) \supset \sim [D(a, x)]), (c \supset \sim d))$ (I. 4)^w [26, 27]
[29] $*, *, *, *, *, (\forall x)(C(x) \supset F(x))$
$\prec H((\forall x)(F(x) \supset \sim [D(a, x)]), (c \supset \sim d))$ (I. 4)^w [24, 28]
[30] $(c \supset \sim d) \prec (\forall x)(C(x) \supset \sim [D(a, x)])$ (VI. 10)
[31] $* \prec H((c \supset \sim d), (\forall x)(C(x) \supset \sim [D(a, x)]))$ (II. 29)^w [30]
[32] $H((\forall x)(F(x) \supset \sim [D(a, x)]), (c \supset \sim d)),$
$H((c \supset \sim d), (\forall x)(C(x) \supset \sim [D(a, x)]))$
$\prec H((\forall x)(F(x) \supset \sim [D(a, x)]), (\forall x)(C(x) \supset \sim [D(a, x)]))$ (II. 13)^w
[33] $*, H((\forall x)(F(x) \supset \sim [D(a, x)]), (c \supset \sim d))$ (I. 4)^w
$\prec H((\forall x)(F(x) \supset \sim [D(a, x)]), (\forall x)(C(x) \supset \sim [D(a, x)]))$ [31, 32]
[34] $*, *, *, *, *, *, (\forall x)(C(x) \supset F(x))$
$\prec H((\forall x)(F(x) \supset \sim [D(a, x)]), (\forall x)(C(x) \supset \sim [D(a, x)]))$ (I. 4)^w [29, 33]

The contraposition rule can be applied to the conclusion:

[35] $H((\forall x)(F(x) \supset \sim [D(a, x)]), (\forall x)(C(x) \supset \sim [D(a, x)]))$
$\prec H(N(\forall x)(C(x) \supset \sim [D(a, x)]), N(\forall x)(F(x) \supset \sim [D(a, x)]))$ (II. 8)^w
[36] $*, *, *, *, *, *, *, (\forall x)(C(x) \supset F(x))$
$\prec H(N(\forall x)(C(x) \supset \sim [D(a, x)]),$
$N(\forall x)(F(x) \supset \sim [D(a, x)]))$ (I. 4)^w [34, 35]

Both clauses of the conclusion can be transformed into truth-functions:

[37] $\sim (\forall x)(C(x) \supset \sim [D(a, x)])$
$\prec N(\forall x)(C(x) \supset \sim [D(a, x)])$ (VI. 2)
[38] $* \prec H(\sim (\forall x)(C(x) \supset \sim [D(a, x)]),$
$N(\forall x)(C(x) \supset \sim [D(a, x)]))$ (II. 29)^w [37]
[39] $H(\sim (\forall x)(C(x) \supset \sim [D(a, x)]), N(\forall x)(C(x) \supset \sim [D(a, x)])),$
$H(N(\forall x)(C(x) \supset \sim [D(a, x)]), N(\forall x)(F(x) \supset \sim [D(a, x)]))$
$\prec H(\sim (\forall x)(C(x) \supset \sim [D(a, x)]),$
$N(\forall x)(F(x) \supset \sim [D(a, x)]))$ (II. 13)^w
[40] $*, H(N(\forall x)(C(x) \supset \sim [D(a, x)]), N(\forall x)(F(x) \supset \sim [D(a, x)]))$
$\prec H(\sim (\forall x)(C(x) \supset \sim [D(a, x)]),$
$N(\forall x)(F(x) \supset \sim [D(a, x)]))$ (I. 4)^w [38, 39]
[41] $*, *, *, *, *, *, *, (\forall x)(C(x) \supset F(x))$
$\prec H(\sim (\forall x)(C(x) \supset \sim [D(a, x)]),$ (I. 4)^w
$N(\forall x)(F(x) \supset \sim [D(a, x)])$ [36, 40]

[42]	$N\,(\forall\,x)\,(F\,(x) \supset \sim [D\,(a,x)]) \prec \sim (\forall\,x)\,(F\,(x) \supset \sim [D\,(a,x)])$	(VI. 2)
[43]	$^* \prec H\,(N\,(\forall\,x)\,(F\,(x) \supset \sim [D\,(a,x)]),$	
	$\sim (\forall\,x)\,(F\,(x) \supset \sim [D\,(a,x)]))$	(II. 29)^W [42]
[44]	$H\,(\sim (\forall\,x)\,(C\,(x) \supset \sim [D\,(a,x)]),\,N\,(\forall\,x)\,(F\,(x) \supset \sim [D\,(a,x)])),$	
	$H\,(N\,(\forall\,x)\,(F\,(x) \supset \sim [D\,(a,x)]),\,\sim (\forall\,x)\,(F\,(x) \supset \sim [D\,(a,x)]))$	
	$\prec H\,(\sim (\forall\,x)\,(C\,(x) \supset \sim [D\,(a,x)]),$	
	$\sim (\forall\,x)\,(F\,(x) \supset \sim [D\,(a,x)]))$	(II. 13)^W
[45]	$^*, H\,(\sim (\forall x)\,(C\,(x) \supset \sim [D\,(a,x)]),\,N\,(\forall x)\,(F\,(x) \supset \sim [D\,(a,x)])$	
	$\prec H\,(\sim (\forall\,x)\,(C\,(x) \supset \sim [D\,(a,x)]),$	(I. 4)^W
	$\sim (\forall\,x)\,(F\,(x) \supset \sim [D\,(a,x)]))$	[43, 44]
[46]	$^*, ^*, ^*, ^*, ^*, ^*, ^*, ^*, (\forall\,x)\,(C\,(x) \supset F\,(x))$	
	$\prec H\,(\sim (\forall\,x)\,(C\,(x) \supset \sim [D\,(a,x)]),$	(I. 4)^W
	$\sim (\forall\,x)\,(F\,(x) \supset \sim [D\,(a,x)]))$	[41, 45]

Finally, the hypothetical conclusion can be transformed into a generalized truth function:

[47]	$H\,(\sim (\forall\,x)\,(C\,(x) \supset \sim [D\,(a,x)]),\,\sim (\forall\,x)\,(F\,(x) \supset \sim [D\,(a,x)]))$	
	$\prec (\sim (\forall\,x)\,(C\,(x) \supset \sim [D\,(a,x)]) \supset \sim (\forall\,x)\,(F\,(x) \supset \sim [D\,(a,x)]))$	(VI. 1)
[48]	$\sim (\forall\,x)\,(C\,(x) \supset \sim [D\,(a,x)]) \supset \sim (\forall\,x)\,(F\,(x) \supset \sim [D\,(a,x)])$	
	$\prec (\forall\,y)\,(\sim (\forall x)\,(C\,(x) \supset \sim D\,(y,x)) \supset \sim (\forall x)\,(F\,(x) \supset \sim D\,(y,x)))$	(VI. 10)
[49]	$^*, ^*, ^*, ^*, ^*, ^*, ^*, ^*, (\forall\,x)\,(C\,(x) \supset F\,(x))$	
	$\prec (\forall y)\,(\sim (\forall x)\,(C\,(x) \supset \sim D\,(y,x)) \supset \sim (\forall x)$	(I. 4)^W
	$(F\,(x) \supset \sim D\,(y,x)))$	[46, 47, 48]
[50]	$^*, (\forall x)\,(C\,(x) \supset F\,(x)) \prec$	
	$(\forall y)\,(\sim (\forall x)\,(C\,(x) \supset \sim D\,(y,x)) \sim (\forall x)\,(F(x) \supset \sim D\,(y,x)))$	(II.)^W [49]

Since $(\exists\,v)\,A\,(v)$, according to (VI. 26) and (VI. 27), is an abbreviation for '$\sim (\forall\,x) \sim A\,(v)$' and '$\sim (\ldots \& \sim \ldots)$' is equivalent to '$\ldots \supset \ldots$', the consequence in line [50] is equivalent to:

$(\forall\,x)\,(C\,(x) \supset F\,(x))$
$\prec (\forall\,y)\,((\exists x)\,(C\,(x)\,\&\,D\,(y,x)) \supset (\exists x)\,(F\,(x)\,\&\,D\,(y,x)))$.[225]

Second example:

There is something of which everything consists.
Therefore: everything consists of something.

---

[225] If we replace '$\ldots \prec \ldots$' with '$\ldots \therefore \ldots$', we then get the – somewhat less accurate – expression which Quine (1959, § 30) offers for the inference, which has been much-discussed since the medieval period (as an example of a non-syllogistic consequence), 'All circles are figures; therefore, all who draw circles, draw figures'.

2 Derived Formulas § 76

The validity of this inference is provable if it is specified as follows, letting '$F(x, y)$' abbreviate for 'x consists of y':

$$(\exists y)(\forall x) F(x, y) \prec (\forall x)(\exists y) F(x, y)$$

Although in this inference, unlike in the first example, no truth functions occur directly but only an exchange of quantifiers, its validity can be proven on the assumption of rules whose validity is postulated according to § 72 or according to § 74 or § 75, which rely on § 72. As the following proof shows, these are the rules (VI. 1), (VI. 2), (VI. 4), (VI. 5), (VI. 10), and (VI. 15). Because of these rules, the sign '$\prec$' should not be replaced with '$\therefore$'.

[1]	$N A\,(('x)\,(\exists y)\,F(x, y),\,\xi_1) \prec I\,(('x)\,N\,(\exists y)\,F(x, y),\,\xi_1)$	(VI. 5)
[2]	$I\,(('x)\,N\,(\exists y)\,F(x, y),\,\xi_1) \prec A\,(('x)\,N\,(\exists y)\,F(x, y),\,\zeta_1)$	(III. 3)^W
[3]	$A\,(('x)\,N\,(\exists y)\,F(x, y),\,\zeta_1) \prec \underset{\sim}{A}\,(('x)\,N\,(\exists y)\,F(x, y),\,\zeta_1)$	(III. 11)^W
[4]	$\underset{\sim}{A}\,(('x)\,N\,(\exists y)\,F(x, y),\,\zeta_1) \prec N\underset{\sim}{A}\,(('x)\,(\exists y)\,F(x, y),\,\zeta_1)$	(V. 9)
[5]	$[(\exists y)\,F(a, y)] \prec \underset{\sim}{A}\,(('x)\,(\exists y)\,F(x, y),\,\zeta_1)$	(V. 1)
[6]	$N\underset{\sim}{A}\,(('x)\,(\exists y)\,F(x, y),\,\zeta_1) \prec N\,[(\exists y)\,F(a, y)]$	(I. 2)^W [5]
[7]	$N A\,(('x)\,(\exists y)\,F(x, y),\,\xi_1) \prec N\,[(\exists y)\,F(a, y)]$	(I. 4)^W [1, 2, 3, 4, 6]
[8]	$I\,(('y)\,F(a, y),\,\xi_2) \prec (\exists y)\,F(a, y)$	(V. 3)
[9]	$N\,[(\exists y)\,F(a, y)] \prec N I\,(('y)\,F(a, y),\,\xi_2)$	(I. 2)^W [8]
[10]	$N I\,(('y)\,F(a, y),\,\xi_2) \prec N A\,(('y)\,F(a, y),\,\xi_2)$	(III. 14)^W
[11]	$N A\,(('y)\,F(a, y),\,\xi_2) \prec I\,(('y)\,N F(a, y),\,\xi_2)$	(VI. 5)
[12]	$I\,(('y)\,N F(a, y),\,\xi_2) \prec A\,(('y)\,N F(a, y),\,\zeta_2)$	(III. 3)^W
[13]	$A\,(('y)\,N F(a, y),\,\zeta_2) \prec \underset{\sim}{A}\,(('y)\,N F(a, y),\,\zeta_2)$	(III. 11)^W
[14]	$\underset{\sim}{A}\,(('y)\,N F(a, y),\,\zeta_2) \prec N\,[F(a, b)]$	(I. 4)^W [14, 16]
[15]	$N A\,(('x)\,(\exists y)\,F(x, y),\,\xi_1) \prec N\,[F(a, b)]$	(I. 4)^W [7, 9, 10, 11, 12, 13, 14]
[16]	$(\forall x)\,F(x, b) \prec [F(a, b)]$	(VI. 15)
[17]	$N\,[F(a, b)] \prec N\,(\forall x)\,F(x, b)$	(I. 2)^W [16]
[18]	$N\,(\forall x)\,F(x, b) \prec {\sim}(\forall x)\,F(x, b)$	(VI. 2)
[19]	${\sim}(\forall x)\,F(x, b) \prec (\forall y)\,{\sim}(\forall x)\,F(x, y)$	(VI. 10)
[20]	$N\,[F(a, b)] \prec (\forall y)\,{\sim}(\forall x)\,F(x, y)$	(I. 4)^W [17, 18, 19]
[21]	$N A\,(('x)\,(\exists y)\,F(x, y),\,\xi_1) \prec (\forall y)\,{\sim}(\forall x)\,F(x, y)$	(I. 4)^W [15, 20]
[22]	$(\forall y)\,{\sim}(\forall x)\,F(x, y) \prec NN A\,(('x)\,(\exists y)\,F(x, y),\,\xi_1)$	(I. 2)^W [21]
[23]	${\sim}(\forall y)\,{\sim}(\forall x)\,F(x, y) \prec N\,(\forall y)\,{\sim}(\forall x)\,F(x, y)$	(VI. 2)
[24]	${*}{\prec}\,(\exists y)\,(\forall x)\,F(x, y) \supset {\sim}(\forall y)\,{\sim}(\forall x)\,F(x, y)$	(VI. 27)
[25]	$((\exists y)\,(\forall x)\,F(x, y) \supset {\sim}(\forall y)\,{\sim}(\forall x)\,F(x, y))$	
	$\prec H\,((\exists y)\,(\forall x)\,F(x, y),\,{\sim}(\forall y)\,{\sim}(\forall x)\,F(x, y))$	(VI. 1)
[26]	${*}{\prec} H\,((\exists y)\,(\forall x)\,F(x, y),\,{\sim}(\forall y)\,{\sim}(\forall x)\,F(x, y))$	(I. 4)^W [24, 25]
[27]	${*},\,(\exists y)\,(\forall x)\,F(x, y) \prec {\sim}(\forall y)\,{\sim}(\forall x)\,F(x, y)$	(II. 30)^W [26]
[28]	$NN A\,(('x)\,(\exists y)\,F(x, y),\,\xi_1) \prec A\,(('x)\,(\exists y)\,F(x, y),\,\xi_1)$	(VI. 4)
[29]	$A\,(('x)\,(\exists y)\,F(x, y),\,\xi_1) \prec (\forall x)\,(\exists y)\,F(x, y)$	(V. 2)
[30]	$(\exists y)\,(\forall x)\,F(x, y) \prec (\forall x)\,(\exists y)\,F(x, y)$	(I. 4)^W [27, 23, 22, 28, 29]

Within the framework of the calculus of functions (i.e., in classical predicate logic) there are of course much shorter and simpler methods for the validity proofs of the two examples of contentful inference discussed here. Here, in § 76, it is not supposed to be shown that there is a more cumbersome and complicated method. Rather, the examples should make clear that even for categorical propositions with a low complexity of conceptual content, the number of logical steps underlying inferences related to this content can be very great. In the shorter and simpler methods used in classical predicate logic these steps take place covertly.

Section Seven
Provability and Derivability within the Logical Calculus of Functions

§ 77 Notation

The system of the extended deductive logic, as far as I have unfolded it in Section Six, contains a series of transformation rules and meaning rules which allow us to present this system in a reduced symbolic language, in which no syllogistic rule can be expressed but rules which do not belong to the syllogistic can be. This reduction of the symbolic language consists in restricting its use to a relatively small set of descriptive and logical signs.

Concerning the descriptive signs, in this reduced language all symbols which are used directly to present a conceptual content are set aside. On the basis of the abbreviations introduced above for propositions whose conceptual content can be rendered with logical functional expressions (in the sense of § 71, def. 2), rules of the extended deductive logic can be presented in a way which makes all the concept variables introduced in § 51 dispensable. All conceptual constants introduced in § 64 are dispensable in this manner of presentation as well. The same holds, finally, for all kinds of concept expressions which were defined in § 65 and § 71 and which rely on the use of a prefix, namely on the use of the predicator, which has thus now become superfluous as well.

We can also significantly reduce the arsenal of signs with respect to the remaining prefixes. On the basis of the logical relations between the universal and existential quantifier (assuming postulates (VI. 5) and (VI. 6)), it is possible to do without one of these two quantifiers entirely. Thus, '($\exists$ x) ( )' may be replaced everywhere with '~ ($\forall$ x) ~ ( )' (on the basis of (VI. 26) and (VI. 27)).

In addition, on the assumption of postulates (VI. 3) and (VI. 4) it has become possible to replace the sign for elementary negation everywhere with truth-functional negation. The logical constants that denote hypothetical and disjunctive propositions are also replaceable with truth-functional signs on this assumption. The type and number of truth-functional signs which must be in use for this replacement depends of course on which modes of abbreviation are to be utilized. In Section Six, ' . . . $\supset$ . . .' and '~ . . .' were introduced as the only truth-functional signs. One could now use 'A & B' to abbreviate '~ (A $\supset$ ~ B)' and replace 'A $\supset$ B' with '~ (A & ~ B)'. Moreover, additional abbreviations could be introduced, for example, 'A $\vee$ B' for '~ A $\supset$ B', or 'A $\equiv$ B' for '(A $\supset$ B) & (B $\supset$ A)', or 'A | B' for '~ (A & B)'. In any case, one could make do with two connectives. Since '~ A' is equivalent to 'A | A' and '(A & B)' to '(A | B) | (A |

B)', it would even be possible to get by with a single connective (i.e., the Sheffer stroke).

Formulas which contain only signs of the just described simplified and reduced language of the expanded deductive logic will be designated in what follows by metalogical signs $\mathfrak{A}_1, \mathfrak{A}_2, \ldots, \mathfrak{A}_n$, or $\mathfrak{A}, \mathfrak{B}, \mathfrak{C}$. $\mathfrak{A}$ will thus be a formula in which only functional expressions and propositional letters ('p', 'q', 'r', etc.) occur as descriptive signs, only simplified (i.e., appearing without square brackets and without quantifiers) expressions of the form $\mathfrak{B}(t)$ or $\mathfrak{B}(v)$ occur as expressions for non-quantified or singular propositions, and finally only quantifiers or truth-functional connectives occur as logical signs. The reduced language to which these formulas belong I call the *language of the logical calculus of functions*. All axiomatic systems of the logical calculus of functions make use of such a language. They differ essentially from each other only by making use of different numbers and different kinds of quantifiers and connectives.

As for the remaining metalogical signs, the signs '(. . .) ⊢ . . .' and '(. . .) ⊨ . . .' are both needed in what follows; their meaning will be defined below, in § 79 and § 81.

§ 78 An Axiomatic System of the Logical Calculus of Functions

In the reduced language of the logical calculus of functions, logical rules can no longer be derived from principles in the same way as I have done up to now (in §§ 45–75). My derivation procedure to this point consisted essentially in applying metarules to rules, and ultimately to basic rules. Above, I called this procedure the *syllogistic* method of derivation. The *axiomatic* derivation procedure differs from this method in that it assumes a certain number of basic formulas (which do not express rules) as a system of axioms or axiom schemata, in order to apply appropriate derivation rules to these basic formulas and to derive other formulas from them. The only rules that are considered appropriate derivation rules are those which, first, are not metarules and, second, are formulated in the same language in which the axioms or axiom schemata are formulated as well.

As for the system of basic formulas to which the axiomatic derivation procedure is applied, Frege was the first to establish such a system in his *Begriffsschrift* of 1879. It encompasses (apart from two axioms which have identity relations as their content) in total seven axioms, the content of which corresponds to the content of the formulas (VI. 17) to (VI. 22) and (VI. 24), as developed above (see § 75), but with the difference that Frege's axioms contain propositional letters or functional expressions instead of the metalogical signs 'A', 'B', and 'C'. Consequently, his logical system requires establishing substitution rules, which would be superfluous if, instead of

Frege's expressions, axiom schemata were used as basic rules, i.e., expressions that correspond formally precisely to the formulas (VI. 17) to (VI. 22) and (VI. 24) as well.

It has been shown that Frege's axiom system can also be simplified in another respect. Frege's third axiom (see Frege 1879/1967, § 16), which corresponds to formula (VI. 19), has turned out to be superfluous, after Jan Łukasiewicz (1935, 111–31, especially 126) showed that it is derivable from the first two axioms, which correspond to the formulas (VI. 17) and (VI. 18). Moreover, it has been shown that formula (VI. 23) is suitable to replace the formulas (VI. 20), (VI. 21), and (VI. 22), which correspond, in sequence, to the fourth, fifth, and sixth axioms in Frege's system (see *Begriffsschrift* §17 to § 19). Frege's system of axioms can thus be replaced by the following system of four axiom schemata in total, of which the fourth corresponds on the one hand to Frege's ninth axiom, on the other hand to formula (VI. 24) (see Frege 1879/1967, § 22):[226]

$\mathfrak{A} \supset (\mathfrak{B} \supset \mathfrak{A})$	(VI. 17)*
$(\mathfrak{A} \supset (\mathfrak{B} \supset \mathfrak{C})) \supset ((\mathfrak{A} \supset \mathfrak{B}) \supset (\mathfrak{A} \supset \mathfrak{C}))$	(VI. 18)*
$(\sim \mathfrak{A} \supset \sim \mathfrak{B}) \supset (\mathfrak{B} \supset \mathfrak{A})$	(VI. 23)*
$(\forall v)\, \mathfrak{A}\,(v) \supset \mathfrak{A}\,(t)$.	(VI. 24)*

Concerning the derivation rules which are needed to be able to deduce other formulas from this system of formulas, one can make do with two rules in total. We can gain these rules, just like the four axiom schemata (VI. 17)* to (VI. 24)*, by merely transforming expressions which I have already introduced above. Namely, from formula (VI. 8) we get the formula (VI. 8),* as the expression for a rule which is called a 'detachment rule' in traditional nomenclature:

$\mathfrak{A},\ \mathfrak{A} \supset \mathfrak{B} \prec \mathfrak{B}$.	(VI. 8)*

We gain the second detachment rule on the basis of (VI. 11). It is usually called the 'rule of posterior generalization':

In case *t* only occurs in the argument places of $\mathfrak{B}\,(t)$, then:

$(\mathfrak{A} \supset \mathfrak{B}\,(t)) \prec (\mathfrak{A} \supset (\forall v)\, \mathfrak{B}\,(v))$.	(VI. 11)*

Both the detachment rule as well as the rule of posterior generalization are utilized in Frege's *Begriffsschrift* as derivation rules (see Frege 1879/1967, § 6 and § 11). In addition, Frege utilizes a still further generalization rule. This one corresponds to rule (VI. 10) (see Frege 1879/1967, § 11):

In case *t* only occurs in the argument places of $\mathfrak{A}\,(t)$, then:

---

[226] Cf. on this system the presentation by Ansgar Beckermann (1997, 272–301). On the history of the simplification of Frege's logical system, see Kneale & Kneale 1975, 534–35.

$\mathfrak{A}(t) \prec (\forall v) \mathfrak{A}(v).$ (VI. 10)*

But (VI. 10)* can be derived, like all the remaining rules that are admissible within the calculus of functions, with the aid of derivation rules (VI. 8)* and (VI. 11)* from the system of the four formulas (VI. 17)*, (VI. 18)*, (VI. 23)*, and (VI. 24)*. What it means for a rule to be admissible within the calculus of functions will come through with the definitions. These definitions fix the structure for the axiomatic calculus that is based on the system of four axiom schemata and two derivation rules just sketched.[227] This axiomatic calculus is to be called *FC*.

§ 79 Definitions

1. If $\mathfrak{A}$, $\mathfrak{B}$, and $\mathfrak{C}$ are propositions or logical functional expressions in the language of the calculus of functions, then the formulas

$\mathfrak{A} \supset (\mathfrak{B} \supset \mathfrak{A})$	(VI. 17)*
$(\mathfrak{A} \supset (\mathfrak{B} \supset \mathfrak{C})) \supset ((\mathfrak{A} \supset \mathfrak{B}) \supset (\mathfrak{A} \supset \mathfrak{C}))$	(VI. 18)*
$(\sim \mathfrak{A} \supset \sim \mathfrak{B}) \supset (\mathfrak{B} \supset \mathfrak{A})$	(VI. 23)*
$(\forall v) \mathfrak{A}(v) \supset \mathfrak{A}(t)$	(VI. 24)*

   are the *axioms of FC*.
2. The detachment rule, according to which it holds that: $\mathfrak{A}, \mathfrak{A} \supset \mathfrak{B} \prec \mathfrak{B}$ (VI. 8)*, and the rule of posterior generalization, according to which, in case t only occurs in the argument places of $\mathfrak{B}(t)$, it holds that: $(\mathfrak{A} \supset \mathfrak{B}(t)) \prec (\mathfrak{A} \supset (\forall v) \mathfrak{B}(v))$ (VI. 11)*, are the *derivation rules of FC*.
3. A finite sequence $\mathfrak{A}_1, \mathfrak{A}_2, \ldots, \mathfrak{A}_n$ of formulas is a *proof in the calculus of functions* for a formula $\mathfrak{A}_n$ if and only if, for all i with $1 \leq i \leq n$, the following holds: $\mathfrak{A}_i$ is an axiom of *FC*, or $\mathfrak{A}_i$ is deducible from one of the preceding formulas $\mathfrak{A}_{i-1}$ with the help of the detachment rule or the rule of posterior generalization.
4. A formula $\mathfrak{A}$ is a *theorem of the calculus of functions* (symbolically expressed: $\vdash \mathfrak{A}$) if and only if there is a proof for $\mathfrak{A}$ in the calculus of functions.
5. A finite sequence $\mathfrak{A}_1, \mathfrak{A}_2, \ldots, \mathfrak{A}_n$ of formulas is a *deduction from a set of formulas Γ of the calculus of functions* if and only if, for all i with $1 \leq i \leq n$, the following holds: $\mathfrak{A}_i$ is an axiom of *FC*, or $\mathfrak{A}_i$ is an element of the set Γ, or $\mathfrak{A}_i$ is deducible from one of the preceding formulas $\mathfrak{A}_{i-1}$ with the help of the detachment rule or the rule of posterior generalization.

---

[227] Compare with the following Beckermann 1997, 134–67 and 272–301.

6. A formula $\mathfrak{A}$ is *deducible in FC from a set of formulas* Γ (symbolically expressed: $\Gamma \vdash \mathfrak{A}$) if and only if there is a deduction of $\mathfrak{A}$ in *FC* from Γ.
7. If the formula $\mathfrak{A}$ is deducible, so that it holds that: $\mathfrak{A}_1, \mathfrak{A}_2, \ldots, \mathfrak{A}_n \vdash \mathfrak{A}$, then the rule $\mathfrak{A}_1, \mathfrak{A}_2, \ldots, \mathfrak{A}_n \prec \mathfrak{A}$ is called *admissible in FC*.

§ 80 Theorems of the Calculus of Functions

Because of these seven definitions, there is an essential difference in what was called a proof in §§ 45–75 and what may be called a proof within an axiomatically constructed logical calculus. We can illustrate this difference by presenting some theorems and derivability claims which can hold as provable in the framework of *FC*.

First of all, each of the formulas (VI. 17)* to (VI. 24)* (in § 78) is *per definitionem* a theorem in the sense of § 79, definition 4. For any law-formula of this kind – call it $\mathfrak{A}$ – can be derived from itself by means of the rule of detachment, since $\mathfrak{A}$ is derivable from $\mathfrak{A}$ and $\mathfrak{A} \supset \mathfrak{A}$. Therefore, we may regard the axioms (VI. 17)* to (VI. 24)* as theorems as well and may thus at once write:

$\vdash \mathfrak{A} \supset (\mathfrak{B} \supset \mathfrak{A})$ (1)

$\vdash (\mathfrak{A} \supset (\mathfrak{B} \supset \mathfrak{C})) \supset ((\mathfrak{A} \supset \mathfrak{B}) \supset (\mathfrak{A} \supset \mathfrak{C}))$ (2)

$\vdash (\sim \mathfrak{A} \supset \sim \mathfrak{B}) \supset (\mathfrak{B} \supset \mathfrak{A})$ (3)

$\vdash (\forall v) \, \mathfrak{A}(v) \supset \mathfrak{A}(t)$ (4)

From these first four theorems, further formulas can be derived, with the application of the detachment rule and the rule of posterior generalization, which are partly theorems and partly express the deducibility of one formula from one or more other formulas; for example, the following:

$\vdash \mathfrak{A} \supset \mathfrak{A}$ (5)

Proof:
[1] $\mathfrak{A} \supset ((\mathfrak{A} \supset \mathfrak{A}) \supset \mathfrak{A})$ (1)
[2] $(\mathfrak{A} \supset ((\mathfrak{A} \supset \mathfrak{A}) \supset \mathfrak{A})) \supset ((\mathfrak{A} \supset ((\mathfrak{A} \supset \mathfrak{A})) \supset (\mathfrak{A} \supset \mathfrak{A}))$ (2)
[3] $(\mathfrak{A} \supset ((\mathfrak{A} \supset \mathfrak{A})) \supset (\mathfrak{A} \supset \mathfrak{A})$ (VI. 8)* [1, 2]
[4] $\mathfrak{A} \supset (\mathfrak{A} \supset \mathfrak{A})$ (1)
[5] $\mathfrak{A} \supset \mathfrak{A}$ (VI. 8)* [3, 4]

$\mathfrak{A} \supset \mathfrak{B}, \mathfrak{B} \supset \mathfrak{C} \vdash \mathfrak{A} \supset \mathfrak{C}$ (6)

Proof:
[1] $\mathfrak{A} \supset \mathfrak{B}$ Premise
[2] $\mathfrak{B} \supset \mathfrak{C}$ Premise

[3] $(\mathfrak{B} \supset \mathfrak{C}) \supset (\mathfrak{A} \supset (\mathfrak{B} \supset \mathfrak{C}))$ *(1)*
[4] $\mathfrak{A} \supset (\mathfrak{B} \supset \mathfrak{C})$ (VI. 8)* [2, 3]
[5] $(\mathfrak{A} \supset (\mathfrak{B} \supset \mathfrak{C})) \supset ((\mathfrak{A} \supset \mathfrak{B}) \supset (\mathfrak{A} \supset \mathfrak{C}))$ *(2)*
[6] $(\mathfrak{A} \supset \mathfrak{B}) \supset (\mathfrak{A} \supset \mathfrak{C})$ (VI. 8)* [4, 5]
[7] $\mathfrak{A} \supset \mathfrak{C}$ (VI. 8)* [1, 6]

$\mathfrak{A} \supset (\mathfrak{A} \supset \mathfrak{B}) \vdash \mathfrak{A} \supset \mathfrak{B}$ **(7)**

Proof:
[1] $\mathfrak{A} \supset (\mathfrak{A} \supset \mathfrak{B})$ *Premise*
[2] $(\mathfrak{A} \supset (\mathfrak{A} \supset \mathfrak{B})) \supset ((\mathfrak{A} \supset \mathfrak{A}) \supset (\mathfrak{A} \supset \mathfrak{B}))$ *(2)*
[3] $(\mathfrak{A} \supset \mathfrak{A}) \supset (\mathfrak{A} \supset \mathfrak{B})$ (VI. 8)* [1, 2]
[4] $\mathfrak{A} \supset \mathfrak{A}$ *(5)*
[5] $\mathfrak{A} \supset \mathfrak{B}$ (VI. 8)* [3, 4]

$\vdash \sim \mathfrak{A} \supset (\mathfrak{A} \supset \mathfrak{B})$ **(8)**

Proof:
[1] $\mathfrak{A} \supset (\sim \mathfrak{B} \supset \sim \mathfrak{A})$ *(2)*
[2] $(\sim \mathfrak{B} \supset \sim \mathfrak{A}) \supset (\mathfrak{A} \supset \mathfrak{B})$ *(3)*
[3] $\sim \mathfrak{A} \supset (\mathfrak{A} \supset \mathfrak{B})$ *(6)* [1, 2]

$\sim \mathfrak{B} \supset \sim \mathfrak{A} \vdash \mathfrak{A} \supset \mathfrak{B}$ **(9)**

Proof:
[1] $\sim \mathfrak{B} \supset \sim \mathfrak{A}$ *Premise*
[2] $(\sim \mathfrak{B} \supset \sim \mathfrak{A}) \supset (\mathfrak{A} \supset \mathfrak{B})$ *(3)*
[3] $\mathfrak{A} \supset \mathfrak{B}$ (VI. 8)* [1, 2]

$\vdash \sim \sim \mathfrak{A} \supset \mathfrak{A}$ **(10)**[228]

Proof:
[1] $\sim \sim \mathfrak{A} \supset (\sim \mathfrak{A} \supset \sim \sim \sim \mathfrak{A})$ *(8)*
[2] $(\sim \mathfrak{A} \supset \sim \sim \sim \mathfrak{A}) \supset (\sim \sim \mathfrak{A} \supset \mathfrak{A})$ *(3)*
[3] $\sim \sim \mathfrak{A} \supset (\sim \sim \mathfrak{A} \supset \mathfrak{A})$ *(6)* [1, 2]
[4] $\sim \sim \mathfrak{A} \supset \mathfrak{A}$ *(7)* [3]

$\vdash \mathfrak{A} \supset \sim \sim \mathfrak{A}$ **(11)**

Proof:
[1] $\sim \sim \sim \mathfrak{A} \supset \sim \mathfrak{A})$ *(10)*
[2] $\mathfrak{A} \supset \sim \sim \mathfrak{A}$ *(9)* [1]

---

228 The content of postulate (VI. 4) can easily be confused with the content of theorem *(10)*. It can thus look as if the content of postulate (VI. 4) is provable within the calculus of functions. To avoid this confusion, one must notice the distinction between simple negation *N* A and truth-functional negation, ~ A.

$\mathfrak{A} \supset \mathfrak{B} \vdash \sim \mathfrak{B} \supset \sim \mathfrak{A}$ (12)

Proof:
[1]	$\mathfrak{A} \supset \mathfrak{B}$	*Premise*
[2]	$\sim \sim \mathfrak{A} \supset \mathfrak{A}$	(10)
[3]	$\sim \sim \mathfrak{A} \supset \mathfrak{B}$	(6) [1, 2]
[4]	$\mathfrak{B} \supset \sim \sim \mathfrak{B}$	(11)
[5]	$\sim \sim \mathfrak{A} \supset \sim \sim \mathfrak{B}$	(6) [3, 4]
[6]	$\sim \mathfrak{B} \supset \sim \mathfrak{A}$	(9) [5]

$\vdash \mathfrak{A}(t) \supset \sim (\forall v) \sim \mathfrak{A}(v)$ (13)

Proof:
[1]	$(\forall v) \sim \mathfrak{A}(v) \supset \sim \mathfrak{A}(t)$	(4)
[2]	$((\forall v) \sim \mathfrak{A}(v) \supset \sim \mathfrak{A}(t)) \supset$	
	$(\sim \sim \mathfrak{A}(t) \supset \sim (\forall v) \sim \mathfrak{A}(v))$	(12)
[3]	$\sim \sim \mathfrak{A}(t) \supset \sim (\forall v) \sim \mathfrak{A}(v)$	(VI. 8)* [1, 2]
[4]	$\mathfrak{A}(t) \supset \sim \sim \mathfrak{A}(t)$	(11)
[5]	$\mathfrak{A}(t) \supset \sim (\forall v) \sim \mathfrak{A}(v)$	(6) [3, 4]

In case t only occurs in the argument places of $\mathfrak{A}(t)$,
$\mathfrak{A}(t) \vdash (\forall v) \mathfrak{A}(v)$ (14)

Proof:
[1]	$\mathfrak{A}(t)$	*Premise*
[2]	$\mathfrak{A}(t) \supset ((\mathfrak{B} \supset \mathfrak{B}) \supset \mathfrak{A}(t))$	(1)
[3]	$(\mathfrak{B} \supset \mathfrak{B}) \supset \mathfrak{A}(t)$	(VI. 8)* [1, 2]
[4]	$(\mathfrak{B} \supset \mathfrak{B}) \supset (\forall v) \mathfrak{A}(v)$	(VI. 11)* [3]
[5]	$\mathfrak{B} \supset \mathfrak{B}$	(5)
[6]	$(\forall v) \mathfrak{A}(v)$	(VI. 8)* [4, 5]

The derivability claim (14) corresponds, as said before (see § 78), to the generalization rule (VI. 10).

$\vdash \sim (\forall v) \sim (\forall x) \mathfrak{A}(x) \supset \mathfrak{A}(v))$ (15)

Proof:
[1]	$(\forall x) \mathfrak{A}(x) \supset [\mathfrak{A}(t)]$	(4)
[2]	$((\forall x) \mathfrak{A}(x) \supset [\mathfrak{A}(t)])$	
	$\supset (\sim (\forall v) \sim ((\forall x) \mathfrak{A}(x) \supset \mathfrak{A}(v)))$	(13)
[3]	$\sim (\forall v) \sim ((\forall x) \mathfrak{A}(x) \supset \mathfrak{A}(v))$	(VI. 8)* [1, 2]

$(\forall v)(\mathfrak{A}(v) \supset \mathfrak{B}(v)) \vdash (\forall v) \mathfrak{A}(v) \supset (\forall v) \mathfrak{B}(v)$ (16)

Proof:

[1] $(\forall v)(\mathfrak{A}(v) \supset \mathfrak{B}(v))$ *Premise*
[2] $(\forall v)(\mathfrak{A}(v) \supset \mathfrak{B}(v)) \supset (\mathfrak{A}(t) \supset \mathfrak{B}(t))$ (4)
[3] $(\mathfrak{A}(t) \supset \mathfrak{B}(t)$ (VI. 8)* [1, 2]
[4] $(\forall v)\mathfrak{A}(v) \supset \mathfrak{A}(t)$ (4)
[5] $(\forall v)\mathfrak{A}(v) \supset \mathfrak{B}(t)$ (6) [4, 3]
[6] $(\forall v)\mathfrak{A}(v) \supset (\forall v)\mathfrak{B}(v)$ (VI. 11)* [5]

Instead of assuming the validity of the rule of posterior generalization in an axiomatic logical calculus in order to be able to carry out derivations within the calculus, it is just as possible to assume the validity of the generalization rule *(14)* and carry out the corresponding proofs with it. The validity of the rule of posterior generalization can be proven on this basis. This rule corresponds, as said before, to the following derivability claim:

> In case t occurs only in the argument places of $\mathfrak{B}(t)$,
> $(\mathfrak{A} \supset \mathfrak{B}(t)) \vdash (\mathfrak{A} \supset (v)\mathfrak{B}(v))$ **(VI. 11)***

Proof:

[1] $\mathfrak{A} \supset \mathfrak{B}(t)$ *Premise*
[2] $\mathfrak{A}$ *Premise*
[3] $\mathfrak{B}(t)$ (VI. 8) [1, 2]
[4] $(\forall v)\mathfrak{B}(v)$ (VI. 10) [3]
[5] $\mathfrak{A} \supset (v)\mathfrak{B}(v)$

Admittedly, to justify the move from line [4] to [5], a supposition must be brought in which for its part needs a proof; and it is provable within the framework of an axiomatic system that differs from *FC* only by assuming rule *(14)* instead of (VI. 11)*. This proof may be left aside here because of its complexity.[229] The supposition that we must make is the deduction theorem (introduced by Tarski and so named by him). It can be formulated in the following way:

> If the formula $\mathfrak{B}$ is deducible from the elements of a set Γ of formulas of the calculus of functions and a formula $\mathfrak{A}$, so that it holds that: $\Gamma, \mathfrak{A} \vdash \mathfrak{B}$, and so that it also holds that: $\Gamma \vdash \mathfrak{A} \supset \mathfrak{B}$, then the deducibility of $\mathfrak{B}$ from $\mathfrak{A}$ and the elements of Γ does not rest on an application of the generalization rule *(14)* to a formula $\mathfrak{C}(t)$, for which it holds that: $\mathfrak{C}(t)$ depends on $\mathfrak{A}$ and t occurs in $\mathfrak{A}$.

Since, as line [3] of the preceding proof implies, $\mathfrak{B}(t)$ is derivable according to the detachment rule from $\mathfrak{A} \supset \mathfrak{B}(t)$ and $\mathfrak{A}$, the deduction theorem permits deriving

---

[229] One can find the proof laid out in Beckermann 1997, 279.

the formula $\mathfrak{A} \supset (v) \mathfrak{B} (v)$ in line [5] from the formula $\mathfrak{A} \supset \mathfrak{B} (t)$ in line [1] in case t only occurs in the argument places of $\mathfrak{B} (t)$. This permission corresponds precisely to what is allowed by the rule of posterior generalization.

§ 81 Soundness and Completeness

The fact that for the formulas (1) to (16) just considered, as for other formulas of the calculus of functions, there is an axiomatic, non-syllogistic proof still says nothing about whether there are also among these formulas such which are logically true or follow logically from other formulas. Rather, such a claim is usually made with two theorems, both of which in turn require a proof. The first of these theorems is the so-called soundness theorem. In its typical formulation, it is supposed to determine under which conditions a theorem that can be proven within a certain axiomatic calculus of functions is also *logically true*, and under which conditions a formula *follows logically* from another formula. In this formulation, with reference to the axiomatic system *FC*, it reads:

> The axiomatic calculus of functions *FC* is *sound*, i.e., it holds for arbitrary formulas $\mathfrak{A}, \mathfrak{A}_1, \ldots, \mathfrak{A}_n$:
> (a) If $\mathfrak{A}$ is a theorem of *FC*, so that it holds that $\mathfrak{A}$ is provable (symbolically expressed: $\vdash \mathfrak{A}$), then $\mathfrak{A}$ is *logically true* (symbolically expressed: $\vDash \mathfrak{A}$).
> (b) If $\mathfrak{A}$ is derivable from the formulas $\mathfrak{A}_1, \ldots, \mathfrak{A}_n$ in *FC* (if it thus holds that: $\mathfrak{A}_1, \ldots, \mathfrak{A}_n \vdash \mathfrak{A}$), and if in addition in at least one deduction of $\mathfrak{A}$ from $\mathfrak{A}_1, \ldots, \mathfrak{A}_n$ the rule of posterior generalization is not applied to a formula $\mathfrak{B} \supset \mathfrak{C} [a_i]$, which in this deduction depends on a premise in which the individual constant a_i occurs, then $\mathfrak{A}$ *follows logically* from $\mathfrak{A}_1, \ldots, \mathfrak{A}_n$ (i.e., symbolically expressed, it holds that: $\mathfrak{A}_1, \ldots, \mathfrak{A}_n \vDash \mathfrak{A}$).

The second theorem is the completeness theorem, which contains the inverse of the claims of the soundness theorem. In one of its usual formulations, it reads:

> The axiomatic calculus of functions is *complete*, that is, for arbitrary formulas $\mathfrak{A}, \mathfrak{A}_1, \ldots, \mathfrak{A}_n$, it holds that:
> (a) If $\mathfrak{A}$ is *logically true*, then $\mathfrak{A}$ is provable in *FC*, i.e., $\mathfrak{A}$ is a theorem in *FC*. (Symbolically expressed: if $\vDash \mathfrak{A}$, then also $\vdash \mathfrak{A}$)
> (b) If $\mathfrak{A}$ *follows logically* from $\mathfrak{A}_1, \ldots, \mathfrak{A}_n$, then $\mathfrak{A}$ is derivable in *FC* from the formulas $\mathfrak{A}_1, \ldots, \mathfrak{A}_n$. (Symbolically expressed: if $\mathfrak{A}_1, \ldots, \mathfrak{A}_n \vDash \mathfrak{A}$, then $\mathfrak{A}_n \vdash \mathfrak{A}$)

Here, too, I will leave aside the proofs that can be carried out for both theorems.[230] It is assumed here that they can be carried out in all strictness.

The concepts of logical truth and logical consequence as introduced here are called 'syntactic concepts'. They are called syntactic because they are used to determine logical truth and logical consequence without referring to anything other than the syntactic relations within the axiomatic system we have considered. They coincide, however, with the so-called 'semantic concepts' of logical truth and logical consequence, since according to the latter concepts the same theorems can be understood as logically true and the same rules can be understood as rules of logical consequence. The latter concepts are called semantic because they refer only to the meaning attached to the logical vocabulary used in the logical calculus of functions to determine logical truth and consequence. Thus, according to this determination, the logical truth of theorems of *FC*, as well as the logical consequence according to the rules of *FC*, is based on the meaning of the logical signs '~ . . .', '. . . ⊃ . . .', and '(∀ . . .) . . .', which occur in these theorems and rules. However, this meaning depends exclusively on the content of the empty places within these expressions, namely, on a certain distribution of truth values to these places. Thus, the following holds for the three logical signs in *FC*:

> If $\mathfrak{A}$ is a *truth-functional negation*, i.e., a proposition of the form ~ $\mathfrak{B}$ (in words: 'not $\mathfrak{B}$'), then $\mathfrak{A}$ is true if and only if $\mathfrak{B}$ is false.
> If $\mathfrak{A}$ is a *truth-functional conditional* proposition, i.e., a proposition of the form $\mathfrak{B} \supset \mathfrak{C}$ (in words: '$\mathfrak{B}$, not unless $\mathfrak{C}$'), then $\mathfrak{A}$ is true if and only if $\mathfrak{B}$ is false or $\mathfrak{C}$ is true.
> If $\mathfrak{A}$ is a *universal* proposition, i.e., a proposition of the form (∀ v) $\mathfrak{B}$ (v) (in words: 'For every v $\mathfrak{B}$ (v) holds'), then $\mathfrak{A}$ is true if and only if an individual variable v bound by the quantifier can be assigned objects of a non-empty domain of individuals in such a way that $\mathfrak{B}$ (v) is a true proposition.

According to the semantic concepts of logical truth and logical consequence, the corresponding points hold in *FC*:

> A proposition $\mathfrak{A}$ is *logically true* (symbolically expressed: ⊨ $\mathfrak{A}$) if and only if its truth results exclusively from the occurrence of the logical constants '~ . . .', '. . . ⊃ . . .', and '(∀ . . .)' in $\mathfrak{A}$.
> A proposition A *follows logically* from arbitrary propositions (symbolically expressed: $\mathfrak{A}_1, \ldots, \mathfrak{A}_n$ ⊨ A) if and only if its truth results exclusively from the occurrence of the logical constants '~ . . .', '. . . ⊃ . . .', and '(∀ . . .)' in $\mathfrak{A}_1, \ldots, \mathfrak{A}_n$ and A.

What should be maintained about the concepts of logical consequence and logical truth as used here? Let us consider them separately.

Now, it is obvious that neither the syntactic nor the semantic concept of logical consequence in *FC* coincides with the concept of logical consequence in § 43.

---

230 Compare here again Beckermann 1997, 287–301.

The symbolic expression '$\mathfrak{A}_1, \ldots, \mathfrak{A}_n \models \mathfrak{A}$' does not represent the same kind of logical consequence as '$\mathfrak{A}_1, \ldots, \mathfrak{A}_n \therefore \mathfrak{A}$'. This discrepancy is due to the fact that the language of the axiomatic calculus of functions differs from the language of the extended deductive logical system (presented in §§ 70 to 76) in that the logical vocabulary of the syllogistic no longer occurs in FC. Consequently, this calculus does not let one recognize that its axioms, theorems and rules of derivation agree in their content with expressions derived in §§ 70 to 76 from syllogistic principles, partly according to syllogistic rules, partly by means of the rules whose validity has been postulated in § 72. For this derivation it was appropriate to transform rules of logical consequence according to § 43 (by 'weakening') into rules of merely regular consequence (see §§ 71 and 73) in order to make the relations of regular consequence expressed by the postulates of § 72 transitive and to make syllogistic rules of logical consequence applicable to them. This transformation 'by weakening' in no way suspends the validity of syllogistic rules of logical consequence. Rather, the occurrence of syllogistic rules called 'weakened' indicates that the system of extended deductive logic presupposes the validity of syllogistic rules according to which logical consequence in the sense of § 43 takes place. This means that the axiomatic calculus of functions also presupposes this validity, just as it depends on the rules of merely regular consequence postulated as valid in § 72.

Therefore, since this calculus depends not only on syllogistic principles, but also on the postulates in § 72, its use of an expression of the form '$\mathfrak{A}_1, \ldots, \mathfrak{A}_n \models \mathfrak{A}$' does not express that $\mathfrak{A}$ follows logically from $\mathfrak{A}_1, \ldots, \mathfrak{A}_n$ in the sense of § 43. If it did, the reasons for logical consequence here would have to be the same as those reasons on which '$A_1, \ldots, A_n \therefore A$' holds. The relation indicated by '$\ldots \models \ldots$' is only a sub-kind of logical consequence, which could be called 'logical consequence in FC'. This label is appropriate because there are different kinds of logical consequence. For there are different axiomatic logical *calculi*, and these differ from each other by not accepting each of the postulates of § 72 (see appendix 6).

As regards the syntactic as well as the semantic concept of *logical truth*, the axiomatic *calculus of functions* is characterized by the fact that its propositional vocabulary is truth-functional. The meanings of the signs for negation and conditionality can therefore be defined directly by truth tables, namely in this way:

$\mathfrak{A}$	$\sim \ldots$
T	F
F	T

$\mathfrak{A}\mathfrak{B}$		$\ldots \supset \ldots$
T	T	T
T	F	F
F	T	T
F	F	T

These tables show that the meanings of '~ ...' and '... ⊃ ...', as functional values, depend on nothing else than the content of the empty places in each case, namely on a certain distribution of truth values to them. In this respect the logical vocabulary of the axiomatic calculus of functions differs from that of the syllogistic. There can be nothing in the syllogistic that corresponds to the symbolism (inspired by Frege's use of the sign '⊢')[231] according to which '⊨ 𝔄' means: '𝔄 is logically true'. To be sure, '*∴ ...' has been used in Part II of this essay in a similar way as '⊨ ...' (as well as the weakened form '*< ...'). For as a sign for the logical consequence of A from the empty set of premises, '*∴ A' represents logically valid expressions which have been formed by conditionalizing logically valid inference forms of the syllogistic. But such expressions do not represent a logically true proposition. Conformity to these forms is not a sufficient but only a necessary condition of truth.[232]

The occurrence of logical truth in *FC*, like that of logical consequence in *FC*, presupposes both the validity of syllogistic rules of logical consequence and the validity of the basic rules (VI. 3) to (VI. 6) postulated in § 72.[233] Since each of these postulates is dispensable for logic and can either be omitted or replaced by another one, *alternatives to the axiomatic calculus of functions* are possible, by which the syntactic, though not the semantic concept of logical truth is maintained. The semantic concept is bound to the occurrence of truth functions, which presupposes the validity of

---

[231] Frege calls the sign '⊢' the "common predicate for all judgments", because it represents the expression "is a fact" (1879, 4, § 3 [1967, 13]). It is composed of the (vertical) "judgement stroke" and the (horizontal) "content stroke" (1879, 2, § 2 [1967, 12]). These names show that Frege, unlike his successors, did not consider his logic to be a 'formal logic' in Kant's sense. ("I was not trying to present an abstract logic in formulas; I was trying to express contents in an exacter and more perspicuous manner than is possible in words, by using written symbols." Frege 1882a, 1 [1968, 89].)
[232] Kant, *CPR* A 59/B 84–85 f. and A 796/B 824.
[233] Logical truth in *FC* therefore presupposes, by virtue of (VI. 5) and (VI. 6), a non-empty universe of discourse and depends to that extent on postulates as they are characteristic of mathematics (see § 72, *Scholium*). Bertrand Russell and others have held the view that truth that depends on the universe not being empty cannot be *logical truth*, since it is true, but not *logically true* that the universe is not empty. See Russell 1919b, 194–206; Langford 1927, 342–346. This view was rejected by W.V.O. Quine. In a polemic (Quine 1963, 160–67), he argued: "from the point of view of utility in application it would be folly [. . .] to want to limit the laws of quantification theory in this way" (1963, 162), i.e., it would be foolish to limit the laws of the calculus of functions to those laws which were valid for every universe, including even an empty universe. Instead, it is recommended (in Quine's view) to leave out of consideration the case of the empty universe, which is relatively useless from the perspective of application (1963, 161). Quine has thus admitted that the range of application of the calculus of functions is essentially a non-empty universe and could have agreed with Russell that logical truth in *FC* can, with equal right, be called 'mathematical'.

postulates (VI. 3) and (VI. 4) (see § 71 above) and to which the logical calculus of functions owes its name. Hence there are axiomatic logical calculi which are not truth-functional. For example, the theorems of soundness and completeness established above can be applied without restriction to the intuitionistic axiomatic system of propositional calculus established by Arend Heyting (1930, 42–56). Since in Heyting's system the simple detachment rule (VI. 8) remains valid, it is even possible to derive all axioms of his system (like those of the axiomatic calculus of functions) (see § 80) from itself and to regard them as theorems of this system as well.

Conclusion

§ 82 Principles and Rules on Which the Complete System of the Calculus of Functions Depends

According to § 78, the complete system of axioms and derived rules of the calculus of functions depends directly on the rules (VI. 8), (VI. 11), (VI. 17), (VI. 18), (VI. 23), and (VI. 24). If one considers the proofs which were given above (in § 74 and § 75) for the validity of these rules, and if one traces the principles which are used either directly or indirectly in these proofs, one will find that – disregarding the weakened or non-weakened versions of the three meta-rules (I. 2), (I. 3), and (II. 1), as well as the meta-rule (VI. 7) (which are used directly or indirectly for derivation) – the validity of the complete system of axioms and derived rules of the calculus of functions depends on *eight syllogistic* and *three non-syllogistic basic rules* in total. The syllogistic basic rules are

(I. 1) The rule of double negation as a result of an affirmation
(II. 2) *Modus ponendo ponens*,
(III. 1) *Dictum de omni*,
(III. 3) The first exposition rule,
(III. 7) Subalternation in the weak logical square,
(III. 8) Basic rule of the universal limitative proposition,
(III. 9) Basic rule of the particular limitative proposition,
(III. 10) Basic rule of the singular limitative proposition.

For non-syllogistic basic rules, the three postulates of the extended deductive logic are needed, namely

(VI. 3) The postulate of the arbitrary sufficient reason
(VI. 4) The postulate of the affirmative use of double negation
(VI. 5–6) The postulate of non-empty domains.

I had already taken as an assumption in Part I of this essay that these three postulates are *non-syllogistic* basic rules – namely, rules whose validity must not be claimed within the elementary syllogistic. But only now that I have, in Part II, let the main features of the structure of the syllogistic systematically confront the main features of the structure of the calculus of functions should it become clear that the elementary syllogistic can be described as that sphere of deductive logic in which the validity of the three mentioned postulates does *not* need to be assumed.

Since, conversely, syllogistic principles must be assumed as valid within the sphere of the calculus of functions, the elementary syllogistic has, in comparison to the calculus of functions, proved to be the *more fundamental* region of deductive logic: the calculus utilizes, at least implicitly, syllogistic rules, while the elementary syllogistic is for its part entirely independent of the rules and laws of the calculus.

The systematic relationship between the elementary syllogistic and the calculus of functions can be described somewhat more precisely by considering still more closely theorem (4) as mentioned in § 80, one of the axioms of the calculus of functions. According to § 78, the validity of this theorem depends on the singularization rule (VI. 15) being valid, from which the law of singularization (VI. 24) in § 75 was derived. The proof that is carried out for this law in § 74 only came off by bringing into play not only expressions with concept variables, but also expressions with conceptual constants. This proof thus relies (directly or indirectly by means of the rules (VI. 12) and (VI. 14)) on the substitution of ζ and ξ in expressions of rules which can be formulated in the syllogistic language. In this way, we can see that theorem (4) is dependent on rules of contentful inference. The case is just the same for the generalization rules (VI. 10)* and (VI. 11)* of the calculus of functions, whose validity is proven in § 74 with rules (VI. 10) and (VI. 11). There are thus good reasons not to count the calculus of functions among the *formal part* of deductive logic but rather as a special division within the *theory of contentful inference*. Of course, since it presupposes the standing of more particular, non-syllogistic principles, it is not to be regarded as a calculus of contentful *syllogistic inference*, which I have described in Section Five of Part II.

The syllogistic differs from the calculus of functions not only by its rules' being *more fundamental* but also by their *more formal* character. The syllogistic is, as can now be seen with great exactness, *formal logic* (in a narrower, more precise sense of this expression). The equation of formal logic and the logic of the classical functional or predicate calculus (including its non-classical derivatives), which is very widespread and almost customary nowadays, clearly rests on a profound lack of insight into the logical presuppositions of this logic. The rules of the classical calculus of functions or predicates are better seen as rules of *informal deductive inference*.

Connected with the syllogistic's status of being a *more fundamental* and *more formal* part of deductive logic is the fact that syllogistic rules are valid for all deductive inference. For this reason, the syllogistic is to be regarded as *general logic*, or more precisely, the *general part of deductive logic*. The phrase 'general part of deductive logic' has the advantage of not letting the misunderstanding arise that the syllogistic could contain *all* rules of deductive inference, rather than the rules of all deductive inference. In truth, syllogistic rules make up only an extremely small part of the totality of deductive rules – which is already evident from the fact that the syllogistic does not contain *all principles* which can be assumed in deductive inference.

§ 83 Logical Form: A Review of the Results Attained

It is now time to summarize some results of this essay and to highlight more clearly those which are especially important and interesting from a philosophical point of view. The most important of them is contained in the response to the question: What does the *logical form* of a statement consist in? It cannot be said that the answer we have discovered delivers an insight that is completely new in every respect. But precisely the fact that here something well-known appears in a new light may in the eyes of some readers have something surprising to it, if not even something altogether provocative.

The answer we have discovered can be summarized as follows:

The logical form of a statement is precisely what is expressed in the syllogistic propositional schema corresponding to this statement. It is, in other words, precisely that in a statement which is left over when its conceptual content (i.e., what concept variables stand for) is left out of consideration. Behind this answer is concealed the old idea that the logical form of a statement is a constellation of statement-properties which do not exceed the dozen that Kant's table of judgments enumerates in a symmetrical arrangement and contains "no more than what Aristotle and his direct students have regarded as the main logical moments in the theory of judgment and inference" (Reich 2001, 4–5). Of course, the old idea needs to be made precise in two respects if it is supposed to be correct and tenable, and this precision is, as it were, the light in which the well-known appears in a new way.

First: the qualitative, relational, and modal statement-properties, insofar as they contribute to logical form, should not be interpreted truth-functionally or understood as properties which are interpretable with the aid of a truth-functional explication; distinct types of truth-functions have something to do with distinctions of logical form only indirectly, since truth-functional expressions – *including* expressions of negation – are structures which, as I have shown above, admit a logical analysis in which they are equivalent to expressions composed of non-truth-functional expressions. *Second*: quantitative properties, insofar as they contributed to the logical form of a statement, should not be confused with various kinds of saturation of propositional functions. Distinctions of logical form do depend on whether empty places in a functional expression are filled by individual constants or bound individual variables. But nevertheless particular conceptual contents, which can be clearly distinguished from the logical form, are connected to the use of these signs. As has been shown, these signs admit an analysis in which they are equivalent to phrases that contain only concept expressions and the logical vocabulary of the syllogistic.

The question of logical form was one of the central questions in twentieth-century philosophy. Bertrand Russell and the young Ludwig Wittgenstein – who were even ready to equate the logical form of statements with the subject-matter of philosophy as such – had seen that the logical form of expressions of the type '$F(a)$' is not apparent on their surface. At the same time, they were proponents of the view that giving a logical analysis of linguistic expressions always requires a reduction to truth- and propositional functions. Such a constellation of positions naturally had the consequence that the question of logical form had to become a philosophical riddle of the first order. To be sure, this riddle has given some impetus to the analytic philosophy of language, especially its attempts to ascertain the essence of expressions for which the 'a' in '$F(a)$' stands – the essence of proper names and so-called singular terms. But the riddle itself has found no satisfactory solution in these attempts. We have seen that even the distinction between singular and general terms rests on mistaken assumptions and that no clarity is secured for the question of the essence of proper names so long as the question of the essence of logical form has found no suitable answer.

An explanation of what a *logical consequence* is and what *logical validity* is also depends on this answer.[234] On these two questions, too, the present essay has achieved an important result: a proposition *p follows logically* from one or more propositions if and only if the occurrence of one or more than one logical constants of the syllogistic makes it impossible that *p* is false and each of the remaining propositions involved is true. A proposition is *logically valid* if and only if it is equivalent to a hypothetical proposition that can be generated by conditionalizing a rule according to which a proposition logically follows from one or more propositions.

Accordingly, tautologies are not just as such logically valid. Thus, a tautological proposition of the form 'every α is an α' can well be false, and indeed it is false if α is an empty concept, so that there is no object with which the proposition (as an affirmative proposition) could correspond. A tautology of the form 'if A, then A' (consisting of identical clauses) does not express a logical truth either. For it depends on the *content* of the proposition A whether its truth is incompatible with the truth of *N* A, so that A follows from A. If one replaces A in both places with *N* A, there is no such incompatibility. Thus, a proposition of the form 'if *N* A, then *N* A' can be false.

---

[234] I have shown in § 81 that within the calculus of functions there is a way of using the expressions 'logically true' and 'follows logically' that clashes with the concepts of logical validity and logical consequence developed above, but that this clash can be eliminated with a suitable terminology.

Only the logical form (in the sense given to this expression) can decide whether a proposition is logically valid or logically follows from other propositions. Theorems of a logical calculus, of which one may be able to say (according to § 81) that they are 'logically true' or 'logically follow' from other theorems *in this calculus*, presuppose the universal validity of rules and laws whose logical form can be represented only in the syllogistic.

§ 84 Stages in the History of Logic

> If one wants to be an innovator,
> then one longs to be the first;
> if one wants only truth,
> one longs for predecessors.
> (Kant, Refl. 2159)

That the old appears in a new light means that what is past must be seen in a new way. – Kant writes in the second edition of the *Critique of Pure Reason* of 1787, that "logic" has

> since the time of Aristotle [. . .] not had to go a single step backwards, unless we count the abolition of a few dispensable subtleties or the more distinct determination of its presentation, which improvements belong more to the elegance than to the security of that science. What is further remarkable about logic is that until now it has also been unable to take a single step forward, and therefore seems to all appearance to be finished and complete. [. . .] It is not an improvement but a deformation of the sciences when their boundaries are allowed to run over into one another; the boundaries of logic, however, are determined quite precisely by the fact that logic is the science that exhaustively presents and strictly proves nothing but the formal rules of all thinking (whether this thinking be empirical or *a priori*, whatever origin or object it may have, and whatever contingent or natural obstacles it may meet with in our minds). / For the advantage that has made it so successful logic has solely its own limitation to thank, since it is thereby justified in abstracting – is indeed obliged to abstract – from all objects of cognition and all the distinctions between them; and in logic, therefore, the understanding has to do with nothing further than itself and its own form. (*CPR* B viii–ix)

This passage is gladly quoted in modern books on logic and the history of logic in order to show, on the one hand, how great and lasting the influence that Aristotle's logic had exercised for centuries, and, on the other hand, how biased even great philosophers had been under this influence when it came to assessing the actual value of Aristotelian logic and its place within the history of logic. As the quotation shows, Kant does not only not anticipate the possibility of substantial progress beyond Aristotle, he was apparently even ready to definitively exclude such a possibility. According to the image promoted by modern handbooks and standard works of the history of logic, Kant would not have had to wait even a hundred years to see his view refuted by the facts.

According to this image, the history of logic can be divided into two great main epochs. The first begins with Aristotle's (382–322) *Analytica priora*, the second with Frege's (1848–1925) *Begriffsschrift* published in 1879. The division of *traditional* and *modern logic* is used today such that it corresponds to the division within logic before and after 1879.

"Logic is an old subject, and since 1879 it has been a great one" (Quine 1959, vii). – With Frege's work a dramatic upswing began, which allowed the initially small sphere of logic, which could be treated between two book covers on a few pages, to become a branch of science which today can hardly be surveyed even by experts. A development which was already initiated by scattered predecessors of Frege has ultimately led to the establishment of modern logic as a many-branched area of mathematical research. *Modern* and *mathematical logic* have basically become synonyms. Modern logic is called mathematical for two reasons: firstly, it has itself become the object of mathematical investigations; secondly its language is suited to seamlessly present mathematical proofs. Traditional logic was not actually in a position to do this.

Now, the fact that the field of logic has since 1879 strongly enlarged itself and grown into mathematics admits of two different readings.

According to the first reading, the historical process can be read as though in the course of expanding the region of logic there was at the same time a reconfiguration of its foundations, in which the syllogistic as the standalone region of logic dissolved and something else took its place. From this perspective, which is today the reigning opinion of logicians and historians of logic, a *revolution within logic* took place in 1879, whereby the Aristotelian syllogistic was "dissolved" "as a paradigm".[235] *After* the revolution, the syllogistic could only claim validity for special cases of deductive inference.[236] Incidentally, Frege himself prepared the way for the revolutionary reading of the events since 1879: he advanced the view in his *Begriffsschrift* that the logical laws which can be derived within that system, would "take the place of the Aristotelian modes of inference" (Frege 1879, 10, § 6 [1967, 17]).

This view, as has hopefully been shown clearly enough in this book, cannot be maintained. In any case, not insofar as one can interpret the Aristotelian doctrine of inference as a theory which deals in its essentials with the forms of syllogistic argumentation as they have been presented systematically in Section One

---

[235] This is how, e.g., Wolgang Künne (1996, 325) sees it.
[236] See on this the article "Logic" in Blackburn (1994, 221): "Syllogistic is now generally regarded as a limited special case of the forms of reasoning that can be represented within the propositional and predicate calculus. These form the heart of modern logic."

of Part I and in the first four Sections of Part II of this essay. These forms have been definitively established as basic forms of deductive inference.

It thus stands to reason that the revolutionary reading of modern logic should be given up and replaced by a description that does not comport with its self-image.

According to this rival description, it was merely an expansion of the region of deductive logic which occurred with the emergence and branching-out of mathematical logic, without in the process compromising the autonomy of its core region, namely, the independence of the syllogistic. Considered in this way, new non-syllogistic sub-spheres of logic, which did not exist or only rudimentarily prior to 1879, have been added on to the core sphere of logic, which coincides in its essentials with the traditional syllogistic tracing back to Aristotle.

This description comports with a perspective which in its basics is completely compatible with the assessment that Kant made of the history of logic since Aristotle in the passage quoted above. It comports with this perspective especially insofar as Kant was also ready to regard the syllogistic, which he called "formal logic," as only a *part*, namely, as the general (pure) part of deductive logic, and to distinguish from it other, more specific parts which he called logics of the "special use of the understanding", among which he counted mathematical logic (which was in his lifetime admittedly still stuck in its very first beginnings).[237] As the last sentence of the passage quoted at the beginning of this § indirectly shows, Kant refers there only to a part of logic which has to do with the *general* use of the understanding (cf. *CPR* A 52, B 76).

How could it nevertheless come about that Frege's innovations have been received by experts almost unanimously as if they were a revolution within deductive logic and not its mere expansion with a specific sphere (however large and extraordinarily important for mathematics it may be) of the theory of contentful deductive inference?

This question will not be able to be satisfactorily answered without accounting for the fact that the enduring lack of insight into the systematics of deductive logic is not due only to the self-image of modern logic as shaped by Frege, but also to the lack of an exact logical analysis of past systems of the syllogistic systems, which because of their predominantly verbal form have made it less clear than modern logical systems that they make up no more than one part of deductive logic. For this a more exact semantic comparison of the differences in the logical vocabulary of syllogistic and modern systems was needed. Lacking such an analysis, it could always look as if traditional syllogistic systems were merely imperfect precursors to what is commonly called modern logic.

---

237 Cf. M. Wolff 1995, 204–30. A second, improved edition of this book is in preparation.

If it was Kant's view that already Aristotle had brought the syllogistic to a scientific level in such a way that a "more distinct determination of its presentation" was either ruled out or could only still lead to such "improvements" as "belong more to the elegance than to the security of that science" (see the first sentence of the passage quoted at the beginning of this §), then he was obviously not right in this opinion. It suffices to recall questions about the validity of the rules of the logical square or the modal syllogistic – which began first to take off in the 19th and 20th centuries in their full acuity – to see that the 'security of science' with respect to the traditional syllogistic was *no lesser* a desideratum than 'elegance'. But it could have achieved security only on the basis of a suitably comprehensive system of sufficiently precise and elaborate definitions which fix the meaning of expressions in its logical vocabulary, and this in sharp delimitation to the meaning of expressions of the calculus of functions. Neither Aristotle nor Kant were in a position to carry out such a delimitation, simply because there was no calculus of functions in their time. Neither Aristotle nor Kant could have left behind a comprehensive system of explicit definitions that fix the meaning of logical constants sufficiently precisely and elaborately, which why only starting attempts at such definitions can be found in their work. The need to establish an appropriate system of definitions – and thus to make a start at a modernized syllogistic – could naturally only appear after a logical calculus of functions was fully formed.

Appendix 1
On the Completeness of a Syllogistic without Logical Conjunction

(To § 40)

The elementary conjunction represented by '(..., ...)' – also called a conjunction of premises above – does not belong to the logical vocabulary which is needed to present the elementary syllogistic in Parts I and II of this essay. In what follows, I will call the language which contains only this logical vocabulary and which I have called the 'elementary language of the syllogistic' at the end of § 15, 'language 1'. I will distinguish from this language a 'language 2' whose vocabulary contains not only the logical vocabulary of language 1 but in addition the logical constant '(..., ...)'. Finally, we can think of a third language which relates to language 2 just like language 1 relates to language 2, because it differs from the latter just by the fact that the logical constant 'H (..., ...)' does not occur in it. I call this language 'language 3'.

We should compare languages 1 and 3 with respect to their capability. For this one needs the superordinate language 2. For only in this language can rules be formulated so that expressions of language 1 can be put into a logical relation with expressions of language 3 and compared with each other. The expressions that matter for the desired comparison are of course expressions of the basic rules which can only be rendered in the languages we are comparing. Concerning language 1, the basic rules which belong to it are first of all those I introduced above in §§ 44 and 48. As for the capability of language 1, we must ask whether there are for the hypothetical expressions which occur in the basic rules of hypothetical inference expressions of language 3 of the same logical strength; and conversely: whether there is for every expression of language 3 an expression of the same logical strength in language 1. By expressions of the same logical strength I mean just those expressions for which there are rules in language 2 according to which the one expression is derivable from the other, and conversely. We can say that the capabilities of languages 1 and 3 are equally great (in a certain respect) if there is for every expression in one language an expression in the other with the same logical strength.

The question which must now be posed is: what are the valid rules which put expressions of languages 1 and 3 in a logical relation that can be formulated in language 2? To be able to answer this question, we must go back to the definitions from which result each of the basic rules that hold for the expressions of the languages we are comparing. These are the definitions of the hypothetical proposition and of the conjunction of premises. According to the definition in § 47, a hypothetical proposition of the form H (A, B) is true if and only if B follows regularly from A; and according to the definition of regular consequence in § 43, B follows regularly from A if and only if A and C, with C = N B and B = N C, are incompatible. Now the incompatibility of two propositions A and C can be immediately defined as a relation which obtains if and only if NM (A, C) is true (see *Appendix 4* below). From this it results that besides the basic rules of § 48, both of the following rules hold as well and can be formulated in language 2:

H (A, B) : : NM (A, N B), (2. 1)
H (A, N B) : : NM (A, B). (2. 2)

By contrast, no rule which could be rendered in language 2 and in which a logical relation to the form of hypothetical propositions would be expressed, could be based directly on the definition of the conjunction of premises which I established in § 30. For according to this definition, the meaning of a conjunction of premises

'(. . ., . . .)'

is fixed such that for every interpretation in which A and B are true or false propositions, it holds that:

> (1) (A, B) is true if A and B are both true or N (A, B) is false; and (2) (A, B) is false if it is possible that A or B is false and thus that N A or N B is true.

From this definition, no logical relation to the form of hypothetical propositions directly results. Rather, only the following three basic rules (belonging to language 3) can be directly based on this definition:

A, B ∴ (A, B), (3. 1)
B, A ∴ (A, B), (3. 2)
NN (A, B) ∴ (A, B). (3. 3)

Now, it can be shown on the basis of the rules (2. 1), (2. 2), and (3. 1) that for certain expressions of the form H (A, B), there is a certain expression of the same logical strength in language 3, and conversely for a certain expression of the form (A, B) there is a certain expression of the same logical strength in language 1 as well. That is, two further rules hold in language 2:

H (A, B) : : N (A, C) (with C = N B or B = N C), (2. 3)
(A, B) : : NH (A, C) (with C = N B or B = N C). (2. 4)

To prove the validity of both these rules, one must provide separate proofs for the sub-rules they contain. Here, first, are the proofs for the four sub-rules which are summarized by (2. 3):

H (A, B) $\therefore$ N (A, N B) (2. 3. 1)

Proof:
[1] H (A, B) $\therefore$ NM (A, N B)   (2. 1)
[2] NM (A, N B) $\therefore$ LN (A, N B) (IV. 4)
[3] LN (A, N B) $\therefore$ N (A, N B)   (IV. 1)
[4] H (A, B) $\therefore$ N (A, N B)   (I. 4) [1, 2, 3]

N (A, N B) $\therefore$ H (A, B) (2. 3. 2)

Proof:
[1] A, N B $\therefore$ (A, N B)   (3. 1)
[2] N (A, N B), A $\therefore$ NN B   (I. 2) [1]
[3] N (A, N B) $\therefore$ H (A, NN B)   (II. 1) [2]
[4] H (A, NN B) $\therefore$ NM (A, N B)   (2. 2)
[5] NM (A, N B) $\therefore$ H (A, B)   (2. 1)
[6] N (A, N B) $\therefore$ H (A, B)   (I. 4) [3, 4, 5]

H (A, N C) $\therefore$ N (A, C) (2. 3. 3)

Proof:
[1] H (A, N C) $\therefore$ NM (A, C)   (2. 2)
[2] NM (A, C) $\therefore$ LN (A, C)   (IV. 6) [1]
[3] LN (A, C) $\therefore$ N (A, C)   (IV. 1) [2]

N (A, C) $\therefore$ H (A, N C) (2. 3. 4)

Proof:
[1] A, C $\therefore$ (A, C)   (3. 1)
[2] N (A, C), A $\therefore$ N C   (I. 2) [1]
[3] N (A, C) $\therefore$ H (A, N C)   (II. 1) [2]

Likewise, the four sub-rules which are summarized in (2. 4) can be proved. For this it is necessary to assume the validity of the rules (2. 3. 1 to (2. 3. 4):

(A, B) $\therefore$ NH (A, N B) (2. 4. 1)

Proof:
[1] H (A, N B) $\therefore$ N (A, B)   (2. 3. 3)
[2] NN (A, B) $\therefore$ NH (A, N B)   (I. 2) [1]

[3] (A, B) ∴ NN (A, B)	(I. 1)
[4] (A, B) ∴ NH (A, N B)	(I. 4) [3, 2]

NH (A, N B) ∴ (A, B)	**(2. 4. 2)**

Proof:

[1] N (A, B) ∴ H (A, N B)	(2. 3. 4)
[2] NH (A, N B) ∴ NN (A, B)	(I. 2) [1]
[3] NN (A, B) ∴ (A, B)	(3. 3)
[4] NH (A, N B) ∴ (A, B)	(I. 4) [2, 3]

(A, N C) ∴ NH (A, C)	**(2. 4. 3)**

Proof:

[1] H (A, C) ∴ N (A, N C)	(2. 3. 1)
[2] NN (A, N C) ∴ NH (A, C)	(I. 2) [1]
[3] (A, N C) ∴ NN (A, N C)	(I. 1)
[4] (A, N C) ∴ NH (A, C)	(I. 4) [3, 2]

NH (A, C) ∴ (A, N C)	**(2. 4. 4)**

Proof:

[1] N (A, N C) ∴ H (A, C)	(2. 3. 2)
[2] NH (A, C) ∴ NN (A, N C)	(I. 2) [1]
[3] NN (A, N C) ∴ (A, N C)	(3. 3)
[4] NH (A, C) ∴ (A, N C)	(I. 4) [2, 3]

These eight proofs show, *first*, that every negated and non-negated expression of the form H (A, B) from language 1 (with arbitrary substitutions for A and B) is replaceable by an equivalent expression from language 3, and, *second*, that conversely every negated and non-negated expression of the form (A, B) from language 3 (with arbitrary substitutions for A and B) is replaceable by an equivalent expression from language 1 as well. Because of the equivalence of these expressions, one may also assume with Alexander of Aphrodisias that they can be translated into one another without loss of meaning, so that, e.g., 'H (A, B)' and 'N (A, N B)' are equivalent to 'A is incompatible with N B'.[238]

However, this cannot mean that languages 1 and 3 are entirely substitutable for each other. The logical vocabulary that is needed for a given logical system, such as the syllogistic, depends decisively on the language which is used for the establishment of its basic rules. Such rules include not only inference forms from which other inference forms are to be derived and which themselves do not need

---

[238] Alexander of Aphrodisias, *In an. pr.* 264, 14–17 and 264, 33. Compare Frede 1974, 251–52.

any derivation, since they (like, e.g., *modus ponendo ponens*) are valid on the basis of the meaning of the logical vocabulary which is used in them. The basic rules also include the metalogical rules according to which forms of inference are derived from other forms of inference.

It can be seen from the proofs of the validity of the eight rules (2. 3. 1) to (2. 4. 4) in language 2 that there is no metalogical rule from language 3 which would be applied here, but there is one from language 1, namely the principle of conditionalization (II. 1). As one can see, the proofs for the validity of (2. 3. 2) and (2. 3. 4) depend on this principle, and those for (2. 4. 2) and (2. 4. 4) depend on it indirectly. This principle is needed here to transform the form of an inference from two premises into a form in which one of the two premises becomes the antecedent of a hypothetical conclusion. This principle is generally valid because the regular consequence of a conclusion B from one of several premises, A, means the same as $H(A, B)$ (see § 48). Since *all* logical consequence is regular consequence, this principle can be used in general to derive modes of inference from other modes of inference.

However, unlike '$H(\ldots, \ldots)$', the expression '$(\ldots, \ldots)$' is incapable of rendering the existence of a consequence relation which must occur in every form of inference from which another form of inference is derived. For this reason, language 3 contains no expression with which the metalogical rule for deriving inference forms from other inference forms can be established. And from this it results that, concerning the logical vocabulary for the basic rules of the elementary syllogistic, language 1 can be replaced only partially, but not completely by language 3. Yet in the opposite direction a complete substitution is possible, as is demonstrated by the use of language 2 described in this *Appendix*.

Appendix 2
Mathematical Induction without Higher-Level Predicate Logic

(To § 28 and § 37)

The principle of complete induction can be presented as the following propositional schema:

$$(A(0) \supset ((\forall n)(A(n) \supset A(n+1)) \supset (\forall n) A(n))), \text{ for } n \in \mathbb{N}.$$

With this is assumed that A is one of the logical function expressions $F_1(x), \ldots, F_m(x)$, with $m > 1$, and that each of these expressions is an abbreviation for some concrete open proposition, for example for a proposition like '$x + x = 2x$', among others. The above proposition schema is thus equivalent to the proposition schema

$$(F_i(0) \supset ((\forall n)(F_i(n) \supset F_i(n+1)) \supset (\forall n) F_i(n))), \text{ for } n \in \mathbb{N},$$

with $n \geq i \geq 1$. In a more logically precise way, we could also write instead:

$$[n \in \mathbb{N}] \supset (F_i(0) \supset ((\forall n)(F_i(n) \supset F_i(n+1)) \supset (\forall n) F_i(n))).$$

Frege carried out a proof for the validity of the principle of mathematical induction in his *Begriffsschrift*, in which he made use of the second-level calculus of functions. In the following, it will be shown how this can be avoided.

Frege's proof relies on three definitions. The first definition (see Frege 1879, 55, § 24, def. 69 [1967, 55]) is supposed to establish what it means that one property is heritable in a certain series of bearers of that property. The *definiendum* of this definition is

> the property F is hereditary in the f-series,

and the relevant *definiens* is clothed in a formula in the concept-script which corresponds to the following expression:

$$(\forall y)(F(y) \supset (\forall x)(f(y, x) \supset F(x))).$$

Roughly, the sub-expressions '$F(x)$' and '$F(y)$' in this formula mean the same as '$F_i(x)$' and '$F_i(y)$'. That is, these sub-expressions are not abbreviations for certain concrete open propositions, but rather schematic expressions which play the role of a substitute for an arbitrary abbreviation of that type. Accordingly, the talk of a "property F" serves Frege as generic designation for all those properties which one would ascribe to an object a, if one replaced $F_i(x)$ with one of the open propositions $F_1(x), \ldots, F_n(x)$ and in each of these propositions replaced x with a. Hence, what Frege calls "property F" is, expressed in my preferred formula language, the same as the property $('x)\, F_i(x)$.[239] In this way, Frege's first definition is designed to make the expression

> the property $('x)\, F_i(x)$ is hereditary in the f-series

replaceable by the formula

$$(\forall y)\, (F_i(y) \supset (\forall x)\, (f(y, x) \supset F_i(x))).$$

The second definition on which Frege's proof relies (see Frege 1879, 60–62, § 26, def. 76 [1967, 59]) has the task of explaining what it means for an object y to follow an object x in the f-series. In other words, the *definiendum* is here:

> y follows x in the f-series.

Frege recommends as *definiens* an expression which is formulated in the language of the second-level calculus of functions. This expression corresponds to the following formula:

$$(\forall \Phi)\, ([\Phi \text{ is hereditary in the f-series}] \supset ((\forall x)\, (f(w, x) \supset \Phi(x)) \supset \Phi(y))).$$

In words, this formula could be rendered in this way: 'For every property Φ, Φ is not hereditary in the f-series unless $((\forall x)\, (f(w, x) \supset \Phi(x)) \supset \Phi(y))$'.

What is meant here by 'property Φ', in contrast to what Frege calls 'property F'? Essentially, properties Φ can mean nothing else than properties which can be enumerated in the series $('x)\, F_1(x), \ldots, ('x)\, F_m(x)$, with $m > 1$, thus properties which are summarized with the expression $('x)\, F_i(x)$, with $m \geq i \geq 1$'. For precisely these are the properties which, according to what was said above, can be considered heritable. The expression $('x)\, F_i(x)$, with $m \geq i \geq 1$' can refer to any of these properties. However, because Frege avails himself of no index-notation but just his concept-script, he finds himself having to introduce the *universally quantified function variable* Φ[240] to be able to refer to all properties $('x)\, F_i(x)$, with $m \geq i \geq 1$, in the series $('x)\, F_1(x), \ldots, ('x)\, F_m(x)$, with $m > 1$. The transition to an expression of the so-called higher-level calculus of functions, i.e., the replacement of '$F(x)$' and '$F(y)$' with universally quantified function variables '$\Phi(x)$' and '$\Phi(y)$' in the *definiens*

---

[239] For discussion of this expression, see § 27 and §§ 64–65 above.
[240] Instead of 'Φ', Frege uses an upper-case Fraktur letter.

of the definition of 'y follows x in the f-series' is explained by Frege's aspiration to attain a sound definition of the latter expression. If the *definiens* of this definition consisted in the formula

[F is hereditary in the f-series] ⊃ (($\forall$ x) (f (w, x) ⊃ F (x)) ⊃ F (y)),

then the letter F in this formula could only be either a constant or a substitute for constants, i.e., a variable or a schematic letter. In the first case, the content of this formula would be too specific to be equivalent to the *definiendum*. For in this case, only just one of the many properties ('x) F_i (x), . . ., ('x) F_m (x) would be understood as heritable with 'F'. In the other case, the definition would be unsound for a different reason. For the *definiens* of a sound definition can only contain a free variable if it occurs free in the corresponding *definiendum*. Otherwise, the defining expression would not be equivalent to the defined expression. Hence, 'F (x)' and 'F (y)' in the formula of the *definiens* need to be replaced by expressions which are neither too specific nor involve an inadmissible multiplication of free variables. Incidentally, a formula like

[('x) F_i (x) is hereditary in the f-series] ⊃ (($\forall$ x) (f (w, x) ⊃ F_i (x)) ⊃ F_i (y))

does not deliver a sound definition either. With 'i', the *definiens* would contain a free variable which did not also occur free in the corresponding *definiendum*. But 'F_i' is not a constant; it rather plays the role of a sign which only becomes a constant if one puts a definite numeral in place of the index letter i. As for Frege's solution to the problem, it consists in replacing 'F (x)' and 'F (y)' with 'Φ (x)' and 'Φ (y)', respectively, and connecting with them a universal quantifier, the prefix '($\forall$ Φ) . . .'. This quantifier makes it so that x and y in the *definiens* and *definiendum* of the definition are the only free variables.

For reasons which I described in § 28 above, however, one should see this solution only as a stopgap. The view at the basis of this solution – that one may regard open propositions of the form F (x) as expressions for properties, so that these expressions may be represented by variables over which one may quantify, even though they are only unsaturated expressions of the form Φ (x) (and thus meaningless on their own) – is untenable. It thus remains the case that the properties which are treated as heritable properties in Frege's definition cannot be adequately designated with signs like 'F', 'Φ', 'property F', or 'property Φ', though they can be enumerated in sequence with '('x) F_i (x), . . ., ('x) F_m (x), with m > 1' and can be designated by the expression '('x) F_i (x), with $m \geq i \geq 1$'.

'F_i' plays the role of a schematic expression only so long as i is something like a free variable. However, one can bind i by explicitly stipulating as a condition that

($\forall$ i) ($i \geq 1$). We then obtain a suitable definition for 'y follows x in the f-series' by replacing the formula last considered with an expression which contains an explicit stipulation of that sort, namely by writing:

($\forall$ i) ($i \geq 1$) ⊃ ([('x) F_i (x) is hereditary in the f-series] ⊃ (($\forall$ x) (f (w, x) ⊃ F_i (x)) ⊃ F_i (y))).

Frege would not have been able to admit such a definition into the framework of his logicistic program, which was designed to reduce the language of arithmetic to a language of the concept-script. For '$i \geq 1$' is clearly not an expression from the concept-script, but from arithmetic. To avoid having to demolish the framework of the formula language of the concept-script, Frege had to condone treating function variables by analogy with individual variables, as if function variables did not carry with them empty places for constants and as if it would thus be possible to bind such variables with a quantifier without difficulty.

Let us see what results for the proof of the validity of the principle of mathematical induction if we abstain from bringing a second-level calculus of functions into a play. The proof can be based on the formula which I last proposed as an alternative to the expression which, according to Frege's second definition, is supposed to take the place of 'y follows x in the f-series'. The formula is:

($\forall$ i) ($i \geq 1$) ⊃ ([('x) F_i (x) is hereditary in the f-series] ⊃ (($\forall$ x) (f (w, x) ⊃ F_i (x)) ⊃ F_i (y))).

To simplify[241] the presentation of the proof a bit, I will use the one-place functional expression 'φ (y)' in place of the two-place functional expression 'f (y, x)'. In this way, I simplify the expression for the *definiens* of the first definition by replacing '($\forall$ y) (F_i (y) ⊃ ($\forall$ x) (f (y, x) ⊃ F_i (x)))' with '($\forall$ y) (F_i (y) ⊃ ($\forall$ x) (φ (y) ⊃ F_i (x)))'. We can further simplify this expression by replacing its sub-formula '(x) (φ (y) ⊃ F_i (x))' with 'F_i (φ (y))'. The *definiens* of the first definition, i.e., the expression which can take the place of 'the property ('x) F_i (x) is hereditary in the f-series', then has the short form:

($\forall$ y) (F_i (y) ⊃ F_i (φ (y))).

With the same kind of simplification, we can obtain a short form of the *definiens* of the second definition, i.e., the expression which can take the place of 'y follows x in the f-series': I replace the sub-formula '($\forall$ x) (f (w, x) ⊃ F_i (x))' which occurs

---

[241] The simplifications utilized in the following correspond to those used by Ulrich Nortmann. Compare Nortmann 1998, 417.

there with an abbreviated expression '$F_i(\varphi(x))$'. After applying the importation rule, the *definiens* of the second definition then has the simplified form:

$$((\forall i)(i \geq 1) \& [('x) F_i(x) \text{ is hereditary in the } \varphi\text{-series}] \& F_i(\varphi(x))) \supset F_i(y).$$

Accordingly, it follows from the second definition that:

(1) [y follows x in the φ-series] $\supset$
    $((\forall i)(i \geq 1) \& [('x) F_i(x) \text{ is hereditary in the } \varphi\text{-series}] \& F_i(\varphi(x))) \supset F_i(y)$.

By exportation and antecedent exchange, a formula resuls from (1) that corresponds to Frege's theorem 78 (Frege 1879, 63, § 27 [1967, 61]):

(2) [$('x) F(x)$ is hereditary in the φ-series]
    $\supset (F_i(\varphi(x)) \supset ([y \text{ follows } x \text{ in the } \varphi\text{-series}] \supset ((\forall i)(i \geq 1) \supset F_i(y)))))$.

From the first definition, by substituting y for x, one attains in an analogous way:

(3) $[('x) F_i(x) \text{ is hereditary in the } \varphi\text{-series}] \supset (F_i(x) \supset F_i(\varphi(x)))$.

According to Frege's second axiom, the law of propositional logic '$(p \supset (q \supset r)) \supset ((p \supset q) \supset (p \supset r))$', a formula results from (2) which corresponds to Frege's theorem 79 (Frege 1879, 63 [1967, 61]):

(4) $([('x) F(x) \text{ is hereditary in the } \varphi\text{-series}] \supset F(\varphi(x))) \supset ([('x) F_i(x) \text{ is hereditary in the } \varphi\text{-series}] \supset ([y \text{ follows } x \text{ in the } \varphi\text{-series}] \supset ((\forall i)(i \geq 1) \supset F_i(y))))$.

After an antecedent exchange in (3), a formula corresponding to Frege's theorem 81 follows from (3) and (4), by an inference according to the rule of detachment (Frege 1879, 63 [1967, 61]):

(5) $F_i(x) \supset ([('x) F_i(x) \text{ is hereditary in the } \varphi\text{-series}] \supset ([y \text{ follows } x \text{ in the } \varphi\text{-series}] \supset ((\forall i)(i \geq 1) \supset F_i(y))))$.

(5) is thus a formula that depends on both definitions.

As Frege (1879, 64 [1967, 62]) remarks, Bernoullian induction "rests" upon theorem 81.[242] The transition to the proof-principle for mathematical induction can be made in a corresponding way, starting from formula (5). By generalization over x and with a subsequent instantiation of the numeral 0, we get from (5):

(6) $F_i(0) \supset ([('x) F_i(x) \text{ is hereditary in the } \varphi\text{-series}] \supset ([y \text{ follows } 0 \text{ in the } \varphi\text{-series}] \supset ((\forall i)(i \geq 1) \supset F_i(y))))$.

---

[242] Jakob Bernoulli uses the mode of inference of mathematical induction in 'Demonstratio rationum etc.' (1686). Reprinted in Bernoulli 1744, Vol. 1, 282–83.

To the sub-expression '[y follows 0 in the φ-series]', the expression '∨ y = 0' can be appended, since the first sub-expression '$F_i(0)$' says that $F_i(y)$ holds if $y = 0$. Moreover, (6) can be generalized over y, in which case a two-fold posterior generalization is admissible, since the variable y does not occur free either in '$F_i(0)$' or in '(′x) $F_i(x)$ is inherited in the φ-series]'. Hence, after replacing '(′x) $F_i(x)$ is inherited in the φ-series' with the expression that defines it, we get from (6):

(7) $F_i(0) \supset ((\forall y)(F_i(y) \supset F_i(\varphi(y)))) \supset (\forall y)(([y \text{ follows } 0 \text{ in the } \varphi\text{-series}] \vee y = 0) \supset ((\forall i)(i \geq 1) \supset F_i(y))))$.

After an antecedent exchange, the following results:

(8) $(\forall i)(i \geq 1) \supset ((\forall y)([y \text{ follows } 0 \text{ in the } \varphi\text{-series}] \vee y = 0) \supset (F_i(0) \supset ((\forall y)(F_i(y) \supset F_i(\varphi(y))) \supset (\forall y) F_i(y))))$.

Now, I define with Frege (1986/1950, § 83) the concept of a natural number:[243] if n belongs to the S-series, beginning with zero, or equals zero, then I say 'n is a natural number'. Thus, '(′x) $S(x)$' stands for successorhood, so that $S(n) = n + 1$. The same in partially symbolic notation:

$([n \text{ follows } 0 \text{ in the } S\text{-series}] \vee y = 0)^{244} =_{\text{def.}} [n \text{ is a natural number}]$.

Now, from (8) we get, after an instantiation of S and n:

(9) $(\forall i)(i \geq 1) \supset ((\forall n)([n \text{ follows } 0 \text{ in the } S\text{-series}] \vee n = 0) \supset (F_i(0) \supset ((\forall n)(F_i(n) \supset F_i(n + 1)) \supset (\forall n) F_i(n))))$.

The sub-expression '[n follows 0 in the S-series] $\vee n = 0$' is equivalent to '$n \in \mathbb{N}$'. For this reason, formula (9) corresponds to the principle of mathematical induction, which can now be formulated as follows:

$(\forall i)(i \geq 1) \supset ([n \in \mathbb{N}] \supset (F_i(0) \supset ((\forall n)(F_i(n) \supset F_i(n + 1)) \supset (\forall n) F_i(n))))$;

---

[243] Natural numbers are called 'finite numbers' in Frege.
[244] The expression in round brackets here corresponds to the *definiens* in concept-script which Frege introduces with formula 99 in § 29 of the *Begriffsschrift* for 'y belongs to the f-series beginning with x'. – On Frege's path to derive the induction principle, see also §§45–46 of *Basic Laws of Arithmetic*, Vol. 1 (Frege 1893/2013). These paragraphs show, just like §§ 79–83 of *Foundations of Arithmetic* (Frege 1986/1950), that for his proof Frege makes use of the definition of belonging to a φ-series beginning with x, which was introduced by formula 99 in § 29 of the *Begriffsschrift*.

or somewhat more informally expressed:

$$F_i(0) \supset ((\forall n)(F_i(n) \supset F_i(n+1)) \supset (\forall n) F_i(n)), \text{ with } i \geq 1 \text{ and } n \in \mathbb{N}.$$

Closing remark: Frege was barred from the path to explaining the validity of the principle of mathematical induction recommended here. In order to avoid using numerals, he was dependent on the step (carried out in § 26 of the *Begriffsschrift*) into a higher-level predicate logic, which was defective according to his own semantic standards. But using numerals was contrary to the logicist program, which was supposed to be carried out in the *Foundations of Arithmetic* (which in its § 79 repeats the step into higher predicate logic from the *Begriffsschrift* § 26); thus, such use was ruled out from the start. It was thus ultimately a 'philosophical' motive (namely, that of logicism and the connected aim of demonstrating against Kant the analytic character of arithmetic) which inspired Frege's attempt to initiate a higher-level predicate logic. And it was this attempt that provided the basis for Russell's paradox (see § 28 above).

Appendix 3
Reduction of Truth-Functional Expressions to Non-Truth-Functional Expressions

(To § 30)

In § 30 I showed that all truth functions can be presented with three operators, namely '(. . ., . . .)', 'N . . .', and 'H (. . ., . . .)'. Even two operators, 'H (. . ., . . .)' and 'N . . .' suffice to present all truth functions. For expressions of the same logical strength can replace each other, and both the pair of formulas H (A, B) and N (A, C) as well as the pair of formulas NH (A, B) and (A, C), with C = N B or B = N C, are pairs of expressions of the same logical strength (see *Appendix 1*). In the following I will limit myself to showing how to present all dyadic truth functions with '(. . ., . . .)', 'N . . .', and 'H (. . ., . . .)'.

For combinatorial reasons, exactly 16 different distributions of truth functions are possible with dyadic truth functions. They correspond to sixteen different propositional connections which can be presented exclusively with '~ . . .' and '. . . & . . .':

Table 4

	Value Distribution	Truth Function
(1)	TTTT	~ (p & ~ p)
(2)	TTTF	~ (~ p & ~ q)
(3)	TTFT	~ (~ p & q)
(4)	TFTT	~ (p & ~ q)
(5)	FTTT	~ (p & q)
(6)	TTFF	p & p
(7)	TFTF	q & q
(8)	FTTF	~ (p & q) & ~ (~ p & ~ q)
(9)	TFFT	~ (p & ~ q) & ~ (~ p & q)
(10)	FTFT	~ q & ~ q
(11)	FFTT	~ p & ~ p
(12)	TFFF	p & q
(13)	FTFF	p & ~ q
(14)	FFTF	~ p & q
(15)	FFFT	~ p & ~ q
(16)	FFFF	p & ~ p

Each formula in the right column of this table can be transformed into an equivalent non-truth-functional expression. For if A, B, and C are formulas which stand within the scope of '~ . . .' and '. . . & . . .', and if we (as per § 30) replace in Table 4 every formula A & B with the conjunctive formula ((A, B), (H ((A, B), A), H ((A, B), B))) and every formula ~ C with the conjunctive formula (N C, H (NN C, C)), then there results for every row of the table a formula which is equivalent with the original formula of that row. Table 4 contains, so to speak, only abbreviations of non-truth-functional expressions.

To explain and justify this claim I would like to compare the meaning of the expressions (i) 'A & B' and (ii) '~ C' with the meaning of the corresponding non-truth-functional expressions, i.e., with '((A, B), (H ((A, B), A), H ((A, B), B)))' and with '(N C, H (NN C, C))', respectively.

(i) Concerning first the meaning of the truth-functional '. . . & . . .', it results from the truth table for 'A & B' (see § 30 and line (12) of Table 4). The same meaning belongs to the expression '((A, B), (H ((A, B), A), H ((A, B), B)' as well. That is, this expression is also true for every interpretation in which both A and B are true or false propositions if and only if both A and B are true, and false if and only if A or B is false. To see this, it is enough to note that the pair of formulas '(H ((A, B), A)' and 'H ((A, B), B))' presupposes the validity of the postulate of arbitrary sufficient reason from § 72. This postulate stipulates that according to the rule (VI. 3),

$$A, B \prec A,$$

the conclusion A is impossibly false if the premises A and B are both true. Since the order of the premises A and B is irrelevant for the validity of this rule, it equally expresses that it is impossible that B is false if A and B are both true. According to § 30, however, the meaning of *elementary* conjunctions of the form (A, B) is determined in such a way that they are true only if it is not possible that A or B is false. According to this determination, assertoric inferences cannot have a premise which is assumed to be possibly false. The postulate of § 72, on the other hand, requires that we abandon this determination and assume instead that for each premise of assertoric inferences, if it is assumed to be true, it is impossibly false (so that not universally valid propositions of the form H (A, H (B, A)) and H (A, H (B, B)) are valid, no matter what proposition B stands for). The formula '((A, B), (H ((A, B), A), H ((A, B), B))' thus expresses that what according to postulate (VI. 3) should be true for two premises A and B should also be true not only for a premise A & B, but also for an elementary conjunction of the form (A, B), namely, that if it is assumed to be true (e.g., as a true premise of an assertoric inference), then each of its conjunctive members impossibly has the value F. This shows that expressions of the form ((A, B), (H ((A, B), A), H ((A, B), B)) are equivalent to expressions of the form A & B.

(ii) What I have shown for '... & ...' can now be shown in a quite similar way for '~ ...'. The meaning of '~ C' results from the truth table for ~ C (see § 30). The same meaning belongs to the expression '(N C, H (NN C, C))' as well. That is, this expression is true for any interpretation in which C is a true or false proposition if and only if C is false, and false if and only if C is true. To see this, it is enough to note that a proposition of the form H (NN C, C) presupposes the validity of the postulate of the affirmative use of double negation from § 72. This postulate stipulates with rule (VI. 4),

$$NN\ C \prec C,$$

that we assume that if the negation of N C is true, then C cannot be false. Rule (VI. 4) is not universally valid (according to the meaning established in § 43), since there are cases in which N C is compatible with NN C. However, the validity of the syllogistic rule (I. 1),

$$C \therefore NN\ C,$$

according to which if C is true, the negation of N C cannot be false, rests on logical grounds and must therefore be assumed. The postulate from § 72 presupposes the validity of this rule, but rule (VI. 4) requires in addition rejecting the definitional determination of the meaning of 'N C' according to § 43, so that the truth value of propositions of the form N C is determined by the value of C alone, and N C is false if and only if C is true. If we now assume for conjunctions of the form (..., ...) that expressions of the form ((A, B), (H ((A, B), A), H ((A, B), B))) mean the same as expressions of the form A & B, as has just been shown, then we can finally show that conjunctive expressions of the form (N C, H (NN C, C)) are equivalent to truth-functional expressions of the form N C & NN C, C and therefore equivalent to truth-functional expressions of the form ~ C.

Conclusion: Both the pair of formulas 'A & B' and '((A, B), (H ((A, B), A), H ((A, B), B)))' as well as the pair of formulas '~ C' and '(N C, H (NN C, C)' consist of equivalent expressions. QED.

It can be shown in a similar way that there is for each of the remaining formulas of the right column of Table 4 an equivalent non-truth-functional expression in which no logical constants occur besides '(..., ...)', 'N ...', and 'H ...'.

Appendix 4
Compatibility and Incompatibility

(To § 30)

We speak of the compatibility of two propositions or two states of affairs when it is possible that they are both true or both obtain. In the common (everyday) understanding, two logically compatible propositions can both be false, indeed even necessarily false. For example, one will not necessarily have to regard it as a logical error if someone believes the two propositions 'Triangles have four angles' and 'The sum of 2 and 1 is 4' are indeed both false or even necessarily false, yet still compatible *with each other*. One can mention in favor of accepting the compatibility of both propositions that the proposition 'If the sum of 2 and 1 is 4, then triangles have four angles' is not (or at least not in all circumstances) false. On the contrary, it represents one state of affairs (that does not obtain) following from another (which likewise does not obtain). That both states of affairs do not obtain *on their own*, does not preclude that *taken together*, and perhaps even *only* taken together, they *could* obtain after all and in this sense are compatible with each other. On the contrary, the statement that the one state of affairs follows from the other says precisely that the obtaining of the one state of affairs is incompatible with the non-obtaining of the other. For a proposition of the form, 'if p, then q' says the same thing as the proposition 'it is impossible that p and not q' (see § 30 above).

Corresponding to the broad sense of logical compatibility just discussed, there is a relatively strict concept of logical incompatibility. For the same reason that one typically does *not* suppose that every arbitrary declarative proposition follows from a false declarative proposition (*ex falso quodlibet*), or that every true declarative proposition follows from every arbitrary true proposition (*verum ex quolibet*), one does not typically suppose that a proposition which is already taken to be false or necessarily false or contradictory is incompatible with arbitrary other propositions. One does not typically suppose, for example, that an empirically false proposition like 'On the 30th of March, 2009, it snowed in Bielefeld' is incompatible with arbitrary propositions, so that the negation of arbitrary propositions follows from it.

Yet in modern modal logic the concepts of compatibility and incompatibility often tend to be dealt with differently. To be sure, compatibility and incompatibility are customarily defined by assuming that both the expressions 'p is compatible with q' and 'it is possible that p and q' and that both the expressions 'p is incompatible with q' and 'it is not possible that p and q' are equivalent (where this assumption still completely corresponds to the common understanding). But primarily (outside of paraconsistent, e.g., relevant-logical, systems) the propositional conjunction occurring in these expressions, '... and ...', is read either as a truth-functional conjunction or it is supposed (as an axiom or on the basis of an axiom) that for expressions of the type 'p and q' a rule holds which corresponds to the simplification rule

$$\frac{p, q}{p}$$

(the same as rule (VI. 3) in § 72), which says that p follows from p & q.[245] With this rule it is at the same time supposed (by the contraposition rule) that $\sim q$ follows from a contradictory propositional conjunction p & $\sim p$, where q can be an arbitrary true or false proposition, thus also a proposition $\sim r$. If one supposes in addition that r follows from $\sim \sim r$, that means one supposes that any arbitrary proposition follows from a contradictory propositional conjunction.[246] The relation of one proposition following from other propositions is often understood in modal logic as the relation of *strict implication*. In this conception, $\sim q$ follows from p & $\sim p$ if and only if it is not possible that $(p$ & $\sim p)$ & $\sim \sim q$ is true, if thus $(p$ & $\sim p)$ is incompatible with $\sim \sim q$. If one accepts the simplification rule, then it is immediately supposed along with this conception that arbitrary double negated propositions are incompatible with a contradictory propositional conjunction. If one accepts in addition that (according to rule (VI. 4) (see § 72)) from a double negated proposition the same non-negated proposition follows, then one ultimately supposes that *every* arbitrary proposition follows from a contradictory propositional conjunction.

The basic assumption behind this supposition is snuck into the understanding of the connective '... and ...' as an expression whose meaning makes accepting the simplification rule unavoidable. This assumption can be given up only if one recognizes that this meaning of '... and ...' is not the only one possible, since it also admits a reading which corresponds to the definition set up above in § 30 (as well as in *Appendix 1*) of the conjunction of premises, according to which the simplification rule does not need to be assumed as a *universally valid* rule. If one assumes this definition and, to avoid misunderstandings, uses the logical constant '(..., ...)' for the connective it defines, then the concepts of logical compatibility and incompatibility can be fixed by a definition that corresponds to the common everyday understanding. This definition says:

---

[245] In intuitionistic logic, the axiom A ⊃ (B ⊃ A) corresponds to this supposition. See Heyting 1930, 191.

[246] To be sure, in intuitionistic logic it is not supposed that A follows from $\sim \sim$ A, but is assumed as an axiom that $\sim$ A ⊃ (A ⊃ B). See Heyting 1930, 191. This axiom expresses the same thing as the supposition *ex falso sequitur quodlibet*.

Two propositions *p* and *q* are *compatible* if and only if it is possible that (*p*, *q*) is true; *p* and *q* are *incompatible* if and only if it is not possible that (*p*, *q*) is true.²⁴⁷

It accords with this definition – since the simplification rule for the conjunction of premises does not hold, so that *p* does not follow from (*p*, *q*) (see § 30) – that no universally valid rule exists according to which it would be admissible (say, on the basis of (IV. 29)) to derive *M p* from *M* (*p*, *q*) or *NM* (*p*, *q*) from *NM p*.²⁴⁸ In other words: on this conception, the possible truth of a proposition is not a necessary condition for its being incompatible with another proposition; and it is likewise not at all sufficient for its incompatibility with other propositions that a proposition is impossibly true *taken on its own*. Rather, one should say according to this conception that e.g., the two propositions 'Triangles have four corners' and 'The sum of 2 and 1 is 4' are completely compatible, *without* then also having to suppose that it is possible that one of the two propositions is true *taken on its own*. Likewise, it is not false to say that the hypothetical proposition 'If triangles have four corners, then the sum of 2 and 1 is 4' is true and accordingly the propositions 'Triangles have four corners' and 'The sum of 2 and 1 is *not* 4' are incompatible, *without* having to suppose for that reason that the impossibility of the proposition 'Triangles have four corners' being true is already a *sufficient* condition for this incompatibility.

Due to the restriction of the concept of compatibility that we have carried out by means of the concept of the conjunction of premises, the relation of regular consequence can be explained by means of the relation of incompatibility, without needing to involve the unwelcome supposition that every arbitrary declarative proposition follows from a declarative proposition which is impossibly true, or that an impossibly false proposition follows from every arbitrary declarative proposition.

---

247 Since *H* (*p*, *N q*) is equivalent to *NM* (*p*, *q*) and *NH* (*p*, *N q*) is equivalent to *M* (*p*, *q*), one could define the compatibility and incompatibility of propositions just as well using hypothetical propositions. From the fact that *H* (*p*, *N q*) is also equivalent to *N* (*p*, *q*) and *NH* (*p*, *N q*) to (*p*, *q*) (see § 40 as well as *Appendix 1*, rules (2. 4) and (2. 5)), the noteworthy fact results that *N* (*p*, *q*) is logically equivalent to *NM* (*p*, *q*) and (*p*, *q*) to *M* (*p*, *q*). In other words: *N* (*p*, *N q*) and *M* (*p*, *q*) are only *apparently* logical weakenings of *NM* (*p*, *N q*) and (*p*, *q*), respectively.

248 Among the systems of modal logic set up by C.I. Lewis, the so-called S1 is distinguished by its lacking the axiom $\Diamond\ (p\ \&\ q) \to \Diamond\ p$. Lewis calls this axiom the 'consistency postulate' and thus indicates that only a statement that is without contradiction and to that extent possible can be part of a conjunction that is without contradiction and to that extent possible. See Lewis & Langford 1932, 166–67.

Appendix 5
Modern Non-Syllogistic Systems of Modal Logic in Their Relationship to Modal Syllogistic

(To §§ 58 to 63)

1. The system of modal logic that was presented above in §§ 58 to 63 as a subsystem of the elementary syllogistic is distinguished by its strict universal validity from systems of modal logic which have been constructed on the basis of rules of propositional logic and laws of the logical calculus of functions. In the following, I would like to indicate the systematic relationship between the basic modal-logical rules established in § 60 and these other systems. In doing so, I will draw attention to logically relevant distinctions that appear in the four most famous of these systems (the systems T, S4, S5, and the Brouwerian system (B)).

For that purpose, it is first necessary to specify how the meanings of the logical constants M and L are related to the meanings given by the expressions 'it is possible that . . .' and 'it is necessary that . . .', when they are used in connection with truth-functional expressions.

According to rules (IV. 5), (IV. 20), and (IV. 21) (see § 60 and § 61 above), L A is logically equivalent both to NMN A and to LNN A. Just so is M A, according to rules (IV. 3), (IV. 30), and (IV. 31), logically equivalent to NLN A and MNN A. If we replace 'N A' and 'NN A' in the expressions used in these rules with the corresponding truth-functional expressions, namely with '~ A' and '~ ~ A' respectively, the logical equivalence relations are not preserved. For according to § 71, definition 4, as well as *Appendix 3* (cf. also § 30), '~ A' is not equivalent to 'N A', but rather to '(N A, H (NN A, A)'.

Hence, M A is logically equivalent neither to NL ~ A, nor to M ~ ~ A. But by means of a new sign, – I will use the diamond sign '◇ . . .' introduced by C.I. Lewis,[249] which has been customary in modal logic ever since – we can formulate two new basic rules, according to which it holds that:

◇ A >< NL ~ A,	(M. 1)
◇ A >< M ~ ~ A.	(M. 2)

These rules of course do not render a *logical* but rather only a *regular* equivalence, namely, an equivalence which obtains between ◇ A on the one hand and NL ~ A

---

[249] The sign '◇' occurs first in Lewis' and Langford's *Symbolic Logic* in 1932.

and $M \sim \sim A$ on the other, if and only if the postulate of the affirmative use of double negation (VI. 4) (see § 72) is assumed as valid. For on this assumption the meaning of '$\sim \ldots$' turns into the meaning of '$N \ldots$' (see the corollary to definition 4 in § 71; cf. also § 10 and § 30, as well as *Appendix 3*). Consequently, on precisely this assumption the meaning of '$\diamond \ldots$' likewise turns into the meaning of '$M \ldots$'. The expression '$\diamond$ A' as it appears in (M. 1) and (M. 2) may thus be read just like 'M A': 'It is possible that A'. But it should be noted that this reading is ambiguous, since the meanings of '$\diamond$ A' and 'M A' must be logically distinguished.

For exactly similar reasons, I utilize the box sign '$\square \ldots$' introduced by Ruth Barcan Marcus, and also customary in modal logic since then, to be able to render two further rules, namely:

$\square A \succ\prec NM \sim A,$ (M. 3)
$\square A \succ\prec L \sim \sim A.$[250] (M. 4)

These equivalence rules hold on the same condition as rules (M. 1) and (M. 2). On this condition, but also only on this condition, one may read the expression '$\square \ldots$' as it appears here as though it means the same thing as '$L \ldots$'.

From (M. 2) and (M. 4), by inference conversion according to rule (I. 2) (see § 44) the equivalence rules

$NM \sim \sim A \succ\prec N \diamond A,$ (M. 5)
$NL \sim \sim A \succ\prec N \square A$ (M. 6)

can be derived. Next, from (M. 1) and (M. 6) and from (M. 3) and (M. 5) respectively the following rules can be derived, if one equates A with $\sim$ B in (M. 1) and (M. 3) and A with B in (M. 5) and (M. 6):

$\diamond \sim B \succ\prec N \square B,$ (M. 7)
$\square \sim B \succ\prec N \diamond B.$ (M. 8)

On the basis of rule (VI. 2) (see § 72), according to which the change from $\sim$ A to N A and conversely from N A to $\sim$ A is permitted, so long as the postulate of the affirmative use of double negation (VI. 4) is valid, the following two rules are also valid:

$\diamond \sim B \succ\prec \sim \square B,$ (M. 9)
$\square \sim B \succ\prec \sim \diamond B.$ (M. 10)

---

[250] The necessity sign '$\square$' first appears in the paper 'A Functional Calculus of First Order Based on Strict Implication', which Ruth C. Barcan Marcus (still under the name Barcan) published in the *Journal of Symbolic Logic* in 1946.

Both these rules are truth-functional analogues to the modal-syllogistic rules (IV. 4) and (IV. 6). By replacing B in (M. 9) and (M. 10) everywhere with ~ A, we then get from these rules together with (M. 2) and (M. 4) truth-functional analogues to rules (IV. 3) and (IV. 5), namely:

$$\Diamond A \mathbin{><} \mathop{\sim} \Box \mathop{\sim} A, \tag{M. 11}$$
$$\Box A \mathbin{><} \mathop{\sim} \Diamond \mathop{\sim} A. \tag{M. 12}$$

The intermodal rules (M. 9) to (M. 12) can, as has just been shown, be derived from the modal-syllogistic intermodal rules (IV. 3) to (IV. 6), though only by assuming that the postulate of the affirmative use of double negation (VI. 4) (see § 72) is valid.

On the same assumption, further analogues to the modal-syllogistic rules can be derived as well. Namely, since according to rule (IV. 1) (see § 60) *a necesse esse valet consequentia* holds, so that ~ ~ A follows logically from L ~ ~ A, since moreover ~ ~ A implies A according to rule (VI. 22) (see § 75), the weakening rule

$$\Box A \prec A \tag{M. 13}$$

can be derived from (M. 4). In the same way, one can derive a further weakening rule from (M. 2), namely

$$A \prec \Diamond A. \tag{M. 14}$$

For A implies ~ ~ A, according to rule (VI. 21) (see § 75), and according to (IV. 25) (see § 61) M ~ ~ A follows logically from ~ ~ A – since *ab esse ad posse valet consequentia* also holds –, so that from M ~ ~ A, according to (M. 2), the transition to $\Diamond$ A is permitted.

In addition, the rule of 'strict detachment' can be derived from detachment rule (VI. 8) (see § 74) together with the weakening rule (M. 13):

$$\Box (A \supset B), A \prec B. \tag{M. 15}$$

Since according to (VI. 21) and (VI. 22) the transition both from A to ~ ~ A as well as conversely from ~ ~ A to A is permitted, according to rule (IV. 19) (see § 61) the transition from L A to L ~ ~ A to L A is permitted as well. For the same reason, according to rule (IV. 29) (see § 61), the transition from M A to M ~ ~ A and conversely from M ~ ~ A to M A is permitted. Hence, on the basis of (M. 2), the rule $\Diamond$ A $\mathbin{><}$ M A holds, and on the basis of (M. 4), the rule $\Box$ A $\mathbin{><}$ L A holds:

$$\Diamond A \mathbin{><} M A \tag{M. 16}$$
$$\Box A \mathbin{><} L A \tag{M. 17}$$

By conditionalization, that is according to rule (II. 1) (see § 48), the rule □ (A ⊃ B) ≺ H (A, B) can be obtained from (M. 15). Since in addition, according to rule (IV. 2) (see § 60), it also holds that L B logically follows from H (A, B) together with L A, the rule □ (A ⊃ B), □ A ≺ □ B follows from (M. 15) together with (M. 17), and from this rule, by conditionalization (according (II. 1)), the rule □ (A ⊃ B) ≺ H (□ A, □ B) follows. From this, according to rule (VI. 7) (see § 71), yet only on the assumption that the postulate of the arbitrary sufficient reason (VI. 3) (see § 72) is valid, the distributive rule

$$□ (A ⊃ B) ≺ (□ A ⊃ □ B) \tag{M. 18}$$

can be derived. Finally, on the same assumption and in a similar way, the rule

$$□ (A ⊃ B) ≺ (◇ A ⊃ ◇ B) \tag{M. 19}$$

can be derived from (M. 15) by conditionalization. For according to rule (IV. 29) it holds that H (M A, M B) follows logically from H (A, B). According to *modus ponendo ponens* (II. 2) (see § 48), M B follows from H (M A, M B) together with M A. Hence, on the basis of (M. 16), □ (A ⊃ B), ◇ A ≺ ◇ B also holds. By conditionalization and subsequent application of rule (VI. 1), we get (M. 19).

The following comparison shows that there is for nine of the just derived formulas (M. 1) to (M. 19) an analogous formula in the modal syllogistic:

Table 5

(M. 13)	□ A ≺ A	(IV. 1)	L B ∴ B
(M. 11)	◇ A ≻≺ ~ □ ~ A	(IV. 3)	M B : : NLN B
(M. 10)	□ ~ B ≻≺ ~ ◇ B	(IV. 4)	NM B : : LN B
(M. 12)	□ A ≻≺ ~ ◇ ~ A	(IV. 5)	L B : : NMN B
(M. 9)	◇ ~ B ≻≺ ~ □ B	(IV. 6)	NL B : : MN B
(M. 14)	A ≺ ◇ A	(IV. 25)	A ∴ M A
(M. 15)	□ (A ⊃ B), A ≺ B	(II. 2')	LH (A, B), A ∴ B
(M. 18)	□ (A ⊃ B) ≺ (□ A ⊃ □ B)	(IV. 19')	LH (A, B) ∴ H (L A, L B)
(M. 19)	□ (A ⊃ B) ≺ (◇ A ⊃ ◇ B)	(IV. 29')	LH (A, B) ∴ H (M A, M B)

In the last three lines of this table, the formulas (II. 2'), (IV. 19'), and (IV. 29') indicate universally valid rules which have not been mentioned so far but which, as one can easily recognize, can be derived directly from formulas (II. 2), (IV. 19), and (IV. 29), with the help of rule (IV. 1). The truth-functional analogues of all ten formulas of this table are not mere translations of one language into another, but rather expressions for a new type of modal-logical rule. The most important distinction between these and the modal-syllogistic rules standing opposite them is that the truth-functional rules are not strictly universally valid. Rather, their validity correlates exactly with the validity of the postulates of the affirmative use of double negation and the arbitrary sufficient reason (VI. 3).

2. Now, the systematic relationship between the modal syllogistic I have presented and the most important or most well-known axiomatic modal-logical systems can be described in the following way. All these systems contain the propositional part of the calculus of functions (described by me above in §§ 77 to 81). They contain it either by the fact that all theorems of the classical propositional calculus are derivable from the axioms of the modal-logical system or by the fact that they explicitly assume the propositional calculus as valid when they expand it through the addition of certain modal-logical axioms and rules. The first mentioned version of an axiomatization of modal logic underlies the various systems which Lewis developed. By contrast, the idea for the second version, to axiomatize modal logic through an extension of classical propositional calculus, stems from Kurt Gödel.[251]

In line with this idea, Robert Feys worked out the so-called 'system T', whose basic features I render here in a modified notation. The only modal-logical axioms of this system (in addition to the axioms of the classical propositional calculus) are the two following:

$\Box p \supset p$, (Necessity Axiom)
$\Box (p \supset q) \supset (\Box p \supset \Box q)$. (Distributive Axiom)

They can be attained directly from rules (M. 13) and (M. 18) by de-conditionalization (according to II. 27) (see § 50) and subsequent transformation into subjunctions (according to (VI. 1) (see § 71)). The first of the three following definitions corresponds to rule (M. 11) in T:

$\Diamond A =_{Def} \sim \Box \sim A$
$A \rightarrowtail B =_{Def} \Box (A \supset B)$
$(A = B) =_{Def} ((A \rightarrowtail B) \& (B \rightarrowtail A))$

The two remaining definitions reduce the use of the signs of strict implication '⊰' and of strict equivalence '=' to the use of '□' and '⊃' and '&'. The necessity rule – according to which it holds that when ⊢ A is a theorem, then ⊢ □ A is a theorem – also holds as a transformation or derivation rule in T (in addition to the rules of substitution and detachment, which are already used in the calculus of functions).

---

[251] On this, compare *Appendix 6* and Hughes & Cresswell 1977, 217–18.

It corresponds to this rule that if *≺ A is a valid law, it is impossible that *≺ L A is invalid.

The so-called Brouwerian System is distinguished from System T only by introducing an additional modal-logical axiom, the so-called Brouwerian Axiom:[252]

$$p \supset \Box \sim \Box \sim p. \tag{B}$$

There are two alternatives to the Brouwerian System, namely the systems set up by Lewis under the names S4 and S5.[253] They, too, can be characterized by the fact that they each add to the axioms of System T an additional axiom. In S4, the axiom

$$\Box p \supset \Box \Box p, \tag{S4}$$

takes the place of the Brouwerian Axiom, while in S5 the axiom

$$\Diamond A \supset \Box \sim \Box \sim A.^{254} \tag{S5}$$

takes the place of the Brouwerian Axiom.

In the modal syllogistic I have described, there are analogues neither to the Brouwerian Axiom nor to the Axioms S4 and S5. That is, according to the definitions of the modal-logical constants '$M \ldots$' and '$L \ldots$' there is no valid basic rule from which one of the three following rules can be derived: (1) A ∴ LNLN A, (2)

---

[252] Though the name of the Brouwerian Axiom refers to the founder of intuitionistic mathematics Luitzen Egbertus Jan Brouwer, it does not go back to him but rather to Oskar Becker; see Becker 1930, 509. The relation to Brouwer's intuitionism seems somewhat far-fetched, but it stems from the fact that from the intuitionistic perspective, $p \supset \sim \sim p$ but not $\sim \sim p \supset p$ is valid. If one interprets (as recommended by Kurt Gödel (see *Appendix 6*)) the negation sign here (the meaning of which is not defined in the intuitionistic axiomatic system developed by Brouwer's student Arend Heyting) as an abbreviation for '$\Box \sim$', then the result is that $\sim \sim p \supset p$ becomes the formula $\Box \sim \Box \sim p \supset p$, which is not regarded as valid in any of the Systems T, S4, and S5, while $p \supset \sim \sim p$ transforms into the formula $p \supset \Box \sim \Box \sim p$, which is equivalent to $p \supset \Box \Diamond p$.

[253] The letter 'S' stands for 'strict' in these labels. The connected numerals indicate that there is a sequence of axiomatically constructed systems beginning with S1 in which each system $n + 1$ contains each system n.

[254] Lewis himself attained the systems S4 and S5 not by starting from system T and adding the axioms designated as (S4) and (S5) to it, but rather by starting from a system called S3 and adding to it in S4 the axiom $\sim \Diamond (\sim p) \dashv \sim \Diamond \sim (\sim \Diamond (\sim p))$ and in S5 the axiom $p \dashv \sim \Diamond (\sim \Diamond p)$. The system S3 is similar to system T inasmuch as it contains the axiom $\sim \Diamond p \dashv \sim p$ instead of the necessity axiom and the axiom $(p \dashv q) \dashv (\sim \Diamond q \dashv \sim \Diamond p)$ instead of the distributive axiom. On the construction of the Lewis-systems, compare the section "The Lewis-Systems" in Hughes & Cresswell 1977, 213–54.

L A ∴ *LL* A, or (3) *M* A ∴ *LNLN* A. This situation requires an explanation, which I will provide in what follows.

3. The definitions established in § 59 fix the uses of '*L* . . .' and '*M* . . .' so that they are not restricted to certain specific contexts in terms of content. Likewise, the colloquial uses of 'it is possible that . . .' and 'it is necessary that . . .' are not restricted to specific contexts either. Rather, they are unrestricted in the same way as the use of the hypothetical proposition 'if . . ., then . . .', which indeed may be understood as equivalent to '*LN* (. . ., *N* . . .)' and '*NM* (. . ., *N* . . .)' and whose meaning can be fixed so that it is suitable to represent an *arbitrary* 'if-then'-relation, i.e., an *arbitrary* relation of regular consequence. I have fixed the meaning of '*H* (. . ., . . .)' in § 47 so that it is applicable to hypothetical propositions of arbitrary content. Because of this, the meanings of '*LN* (. . ., *N* . . .)' and '*NM* (. . ., *N* . . .)' are also fixed so that the rules whose validity can be rendered by means of these expressions are rules of arbitrary content (whether they are, e.g., conventions whose scope is restricted to an arbitrarily small set of individuals, or rules with a regional or temporary scope, or rules which are derivable from laws of nature but are valid only within the bounds of prior experiences, or logical rules whose scope encompasses all possible worlds, etc.).[255]

Accordingly, the necessity which can be rendered by propositions of the form *H* (*p*, *q*), *LN* (*p*, *N p*), and *NM* (*p*, *N q*), is not a special kind of absolute or relative necessity, but rather a modality which lies at the common basis of all special types of absolute and relative necessity. '*L* . . .' (in the sense of 'necessarily (true that) . . .') thus means the same thing as 'in all thinkable circumstances (it is true that) . . .' (cf. § 59, def. 2), whereby it depends on the context which universe of discourse of thinkable circumstances the expression 'in all thinkable circumstances' tacitly assumes (as a non-empty domain). Though this expression can, it need not mean the same thing as 'in all possible worlds'. Hence, the assumed universe of discourse of thinkable circumstances need not coincide with the total content of all possible worlds. Rather, this domain coincides in each case with the totality of circumstances which the rules at issue in the given context refer to or to which they can be applied. The domain coincides with the scope of these rules in each case, which need not coincide with the domain which encompasses all possible worlds.

---

[255] For this reason, propositions like 'If I have the desire tomorrow evening, I will go to the cinema', 'If one does not comply with a no-passing zone, then one may receive a fine', 'If a castling is performed, then the rook jumps over the king', or 'If something is necessarily true, then it also actually true' should be understood as propositions of the same logical form and transformed into propositions of the form *LN* (*p*, *N q*).

Thus, e.g., the proposition, 'Necessarily, the square on which the knight stands changes color with every move', means that under all thinkable circumstances (that fall within the scope of the rules of chess which are tacitly assumed to be valid) the color of the square of the knight changes from white to black or from black to white when it is played. The thinkable circumstances here are the moves which are thinkable according to the rules of chess as they are assumed to be valid. In just the same way, the proposition 'It is possible that a pawn jumps over a square' means that (according to the assumed rules of chess) there is a thinkable circumstance in which a pawn's jumping over a square occurs. Here again it is the totality of possible chess moves that implicitly constitutes the scope of the assumed rules and the domain of thinkable circumstances for which these rules have validity, which includes the opening move in a game of chess. The proposition 'It is impossible that a castling is performed and the rook does not jump over the king' says that the given domain contains no element which has the property of being a castling where a rook does not jump over the king.

These examples deal with necessity, possibility, and impossibility by assuming a totality of thinkable circumstances as an application domain for valid rules, without this totality being equated immediately with the totality of possible worlds. If the proposition that a change in square color is necessary with every move of a knight were understood as if it stated that this change took place in all possible worlds, then it would be false, since, e.g., a world is readily thinkable with a chess rule according to which an opening move is possible in which a knight is moved without changing square colors. Likewise, the impossibility of a castling in which the king is not jumped over is not due to there being no possible world in which such a castling occurs, since a world is readily thinkable where a castling involves a king jumping over a rook and not the opposite. Finally, the possibility that a pawn jumps over a square does not depend on the fact that there is a world among all possible worlds in which such a jump takes place. Instead, the statement that it is possible to allow the pawn to jump over a square is already false if, e.g., with the introduction of a new opening rule the supposition on which the truth of that statement depends is abolished – although even after this abolishment it would remain totally thinkable that there is a world in which a pawn jumps over a square.

Rather than choosing my example propositions from the context of chess, I could have selected them from any other context (from the fields of mathematics, psychology, physics, logic, and other sciences, as well as from the fields of everyday habits as from political life and otherwise), to elucidate the connection that exists between the modalities of necessity, possibility, and impossibility on the one hand and on the other hand the domains thinkable circumstances that are assumed with them in each case, to which the relevant rules refer.

When specifically *logical* necessity, *logical* possibility, or *logical* impossibility is at issue, here too, as with the other use of the modal expressions ('necessarily', 'possibly', and 'impossibly'), the modality is at issue *only with respect to rules*. Yet in this case they are specifically *logical* rules, which, provided they are strictly universally valid, are rules which can refer in their scope and domain of application to a universe of discourse of thinkable circumstances that can also be interpreted as the totality of possible worlds. For strictly universally valid logical rules can be transformed into 'if-then'-propositions and hence also into propositions involving necessity, from which propositions involving possibility are ultimately derivable. To be sure, the modality rendered by '*L* . . .' and '*M* . . .' in these propositions can again be interpreted here so that '*L* . . .' is equivalent to 'in all thinkable circumstances (it is true that) . . .' and '*M* . . .' to 'in some thinkable circumstances (it is true that) . . .'. But the universe of discourse of thinkable circumstances to which strictly universally valid logical rules refer encompasses the universe of all possible worlds and hence permits equating what is true in all thinkable circumstances with what is true in all possible worlds and permits understanding 'true in some circumstance' in the sense of 'true in some possible world'.

Now of course the rules of modal logic do not necessarily need to consider distinctions in the meaning and use of the modal expressions 'necessarily' and 'possibly' which stem from a given universe of discourse. Rather, if the use of these expressions is supposed to be strictly universally valid, they must abstract completely from these distinctions. Namely, as strictly universally valid rules they are (as per § 82 and § 83) *formal-logical* rules, i.e., rules which abstract from distinctions in content between propositions and whose validity depends only on the meaning of the logical constants that occur in the propositions to which they are related. The modal syllogistic that I described in §§ 58 to 63 only contains rules which are *formal* and *abstract* in *this* sense.

This is the reason why the modal syllogistic recognizes only very few rules for so-called *iterated* modalities, i.e., for sequences of operators (as in '*LL* . . .' or '*LNLN* . . .'), as strictly universally valid. In this respect, only those rules are universally valid which rely on the mere substitution of a modally definite expression (as '*L* B') in the expression of a universally valid rule (e.g., '*L* A ∴ A'). That is, though the rules *LL* B ∴ *L* B and *M* B ∴ *MM* B are valid, it is because the rules *L* A ∴ A and A ∴ *M* A are valid. Yet the rules *L* A ∴ *LL* A and *M* A ∴ *LNLN* A, which are analogous to the S4- and S5-axioms, respectively, are invalid. The invalidity of these rules can be proved through examples as follows.

Let *L p* stand for a valid rule of chess, according to which the proposition 'It is necessary that with the change of the square on which a knight stands, the color of the square changes' is true. However, if *L p* is true, the proposition *LL p* need not also be true. That is, if it is true that in all thinkable circumstances (according to the rules of chess assumed as valid), moving a knight involves changing the square color, it need not also be true that in all circumstances there must be circumstances the rules of chess remain valid according to which a knight's move must be tied to the change of a square's color. To see this, it suffices to recall that rules of play are changeable, so that circumstances are thinkable in which even the thinkable circumstances as they are assumed in the rules of chess can change. There is thus also a thinkable circumstance in which the rule of chess rendered by $L\ p$ is invalid. Namely, it is invalid when, e.g., after the introduction of a new rule for the opening moves of a knight, an exception to the old rule is permitted. Thus, if $L\ p$ is true, it is nonetheless thinkable that $LL\ p$ is false and thus $MNL\ p$ true. Hence, the inference (analogous to the S4-axiom) from $L\ p$ to $LL\ p$ is not universally valid.

A second example: let $M\ p$ stand for the proposition 'It is possible that a pawn jumps over a square'. This proposition is true if the rules of chess from which it follows are valid. However, if it is true, the proposition $LNLN\ p$ need not also be true. Namely, $LNLN\ p$ is equivalent to $LM\ p$, i.e., equivalent to the proposition 'It is necessary (or true in all thinkable circumstances) that (according to the rules of chess assumed as valid) it is possible that a pawn jumps over a square'. This proposition is false. For in no way is it true in all thinkable circumstances (according to the rules of chess assumed as valid) that it is possible that a pawn jumps over a square. Instead, a circumstance is thinkable in which this is not possible. Such a circumstance obtains when, by changing the rules of the game, the currently valid exception to the rule that a pawn can never jump over a square is no longer permitted. Thus, if $M\ p$ is true, it is nonetheless thinkable that $M\ p$ is false. The inference (analogous to the S5-axiom) from $M\ p$ to $LM\ p$ is hence not universally valid.

Neither may one infer, without any further addition, from p to $LM\ p$ (analogous to the B-axiom). This can be seen in the following way: let p stand for the proposition 'A white knight takes a black pawn in the first two moves'. Let this proposition be true and let it describe an actual move in chess that has just been performed. Yet it does not follow from the fact that it is true that the proposition $LM\ p$ is also true. Namely, it is not true in all thinkable circumstances that the move just played (according to the rules of chess assumed as valid) is possible. Rather, a circumstance is thinkable in which it is not possible, namely, e.g., in the just described circumstance where the currently valid exception to the old rule that a pawn can never jump over a pawn is no longer permitted, while all other rules remain. In this circumstance, openings moves are regulated so that a white knight cannot make a play on a black pawn in the first two moves. Hence, if p is true, $LM\ p$ need not also be true.

Accordingly, the rule A ∴ $LNLN$ A is invalid as well. Hence, among the modal-syllogistic rules there is no universally valid rule which could be considered an analogue to the Brouwerian axiom.

4. Incidentally, we can also see here that the rules of the modal syllogistic differ in another way from the basic assumptions of the Brouwerian system and systems S4 and S5, as well as those of the system T. The system T differs from the modal syllogistic (as has been shown above in sections 1 and 2 of this appendix) only by assuming the validity of the classical propositional calculus. By contrast, the other three systems differ from the modal syllogistic still further by assuming for the axioms peculiar to each,

$p \supset \Box \sim \Box \sim p$, (B)
$\Box p \supset \Box \Box p$, and (S4)
$\Diamond p \supset \Box \sim \Box \sim p$, (S5)

special interpretations of the concepts of necessity and possibility.

We can gain insight into the validity of the S5-axiom – thus indirectly that of the Brouwerian and the S4-axiom –, first, by assuming that necessity is the same as truth in all possible worlds and that possibility is the same as truth in at least one possible world, and, second, by supposing that the totality of possible worlds coincides with the totality of thinkable worlds, and the thinkability of one world places demands on the thinking ability of the inhabitants of all possible worlds, which they equally satisfy. For on these assumptions the S5-axiom states that there is *no* possible world in which p is true unless it is true in *all* possible worlds, that there *is* a possible world in which p is true. According to the assumed interpretation, this means that there is (for the thinking ability of the inhabitants of all possible worlds) a thinkable world in which p is true. But then it must also hold that $\Box \sim \Box \sim p$. For $\Box \sim \Box \sim p$ means, according to the assumed interpretation, that it is true in every thinkable world (for the thinking ability of the inhabitants of all possible worlds) that a world is thinkable (for these inhabitants) in which p is true.

As Saul A. Kripke first showed, one can modify the interpretation of the concepts of necessity and possibility assumed here so that the S5-axiom is invalid but the validity of the S4-axiom or the Brouwerian axiom remains intact.[256] This modification requires giving up the strong assumption that the inhabitants of all possible worlds satisfy in the same way the demands which the thinkability of a world places on the thinking ability which is present in that world itself and in the rest of the possible worlds. This assumption can be replaced by a weaker one, namely, that the thinkability of a world is only a reflexive and transitive, but not a symmetrical relation. According to this assumption, for arbitrary possible worlds W1, W2, and W3, if W3 is thinkable in W2, and W2 in W1, then W3 is thinkable in

---

[256] A relatively accessible presentation of the basics of the modal semantics developed by Kripke is given by Hughes & Cresswell 1977, 75–80.

W1 as well. It also holds on this assumption that in each possible world that world itself is thinkable, but that when one of them (say, W1) is thinkable in another world (say, W2), then also the latter world is always thinkable in the former. For on this assumption, whatever holds for W1 holds for each of these worlds. Thus, the proposition that $\Box\, p$ is true means for W1 the same as that p is true in all worlds thinkable in W1. According to the assumption just described, even the worlds that are thinkable in the worlds thinkable in W1 belong to those worlds thinkable in W1. Thus, if p is true in all worlds thinkable in W1, there is no world thinkable in W1 in which it is not also true that p is true in all worlds thinkable in W1. Hence, if it is true in W1 that $\Box\, p$, it is also true in W1 that $\Box\,\Box\, p$. Hence, on this assumption the S4-axiom is valid. By contrast, on this assumption, neither the S5-axiom nor the Brouwerian axiom is valid. For if it is true in W1 that $\Diamond\, p$ or that p, this means that in one of the worlds thinkable in W1 or in W1 itself it is true that p. But neither this world thinkable in W1 nor W1 itself need be thinkable in each of the worlds thinkable in W1. Hence, on this assumption $\Box \sim \Box \sim p$ follows neither from $\Diamond\, p$ nor from p.

Yet if one supposes as an alternative to this assumption that the thinkability of a world is not a transitive but rather a symmetrical and reflexive relation, then the Brouwerian axiom, though not the S4- or S5-axiom, seems to be valid. In that case, one merely supposes that, for any possible worlds W1 and W2, if W2 is thinkable in W1, then W1 is thinkable in W2, and that any possible world is thinkable in itself. On this assumption, the supposition that p is true means the same for W1 as that p is true in W1. Now if p is true in W1, it is at the same time also possible that p. For there is then for W1 a thinkable world in W1 in which p is true, namely W1. Moreover, among the worlds thinkable in W1, there are none in which it would not also be true that there is a thinkable world in which p is true. For W1 belongs, as we assumed, among the worlds which are thinkable in all the worlds thinkable in W1. Hence, if p is true in W1, it is also true in W1 that it is necessarily possible that p. In other words, $\Box \sim \Box \sim p$ follows from p. Hence, on the assumption we mentioned, the Brouwerian axiom is valid. Yet the S5-axiom, according to which $\Box \sim \Box \sim p$ follows from $\Diamond\, p$, is not thereby valid as well. Namely, if it is true that $\Diamond\, p$, and consequently that there is in W1 a thinkable world in which p is true, it does not follow from this that this world is also thinkable in every world which is thinkable in W1.

As these considerations show, quite special interpretations of the concepts of necessity and possibility lie at the basis of the systems B, S4, and S5.

5. The question is sometimes raised about which modal-logical system is really 'the correct' one. If one relates this question only to the systems which assume classical predicate logic as valid, which includes the Brouwerian system and the systems T, S4, and S5, then the answer apparently depends merely on what

meaning one wants to give to the expressions '□ . . .' and '◇ . . .'. For this meaning varies with the strength and weakness of each system, depending on the axioms and basic rules which are supposed to hold in it. The semantics of possible worlds developed by Kripke, which I sketched in its rudiments above, has contributed to making these distinctions in meaning more precise.

Yet if one considers the complex meaning which the expressions '□ . . .' and '◇ . . .' have even in the weakest of these systems, and then factors into the assessment the modal-logical system I have described, it will emerge that only the latter satisfies the demands of strict universal validity. For only this system is independent of the specific assumptions on which the classical predicate logic depends, insofar as it accepts the postulates of the affirmative use of double negation (VI. 4) and arbitrary sufficient reason (VI. 3) (see § 72). As for the four systems considered above, T, S4, S5, and the Brouwerian system, the system T is closer to the modal syllogistic than the rest. For one already gets from the modal syllogistic to system T simply by assuming postulates (VI. 3) and (VI. 4) as valid.

Yet by making such assumptions, modal logic loses its strict universal validity and thus its proximity to the rules and laws which lie at the basis of all thought. This loss is manifested by the fact that on the assumption of postulates (VI. 3) and (VI. 4) the so-called paradoxical theorems of strict implication, namely the theorems '(A & ~ A) ⥽ B' and 'B ⥽ (A ∨ ~ A)', are derivable in modal logic. These theorems are called 'paradoxical' not because they are invalid in all circumstances – this of course is not the case. They are rather called 'paradoxical' because their derivability was precisely what Lewis had originally wanted to avoid with his invention of systems of strict implication.

Appendix 6
Non-Classical Systems of Logic in Their Relationship to the Logical Calculus of Functions

The formulas derived in § 75,

$*\prec A \supset (B \supset A)$,	(VI. 17)
$*\prec (A \supset (B \supset C)) \supset ((A \supset B) \supset (A \supset C))$,	(VI. 18)
$*\prec (\sim B \supset \sim A) \supset (A \supset B)$, and	(VI. 23)
$*\prec (\forall v) A (v) \supset A (t)$,	(VI. 24)

together with the formulas which are derivable from them according to the simple detachment rule (VI. 8) and one of the two generalization rules (VI. 10) and (VI. 11), form the system of the basic laws of the logical calculus of functions, which is usually simply called 'classical logic' today. Since underlying this system is the assumption that the four rules

$A, B \prec A$,	(VI. 3)
$NN A \prec A$,	(VI. 4)
$N A (('v) A (v), \alpha) \prec I (('v) N A (v), \alpha)$, and	(VI. 5)
$N A (('v) N A (v), \alpha) \prec I (('v) A (v), \alpha)$	(VI. 6)

are valid, alternatives to classical logic (and thus systems of so-called 'non-classical logic') result by taking one of two measures: either (1) dispensing with the supposition of the unrestricted validity of at least one (if not all) of these four rules, or (2) retaining this supposition but assuming in addition the validity of at least one further rule or further law.

Among the systems which arise from measure (2) belongs the system of strict implication, but also other modal-logical systems, such as, e.g., the system T and the so-called Brouwerian system. (I discussed all these systems in *Appendix 5*.)

To provide examples for the first type of non-classical logical systems as well, which arise from measure (1), I mention in what follows the systems of 'paraconsistent', 'free', and 'intuitionistic' logic and will briefly describe them in turn from the point of view of interest here. From this point of view, all the non-classical logical systems mentioned here have one core stock of logical rules in common. This core stock coincides with the rules of syllogistic I have described, which also (as has been shown in this book) underlie classical logic.

A logical system is called 'paraconsistent' when the principle that from two contradictory statements an arbitrary statement follows (*ex contradictione quodlibet sequitur*) is not recognized as valid.²⁵⁷ This principle presupposes the validity of rules (VI. 3) and (VI. 4) (see § 72), according to which A follows from A and B, and A follows from *NN* A (with arbitrary propositions A and B). Namely, by inference conversion (according to rule (I. 2) (see § 44)) it can be immediately derived from (VI. 3) (with B = *N* C and arbitrary C) that *NN* C (with arbitrary B) follows from A and *N* A. And then according to (VI. 4) *NN* C may equal C and ~ A may take the place of *N* A (see § 71). Thus, if one presupposes that rules (VI. 3) and (VI. 4) are valid, then it also holds that from A and ~ A an arbitrary proposition C follows. This means that paraconsistent systems of logic which do not recognize the principle *ex contradictione quodlibet* assume that at least one of the rules (VI. 3) and (VI. 4) is invalid. Assuming the invalidity of (VI. 4) forces paraconsistent logic into an understanding of the negation sign '~' as equivalent to '*N*' or into a modal-logical reading of the negation '~' as well as the expression 'it is false that . . .'.²⁵⁸ Assuming the invalidity of rule (VI. 3) must not lead to an elimination of this rule without replacement, but rather always permits the mere restriction of the validity of this rule, so that it remains valid in the case in which B is the empty set of premises in A, B ≺ A, so that A ≺ A is a valid rule.²⁵⁹

As for so-called free logic, it results from the implicit renunciation of the validity of rules (VI. 5) and (VI. 6) and from the implicit retention of the validity of rules (VI. 3) and (VI. 4) (see § 72). Free logic differs from classical logic precisely in that it allocates no object in the model of the system to the individual constants, free

---

257 The designation 'paraconsistent' was suggested by M. Quesada at a Latin American symposium on mathematical logic for logical systems in which the principle *ex contradictione quodlibet* does not hold. Cf. Anderson, Belnap & Dunn 1992, vol. 2. In the sense of this designation, all so-called relevant-logical systems are paraconsistent. They are labeled this way because they insist that it does not suffice for the truth of a conditional proposition that its antecedent is false; rather, it must also be 'relevant' for the succedent. The system of the elementary syllogistic I have presented in this book is also paraconsistent. This system traces the invalidity of the principle *ex contradictione quodlibet* as well as the principle *ex falso quodlibet* back to the truth-ambivalence of expressions of the form *N* A. Because of this ambivalence, the rule according to which propositions follow from themselves is not universally valid. For the same reason, a proposition A is neither equivalent in all circumstances nor logically equivalent to the proposition 'It is true that A'.
258 The resort to modal logic was taken by authors like Stanislaw Jaśkowski (1969) and Richard Routley (1977). The reading of negation recommended by Da Costa (1974) essentially amounts to an equation of '~' with '*N*'.
259 A logical system is called 'monotonic' when it allows that nothing changes in the validity of a consequence when one adds a premise to it which contributes nothing to the validity of the consequence. Classical logic is monotonic because it assumes the validity of (VI. 3). By contrast, a paraconsistent logical system is non-monotonic if it restricts the validity of (VI. 3) in the manner described.

variables, or individual identifiers (definite or indefinite descriptions).²⁶⁰ When one makes the renunciation just mentioned, it results that neither the law of instantiation (VI. 24) nor the rules of generalization ((VI. 10) and (VI. 11)), particularization (VI. 12), or singularization (VI. 15) are valid for free logic. Indeed, all these rules depend on rules (VI. 5) and (VI. 6), as can be easily gathered from the relevant proofs in § 74 and § 75.²⁶¹

Finally, intuitionistic logic can likewise be regarded as an example of the first type of non-classical system, namely, as a system of logic that dismisses rule (VI. 4) as invalid, but at the same time continues to accept rules (VI. 3), (VI. 5), and (VI. 6).²⁶² The validity of the law-formula (VI. 21) derived in § 75 depends on the validity of rule (VI. 4), as the relevant proof shows. Though Heyting's intuitionistic formula language is consciously demarcated from the classical formula language, if one interprets his preferred though uninterpreted sign '¬' so that it corresponds to the negation sign '∼' used in classical logic, it turns out that the intuitionistic propositional calculus contains the classical predicate calculus as a proper sub-system, in which the law rendered by formula (VI. 21), ∼ ∼ A ⊃ A, is invalid (cf. Gödel 1933b, 34–8).

Yet one can also interpret intuitionistic logic so that it is an example of taking measure (2) mentioned above, so that it then belongs among non-classical logical systems which arise from classical logic not by implicitly omitting but rather by implicitly adding validity assumptions. Namely, intuitionistic logic in the form sketched by Heyting leaves the sign '¬' and all logical propositional connectives undefined yet at the same time explicitly understands the formula '¬ ¬ p ⊃ p' so that it does not mean exactly the same thing as the formula ∼ ∼ p ⊃ p in classical logic, but rather has a meaning colored by modal logic, according to which it says: 'If it is impossible that p can be false, then it is correct' (Heyting 1930, 189). On this account, the intuitionistic propositional calculus appears as a mere variant of a modal-logical system in which the classical propositional calculus is

---

260 The earliest recommendation of a corresponding revision to classical quantificational logic stems from Henry Leonard (1956). The name 'free logic' was introduced by Karel Lambert as an abbreviation for 'logic free of existence assumptions with respect to both its general terms and its singular terms'. A systematic presentation of the basics of free logic is given in Bencivenga 1986.
261 Karel Lambert (1998, 740) writes: "Indeed, free logic is the culmination of a long historical trend to rid logic of existence assumptions with respect to its terms." Regarding the history of logic as a whole, this singling-out of free logic as a "culmination" is a massive distortion of the facts. Since in the framework of the Aristotelian syllogistic, existence assumptions with respect to concept expressions are entirely unnecessary, it never needed to "rid" itself of these assumptions.
262 The earliest elaboration of an intuitionistic logical calculus stems from Arend Heyting (1930), published under the title "Die formalen Regeln der intuitionistischen Logik".

contained as a sub-system. Kurt Gödel (1933c, 39–40) carried out a corresponding interpretation of this calculus.[263]

According to Gödel, one can interpret the sign '¬' and the logical propositional connectives of this calculus so that its system contains not only the classical propositional calculus as a sub-system, but also a modal-logical system S, which is an exact analogue of the system T, extended with the S4-axiom.[264] System S differs from the latter only by everywhere using the concept of provability in place of the concept of necessity. Since provability is supposed to mean either the same as necessary truth or a certain *kind* of necessary truth,[265] one can say that system S is not only an exact analogue to system T extended with the S4-axiom. It is rather precisely the same as system T, yet related to cases in which the operator '□ . . .' ('it is necessary that . . .') takes the special (or only specially colored) meaning of 'it is provable that . . .'. Gödel uses the abbreviation 'B . . .' for 'it is provable that . . .'. If one translates the Heytingian expressions '¬ . . .', '. . . ⊃ . . .', '. . . ∨ . . .', and '. . . ∧ . . .' in turn into the expressions, '∼ B . . .', 'B . . . ⊃ B . . .', 'B . . . ∨ B . . .', and '. . . & . . .' (whereby the signs used in the translation ∼, ⊃, ∨, and & render in turn truth-functional negation, subjunction, adjunction, and conjunction, as in the classical propositional calculus), then the formulas which are valid in Heyting's system (but also only them) transform into formulas which are derivable from the system S.[266] By contrast, the Gödelian translation of the formulas ¬ ¬ $p \supset p$ and $p \vee \neg p$ is not derivable. Quite generally, no formula of the form B A ∨ B B follows from S unless either B A or B B is already provable from S (Gödel 1933c, 201).

One *can* understand both formulas ¬ ¬ $p \supset p$ and $p \vee \neg p$ so that they express the principle of affirmation by (double) negation (which is often identified with the principle of excluded middle by intuitionists). Indeed, if one says that intuitionistic logic rejects this principle as invalid, one cannot have in mind the intuitionistic propositional calculus in the *modal-logical* interpretation *just described*.

---

263 Gödel's interpretation refers to Heyting's 1930 calculus.
264 Gödel himself could admittedly not yet have in view the system T, which was first set up by Robert Feys (1937), as he undertook his modal-logical interpretation of the intuitionistic propositional calculus. In *Appendix 5*, I have described the system T extended with the S4-axiom inasmuch as it is of interest here.
265 Edward John Lemmon has pointed out that if '□ . . .' means the same as 'it is informally provable in mathematics that . . .', S4 is the correct modal system. See E.J. Lemmon 1959.
266 The translation described here is not the only one which leads to this result. Rather, the desired derivability can also be achieved by translating '¬ . . .' and '. . . ∧ . . .' with 'B ∼ ◇ . . .' and with 'B . . . & B . . .', respectively. See Gödel 1933c, 39. – Gödel uses the Hilbertian notation, i.e., the arrow and the point, for truth-functional subjunction and truth-functional conjunction, respectively.

For according to this interpretation, the intuitionistic propositional logic allows the classical propositional logic to hold unrestrictedly, so that even the postulate of the affirmative use of double negation fundamental to the latter (VI. 4) (see § 72 above) and the formula (VI. 22), ∼ ∼ A ⊃ A, which follows from this principle, remain valid in it.[267]

---

267 As Kurt Gödel has proved, the Heytingian propositional calculus is not the only one which differs from the classical version by rejecting *tertium non datur*. Rather, there are infinitely many calculi which lie as it were *between* these two calculi and are designated as 'intermediary' systems of logic. Indeed, the invalidity of $p \vee \neg p$ does not necessarily preclude that, e.g., $\neg p \vee \neg \neg p$ is valid and can be established as an axiom in one of these calculi. Cf. Gödel 1932, 65. There is no reason to assume that one of these infinitely many calculi is set apart from the others. Yet the Heytingian calculus is set apart from these and from the classical propositional calculus by admitting an interpretation according to which it rejects postulate (VI. 4), which is not logically universally valid, without replacing it with another assumption that is not logically universally valid.

Appendix 7
The Barcan Formula

The Barcan formula

$$\Diamond (\exists x) A (x) \dashv (\exists x) \Diamond A (x)$$

renders an axiom with which axiomatic modal propositional logic can be extended into a modal predicate logic. The name of this formula refers to Ruth Barcan Marcus, who introduced this axiom in 1946 (see Barcan 1946). It has become a controversial starting point for philosophical discussions, since it suggests an interpretation according to which it entails the supposition (which is not very plausible) that it follows from the fact that it is *possible* that objects with a certain property exist that objects (actually) exist which possibly have this property. Ruth Barcan Marcus herself rejected this interpretation and replaced it with a so-called 'substitutional' interpretation. According to the latter interpretation, the Barcan formula is supposed merely to state that if it is possible that there is a substitution instance for x which transforms an expression of the form $A(x)$ into a true expression of the form $A(a)$, there is then a substitution instance for x which transforms an expression of the form $\Diamond A(x)$ into a true expression of the form $\Diamond A(a)$. The substitutional interpretation gives the existential quantifier a reading which departs from the 'classical' one and can be applied to non-modalized classical quantificational logic as well. According to this reading

$$\sim (\exists x) A (x) \supset (\exists x) \sim A (x)$$

does not mean that from a statement of the form $\sim (\exists x) A (x)$ it follows that something, namely x, exists, to which $A(x)$ does not apply, but rather only that from a statement of the form $\sim (\exists x) A (x)$ no true statement can arise by replacing '$(\exists x) \ldots (x)$' with the specification of a suitable singular case, unless by the same replacement a true statement also arises from $(\exists x) \sim A (x)$. In this way, in place of the classical assumption that there is for every true particular proposition of the form $(\exists x) A (x)$ an existing object, the substitutional interpretation prefers the assumption that there is for every such proposition a true singular proposition even if the object which it treats does not exist.

Yet this assumption is hardly less problematic than the classical one. For singular propositions which deal with an object that does not exist (or, more precisely, which does not belong to the domain of individuals, i.e., a "world of attributions", which is assumed to be satisfied (see § 20 above)) will not ordinarily be regarded as true (except in the case of certain negative propositions). This ordinary view, which agrees with the principle of qualitative existential import, is accommodated by the definition of the singular categorical proposition I established in § 52.

If one places this definition at the basis of universally valid rules and laws of logic, one cannot expect the Barcan formula to express a universally valid logical law. One cannot even expect that the expression analogous to the Barcan formula,

$$H\,(M\,I\,(('x)\,A\,(x), \xi), I\,(('x)\,M\,A\,(x), \xi)),$$

renders a universally valid law of modal logic. Rather, the degree of validity of the axiom that renders the Barcan formula corresponds at best to the degree of validity which can be ascribed to the S4- and S5-axioms. (See *Appendix 5*.)

One can consider the expression $(\exists\,x) \Diamond A\,(x)$, occurring on the right side of the Barcan formula, as an expression of a *pure de re* modality. For it is a *de re* expression which is not (like syllogistic expressions of modality (see § 6 and § 59)) *equivalent* to a *de dicto* expression of the same modality. Considered in this way, the Barcan formula renders the law (which is not universally valid) that the *de dicto* possibility which is stated by a problematic particular proposition implies a pure *de re* possibility.

According to §§ 31–32 and §§ 64–65, the expression $(\exists\,x) \Diamond A\,(x)$ is only an abbreviation for

$$`I\,(('x) \Diamond A\,(x), \xi)`.$$

The modality indicated by '$\Diamond$' here belongs only to the *content* of a *concept*, namely the *logical* predicate $('x) \Diamond A\,(x)$. It alters nothing in the *assertoric affirmative form*, which the formula '$I\,(('x) \Diamond A\,(x), \xi)$' renders as the logical form of an affirmative proposition. A proposition of this form has existential import that is unrestricted and independent of its conceptual content. The existential import of an affirmative proposition is restricted, however, if the prefix '$\Diamond$' (or '*M*') is placed in front of it, as in '$\Diamond I\,(('x) A\,(x), \xi)$'. This prefix decreases its modal-logical strength. And a proposition of greater logical strength cannot follow from a proposition of lesser logical strength. For this reason, it is not universally valid that '$I\,(('x) \Diamond A\,(x), \xi)$' follows from '$\Diamond I\,(('x) A\,(x), \xi)$', nor that '$(\exists\,x) \Diamond A\,(x)$' follows from '$\Diamond (\exists\,x) A\,(x)$'.

Appendix 8
On Bivalence

(To §§ 6 to 9)

From the perspective of 'logical pluralism' (Beall & Restall 2006) there is no reason to single out a two-valued logic from any many-valued logic. But one will have to decide in favor of a two-valued logic if one understands the basis of the bivalence principle, and if one demands that logic be formal in a narrow, clear, and clearly explicable sense (as I have specified it above in § 82 and § 83). In what follows, I first (1) attend to the question of the grounds of the validity of the bivalence principle. I then (2) turn to the connection between bivalence and formality.

(1) The bivalence principle is to be understand so that it states that for expressions which as declarative propositions are used as judgments there are exactly two truth values: the true (T) and the false (F). The supposition that there are no more than these two values does not rest on some profound discovery, but rather merely on a linguistic stipulation of the meaning of 'true' and 'false'. The bivalence principle *consists* in this stipulation. It stipulates that a proposition may be taken as false if and only if it is not true.[268] Even a meaningless proposition like 'Ten is a wicked number' (which as a meaningless proposition is not true) is to be regarded as false according to this stipulation. If one prefers to say that, because it is meaningless, it is rather *neither* true *nor* false, then one has decided on a different use of the word 'false' and has with this use already assumed that there is a third truth value (namely, that of the meaningless) and thus that the bivalence principle should not hold.

According to the bivalence principle, 'true' should not be understood as implying a *time-dependent* but rather a *timeless* being the case or truth.[269] According to this principle, what is true today will not be false tomorrow, and what is not true today will still be false tomorrow. This means that the truth of even time-related statements, e.g., true predictions, is not time-dependent. If one says of a prediction that it has *become* true, then one helps oneself to a usage according to which 'true' means a time-dependent truth, which the bivalence principle excludes. Connected with this alternative usage is the notion that the truth of a predictive statement as it were matures with time and comes to completion only

---

[268] The bivalence principle thereby also stipulates that a proposition is not false if and only if it is true.
[269] For a discussion of the distinction between time-dependent and timeless truth, compare von Wright 1974, esp. 174–77.

with the arrival of the foretold event; only with the event does it become *actual* and as it were complete and mature truth. If one says that a prediction has *become* true, that is not supposed to mean that it was false up to the arrival of the event it foretold and then immediately changes to a true statement. Rather, it is supposed to mean that there is a time at which it is *neither* (entirely) true *nor* (entirely) false. To think in this way that a time-dependent statement about the future can have the property of being neither true nor false is certainly allowable and not perverse. Yet in thinking this way one has given the word 'true' a meaning which it does not have according to the bivalence principle. To this extent, 'many-valued' logics do not invalidate the validity of the bivalence principle and give no cause to call in question the 'correctness' of two-valued systems of logic.

Yet 'many-valued' logics have been developed *precisely in the opinion* that the bivalence principle can have no or only a restricted validity, since statements which refer to future contingents (*contingentia futura*) are capable of being neither true nor false. Underlying this opinion is the conviction that if one accepts the principle of two-valuedness for statements about the future and believe that what is true tomorrow is also already true today, then one will have to suppose that the future is inescapably predetermined by the past.[270] According to this conviction, logic oversteps its domain of competency, since in assuming the bivalence principle, it commits itself to a deterministic picture of the world.

In truth, however, the bivalence principle is perfectly compatible with indeterminism. In order to see this, one need only assume for the sake of argument that determinism is false. On this assumption, the statement that *as a result of an event that was not predetermined* a sea battle will take place tomorrow is, according to the bivalence principle, true or false. If this statement is not false, according to the bivalence principle it is true, and this entirely independently of what time it is made. But if it is true, indeterminism is true as well, since along with the statement it is indeed supposed that there is an event that is not predetermined which results in the sea battle having taken place. Hence, even if one is unsympathetic to determinism, one need not abandon the bivalence principle. Statements about *contingentia futura* do not require us to introduce a logic which accepts, in

---

[270] According to a reading that Ockham (1957) in his *Tractatus de Praedestinatione Dei et de Futuris Contingentibus* gave to chapter nine of Aristotle's *De Interpretatione*, Aristotle had there rejected the principle of two-valuedness with respect to statements about the future. The development of a many-valued logic by Jan Łukasiewicz in the 1920s was based on the idea that the bivalence principle must favor fatalism. See Łukasiewicz 1970, especially the essays "On Three-Valued Logic" (1920), "On Determinism" (1922), and "Philosophical Remarks on Many-Valued Systems of Propositional Logic" (1930).

addition to the values 1 (= T) and 0 (= F), an intermediate value like the indefinite (= ½) or probability values.

The *time-dependent* truth of a predication precisely does not consist in its being always already *fixed* in advance that it will be the case. An event's being fixed in advanced (or *predetermined*) means of course that its arrival follows unavoidably from preceding events on the basis of natural laws or that its arrival cannot be prevented by a decision, no matter how powerful. 'It is already fixed today that p' is thus neither equivalent to, nor even entailed by, the statement 'It is true that p'. To be sure, preceding events on the basis of natural laws are causally relevant for the truth of p, but whether the arrival (and truth) of p *already* follows *solely* on the basis of natural laws from preceding events, or whether there are *additional* factors on which this arrival depends according to rules which are not natural laws but of another kind instead (rules of traffic, war, convention, morality, etc.), is not yet settled simply on the basis of the truth of p. The proposition 'What is true tomorrow is already true today' can thus be understand so that it is free from any deterministic inflection and says simply, for any arbitrary statement p: if it is true tomorrow that tomorrow it will be the case that p, this means that the statement that, on the day that is (today) called 'tomorrow', it is the case that p is true, and it is true not only tomorrow and today but entirely independently of the time at which it is stated.

Even if the statement contains a relative time specification like 'tomorrow', this does not alter the fact that it has a timeless truth value all the same. For statements with relative time specifications get their meaning from the point in time within which they are positioned and can be transformed into equivalent statements with absolute time specifications, i.e., into statements with a specification of the type 'On January 15, 2009 . . .'. To that extent, even statements with relative time specifications have a time-independent truth value.[271] The fact that these time specifications can refer to the future does not make it necessary to assume more than two timeless truth values. But these values must be understood as timeless if one accepts the bivalence principle in its complete generality.

By way of summary, one can say that the bivalence principle only stipulates a certain usage, by stipulating that 'false' is equivalent to 'not true' and that 'truth' means a timeless being the case of statements. In light of the fact that the words 'true' and 'false' can also be used differently, one should not hope to decide

---

[271] That there are declarative propositions whose truth value can only be decided in the future does not need to mean that they have up until this decision either no truth value at all or only a truth value lying between true and false or a probability value. Rather, according to the bivalence principle, if a decision about the truth value of a declarative proposition has not yet been made, or will never be made, or is not even possible, this value may be unknown, but it is not indefinite.

which usage is 'the correct' one. For one can use words as one pleases, so long as one sticks to the meaning that one has given them (see § 8 above). Whether the bivalence principle should hold or not is to that extent only a question of linguistic convention.

As a principle of propositional logic, it can remain safely in effect.

(2) Yet as a principle of a *strictly formal* propositional logic, it *should* remain in effect. This can be seen in the following way.

Variables in propositional logic are characterized by the fact that they stand for *arbitrary* declarative propositions. From a logical point of view, arbitrary declarative propositions have the property of being true or false. For only by reference to this property can it be said what a valid inference from declarative propositions consists in at all. The values T and F must therefore be taken into account in every logic. But in *formal* logic, no *more than* these two values can be taken into account. For if one wanted to demand of formal logic that it distinguishes declarative propositions which are neither true nor false from those which are true or false, one would have to ascribe to it a capability of specifying criteria according to which the sphere of non-true declarative propositions could be further divided into false and non-false propositions, so that the designation 'false' would apply only to a *part* of non-true propositions. However, formal propositional logic has no such criteria at its disposal. For as *formal* propositional logic, it does not bring into consideration actual declarative propositions but only variables which stand for arbitrary declarative propositions. In order to distinguish, e.g., false from meaningless or false from indefinite or false from probable declarative propositions, formal logic would have to abandon its formal standpoint and bring into consideration declarative propositions with respect to properties from which it precisely abstracts in its propositional variables. That is, it would have to apply criteria for dividing declarative propositions which concern the *content* of propositions, which are not at its disposal due to its formal standpoint. Thus, one cannot reasonably demand of a *strictly formal propositional logic* that it goes beyond the distinction between true and false.

The same thing holds for a *strictly formal predicate logic*. To be sure, as predicate logic it goes beyond propositional logic insofar as it considers the truth of statements as an *applying to* something, namely, an applying to that *about which* statements say *something*, i.e., an applying of predicates to subjects of statements (see § 27, § 33, and § 65, remark). A strictly formal predicate logic does not go beyond the dissection of declarative propositions into predicates and subjects. For this reason, the concept variables it uses, α, β, etc., can stand for *arbitrary* and thus even *empty* concepts. And the bivalence principle *suffices* for the assessment of statements with empty concepts.[272] That is, in a strictly formal predicate logic, unlike in the ('classical') predicate logic of the calculus of functions, such statements do not need to be eliminated from consideration from the outset (see § 35); they can rather simply be treated as false. The task of distinguishing between false and meaningless (or nonsensical) singular statements only arises by introducing the postulate of non-empty domains, i.e., by introducing the not universally valid (and not formal) rules (VI. 5) and (VI. 6) (see § 72). The validity of these rules is assumed in the predicate logic of the logical calculus of functions, but not in a strictly formal predicate logic.

In this way, the unrestricted recognition of the bivalence principle belongs among the marks by which formal logic, both in its propositional as well as its predicate-logical parts, is distinguished quite essentially from non-formal logics. In this respect, it is not a matter of 'arbitrary' decision but is rather tied inseparably to the formality of formal logic.[273]

---

[272] Aristotle seems to have assessed the situation similarly. He formulates the bivalence principle in *De Interpretatione* 8. 18 a 34 ff. by saying that every affirmative and negative proposition is either true or false. It is consistent with this that he means that one says either something true or something false when one says something *about something* (*Metaphysics* 4. 7, 1011 b 27 ff.), and that one must either ascribe or deny some predicate to an object (*Metaphysics* 4. 7, 1011 b 24); a predicate either applies or does not apply to an object (*De Interpretatione* 18 a 35 ff.). Christopher Kirwan (1971, 118) comments on the cited passage in *Metaphysics* 4. 7 with the following words: "'The present King of France is neither wise nor not wise; for the expression "the present King of France" is not being, or on the occasion of utterance cannot correctly be, used to refer to anyone': Aristotle nowhere comments on this kind of case, but he might have held that the sentence makes no assertion, or asserts nothing 'of one thing', and is therefore no exception to the rule that we must assert or deny one thing of one thing (cf. *De Interpretatione* 8)."

[273] Compare here the concerns with Ignacio Angelelli (2005, 445) has raised in his review of the first edition of the present book, published in the *Bulletin of Symbolic Logic*.

Appendix 9
Absolute Logical Constants

> Symbols hold the selfsame significance for thinking as did the discovery of using the wind to sail cross-wind for navigation. Let no one be contemptuous of signs! A good deal depends on a practical selection on them.
> (Frege 1882b, 107 [1964b, 156])

The question of which expressions should be regarded as logical constants can only be stated relatively, namely, always only in relation to the respective logical system in which they are used – unless they are expressions of logical vocabulary which express the *logical form* of propositions (in the sense of § 83) and are needed to render rules and laws which belong to the common core of *all* logical systems. These expressions could reasonably be called 'absolute logical constants'.

If one asks for secure criteria by which it is possible to decide whether an expression is an *absolute* logical constant and belongs to the vocabulary that is suitable to fix and express the logical form of propositions, it suffices to point out four marks which such an expression must exhibit:

1. An absolute logical constant is an expression with one or more than one empty place, such that all these places are suited to be filled either by a concept expression or by a declarative proposition, and by filling all empty places in each case a declarative proposition arises.
2. An absolute logical constant is, as a component of a declarative proposition, capable of fixing simply through its meaning that this proposition follows regularly from other declarative propositions or that other declarative propositions follow regularly from it, regardless of the content of all the components that take the place of concept- or propositional variables in this proposition. (Here regular consequence is meant in the sense explained in § 43, definition 4.)
3. An absolute logical constant is an expression which can be used to render a stable hierarchical conceptual relation (in line with *Figure 1* of § 1 and § 6) with a declarative proposition which makes explicit what the proposition applies to if it is true.
4. Expressions which satisfy the first three criteria can only count as absolute logical constants if an analysis of their meaning does not show them to be composed of expressions of which at least one already satisfies one of the first three criteria. –

Comment: According to these four criteria, e.g., the expressions '... is greater than ...', '... is equal to ...', '... is identical with ...' are not absolute logical constants. All three satisfy the second criterion. For whether a proposition of the form 'if x is greater than y, then z is greater than y' follows regularly from a proposition of the form 'z is greater than x' rests only on the meaning of '... is greater than ...', regardless of what the variables 'x', 'y', and 'z' stand for. But since these variables can be taken neither as concept variables nor as propositional variables, the *first criterion* is not satisfied. (The reasons why the *third* and *fourth criteria* are not satisfied either can be easily seen as well.)

One might have supposed that expressions like 'most ... are ...' or 'only a few ... are ...' belong to the vocabulary of formal logic in the narrow sense. They do satisfy the *first two criteria*, since, e.g., a proposition of the form 'only a few α are not β' follows regularly from a proposition of the form 'most α are β', and both 'α' and 'β' are concept variables. For this reason, they are treated as logical constants in an *extended* syllogistic. Yet we can see that they do not satisfy the *fourth criterion* by analyzing the meaning of propositions of the form 'most α are β'. Such an analysis shows that these propositions do not only contain statements about the relative amount of objects that fall under the concepts α and β or under the concepts α and not-β, respectively, but they also contain statements which can be rendered by two propositions of the form 'some α are β' and 'some α are not β', whose logical constants each satisfy the *first three criteria*.

Expressions which tend to be treated as logical constants in so-called deontic logic – namely, the (deontic) modal expressions 'it is required that ...', 'it is forbidden that ...', and 'it is permitted that ...' – should also be subjected to an analysis of this kind. It is clear first of all that they satisfy the *first two criteria*, since for arbitrary interpretations of the propositional variable 'p' it holds, e.g., that a proposition of the form 'it is not permitted that not p' follows regularly from 'it is required that p'. However, one can easily see that these expressions only abbreviate more complex logical expressions which are tied to a specific content. This content stems from the way each of these expressions points implicitly to the validity of a tacitly assumed norm, whether it be a moral principle, a legal injunction, or a command. Thus, 'it is required that p' has the form of a necessary proposition and is equivalent to 'L [if the norm in question is not violated, then p]'. Similarly, 'it is forbidden that p' means the same as 'L [if the norm in question is not violated, then $N\,p$]', and 'it is permitted that p' means the same as 'NL [if the norm in question is not violated, then p]'. It is due to this meaning that, while p follows logically from $L\,p$ (as per § 60, rule (IV. 1)), a proposition p follows *neither* logically *nor* regularly from a proposition of the form 'it is required that p'. Rather, p only follows regularly from this requirement if the norm which it implicitly points to is not violated but is obeyed.

Finally, hypothetical propositions of a specific content also hide behind expressions which are treated as elementary logical constants in so-called temporal logic, namely, the (temporal) modal expressions 'it has always been the case that ...' and 'it will always be the case that ...'.[274] Thus, 'it has always been the case that p' is equivalent to 'L [if p is in the past, then p]'. Similarly, 'it will always be the case that p' is equivalent to 'L [if p is in the future, then p]'. p can only be derived from both formulas if the assumption expressed by the respective 'if'-clause of these formulas is satisfied.

According to a widespread doctrine, the most important logical constants in modern predicate logic are the so-called quantifiers '∀ ... (...)' ('for every ... it holds that: ...') and '∃ ... (...)' ('there is a ... such that: ...'). That these expressions are likewise abbreviations of more complex expressions I have shown in §§ 31 to 35 (cf. § 64 and § 65).

---

274 The expressions (a) 'it has always been the case that ...' and (b) 'it will always be the case that ...' are elementary expressions of temporal logic insofar as one can trace back to them (c) 'it has been the case that ...' and (d) 'it will be the case that ...', respectively, since (c) is equivalent to 'N (a) N ...' and (d) is equivalent to 'N (b) N ...'.

Index of Symbols Used

1 Signs of the Functional Calculus (FC)

$a, b, c \ldots, a_1, a_2, \ldots a_n$	Individual constants
$x, y, z \ldots, x_1, x_2, \ldots x_n$	Individual variables
v, t	Metavariables for individual variables and for individual constants (respectively)
$F(\ ), G(\ ), \ldots, F_1(\ ), F_2(\ ), \ldots$	Functional constants with empty places
$A(\ ), B(\ ), \ldots, \Phi(\ ), \Psi(\ )$	Functional variables with empty places
$(\forall v) A(v)$	'for all v, let it hold that $A(v)$'
$(\exists v) A(v)$	'there is a v such that $A(v)$ holds'
$[A(t)]$	't is an individual v, for which it holds that $A(v)$'
$\sim A$	'it is false that A'
$A \& B$	'A and B'
$A \supset B$	'not A unless B'
$A \vee B$	'A or B'
$\mathfrak{A}, \mathfrak{B}, \mathfrak{C} \ldots, \mathfrak{A}_1, \mathfrak{A}_2, \ldots, \mathfrak{A}_n$	Metavariables for formulas of FC
$\vdash \mathfrak{A}$	'$\mathfrak{A}$ is a theorem of the functional calculus'
$\mathfrak{A}_1, \ldots, \mathfrak{A}_n \vdash \mathfrak{A}$	'$\mathfrak{A}$ is provable in FC with $\mathfrak{A}_1, \ldots, \mathfrak{A}_n$'
$\vDash \mathfrak{A}$	'$\mathfrak{A}$ is true in FC'
$\mathfrak{A}_1, \ldots, \mathfrak{A}_n \vDash \mathfrak{A}$	'$\mathfrak{A}$ follows from $\mathfrak{A}_1, \ldots, \mathfrak{A}_n$ in FC'

2 Signs of the Calculus of Classes and Set Theory

$a, b, c \ldots$	Variables for sets or classes
$\bar{a}$	'the complement class of a'
$\{a, b\}$	'the set that consists of a and b'
$\emptyset$	'the null class'
$\{x: \Phi(x)\}$	'the set of x which satisfy the condition $\Phi(x)$'
$a \subset b$	'a contains b'
$a \cup b$	'the union of a and b'
$a \cap b$	'the intersection of a and b'
$a \in b$	'a is an element of b'

3 Signs of Truth-Functional Modal Logic

$A \dashv B$	'A strictly implies B'
$\Diamond A$	'possibly (it is true that) A'
$\Box A$	'necessarily (it is true that) A'
$\bigcirc A$	'contingently (it is true that) A'

4 Syllogistic Signs

$\alpha, \beta, \gamma \ldots, \alpha_1, \alpha_2, \ldots, \alpha_n$	Concept variables
$A, B, C \ldots, A_1, A_2, \ldots, A_n$	Metavariables for formulas
ε_0	Conceptual constant for 'element of the null class'
ζ	Conceptual constant for 'individual t'
ξ	Conceptual constant for 'element v of the given domain of individuals'
$(′v)\, A\,(v)$	'individual v, for which $A\,(v)$'
$A\,(\alpha, \beta)$	'every β is an α'
$E\,(\alpha, \beta)$	'no β is an α'
$I\,(\alpha, \beta)$	'some β is an α'
$O\,(\alpha, \beta)$	'not every β is an α'
$\underline{A}\,(\alpha, \beta)$	'that β is an α'
$\underline{E}\,(\alpha, \beta)$	'that β is not an α'
$^N\alpha_n$	'not-α_n'
$N\,A$	'not A'
$M\,A$	'possibly (it is true that) A'
$L\,A$	'necessarily (it is true that) A'
$K\,A$	'contingently (it is true that) A'
(A, B)	'both A and B'
$H\,(A, B)$	'if A, then B'
$D\,(A, B)$	'either A, or B'
$A_1, \ldots, A_n \therefore B$	'$A_1, \ldots, A_n$; therefore, on logical grounds, B'
$A_1, \ldots, A_n \prec B$	'$A_1, \ldots, A_n$; therefore, B'
$A_1, \ldots, A_n / A_{n+1}$	'an inference of the form A_{n+1} is reducible to inferences of the form $A_1, A_2, \ldots$ und A_n'
$\ast \therefore A$	'A follows logically from the empty set of premises'
$\ast \prec A$	'A follows regularly from the empty set of premises'
$A_1, \ldots, A_n \therefore B_1, \ldots, B_n$	Abbreviation for: $A_1, \ldots, A_n \therefore B_1; A_1, \ldots, A_n \therefore \ldots; A_1, \ldots, A_n \therefore B_n$
$A_1, \ldots, A_n \prec B_1, \ldots, B_n$	Abbreviation for: $A_1, \ldots, A_n \prec B_1; A_1, \ldots, A_n \prec \ldots; A_1, \ldots, A_n \prec B_n$
$A_1, \ldots, A_n ∷ B_1, \ldots, B_n$	Abbreviation for: $A_1, \ldots, A_n \therefore B_1, \ldots, B_n; B_1, \ldots, B_n \therefore A_1, \ldots, A_n$
$A_1, \ldots, A_n \succ\!\!\prec B_1, \ldots, B_n$	Abbreviation for: $A_1, \ldots, A_n \prec B_1, \ldots, B_n; B_1, \ldots, B_n \prec A_1, \ldots, A_n$

Outline of the Rules Used Mainly in the Proofs of Part II

(with reference to the page on which each is introduced)

(I. 1)	Double negation as a result of an affirmation	p. 153
(I. 2)	*Reductio ad absurdum*	p. 153
(I. 3)	Peripatetic inference chain rule	p. 154
(I. 4)	Simple transitivity in an inference chain	p. 154
(I. 5)	Complex transitivity in an inference chain	p. 155
(I. 6–8)	Derived negation rules	pp. 155–56
(II. 1)	Principle of conditionalization	p. 164
(II. 2)	*Modus ponendo ponens*	p. 164
(II. 3)	Reduction of two-member disjunctions	p. 164
(II. 5)	Deconditionalization of a conclusion	p. 165
(II. 6)	Idempotency rule	p. 164
(II. 7)	*Modus tollendo tollens*	p. 166
(II. 9)	*Peritrope*	p. 166
(II. 13)	Basic form of purely hypothetical syllogisms	p. 168
(II. 21)	*Modus ponendo tollens*	p. 170
(II. 22)	*Modus tollendo ponens*	p. 171
(II. 29)	Generalized conditionalization	p. 174
(II. 30)	Deconditionalization	p. 175
(III. 1)	*Dictum de omni*	p. 182
(III. 2)	*Dictum de nullo*	p. 182
(III. 3–4)	Exposition	p. 182
(III. 5–6)	Contradiction rule	p. 183
(III. 7)	Subalternation	p. 184
(III. 8–10)	Basic rules of limitative propositions	p. 184
(III. 11)	Subordination	p. 185
(III. 13–14)	Derived subalternation	p. 186
(III. 15)	Derived subcontrariety	p. 186
(III. 16)	Contrariety	p. 187
(III. 17–18)	Simple conversion (*conversio simplex*)	pp. 187–88
(III. 19)	Conversion *per accidens*	p. 188
(III. 20)	*Barbara*	p. 191
(III. 21)	*Celarent*	p. 192
(IV. 1)	*A necesse esse ad esse valet consequentia*	p. 210
(IV. 2)	Modal version of *modus ponendo ponens*	p. 210
(IV. 3–8)	Six modal-syllogistic basic rules	p. 210
(IV. 9–11)	Modal-syllogistic versions of *dictum de omni*	p. 211
(IV. 12–14)	Modal-syllogistic versions of *dictum de nullo*	p. 211
(IV. 15–18)	Modal-syllogistic expositions rules	p. 212
(IV. 25)	*Ab esse ad posse valet consequentia*	p. 213
(IV. 47–50)	'Complementary conversion'	p. 219
(IV. 51–60)	Modal conversion rules	pp. 220–25
(IV. 61–77)	Perfect modal syllogisms	pp. 226–35

Outline of the Rules Used Mainly in the Proofs of Part II

(V. 1)	Abbreviation for singular categorical formulas	p. 267
(V. 2)	Abbreviation for universal categorical formulas	p. 267
(V. 3)	Abbreviation for particular categorical formulas	p. 268
(V. 5–6)	Additional abbreviation rules	p. 270
(V. 7–9)	Variation of rules for limitative propositions	p. 270
(VI. 1)	Transformation of conditional schemata	p. 272
(VI. 2)	Transformation of negative schemata	p. 272
(VI. 3)	Postulate of the arbitrary sufficient reason	p. 272
(VI. 4)	Postulate of the affirmative use of double negation (*duplex negatio affirmat*)	p. 273
(VI. 5–6)	Postulate of non-empty domains	p. 273
(VI. 7)	Weakening of logical consequence	p. 276
(VI. 8)	Simple detachment rule	p. 277
(VI. 9)	Complex detachment rule	p. 277
(VI. 10)	Rule of generalization	p. 278
(VI. 11)	Rule of posterior generalization	p. 279
(VI. 13)	Particularization rule	p. 279
(VI. 15)	Singularization rule	p. 280
(VI. 20)	Truth-functional contraposition	p. 282
(VI. 21–22)	Truth-functional negation rules	p. 283
(VI. 23)	Transformation of truth-functional contraposition	p. 283

Index of Metalogical Rules Used in the Proofs of Part II

(Notation according to § 42)

(I. 2)	*Reductio ad absurdum* (inference conversion): $(A_1, \ldots, A_n \therefore A) /$ $(N A, A_2, \ldots, A_n \therefore N A_1), \ldots, (N A, A_1, \ldots, A_{n-1} \therefore N A_n)$ (with $n \geq 1$)	p. 153
(I. 3)	Peripatetic inference chain rule: $(A_i, \ldots, A_k \therefore B), (B, C_m, \ldots, C_n \therefore D) /$ $(A_i, \ldots, A_k, C_m, \ldots, C_n \therefore D)$ (with $i \geq 0, k \geq i, m \geq 0$ and $n \geq m$)	p. 154
(I. 4)	Simplified inference chain rule: $(A_i, \ldots, A_k \therefore B), (B, C \therefore D) / A_i, \ldots, A_k, C \therefore D$ (with $i \geq 0, k \geq i$)	p. 154
(I. 5)	Complex inference chain rule: $(A_i, \ldots, A_k \therefore A), (A_{k+1}, \ldots, A_n \therefore B_1), (A, B_1 \therefore D) / A_1, \ldots, A_n \therefore D$ (with $i \geq 0, k \geq i, n \geq k+1$)	p. 155
(II. 1)	Conditionalization principle: $A_i, \ldots, A_k, B \therefore C / A_i, \ldots, A_k \therefore H(B, C)$ (with $i \geq 0$ and $k \geq i$)	p. 164
(II. 5)	Deconditionalization of a conclusion: $A_i, \ldots, A_k \therefore H(B, C) / A_i, \ldots, A_k, B \therefore C$ (with $i \geq 0$ and $k \geq 0$)	p. 165
(II. 6)	Idempotency rule: $A_i, \ldots, A_k, A_1, A_1 \therefore D / A_1, A_i, \ldots, A_k \therefore D$ (with $i \geq 0, k \geq i$)	p. 164
(II. 28)	Conditionalization rule: $*, B \therefore C / * \therefore H(B, C)$	p. 174
(II. 29)	Generalized conditionalization rule: $A_1, A_i, \ldots, A_n \therefore B / * \therefore H(A_1, H(A_i, H(\ldots, H(A_n, B)))\ldots)$ (with $i \geq 1, n \geq i$)	p. 174
(II. 30)	Deconditionalization: $* \therefore H(A_1, H(A_i, H(\ldots, H(A_n, B)))\ldots)$ $/ *, A_1, A_i, \ldots, A_n \therefore B$ (with $i \geq 1, n \geq i$)	p. 175
(VI. 7)	Weakening of logical consequence: $A_1, \ldots, A_n \therefore B / A_1, \ldots, A_n \prec B$ (with $n \geq 1$)	p. 276

Index of Syllogistic Rules Used Directly in the Validity Proofs of Assertoric Syllogisms (in § 56)

(Notation according to § 42, § 46, and § 51)

(II. 13)	$H(A, B), H(B, C) \therefore H(A, C)$ (Hypothetical syllogism)	p. 168
(III. 1)	$A(α, β) :: I(β, β), H(I(β, γ), A(α, γ))$ (Dictum de omni)	p. 182
(III. 2)	$NI(α, β) :: H(I(β, γ), NA(α, γ))$ (Dictum de nullo)	p. 182
(III. 3)	$I(α, β) \therefore A(α, γ), A(β, γ)$ (Exposition rule)	p. 182
(III. 4)	$NA(α, β) \therefore NI(α, γ), H(I(β, β), A(β, γ))$ (Exposition rule)	p. 182
(III. 6)	$NNI(α, β) \therefore I(α, β)$ (Logical square)	p. 183
(III. 7)	$A(α, β) \therefore I(α, β)$ (Weak logical square)	p. 184
(III. 12)	$NA(α, β) \therefore NA(α, β)$ (Weak logical square)	p. 185
(III. 13)	$A(α, β) \therefore I(α, β)$ (Logical square)	p. 186
(III. 14)	$NI(α, β) \therefore NA(α, β)$ (Logical square)	p. 186
(III. 16)	$A(α, β) \therefore NNI(α, β)$ (Logical square)	p. 187
(III. 17)	$NI(α, β) \therefore NI(β, α)$ (Conversio simplex)	p. 187
(III. 18)	$I(β, α) \therefore I(α, β)$ (Conversio simplex)	p. 188
(III. 19)	$A(α, β) \therefore I(β, α)$ (Conversio per accidens)	p. 188
(III. 20)	$A(α, β), A(β, γ) \therefore A(α, γ)$ (Barbara)	p. 191
(III. 21)	$NI(α, β), A(β, γ) \therefore NI(α, γ)$ (Celarent)	p. 192
(III. 22)	$A(α, β), I(β, γ) \therefore I(α, γ)$ (Darii)	p. 193
(III. 23)	$NI(α, β), I(β, γ) \therefore NA(α, γ)$ (Ferio)	p. 193
(III. 24)	$NI(β, α), A(β, γ) \therefore NI(α, γ)$ (Cesare)	p. 194
(III. 25)	$A(β, α), NI(β, γ) \therefore NI(α, γ)$ (Camestres)	p. 194

Index of Modal-Syllogistic Rules Used Directly in the Validity Proofs of Modal Syllogisms (in § 63)

(Notation according to § 42, § 43, and § 58)

(IV. 1)	L B ∴ B (*A necesse esse ad esse*)	p. 210
(IV. 2)	L B, H (B, C) ∴ L C (Variant on *modus ponendo ponens*)	p. 210
(IV. 3)	M B :: NLN B (Intermodal rule)	p. 210
(IV. 4)	NM B :: LN B (Intermodal rule)	p. 210
(IV. 6)	NL B :: MN B (Intermodal rule)	p. 210
(IV. 7)	K Y (α, β) :: M Y (α, β), M Z (α, β) (with Y = A, I, or $Ą$ and with Z = N A, N I, or N $Ą$ respectively, with the same quantity as Y)	p. 210
(IV. 8)	K Z (α, β) :: M Y (α, β), M Z (α, β) (with Y = A, I, or $Ą$ and with Z = N A, N I, or N $Ą$ respectively, with the same quantity as Y)	p. 210
(IV. 9)	L A (α, β) :: I (β, β), H (I (β, γ), L $Ą$ (α, γ)) (Variant on *dictum de omni*)	p. 211
(IV. 10)	M A (α, β) :: I (α, α), I (β, β), H (M I (β, γ), M $Ą$ (α, γ)) (Variant on *dictum de omni*)	p. 211
(IV. 11)	K A (α, β) :: I (α, α), I (β, β), H (I (β, γ), M $Ą$ (α, γ)), H (I (β, γ), MN $Ą$ (α, γ)) (Variant on *dictum de omni*)	p. 211
(IV. 13)	NM I (α, β) :: H (M I (β, γ), LN $Ą$ (α, γ)) (Variant on *dictum de nullo*)	p. 211
(IV. 14)	NM I (α, β) :: H (M I (β, β), LN $Ą$ (α, β)) (Variant on *dictum de nullo*)	p. 211
(IV. 16)	M I (α, β) ∴ M $Ą$ (α, γ), M $Ą$ (β, γ), I (α, α), I (β, β) (Exposition rule)	p. 212
(IV. 25)	A ∴ M A. (*ab esse ad posse*)	p. 213
(IV. 26)	L A ∴ M A (*a necesse esse ad posse*)	p. 213
(IV. 29)	H (A, B) ∴ H (M A, M B) (Analogy rule)	p. 214
(IV. 33)	MN $Ą$ (α, γ) ∴ MN A (α, γ) (Variant on the logical square)	p. 215
(IV. 34)	M $Ą$ (α, γ) ∴ M I (α, γ) (Variant on the logical square)	p. 215
(IV. 36)	K A (α, β) ∴ H (M I (β, γ), M $Ą$ (α, γ))	p. 215
(IV. 37)	K A (α, β) ∴ H (M I (β, γ), MN $Ą$ (α, γ))	p. 216
(IV. 41)	H (M I (β, γ), M $Ą$ (α, γ)), H (M I (β, γ), MN $Ą$ (α, γ)), I (α, α), I (β, β) ∴ K A (α, β)	p. 216
(IV. 43)	K A (α, β) ∴ H (I (β, γ), M $Ą$ (α, γ))	p. 218
(IV. 47)	K A (α, β) ∴ KN I (α, β) ('Complementary conversion')	p. 219
(IV. 48)	KN I (α, β) ∴ K A (α, β) ('Complementary conversion')	p. 219
(IV. 49)	K I (α, β) ∴ KN A (α, β) ('Complementary conversion')	p. 219
(IV. 50)	KN A (α, β) ∴ K I (α, β) ('Complementary conversion')	p. 219
(IV. 51)	LN I (α, β) ∴ LN I (β, α) (Conversion)	p. 220
(IV. 52)	L I (α, β) ∴ L I (β, α) (Conversion)	p. 221

(IV. 53)	$L\,A\,(α, β) \therefore L\,I\,(β, α)$ (Conversion)	p. 223
(IV. 54)	$MN\,I\,(α, β) \therefore MN\,I\,(β, α)$ (Conversion)	p. 223
(IV. 55)	$M\,I\,(α, β) \therefore M\,I\,(β, α)$ (Conversion)	p. 223
(IV. 57)	$K\,I\,(α, β) \therefore K\,I\,(β, α)$ (Conversion)	p. 224
(IV. 58)	$K\,A\,(α, β) \therefore K\,I\,(β, α)$ (Conversion)	p. 224
(IV. 59)	$KN\,A\,(α, β) \therefore KN\,A\,(β, α)$ (Conversion)	p. 224
(IV. 62)	$LN\,I\,(α, β), L\,A\,(β, γ) \therefore LN\,I\,(α, γ)$ (Celarent LLL)	p. 226
(IV. 63)	$L\,A\,(α, β), L\,I\,(β, γ) \therefore L\,I\,(α, γ)$ (Darii LLL)	p. 227
(IV. 64)	$LN\,I\,(α, β), L\,I\,(β, γ) \therefore LN\,A\,(α, γ)$ (Ferio LLL)	p. 227
(IV. 65)	$L\,A\,(α, β), A\,(β, γ) \therefore L\,A\,(α, γ)$ (Barbara LXL)	p. 228
(IV. 66)	$LN\,I\,(α, β), A\,(β, γ) \therefore LN\,I\,(α, γ)$ (Celarent LXL)	p. 229
(IV. 67)	$L\,A\,(α, β), I\,(β, γ) \therefore L\,I\,(α, γ)$ (Darii LXL)	p. 230
(IV. 68)	$LN\,I\,(α, β), I\,(β, γ) \therefore LN\,A\,(α, γ)$ (Ferio LXL)	p. 230
(IV. 74)	$K\,A\,(α, β), K\,I\,(β, γ) \therefore K\,I\,(α, γ)$ (Darii KKK)	p. 233
(IV. 75)	$K\,A\,(α, β), A\,(β, γ) \therefore K\,A\,(α, γ)$ (Barbara KXK)	p. 234
(IV. 76)	$K\,A\,(α\,β), I\,(β, γ) \therefore K\,I\,(α, γ)$ (Darii KXK)	p. 235
(IV. 79)	$L\,A\,(β, α), LN\,I\,(β, γ) \therefore LN\,I\,(α, γ)$ (Camestres LLL)	p. 236
(IV. 81)	$L\,A\,(β, α), LN\,A\,(β, γ) \therefore LN\,A\,(α, γ)$ (Baroco LLL)	p. 237
(IV. 84)	$LN\,I\,(α, γ), L\,I\,(β, γ) \therefore LN\,A\,(α, β)$ (Ferison LLL)	p. 238
(IV. 90)	$A\,(α, β), K\,A\,(β, γ) \therefore M\,A\,(α, γ)$ (Barbara XKM)	p. 242
(IV. 91)	$N\,I\,(α, β), K\,A\,(β, γ) \therefore MN\,I\,(α, γ)$ (Celarent XKM)	p. 244
(IV. 92)	$A\,(α, β), K\,I\,(β, γ) \therefore M\,I\,(α, γ)$ (Darii XKM)	p. 244
(IV. 95)	$LN\,I\,(α, β), K\,A\,(β, γ) \therefore N\,I\,(α, γ)$ (Celarent LKX)	p. 245
(IV. 96)	$LN\,I\,(α, β), K\,I\,(β, γ) \therefore N\,A\,(α, γ)$ (Ferio LKX)	p. 245
(IV. 97)	$L\,A\,(α, β), K\,I\,(β, γ) \therefore M\,I\,(α, γ)$ (Darii LKM)	p. 246
(IV. 105)	$K\,A\,(α, γ), K\,A\,(β, γ) \therefore K\,I\,(α, β)$ (Darapti KKK)	p. 251
(IV. 106)	$K\,A\,(α, γ), K\,I\,(β, γ) \therefore K\,I\,(α, β)$ (Datisi KKK)	p. 252
(IV. 109)	$KN\,I\,(α, γ), K\,I\,(β, γ) \therefore KN\,A\,(α, β)$ (Ferison KKK)	p. 252
(IV. 126)	$L\,I\,(α, γ), K\,A\,(β, γ) \therefore K\,I\,(α, β)$ (Disamis KLX)	p. 257

Index of Logical Rules Used Directly for the Derivation of Truth-Functional Rules and Laws (in § 74 and § 75)

(Notation according to § 42, § 46, § 51, § 58, § 64, and § 70)

(II. 2)	A, H (A, B) ∴ B (Modus ponendo ponens)	p. 164
(II. 7)	N B, H (A, B) ∴ N A (Modus tollendo tollens)	p. 166
(II. 13)	H (A, B), H (B, C) ∴ H (A, C) (Hypothetical syllogism)	p. 168
(III. 3)	I (α, β) ∴ A (α, γ), A̸ (β, γ) (Exposition rule)	p. 182
(III. 7)	A̸ (α, β) ∴ I (α, β) (Weak logical square)	p. 184
(III. 11)	A (α, β) ∴ A̸ (α, β) (Subordination rule)	p. 185
(III. 14)	N I (α, β) ∴ N A (α, β) (Subalternation rule)	p. 186
(V. 1)	A̸ (('v) A (v), ζ) >< [A (t)] (Transformation rule)	p. 267
(V. 2)	A (('v) A (v), ξ) >< (∀ v) A (v) (Transformation rule)	p. 267
(V. 3)	I (('v) A (v), ξ) >< (∃ v) A (v) (Transformation rule)	p. 268
(V. 7)	A (('v) N A (v), β) < N I (('v) A (v), β) (Transformation of (III. 8))	p. 270
(V. 8)	I (('v) N A (v), β) < N A (('v) A (v), β) (Transformation of (III. 9))	p. 270
(V. 9)	A̸ (('v) N A (v), β) < N A̸ (('v) A (v), β) (Transformation of (III. 10))	p. 270
(VI. 1)	H (A, B) >< A ⊃ B (Transformation rule)	p. 272
(VI. 2)	N A >< ~ A (Transformation rule)	p. 272
(VI. 3)	A, B < A (Postulate)	p. 272
(VI. 4)	NN A < A (Postulate)	p. 273
(VI. 5)	N A (α, β) < I (ᴺα, β) (Postulate)	p. 273
(VI. 6)	N A (ᴺα, β) < I (α, β) (Postulate)	p. 273
(VI. 8)	A ⊃ B, A < B (Simple detachment rule)	p. 277
(VI. 9)	(A ⊃ B), (B ⊃ C), A < C (Complex detachment rule)	p. 277
(VI. 10)	In case t occurs only in the argument places of A (t), then: A (t) < (∀ v) A (v) (Generalization rule)	p. 278
(VI. 12)	(∀ v) B (v) < A (('v) NN B (v), ξ) (Negation rule)	p. 279
(VI. 13)	B (t) < (∃ v) B (v) (Particularization rule)	p. 279
(VI. 15)	(∀ v) B (v) < B (t) (Subordination rule)	p. 280
(VI. 20)	*< (A ⊃ B) ⊃ (~ B ⊃ ~ A) (Law of contraposition)	p. 282
(VI. 21)	*< A ⊃ ~ ~ A (Negation rule)	p. 283
(VI. 24)	*< (∀ v) A (v) ⊃ A (t) (Law of instantiation)	p. 284
(VI. 25)	*< B (t) ⊃ (∃ v) B (v) (Law of particularization)	p. 285

Bibliography

Ackermann, Wilhelm. 1956. "Begründung einer strengen Implikation." *Journal of Symbolic Logic* 21: 113–28.
Alexander of Aphrodisias. 1881. *In Aristotelis Topicorum Libros Octo Commentaria*. In *Commentaria in Aristotelem Graeca*, Vol. II. 2, ed. Maximillian Wallies. Berlin.
Alexander of Aphrodisias. 1883. *In Aristotelis Analyticorum Priorum Librum I Commentarium*. In *Commentaria in Aristotelem Graeca*, Vol. II. 1, ed. Maximillian Wallies. Berlin: Reimer.
Anderson, Alan Ross, Nuel D. Belnap, and J. Michael Dunn. 1992. *Entailment*, vol. 2. Princeton: Princeton University Press.
Angelelli, Ignacio. 2005. "Review: Michael Wolff, *Abhandlung über die Prinzipien der Logik*." *The Bulletin of Symbolic Logic* 11: 444–45.
Apuleius, Madaurensis. 1908. "Peri hermeniae." *Opera quae supersunt*, vol. 3. Edited by Paul Thomas. Leipzig: Teubner.
Apuleius, Madaurensis. 1987. *The Logic of Apuleius*. Edited by David Londey and Carmen Johanson. Leiden: Brill.
Aristotle. 1886. *Fragmenta*. Collected by Valentini Rose. Leipzig: Teubner.
Aristotle. 1949. *Prior and Posterior Analytics*. Revised text with introduction and commentary by W.D. Ross. Oxford: Clarendon Press.
Aristotle. 1984. *The Complete Works of Aristotle*. 2 volumes. Edited by Jonathan Barnes. Princeton: Princeton University Press.
Aristotle. 1989. *Prior Analytics*. Translated by Robin Smith. Indianapolis: Hackett Publishing.
Aristotle. 2002. *Peri hermeneias. Werke in deutscher Übersetzung*. Vol. 1, part 2. Edited by Hermann Weidemann. Darmstadt: Wissenschaftliche Buchgesellschaft.
Aristotle. 2007. *Analytica priora, Buch I. Werke in deutscher Übersetzung*. Vol. 3, part I. Translation and commentary by Theodor Ebert and Ulrich Nortmann. Darmstadt: Wissenschaftliche Buchgesellschaft.
Aristotle. 2016. *Metaphysics*. Translated by C.D.C. Reeve. Indianapolis: Hackett Publishing.
Barcan, Ruth C. 1946. "A Functional Calculus of First Order Based on Strict Implication." *Journal of Symbolic Logic* 11: 1–16.
Barnes, Jonathan. 1982. *The Presocratic Philosophers*. London: Routledge.
Barnes, Jonathan. 1996. "Grammar on Aristotle's Terms." In *Rationality in Greek Thought*, edited by Michael Frede and Gisela Striker. Oxford: Clarendon Press.
Beall J.C. and Greg Restall. 2006. *Logical Pluralism*. Oxford: Clarendon Press.
Becker, Oskar. 1930. "Zur Logik der Modalitäten." *Jahrbuch für Philosophie und phänomenologische Forschung* 11: 497–548.
Beckermann, Ansgar. 1997. *Einführung in die Logik*. Berlin: De Gruyter.
Bencivenga, Ermanno. 1986. "Free Logics." In *Handbook of Philosophical Logic*, vol. 3, edited by Dov Gabbay and Franz Guenther, 373–426. Dordrecht: Reidel.
Bencivenga, Ermanno. 1998. "Free Logics." In *Routledge Encyclopedia of Philosophy*, edited by Edward Craig, vol. 3. London: Routledge.
Berka, Karel and Lothar Kreiser (eds.). 1983. *Logik-Texte, kommentierte Auswahl zur Geschichte der Logik*. Third edition. Berlin: Akademie-Verlag.
Bernoulli, Jakob. 1744. *Opera*, vol. 1. Geneva: Cramer & Philbert.
Bolzano, Bernard. 1829–31. *Wissenschaftslehre*, 4 vols. Edited by W. Schulz. Reprint 1970, Aalen: Scientia Verlag.

Blackburn, Simon (ed.). 1994. *The Oxford Dictionary of Philosophy*. Oxford: Oxford University Press.
Boole, George. 1854. *An Investigation of the Laws of Thought on Which are Founded the Mathematical Theories of Logic and Probabilities*. London: Walton & Maberly.
Bury, Robert G. 1933–49. *Sextus Empiricus*. 4 vols. Loeb Classical Library. London: Heinemann.
Capella, Martianus. 1983. *De nuptiis Philologiae et Mercurii*. Edited by J. Willis. Leipzig: Teubner.
Carnap, Rudolf. 1934. *Die logische Syntax der Sprache*. Wien: Springer.
Carnap, Rudolf. 1947. *Meaning and Necessity*. Chicago: The University of Chicago Press.
da Costa, Newton C.A. 1974. "On the Theory of Inconsistent Formal Systems." *Notre Dame Journal of Formal Logic* 15: 497–510.
Diogenes Laertius. 1999. *Diogenis Laertii Vitae philosophorum*. Edited by M. Marcovich. Stuttgart: Teubner.
Ebert, Theodor. 1991. *Dialektiker und frühe Stoiker bei Sextus Empiricus*. Göttingen: Vandenhoeck & Ruprecht.
Ebert, Theodor and Ulrich Nortmann. 2007. *Aristoteles, Analytica priora, Buch I. Werke in deutscher Übersetzung*. Vol. 3, part I. Darmstadt: Wissenschaftliche Buchgesellschaft.
Feys, Robert. 1937. "Les Nouvelles logiques des modalités." *Revue Néoscholastique de Philosophie* 40: 517–53.
Frede, Michael. 1974. *Die stoische Logik*. Göttingen: Vandenhoeck & Ruprecht.
Frede, Michael. 1987. *Essays in Ancient Philosophy*. Minneapolis: University of Minnesota Press.
Frege, Gottlob. 1879. *Begriffsschrift. Eine der arithmetischen nachgebildete Formelsprache des reinen Denkens*. Halle: Nebert.
Frege, Gottlob. 1882a. "Über den Zweck der Begriffsschrift." In *Sitzungsberichte der Jenaischen Gesellschaft für Medizin und Naturwissenschaft für das Jahr 1882*. Jena: G. Fischer 1883, 1–10. Reprinted in Frege 1964a, 97–106.
Frege, Gottlob. 1882b. "Über die wissenschaftliche Berechtigung einer Begriffsschrift." *Zeitschrift für Philosophie und philosophische Kritik* 81: 48–56. Reprinted in Frege 1964a, 106–14.
Frege, Gottlob. 1893. *Grundgesetze der Arithmetik, begriffsschriftlich abgeleitet*. Vol. 1. Jena: H. Pohle.
Frege, Gottlob. 1950. *Foundations of Arithmetic*. Translated by J.L. Austin. Oxford: Basil Blackwell.
Frege, Gottlob. 1960. *Translations from the Philosophical Writings of Gottlob Frege*. Edited by Peter Geach and Max Black. Oxford: Basil Blackwell.
Frege, Gottlob. 1964a. *Begriffsschrift und andere Aufsätze*, 2nd ed. Edited by I. Angelelli. Darmstadt.
Frege, Gottlob. 1964b. "On the Scientific Justification of a Concept-Script." Translated by James M. Bartlett. *Mind* 73, no. 290: 155–60.
Frege, Gottlob. 1967. *Begriffsschrift, a formula language, modelled on that of arithmetic, for pure thought*. Translated by S. Bauer-Mengelberg. In *From Frege to Gödel: A Source Book in Mathematical Logic, 1879–1931*, edited by Jean van Heijenoort, 1–82. Cambridge, MA: Harvard University Press.
Frege, Gottlob. 1968. "On the Purpose of the Begriffsschrift." Translated by Victor H. Dudman. *Australasian Journal of Philosophy* 46, no. 2: 89–97.
Frege, Gottlob. 1971. *Schriften zur Logik und Sprachphilosophie*. Edited by Gottfried Gabriel. Hamburg: Meiner.
Frege, Gottlob. 1976. *Wissenschaftlicher Briefwechsel*. Edited by G. Gabriel, H. Hermes, F. Kambartel, C. Thiel, and A. Veraart. Hamburg: Meiner.
Frege, Gottlob. 1979. *Posthumous Writings*. Translated by Peter Long and Roger White, with Raymond Hargreaves. Oxford: Basil Blackwell.
Frege, Gottlob. 1980. *Philosophical and Mathematical Correspondence*. Abridged by Brian McGuiness and translated by Hans Kaal. Oxford: Basil Blackwell.

Frege, Gottlob. 1983. *Nachgelassene Schriften*. Second edition. Edited by H. Hermes, F. Kambartel, and F. Kaulbach, in cooperation with G. Gabriel and W. Rödding. Hamburg: Meiner.

Frege, Gottlob. 1984. *Collected Papers on Mathematics, Logic, and Philosophy*. Translated by Max Black, V.H. Dudman, Peter Geach, Hans Kaal, E.-H.W. Kluge, Brian McGuiness, and R.H. Stoothoff. Oxford: Basil Blackwell.

Frege, Gottlob. 1986. *Die Grundlagen der Arithmetik. Eine logisch-mathematische Untersuchung über den Begriff der Zahl*. Edited by C. Thiel. Hamburg: Meiner.

Frege, Gottlob. 1990. *Kleine Schriften*. Edited by Ignacio Angelelli. Hildesheim: Olms.

Frege, Gottlob. 2013. *Basic Laws of Arithmetic*. Volume 1. Translated and edited by Philip A. Ebert and Marcus Rossberg. Oxford: Oxford University Press.

Galenus, Claudius. 1896. *Institutio logica*. Edited by C. Kalbfleisch. Leipzig: Teubner.

Gödel, Kurt. 1932. "Zum intuitionistischen Aussagenkalkül." *Anzeiger der Akademie der Wissenschaften in Wien, mathematisch-naturwissenschaftliche Klasse* 69: 65–66. Reprinted in: Berka & Kreiser 1983, 199–200.

Gödel, Kurt. 1933a. "Zum Entscheidungsproblem des logischen Funktionenkalküls." *Monatshefte für Mathematik und Physik* 40, 433–43.

Gödel, Kurt. 1933b. "Zur intuitionistischen Arithmetik und Zahlentheorie." *Ergebnisse eines mathematischen Kolloquiums* 4: 34–38. Reprinted in: Berka & Kreiser 1983, 201–2.

Gödel, Kurt. 1933c. "Eine Interpretation des intuitionistischen Aussagenkalküls." *Ergebnisse eines mathematischen Kolloquiums* 4: 39–40. Reprinted in: Berka & Kreiser 1983, 200–1.

Gödel, Kurt. 1944. "Russell's Mathematical Logic." In *The Philosophy of Bertrand Russell*, edited by P. A. Schilpp. Evanston, IL: Northwestern University Press.

Halmos, Paul R. 1976. *Naive Mengenlehre*. 4th edition. Göttingen: Vandenhoeck & Ruprecht.

Hegel, G.W.F. 1981. *Wissenschaft der Logik, zweiter Band: Die subjective Logik* [1816]. In *Gesammelte Werke*, vol. 12. Hamburg: Meiner.

Heyting, Arend. 1930. "Die formalen Regeln der intuitionistischen Logik." In *Sitzungsberichte der Preußischen Akademie der Wissenschaften, Physikalisch-mathematische Klasse*, vol. II: 42–56. Reprinted in: Berka & Kreiser 1983.

Hilbert, David and Wilhelm Ackermann. 1950. *Principles of Mathematical Logic*. Translated by Lewis M. Hammond, George G. Leckie, and F. Steinhardt. New York: Chelsea Publishing.

Hilbert, David and Wilhelm Ackermann. 1967. *Grundzüge der theoretischen Logik*. 5th edition. Berlin: Springer.

Hintikka, Jaakko. 1992. "Kant on the Mathematical Method." In *Kant's Philosophy of Mathematics: Modern Essays*, edited by Carl C. Posy. Dordrecht: Kluwer Academic Publishers.

Hoyningen-Huene, Paul. 1998. *Formale Logik. Eine philosophische Einführung*. Stuttgart: Reclam.

Hughes, George E. and Maxwell J. Cresswell. 1977. *An Introduction to Modal Logic*. London: Methuen.

Jaśkowski, Stanislaw. 1969. "Propositional Calculus for Contradictory Deductive Systems." *Studia Logica* 24: 143–57.

Kant, Immanuel. 1900– (Ak. + vol). *Kants gesammelte Schriften*. Edited by the Königlich Preussische Akademie der Wissenschaften, subsequently the Deutsche and then Berlin-Brandenburg Akademie der Wissenschaften. 29 volumes. Berlin: de Gruyter.

Kant, Immanuel. 1998 (*CPR*). *Critique of Pure Reason*. Translated by Paul Guyer and Allan Wood. Cambridge: Cambridge University Press.

Keynes, John Neville. 1928. *Studies and Exercises in Formal Logic*. Fourth edition. London: Macmillan.

Kirwan, Christopher. 1971. *Aristotle's Metaphysics, Books Γ, Δ, E*, translated with notes. Oxford: Clarendon.

Kneale, William and Martha Kneale. 1975. *The Development of Logic*. Oxford: Clarendon.

Kripke, Saul. 1980. *Naming and Necessity*. Oxford: Basil Blackwell.
Künne, Wolfgang. 1996. "Gottlob Frege (1848–1925)." In *Klassiker der Sprachphilosophie*, edited by T. Borsche, 325–45. München: Beck.
Lambert, Johann Heinrich. 1764. *Neues Organon*. Two volumes. Leipzig. Reprinted in: Lambert, J.H., *Philosophische Schriften*, volumes 1 and 2. Hildesheim: Olms, 1969.
Lambert, Karel. 1998. "Free logics, philosophical issues in." In *Routledge Encyclopedia of Philosophy*, edited by Edward Craig. London: Routledge.
Langford, Cooper H. 1927. "On Propositions Belonging to Logic." *Mind* 36: 343–46.
Leibniz, G.W. 1840. *Nouveaux Essais sur l'entendement human*. In *Opera philosophica quae extant*, ed. J.E. Erdmann. Berlin
Lemmon, Edward John. 1959. "Is There Only One Correct System of Modal Logic?" *Aristotelian Society Supplementary* 23: 23–40.
Leonard, Henry. 1956. "The Logic of Existence." *Philosophical Studies* 7: 49–64.
Lewis, Clarence I. and Cooper H. Langford. 1932. *Symbolic Logic*. Reprint 1959, New York: Dover Publications.
Łukasiewicz, Jan. 1935. "Zur Geschichte der Aussagenlogik." *Erkenntnis* 5: 111–31.
Łukasiewicz, Jan. 1970. *Selected Works*. Edited by L. Borkowski. Amsterdam: North Holland.
MacColl, Hugh. 1903. "Symbolic Reasoning." *Mind* 12: 355–64.
MacFarlane, John. 2000. *What Does It Mean to Say that Logic is Formal*. Dissertation, University of Pittsburgh.
MacFarlane, John. 2002. "Kant, Frege, and the Logic of Logicism." *The Philosophical Review* 111: 25–65.
Marciszewski, Witold. 1981. "Definite Descriptions." In *Dictionary of Logic as Applied in the Study of Language*. Dordrecht: Springer.
Mates, Benson. 1973. *Stoic Logic*. Berkeley, CA: University of California Press.
Mates, Benson. 1996. *The Skeptic Way*. Sextus Empiricus's Outlines of Pyrrhonism. Translated, with introduction and commentary. Oxford: Oxford University Press.
Mautner, Thomas (ed.). 1996. *A Dictionary of Philosophy*. Cambridge: Wiley-Blackwell.
Menne, Albert. 1985. *Einführung in die formale Logik*. Darmstadt: Wissenschaftliche Buchgesellschaft.
Mill, John Stuart. 1843. *A System of Logic, Ratiocinative and Inductive*. Vol. 1. London: John W. Parker.
Nortmann, Ulrich. 1996. *Modale Syllogismen, mögliche Welten, Essentialismus. Eine Analyse der aristotelischen Modallogik*. Berlin: De Gruyter.
Ockham, Guilelmus de. 1957. *Summa Logicae*. Edited by P. Boehner. St. Bonaventure, N.Y.: Franciscan Institute Nauwelaerts.
Patzig, Günther. 1963. *Die aristotelische Syllogistik*. Second edition. Göttingen: Vandenhoeck & Ruprecht.
Patzig, Günther. 1969. *Die aristotelische Syllogistik*. Third edition. Göttingen: Vandenhoeck & Ruprecht.
Patzig, Günther. 1970. *Sprache und Logik*. Göttingen: Vandenhoeck & Ruprecht.
Patzig, Günther. 1994. "Die logischen Formen praktischer Sätze in Kants Ethik." In Günter Patzig, *Gesammelte Schriften I*, 209–33. Göttingen: Wallstein.
Philoponus, Ioannes. 1905. *In Aristotelis Analytica Priora Commentaria*. In *Commentaria in Aristotelem Graeca*, XIII. 2. Edited by Maximilian Wallies. Berlin: Reimer.
Plutarch. 1895. "De Sollertia Animalium." *Plutarchi Moralia*, vol. 6. Leipzig: Teubner.
Prantl, Carl. 1855. *Geschichte der Logik im Abendlande*. Volume 1. Reprint of volumes 1–4, 1997, Hildesheim: Olms.
Prior, Arthur N. 1967a. "Existence." In *Encyclopedia of Philosophy*, vol. 3, edited by P. Edwards. New York: Macmillan.

Prior, Arthur N. 1967b. "The Heritage of Kant and Mill." In *Encyclopedia of Philosophy*, vol. 5, edited by P. Edwards. New York: Macmillan.
Purtill, Richard. 1995a. "Principle of Bivalence." In *The Cambridge Dictionary of Philosophy*, edited by Robert Audi, 644. Cambridge: Cambridge University Press.
Purtill, Richard. 1995b. "Principle of Excluded Middle." In *The Cambridge Dictionary of Philosophy*, edited by Robert Audi, 645. Cambridge: Cambridge University Press.
Quine, Willard V.O. 1959. *Methods of Logic*. Revised edition. New York: Holt, Rinehart & Winston.
Quine, Willard V.O. 1963. *From a Logical Point of View*. Second edition. New York: Harper.
Reich, Klaus. 2001. *Gesammelte Schriften*. Hamburg: Meiner.
Routley, Richard. 1977. "Ultralogic as Universal?" *Relevance Logic Newsletter* 2: 50–90.
Russell, Bertrand. 1903. *The Principles of Mathematics*. Cambridge: Cambridge University Press.
Russell, Bertrand. 1919a. "The Philosophy of Logical Atomism." *The Monist* 28, no. 4: 495–527.
Russell, Bertrand. 1919b. *Introduction to Mathematical Philosophy*. London: George Allen & Unwin.
Russell, Bertrand. 1957. "Mr. Strawson on Referring." *Mind* 66: 385–89.
Russell, Bertrand. 1960. *Our Knowledge of the External World*. London: Routledge.
Schmid, Carl Christian Erhard. 1798. *Wörterbuch zum leichtern Gebrauch der Kantischen Schriften*. Jena.
Schmidt, Jürgen. 1966. *Mengenlehre. Einführung in die axiomatische Mengenlehre*. Volume I: *Grundbegriffe*. Mannheim: Bibliographisches Institut.
Schmidt, Klaus J. 2000. *Die modale Syllogistik des Aristoteles. Eine modalprädikaten-logische Interpretation*. Paderborn: Mentis.
Schröder, Ernst. 1890–95. *Vorlesungen über die Algebra der Logik. Exakte Logik*. 3 volumes. Leipzig: Teubner.
Sextus Empiricus. 2000. *Outlines of Scepticism*. Translated by Julia Annas and Jonathan Barnes. Cambridge: Cambridge University Press.
Sextus Empiricus. 2005. *Against the Logicians*. (Adversus Mathematicos VII and VIII). Translated by Richard Bett. Cambridge: Cambridge University Press.
Sigwart, Christoph. 1889. *Logik*. Second edition. Tübingen: H. Laupp'sche Buchhandlung.
Sommers, Fred. 1982. *The Logic of Natural Language*. Oxford: Clarendon Press.
Stekeler-Weithofer, Pirmin. 1992. "Satz vom ausgeschlossenen Dritten." In *Historisches Wörterbuch der Philosophie*, vol. 8, 1198–1202. Basel: Schwabe.
Strawson, Peter F. 1950. "On Referring." *Mind* 59: 320–44.
Strawson, Peter F. 1952. *Introduction to Logical Theory*. London: Methuen.
Strawson, Peter F. 1959. *Individuals: An Essay in Descriptive Metaphysics*. London: Methuen.
Strawson, Peter F. 1982. "Review: The Logic of Natural Language." *The Journal of Philosophy* 79: 786–90.
Strobach, Niko. 2001. "Schlüsse aus Annahmen bei Aristoteles. Eine argumentationstheoretische Deutung des *syllogismos ex hypotheseôs*." *Zeitschrift für philosophische Forschung* 55: 248–57.
Stuhlmann-Laeisz, Rainer. 1995. *Gottlob Freges 'Logische Untersuchungen'*. Darmstadt: Wissenschaftliche Buchgesellschaft.
Tarski, Alfred. 1935. *Der Wahrheitsbegriff in den formalisierten Sprachen*. Reprinted in: Berka & Kreiser 1983, 445–546.
Tarski, Alfred. 1936. "Über den Begriff der logischen Folgerung." *Actes du Congrès Internationale de Philosophie Scientifique* 7: 1–11. Reprinted in: Berka & Kreiser 1983, 404–13.
Thompson, Manley. 1953. "On Aristotle's Square of Opposition." *The Philosophical Review* 62: 251–65. Reprinted in: *Aristotle: A Collection of Critical Essays*, edited by J.M.E. Moravcsik, 51–72. South Bend, IN: Notre Dame University Press, 1968.
Tugendhat, Ernst and Ursula Wolf. 1983. *Logisch-semantische Propädeutik*. Stuttgart: Reclam.

von Wright, Georg Henrik. 1974. "Determinismus, Wahrheit und Zeitlichkeit. Ein Beitrag zum Problem der zukünftigen kontingenten Wahrheiten." *Studia Leibnitiana* 6: 161–78.
Wedin, Michael. 1990. "Negation and Quantification in Aristotle." *History and Philosophy of Logic* 11: 131–50.
Wieland, Wolfgang. 1966. "Die aristotelische Theorie der Notwendigkeitsschlüsse." *Phronesis* 11: 35–60.
Wolff, Christian. 1740. *Philosophia Rationalis sive Logica*. Frankfurt & Leipzig.
Wolff, Michael. 1995. *Die Vollständigkeit der Kantischen Urteilstafel. Mit einem Essay über Freges 'Begriffsschrift'*. Frankfurt: Klostermann.
Wolff, Michael. 1998. "Prinzipien und expositorische Beweise in Aristoteles' Syllogistik." In *Philosophiegeschichte und logische Analyse*, vol. 1: 131–70.
Wolff, Michael. 2006. "Frege und das traditionelle Bild der Syllogistik." In *Von der Logik zur Sprache*, edited by R. Bubner and G. Hindrichs, 272–85. Stuttgart: Klett-Cotta,
Wolff, Michael. 2007. "Die Reinheit der Logik: Kant und Frege." In *Kant und der Gegenwart*, edited by J. Stolzenburg, 53–70. Berlin: De Gruyter.
Wolff, Michael. 2013. "Viele Logiken – Eine Vernunft. Warum der Logische Pluralismus ein Irrtum ist." *Methodus* 7: 79–134.

Subject Index

a necesse esse ad esse valet consequentia 17, 210, 339
a necesse esse ad posse valet consequentia 213
ab esse ad posse valet consequentia 17, 103, 213, 339
adjunction 67, 221, 354
– comparison with inclusive disjunction 163
affirmative / affirmation 7, 10, 11, 26, 27, 30, 31, 36, 38, 50–53, 55, 57, 59, 62, 64, 97, 100–3, 105, 106, 116, 120–22, 124, 135–38, 145, 153, 209, 272, 273, 306, 331, 338, 339, 341, 349, 354, 355, 358
– affirmative proposition 26, 55, 206, 358
algebra
– Boolean 41
– logical 41
– mathematical 130, 131
anaphoric
– anaphoric expressions 39, 114
– anaphoric and kataphoric use of logical constants in singular propositions 39
antonym 9, 11, 42, 184
apodictic 15–19, 21, 22, 204, 206, 207, 209, 212, 219–22, 226, 228, 238–42, 247, 248, 255
– apodictic proposition 16–19, 206, 207, 209
arithmetic vii, 88–89, 131–34, 274, 324
assertoric 15, 16, 18–21, 33, 34, 38, 43, 44, 88
– assertoric opposition 31, 33, 34, 38, 43, 106, 243, 244, 253, 330, 358
– assertoric proposition 19
– assertoric syllogistic ix, x, 3, 6, 8
axiom (logical) vi, vii, ix–xi, 89, 281–83, 294
– of the calculus of classes: axiom of choice 54
  – axiom of extensionality 54, 56
– of the calculus of functions 295
– of modal logic: B-axiom 342, 346
  – S4-axiom 342, 347–49
  – S5-axiom 342, 347–49
  – T-axiom 341
  – Barcan-formula 351
axiom schemata 294, 295

basic rules ix, 145, 146, 153, 154, 164, 166, 182–84, 190, 192, 203, 217, 259, 274, 275, 294, 304, 315–19, 337, 342, 349
– metalogical 154, 275
– syllogistic b.r. as depending on meaning of logical constants 135, 136, 264, 306
bisubtraction 163
bivalence principle 19, 21, 24–27, 118, 120–24, 359–63

calculus of classes 41–43, 45, 63
calculus of functions (logical) 70, 122, 145, 261, 262, 296
– as axiomatic system 295, 305
– axioms of *FC* 296, 303–5
– derivability in 294, 295
– derivation rules of *FC* 295, 296, 303
– second level 321, 323
– theorems of *FC* 297, 301–4
categorical 12–15, 17, 21, 38, 40, 41, 47–53, 58, 59, 73, 80, 91, 92, 105–10, 158, 168, 178, 179, 181, 182, 194–96, 200–2, 204–6, 210, 263, 264, 267–69, 286, 292
– c. form 12, 15, 17, 105, 107, 108, 269
– as form of logically simple and logically independent propositions 13–17
– in the language of the calculus of functions 105
class 41, 42
– empty (see *null class*)
class constants 69
class inclusion (see *inclusion*)
class-logical relations 50, 51, 62
class variables 42, 43, 45, 46, 50, 53, 66, 68, 69
compatible / compatibility viii, ix, 13, 25, 28, 29, 48, 55, 56, 92, 98, 102, 141, 151, 156, 157, 222, 230, 236, 309, 312, 316, 318, 331, 333–35
complementary class 42, 54, 56
complementary conversion 248, 252, 254, 256–58

388 — Subject Index

concept xix, xx
- first and second level (according to Frege) 87, 88
- according to Frege's function theory (see also: *propositional function, unsaturated monadic*) 74–90, 264, 65
- as limit cases of relations (according to Frege) 77

concept expression, syllogistic: see *term*
concept expression schema 10, 82
concept pyramid viii, 3, 8
conceptual constant 226–68, 293, 307
- 'bearer of the name *t*' as c.c. 113, 263
- 'element of the null class' as c.c. 60
- 'individual ('object') as c.c. 104, 105, 263
conceptual division 9, 17
- analytic c.d. 9
conceptual hierarchies 3, 9, 17, 38
conceptual relations xix, xx
- in distinction from classical relations 47, 58
- Frege's program to reduce all c.r. 72–74, 89, 90, 105, 107, 108, 125, 126
- hierarchical 3, 9, 11, 17, 38
conceptual scope 10
- empty c.s. 54, 56
- scope (extension) of concepts in class logic 42–47, 53–58, 66
concept variable
- only object variable in the syllogistic 5, 6, 8, 11, 40
- as placeholder for a term 5, 6, 54, 81, 87, 89, 307
concept word 79, 83, 86, 114, 194, 263
- in Frege xx
conditionalization 138, 174, 176, 201, 274, 275, 304, 309, 340, 371
- generalized rule of 174
- principle of 147, 165, 275, 276, 319
- rule of 174, 175, 277, 373
conjunction, logical
- conjunction of premises (see *elementary*)
- elementary 94, 98–100, 125, 135, 139–42, 315, 316, 330, 331
- non-truth-functional (see *elementary*)
- truth-functional 95, 333–35, 354
conjunction of premises (see *conjunction, elementary logical*)

connective
- hypothetical 40, 102, 177
- syllogistic 92, 103
- truth-functional 67, 68, 70, 102
consequence (following) 69, 96, 99, 141, 151, 156, 157, 160, 161, 184, 185, 244, 254, 287, 352, 357
- expressed by a hypothetical connective 7, 8, 13, 22, 160, 162, 319
- logical c. viii, 16, 19, 141, 149, 151, 152, 156, 157, 164, 174, 186, 209, 275, 176, 301–3, 309, 337, 367
- logical c. in calculus of functions 301–5
- regular c. 146, 149, 151, 152, 156, 157, 159, 161, 162, 164, 174, 204, 273, 275, 276, 278, 303, 316, 319, 343, 365–67
- c. rules 95, 96, 138, 212, 213, 215
- semantic concept of logical c. 301–3
- syntactic concept of logical c. 301–3
- weakening of logical c. 276, 371, 372
constants, logical
- of the calculus of classes 65–68
- of the functional calculus 145, 146 (see also *propositional connective*)
- of the syllogistic 8, 11, 37, 60
construction, symbolic vi, 129–31, 133
content, conceptual 6, 60, 66, 83, 88–89, 109–13, 117, 138, 261, 293, 308, 358
context principle 119
contingent / contingently 18–22, 35, 57, 204–8, 210, 215–17, 224, 232, 234, 235, 243, 246–49, 251, 253, 255, 360
contingentia futura 360
contradictoriness 26, 27, 30–35, 44, 45, 48–51, 61, 62, 120, 121, 190
contraposition 166, 169, 282–83, 289, 372
contrariety 48, 49, 51, 186, 187, 371
- rule of 117
conversion (see also *complementary conversion*) 43, 187–89
- modal-syllogistic conversion rules 219, 220 (see also *complementary conversion*)
- *per accidens* 36, 43, 188, 189
- rules of 10, 43, 80, 187–90, 219, 220, 225
- simple (*conversio simplex*) 43, 187, 188
copula (auxiliary word) 80, 84, 86

de dicto/de re use of expressions
- *de dicto/de re* contingency 19, 20
- *de dicto/de re* necessity 17, 229, 250
- *de dicto/de re* negation (see *negation*)
- *de dicto/de re* possibility 17, 358
deconditionalization 165, 175, 277, 341
deduction theorem 300
definition
- as basis of syllogistic method of derivation 145–46
- use def. 27
derivation method (see also *reduction, synthetic method*)
- axiomatic 146, 294–96
- syllogistic, as a method for inference chain abbreviation 147, 269, 294
detachment rule
- complex 277
- simple 277
- as derivation rule 295, 296, 300, 305, 325, 339, 349
determinism/indeterminism 419
dictum de omni et nullo 91, 109, 190
- *dictum de omni* 91, 109, 182, 183, 189, 190, 306, 371, 375, 377
- *dictum de nullo* 182, 189, 371, 375, 377
dilemma
- constructive 64, 172
- destructive 171
- weak constructive 171
disjunctive/disjunction 7, 9, 12–15, 40, 59, 67, 158, 160, 162–164, 170–73, 293
- complete disjunction 163
- disjunctive proposition 40, 163
- exclusive and inclusive d. 59, 67, 163
domain of individuals (universe of discourse) 52, 56, 68, 120–22, 127–29, 239, 249, 273, 274, 343–45, 357 (see also *postulate*)

ex contradictione quodlibet 351, 352
ex falso quodlibet sequitur 55, 96, 97, 273, 333, 334, 352
existential import 47, 48, 50–53, 55, 57, 58, 106, 120, 125, 138, 129, 179, 180, 206, 210, 358

existence
- as belonging to a non-empty domain of individuals 52, 53, 57, 58, 138, 139, 274, 357
existential quantifier 68, 115–17, 263, 293, 357
- substitutional interpretation of 357
exposition (*ekthesis*) 182, 187, 190, 193, 194, 199, 225, 237, 371
- first exposition rule 182
- second exposition rule 182
ex quolibet verum sequitur 273, 333
extensionalism 136

form, logical 4, 6, 7, 14–17, 21, 66, 77, 91, 119, 124, 159, 205, 206, 220, 221, 229, 230, 240, 241, 250, 269, 307–10, 358, 365
formality of formal logic 25, 126, 359, 365
function vii–viii, 14, 68, 70, 74–78, 82, 83, 85, 87–90 (see also *propositional function, truth function*)
functional expression (logical) 17, 68–73, 76, 77, 82–84, 94, 107, 112, 261, 262, 272, 294–96
- number of empty places not the same as number of arguments 76, 77
function variable
- bound 87
- comparison with syllogistic concept variables 74
- universally quantified 322

grammar xix, 14, 211

hypothetical viii, 7, 8, 12–15, 22, 23, 37, 38, 40, 59, 62, 67, 91–94, 96, 102–5, 108, 109, 130, 138, 141, 142, 147, 158–62, 164, 166–70, 175–77, 269, 271, 276, 286, 288, 290, 315, 316, 335, 343, 367
- h. connective (see *propositional connective*)

identifier, individual 112–14, 123, 128
- definite description 123
identity of sets or classes 41, 56, 65, 66
identity sign 130
implication (see *strict implication*)
impredicative proposition 181

inclusion of sets or classes 41, 42, 59
incompatible / incompatibility (see *compatible / compatibility*)
inconsistency 139, 274 (see also *contrariety*)
individual constant 70, 110, 115, 119, 121, 122, 127, 261, 262, 274, 301, 352, 369
individual variable 67–70, 73–76, 88, 103, 104, 115, 125, 127, 131, 262, 263
inference (deductive)
– contentful 152, 264, 286
– contentful syllogistic 261
– 'natural' 147
– theory of contentful i. 307
inference conversion 153, 338, 373
informal inference (see *inference*)
intermodal rules 210, 339
intersection 41, 57, 65, 66
intuition (according to Kant) 128, 129
intuitionism / intuitionistic x, 305, 334, 342, 351, 353–55
intuitive 129–31
– according to Frege 126–28

judgment
– of attribution 5
– theory of 83
– unity of 83, 84

Kantian table of judgments viii, 7, 21, 142, 308
kataphoric 39, 114

language(s):
– of the calculus of classes 41–43, 46, 50, 53, 54, 58, 65–67, 70, 72, 135
– of the (logical) calculus of functions 65, 70, 72, 74, 83, 90, 102, 103, 105, 115, 119–22, 124–26, 129, 132, 133, 135, 136, 139, 140, 145, 179, 260, 261, 286, 293, 294, 296
– elementary l. of the syllogistic (as symbolic l.) 40, 47, 66, 102, 103, 119, 125–27, 142, 145–47, 315 (see also *universal language*)
– extended l. of the syllogistic 40, 105, 109
– non-truth-functional 105, 135
– non-extensional 136
– of the syllogistic ix, x, xix, xx, 5, 6, 8, 11, 37, 38, 46, 58, 60, 65, 66, 74, 102, 103, 115, 135, 140, 260, 271, 322
– truth-functional 37, 40, 136
language analysis xix, xx, 133
laws
– algebraic 130
– of the calculus of functions 136, 140, 304, 305
– De Morgan's 67
– logical (valid on logical grounds) 138, 139, 311
– of thinking (Frege) 134
– truth-functional 281
limitative / limitation 10, 11, 21, 40, 120, 181, 184, 206, 306
logic
– deductive xix, 4–6, 22, 41, 72, 135, 136, 138, 174, 176, 267, 271, 272, 274, 277, 281, 293, 294, 303, 306, 307, 312
– deontic 15, 366
– formal xix, 25, 55, 84, 96, 97, 126, 127, 273, 304, 307, 312, 345
– free x, 50, 352, 353
– general v–vi, viii–ix, xi, 127, 260, 307
– history of 13, 310–13, 353
– intuitionistic x, 305, 334, 342, 351, 353–55
– mathematical vii, xi, 41, 50, 106, 126, 179, 311, 312, 352
– modal logic (see entry)
– modern v, 6–8, 22, 50, 263, 311, 312, 333
– of normal language 50
– paraconsistent x, 16, 29, 333
– pure vi, 89, 126, 127, 129, 133, 134
– relevance x, 333, 352
– revolution in 311
– temporal 367
– traditional (syllogistic) 33, 41, 63, 311, 303
logical calculus
– axiomatic 296, 301–5
– intuitionistic 354

material, logical (as conceptual content of judgment) 6
mathematics vi, vii, xi, 89, 111, 134, 152, 274, 275, 304, 311, 312, 342, 344, 354
mathematical (complete) induction vi, 70, 89, 133, 135, 145, 321–27
metalogical rules 146, 147, 153–56, 164, 165, 174, 175, 185, 271, 275–77, 319
metavariable 40, 107, 154
modal expressions

- deontic 15, 366
- epistemic 15
- negative 21
- temporal 367
modality 20, 22, 152, 343–45, 358
- alethic 15, 22
- *de dicto* / *de re* 17, 22, 203, 206, 358 (see also *de dicto* / *de re use of expressions*)
modal logic ix, x, xx, 203, 220, 234, 259, 333, 334, 337, 339, 340, 345, 348, 349
- axiomatic ix, x, 22, 23
- Brouwerian system of 230, 337, 342, 346–49
- modal predicate logic 357
- modal syllogistic (see *syllogistic*)
- S4-system 243, 254, 337, 342, 345–49, 354, 358
- S5-system 221, 234, 241, 255, 337, 342, 345–49, 358
- T-system 337, 341, 342, 347, 349, 354
modus Barbara viii, 15, 64, 191, 192, 235, 36
modus ponendo ponens viii, 8, 13, 98, 108, 158–59, 162, 164–66, 176, 184, 185, 277, 306, 319, 340, 371–74

negation viii, 7, 11, 16, 19, 23, 24–27, 29–31, 36, 45, 53, 57, 62, 100, 101, 106, 109, 116, 120–22, 124, 125, 137, 138, 141, 151, 152, 161, 162, 168, 180, 194, 211, 225, 271, 298, 303, 306, 331, 333, 338, 339, 342, 352–55
- *de dicto* negation 19, 24, 25
- *de re* negation 19, 24, 25
- elementary 30, 102, 116, 150
- expressions of 24
- negative categorical statements 50
- non-truth-functional 27, 28, 30, 32–36, 51, 52, 57, 100, 101, 141
- syllogistic viii, 24
- truth-functional 24, 27, 29–31, 42, 53, 57, 59, 68, 70, 91, 101, 116, 178, 271, 294, 302
necessity 16, 204, 206, 250, 342
- absolute / relative 343
- logical 344
null class (null set) 44–46, 53–60, 62, 66, 93

object of the proposition 79
object variable 5, 8, 11
open proposition 76, 78, 81, 86, 123, 263, 265, 321

open term (see *term*)
opposition, logical 43, 49

paraconsistent x, 16, 29, 333
particular 7, 20, 30–34, 38, 48, 49, 104, 109, 159, 178, 180, 189, 193, 207, 208, 211, 221, 222, 240, 254
peritrope (*lex clavii* / *lex mirabilis*) 166, 167, 169, 187, 220
- inverse of 167, 169
possibility, logical 345
- one-sided 20
- two-sided 20, 205
postulate (logical, non-syllogistic) 118, 137–39, 272, 273, 298, 304, 305, 340–44, 330, 331, 335, 338–41, 354, 355
- of extended deductive logic ix, x, 304, 305, 309, 313
- p. (or principle) of the affirmative use of double negation (*duplex negatio affirmat*) 30, 36, 57, 50, 62, 64, 97, 100–3, 105, 116, 120–22, 124, 125, 135–38, 145, 272, 273, 306, 331, 338, 339, 341
- p. (or principle) of the arbitrary sufficient reason 97, 98, 100–3, 105, 125, 135–7, 138, 145, 272, 306, 330, 340, 341, 349, 372
- p. (or principle) of non-empty domains 125, 135–39, 145, 273, 274, 302, 306, 363
predicate
- grammatical 14, 79–82, 90, 264 (see also *open proposition*)
- logical 14, 15, 79, 80, 88
- predicate concept 14, 15, 47, 48, 51, 78, 84, 88, 89, 107, 111, 112, 132, 184
- predicate prefix (see *predicator*)
- predicate name 79–81
- predicate of predicates 88
predicator (predicate prefix) 82, 261, 263, 293, 358
prefix 16, 67, 68, 82, 261, 263, 264, 323
- predicate (see *predicator*)
- privative 11
- quantifier p. (see *quantifier, universal, existential*)
- ∇-prefix as quantifier prefix of singular quantified proposition 114, 261, 263
presuppositional inference (syllogism *ex hypothesi*) 158, 59

principle of excluded middle (*tertium non datur*) 25–27, 29, 354
principle of mathematical (complete) induction vi, 89, 321–27
– generalized 89, 135
principle of qualitative existential import 50–53, 55, 57, 58, 106, 120, 125, 138, 179, 206, 358
problematic 15–22, 204, 205, 207, 213, 217, 223
– problematic proposition 17–22, 204
proper names:
– according to Frege xx
– 'bundle' theory 123
– 'causal theory' 123
– in the narrow sense 110
– legitimately formed (Frege) 118
– logically p.n. (Russell) 122
– pseudo p.n. (Frege) 118
– p.n. and the logical form of singular propositions 39, 70, 110–14, 118,122, 123, 127, 309
– 'use theory' 123
propositional function 68, 72, 74–78, 80, 87–90, 114, 135
– complex 70
– monadic 72, 74, 84, 88
– polyadic 70
– unsaturated monadic (the same as Fregean concept) 74–89, cf. 114, 327
propositional schema 4–6, 8–11, 16, 19–22, 31, 35, 40, 42, 44, 46, 47, 58, 59, 66, 68, 73, 91, 92, 104, 105, 109, 113, 146, 174, 201, 272, 321
– class-logical 59, 66
– syllogistic 3–6, 8, 10, 17, 18, 21, 22, 35, 47, 54, 58, 60, 72, 73, 133, 308
– universally valid 176, 201

quality (logical) 7, 10, 21, 50, 51, 217
quantity (logical) 7, 20, 50, 79, 180, 181, 184, 205, 210, 217, 268
quantifier 67–70, 115, 116, 120, 263, 302, 323, 324
quantifier rules 115–17, 119, 120, 138, 139
– elimination of universal quantifier 116
– existential generalization 116
– introduction of existential quantifier 116
– posterior generalization 279, 295–97, 300, 301
– universal instantiation 116

reduction 164, 293
– *reductio ad absurdum* (*reductio ad impossibile*) 97, 117, 140, 147, 153, 187, 190, 225, 275, 371, 373
reference (to objects) 26, 39, 40, 52, 88, 104, 111–14, 117, 119–24, 127
relations 47, 58
– between concepts (see also *conceptual relations*)
– in class logic 110, 118
– of the logical square 31–33, 44, 46–51
– r. and relational concepts in Frege 77
relation, logical (between parts of a statement) 7, 14, 83, 178, 186, 188, 308
– elementhood 41, 67, 68
– set theoretical 68, 69
– syllogistic concept relations 73, 267, 268
relational constant 38–40
relational expression 41, 159
relevance logic / relevant-logical x, 333, 352
Russell's paradox 87–89, 327

semantics 22, 39, 112, 203, 347
– possible worlds s. 347, 449
set 41
– empty (see *null class*)
– set as element 54
set theory 41, 42, 45
– axiomatic 56
singular proposition (see *proposition*)
singular 6, 7, 10, 20, 38, 39, 41, 77, 79, 83–85, 90, 110–15, 117–19, 178, 181, 200, 207, 208, 248, 261, 267, 268, 274, 294, 357
– name 110, 111, 114, 118
– proposition 26, 27, 33, 34, 104, 109, 117, 120–25, 138
– term 110, 111 (see *term*)
– types of 111 (see *proper name*)
square, logical 34, 44, 46–51, 53, 72, 73, 105–7, 109, 120, 139, 183–86, 173, 306
– weak 33, 34, 57, 88, 115, 185
– strong 31, 34, 43, 44, 186
– assertoric opposition 31, 106
– modal opposition 34
strict implication 22, 23, 36, 37, 67, 94, 101–3, 161, 334, 338, 341, 349
– according to Ackermann 177

- paradoxical theorems of 349
subalternation /subaltern 32–35, 43–45, 48–51, 184–86, 189, 192, 306
subject
- grammatical 13–15, 76, 79–81, 90, 111–13, 115, 127, 263
- logical 13–15, 79, 80
- subject concept 14, 15, 45, 47–51, 53, 79, 84, 88, 89, 107
subjunction 8, 67, 91–93, 103–6, 177, 271, 272, 341, 354
- universally quantified 73, 91–93, 103–6
subcontrariety / subcontrary 32, 34, 35, 44, 48, 49, 51, 186
subordination vii, 4, 9, 17, 21, 38, 73, 74, 82, 90, 91, 93, 108–10, 251
- kinds of subordination 109
- subordination rule 185
substitution 155, 156, 174, 262
- substitutional interpretation of existential quantifier (see *existential quantifier*)
- substitution rule 294
subsumption 73, 74, 80, 87, 89, 108, 110, 114, 124, 127
syllogism viii, 4, 63, 152, 158, 159, 168, 169, 171, 189–91, 193, 194, 200, 225, 226, 228, 239–41, 248
syllogistic
- Aristotelian 19, 20, 29, 147, 153, 154, 179, 182, 183, 189, 190, 193, 194, 206, 220, 240, 260, 310
- elementary 38–40, 59, 102, 103, 127, 133, 142, 145, 149, 202, 203, 260, 274, 306–8, 315, 318, 319, 337, 352
- as formal and pure logic 127, 128
- language of (see *language*)
- logical vocabulary of viii–x, xix–xi, 6–8, 18–20, 22–24, 67, 72, 303, 304, 308, 309
- Megarian 161, 164, 171
- modal x, 18, 19, 22, 23, 74, 75, 203, 204, 209, 250, 254, 259, 260, 337
- 'new syllogistic' 125
- Stoic 140–42, 154
- as sub-domain of deductive logic 5, 6
- traditional v, xix–xi, 11, 18, 19, 83, 84, 91, 312, 313

symbolic construction vi, 129–31
synthetic (non-analytic) 134, 135, 139, 146, 147, 154, 274
- synthetic propositions *a priori* in arithmetic 133, 134
synthetic method 145, 146
synthetic theorem (peripatetic inference chain rule) 145, 46, 154

tautology (tautological proposition) 202, 309
term (as syllogistic concept expression) 6, 74, 75
- general 6, 110–13, 309
- open proposition 75
- singular 6, 110–13, 309
tertium non datur (see *principle of excluded middle*)
thought, pure 129
transformation rules xxi, 268, 293
truth
- analytic 52, 58, 123, 134
- as (timeless) application of a predicate to an object 51, 359, 361–63
- logical vii–viii, xi, 8, 175, 301, 302, 304, 310
- logical t. in *FC* 304
- semantic concept of 301–4
- syntactic concept of 301–4
- time-dependent 359–61
- timeless 359
truth, logical vii, 8, 175, 301, 302, 304, 310
- semantic concept of 301–4
- syntactic concept of 301–4
truth-ambivalence 16, 29, 151, 352
truth function vii–viii, xi, 67, 71, 94, 98–101, 151, 160–65, 287–88, 329, 330
- dyadic 37, 68, 71, 101, 329, 330
- monadic (see *negation*)
truth-functional connective 68, 72, 102, 103, 98
truth value vii–viii, x, 8, 19, 23, 25, 26, 28, 29, 68, 71, 75, 76, 90, 100, 122, 151–53, 160, 311, 359, 361
- the true / the false 76, 359

universal 7, 20, 21, 26, 30–33, 38, 48–50, 73, 90–94, 108, 109, 137–39, 178–80, 189, 193, 206–8, 222, 241, 263

universal language of deductive logic x, 55, 135
universe of discourse (see *domain of individuals*)
universal class 66, 179
– absolute 56
universal quantifier 67, 103, 104, 263, 322
– Frege's view of 92, 103

validity, logical 95–98, 100, 175, 176, 261, 304, 309

weakening of logical consequence as a metalogical rule 276, 373
world of attribution 52, 179, 357

Name Index

Ackermann, Wilhelm ix, 41–48, 50, 51, 53, 58, 59, 63, 65, 70, 105, 177, 196
Alexander of Aphrodisias 141, 142, 153, 154, 158, 164, 168, 180, 243, 318
Angelelli, Ignacio 363
Apuleius Madaurensis 7, 79, 153
Aristotle v, vi, viii–x, xix, xxi, 4, 6, 18, 20, 25, 26, 34, 38, 44, 45, 51, 141, 146, 147, 152, 158–59, 162, 164, 166, 168, 169, 171, 172, 179–82, 184, 185, 187–97, 199, 200, 203–5, 209, 210, 211, 212, 214, 217, 219–23, 225, 226, 228, 230, 233–41, 243–46, 248–50, 252–54, 258, 260, 308, 310–13, 360, 363

Barcan, Ruth 24, 338, 357, 358
Barnes, Jonathan 84, 167
Beall, J.C. 359
Becker, Albrecht 203
Becker, Oskar 342
Beckermann, Ansgar 295, 296, 300, 302
Bencivenga, Ermanno 50, 353
Bernoulli, Jakob 325
Bolzano, Bernhard 167
Boole, George 52, 93

Capella, Martianus 79
Carnap, Rudolf 82, 136, 174
Chomsky, Noam 125
Chrysippus 140–42, 153, 161
Cresswell, Maxwell J. 23, 24, 341, 342, 347

da Costa, Newton C.A. 352
De Morgan, Augustus 67
Diogenes Laertius 153, 161

Ebert, Theodor 18, 147, 158, 159, 161, 185, 188, 189, 191, 193, 203, 206, 209, 220, 221, 223, 225, 228–30, 234, 236, 240–44, 250, 254, 255, 257, 259
Eudemus of Rhodes 158

Feys, Robert 341, 354
Frede, Michael 141, 153–55, 158–66, 168, 169, 171, 175, 318

Frege, Gottlob vi, vii, ix, xix, xx, 8, 12, 14, 33, 72–94, 105–10, 114, 116–22, 124–26, 128, 129, 131–35, 145, 264, 277, 281–84, 294, 295, 304, 311, 312, 321–27, 365

Gabriel, Gottfried 77
Galen 141, 142
Gentzen, Gerhard 147
Gödel, Kurt xi, 70, 341, 342, 353–55

Halmos, Paul R. 42, 54
Hegel, G.W.F. 84, 112, 216
Heyting, Arend 305, 334, 342, 353–55
Hilbert, David ix, xx, 41–47, 50, 51, 53, 58, 59, 63, 65, 70, 105, 177, 196, 354
Hoyningen-Huense, Paul 97, 273

Jaśkowski, Stanislaw 352
Jevons, William Stanley 48

Kant, Immanuel v–ix, xi, 7–10, 13, 21, 33, 50, 58, 78, 84, 112, 126–29, 131, 133, 134, 142, 163, 304, 308, 310–13, 327
Keynes, John Neville 47–50
Kirwan, Christopher 363
Kneale, Martha & William viii, 3, 23, 33, 82, 168, 169, 295
Kripke, Saul A. 123, 347, 349
Künne, Wolfgang 311

Lambert, Johann Heinrich 167
Lambert, Karel 50, 353
Langford, Cooper H. 23, 161, 304, 335
Leibniz, G.W. 33, 197
Lemmon, Edward John 354
Leonard, Henry 353
Lewis, Clarence I. x, 22, 23, 37, 67, 102, 161, 335, 337, 341, 342, 349
Łukasiewicz, Jan 175, 189, 295, 360

MacColl, Hugh 22
MacFarlane, John 126
Marciszewski, Witold 119
Mates, Benson 141, 153, 163, 175

Mautner, Thomas 38
Mill, John Stewart 6, 48, 111, 112

Nortmann, Ulrich 18, 147, 159, 185, 188–89, 191, 193, 203, 206, 209, 220, 221, 223, 225, 228–30, 234, 236, 240–44, 248, 250, 251, 254, 255, 257, 259, 324

Ockham, William of 200, 360

Patzig, Günther 8, 13, 25, 179, 183, 189, 191, 205, 260
Peano, Giuseppe xi, 33
Peirce, Charles S. 50
Philo of Megara 161
Philoponus, Ioannes 153
Plato viii, 3, 167
Plutarch 163
Prantl, Carl 13
Prior, Arthur 21, 50
Purtill, Richard 26

Quine, W.V.O. 6, 39, 83, 274, 290, 304, 311

Reich, Klaus 308
Restall, Greg 359
Ross, William David 180, 219
Russell, Bertrand vii, ix, 33, 46, 75, 87–89, 122–24, 196, 197, 304, 309, 327

Schmid, C.C.E. 10
Schmidt, Jürgen 55
Schmidt, Klaus J. 230, 234–36, 240, 241, 243
Schröder, Ernst 41, 42, 45–47
Sextus Empiricus 96, 141, 160, 61, 167, 175, 200
Sigwart, Christoph 10
Smith, Robin 189
Sommers, Fred 24, 25, 39, 113, 124, 125
Stekeler-Weithofer, Pirmin 25
Strawson, Peter F. 50, 79, 106, 123, 126
Strobach, Niko 158, 159
Stuhlmann, Laeisz, Rainer 91

Tarski, Alfred 16, 151, 152, 300
Theophrastus 158, 162, 168
Thompson, Manley 50
Tugendhat, Ernst 111, 112

Ueberweg, Friedrich 50

Venn, John 48
von Wright, Georg Hendrik 359

Wedin, Michael 180
Weidemann, Hermann 180
Whitehead, Alfred North ix
Wieland, Wolfgang 18
Wittgenstein, Ludwig 309
Wolf, Ursula 111, 112
Wolff, Christian 91, 167

www.ingramcontent.com/pod-product-compliance
Lightning Source LLC
Chambersburg PA
CBHW021758220426
43662CB00006B/108